READINGS IN MANAGEMENT ACCOUNTING

Second Edition

READINGS IN MANAGEMENT ACCOUNTING

S. Mark Young
University of Southern California

 PRENTICE HALL, Upper Saddle River, New Jersey 07458

Project editor: Richard Bretan
Acquisitions editor: P.J. Boardman
Associate editor: Natacha St. Hill
Manufacturing buyer: Paul Smolenski

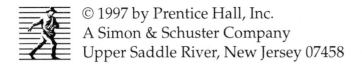 © 1997 by Prentice Hall, Inc.
A Simon & Schuster Company
Upper Saddle River, New Jersey 07458

Printed in the United States of America

10   9   8   7   6   5   4

ISBN 0-13-491911-4

Prentice-Hall International (UK) Limited, *London*
Prentice-Hall of Australia Pty. Limited, *Sydney*
Prentice-Hall Canada Inc., *Toronto*
Prentice-Hall Hispanoamericana, S.A., *Mexico*
Prentice-Hall of India Private Limited, *New Delhi*
Prentice-Hall of Japan, Inc., *Tokyo*
Simon & Schuster Asia Pte. Ltd., *Singapore*
Editora Prentice-Hall do Brasil, Ltda., *Rio de Janeiro*

TABLE OF CONTENTS

PREFACE

While this book can be used to supplement any management or cost accounting text, the readings have been designed to accompany Anthony Atkinson, Rajiv Banker, R. S. Kaplan and S. Mark Young's textbook, *Management Accounting, 2nd Edition* (Prentice Hall, 1996).

TO STUDENTS

For each textbook chapter there is a corresponding set of readings that highlights text material and introduces you to applications of the material in a wide variety of contexts. At the end of each reading, questions test your understanding of what you have read. The readings are taken from many sources including the *Wall Street Journal, Management Accounting, Journal of Cost Management, Fortune, Harvard Business Review* and others. They represent very current thinking on each of the topics covered in the text.

Probably the best way to use this book is to read each assigned article in one sitting. Then, read the article a second time taking notes and asking yourself how the article extends your understanding of the text material. In some cases, your instructor may assign specific questions that follow each of the readings. Taking the time to answer these questions thoughtfully will improve your understanding of the material. I hope you find the material stimulating and thought-provoking.

TO INSTRUCTORS

Readings in Management Accounting, Second Edition contains forty-eight articles representing state-of-the-art thinking and examples on a wide variety of management accounting topics in many types of service and manufacturing contexts. The second edition has been updated from the first with the inclusion of twenty new, recently published articles.

Readings in Management Accounting, Second Edition is designed primarily to be used with Atkinson, Banker, Kaplan and Young's text, *Management Accounting, Second Edition* (Prentice Hall, 1996). After publication of the first edition, however, I discovered that a number of instructors who had adopted a different textbook had chosen to use *Readings in Management Accounting* as a supplementary text, or in some cases as a standalone text. To aid these instructors, I have written a separate *Instructor's Manual* (available from Prentice Hall) which keys the readings in this book to chapters in a number of other leading texts. Thus, suggested solutions to the questions in this book can be found in both the *Instructor's Manual* to the text *Management Accounting* as well as in the separate *Instructor's Manual* prepared for *Readings in Management Accounting*. While the each of the readings has been listed for a specific chapter, in many cases, a reading may successfully applied to several chapters. As an example, Reading 2.3, G. Foster and C. T. Horngren's "Cost Accounting and Cost Management in a JIT Environment," can be used for both Chapters 2 and 8 depending on the instructor's predilections. Finally, if you have a favorite reading that is not contained in this book, please send me a copy and I will gladly consider it for the next edition. Thank you very much.

S. Mark Young
Leventhal School of Accounting
University of Southern California
June, 1996

ACKNOWLEDGMENTS

I would like to thank Natacha St. Hill for her editorial assistance and P. J. Boardman for her encouragement and support of the project. Also, I would like to thank Bob Kaplan, Harvard University, Gerald Meyers, Pacific Lutheran University, and Mike Shields, University of Memphis for sending me their reading lists. I would like to especially thank Ella Mae Matsumura, University of Wisconsin, Madison for her very thoughtful critique of the first edition of this book.

S. Mark Young
Leventhal School of Accounting
University of Southern California

ABOUT THE AUTHOR

S. Mark Young, Professor of Accounting at the Leventhal School of Accounting at the University of Southern California, is Associate Editor of the *Journal of Management Accounting Research* and past Associate Editor of *The Accounting Review.* He also serves on several other major editorial boards including *Accounting, Organizations and Society.* Young received an A.B. from Oberlin College, an M.Acc. from The Ohio State University, and a Ph.D. from the University of Pittsburgh. He is the recipient of four outstanding teaching awards at the undergraduate and graduate levels, including the Golden Apple Teaching Award from the MBA Program at USC. He has published over 40 papers and made over 100 presentations of his research in Europe, Asia, Australia and the United States. Young has been a KPMG Peat Marwick Faculty Fellow and has received research grants from the National Science Foundation, The Institute of Management Accountants, the Consortium for Advanced Manufacturing International, The Institute of Internal Auditors and the Center for Innovation Management Studies. In 1994, together with coauthor Frank Selto, Young won the Management Accounting Section's (AAA) Notable Contribution to the Management Accounting Literature Award. Most recently, Dr. Young has conducted research or consulted with Nevada Power Company, Texas Instruments, the Economic Analysis Corporation, First Data Corporation, Chrysler and General Motors.

CHAPTER 1

Management Accounting: Information That Creates Value

The readings in Chapter One all emphasize the changing role of management accounting information in today's business organizations. The first article (Reading 1.1) is Peter Drucker's *"Be Data Literate—Know what to Know."* Drucker's article argues that there are three informational challenges facing executives. The first is to become information literate to know what information they need, when, and in what form. The second challenge is how to obtain, test, and combine information and integrate it into the existing information system. The final challenge, which is central to the study of management accounting, is that the data processing and accounting systems need to be brought together to decrease redundancy and increase compatibility. Drucker discusses the many new roles for accounting information and states: "Accounting has become the most intellectually challenging area in the field of management, and the most turbulent one."

The second article, *"What Production Managers Really Want to Know Management Accountants Are Failing to Tell Them"* by Shannon McKinnon and William Bruns (Reading 1.2), continues with the theme established by Drucker that management accounting information can be highly relevant to any modern organization, but it must be responsive to specific user needs. McKinnon and Bruns conducted in-depth surveys of 73 top managers in production, sales, marketing, general management, and information systems in 12 firms in the U.S. and Canada. An interesting finding from this research is that production managers tend to make more use of physical unit data than dollar or financial data in the daily control of their operations, although financial measures play a central role in decision making over longer time periods. The article reports that many managers surveyed have developed their own information networks due to the inadequacies of many current accounting systems. To remedy this situation, they suggest that management accountants expand their role to include providing managers with more physical unit data, facilitating more information flows between sales and production and taking the lead to further integrate their organization's information system.

In Reading 1.3, *"Let's Reengineer Cost Accounting,"* D. Keegan and R. Eiler take the position that there may be a compromise between completely abandoning traditional cost accounting systems and embracing activity based costing systems (ABC). Based on their consulting experience the authors cite instances where organizations have not been able to integrate ABC information into their financial reporting system. Since many types of organizational stakeholders rely on external financial reports in order to make investment decisions, ABC and traditional systems are still disconnected in some organizations leading to confusion and indecision. The authors suggest ways in which traditional costing systems can be reengineered to take advantage of, and incorporate, the insights and understanding that ABC can provide.

1.1 Be Data Literate—Know What to Know

By Peter F. Drucker

Executives have become computer literate. The younger ones, especially, know more about the way the computer works than they know about the mechanics of the automobile or the telephone. But not many executives are information-literate. They know how to get data. But most still have to learn how to use data.

Few executives yet know how to ask: What information do I need to do my job? When do I need it? In what form? And from whom should I be getting it? Fewer still ask: What new tasks can I tackle now that I get all these data? Which old tasks should I abandon? Which tasks should I do differently? Practically no one asks: What information do I owe? To whom? When? In what form?

A "database," no matter how copious, is not information. It is information's ore. For raw material to become information, it must be organized for a task, directed toward specific performance, applied to a decision. Raw material cannot do that itself. Nor can information specialists. They can cajole their customers, the data users. They can advise, demonstrate, teach. But they can no more manage data for users than a personnel department can take over management of the people who work with an executive.

THE FIRST CHALLENGE

Information specialists are toolmakers. The data users, whether executive or professional, have to decide what information to use, what to use it for and how to use it. They have to make themselves information-literate. This is the first challenge facing information users now that executives have become computer-literate.

But the organization also has to become information literate. It also needs to learn to ask: What information do we need in this company? When do we need it? In what form? And where do we get it? So far, such questions are being asked primarily by the military, and even there mainly for tactical, day-to-day decisions. In business such questions have been asked only by a few multinationals, foremost among them the Anglo-Dutch Unilever, a few oil companies such as Shell, and the large Japanese trading companies.

The moment these questions are asked, it becomes clear that the information a business most depends on are available, if at all, only in primitive and disorganized form. For what a business needs the most for its decisions—especially its strategic ones—are data about what goes on outside of it. It is only outside the business where there are results, opportunities and threats.

So far, the only data from the outside that have been integrated into most companies' information systems and into their decision-making process are day-to-day market data: what existing customers buy, where they buy, how they buy. Few businesses have tried to get information about their noncustomers, let alone have integrated such information into their databases. Yet no matter how powerful a company is in its industry or market, noncustomers almost always outnumber customers.

American department stores had a very large customer base, perhaps 30% of the middle-class market, and they had far more information about their own customers than any other industry. Yet their failure to pay attention to the 70% who were not customers largely explains why they are today in a severe crisis. Their noncustomers increasingly were the young affluent, double-earner families who were the growth market of the 1980s.

The commercial banks, for all their copious statistics about their customers, similarly did not realize until very late that more and more of their potential customers had become noncustomers. Many had turned to commercial paper to finance themselves instead of borrowing from the banks.

When it comes to nonmarket information—demographics; the behavior and plans of actual and potential competitors; technology; economics; the shifts signaling foreign-exchange fluctuations to come and capital movements—there are either no data at all or only the broadest of generalizations. Few attempts have been made to think through the bearing that such information has on the company's decisions. How to obtain these data; how to test them; how to put them together with the existing information system to make them effective in a company's decision process—this is the second major challenge facing information users today.

It needs to be tackled soon. Companies today rely for their decisions either on inside data such as costs or on untested assumptions about the outside. In either case they are trying to fly on one wing.

Finally, the most difficult of the new challenges: We will have to bring together the two information systems that businesses now run side by side—computer-based data processing and the accounting system. At least we will have to make the two compatible.

People usually consider accounting to be "financial." But that is valid only for the part, going back 700 years, that deals with assets, liabilities and cash flows; it is only a small part of modern accounting. Most of accounting deals with operations rather than with finance, and for operational accounting money is simply a notation and the language in which to express nonmonetary events. Indeed, accounting is being shaken to its very roots by reform movements-aimed at moving it away from being financial and toward becoming operational.

There is the new "transactional" accounting that attempts to relate operations to their expected results. There are attempts to change asset values from historical cost to estimates of expected future returns. Accounting has become the most intellectually challenging area in the field of management, and the most turbulent one. All these new accounting theories aim at turning accounting data into information for management decision-making. In other words, they share the goals of computer-based data processing.

Today these two information systems operate in isolation front each other They do not even compete, as a rule. In the business schools we keep the two apart with separate departments of accounting and of computer science, and separate degrees in each.

The practitioners have different backgrounds, different values, different career ladders. They work in different departments and for different bosses. There is a "chief information officer" for computer-based data processing, usually with a background in computer technology. Accounting typically reports to a "chief financial officer," often with a background in financing the company and in managing its money. Neither boss, in other words, is information-focused as a rule.

The two systems increasingly overlap. They also increasingly come up with what look like conflicting—or at least incompatible—data about the same event; for the two look at the same event quite differently. Till now this has created little confusion. Companies tended to pay attention to what their accountants told them and to disregard the data of their information system, at least for top-management decisions. But this is changing as computer-literate executives are moving into decision-making positions.

UP FOR GRABS

One development can be considered highly probable: Managing money—what we now call the "treasury function"—will be divorced from accounting (that is, from its information component) and will be set up, staffed and run separately. How we will otherwise manage the two information systems is up for grabs. But that we will bring them together within the next 10 years, or at least sort out which system does what, can be predicted.

Computer people still are concerned with greater speed and bigger memories. But the challenges increasingly will be not technical, but to convert data into usable information that is actually being used.

Mr. Drucker is professor of social sciences and management at the Claremont Graduate School in California.

From P. Drucker, "Be Data Literate—Know What to Know," *Wall Street Journal* (December 1, 1992): 14. Reprinted with permission.

Question

1.1 What does Drucker mean when he says: "be data literate?"

1.2 What Production Managers Really Want to Know . . .
Management Accountants Are Failing to Tell Them

By Sharon M. McKinnon, CMA, and William J. Bruns, Jr.

Does the information management accountants provide to functional areas such as manufacturing and sales represent a major chunk of the most valuable information for daily operation control? Is it important to increase the speed with which operating reports reach managers' desks or perhaps to increase the precision of financial measurements?

We recently conducted a study[1] to determine the usefulness of accounting information. We found that the actual information used for daily operating control usually does *not* come from the accounting area.

Years of teaching in executive programs has taught us that numerous successful executives do not have a basic understanding of accounting concepts and principles. Consequently, we began to wonder what information managers were really using on a day-to-day basis.

73 MANAGERS INTERVIEWED

We interviewed 73 top managers of production, sales and marketing, general management, and information systems in 12 manufacturing companies. Six operate in the United States and six in Canada. We asked these managers about their daily activities, the types of information they need to fulfill these activities, and how they gather or receive the information. Table 1 describes the firms in the study and the positions of the managers concerned with production and manufacturing.

Manufacturing and production encompass numerous supportive activities such as research and development, maintenance, safety, and quality control. The major activity areas, however, can be defined as the actual production of

---

TABLE 1
FIRMS AND MANAGERS IN THE STUDY

Firms (in order of size)
- Manufacturer, seller, and servicer of computer hardware and software.
- Producer, refiner, and marketer of petroleum materials and products.
- Manufacturer and distributor of branded consumer food products.
- Producer and distributor of industrial chemicals, coatings, and explosives.
- Iron and steel manufacturer for construction and manufacturing industries.
- International manufacturer of communications equipment.
- Specialty producer of rubber, latex, and polymer products.
- Manufacturer and distributor of wire and cable products to industrials.
- Producer and seller of specialized lines of branded consumer foods.
- Producer of electronic instruments for sales to worldwide market.
- World competitor in creation, sales, support in computer-aided design.
- Major supplier of paper filters for air and fluid systems.

Positions Held by Production Managers

Distribution Manager (2)	Plant Manager (4)
Division Manufacturing Manager	VP Steel Operations
General Foreman-Steelmaking	Production Manager
Manager, Coke/Iron Production	Purchasing Manager
Manager, Distribution/Transportation	Regional Manufacturing Manager
Manager, Engineering Services	VP Logistics
Manager, Engineering/Maintenance	VP Operations (3)
Manufacturing Manager	VP Product Manufacturing (2)
	VP Quality
	VP Regional Manufacturing (2)
	VP Technology

---

products, purchase of raw materials, and distribution of finished products. Although we talked to managers involved with all of these activities, we will focus on the three major activities concerning information needs.

INFORMATION FOR DAILY MANUFACTURING

The needs of a manager who is responsible for the efficient daily operations of a manufacturing facility are affected by:

- The production factors that are most significant to the process in terms of cost, quality, and availability:
- The time frame in which the information is needed; and
- The channels of communication through which the information flows from the floor to the manager and back.

The level of finished goods inventory maintained and available to fill orders is a major factor in determining the most valuable information for daily manufacturing control. In companies that maintain significant levels of ending inventory, manufacturing operations are spared many of the shocks of frequent changes in production plans and disruptions of schedules.

Table 2 displays the categories of plant we encountered in our study and their inventory levels in relation to one another. Companies try to maintain low inventory levels for many reasons. Even those labeled as high-inventory plants try to maintain as low a level of inventory as possible to avoid tying up much of their working capital in inventory. Investment or expense for storage facilities, product obsolescence, and problems with physical deterioration of products are other reasons companies try to minimize inventory levels regardless of their production strategy.

High-inventory companies in our study fall into two subgroups: those that produce large quantities of standard unit output, and those in which conversion of raw materials produces products that are relatively easy to store. Low inventory companies also can be divided into two groups: those that use continuous manufacturing processes with highly volatile, frequently toxic products that are difficult and expensive to store and those that produce specialty products, a good many of which are tailored to a customer's detailed specifications.

Companies with relatively *high finished goods inventory levels* work less to everyday orders. Instead, they place more emphasis on following a master production plan, usually prepared annually, with rolling revisions monthly or quarterly. Usually there is some reporting of what is happening on the floor on a daily basis. The reports may run the spectrum from computer printouts of process yields to handwritten memos on minutes of downtime. In our study, the common characteristic of the information deemed most valuable by the production managers in these companies was

TABLE 2
KEY PRODUCTION CONTROL INFORMATION

High Levels of Finished Goods

Branded Food Products	Labor counts; units of output
Filters	Labor counts; units of output; scrap
Steel	
Cable	Output; quality Scrap; labor time

Low Levels of Finished Goods

Latex	Order quantity; product specifications
Chemicals and Explosives	Order quantity; inventory availability
Petroleum Products*	Order quantity; inventory availability
Electronic and Telecommunications Equipment	Order quantity, product specifications quality
Software	Order quantity; specifications; quality

*Note: Although petroleum refiners often hold large inventories of some finished products, the diversity of products and specifications often leads to situations where product must be produced or blended to fill a specific order. In addition, the use of large transportation vehicles, such as tanker ships, creates a need to create enough product for shipment at a specified time to achieve economies of scale in transport utilization.

the emphasis placed on controlling or monitoring what we will call the "key production limiting factor."

John F. Rockart described a concept known generally as the "critical success factor" (CSF) approach to providing information to executives.[2] If this approach is followed, a company's information system should be focused to ensure that the few areas vital to the success of corporate goals are reported on an accurate, timely basis. Our key production control factors, related directly to this CSF concept in that each defines a vital production factor that must be monitored daily to meet the annual production plan.

Many production control factors for high-inventory companies revolve around ensuring continuous output. Labor, materials, and some other costs are a function of the number of units produced. Those managers in our study who focused on daily output measures relied solely on primary measures, or counts, rather than on financial data. Output measures such as tons of steel produced or numbers of air filters assembled were considered vital, and physical measures also frequently were used to assure the continuous output of product, regardless of its nature. Downtime per shift or per machine was a common such measure.

Low-automation companies often find that the limiting factor defining output is tied to labor costs. The "cost" of labor proves a difficult item to track on an immediate basis. The daily labor measures used most frequently are basic

counts of how many personnel worked on production during recent shifts. These counts enable production managers to estimate effects on output and costs and to take steps to increase the number or change the mix or workers.

In other factories, we found that the cost of materials running through the plant dwarfed the other factors of production and became the single most important factor watched on a daily basis. Yet like labor costs, materials costs themselves are tracked on a short-term basis by counts of scrap or reworked materials.

Whether unit output, downtime, scrap, or some other measure is the vital daily data item, these companies are similar in that their daily operations are driven more by a long-range production plan than by a response to daily sales. This is not to say that sudden changes in sales circumstances have no impact. They frequently do, and they call for immediate action. But the usual mode of operation in these companies is steady production in conformance to a plan. When production volume and effort remain fairly constant over a period of time, sales and finished goods inventories may differ from plan, which leads to the need for the higher-volume inventories that characterize this group of firms and that separate them from low-inventory companies.

Even companies that keep *low finished goods inventories* generally work from a long-range production plan. These plans, however, are subject more frequently to revision on a short-term basis. When inventories are low, there must be more flexibility to change operations to meet immediate needs.

Several characteristics of production processes lend themselves to low inventory levels. The nature of the product frequently demands quick distribution—perishable goods being the obvious example. In our study, three companies produce liquid or semi-liquid products that are not only difficult to store but have toxic properties that dictate fast, safe, and efficient movement from source to customer.

A second product characteristic leading to low inventories is the specialization typical in high-technology, low-volume industries.

The third results when the product is tailored to the customer's needs. This leads to a much closer relationship between production and customer in terms of both specifications and time between order, production, and delivery.

The information needs of production managers in low-inventory companies are not totally different from those of managers in companies with larger inventories, particularly in the need to monitor key production limiting factors. However, in low-inventory companies the key production control factors tend to be related less to volume. What most characterized managers' need for information here is their daily interest in and reliance on some measure of bookings or orders. This reliance introduces a major issue into the need for information, that of interdepartmental communication and cooperation.

5

When production is a high-volume process, this communication and cooperation must exist on a daily basis, to the extent that, in some firms, production levels actually may be set by managers in nonproduction departments. For example, we found marketing managers determining output levels in a chloralkali plant because of the need to balance sales with two byproducts of the same process. When specialized orders must be filled on short notice, plant managers must depend on the immediate availability of knowledge about customer quality specifications and time requirements, inventory levels, plant capacity, and distribution schedules. Naturally, much of this information is found in a plant's databases, but the nature of the immediate need depends on communication with and through the sales force.

In other low-inventory companies, the production cycle is more lengthy because large specialized products are tailored to customer specifications. Production cycles often span days or weeks. In such cases, reports of daily production quantities are supplemented by fuzzier measures that show how orders, projects, or products are generally progressing. Although production is still driven by orders, there is no need for daily changes in production because each order takes longer to fill. The importance of daily production or sales reports is diminished, while other measures take on more significance. Particular emphasis goes to measures that ensure customer satisfaction, such as quality and product innovation.

DAILY PURCHASING ACTIVITIES

Control of production is tied inextricably to two other major functions: purchasing the raw materials needed to ensure a continuing production process and distributing the finished products. Purchasing managers rely on many different types of information to achieve their objectives. Some of these data are similar in nature to information for production control. For example, needs, orders, and promises are expressed in the form of physical counts. The key financial indicator of material prices as an operating control accounts for the major difference between the type of information valued most by purchasing managers versus production managers on a daily basis.

The nature of purchasing is such that dealing with prices and transportation costs is an integral part of the job description. Purchasing managers are evaluated on price efficiencies and must deal with prices in addition to quantities on a day-to-day basis. The importance of price and quantity information to a purchasing manager is a function of relationships displayed in Figure 1.

Six major categories of information are necessary to run a purchasing department in support of a production facility. Although all these items are necessary to purchasing, some are more vital than others to everyday control.

1. A production plan outlines the intent to produce certain products at certain times;

2. A bill of materials defines the materials required for production of each product;
3. Knowledge of the production cycle indicates when and where in the process the material is needed;
4. Inventory levels provide cues as to when more materials should be purchased;
5. Knowledge of supplier lead time enables materials to be ordered in time; and
6. Knowledge of the prices of materials allows choice of low-cost suppliers and subsequent analysis of the effectiveness of the purchasing function.

Production plans, bills of materials, and knowledge of cycle times and supplier lead times all can be characterized as part of a generally stable, slowly changing knowledge base. The remaining two information categories, inventory levels and prices, comprise the most valuable information for everyday control of purchasing because of their changing nature and because the purchasing manager can affect the cost of operations directly by controlling them.

In any production operation, the major challenge to a purchasing manager is maintaining an appropriate amount of materials inventory. Interlocking goals put into play opposing forces: Too much inventory will tie up capital, and too little inventory can result in losses. The relative importance of each force and the value of the information associated with inventory levels and prices are a function of the nature of the production process and the cost and nature of the raw materials.

A relatively stable production process is characterized by predictability of future materials requirements. Production plans are changed infrequently, and needs are known in time to be satisfied easily. Stable production schedules lend themselves well to purchasing through a materials require-

FIGURE 1
FACTORS AFFECTING THE VALUE
OF INFORMATION USED
IN THE PURCHASING FUNCTION

Key Information Items
Inventory Levels (counts) and Material Prices

Key Considerations

Cost of Running
Out of Materials

Cost of Maintaining
Materials Inventory

Nature of Production
Processes
(stable vs. unstable)

Cost of Raw Materials
(high/volatile vs. low)

Nature of Raw Material
(stable/homogeneous vs.
unstable/heterogeneous)

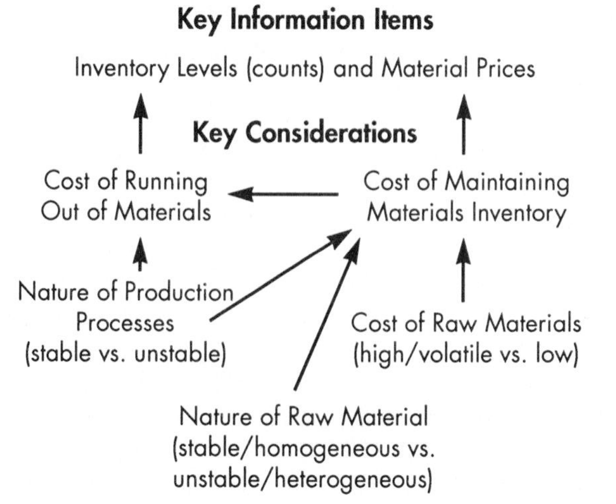

ments planning (MRP) system, which keeps track of inventories and forecasts needs for purchases with enough lead time to negotiate contracts and prices well in advance.

We talked to purchasing managers in several companies who enjoy these circumstances. In each, the key information needed daily was knowledge of open purchase orders—material that had been purchased but not yet received. Overdue shipments represented a tangible data item on which action could be taken that would have an immediate effect in ensuring that inventory levels remained at necessary levels. Prices were monitored over longer horizons because of the ability to forecast and plan. Less stable production environments shorten the horizon for monitoring inventory and prices.

Several of the managers in our study emphasized the importance of the relative cost of raw materials as a key factor in whether they maintained high inventories. When raw materials are commodities, their value fluctuates with market conditions, and this volatility leads to minimization of inventories where possible, with a continuing eye on the market price in order to take advantage of perceived opportunities.

When materials are particularly expensive, more attention is paid to minimizing the levels. Not only do expensive materials tie up capital, but they also are more susceptible to loss the longer they remain unused in storage.

In our study, purchasing managers dealing with expensive materials, such as some materials used in semiconductor test systems, focused on daily observation of the level of expensive components. Despite the significance of the cost, the actual cost was a long-range factor compared to assurance of immediate availability. When inventory items are inexpensive, the emphasis of the purchasing function appears to be ensuring their continued supply with the least effort. A good system which automatically puts in place a purchasing process obviates the need for everyday control by purchasing managers.

In summary, the importance of certain types of information in the daily control of a purchasing function is dependent on several factors. Continuous planned production processes with stable suppliers and relatively low-cost homogeneous raw materials form one end of the spectrum of circumstances for purchasing. In this situation, daily actions are geared to those that will help keep an MRP system functioning smoothly and are typified by close scrutiny of open purchase orders. Continuous planned production processes with volatile or perishable materials require close control over inventory levels and prices. When production processes use high-cost materials or consume large quantities of commodity materials, greater efforts are made to reduce the investment in inventories through coordination of deliveries at the right time. Emphasis varies from prices to inventory levels depending on the nature of the process and materials.

We found that financial data about the effectiveness of purchasing was used more and more as the time horizon was extended. In particular, purchase price variances on a per-unit basis were seen as significant for evaluating short-term suc-

cess, but most managers found that monthly total variance analysis was necessary for a realistic assessment of the effectiveness of purchasing. Routine efforts were devoted to minimizing daily price increases, while most non-routine efforts were concerned with evaluating how total cost variances above budget could be minimized over longer time periods.

DAILY DISTRIBUTION ACTIVITIES

The types of information used to coordinate daily distribution activities can be categorized in several ways. Distribution managers are highly focused on the levels of finished goods inventory and the logistics through which this inventory reaches the customer. Figure 2 displays a matrix of some of the types of data that are associated with inventory levels and logistics, divided into two major categories: customer service and distribution costs.

FIGURE 2
INFORMATION USED IN DISTRIBUTION

	FG Inventory	Logistics
Customer Service	Days in Inventory Availability Back orders	Location of carriers Fill rates Due dates
Distribution Costs	Financial decisions Space constraints	Freight rates Lease versus buy

Customer service. Daily information needs are dominated by customer service demands, particularly in those industries characterized by a rigorous competitive environment. Managers are involved in a highly complex logic problem. When solved successfully, the finished goods inventory is available in a timely manner, orders are filled completely and shipped to customers at their desired date by the least expensive, reliable carrier. At each stage in this process, problems can produce bottlenecks that have ramifications through the systems.

The level of finished goods inventory is one factor affecting what information is vital for distribution control. Companies that produce large, discrete products, frequently to order, have low finished goods and compete mainly on the quality of their products. Neither distribution costs nor highly reliable delivery services serve as major determinants of profitability. Therefore, distribution activities play a minor role in operations management. At the other end of the low inventory spectrum is a process company (for example, chemicals) that produces volatile products that are difficult or dangerous to store. Finished goods exist mainly in transit. The present and prospective future location of trucks or railroad cars is the most important daily information for the distribution manager.

Companies that have higher levels of finished goods inventory face unique problems. Inventory is expensive to maintain, so even companies with relatively high levels face the challenge of availability, particularly if they produce "lots of different things" such as soup varieties or filter sizes. Risks associated with a failure to fill a customer's order when desired vary with the size of the customer and competitive situation.

Distribution costs. In some companies, control of distribution costs is the key to profitability, particularly if there is a low contribution margin percentage and transportation is expensive or complex. When numerous backorder situations exist, there is a high potential for an order actually to be unprofitable. Distribution costs also assume added importance when alternative transport opportunities exist and there is a highly competitive market for the product.

Despite these scenarios, the actual costs themselves are not followed extensively on a daily basis, even in companies where they are "make-or-break." Instead, managers try daily to minimize costs through physical surrogates that can be controlled, such as decisions on rail car movements between plants or judgments about which orders to delay or fill. Often these decisions are based on experience as to what the underlying cost consequences will be. Daily variations in costs may be caused by special circumstances that level out over time, and it is over time that cost analysis becomes a major activity.

WHAT IS USEFUL?

According to our research, production managers make more use of physical unit data than dollar or financial data in their control of daily operations. In 12 varied manufacturing companies, we found no instance of a key daily production indicator being a cost or financial number. This was as true in the three companies that had embraced activity-based costing systems as in the others.

What we did find, however, was that financial numbers do play a significant role in production control. First, there is an underlying knowledge of the financial implications of physical counts and counting data implicit in the analyses and actions of many managers. Second, when considered on a longer time dimension, financial indicators transcend physical counting measures in the importance managers place on them.

Many plant managers have a seemingly odd pattern of responses to our questions on useful data. They talked about daily control of operations as their most important tasks and about the physical measures they follow each day. When asked later about their "most valuable report in general," however, they cited a monthly income or expense report. One plant manager explained this seeming contradiction:

"At this company you live or die by the numbers. One of the reasons I've been successful is that I know how to move and groove and bake and shake the numbers I know what affects them. I don't mean that I play with the numbers . . .

but when you push something down I know where it pops up. The reason I talk about production in terms of quantities is that I know the underlying effect of quantities on the dollars and cents and how volume covers the overhead in this plant."

Operating managers will take action on variables that have two major characteristics: The variables are significant in terms of moving toward a desired goal, and the variables can be altered or controlled by the manager. If production managers or their units are evaluated on a basis that includes profits. the managers will seek opportunities to increase the profitability of operations under their influence. Yet it is the physical units that managers can actually control and relate to on a daily basis.

Three characteristics are required to make information useful: timeliness, accuracy, and relevance. This is nothing new, and yet the failure of much information circulated within firms to fulfill these three criteria continues to plague managers.

We found that, in their attempts to obtain information that meets these criteria, managers have constructed their own networks to supplement those created by management accountants and information specialists. These networks are composed of both formal and informal information items and channels such as:

- Internally generated—often handwritten—reports of daily activities such as downtime or units produced;
- Personally designed spreadsheets managers use to massage the data they receive or collect themselves;
- Personal observation through walking around or calling individual managers; and
- Personal or supervised collection of external environmental or economic information.

Why has traditional accounting failed to meet the daily needs of production managers? After all, accuracy, timeliness, and relevance are primary characteristics specified in the conceptual framework of accounting project of the Financial Accounting Standards Board. It would seem that accounting information, properly prepared, would indeed fulfill these characteristics. But there are numerous reasons why this is not the case.

First, many accounting data are considered old news by the time they are reported to operating managers. Accounting recognition and measurement criteria delay recognition of events until uncertainties have been resolved.

Second, accounting information is frequently organized and presented in forms that limit its usefulness. Aggregations and allocations tend to obscure details that managers consider important.

Third, most accounting data continue to be reported on a dollar or cost basis. Operating managers, however, take actions daily based on physical units.

Fourth, many companies' accounting or controllership departments have ceded the responsibility for providing daily operating data to either individual plants or factories themselves or to an information systems function within the firm. Thus, the link between the eventual financial reports and the operations that formed their genesis has been partially or completely severed.

WHAT SHOULD YOU DO?

Based on what information production managers say they use and our observations about the inadequacies of management accounting, we can make several recommendations. Some are specific and some general.

Management accountants should aid in providing physical unit data to managers.

Inventory levels appeared repeatedly as vital information items in our study. Finished goods levels determined short-term production changes and the ability to coordinate distribution and sales quickly. Despite this fact, most information on finished goods inventory was provided to managers on a piecemeal basis or a monthly basis. Managers complained consistently that accounting reports on inventories suffered by being out-of-date and frequently inaccurate or poorly classified.

Some managers complained that the accounting function tried to impose its financial accounting responsibilities on the management reports with conventions (such as valuation methods) that obscured either the time periods or physical flow useful for them. Most had simply given up on formal accounting reports and developed their own systems.

These observations about inventories imply that there is a void in many companies that accountants are uniquely qualified to fill, if they will break from some traditional reporting molds. Many accountants express the belief that speeding up the monthly closing process is the most valuable improvement they can make in reporting to their managers. We believe if management accountants truly want to help production managers, they should play major roles in metering and measuring physical flows and supervising their communication.

Management accountants should play major roles in assuring effective interdepartmental communication flows between sales and production.

The links between these two functions were important in most of the companies where we interviewed. Yet frequent problems exist in several areas.

First, information flows tend to be irregular or informal even in circumstances where fast, accurate flows are vital to daily production scheduling. Some of these informal channels were very effective, but they tended to depend upon individuals themselves and suffered from problems when the individuals were unavailable either temporarily or through leaving the position.

Second, even when formal daily reporting between sales and production existed, it often suffered from incompatibility of data from one function to another because of distributed databases. Our recommendation that management accountants become involved in improving communication between these two vital areas is closely tied to our belief that management accountants should regain their roles as information specialists in companies.

Management accountants should redefine their roles to include management of information systems development and implementation.

Traditionally, the management accountant *was* the information specialist. As computer technology evolved, many accounting functions allowed the primary responsibilities for developing information channels to slip into the hands of computer information systems departments. Too frequently, their inherent biases were toward the technology rather than the information content.

Extensive resources have been expended toward computerized information flows between managers and functions with varying degrees of success. Management accountants have the expertise in terms of information content to improve systems development. In most companies they already have responsibilities to collect, maintain, and distribute financial information to others. Optimally, they are trained to understand the relationship between managerial actions and the desired outcomes expressed as measures of financial performance.

REAL TIME DATABASE

According to the operating managers we interviewed, management accountants need to enhance the capture of operating data and speed the process by which this information is made available to production managers. If they do this, they will regain their place as primary information providers.

None of the 12 companies we visited had a comprehensive corporate management accounting system designed to provide the day-to-day information needs of operating managers. To be effective, such a system would need to be built around the identified information needs of particular operating managers in each company. Information would need to be collected by a means as timely as the personal reports of participants in function activities. It would have to be available to managers on command.

To capture operating data more quickly, management accounting systems have to be linked to measuring devices that will report activity as it takes place. In plants, meters might be used to provide continuous information on production activity, output rates, and inventory levels. Measurements of daily activity can be collected easily or distributed by telephone or electronic mail.

This suggests to us that the management accounting system of the future should include a large, real time database into which information is flowing continually. It must be accessible and friendly and must allow managers to format output in any desired relationships. The goal should be to enable any manager to work with the data in any way he or she chooses with full confidence that the information obtained will be current and reliable.

The failure of accountants and controllers to break from the accounting paradigms of information and financial reporting has led to separate management information departments in many firms. In these companies, careful coordination and reintegration will be required between the accountants or meters and monitors from whom the raw data originate and the technology specialists who send them through the system.

It is impossible for management accountants to provide for the information needs of managers unless they are directly involved with the operation of the data collection and reporting system. If specialists are required because of the nature of communication and electronic data processing equipment, the management accountant must not relinquish responsibility for the data collection or output functions to the technology specialists.

Management accountants should be at the center of every management information system. Understanding data processing and communication technologies is critical because the value of even the right information is conditional on the medium through which it is received.

This belief has implications for the education of management accountants in the future. The line between the data and their transmission has blurred to the point that accountants can no longer afford to be technologically ignorant. The management accountant of the future must be skilled in both systems strategy and technology, in addi-

tion to being proficient in the collection and interpretation of data. Only then can the artificial and costly separation of the management accounting and information operations be eliminated successfully.

Sharon M. McKinnon, Ph.D., CMA, is associate professor at Northeastern University. William J. Bruns, Jr., Ph.D., is professor of Business Administration at Harvard University. They are members of IMA's Boston Chapter.

Notes

1. This research was funded by the Society of Management Accountants of Canada and the Division of Research of the Harvard Business School. Material forming the basis for this article is part of the book. *The Information Mosaic,* published by the Harvard Business School Press, May 1992.

2. John F. Rockart, "Chief Executives Define Their Own Data Needs," *Harvard Business Review,* March–April 1979, pp. 81–93.

From W. Bruns and S. McKinnon, "What Production Managers Really Want to Know, Management Accountants Are Failing to Tell Them," *Management Accounting* (January 1993): 29–35. Reprinted with permission.

Question

1.2 According to McKinnon and Bruns, what should management accountants do to provide better information?

1.3 Let's Reengineer Cost Accounting
We need to synthesize the old with the new.

By Daniel P. Keegan and Robert G. Eiler

Lybrand Gold Medal Winner, 1993–94

The 19th century German philosopher Georg Friedrich Hegel explored the evolution of thought. He wrote that ideas follow a predictable path:

- First, there is Thesis—the established way of thinking.
- Second comes Antithesis—a radical departure from the established thought.
- And, finally, there is Synthesis—a blending of the original ideas with the new.

It's time for a little synthesis of cost management thought!

Companies are holding on to their old, traditional cost accounting systems (thesis) while proponents of change shape all new thought toward activity-based costing (antithesis). Neither of these approaches fully meets the needs of a business. Companies are right to experiment with ABC, but this

analytical technique is not an end in itself. It should be one step in reengineering the company's traditional cost system.

A DECADE LONG EVOLUTION

We explored the problems of cost accounting in an article published in the *Harvard Business Review* more than 10 years ago.[1] This article sparked considerable debate in the academic community. It stated, 'Traditional cost systems have become obsolete because of the changed proportion of labor, material and overhead. The overriding focus of a revised system should be product costing . . . This effort will require concentration on that somewhat mystifying pool of costs called overhead."

Conventional wisdom having been challenged, new thought emerged: A company should understand its cost drivers—and apply these drivers to the cost of products in proportion to the volume of activity that a product consumes. This powerful thought became popularized under the name activity-based costing (ABC).

Over the last several years, professional literature has been filled with articles on ABC. Of more importance, many companies have adopted activity-based costing methodology. A private survey of Price Waterhouse clients in indicates that more than half of American manufacturing companies list ABC as one of their current buzzwords. About one-third of service companies have experimented with the approach. In addition, the technique of activity-based costing is spreading quickly to Pacific Rim and European-based companies.

The increased knowledge of "cost drivers" has prompted many companies to reengineer their business processes in an attempt to reduce expense levels. The original term, activity-based costing, is giving way to a broader concept called *activity-based management,* in which companies monitor each of their activities and eliminate those that are of marginal value. Antithesis has reigned supreme. For a time, anyone who dared to address the still remaining problems of cost accounting seemed to be locked in a time warp.

SYNTHESIS IS NEEDED

Some have come to question whether Emperor ABC actually is wearing any royal garments. In many companies you can hear the following comments:

- "Too academic. It's just a model. What do we do with the results?"
- "There must be some easier way to get the benefits. It takes too long to conduct an ABC analysis."
- "It doesn't tie to the P&L. And that's what I'm judged on."
- "How do we embed the system? It needs to be part of our measurement process."

As the Hegelian triad would predict, *both the proponents and detractors of ABC overstate their case.* We need to synthesize the old with the new. Activity-based costing is only a part of the answer for several reasons.

First, activity-based costing is a technique, not a system. The technique is directed toward improving product costing. It provides information for strategic pricing, process improvement, and market positioning. An ABC analysis can—and does—provide useful insight concerning the relationship between indirect costs and products. ABC is most valuable to a company that has not allocated its overhead properly—or that needs to understand how its selling, general, and administrative (SG&A) expenses relate to products or product lines. (Allocation is a forbidden word to the ABC practitioner. Yet we think Shakespeare, hearing this protestation, would pen some lines about roses and names.)

When used properly, ABC is an effective tool of management, supplying insights to guide product strategy. For example, one of our clients believed that its distributor sales channel was its most profitable business segment. Distributor gross margins convinced management of this fact. An ABC analysis showed, however, that direct sales to large chains such as Wal-Mart actually were much more profitable than sales through distributors. Although retailers negotiated prices with a vengeance, the analysis showed management that it was less expensive overall to sell through retailers. The consumer channel needed only a small sales force; just a few large orders produced significant volume. In addition, this channel did not need an elaborate catalog—and fewer product returns were disputed. ABC pierced below the gross margin line. It provided invaluable information to executive management. The distributor channel no longer gets the lion's share of capital.

FIX THE INEFFECTIVE ACCOUNTING SYSTEM

ABC does not overcome the problems of an ineffective cost accounting system, however. The nonintegrated nature of an ABC analysis does, in fact, limit its usefulness. Because activity-based costing information usually is not reflected in the books of account, there is a credibility gap between ABC and "official" financial reporting. The proponents of activity-based costing dismiss this problem, but it is very real. Until management integrates activity-based costing into the company's formal system of reporting, ABC is in danger of remaining a sideshow exercise championed by staff groups and consultants but of little real meaning to the day-to-day operations of the company.

For example, a division of a large organization began to understand that the proliferation of models and options added complexity to the product line—and drove product cost higher. Division management therefore curtailed the options and simplified the offerings. The managers expected to see decreased product costs and higher profits.

A sister division, which produced; similar items, was not so well informed. It continued to offer options—and it increased market share at the expense of its more informed sibling. What was worse, the "official" product costs of the informed division did not fall. The company's cost system simply did not react as rationally as the ABC proponents said it would. Possibility, if divisional management had given the situation more time, the expected cost reduction might have occurred. But in this company, market share was a very important measurement that could not be ignored. Worse, lower-level operating managers groused that the "official" scorekeeping system continued to state that the ABC answers were wrong. The enlightened division abandoned its simplification strategy and reverted to its old ways.

The advocates of activity-based costing would cite the company's ineffective measurement system and reject this case example out of hand. Many companies should change their performance measurements, so this; argument has a ring of truth[2]. Yet it is doubtful that any organization will abandon gross margin or profitability as key measures of performance and instead believe its computer models. Because a company's cost accounting system plays such a predominant role in determining product margins, management cannot ignore the official cost system for very long. Each month it turns out reports that prompt questions.

We need *synthesis*. We need to incorporate what we have learned from activity-based costing into the company's formal management systems. It is naive to expect managers to ignore product gross margin and profitability reports and rely instead on the results of an ABC analysis. Even if they did, external investment analysts, the board of directors. and the executive committee might have some different ideas.

Company eyes now are turning back to the cost accounting system. These systems on the whole have not become any better over the last decade. They still apply overhead on the old traditional basis of direct labor; they still split hairs over fixed and variable expenses; they still result in unpleasant inventory surprises every once in a while; they still are incomprehensible to most operating managers; and they still are very expensive to operate. But they still tell us, officially, the magnitude of product margins and how much profit we have made.

REENGINEER YOUR COST ACCOUNTING SYSTEM

ABC has taught us much, and we can incorporate this knowledge into our formal systems. We can synthesize. We can allocate overhead properly, we can simplify the details of accounting, we can speed up information, and we can use the system to present key performance measures.

You may wish to consider the following principles as you begin this reengineering exercise. Not only can you obtain better information, but reengineering will curtail system expense. Here are a few starter ideas (temper these thoughts if you are a government contractor):

Eliminate labor reporting. For most companies, labor has become a very small part of product cost. It is not really variable in the short run even though the cost system treats it that way. And it isn't particularly important to know that the direct labor force spends, on average, 11.6 minutes per day on cleanup. Labor reporting is very expensive—and it provides little information of real value.

Vest responsibility for controlling labor cost with the first-line supervisor, turning your attention to more important cost elements such as purchased material or manufacturing overhead. One $700 million company estimated that it would save $1.6 million per year by eliminating its labor distribution system, a system that no one paid much attention to anyway. While there was some anguish along the way from staff groups that had a vested interest in labor efficiency and utilization information (because it was their

job to collect and report it), the company has learned to live without this information.

Streamline job order costing. Unless your company manufactures predominately custom products, management should consider modifying the company's job order costing system to make it less complex—or completely abandon it. In some environments it is nearly impossible to get job order costing right. A person on the shop floor is always borrowing material from one job to use on another—or citing an erroneous job number when reporting production. Costly shop floor data collection systems merely report this bad information faster. In many organizations, plant analysts and industrial engineers spend high-cost hours poring over yesterday's reports to correct the input. Despite these efforts, the inventory records are in a constant state of disrepair, and material losses become a problem of the cost accounting department, not the first-line manager.

Of even more significance, as manufacturing companies become cellular, job order costing may not even reflect the operating environment very well. Cellular companies strive for continuous flow production and quick changeovers. Management concentrates on fine-tuning the production processes to increase throughput speed and improve quality. The job order is no longer the focus of the plant.

We have found that when a job order system cannot be abandoned, reducing the number of data collection points, going to milestone reporting of production, and using predetermined estimates of cost will make the system less expensive and more relevant.

Ask yourself how much it costs to accumulate data by job order—and what value you receive from all this effort? Do you budget by job order? Do you hold anyone responsible for job order variances? Do you price by job order? Can you streamline the job order system to make it less complex? And the key question: Can you abandon it completely?

Charge first-line management with inventory responsibility. Use your computer systems to accumulate accurate work-in-process inventory balances in each department or for each major section of the plant. Plot days' supply of inventory for every one of these operating units, and ask the first-line supervisor to comment on the difference between actual and goal (see Figure 1, a sample Days' Supply of Inventory measurement chart). In a "pull" manufacturing environment, the amount of in-process inventory tends to be so small that any variation will show up immediately on the measurement chart. By focusing on days' supply of inventory at this discrete level, management will be riveting attention on material costs, sidestepping the compulsion to reduce labor costs only. Furthermore, by concentrating on in-process inventory, you will minimize its amount. The capital cost thus saved will probably more than pay for your new system.

Eliminate actual costing (except in cases where you have a very simple manufacturing process or product line). Base your cost accounting system on pre-

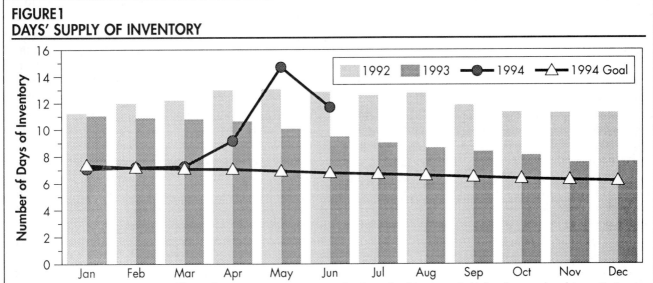

FIGURE 1
DAYS' SUPPLY OF INVENTORY

As noted on our two previous goal-focused management reports, our days' supply of inventory is higher than goal and is continuing to deteriorate. Two months ago, we empowered an Engineering Team to investigate all aspects of the Board Population Department's activities and determine the root cause problems. There are a number of factors present including new designs that were not fully functional, diodes that were not consistently within specifications, and insufficient training of second shift technicians.

determined estimates of anticipated actual cost. Actual cost systems are slow to present information, and they are very expensive to operate. Most companies cannot even define the term "actual" with any degree of precision.

Even when it is practical to determine actual cost, such information tends to frustrate performance measurement. Actual cost information is unstable. It is influenced by factors such as workdays in the month, a spot purchase of low-cost raw material, or an unusually high volume of production. Because of this instability, companies often will average their monthly "actual" costs to see trends. In doing so, the company chips through variations and obtains some of the same information that a system of predetermined estimates routinely provides. However, the averaged information developed in this way shows only history. A well-designed system of predetermined estimates looks toward the future.

We have deliberately not used the words "standard cost." Too much emotion is associated with this term. However, an accounting system based on budgets and rates (standards) can provide very useful information at a relatively low cost. Even defense contractors, who traditionally have attempted to make an actual cost system work, are beginning to realize that such a system is too expensive.

Subdivide and group cost centers. A company can obtain many of the benefits of activity-based costing with much less work by simply dividing its cost centers into logical groupings. This step eliminates the product cost distortion associated with spreading overhead in a gross, non-precise manner.

Sometimes an ABC analysis confirms that a company has computed product cost accurately using traditional approaches. In other cases, the ABC analysis will indicate significant distortions. When the company's product costs are wrong, a root-cause inquiry often targets the plant's cost center groupings as a prime culprit. By simply changing these groupings—and by distributing budgeted service center expenses using better drivers—management can improve its cost information significantly without revamping the underlying system.

Use ABC to allocate budgeted costs. Companies prepare a budget every year. With just a little additional effort, they could allocate overhead and SG&A expenses in a much more precise manner to products, product lines, or channels of distribution. Build ABC techniques into the budgeting process. In this way, you can obtain the insights of an ABC analysis at almost no incremental expense. By incorporating these distributions into the rates you use to develop "official" product costs, product gross margins will reflect ABC information.

The approach is simple. Just add an additional section to the budget worksheet, and ask the manager to indicate the department's activities and the recipients of these activities. Accumulate this information and distribute the activity rates to the appropriate cost center or product. If you want to add some spice to the process, ask the receiver of the activity if he or she agrees with the budgeted consumption. Possibly not.

Expand the number of elements in your product cost buildup. An ABC analysis may generate hundreds of cost drivers. They are too complex for the formal system—and probably too complex for discussion with management. Yet the traditional product cost buildup consisting of labor, material, and overhead is not the answer either.

Such a buildup clearly is too aggregated for product cost decision making. Strike a balance—find five to 10 significant, product cost elements by summarizing the ABC budget into a few activity pools. The revised approach probably will retain labor and material in the product cost buildup. However, you also may wish to include the cost of moving parts through the plant, the cost of process engineering, the cost of shop paperwork, and items such as inspection, maintenance, and freight. The objective is to highlight significant expenses that vary among products so as to reflect them in product cost—or better, to eliminate them.

You can close the budget-actual loop by crediting the activity pool for the actual drivers consumed. (We produced 10,000 widgets, and the product cost buildup includes one quality control inspection per 1,000 widgets.) You could further distribute the budget-actual drivers back to the originating departments if you like-but the value of this approach is probably not worth the work. Instead, use the activity pool information to reduce cost: reengineer expensive activities. For example, create work cells to eliminate the cost of moving material and establish focused factories to reduce interunit freight.

Simplify variance reporting. Classify the difference between budgeted and actual costs into a very few categories such as purchasing, volume, and spending. Too much variance detail obscures the real picture. The problem is that volume is lower than planned—or that costs are higher than they should be. Possibly, the plan was wrong. Possibly, performance is unsatisfactory. Rather than complicate the cost accounting system in an attempt to get the computer to ferret out the right conclusion. simply ask the department manager what happened. Develop a balanced set of performance measures and use them to spark communication.

Link into the manufacturing system for value-adding transactions. Most companies already have this link, but if you have a standalone cost accounting system, integrate it with your production control transactions. It is hard enough to make one of these systems work properly and almost impossible to reconcile two of them. Both systems need the same data: Manufacturing cares about quantities, accounting about dollars—two sides of the same coin.

It generally is becoming more uncommon to find non-integrated cost accounting/manufacturing control systems in today's business world. Yet we recall several cases where shop floor transaction pricing was "an accounting matter," never to be modified without approval. Because approval seldom was forthcoming, the manufacturing control systems evolved from traditional MRP into just-in-time tracking systems—but the accounting system remained as it had been designed 30 years earlier.

We often cite one company where more than one-quarter of all computer system maintenance requests came from the cost accounting staff. The cost system did not reflect the shop floor. It had to be modified constantly so it could be reconciled to the material control system. Operating management had lost all faith in cost system outputs and were lobbying for an actual ABC system. They were not sure what such a system really did, but they assumed it had to be better. For a long time. instead of scrapping the old system and starting over, the accounting staff continued to patch and patch. Eventually, executive management decided that something had to be done. All meetings were becoming a series of debates about the cost system.

A quick study showed that a reengineered cost system would have a payback of about a year. It took 18 months to install it, but the new system was far less complex—and month-end closing could take place much more quickly. Executive and operating managers appreciated the more timely scorecard. They also endorsed the hybrid nature of the new system. It had elements of ABC, but it was basically a standard cost system that could be used to pinpoint areas for performance improvement.

While this example benefited from the costly nature of the company's old system, most companies should expect, at worst, a two-year payback from a new cost accounting system—and a quicker payback if shop floor inventory is high.

Prepare channel of distribution/product line operating reports. Use an activity-based budget to distribute costs below the gross margin level. Show the differences between actual SG&A and the budgeted amounts as a variance. Control these variances at the responsibility level, not at the product level.

Many will not agree with this last design thought. Consumer product companies traditionally have distributed all SG&A and overhead to the product line in an attempt to cover these costs through prices. They believed that the product manager would wield a big stick to keep these costs under h control. Or if the costs could not be eliminated, the product manager would raise prices to maintain product margins. Recently, however, even companies with strong brand names have come under pricing attack by generics. Thus, consumer product companies are rediscovering that the ultimate drivers of cost are people and purchases. They are looking at the cost originating departments—as well as the brands—to improve their bottom lines.

If you must spread the actual SG&A to products or to product lines at interim periods. use the same ABC methodology that you developed during the budget. Of course, allocations are never perfectly precise—and the underlying business situation may have changed dramatically. Thus, the budget assumptions may no longer be valid. If it is really important to know product line profitability with precision, it may be necessary to go through a mini re-budget. Usually, however, strategic product line decisions are infrequent, and they are based only partially on cost data. Again, strive for simplicity. Avoid building too much product line information into the formal system. Having the computer slice and homogenize data in an attempt to improve its accuracy adds to system complexity but seldom results in better answers. Keep the formal system focused and simple. Extract data and use spreadsheets when you need a strategic analysis. This approach is much cheaper than building an all-encompassing product line profitability system.

We recall visiting a company that had just completed a study of world-wide product profitability. Determining net margins in Indonesia, Brazil, and Hungary was a daunting task that the company did not want to repeat. So it decided to build a transaction-processing system and accumulate this information routinely each quarter. Unfortunately, the system designers were not empowered to simplify. Their job was to accumulate the needed data, precisely and accurately. . .we need not continue. The resulting project dragged on for years and was killed only after a new chief operating officer (COO), hired by the board to reduce cost, asked, "What would anyone do with this information each quarter even if it were known?" To improve profits, the COO first cut departmental budgets and next reengineered company processes. He presumes that worldwide product costs have fallen.

Augment the cost system with nonfinancial performance measurements. Although cost system results are a very important aspect of the company's overall performance measurements management also should concentrate on other items of performance such as product development lead time, first-time product quality, customer satisfaction indexes, and market share.

Derive your performance measurements from your strategies, and report a balanced set of financial and statistical measures.[3] You can't expect the cost accounting system to provide all the answers. Array 40 to 60 measurements throughout your value chain—from product development through field service. Set goals and use the measurements as a spring board for managerial discussion. Look to the manager for an explanation when there are differences, not to the computer.

It is our experience that the senior financial executives of American companies are fast abandoning the notion that an information system must be expensive to be good. In fact, the financial executives often are the internal champions of cost system reengineering. Historically many companies have felt that changing their cost accounting system would be like touching the third rail of a New York subway line. That is why ABC has been so appealing. It promised a way around all this unpleasant work—and, to some considerable extent, it has been helpful in providing managerial insights. But it is time for synthesis.

SIMPLIFY AND INTEGRATE

What is to be gained from all this? By tailoring the design principles outlined above. you can reengineer your cost accounting system effectively. When you are finished you can expect to have a more focused less expensive system that provides more accurate product costs and helps you control expenses. Because every one will be using the same fact base, there will be no difference between activity-based costing answers and the "official" scorecard.

Let's make synthesis the watchword of the day. We can take what we know from ABC and incorporate this knowledge into the company's formal system.

Let's turn our attention back to these traditional systems. They have been neglected as we pursued activity-based costing. Start with a simplified ABC analysis, if you have not done so already—it will provide a great deal of insight concerning product cost and cost drivers. Then take what you learn and build it into your formal system.

Be particularly careful to avoid getting bogged down in all the ABC detail. We recall a meeting with the senior financial executives of a large Fortune 500 company. The financial executives sat around the mahogany table in the boardroom with their analysts seated behind them. The company had identified its cost drivers carefully and had allocated and reallocated these drivers among the service departments, moving them eventually to the product. The company had a large computer system consisting of more than 2,000 simultaneous equations to perform these calculations.

Management's question to us is, "What should we do now? We are finding it hard to get our product costs understood. Operating managers don't relate well to this information, and executive management won't sit still for all the details." Our answer: "Simplify and integrate."

On a smaller scale, these comments are repeated in almost all companies after they have completed their first ABC analysis. The project team asks, 'Where do we go from here?" Our answer remains, "Simplify and integrate."

As you rework your cost system, adopt the key words of reengineering: customer service, high quality, fast response, and low cost.

- Does your cost system meet customers' needs? Operating management will forcefully say, no.
- Is it of high quality? The marketing staff will cite pricing war stories.
- Is it quick? The financial staff will stare grimly at its closing schedule.
- Is it low cost? Everyone will look away.

Synthesize ABC, and reengineer your cost accounting system. Not only will you make the system better, but your efforts probably will pay for themselves more quickly than you can imagine.

What are the benefits of a new cost system? As the CFO of one company put it:

"We began to understand how little we knew about our product costs when we conducted the first ABC pilot. Next, we started to see that the operating managers were correct. Our system did pump out a lot of useless information. Finally, we realized what the system cost us to operate, and we took action. I don't recall referring to our change project as *reengineering,* but whatever it was, it worked. Our new system is more aerodynamic: It's quicker, it's more responsive, it allows us to close earlier—and, most important, it's *cheaper* We like that."

Daniel P. Keegan is a partner and national director of performance measurement for Price Waterhouse in the Cleveland office. He holds an MBA degree in operations research from the University of Pittsburgh.

Robert G. Eiler is partner and national director of cost management for Price Waterhouse in the Cleveland office. He holds an MBA degree from Washington University. The two authors are members of the Cleveland Chapter, through which this article was submitted. They can be reached at (216) 781-3700.

Notes

1. Robert G. Eiler, Walter K. Goletz, and Daniel P. Keegan, "Is Your Cost Accounting Up to Date?" *Harvard Business Review,* July–August 1982, pp. 133–139.

2. Robert G. Eiler, Charles R. Jones. and Daniel P. Keegan, "To Implement Your Strategies, Change Your Measurements," *PW Review,* No. 1, 1991. For a copy of this article call Daniel P. Keegan at (216) 781-3700. Also see

Daniel P. Keegan, Robert G. Eiler and Charles R. Jones, "Are Your Performance Measures Obsolete?" MANAGEMENT ACCOUNTING®, June 1989, pp. 45–50.

3. Daniel P. Keegan and Susannah W. Pesci, "Why Not Reengineer the Management Process Itself?" *Journal of Cost Management,* Summer 1994, pp. 63–70.

From D. P. Keegan and R. G. Eiler, "Let's Reengineer Cost Accounting," *Management Accounting* (August 1994): 26–31. Reprinted with permission.

Questions

1.3a What are some of the criticisms of ABC systems that Keegan and Eiler say that companies have mentioned. Do you think these criticisms are justified? Explain.

1.3b According to Keegan and Eiler, a number of actions can be taken to reengineer traditional costing systems. Discuss three of these.

CHAPTER 2

The Organization as a System of Activity

John Shank and Vijay Govindarajan's article, *Strategic Cost Management and the Value Chain* (Reading 2.1), begins the series of articles related to Chapter Two. The article discusses the value chain concept as the central building block of strategic cost management. Management accounting methods such as activity-based costing and other tools can be incorporated into the value chain concept. The authors illustrate their method of developing a value chain within an organization and then use a case study of the paper industry to illustrate their argument.

In *ABC and High Technology: A Story with a Moral,* (Reading 2.1), Frank Selto and Dale Jasinski discuss their case study of a small high technology company's experience in attempting to implement activity-based costing. DataCom, a premier supplier of computer communication links to mainframe computer original equipment manufacturers (OEM), was a fast-growing firm. During the late 1980s, the company lost its major OEM partner, which led to a steady decline in its business. In 1992, the company embarked on a new strategic plan to revitalize itself. The plan included the creation of three decentralized business units from the existing centralized operation. Part of this plan involved the implementation of ABC to better analyze and cost support services to all three units. Unfortunately, as the article chronicles, the ABC effort failed due to lack of top management support in the form of necessary resources and the lack of initiative of one of the system's key supporters, the CFO. Selto and Jasinski conclude that unless ABC is truly integrated and accepted as part of the strategic plan, management accounting will always be relegated to its traditional scorekeeping function.

Based on discussions with many managers who have adopted the just-in-time manufacturing philosophy and method, George Foster and Charles Horngren's article, *Cost Accounting and Cost Management in a JIT Environment,* (Reading 2.3), raises a number of issues relating to how management accounting must change to accommodate the use of JIT. Since JIT changes many of the activities that underlie the manufacturing process, management accounting systems have to change in order to provide relevant information for decision-making. For example, JIT can greatly reduce or eliminate the traditional purchasing function, change the flow of production activities, and increase the direct traceability of many indirect costs. If a traditional management accounting system is used with JIT, many of the benefits of the system will be lost. For more background on the behavioral and organizational issues relating to JIT and other Japanese manufacturing practices, a related reading from Chapter Fifteen (Reading 15.4), Mark Young's *"A Framework for Successful Adoption and Performance of Japanese Manufacturing Practices in the United States,"* is recommended.

2.1 Strategic Cost Management and the Value Chain

John K. Shank and Vijay Govindarajan

The value chain for any firm in any business is the linked set of value-creating activities—from basic raw material sources to the ultimate product or service that is delivered to consumers. This article explains how to construct and use value chains. It uses a real-world study from the airline industry to highlight the fact that the strategic cost management (SCM) insights that emerge from value chain analysis are different from—and better than—the insights available from traditional management accounting approaches.

This article begins by defining the value chain concept, contrasting it with the value-added notion, and demonstrating its power. Then, the methodology for constructing and using a value chain is introduced. The case study is presented to illustrate the power of value chain analysis. The final part of the article explains how the value chain concept is the overarching framework for strategic cost management and how activity-based costing and similar cost management tools can be usefully accommodated within the value chain concept.

One of the major themes in strategic cost management (SCM) concerns the focus of cost management efforts: How does a firm organize its thinking about cost management? In the SCM framework, managing costs effectively requires a broad focus that Michael Porter calls the "value chain"—i.e., the linked set of value-creating activities.[1] This focus is external to the firm, with each firm viewed in the context of the overall chain of value-creating activities of which it is only a part, from basic raw material to end-use consumers.

In contrast, traditional management accounting adopts a focus that is largely internal to the firm, with each firm viewed in the context of its purchases, its processes, its functions, its products, and its customers. In other words, management accounting takes a value-added perspective that starts with payments to suppliers (purchases) and stops with charges to customers (sales). The key theme is to maximize the difference (i.e., *the value added*) between purchases and sales. The strategic insights yielded by value chain analysis, however, differ significantly from—and are superior to—those suggested by value-added analysis.

THE CONCEPT

Porter notes that a business can develop a sustainable competitive advantage by following one of two strategies:[2]

- A low-cost strategy; or
- A differentiation strategy.

Low-cost strategy. The primary focus of a low-cost strategy is to achieve low cost relative to competitors (i.e., cost leadership). Cost leadership can be achieved through such approaches as:

- Economies of scale in production;
- Experience curve effects;
- Tight cost control; and
- Cost minimization in such areas as research and development (R&D), service, sales force, or advertising.

Firms that have followed this strategy include Texas Instruments in consumer electronics, Emerson Electric in electric motors, Hyundai in automobiles, Briggs and Stratton in gasoline engines, Black and Decker in machine tools, Commodore in business machines, K-Mart in retailing, BIC in pens, and Timex in wrist watches.

Differentiation strategy. The primary focus of a differentiation strategy is to create something that customers perceive as being unique. Product uniqueness can be achieved through such approaches as brand loyalty (Coca Cola in soft drinks), superior customer service (IBM in computers), dealer network (Caterpillar Tractors in construction equipment), product design and product features (Hewlett-Packard in electronics), or technology (Coleman in camping equipment). Some firms that have followed a differentiation strategy include Mercedes Benz in automobiles, Stouffer's in frozen foods, Neiman-Marcus in retailing, Cross in pens, and Rolex in wrist watches.

Whether or not a firm can develop and sustain cost leadership or differentiation depends fundamentally on how the firm manages its own value chain relative to those of its competitors. Both intuitively and theoretically, competitive advantage in the marketplace ultimately derives from providing better customer value for equivalent cost or equivalent customer value for a lower cost. Thus, value chain analysis is essential to determine exactly where in the firm's segment of the chain—from design to distribution—costs can be lowered or customer value enhanced.

THE VALUE CHAIN FRAMEWORK

The value chain framework is a method for breaking down the chain—from basic raw materials to end-use customers—into strategically relevant activities in order to understand the behavior of costs and the sources of differentiation. As noted earlier, a firm is typically only one part of the larger set of activities in the value delivery system. Suppliers not only produce and deliver inputs used in a firm's value activities, but they importantly influence the firm's cost or differentiation position as well. Similarly, distribution channels have a significant impact on a firm's value activities.

As is discussed more fully below, gaining and sustaining a competitive advantage require that a firm understands the *entire* value delivery system, not just the portion of the value chain in which it participates. Suppliers and distribution channels have profit margins that are important to identify in understanding a firm's cost or differentiation positioning, because end-use customers ultimately pay for all the profit margins throughout the value chain.

STRATEGIC IMPLICATIONS

Exhibit 1 provides a conceptual value chain for the paper industry. The distinct value activities (such as timber, logging, pulp mills, paper mills, and conversion plants) are the building blocks by which this industry creates a product of value to buyers. It is possible to quantify the economic value created at each stage by identifying the costs, revenues, and assets for each activity. Every firm in Exhibit 1—*A, B, C,*

EXHIBIT 1
VALUE CHAIN IN THE PAPER PRODUCTS INDUSTRY

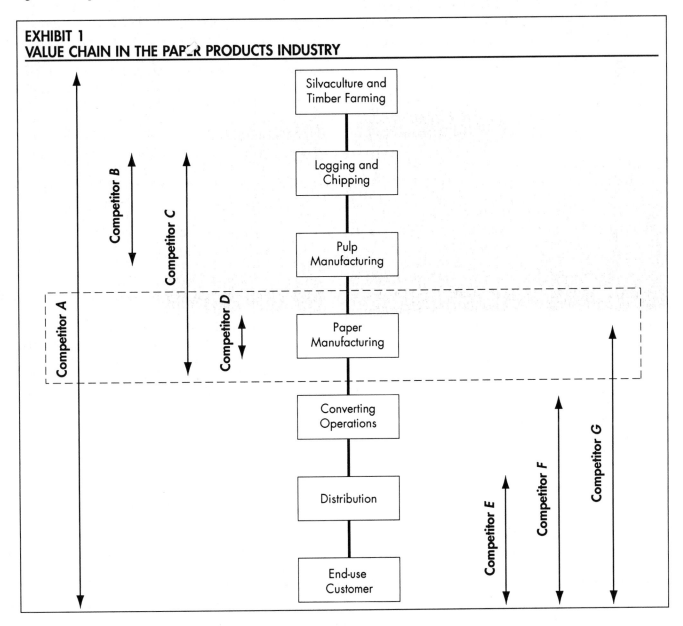

D, E, F, and G—must construct a value chain for the total paper industry, breaking the total value in the chain into its fundamental sources of economic value. Such an analysis has potential strategic implications for every competitor in this industry:

- If competitor A (a fully integrated company) calculates the return on assets (ROA) at each stage of the chain by adjusting all transfer prices to competitive market levels, it could highlight potential areas where the firm could more economically buy from the outside (which is the strategic choice of make versus buy). For example, most "fully integrated" forest product companies still use independent loggers to cut their trees on the way to their mills.
- With a complete value chain, competitors B, C, D, E, F, and G might be able to identify possibilities to integrate forward or backward into areas that can enhance their performance. Westvaco, for example, has stopped manufacturing envelope paper, although it still owns a large envelope converter. Champion International has sold its envelope converting business but still produces envelope paper.
- Each value activity has a set of unique cost drivers that explain variations in costs in that activity.[3] Thus, each value activity has its unique sources of competitive advantage. Companies are likely to face a different set of competitors at each stage: Some of these competitors would be fully integrated companies, and some of them would be more narrowly focused specialists. For example, company D faces competition from A, C, and G in the paper manufacturing stage. Yet A, C, and G bring very different competitive advantage to this stage of the value chain vis-à-vis D. It is possible for D to compete effectively with A, C, and G only by understanding the total value chain and the cost drivers that regulate each activity. For example, if "scope" (vertical integration) is a key structural driver of paper mill cost, A has a significant advantage, and D a significant disadvantage in this marketplace.
- The value chain analysis helps to quantify buyer power (for B, C, and D) and supplier power (for E, F, and G) by calculating the percentage of total profits that can be attributed to each stage in that chain. This calculation can help firms identify ways to exploit linkages with both their suppliers and their customers to reduce costs, enhance differentiation, or both.

VALUE CHAIN VS. VALUE-ADDED ANALYSIS

The value chain concept can be contrasted with the internal focus that typically is adopted in management accounting. Management accounting usually takes a value-added per-

spective, as noted earlier. From a strategic perspective, the value-added concept has two big disadvantages:

1. It starts too late; and
2. It stops too soon.

Starting cost analysis with purchases misses all the opportunities for exploiting linkages with the firm's suppliers. Such opportunities can be dramatically important to a firm.

SUPPLIER LINKAGES

The differences between a value chain perspective and a value-added perspective can be seen clearly in the context of scheduling problems that can arise if a firm ignores the complete value chain. The automobile industry provides a good example.

A few years ago, a major U.S. automobile manufacturer began to implement just-in-time (JIT) management concepts in its assembly plants. Assembly costs represented 30 percent of sales. The company reasoned that use of JIT would eliminate 20 percent of these costs, because assembly costs in Japanese automobile plants were known to be more than 20 percent below those in U.S. plants. As the firm began to manage its factories differently in order to eliminate inventory buffers and waste, its assembly costs began to drop noticeably. But the firm experienced dramatic problems with its major suppliers, who began to demand price increases that more than offset the savings in the assembly plants. The automobile firm's first response was to chide its suppliers and tell them that they, too, needed to embrace JIT concepts for their own operations.

A value chain perspective revealed a much different picture of the overall situation. Of the automobile company's sales, 50 percent were purchases from parts suppliers. Of this amount, 37 percent were purchases by the parts suppliers, and the remaining 63 percent was value added by the suppliers. Thus, suppliers actually were *adding* more manufacturing value to the automobiles than the assembly plants (63 percent × 50 percent = 31.5 percent, versus 30 percent). By reducing buffer inventory and requiring JIT deliveries by suppliers, the company had placed major strains on its suppliers. As a result, the suppliers' aggregate manufacturing costs went up more than the company's assembly costs went down.

The reason, once identified, was very simple. The assembly plants experienced huge and uncertain variability in their production schedules. One week ahead of actual production, the master schedule was more than 25 percent wrong 95 percent of the time. When inventory buffers are stripped away from a highly unpredictable production process, the manufacturing activities of the suppliers become a nightmare. For every dollar of manufacturing cost that the assembly plants saved by moving toward JIT management concepts, the suppliers' plants spent much more than one dollar extra because of the schedule instability.

Because of its narrow, value-added perspective, the automobile company had overlooked the ramifications that its scheduling changes had on its suppliers' costs. Management had ignored the fact that JIT requires a partnership with suppliers. A major factor in the success of JIT at a Japanese automobile assembly plant is stable scheduling for suppliers. Whereas the U.S. plant regularly missed schedules only one week in the future by 25 percent or more, Japanese plants vary by 1 percent—or less—from schedules that are planned four weeks in advance.

A failure to adopt a value chain perspective doomed this major effort to failure; ignorance of supply chain cost analysis concepts on the part of the automobile company's management accountants proved very costly. These scheduling ramifications might have been handled better if management accountants in the automobile industry had been taught value chain concepts somewhere in their accounting education.

Beneficial linkages (i.e., linkages with suppliers and customers that are managed in such a way that all parties benefit) can also be tracked more accurately with value chain analysis rather than with value-added analysis. For example, when bulk chocolate began to be delivered as a liquid in tank cars instead of as ten-pound, molded bars of chocolate, industrial chocolate companies (i.e., the suppliers) eliminated the cost of molding bars and packing them, but they also saved candy makers the cost and trouble of unpacking and melting the solid bars of chocolate.[4]

CUSTOMER LINKAGES

In addition to starting too late, value-added analysis has another major flaw: It stops too soon. Customer linkages can be just as important as supplier linkages; stopping cost analysis at the point of sale eliminates all opportunities for exploiting linkages with customers.

Exploiting customer linkages is the key idea behind the concept of life-cycle costing. *Life-cycle costing* is a costing concept that argues for including all the costs incurred for a product—from the time when a product is conceived until it is abandoned—as part of the product cost. Life-cycle costing thus deals explicitly with the relationship between what a customer pays for a product and the total cost that the customer incurs over the life of the product. A life-cycle costing perspective on the customer linkage in the value chain can lead to enhanced profitability. Explicit attention to post-purchase costs by the customer can lead to more effective market segmentation and product positioning. Designing a product to reduce post-purchase costs of the customer can be a major weapon in capturing competitive advantage. In many ways, the lower life cycle cost of imported Japanese automobiles helps to explain their success in the U.S. market.

There are other examples in which the linkage between a firm and its customer is designed to be mutually beneficial and the relationship with the customer is viewed not as a zero-sum game but as a mutually beneficial one. A case in point is the container industry. Some container producers have constructed manufacturing facilities near beer breweries and deliver the containers through overhead conveyers directly onto the customers' assembly line. This practice results in significant cost reductions for both the container producers and their customers by expediting the transport of empty containers, which are bulky and heavy.[5]

MISSED OPPORTUNITIES

Just as many cost management problems are misunderstood because of failure to see the impact on the overall value chain, many management opportunities are missed in the same way. The paper industry again provides an example of these missed opportunities when a value-added, rather than a value chain, analysis is applied.

In the late 1980s, U.S. suppliers of paper to envelope converters lost profits because they were caught unawares by a significant change in the value chain of the envelope converter. The shift from sheet-fed to roll-fed envelope finishing machines had dramatically changed the raw material specifications for envelope paper.

Although roll-fed machines were not introduced in the United States until around 1980, today they produce more than 60 percent of all domestic envelopes. Roll-fed machines—which are far more expensive to buy, but much less expensive to operate, than sheet-fed machines—can bring substantial overall savings for envelope converters, especially when large volumes of envelopes are produced.

With sheet-fed machines, an envelope company buys large rolls of paper 40–60 inches wide, which are cut into sheets, cut into blanks in die-cutting machines, and finally fed by hand into folding-and-gluing machines. With roll-fed machines, however, the envelope company buys narrow rolls of paper 5–11 inches wide, which are converted directly into envelopes in one combined operation.

Paper manufacturers do not want to complicate their primary manufacturing process by producing the narrow rolls directly on the paper machines. Instead, they use secondary machines called "rewinder slitters" to convert the large rolls of paper from the paper machines into the narrower rolls that the converters who use roll-fed machines now want. Thus, the transition from selling wide rolls to selling narrow rolls has added an additional processing step for the paper manufacturers. The business issue, therefore, is how the change in the customers' (i.e., the envelope company's) value chain should be reflected in paper prices now that manufacturing costs along the value chain have increased because of the envelope company's changed requirements.

Management accounting in the paper industry takes neither value chain analysis nor life-cycle costing into account. Consequently, the additional costs for the rewinder slitter machines are considered just a small part of mill overhead, which is assigned to all paper production on a per-ton basis. For a large, modern paper mill, rewinder slitter cost ranges from 1–7 percent of total cost. The impact on total average cost per ton is less than $10. Little of this cost is variable with incremental production, because the mill always keeps excess capacity in such a small department. (It is only common sense to make sure that $300 million paper machines are never slowed down by a bottleneck at a $2 million rewinder slitter machine.)

The industry norm is to charge $11 per ton extra if the customer wants the rolls slit to the narrow widths (i.e., 11 inches or less). The savings to the envelope converter from roll-fed machines far exceed this extra charge. Unfortunately, the full cost to the paper mill of providing the incremental rewinder slitting service also far exceeds this extra charge. It can cost more than $100 per ton to have an outside subcontractor slit rolls to narrow widths. An external value chain perspective would look at the savings from narrow rolls for the customer and the extra costs to the paper mill and set a price differential somewhere in between. An internal mill costing perspective, however, sees no cost issue at all.

The lack of a value chain perspective contributes to the lack of concern about product costing issues. The $11 surcharge looks like pure extra contribution to profit. The result is an uneconomic price, the impact of which is buried in a mill management accounting system that ignores value chain issues. The opportunity to more accurately price might not have been missed if the management accountants in the paper companies (like their colleagues in the automobile and candy industries) had been exposed to value chain concepts somewhere in their management accounting education.

A FRAMEWORK OF INTERDEPENDENCE

The value chain framework highlights how a firm's products fit into the buyer's value chain. Under this framework, for example, it is readily apparent what percentage the firm's product costs are in relation to the ultimate buyer's total costs. The fact that paper constitutes over 40 percent of the total costs of a magazine is very useful in encouraging the paper mill and the publisher to cooperate on cost-reduction activities.

Unlike the value-added concept, value chain analysis explicitly recognizes the fact that the various activities within a firm are not independent but, rather, interdependent. At McDonald's, for example, the timing of promotional campaigns (one value activity) significantly influences capacity utilization in "production" (another value activity). These linked activities must be coordinated if the full effect of a promotion is to be realized. As another example, Japanese producers of videocassette recorders (VCRs) were able to reduce prices from $1,300 in 1977 to $298 by 1984 by emphasizing the impact of an early step in the chain (product design) on a later step (production) by drastically reducing the number of parts in VCRs.[6]

Conventional management accounting approaches tend to emphasize across-the-board cost reductions. By recognizing interdependencies, however, value chain analysis admits to the possibility that deliberately increasing costs in one value activity can bring about a reduction in total costs. The expense that Procter & Gamble incurred to place order-entry computers directly in Wal-Mart stores, for example, significantly reduced overall order-entry and processing costs for both firms.

THE METHODOLOGY

The value chain concept just described has a unique methodology. Its methodology involves the following steps:

1. Identify the industry's value chain, then assign costs, revenues, and assets to value activities;
2. Diagnose the cost drivers regulating each value activity; and
3. Develop sustainable competitive advantage, either through controlling cost drivers better than competitors or by reconfiguring the value chain.

These steps are considered in greater detail in the following sections.

IDENTIFYING THE VALUE CHAIN

The first step in constructing and using a value chain is to identify the industry's value chain. This step must be executed with the idea of gaining competitive advantage, for competitive advantage cannot be meaningfully examined at the level of the industry as a whole.

A value chain desegregates an industry into its distinct strategic activities. Therefore, the starting point for cost analysis is to define an industry's value chain, then to assign costs, revenues, and assets to the various value activities. These activities are the building blocks with which firms in the industry create a product that buyers find valuable.

Activities should be isolated and separated if they satisfy any or all of the following conditions:

- They represent a significant percentage of operating costs;
- The cost behavior of the activities (or the cost drivers) is different;
- They are performed by competitors in different ways; and
- They are likely to create differentiation.

Each value activity incurs costs, generates revenues, and ties up assets in the process.

After identifying the value chain, operating costs, revenues, and assets must be assigned to individual value activities. For intermediate value activities, revenues should be assigned by adjusting internal transfer prices to competitive

22

market prices. With this information, it should be possible to calculate ROA for each value activity.

DIAGNOSING COST DRIVERS

The second step in constructing and using a value chain is to diagnose the cost drivers that explain variations in costs in each value activity.

In conventional management accounting, cost is primarily a function of only one cost driver: output volume. Cost concepts related to output volume—fixed versus variable cost, average cost versus marginal cost, cost-volume-profit analysis, break-even analysis, flexible budgets, and contribution margin, to name a few—permeate the thinking and the writing about cost.

In the value chain framework, by contrast, output volume per se is seen to capture little of the richness of cost behavior. Rather, multiple cost drivers are usually at work. Further, cost drivers differ across value activities. For example, number of orders received is the cost driver for the receiving activity, number of setups is the cost driver for the production control activity, and number of orders shipped is the cost driver for the shipping activity.

Attempts have been made to create a comprehensive list of cost drivers.[7] In the strategic management literature, in particular, good lists of cost drivers exist.[8] Following these lists, the following list of cost drivers is divided into two categories:

- Structural cost drivers; and
- Executional cost drivers.

These two categories are discussed in the sections below. An attempt is also made below to define which drivers in these two categories can be considered "fundamental" cost drivers.

STRUCTURAL COST DRIVERS

The first category of cost drivers, structural cost drivers, draws on industrial organization literature.[9] *Structural cost drivers* derive from a company's choices about its underlying economic structure. These choices drive cost positions for any given product group. There are at least five strategic choices that a firm must make about its underlying economic structure:

1. *Scale:* What is the size of the investment to be made in manufacturing, R&D, and marketing resources?
2. *Scope:* What is the degree of vertical integration? (Horizontal integration is more related to scale.)
3. *Experience:* How many times in the past has the firm already done what it is doing again?
4. *Technology:* What process technologies are used in each step of the firm's value chain?
5. *Complexity:* How wide a line of products or services is being offered to customers?

Each structural driver involves choices that drive product cost. Given certain assumptions, the cost calculus of each structural driver can be specified.[10]

Recently, much interest has arisen over activity-based costing (ABC).[11] The ABC analysis is largely a framework to operationalize complexity, which is a fundamental cost driver.

EXECUTIONAL COST DRIVERS

The second category of cost drivers, *executional cost drivers,* are those determinants of a firm's cost position that hinge on its ability to "execute" successfully.

Whereas structural cost drivers are not monotonically scaled with performance, executional drivers are. That is, for each of the structural drivers, more is not always better. Thus, for example, there are diseconomies of scale or of scope: A more complex product line is not necessarily better or necessarily worse than a less complex line. Too much experience can be as bad as too little in a dynamic environment. Texas Instruments, for example, emphasized the learning curve and became the world's lowest-cost producer of obsolete microchips. Technological leadership versus "followership" is a legitimate choice for most firms.

In contrast, for each one of the executional cost drivers, more is *always* better. The list of basic executional cost drivers includes at least the following:

- *Work force involvement ("participation"):* Is the work force committed to continuous improvement (*kaizen* in Japanese)?
- *Total quality management (TQM):* Is the work force committed to total product quality?
- *Capacity utilization:* What are the scale choices on maximum plant construction?
- *Plant layout efficiency:* How efficient, against current norms, is the plant's layout?
- *Product configuration:* Is the design or formulation of the product effective?
- *Linkages with suppliers or customers:* Is the linkage with suppliers or customers exploited, according to the firm's value chain?

Quantifying the effects of each of these drivers also involves specific cost-analysis issues. Many strategic planners maintain that SCM is moving quickly away from structural drivers and toward executional drivers because the insights from analyses based on structural drivers are too often obsolete and, hence, ineffective.

FUNDAMENTAL COST DRIVERS

No consensus currently exists on what constitutes "fundamental" cost drivers. One publication, for example, offers two different lists of fundamental cost drivers.[12] Those who see cost behavior in strategic terms, however, agree that output volume alone cannot catch all aspects of cost behavior. Ultimately, how unit costs change because of changes in output volume in the short run is seen as a less interesting question than how a company's cost position is influenced by the firm's comparative position on the various drivers that are relevant in its competitive situation.

Whatever items are on the list of "fundamental" cost drivers, the key ideas are as follows:

1. *Value chain as the broader framework.* The concept of cost drivers is a way to understand cost behavior in each activity in the value chain. Thus, ideas such as ABC are only a subset of the value chain framework.
2. *Volume is not enough.* For strategic analysis, volume is usually not the most useful way to explain cost behavior.
3. *Structural choices and executional skills.* What is more useful in a strategic sense is to explain cost position in terms of the structural choices and executional skills that shape the firm's competitive position. For example, Michael Porter[13] analyzes the classic confrontation in 1962 between General Electric and Westinghouse regarding steam turbines in terms of the structural and executional cost drivers for each firm.
4. *Relevant strategic drivers.* Not all strategic drivers are equally important all the time, though several are probably important in every case. For example, Porter develops a strategic assessment of du Pont's position in titanium dioxide, based primarily on scale and capacity utilization issues.[14]
5. *Cost analysis framework.* For each cost driver, a particular cost analysis framework is critical to understanding the positioning of a firm.
6. *Cost drivers specific to activities.* Different activities in the value chain are usually influenced by different cost drivers. For example, the relevant cost driver for advertising is market share, whereas promotional costs are usually variable. For example, Coca Cola can realize economies of scale in advertising because of its large market share. A price-off by contrast (an example of a sales promotion activity), is strictly a variable cost per unit.

DEVELOPING SUSTAINABLE COMPETITIVE ADVANTAGE

The third step in constructing and using a value chain is to develop sustainable competitive advantage. Once a firm has identified the industry's value chain and diagnosed the cost drivers of each value activity, sustainable competitive advantage can be gained either by controlling those drivers better than competitors or by reconfiguring the value chain.

For each value activity, the key questions to ask about developing sustainable competitive advantage are:

1. Can costs in this activity be reduced, holding value (revenues) constant?

2. Can value (revenue) be increased in this activity, holding costs constant?

COST REDUCTION

By systematically analyzing costs, revenues, and assets in each activity, the firm can achieve both differentiation and low cost. An effective way to accomplish this goal is to compare the value chain of the firm with the value chains of one or two of its major competitors, then identify the actions needed to manage the firm's value chain better than competitors manage their value chains.

VALUE INCREASE

While continuing the focus on managing the existing value chain better than competitors, a company should devote more effort toward identifying where in the value chain payoffs could be significant. For example, in the mature and highly competitive meat packing industry, Iowa Beef Processors has performed exceptionally well by controlling its processing, distribution, and labor costs. It accomplished these cost reductions by redefining the traditional value chain in this industry:

"Earnings per share [of Iowa Beef Processors] have soared at a compound annual rate of over 23 percent since 1973. The company has achieved this remarkable record by never wavering from its strategy and obsession—to be the low-cost producer of beef.

To that end, it rewrote the rules for killing, chilling, and shipping beef. It built plants on a grand scale, automated them to a fare-thee-well, and now spends up to $20 million a year on renovation to keep them operating efficiently. The old-line packers shipped live animals to the abattoirs at such rail centers as Chicago, but Iowa Beef brought the plant to the cattle in the sprawling feedlots of the High Plains and Southwest. This saved on transportation and avoided the weight loss that commonly occurs when live animals are shipped. Iowa Beef also led the industry in cleaving and trimming carcasses into loins, ribs, and other cuts, and boxing the pieces at the plant, which further reduced transport charges by removing excess weight.

The company has fought tenaciously to hold down labor costs. Though some of its plants are unionized, it refused to pay the wages called for in the United Food & Commercial Workers' expensive master agreement, which the elders of the industry have been tied to for forty years. Iowa Beef's wages and benefits average half those of less hard-nosed competitors."[15]

It is not suggested here that constructing a value chain for a firm is easy, as the above details demonstrate. There are several thorny problems to confront: calculating value for intermediate products, isolating cost drivers, identifying linkages across activities, and computing supplier and channel margins, for example. Despite these problems, it is in every firm's self-interest to construct its value chain. The very process of performing the value chain analysis can be quite instructive. Such an exercise forces managers to ask: "How does my activity add value to the chain of customers who use my product or service?"

POWER OF VALUE CHAIN ANALYSIS: A CASE STUDY

This section presents a case to illustrate the value chain concept and methodology. This study also demonstrates how value chain analysis differs from conventional management accounting analysis.

In the study, the cost and differentiation positioning of two firms from the airline industry are contrasted by comparing the cost per seat mile of these two airlines in the different components of their value chains. The analysis offered is based on the published financial statements of the firms discussed.

The value chains of airline competitors are described in both qualitative and quantitative terms. Generally, it can be said that all commercial airlines provide value to customers at the following three stages:

1. By providing reservation information and ticketing services;
2. By operating the aircraft from point A to point B; and
3. By providing other services to passengers before a flight, during a flight, and after a flight arrives.

Each element in the value chain utilizes specific assets and has a specific cost function. Overall return on investment is a result of value added at all three linked stages.

Conventional financial reports reveal nothing about the separate value-creating activities in which the airline is engaged. Exhibit 2 shows a disguised and condensed version of the published income statements and balance sheets of one of the major trunk airlines (which here is fictitiously called Ajax Airlines). The statements clearly reveal much that is interesting about the company—but nothing about the value chain. Combining the financial statements with a du Pont analysis (as shown in Exhibit 3) can yield conventional insights, but not much about business strategy.

PROFIT MARGINS

The du Pont analysis reveals (for one thing) that profit margins at Ajax improved along with sales. That is, the airline was able to sell more tickets, while operating expense declined per dollar of sales. Asset utilization—a critical factor in the airline industry—also improved, as the improved asset turnover (from 0.857 to 0.917 in Exhibit 3) shows. All the while, financial leverage remained constant. So it appears that Ajax Airlines was able to improve both margins and asset utilization, while holding financial risk constant. It would appear that management has done a good job and should continue with its apparently successful growth strategy.

But *how* has Ajax grown? And how has the company been able to earn greater margins at a higher level of sales? Where has Ajax added capacity to improve asset utilization?

EXHIBIT 2
AJAX AIRLINES FINANCIAL DATA

Statements of Income	1988	1987
Sales	$8,800	$7,200
Expenses		
Salaries and benefits	$2,900	$2,400
Aircraft fuel	1,100	1,000
Fleet operations cost (lease and depreciation)	3,900	3,200
Total operating expenses	$7,900	$6,600
Operating income	$900	$600
Interest expense	230	200
Tax	335	200
Net income	$335	$200
Balance Sheets		
Current assets	$2,600	$2,100
Property and equipment	7,000	6,300
Total assets	$9,600	$8,400
Current liabilities	$2,700	$2,000
Long-term debt	3,000	3,000
Equity3,900	3,900	3,400
Total liabilities	$9,600	$8,400

And, finally, what strategy is Ajax pursuing? Financial statement analysis provides no answers to these questions.

TRADITIONAL MANAGEMENT ACCOUNTING ANALYSIS

Traditional management accounting provides additional information about Ajax Airlines, though it also ignores a value chain perspective. Traditional cost accounting would suggest that, in an industry such as the airline industry with high fixed costs, contribution analysis is the key. The argument would be that, because fleet cost and compensation for pilots, flight attendants, and ground personnel do not depend on volume in the short run, the airline strategy should be to fill up capacity by aggressive pricing. Once the break-even point is met, most of every incremental dollar of revenue goes straight to the bottom line, because incremental variable cost is probably confined mainly to fuel and food.

EXHIBIT 3
AJAX AIRLINES DU PONT ANALYSIS

	Net income Sales	×	Sales Assets	×	Assets Equity	=	Net Income Equity
1988	$\frac{\$335}{\$8,800}$	×	$\frac{\$8,800}{\$9,600}$	×	$\frac{\$9,600}{\$3,900}$	=	$\frac{\$335}{\$3,900}$
	0.038	×	0.917	×	2.46	=	0.086
1987	$\frac{\$200}{\$7,200}$	×	$\frac{\$7,200}{\$8,400}$	×	$\frac{\$8,400}{\$3,400}$	=	$\frac{\$200}{\$3,400}$
	0.028	×	0.857	×	2.47	=	0.059

25

EXHIBIT 4
AJAX AIRLINES CONTRIBUTION ANALYSIS

	1988	1987
Additional Information		
Seat miles flown	65,000	57,000
Available seat miles	102,000	89,000
Asset utilization (load factor realized)	64%	64%
Revenue per seat mile flown	$0.135	$0.126
Compensation per seat mile flown	$0.045	$0.042
Fuel per seat mile flown	0.017	0.018
Fleet operations cost per seat mile flown	0.060	0.056
Total $0.122	$0.122	$0.116
Operating profit per seat mile	$0.013	$0.010
Contribution margin per seat mile flown	$0.118	$0.108
Break-even level	$\frac{\$6,800}{\$0.118} = \$57,600$	$\frac{\$5,600}{\$0.108} = \$51,900$
Break-even percent of available capacity	56.5%	58.3%

Given additional information that is usually supplied in the annual report of most major airline companies, the traditional contribution analysis for a firm can be constructed. Exhibit 4 shows that analysis for Ajax Airlines using seat miles flown as the per-unit metric.

Since incremental cost in the short run is very low, traditional managerial accountants would recommend filling up the unused capacity (as shown in Exhibit 4) at almost any price. But the supplementary financial data show that Ajax Airlines did not pursue this objective. Ajax Airlines was able to charge significantly more for each seat mile flown without improving utilization of the available seat miles, because seat miles flown at capacity utilization stayed constant at 64 percent. This conflicts, moreover, with conclusions drawn from Exhibit 3. That analysis shows that asset utilization improved, while traditional management accounting concludes that it remained constant. This conflict resurfaces when other factors are analyzed, as is discussed next.

FURTHER MANAGEMENT
ACCOUNTING ANALYSIS

The management accounting analysis in Exhibit 4 reveals that, for the same capacity utilization, Ajax Airlines was able to charge a higher price per seat mile flown while paying more for compensation and equipment (compensation per seat mile rose from $0.042 to $0.045, while fleet operations cost per seat mile rose from 5.6 cents to 6.0 cents). This suggests that, by improving the quality of service and the quality of equipment used, Ajax was able to charge higher prices. Although this conclusion may correspond to what happened, there is no way to be sure that this was the strategy that Ajax actually pursued. (In fact, it probably is not what happened.) Moreover, how can the contradictory conclusions about asset utilization from the two different analyses be explained? Also, should the extra revenue from the unused seats flow straight to the bottom line (as both analyses would seem to suggest)?

In an attempt to understand these problems, quite different insights can be gleaned from a value chain analysis, as shown in Exhibit 5. Clearly, Ajax Airlines invested heavily in ticketing and reservations (T&R), probably to improve its computerized reservations system. And—despite a 14 percent increase in seat miles flown (i.e., from 57,000 in 1987 to 65,000 in 1988, as Exhibit 4 shows)—T&R cost per seat mile flown held constant at $0.005 (see the "Costs" section near the bottom of Exhibit 5), though T&R cost is hardly a fixed cost. Presumably, Ajax Airlines is willing to

EXHIBIT 5
AJAX AIRLINES VALUE CHAIN ANALYSIS

Sales	1988	1987
	$8,800	$7,200
Tickets and reservations	320	300
Aircraft operations	4,980	3,900
Customer service	2,600	2,400
Total expenses	$7,900	$6,600

Identifiable Property, Plant, and Equipment (PPE) Assets		
Tickets and reservations	$2,000	$1,000
Aircraft operations	5,000	5,300
Customer service	0	0
Total	$7,000	$6,300

	Per Seat Mile Flown		Per Available Mile	
	1988	1987	1988	1987
Costs				
Tickets and reservations	$0.005	$0.005	$0.003	$0.003
Aircraft operations	0.077	0.068	0.049	0.044
Customer service	0.040	0.043	0.025	0.027
Total	$0.122	$0.116	$0.077	$0.074
Assets				
Tickets and reservations	$0.030	$0.020	$0.020	$0.010
Aircraft	0.080	0.090	0.050	0.060
Customer service	0	0	0	0
Total	$0.110	$0.110	$0.070	$0.070

26

increase T&R costs and assets as a strategic investment in better service.

A value chain analysis also shows that operating an aircraft is not purely a fixed cost, as traditional management accounting suggests. While the number of seat miles flown increased by 14 percent, operating expenses increased by 28 percent (i.e., from $3,900 to $4,980, as the line item labeled "Aircraft operations" in Exhibit 5 shows), so this figure is obviously not a fixed cost. Clearly, therefore, cost drivers other than capacity utilization are at work here, and management evidently does not control them.

The reduction in the asset base (see the line item "Aircraft operations" in Exhibit 5 under the category "Identifiable Property, Plant, and Equipment") is presumed to reflect one more year's depreciation on the aging fleet rather than a strategic change in fleet configuration. Also, it is interesting that cost per seat mile flown has risen about 13 percent (i.e., from $0.068 to $0.077—see the line item "Aircraft operations" in Exhibit 5 under the category "Costs" near the bottom of the exhibit). This is an element in the value chain that seems not to translate easily into value to the customer— the part, that is, that simply involves getting from point A to point B. Apparently, Ajax Airlines has raised the price per seat mile flown mostly to compensate for an increase in fleet operating expenses that has no clear strategic justification.

Customer service expense per seat mile flown has dropped from $0.043 to $0.040. As a straight fixed cost, this expense should have dropped to $0.038 ($0.043 ÷ 1.14, where 1.14 adjusts for the 14 percent increase in seat miles flown), so Ajax Airlines is spending a little more on this activity, as adjusted for volume.

Strategically, Ajax Airlines seems to be hoping that a small increase in aggregate (but not per-unit) customer service expenditures and a better T&R system will justify higher prices in an aging fleet. But increased aircraft operations costs offset most of the profit impact of the increase in revenue per seat mile flown from $0.126 in 1987 to $0.135 in 1988 (see "Revenue/seat mile" in Exhibit 4). This result hardly seems to fit the "success story" told by the traditional management accounting analysis. Value chain analysis, however, can yield different insights. The linking of traditional financial analysis with strategic positioning in this way is a critical element in effective financial analysis.

COMPARATIVE ANALYSIS

It should be noted that the ability to present value chain analyses that are comparative across competing firms increases the value of the technique. Exhibit 6 shows a simple example of the comparative value chain perspective. The

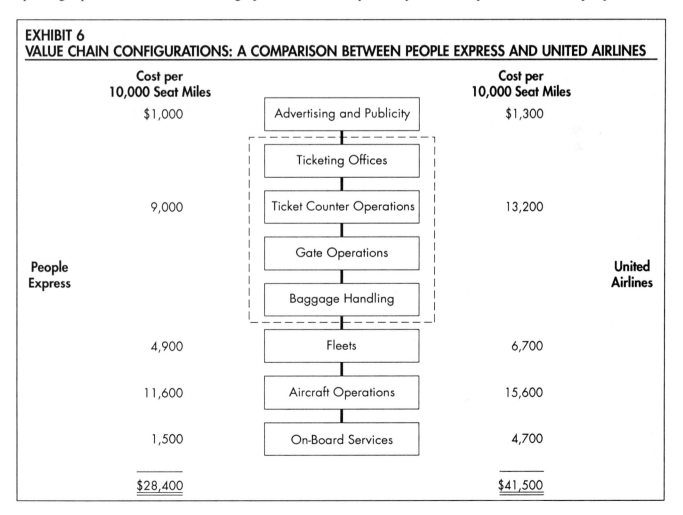

EXHIBIT 6
VALUE CHAIN CONFIGURATIONS: A COMPARISON BETWEEN PEOPLE EXPRESS AND UNITED AIRLINES

People Express — Cost per 10,000 Seat Miles		United Airlines — Cost per 10,000 Seat Miles
$1,000	Advertising and Publicity	$1,300
	Ticketing Offices	
9,000	Ticket Counter Operations	13,200
	Gate Operations	
	Baggage Handling	
4,900	Fleets	6,700
11,600	Aircraft Operations	15,600
1,500	On-Board Services	4,700
$28,400		$41,500

EXHIBIT 7
STRATEGIC INFERENCES FROM THE VALUE CHAINS OF PEOPLE EXPRESS AND UNITED AIRLINES

Value Chain Elements	People Express Less Than United Airlines (Cost per 10,000 Seat Mile)	Strategic Differences	
		People Express	**United Airlines**
Advertising and publicity	$300	Heavy promotion to tout low price/no-frills airline	Heavy promotion of full-service airline
Reservations and Ticketing	$4,200	No ticket offices	Ticket offices in downtown locations
		No separate computer reservation system	Extensive computer reservation system
		Secondary airports and terminals	Full-service
		No ticket counters (check-in only)	
		Tickets purchased on board the aircraft or from machines	
		No interline tickets	
		Few fare options	
		First-come, first-serve seating	Full-service
		No ticketing at gates	
		Carry-on space provided	Free baggage checking
		Charge for checked baggage	
		No interline baggage	
Fleet costs	$1,800	Used aircraft ("budget" airplanes)	New aircraft
Flight operations	$4,000	High-density seating	Union pilots
		Nonunion pilots	Bigger crews
		Smaller crews and more flying hours per day	Crews paid on higher scale
		Flight crews paid on dramatically lower scale	
		Flight crews double on ground duties	
Cabin operations	$3,200	Nonunion flight attendants	Full-service
		Lower pay scale	
		No first class	
		No meals	
		Charge for snacks and drinks served	

exhibit shows a chart that was prepared from publicly available information for two very different major airlines: United Airlines and People Express (in its heyday).

Structured in this way, the difference in strategies between the two airlines becomes obvious. The "no frills" concept of People Express is readily apparent. Specifically, strategic decisions in the five areas listed in the "Value chain elements" column of Exhibit 7 account for the $13,500 difference in the cost per 10,000 seat miles flown between these two airlines.

A STRATEGY FOR COMPETITIVE ADVANTAGE
Traditional cost analysis focuses on the notion of value added (i.e., selling price less the cost of purchased raw materials) under the mistaken impression that this is the only area where a firm can influence costs. This article argues that value chain analysis provides a more meaningful way to explore competitive advantage.

Value added could be quite misleading for at least three reasons:

1. It arbitrarily distinguishes between raw materials and many other purchased inputs. Purchased services, such as maintenance or professional consulting services, are treated differently than raw materials purchased;
2. It does not point out the potential to exploit linkages (whether between a firm and its suppliers or between a firm and its customers) with a view to reducing costs or enhancing product differentiation; and
3. Competitive advantage cannot be fully explored without considering the interaction between purchased raw materials and other cost elements (e.g., purchasing higher-quality and higher-priced raw material can reduce scrap costs, and thus could lower total costs).

The focus of the value chain analysis is external to the firm. Each firm is seen in the context of the overall chain of value-creating activities, of which the firm is likely to be only a small part. (There apparently are no firms that span the entire value chain in which they operate.)

In summary, the methodology for constructing and using a value chain involves the following steps:

1. Identify the industry's value chain, then assign costs, revenues, and assets to each activity;
2. Identify the cost drivers that regulate each value activity; and
3. Build sustainable competitive advantage, either by controlling cost drivers better than competitors or by reconfiguring the value chain.

Efforts to simultaneously reduce costs and enhance differentiation are possible by carefully considering costs, revenues, and assets at each value activity vis-à-vis competitors. Cost driver analysis (of which ABC is a subset) is a part of value chain analysis. In SCM, therefore, the value chain provides the overall framework; topics such as ABC are components of constructing and using value chains.

The case study provided in this article illustrates that the insights derived from value chain analysis are much different from those suggested by more conventional management accounting tools. Exhibit 8 summarizes the key

EXHIBIT 8
VALUE CHAIN VS. CONVENTIONAL MANAGEMENT ACCOUNTING—A SUMMARY

	Traditional Management Accounting	Value Chain Analysis in the SCM Framework
Focus	Internal	External
Perspective	Value-added	Entire set of linked activities from suppliers to end-use customers
Cost driver concept	Single driver ("Volume")	Multiple cost drivers • Structural drivers (e.g., scale, scope, experience, technology, and complexity) • Executional drivers (e.g., participative management, total quality management, and plant layout) A set of unique cost drivers for each value activity
Cost containment philosophy	Application at the overall firm level (cost-volume-profit analysis) "Across the board" cost reductions	View cost containment as a function of the cost driver(s) regulating each value activity Exploit linkages with suppliers Exploit linkages with customers "Spend to save"
Insights for strategic decisions	None readily apparent (this is a large reason why the strategic consulting firms always discard the conventional reports as they begin their cost analyses)	Identify cost drivers at the individual activity level, and develop cost/differentiation advantage either by controlling those drivers better than competitors or by reconfiguring the value chain (e.g., Federal Express in mail delivery and MCI in long-distance telephone) For each value activity, ask strategic questions pertaining to: • Make versus buy • Forward/backward integration Quantify and assess "supplier power" and "buyer power," and exploit linkages with suppliers and buyers

differences between value chain and conventional management accounting.

The value chain perspective can be used to derive the following insights:

- Since virtually no two companies compete in exactly the same set of value activities, value chain analysis is a critical first step in understanding how a firm is positioned in its industry. Building sustainable competitive advantage requires a knowledge of the full, linked set of value activities of which the firm and its competitors are a part.
- Once a value chain is fully articulated, critical strategic decisions (e.g., make-or-buy decisions or forward versus backward integration) become clearer. Investment decisions can be viewed from the perspective of their impact on the overall chain and the firm's position within it.
- The value chain analysis helps to quantify supplier power by calculating the percentage of total profits that can be attributed to suppliers. This activity could help the firm identify ways to exploit linkages with suppliers.
- The value chain framework highlights how a firm's product fits into the buyer's value chain. Given this framework, it is readily apparent what percentage the firm's product costs comprise of the buyer's total costs. This information could be useful in encouraging the firm and buyers to work together in cost reduction activities.
- In the final analysis, the simultaneous pursuit of low cost and differentiation depends on a sophisticated understanding of the drivers of costs, revenues, and assets at each value activity and the interdependencies between value activities.

John K. Shank is Noble Professor of Managerial Accounting and Management Control and Vijay Govindarajan is Professor of Strategy and Control, both at Amos Tuck School of Business Administration, Dartmouth College, in Hanover, New Hampshire.

Notes

1. Michael E. Porter, *Competitive Advantage: Creating and Sustaining Superior Performance* (New York: The Free Press, 1985): 62–67.

2. Michael E. Porter, *Competitive Strategy* (New York: The Free Press, 1980): 34–44.

3. John K. Shank, "Strategic Cost Management: New Wine, or Just New Bottles?" *Journal of Management Accounting Research* (Fall 1989): 47–65.

4. Porter, *Competitive Advantage*, 88.

5. M. Hergert and D. Morris, "Accounting Data for Value Chain Analysis," *Strategic Management Journal* (June 1989): 175–188.

6. *Ibid.*

7. Porter, *Competitive Strategy,* 70–87.

8. Daniel Riley, "Competitive Cost Based Investment Strategies for Industrial Companies," in *Manufacturing Issues* (New York: Booz, Allen & Hamilton Inc., 1987): 27–34.

9. F.M. Scherer, *Industrial Market Structure and Economic Performance,* 2nd ed. (New York: Rand McNally, 1980).

10. Pankaj Ghemawat, *The Arithmetic of Strategic Cost Analysis* (Boston: Harvard Business School Press, 1986).

11. Robin Cooper, "You Need a New Cost System When . . . ," *Harvard Business Review* (January–February 1989): 38–49; Robin Cooper and Robert S. Kaplan, "Measure Costs Right: Make the Right Decisions," *Harvard Business Review* (September–October 1988): 72–91; Robert S. Kaplan and H. Thomas Johnson, *Relevance Lost: The Rise and Fall of Management Accounting* (Boston: Harvard Business School Press, 1987).

12. [no author], *Manufacturing Issues* (New York: Booz, Allen & Hamilton Inc., 1987): 16–31.

13. Michael E. Porter, *du Pont in Titanium Dioxide* (Boston: Harvard Business School Press, 1986).

14. Michael E. Porter, "GE vs. Westinghouse in Large Turbine Generators," *Harvard Business School Case Series* 380–128.

15. A. Stuart, "Meatpackers in Stampede." *Fortune* (July 29, 1981): 67–73.

From J. Shank and V. Govindarajan, "Strategic Cost Management and the Value Chain," *Journal of Cost Management* (Winter 1992): 5–21. Reprinted with permission.

Questions

2.1a What is the difference between the value-added and value chain concepts? Explain.

2.1b What are structural and executional cost drivers and how are they distinguished in Shank and Govindarajan's article?

2.2 ABC and High Technology: A Story with a Moral

By Frank H. Selto and Dale W. Jasinski

Except in some large companies that are well-staffed, well-trained, and well-funded, there is not much evidence that ABC is understood well enough to be designed or implemented successfully as a stand-alone system, let alone one that is integrated with strategy. Even in large firms, widespread success of ABC is not obvious.

Because most job creation and innovative economic activity occur in small firms, we describe here the efforts of an accounting staff to design and implement an activity-based accounting system to support strategic changes in a relatively small, high-technology firm with approximately $100 million in annual sales. The experience has lessons for others who embark on similar tasks.

The company, which chooses to remain anonymous and which we will call DataCom, is an entrepreneurial, privately held, high-technology concern that designs, assembles, and markets computer communication equipment. DataCom has faced challenges of rapid growth and equally rapid changes in both technology and customer needs that beset any high-technology company. Those that survive, and especially those that thrive, must be creative, agile, and quick to the market. DataCom encountered a dramatic change in its business environment that tested its abilities to survive.

Founded in 1985, DataCom quickly built its reputation as a premier supplier of computer communication links to mainframe computer original equipment manufacturers (OEMs) that incorporated DataCom's products without DataCom's name. DataCom enjoyed steady growth and added OEM partners. Founders of the company eagerly anticipated the right opportunity to take the firm public. In 1989, DataCom's primary OEM partner unexpectedly acquired its own mainframe communications technology and did not renew its contract. Sales dropped, but large cash reserves preserved the existence of DataCom.

DataCom's initial response was to redefine its marketing strategy as direct sellers to end users. Lack of name recognition and experience with direct sales, however, prevented significant sales growth. DataCom had no information that would measure the profitability of alternative markets or channels of distribution. DataCom downsized in 1990, primarily by reducing its direct sales force, and it focused on a few key markets. Cost cutting and focused marketing returned profitability in late 1990 and 1991. As a result, the company expanded its direct sales force to seek an increased market share, primarily in Europe where mainframe computing continued to be the technology of choice.

Economic recession in Europe in 1992 and rapid changes in U.S. computing technology to networked personal computers abruptly cut DataCom's already declining sales in half. DataCom had not foreseen the recession and had not expected domestic computing technology to switch so quickly away from mainframes. Although DataCom was not the only myopic firm at this time, in retrospect it was far

more dependent on a dominant technology within a single market than was prudent. DataCom, however, never was blind to technological change and had continued to invest heavily in R&D even when sales first dropped in 1989.

By 1992 the combination of high expenditures for R&D, marketing, and administration had all but eliminated the company's sizable cash reserves, dropping its liquidity ratio from 5.0 to 1.0, with more than 50% of the 1992 numerator as receivables. DataCom found itself with a failing marketing strategy and a dependency on an apparently outmoded technology. It had neglected its creativity and agility and was in danger of being an also-ran in the market. During this threatening time, the accounting function continued to play a scorekeeping role—an increasingly unpleasant task.

STRATEGIC RESPONSE

In 1992, DataCom's executive committee began urgent strategic planning. In the process, it affirmed that its comparative advantages were its abilities to:

1. Anticipate emerging communications technology accurately;
2. Create innovative, value-adding solutions to communications problems in the new technology;
3. Deliver outstanding functional quality.

The executive committee noted that continued investment in R&D had not resulted in significant new products. The causes were identified as diffused engineering efforts directed at putting out fires and making marginal changes to existing products to chase marginal sales. The executive committee sought a structural solution to refocus DataCom's considerable technological talent on its comparative advantages. The solution was to transform the highly centralized company into three distinct business units, each operating within technological boundaries. These business units were to be evaluated individually as profit centers that competed for scarce internal funds for growth.

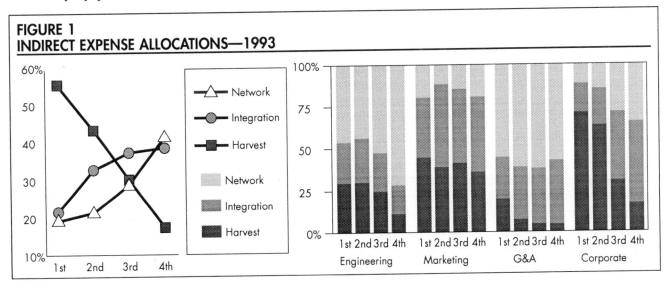

FIGURE 1
INDIRECT EXPENSE ALLOCATIONS—1993

The three business units were Harvest, Integration, and Network.

Harvest: The first unit was dedicated to prolonging the original line of business that connected mainframe computers to remote terminals. It would be operated as a harvest unit that generated cash to fund new product development. Technological risks were negligible, but the company expected that this market would disappear—but not, the company hoped, before new products were brought to market.

Integration: The second unit was designed to develop a complementary line of business that integrated communications among different computing technologies. This unit would extend DataCom's current expertise, but it followed previous R&D efforts. The integration problem is a significant barrier to computer communications and DataCom believed it could develop innovative solutions in this large market. Growth in this market could prove to be steady but might level off within a few years.

Network: The third unit was organized to seek communication solutions to the emerging network computing technology. Though related to DataCom's previous efforts, this technology was sufficiently new to represent significant technological risk. If successful, however, solutions to network communication problems had the potential to repeat or outstrip DataCom's original level of success. This unit's performance would be the "home run" the executive committee sought, if its prediction was realized that networks would be the dominant computing technology of the foreseeable future.

ACTIVITY-BASED INFORMATION

The information needs to manage these three business units were somewhat different, requiring innovative solutions. Common to all three divisions was a need to identify and measure the costs of support activities provided to each unit, including design and test engineering. (Figure 1 shows the history of the shifting allocations over four quarters. As new directions were chosen, each unit was dramatically impacted.)

The Harvest business unit primarily required accurate scorekeeping to monitor profitability, cash flow, and marketing effectiveness—a familiar task for accounting. The new technology units, Integration and Network, weren't generating significant sales, but they did require expertise to evaluate the financial impacts of alternative technology and product development scenarios. The accounting staff was less prepared to fill this need.

Top management believed that an activity-based accounting system would enable them to better identify and cost DataCom's value-adding activities. The CEO, an engineer by training, saw that "as you get narrower (level of detail), you can look at the things that really impact your business. One of the things you find out as you do this is that your information systems may not be adequate to break down costs at the level that you need to make these decisions."

Accordingly, the CFO and the accounting department determined to develop an accounting system that would monitor the operations of the three business units as if they were separate entities and, at the same time, support managers' efforts to allocate resources efficiently. Some employees and activities were identified clearly with specific business units, including several financial staff who were to provide financial modeling assistance to unit managers. The majority of the company's employees still provided support activities from centralized service departments. These indirect expenses were and would continue to be a large percentage of total expenses.

The CFO began tracking service activity and costs to the business units. Interestingly, the CFO would not call this process ABC because of the connotation that ABC systems required special financial expertise and software, which at the time DataCom did not have and could not afford. At the same time, however, engineers in the centralized design unit were accustomed to recording their time, activities, and costs to projects and were well aware of the concepts and practices of ABC.

Despite the executive committee's desire to identify activities and to trace them to business units and products, the CFO never received sufficient resources to complete a thorough study. Because of the costs involved, the CFO never directly requested resources for that purpose. The engineers' comfort with ABC was not repeated in other service areas, and unassigned indirect costs averaged 38% of total expenses during 1993. The CFO allocated these expenses on the basis of revenues and hoped that business unit managers would reject these arbitrary allocations and demand more accurate, activity-based cost assignments—and then supply resources to generate the information. In 1993, based on revenue, the Harvest division received the great majority of the allocation, followed by the Integration division, which began to bring products to market. The Network division was shipping no products and was spared any revenue-based allocation.

Perhaps not surprisingly, the vice president of manufacturing and manager of the Integration business unit believed, "The new financial reporting that we have with the separation of the business units is clearly giving us a view of where the winners are and where the losers are. There have been some complaints from those who are spending time putting all these numbers together, saying, 'Where's the benefit? Where's the beef?', but for those of us who have become accustomed to it, it is a good decision-making tool."

Because the Harvest unit could "afford" the expense allocation and the other units saw no advantage to arguing for larger cost assignments, demand for improved activity-based information never materialized. Business unit managers did demand and receive extensive, centralized marketing services, which were traced only partially. Despite their increasing ABC skills, the accounting staff never got beyond their comfortable scorekeeping role, and they complained (somewhat incorrectly as it turned out): "The frustration from a planning point is—and we can do numbers as well as anybody else—that sometimes you still have to make a decision based upon those numbers, and we haven't made any decisions based on the numbers. We would view it [tracing activities and cost] as sort of a waste of time." (Table 1 displays the different information needs for each unit and the frustrating disparity between the needs of the units and what the accountants were able to provide.)

It was common knowledge that the revenue-based allocations were distorting business-unit profitability and that activity-based information could reveal a different picture: "If you use those [activity-based] numbers, you would discontinue the new products and continue to build the old, because they're making a bundle of money, and the new products are costing you a ton of money. But everyone thinks the future is Network.

"I'm wasting the company's dollars by spending my time tracking it now. . . they're dumping all the dollars in revenue anyway... and putting it into the Harvest business, which in reality has been taking substantially less of my time."

The accounting staff focused on scorekeeping of existing products rather than supporting the company's primary competencies—anticipating technological change, developing innovative solutions, and delivering high quality. The executive committee, however, did make critical decisions without accurate information about the activities necessary to support alternative product scenarios. Harvest was virtually eliminated, and Integration was divested, despite the facts that both generated positive cash flow and both probably were profitable.

Furthermore, the Integration market was growing more than had been anticipated and was receiving larger revenue-based allocations. Both units were judged to be insufficiently profitable to continue. (Integration is profitable under new ownership.)

The executive committee swung for the fence on Network and did hit the home run, as it turned out, while ignoring the high percentage hit that Integration delivered. This may be a defining difference between entrepreneurial, high-technology firms and more mature firms—the penchant for the home run and disdain for more conservative alternatives. Traditional management accounting's focus on scorekeeping may add relatively little value in this setting.

The CFO was sanguine about the prospects of developing improved, activity-based information, knowing that the future of the company rested on predicting the direction of computing technology accurately. The predisposition of the executive committee to go for the home run had been reinforced by misleading business unit profitability: "We have to go forward with the new development on our new product line [Network], which represents the future of business. Since we are trying to fund Network through the Harvest business unit, which happens to be the declining business, the decisions of how quickly to move forward would be the same [depending on cash flow]. So I am not convinced that we [would] have made different decisions [with better activity-based information]."

This comment probably was both rationalization and statement of fact. It was clear from the initial formation of the business units that Network was the executive committee favorite. Financial investigation of alternatives was limited because the CFO was the only member of the executive committee not given an explicit strategy formulation role. If aggregate scorekeeping was all that accounting could provide accurately it could not bring much of value to the strategy table. Indeed, in the subsequent strategic planning process, the executive committee decided to solicit more input from throughout the organization and formed a planning committee of approximately 25 members. Any member of the executive committee could nominate an employee to serve on the committee. The only functional area not to have a representative was finance and accounting.

It seems likely that lack of accounting input will be repeated when DataCom eventually seeks a new home run technology to replace Network. After the sale of Integration, the accounting staff dropped efforts to trace activities and costs to any specific products or projects. An opportunity to add value to strategic decision making by developing activity-based information was missed, and aggregate scorekeeping is still accounting's primary function.

TABLE 1
BUSINESS UNIT—INFORMATION NEEDS

	Harvest	Integration	Network
Strategic Accounting Need	Scorekeeping: ABC system to monitor profitability, cash flow, and marketing effectiveness.	Problem-solving: ABC system to evaluate financial impacts of alternative technology and product development scenarios.	Problem-solving: ABC system to evaluate financial impacts of alternative technology and product development scenarios.
Accounting Information's Actual Impact on Strategy	Misleading (over) allocations led to its elimination.	Misleading (over) allocations masked real contributions and led to its divestiture.	Misleading (under) allocations enabled it to continue to receive resources until market success achieved.

THE MORAL OF THE STORY

Although ABC holds much promise for organizations, it cannot be implemented or evaluated independently of the organization's strategy. Unless ABC is integral to the company's strategy, it is unlikely that management accountants can break through the high-technology glass ceiling and become important members of the strategic planning team. Absent that input, it is clear that the job security of management accountants depends on providing relevant information to support the organization's decision making, and scorekeeping alone may be inadequate. Formulation and implementation of strategy will proceed with or without the accounting staff's contribution.

This research has been supported by the Institute of Management Accountants and the University of Colorado Hart Fellowship Program. We also gratefully acknowledge and appreciate the virtually unlimited access to personnel and information granted to us by our field hosts.

Frank H. Selto, Ph.D., teaches accounting and is chair of the Accounting and Information Systems Division at the College of Business and Administration, University of Colorado at Boulder. Dale W. Jasinski will join the faculty at Idaho State University, Pocatello. Dr. Selto can be reached at (303) 492-1549, and Mr. Jasinski is at (303) 492-1175. This article was submitted through IMA's Boulder Valley (Colo.) Chapter.

From F. H. Selto and D. W. Jasinski, "ABC and High Technology: A Story with a Moral," *Management Accounting* (March 1996): 37-40. Reprinted with permission.

Questions

2.2a Were the information needs of all three divisions of DataCom the same? Explain.

2.2b According to Selto and Jasinski, why did ABC fail at DataCom?

2.3 Cost Accounting and Cost Management in a JIT Environment

George Foster and Charles T. Horngren

The just-in-time (JIT) philosophy and methods are being adopted by an increasing number of organizations. What impact will JIT have on cost accounting, cost management, and management accounting? This article, based on discussions with managers of domestic and foreign organizations that have adopted JIT and on public accounting and consulting firms engaged by such organizations, examines that impact.

In the broadest sense, JIT is a philosophy that focuses on performing activities as they are needed by other internal agents of an organization. Four fundamental aspects of JIT are:

- All activities that do not add value to a product or service are eliminated—This includes activities or resources that are targets for reduction or elimination (e.g., inventory held in warehouses or storage areas and work in process that must be handled and stacked several times before becoming finished goods).
- There is a commitment to a high level of quality—Doing things right the first time is essential when there is no time allowance for rework.
- Continuous improvements in the efficiency of activities are strived for.
- Simplifying and increasing the visibility of value-adding activities are emphasized—This helps identify activities that do not add value. For example, a walk through a JIT plant will instantly reveal if work-in-process inventory has been eliminated.

JIT also refers to operations management methods in such functional areas as purchasing, production, distribution, retailing, and even in such administrative areas as payroll and accounts payable. For example, JIT purchasing is the purchase of goods so that delivery immediately precedes demand or use. JIT production is a system in which each component on a production line is produced as needed by the next step in the production line. JIT purchasing can be adopted by retailers, wholesalers, distributors, and manufacturing organizations; JIT production can be adopted only by manufacturing organizations. Exhibit 1 presents an overview of the ways in which JIT is used.

PURPOSES AND CHOICES IN COST ACCOUNTING

Cost or management accounting systems have two major purposes: product costing, and planning and control. Cost accounting techniques for fulfilling these purposes include:

- Cost/benefit tests for designing and changing management accounting systems—Elaborate systems are expensive and time-consuming, but managers authorize their installation and adaptation only if doing so will sufficiently improve collective operations.
- Product costing and control systems that are tailored to underlying operations, not vice versa.

34

EXHIBIT 1
JIT: A PHILOSOPHY AND A SET OF OPERATING METHODS

JIT: A philosophy that focuses on the undertaking of activities immediately as needed or demanded. This philosophy includes four pivotal aspects:
- Elimination of all activities that do not add value.
- Commitment to a high level of quality.
- Commitment to continuous improvement.
- Emphasis on simplification and increased visibility of all activities that add value.

JIT Purchasing Methods	JIT Production Methods	JIT Distribution Methods	JIT Retailing Methods	JIT Administrative Methods

- Control devices in all product costing systems—These systems include responsibility accounting, budgeting, and variance analysis.
- Various sources of management information in addition to management accounting systems.

JIT is primarily a change in underlying operations, and, as with any significant change in operations, serious consideration should be given to changing the accompanying accounting system. JIT accounting systems are merely applications of long-standing cost accounting concepts. In addition, JIT operations illustrate that the financial measures provided by cost accounting systems are only one means of planning and control.[1]

JUSTIFICATIONS FOR CHANGES IN COST ACCOUNTING SYSTEMS

The changes in cost accounting suggested in this article will yield the following benefits:

- More accurate product cost information—Uses include decisions on pricing, product mix to produce or sell, and cost-based reimbursement contracts. The management accounting system is the primary source of product cost information.
- Better control of cost incurrence—In a JIT environment, the focus is on reducing total costs for the organization as a whole, not individual costs or departmental costs. Changes can take two forms:
  —Fewer or no dysfunctional decisions often associated with the existing cost accounting system.
  —Advantageous comparison of accounting versus non-accounting variables in cost control.

The internal accounting system is only one of several sources of cost control information. Other sources include

personal observation, administrative approval mechanisms, and such nonfinancial measures as setup times and the percentage of defective products.

- Reduced costs of the system—Many existing cost accounting systems are expensive, complex, and time-consuming for both managers and accountants. A key element of JIT is that it simplifies all activities, including cost systems and such operational areas as purchasing and production.

JIT PURCHASING

With JIT purchasing, the acquisition of goods is scheduled in such a way that delivery immediately precedes demand or use. In some industries, JIT purchasing has long been an accepted practice (e.g., industries dealing with such perishables as baked goods, fresh flowers, and fresh fish). Today, JIT purchasing is being adopted by organizations that acquire nonperishables. These organizations previously ordered lots much larger than required by short-run demand or use and often stored inventory in large warehouses for weeks or longer.

Characteristics of operating activities. Organizations that adopt JIT purchasing report a substantial increase in individual deliveries, each containing fewer units. The costs and time associated with purchasing activities have been reduced by:

- Decreasing the number of suppliers and, consequently, the resources devoted to purchase negotiations—For example, Apple Computer reduced its vendors from 400 to 75, and IBM Corp cut its suppliers from 640 to 32.
- Stipulating price and acceptable quality levels in long-term agreements with suppliers, thus eliminating negotiations for each purchase transaction—When purchasing goods, some JIT adopters use an advanced delivery

schedule (ADS) that defines the daily (or even hourly) delivery schedule for a time period (e.g., a month). Clearly, firms using an ADS must have a high degree of certainty regarding demand or production for the time period covered. For example, several Toyota plants freeze the production schedule at least one month in advance.

- Having purchasers establish programs to inform vendors about quality and delivery requirements—These requirements can be stringent, bearing high penalties for nonconformance. For example, Hewlett-Packard has contracts that specify "if [the supplier] misses a four-hour window more than three times in a year, their contract is up for renewal."[2]
- Using shop-ready containers—Activities associated with packing and unpacking are examples of how non-value-added costs are often incurred. Having the correct number of units in individual containers is emphasized, diminishing all facets of material handling (e.g., the use of large material-handling equipment).
- Costs for incoming quality inspection programs are reduced—The number of quality inspectors can be reduced or even eliminated.

The goals set by firms switching to JIT purchasing are ambitious. A consultant gave the following example of how "specific improvement goals are typically very aggressive": supplier productivity and price improvements (30%); total inventory and lead time reduction (90%); quality without inspection (100%); schedule performance (100%).[3]

Implications for cost accounting. JIT purchasing can affect a cost accounting system in one or more of the following ways.

It increases the direct traceability of costs. In a traditional purchasing environment, many material handling and warehouse costs are incurred for multipurpose facilities that service different product lines. Organizations typically classify the costs of operating such facilities as indirect costs. In a JIT purchasing environment, the material handling facilities are often dedicated to a single retail area or a single production line. Such operating costs can be classified as direct costs. Consequently, in a JIT purchasing setting, there can be an increase in the direct traceability of costs to individual retail areas or production lines.

It changes the cost pools that are used to accumulate costs. In traditional purchasing environments, separate cost pools are frequently used for such activities as purchasing, material handling, quality inspection, and warehouse facilities. These costs are allocated to production departments in one of two ways:

- Each cost pool is separately allocated to each production department.
- Purchasing, warehouse, and related costs are collected in one or more aggregate cost pools and are then allocated to each production department.

In an ideal JIT purchasing environment, the warehouse would be eliminated and material handling costs would be reduced. Exhibit 2 summarizes these changes in materials movement. If an organization formerly allocated purchasing, material handling, quality inspection, and warehouse costs separately, the JIT accounting system will reduce the number of such indirect cost pools. At the very least, the warehouse cost pool will vanish. Other cost pools may be combined because of the former pools' diminished materiality.

JIT changes the bases used to allocate indirect costs to production departments. If an organization previously collected purchasing, warehouse, and related costs in a single cost pool, the composition of this pool will change. This has implications for the choice of an allocation base.

Surveys of cost allocation methods report that floor space occupied in a warehouse is a commonly used allocation base for purchasing and material handling costs in traditional purchasing environments. In a pure JIT environment, there is no warehouse; hence, warehouse space is unavailable as an allocation base. Such allocation bases as the dollar value of materials or the number of deliveries may better capture the cause and effect relationship between purchasing and material handling activities and indirect cost incurrence.

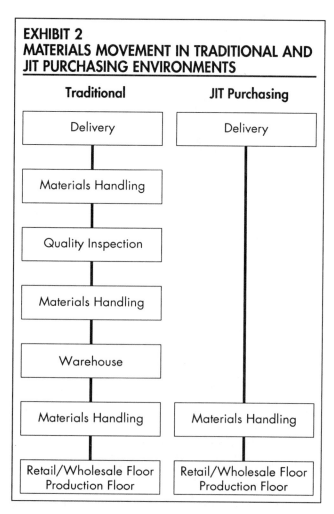

EXHIBIT 2
MATERIALS MOVEMENT IN TRADITIONAL AND JIT PURCHASING ENVIRONMENTS

Traditional	JIT Purchasing
Delivery	Delivery
Materials Handling	
Quality Inspection	
Materials Handling	
Warehouse	
Materials Handling	Materials Handling
Retail/Wholesale Floor Production Floor	Retail/Wholesale Floor Production Floor

It reduces emphasis on individual purchase price variance information. In traditional purchasing environments, many organizations place great emphasis on purchase price variances. Favorable purchasing price variances can sometimes be achieved by buying in larger quantities to take advantage of price discounts or by buying lower quality materials. In JIT environments, the emphasis is on the total cost of operations, not just on purchase price. Such factors as quality and availability are given greater emphasis, even if they are accompanied by higher purchase prices. Firms using JIT purchasing attempt to achieve price reductions by having long-term agreements with suppliers rather than by seeking large quantity, one-time purchases that result in sizeable holdings of materials or subcomponents.

As always, the cost accounting system should be adapted to the underlying operating activity. In JIT purchasing, the underlying process focuses on long-term commitments that reduce total operating costs. Purchase price variances for each delivery have much less significance under JIT.

JIT reduces the frequency or detail of reporting of purchase deliveries in the internal accounting system. In a JIT purchasing environment, the number of deliveries of goods (e.g., raw materials) increases substantially. Organizations have sought to reduce the costs of processing information in the internal accounting system in one or more of the following ways:

- Batching, or summarizing, individual purchase deliveries to avoid a separate transaction for each delivery. When there is an ADS, the transaction may relate to the period of the delivery schedule. When there is no ADS, the individual deliveries may be batched on a weekly basis and only the aggregate of the deliveries recorded as a transaction.
- Using an electronic transfer system in which the initial purchase order (or delivery schedule) automatically sets up electronic data transfers at the delivery date and electronic funds transfers at the payment date.
- Reorganizing the accounts payable department so that it operates as an assembly line. An electronics company initially adopted this approach at one of its plants but subsequently moved to batching purchase deliveries when the reorganized department was splitting at the seams" and was "archiving mountains of documents."[4]

The appendix to this article describes a backflushing costing system that reduces the information recorded in the internal accounting system. Backflushing can be extended to the purchasing function so that the first recording of materials in the internal accounting system occurs when a finished good using those materials is completed.

Exhibit 3 links the justifications for changes in the cost accounting system with each of the specific changes associated with JIT purchasing described in the preceding sections.

JIT PRODUCTION
Characteristics of operating activities. In a JIT production environment, each component is produced as needed by the next step in the production line. Key elements of JIT production include:

- The production line is run on a demand-pull basis, so that activity at each workstation is authorized by the demand of downstream workstations. Work in process at each workstation is therefore held to a minimum.
- Emphasis is placed on reducing the production lead time (the time from the first stage of production to when the finished product leaves the production line). Reduced lead time enables a firm to better respond to changes in demand; it also reduces changes in supplier orders.
- The production line is stopped if work-in-process is defective. In JIT, there are no buffer inventories at each workstation to keep workers busy. Stoppage is counter to traditional economic-lot-size assumptions concerning the length of the production run. Organizations adopting JIT production continually strive to reduce parameters that are assumed constant in economic lot size formulas (e.g., the setup cost for machinery at a workstation).
- Emphasis is on simplifying activities on the production line so that areas in which non-value-added activities occur are highly visible and can be eliminated. Some firms adopting JIT production methods restructured the layout of their plants. Much emphasis is placed on streamlining material handling between successive workstations. A consultant noted that "one of the many benefits will be the elimination of the dinosaurs—the forklift trucks."[5]

Dramatic improvements have been reported by firms adopting JIT production methods. Exhibit 4 presents examples of efficiency improvements at five companies; the values shown are representative of those reported by a diverse

---

EXHIBIT 3
JUSTIFICATIONS FOR COST ACCOUNTING CHANGES FOR JIT PURCHASING

- More accurate product cost information.
  —Changes in direct traceability of costs.
  —Changes in cost pools.
  —Changes in allocation bases.
- Better control of cost incurrence.
  —Reduced emphasis on individual purchasing price variance information, increased emphasis on total cost of operations. (This minimizes dysfunctional operating decisions often associated with existing cost accounting system.)
- Reduced system costs.
  —A reduction in the frequency or detail of purchase delivery reporting.

EXHIBIT 4
EFFICIENCY IMPROVEMENTS WITH JIT PRODUCTION METHODS

	Range of Percentage Improvement for 5 Companies (%)
Manufacturing Lead Time	83 – 92
Inventory: Raw	35 – 73
WIP	70 – 89
Finished Goods	0 –100
Changeover Time	75 – 94
Labor: Direct	0 – 50
Indirect	21 – 60
Space	39 – 80
Cost of Quality	26 – 63
Purchased Material	6 – 11

set of organizations.[6] Significant changes in operations underlie these improvements. Accordingly, major changes in the cost accounting area should be expected.

Organizations adopting a JIT production approach are making one or more of the following changes.

Increasing the direct traceability of some costs. Direct traceability of cost items has been increased in two ways.

Change in underlying production activities. The costs of many activities previously classified as indirect costs have been transferred to the direct cost category in JIT plants. For example, production line workers in JIT plants perform plant maintenance and plant setups. Previously, such activities were often performed by other workers who were classified as indirect labor.

Equipment suppliers to JIT plants are increasingly asked to supply equipment that facilitates high-speed changeover of tools by production workers, on-line monitoring of quality, and on-line packaging and labeling.

For those firms retaining direct labor as a separate cost category, changes in the set of production activities increase the direct traceability of costs to individual product lines. This means that indirect cost pools associated with such activities as plant maintenance and setup are likely to be eliminated (or combined with other cost pools because of the previous pools' diminished materiality).

Change in the ability to trace costs to specific production lines or areas. Even if underlying production activities are unchanged, data may be captured more economically. There is increased use of time clocks, minicomputers, and bar-coded identification codes for production workers (as well as materials, parts, and machines). This has made it more cost-effective to trace costs to specific production lines or areas. Improvements in data bases relating to machine use are also facilitating the development of cost functions that better capture cause and effect relationships at the plant floor level.

IBM is an example of a company that is exploring ways to increase the ratio of directly attributable product costs to total product costs. Controllers at plants where this ratio has been increased said that it improves sourcing decisions and competitive analysis, allows for cost reductions and improves competitiveness, and improves expense information to manage product cost (increases visibility and awareness of expense items). [7]

Eliminating (or reducing) cost pools for indirect activities. This change is related to increased traceability of costs and can be achieved in several ways:

- Change underlying production activities, as described.
- Eliminate activities that do not add value. Prime targets for elimination in a JIT environment are:
  —Storage areas for work-in-process inventory.
  —Storage areas for spoilage, waste, reworked units, and scrap.
  —Material handling facilities for transportation between the production line and storage areas—Machines or workstations are adjacent to each other so that materials and components can be moved by the workers themselves or on short conveyor belts. Increased emphasis also is given to the design and packaging of materials and components so as to reduce the need for large bulk containers that require forklifts.

Elimination of the items listed may result in the elimination of associated cost pools.

Reducing emphasis on individual labor and overhead variances. In many traditional plants, much of the internal accounting effort is devoted to setting labor and overhead standards and to calculating and reporting variances from these standards. Firms implementing JIT production methods report reduced emphasis on the use of labor and overhead variances.

When defined at the production cell level, labor variances create incentives for workers in each production cell to ignore the effect of their actions on other production cells. In JIT plants, the emphasis is on total plant performance, not on the performance of each cell. At one of its semiconductor plants that is run on a JIT production basis, Motorola has eliminated all labor and overhead standards. The benefits reported include reduced dysfunctional aspects associated with focusing on individual production cells and reduced administrative expenses.

Firms retaining variance analysis stress that a change in focus is appropriate in a JIT plant. The emphasis is on variance analysis at the plant level with the focus on trends that may be occurring in the production process rather than on the absolute magnitude of individual variances. (The notion of continuous improvement that underlies a JIT philosophy means that standards will be revised at shorter intervals than in traditional plants.)

Reducing the level of detailed information recorded on work tickets. A key aspect of a JIT philosophy is the simplification of all activities. There are several ways in which work tickets have become simplified in JIT production.

The production process is changed so that there are fewer materials parts per finished product. This can be achieved by redesigning the product so that fewer parts are used or by increasing the percentage of components assembled elsewhere.

Only direct materials are recorded on work tickets; all other costs are expensed to the period. Several JIT plants that produce products with a low percentage of labor costs have adopted this approach.

A job costing system is changed to a process costing or backflush product costing system. Exhibit 5 compares job, operation, process, and backflush costing systems in terms of the level of detail with which individual product information is recorded. Job costing contains the most detailed level of information about individual product units; the individual job is the focus of product costing. Process costing typically has been viewed as being at the other end of the spectrum; an individual process for a given time period is its focus. Job costing typically is associated with batch manufacturing, and process costing with constant-flow manufacturing (often called continuous-flow manufacturing). Operation costing is a hybrid costing system combining elements of job and process costing.

The appendix to this article describes and illustrates the relatively new backflush costing system used at several JIT plants. Exhibit 5 indicates that extreme backflushing is even less detailed than a process costing system in terms of the recordkeeping for each product unit.

Most firms making changes in their basic costing systems for plants using JIT production have adopted one of three approaches:

- Switch from a job costing to a process costing system. The effect of adopting JIT production methods is that the production line is run on a constant-flow basis; not surprisingly, some of these firms are switching to process costing. Another rationale for adopting process costing is that with the increased emphasis on quality in

JIT production plants, there is more homogeneity in the units processed. JIT puts great emphasis on eliminating spoilage and reworked units. Spoilage and reworked units are an important source of heterogeneity in work tickets in non-Jit production plants.

- Switch from a more detailed to a less detailed process costing system. Omark Industries made the following changes in three of its product lines:

	Number of Cost Centers	
Product Line	**Pre-Jit**	**JIT**
Chain Saws	18	4
Sprockets	5	3
Bars	4	1

- Switch from a job- or process-costing system to a backflush costing system. Most firms adopting the backflush approach use two triggers to make entries into the internal accounting system. The first trigger is the purchase of materials or components; the second is the completion of production or the sale of a finished good.

These simplifications have led to sizable reductions in individual accounting entries for product costing in JIT production plants.

The level of detailed information recorded about labor costs is reduced. In many organizations, labor costs are a declining percentage of total manufacturing costs. Organizations adopting JIT production methods have adapted to the declining materiality of labor costs by:

- Retaining direct labor as a separate direct cost category but reducing individual labor classifications. An industrial machine manufacturer reduced labor classifications at one of its plants from 26 to five over a three-year period in which it adopted JIT production methods. This reduction is consistent with a JIT philosophy that emphasizes teams, not individuals. JIT plants train workers for many activities. Such training increases flexibility regarding the assignment of workers to

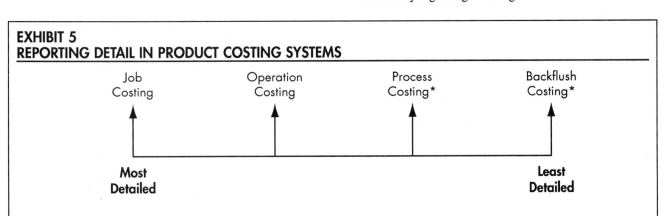

EXHIBIT 5
REPORTING DETAIL IN PRODUCT COSTING SYSTEMS

Job Costing	Operation Costing	Process Costing*	Backflush Costing*

Most Detailed — **Least Detailed**

*Depending on the desire for detailed tracking, some observers would switch the postions of process costing and backflush costing on this continuum. In any event, backflush costing has more characteristics of process costing than of job costing.

individual work cells. (Plants with a high level of union-ization have reported difficulty in negotiating these reductions in labor classifications with unions.)

- Abandoning labor as a separate direct cost category. The alternative treatments of labor costs are:
  —Classification of labor costs as a part of an indirect manufacturing cost pool that is allocated to units of production.
  —Classification of labor costs as a period cost that is immediately expensed.

Of course, abandoning direct labor as a separate cost category precludes the use of direct labor as an allocation base.

One example of altering labor cost reporting is the Milwaukee plant of Harley-Davidson. Direct labor was less than 10% of the product cost. When direct labor was recorded as a separate cost category, 65% of cost accounting efforts were devoted to administrative work related to these labor costs, including the setting of labor standards, the correction of wrong entries associated with labor, and attempts to reconcile the labor reported on job tickets with the total labor time available. Harley-Davidson concluded that the effort did not meet a cost/benefit test, and the company now combines direct labor and overhead costs into a single conversion cost pool.[10]

Piecework payment plans are being eliminated in JIT plants. Therefore, labor costs can be recorded in far less detail. The elimination of piecework plans drastically reduces the transactions reported per worker. Piecework plans create incentives for workers to produce, even though there is no demand for the finished good. In a JIT plant, management prefers workers to be idle rather than to produce for inventory.

Exhibit 6 links the justifications for changes in the cost accounting system to each of the five specific changes associated with JIT production.

COST MANAGEMENT IN A JIT ENVIRONMENT

Cost management in JIT plants includes several activities, many of which also apply to plants not using JIT.

Cost planning. This is undertaken before production commences, and in some cases before the production line is constructed. Plant engineers and product designers play important roles in cost planning. Their aim is to design the product and the production line with a mix of cost, quality, deliverability, and flexibility that reflects senior management's strategy. In the design of production lines for JIT plants, great emphasis is placed on eliminating all activities that do not add value to the product.

Cost reduction. This is undertaken in both the pre-production and production stages. At several Japanese plants that use JIT, cost reduction targets are set for each product (e.g., a 25% cost reduction target for a product in its first

---

EXHIBIT 6
JUSTIFICATIONS FOR COST ACCOUNTING CHANGES FOR JIT PRODUCTION

- More accurate product cost information.
  —An increase in direct traceability of some costs.
  —Elimination (or at least reduction) of several activities classified as indirect.
- Better control of cost incurrence.
  —Reduced emphasis on individual labor and overhead variances, which minimizes dysfunctional operating decisions often associated with existing cost accounting system.
- Reduced system costs.
  —A reduction in the level of detailed information recorded on work tickets.
  —A reduction in the level of detailed information recorded about labor costs.

---

year). Product line workers are all members of cost reduction circles that seek ways to achieve the cost reduction targets. Each year individual workers are required to submit a specific number of cost reduction ideas to be discussed by the cost reduction circle.

Cost control. This is undertaken when production starts. The sources of information for cost control activities include:

- Personal observation by production line workers.
- Financial performance measures (e.g., inventory turnover ratios and variances based on standard costs for materials, labor, and overhead).
- Nonfinancial performance measures (e.g., production lead-time, setup time, percentage of product defects, and schedule attainment).

The general trends at both the shop production-cell level and at the plant level that have been observed in JIT plants are a declining role for financial measures, and an increasing role for personal observation and nonfinancial measures in cost control activities. The reasons for these trends include:

- Production workers play a pivotal role in cost control activities. They directly observe nonfinancial variables on the plant floor. Hence, nonfinancial variables are intuitive and easy to comprehend.
- Dramatic reductions in lead times in JIT plants place a premium on the timeliness of data when controlling costs. Measurements taken on the plant floor are inevitably the most up-to-date data available.
- Increased recognition is being given to early pinpointing and controlling of cost drivers (i.e., the underlying causes of costs). The focus is on before-the-fact, rather than after-the-fact, control. For example, workers are encouraged to reduce setup times, minimize scrap, and minimize the number of reworked units.

- The internal accounting system in a JIT plant typically contains little cost control data about actual product costs at individual production cells. For example, under the backflush costing method, no tracking is made of product cost accumulation as products move through successive work cells.

Inventory turnover measures. Inventory turnover is a key performance measure in JIT plants. For example, at one of its plants using JIT production methods, a consumer products company in England now computes separate inventory turnover ratios for each product line and for raw materials and components, work in process, and finished goods. This company still records work in process with a process costing system. (For companies using extreme backflush costing, cost measures of work in process are not recorded in the internal accounting system.)

Cost reduction target measures. Comparisons of actual product costs with target product costs play an important role in organizations that emphasize cost reduction activities. For example, an automotive company in Japan has targets for the materials costs associated with individual product lines. Separate material costs are accumulated for each product variation in its product line in order to gain insight into how cost reduction ideas are leading to lower product costs.

JIT IS SIMPLIFICATION

There is no single blueprint for cost accounting and cost management in a JIT environment. Rather, there is considerable variation in the changes made—for the cost pools used, allocation bases chosen, costing system adopted (job, operation, process, or backflush), and types of performance measures used. However, the changes observed share an underlying commonality—specifically, a movement toward simplification of cost accounting practices. This commonality is part of the JIT theme: to simplify all activities. Activities that add value can be further improved, and those that do not can be eliminated.

Many organizations reject JIT as inappropriate for them. Nevertheless, JIT methods have proven that any significant change in underlying operations is likely to justify a corresponding change in the accounting system.

If a company's accounting system is still creaking along on outdated engines, managers are probably not being served optimally in their attempts to cope with today's and tomorrow's challenges and operations. Thus, the flurry of attention to JIT is beneficial even if it only prods managers and accountants to make a zero-base review of their existing cost accounting systems, regardless of whether the underlying operations are using JIT purchasing or production methods.

APPENDIX: BACKFLUSH COSTING

A backflush costing system focuses first on the output of an organization and then works backward when applying

costs to units sold and to inventories. The term backflush probably arose because the trigger points for product costing entries can be delayed until as late as sales, when costs finally are flushed through the accounting system. In contrast, conventional product costing systems track costs through work in process (WIP) as the focal account, beginning with the introduction of raw materials into production.

The following three examples demonstrate backflushing. Example 1 illustrates the elimination of a separate WIP inventory account. Examples 2 and 3 are more dramatic departures from widely used product costing systems.

EXAMPLE 1

A hypothetical company, Silicon Valley Computers (SVC), has two trigger points for making entries in the internal accounting system:

- Trigger point 1—The purchase of raw materials and components.
- Trigger point 2—The manufacture of a finished good unit.

SVC manufactures keyboards for personal computers. For the month of April, there are no beginning inventories of raw materials, WIP, or finished goods. The standard material cost per keyboard unit in April is $19. For product costing, SVC combines labor costs and indirect manufacturing costs into a single conversion cost category. The standard conversion cost per keyboard unit in April is $12. SVC has two inventory accounts:

Type of Account	Name
Combined raw materials and WIP	Inventory: raw and WIP
Finished goods	Finished goods

Incurrences of conversion costs are charged to responsibility centers under backflush costing just as in other costing systems. Applications of conversion costs are made to products at various trigger points. Any conversion costs not applied to products are written off immediately as expenses incurred in the period. For example, all unfavorable variances are charged as period expenses.

(For simplicity, Examples 1 to 3 assume that all actual costs and standard costs are the same.)

SVC uses the following steps when applying costs to units sold and to inventories:

Step one. Record the raw materials purchased in the reporting period. Assume that April materials purchases were $1,950,000.

| Inventory: raw and WIP | $1,950,000 | |
| Accounts payable | | $1,950,000 |

Step two. Record the incurrence of conversion costs during the reporting period. Assume conversion costs were $1,200,000.

| Conversion costs | $1,200,000 |
| Accounts payable, accrued payroll | $1,200,000 |

Step three. Determine the number of finished units manufactured during the reporting period. Assume that 100,000 keyboard units were manufactured in April.

Step four. Compute the standard cost of each finished unit. This step typically uses a bill of materials and an operations list, or equivalent records. For SVC, the standard cost per unit is $31 ($19 standard material cost + $12 standard conversion cost).

Step five. Record the cost of finished goods manufactured in the reporting period:

Inventory: finished goods	$3,100,000
(100,000 units @ $31)	
Inventory: raw and WIP	$1,900,000
Conversion costs	1,200,000

Step six. Record the cost of goods sold in the reporting period. Assume that 99,000 units were sold during the month.

Cost of goods sold	$3,069,000
(99,000 units @ $31)	
Inventory: finished goods	$3,069,000

The end of month inventory balance for April are:

Inventory: raw and WIP	$50,000
Inventory: finished goods	
(1,000 units @ $31)	31,000
	$81,000

The elimination of the WIP account considerably reduces the amount of detail in the internal accounting system. (There still may be tracking of units on the production line, but there is no "costs attach" tracking through work tickets in the internal accounting system.

Exhibit 7 provides an overview of the accounts affected in Example 1.

EXAMPLE 2

A variant of Example 1 is a backflush costing system whose second trigger point for making entries into the internal accounting system is the sale, rather than the manufacture, of a finished unit. See Exhibit 8.

Two rationales given for this variant system are:

- To remove the incentive for managers to produce for inventory—Under the "costs attach" assumption implicit in job, operation, and process costing, period expenses can be reduced by producing units not sold and by increasing WIP.
- To increase the focus of managers on a plantwide goal (producing saleable units) rather than on an individual subunit goal (e.g., increase labor efficiency at an individual production center).

This variant has the same effect on net income as the immediate expensing of all conversion costs. Under this approach, the inventory account is confined solely to raw materials (whether they are in storage, in process, or in finished goods). No conversion costs are inventoried. The summary accounting entry is:

Cost of goods sold	$3,069,000
(99,000 units @ $31)	
Inventory	$1,881,000
Conversion costs	1,188,000

At the end of each period, an adjusting entry is made that immediately expenses the conversion costs incurred but not attributed to units sold:

| Period expenses | $12,000 |
| Conversion costs | $12,000 |

The end-of-period inventory account is $69,000 ($50,000 in raw materials still on hand and $19,000 in raw materials embodied in the 1,000 units manufactured but not sold during the period).

Under this variant, there is no account for finished goods inventory because the trigger for making the second set of entries is sale rather than manufacture.

EXAMPLE 3

The simplest version of a backflush product costing system has only one trigger point for making product costing entries in the accounting system. Assume this trigger point is the manufacture of a finished unit. With the same data as in Examples 1 and 2, the summary entry is:

EXHIBIT 7
EXAMPLE 1—AN OVERVIEW OF BACKFLUSH COSTING

	Inventory: Raw and WIP			Inventory: Finished Goods			Cost of Goods Sold	
Direct →	(1) 1,950,000	(3) 1,900,000 →	(3)	1,900,000	(4) 3,069,000 →	(4) 3,069,000		
Materials	Balance 50,000							
	Conversion Costs							
Conversion								
Costs →	(2) 1,200,000	(3) 1,200,000 →	(3) 1,200,000					
			Balance 31,000					

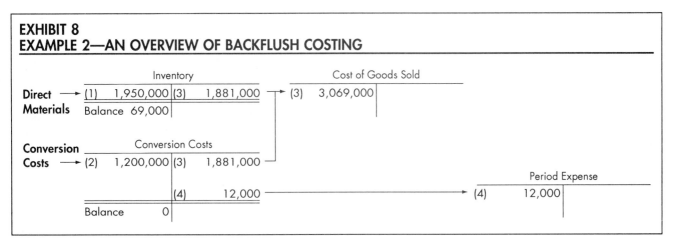

EXHIBIT 8
EXAMPLE 2—AN OVERVIEW OF BACKFLUSH COSTING

Inventory—finished goods	$3,100,000
Accounts payable	$1,900,000
Conversion costs	1,200,000

At the end of the period, the $50,000 of raw materials purchased but not yet manufactured into finished units will not have been entered into the internal product costing system. This variant of a backflush system is less feasible if there are significant inventories of raw materials and WIP.

George Foster and Charles T. Horngren are professors at Stanford University's Graduate School of Business, Stanford CA.

Portions of this paper appeared in the June 1987 issue of *Management Accounting.*

Notes

1. C. Horngren, "Cost and Management Accounting: Yesterday and Today," in E. Bromwich and A. Hopwood (eds.), *Research and Current Issues in Management Accounting* (London: Pitman, 1986), p 37.

2. V. Wright, "The Effect of Zero Inventories on Cost (Just-in-Time)," *Cost Accounting for the '90s: The Challenge of Technologies Change* (Montvale NJ: National Association of Accountants, 1986), p 157.

3. T. Arenberg, "Vendor Support Systems—Partners in Profit." *Readings in Zero Inventory* (American Production and Inventory Control Society, 1984), p 98. Further discussion of JIT purchasing is in C. Horngren and C. Foster, *"Cost Accounting: A Managerial Emphasis,* 6th ed. (Englewood Cliffs NJ: Prentice-Hall, 1987), pp 724–726.

4. Wright, "The Effect of Zero Inventories on Cost (Just-in-Time)," p 158.

5. B. O'Connor, "Just-in-Time Vendors Are Coming," *Readings in Zero Inventory* (American Production and Inventory Control Society, 1984), p 95.

6. H. Johansson, "The Effect of Zero Inventories on Cost (Just-in-Time)," in *Cost Accounting for the '90s: The Challenge of Technological Change* (Montvale NJ: National Association of Accountants, 1986), p 145. Numerous examples of improvements associated with JIT are given in R. Schonberger, *"World Class Manufacturing (*New York: Free Press, 1986).

7. R. Kelder, "CIM and Traditional Cost Accounting Practice" (Presentation at AME Cost Accounting Conference, Chicago: November 1986).

8. An example is the Hewlett-Packard personal computer. The HP150B had 550 part numbers; the next model (HP15OC) had only 120 part numbers. See J. Patell, "Adapting a Cost Accounting System to Just-in-Time Manufacturing: The Hewlett-Packard Personal Office Computer Division" (Working Paper, Stanford University, 1986).

9. C. Sanchez, "Manufacturing Accounting Cost System" (Presentation at AME Cost Accounting Conference, Chicago: November 1986).

10. R. D'Amore and W. Turk, "Just-in-Time Accounting at Harley-Davidson" (Presentation at AME Cost Accounting Conference, Chicago: November 1986).

Recommended Reading

Heard, J. "JIT Accounting." *Readings in Zero Inventory."* American Production and Inventory Control Society, 1984.

Holbrook, W., and Eiler, R. "Accounting Changes Required for Just-in-Time Production." *American Production and Inventory Control Society Conference Proceedings*, 1985.

Horngren, C., and Foster G. *Cost-Accounting: A Managerial Emphasis*, 6th ed. Englewood Cliffs NJ: Prentice-Hall, 1987

Maskell, B. "Management Accounting and Just-in-Time." *Management Accounting* (UK) (September 1986), pp 32–34.

Neumann, B., and Jaouen, P. "Kanban, Zips and Cost Accounting. A Case Study." *Journal of Accountancy* (August 1986).

From G. Foster and C. T. Horngren, "Cost Accounting and Cost Management in a JIT Environment," *Journal of Cost Management* (Winter 1988): 4-14. Reprinted with permission.

Question

2.3 For firms adopting JIT production, what major changes in management accounting systems are being made?

CHAPTER 3

Cost Concepts

Robin Cooper and Robert Kaplan's *Activity-Based Systems: Measuring the Costs of Resource Usage* (Reading 3.1) presents one of the key distinguishing ideas between traditional and activity-based costing systems. Traditional costing systems tend to use allocation bases, such as direct labor and machine hours, that are volume-driven. However, the resource demands of customers and products often are not proportional to the volume of units sold or produced. Thus, traditional systems do not accurately measure the costs of resources used to produce products; rather, they rely on the cost of resources supplied. Activity-based costing systems overcome this problem by focusing on the demands of resources needed to perform activities to produce outputs. The demands derive from variation in the diversity and complexity of products and customer mix.

The second reading (Reading 3.2), *Cost Classification in Unit-Based and Activity-Based Manufacturing Cost Systems,* by Robin Cooper, presents an important advance in the classification of activities in manufacturing processes. Based on an analysis of fifty costing systems representing thirty-one firms, Cooper classifies activities as unit-level, batch-level, product-level and facility-level. For unit-based activities, costs are assigned in strict proportion to production volume; batch level activities work under the assumption that inputs are consumed in direct proportion to the number of batches; product-level activities assume that inputs are consumed to sustain production of the variety of products that an organization produces; and facility-level activities are those common to many products, with allocation done on an arbitrary basis. This classification of activities forms a critical part of the definition of an activity-based costing system.

ABC and Life-Cycle Costing for Environmental Expenditures, by Jerry Kreuze and Gale Newell (Reading 3.3), presents an interesting application of ABC and Cooper's activity classification to environmental costing settings. The article addresses issues related to the costs of hazardous waste disposal, cleaning up polluted water, soil, and buildings, and many other issues. The concept of life-cycle costing also is introduced and is extremely pertinent for dealing with products or processes that may ultimately result in environmental problems. For instance, Kreuze and Newell state that responsibility for dealing with hazardous waste essentially lasts forever. The ABC classification of costs is used very effectively to illustrate how environmental costs can be separated and managed. Life cycle costing will be discussed in depth in Chapter 13 of the ABKY text.

3.1 Activity-Based Systems: Measuring the Costs of Resource Usage

Robin Cooper and Robert S. Kaplan

Robin Cooper is a Professor at the Claremont Graduate School and Robert S. Kaplan is a Professor at the Harvard Business School.

This paper describes the conceptual basis for the design and use of newly emerging activity-based cost (ABC) systems. Traditional cost systems use volume-driven allocation bases, such as direct labor dollars, machine hours, and sales dollars, to assign organizational expenses to individual products and customers. But many of the resource demands by individual products and customers are not proportional to the volume of units produced or sold.[1] Thus, conventional systems do not measure accurately the costs of resources used to design and produce products and to sell and deliver them to customers. Companies, including those with excellent traditional cost systems,[2] have developed activity-based cost systems so that they can directly link the costs of performing organizational activities to the products and customers for which these activities are performed.

I. ABC SYSTEMS AS RESOURCE USAGE MODELS

Activity-based cost systems estimate the cost of resources *used* in organizational processes to produce outputs.[3] Many people have attempted to interpret activity-based costs using their more familiar fixed versus variable cost framework, an interpretation inconsistent with an ABC system's measurements of resource usage costs. The conventional fixed versus variable cost classification arises from an attempt to classify the likely change in spending or *supply* of a resource. The measurement of unused capacity provides the critical link between the costs of resources *used,* as measured by an ABC model, and the costs of resources *supplied* or *available,* as reported by the organization's periodic financial statements.[4] The following equation, defined for each major activity performed by the organization's resources, formalizes this relationship:

Activity Availability = Activity Usage + Unused Capacity

A simple example illustrates the difference between the cost of resources supplied and the cost of resources used to perform activities. Consider a purchasing department in which the equivalent of 10 full-time people [the *resource supplied*] are committed to processing purchase orders [the activity performed]. If the monthly cost of a full-time employee is $2,500,[5] the monthly cost of the activity, "Process Purchase Orders," equals $25,000. Assume that each employee, working at practical capacity, can process 125 purchase orders per month, leading to an estimated cost of $20 for processing each purchase order.[6] Thus, the organization, each month, spends $25,000. This expenditure provides a capability to process up to 1,250 purchase orders [the *activity availability*] during the month. During any particular month, the department may be asked to process fewer purchase orders, say only 1,000. At an estimated cost of $20/purchase order, the ABC system would assign $20,000 of expenses to the parts and materials ordered by the purchasing department that month. The remaining $5,000 of monthly operating expenses represents the cost of unused capacity in the purchase order processing activity.

This example shows why companies need two different reporting systems. The periodic financial statements provide information on the cost of activities supplied each period (the $25,000 monthly expense in the purchasing department); and the activity-based cost system provides information on the quantity (1,000 purchase orders) and the estimated cost ($20,000) of activities actually used in a period. The difference ($5,000) between the cost of activities supplied ($25,000) and the cost of activities used ($20,000) equals the cost of unused capacity (or capacity shortage) during the period. And this difference is measured for each organizational activity, defined by the ABC system.[7]

The two systems provide different types of information for management. The cost of resources supplied is relevant for predicting near-term spending. Spending on many organizational resources will not vary with short-term fluctuations in activity volume and mix. That is why these costs have been classified as "fixed" in numerous accounting systems and textbooks.

But measuring and managing the operating expenses of most organizational resources as fixed in the short-run does not give much insight as to why the resources were acquired, what the resources are currently being used for, and the level of resources that will likely be required in the future. While the cost of supplying the resources may be fixed in the short-run,[8] the quantity of these resources used each period fluctuates based on activities performed for the outputs produced. Activity-based systems measure the cost of using these resources, even though the cost of supplying them will not vary, in the short run, with usage.

The ABC resource usage cost information can be used by managers to monitor and predict the changes in demands for activities as a function of changes in output volume and mix, process changes and improvements, introduction of new technology, and changes in product and process design. As such changes are contemplated, managers can predict where either shortages or excesses of capacity will occur. The managers can then either modify their decisions so that activity demand will be brought into balance with activity supply, or they can change the level of activities to be supplied in forthcoming periods.

For example, if newly designed custom products, with many unique parts and materials, are added to the mix, managers may forecast a much higher demand for the purchasing activity, perhaps now requiring that 2,000 purchase orders a month be processed. With no change in the process or efficiency of the processing purchasing order activity, this increase in demand will exceed available supply by 750 purchase orders per month, a shortage that can be relieved by hiring six more purchasing clerks. The ABC model, in addition, will trace purchasing costs directly to the newly designed custom products that are creating the demand for these additional purchasing resources, enabling managers to determine whether the revenues received fully compensate the organization for the cost of all the resources used to produce and deliver these products.

Of course, supplying additional purchasing clerks is only one possible action that the managers can take to the contemplated activity shortage. The engineering department can be asked to redesign the custom products so that they make more use of existing part numbers, an action that would reduce the amount of additional purchase orders required. Or the managers can search for process improvements or technology that would make the purchase order processing activity more efficient, perhaps raising the monthly output per person from 125 to 200 purchase orders.

Thus, measuring the *costs of resources supplied* indicates to managers the level of current spending (or more generally, expenses) and the capacity to perform activities that this spending has provided. Measuring the *costs of resources used* by individual outputs provides information for managerial actions, as will be discussed more fully subsequently in the paper.

II. ISN'T THE UNUSED CAPACITY CALCULATION JUST A NEW NAME FOR THE VOLUME VARIANCE?

The calculation of unused capacity each period looks, at first glance, suspiciously like the traditional cost accounting volume variance. But the formulas:

Activity Availability = Activity Usage + Unused Capacity

or

Cost of Activity Supplied = Cost of Activity Used + Cost of Unused Activity

differ from the standard cost calculations of a volume variance in several significant ways.

First, and most obviously, volume variances are reported only in aggregate financial terms since traditional cost systems do not identify the **quantity** of overhead resources supplied or used. The activity-based approach reports both the quantity (number of purchase orders not written) and the cost of unused capacity Second, traditional volume variances are often calculated with a denominator volume based on budgeted production, rather than practical capacity. In the activity-based approach, the "denominator volume" must always be the practical capacity of the activity being supplied, not the anticipated volume. And, third, the traditional cost accounting procedure of allocating overhead with a denominator volume is viewed as useful only for inventory valuation, not to provide information relevant for management; e.g.,

> *The preselected production volume level of the application base used to set a budgeted fixed-factory-overhead rate for applying costs to inventory is called the denominator volume.*
>
> *In summary, the production volume variance arises because the actual production volume level achieved usually does not coincide with the production level used as a denominator volume for computing a budgeted application rate for inventory costing of fixed-factory overhead.[9] (emphasis added)*

Note how students are instructed that the calculation involves only the application of (so-called) *fixed*-factory overhead to units of production. Clearly, the volume variance is viewed, at least in textbooks (but not always in practice), as a cost accounting exercise for financial statements that is devoid of managerial significance.

These three differences between volume variances and measurements of unused capacity, while real, are not, however, the most important distinction. The cost accounting calculation that leads to a volume variance uses a measure of activity volume for the period (i.e., the denominator volume, also called the allocation base) that varies with the number of units produced. Direct labor hours, units of production, materials purchases, and machine hours are typical allocation bases used by traditional systems to assign factory expenses to products in production cost centers.[10] Implicitly, this procedure assumes that factory expenses are used by products in proportion to the overhead allocation base, i.e., proportional to volume of units produced. In practice, of course, this assumption is not valid.

Activity-based cost systems use separate activity cost drivers (the ABC generalization of an assignment or allocation base) for each activity. The activity cost drivers are not devices to allocate costs. They represent the demand that outputs make on each activity. For example, the activity cost driver for the setup activity could be the number of setups or the number of setup hours; the activity cost driver for processing purchase orders could be the number of purchase orders; the cost driver for administering and maintaining parts in the system could be the number of active part numbers. While some activity cost drivers are unit-related (such as machine and labor hours), as conventionally assumed, many activity cost drivers are batch-related, order-related, product-sustaining, and customer-sustaining.[11]

Because traditional cost systems use allocation bases that do not represent the demands for support resources by activities, the volume variance for a period can be zero even while substantial shortages or surpluses of capacity exist for many individual activities. For example, if actual production includes an unexpectedly high proportion of mature, standard products, produced in large batches, the demands for many batch and product-sustaining activities will be well below the quantity of resources supplied to perform these activities and much unused capacity will exist during the period. Conversely, if the actual production volume includes a substantial and unexpectedly high number of new, customized products, that are made in very small batches, the demand for batch and product-sustaining activities may exceed the quantity supplied. Shortages, delays, and overtime may occur in the batch and product-sustaining activities even though the total quantity of units produced during the period equaled the budgeted or anticipated amount.

The distinction between the measurement, by activity-based cost systems, of the cost of activities used (and unused) and the traditional cost accounting emphasis on fixed versus variable costs can be reconciled by examining closely the way managers contract for and supply resources to perform organizational activities.

III. RESOURCES THAT ARE SUPPLIED AS USED (AND NEEDED)

Some resources are acquired as needed. For these resources, the cost of resources supplied will generally equal the cost of resources used. For example, materials are usually ordered as needed so that materials expense equals the cost of materials used. And the cost of energy supplied to operate production machines also equals the cost of using that energy. Temporary employees hired on a daily basis from employment agencies and employees who are paid on a piece-work or overtime basis are additional examples. The company contracts with these workers to produce output and the workers are paid only when they are needed to produce output. Capital supplied by lenders is another example where the supply and the usage cost are identical (equaling the interest expense on the amount borrowed).[12]

In general, when the organization acquires a resource from outside suppliers, without long-term commitments, the cost of using the resource can equal the cost of acquiring (and supplying) the resource; for example, when the organization acquires the resource in spot markets. The costs of supplying such resources are apparently what many people have in mind when they refer to "variable costs." Such resources have no unused capacity. Whatever is supplied is used, or, alternatively, whatever is needed is acquired. This causes the costs of supplying the resource to be strongly correlated with the quantity (and hence the cost) of the resource used.

IV. RESOURCES THAT ARE SUPPLIED IN ADVANCE OF USAGE

Organizations commit, however, to making many other resources available whether or not the resources will be fully used for current and future activities. This commitment can take several forms. The organization can make a cash expenditure to acquire a resource that provides service for several periods into the future. The most common example occurs when the company acquires or overhauls buildings and equipment. Such a transaction leads to an expense being recognized in each period during the useful life of the resource, with the organization gaining the capacity provided by the resource during each such period. The expense of supplying the resource will be incurred, each period, independent of how much of the resource is used.[13]

As a second example, the organization can enter into an explicit contract to obtain the use of a resource for several periods in the future. For example, a company leases buildings and equipment, or it guarantees access to energy or key materials through take-or-pay contracts. In this situation, a cash payment will occur and an expense will be recognized in each future period. Again, the amount of the cash payment and associated expense are independent of the actual quantity of usage of the resource in any period.

The third, and most important, example occurs when an organization enters into implicit contracts, particularly with its salaried and hourly employees, to maintain employment levels despite short-term downturns in activity levels. In this case, the spending (and expenses) associated with these employees will remain constant independent of the quantity of work performed by the employees.[14]

In each of the three contracting mechanisms, the organization acquires units of service capacity before the actual demands for the service units are realized. Consequently, the expenses of supplying the service capacity from these resources are incurred (or recognized) independent of usage. This independence in the short-run between the supply (or expense) of these resources and their usage has led this category of expense to be considered "fixed" with respect to current production volume and mix.

The separation between the acquisition of resource capacity and its actual usage arises from economies-of-scale in contracting for resources. For example, some service units come in lumpy amounts (e.g., physical capacity of machines, or the services provided by individual employees). Managers also find it less expensive to acquire some resources on a long-term commitment basis rather than to contract continually in spot markets to acquire resource capacity as needed.[15] These issues have been discussed at some length by scholars, such as Coase, Chandler, and Williamson.

Through any or all of these three contracting mechanisms, the organization acquires a capability or capacity to perform activities, and an associated expense of providing that capacity. The first step, therefore, in an activity-based analysis is to estimate both the expense of providing the capacity to perform an activity (the $25,000 monthly expense to process purchase orders), and the capacity or number of units of service activity that can be practically delivered (the 1,250 purchase orders per month) by the resources supplied. The expense of providing the activity capacity is divided by the number of available service units to obtain an estimate of the cost of supplying a unit of service of the activity (the $20 per purchase order cost).

V. MEASURING COSTS OF RESOURCES USED IN A PERIOD: THE ROLE FOR ACTIVITY-BASED COST SYSTEMS

The distinction between resources supplied as needed and resources supplied prior to (but in anticipation of) usage suggests that a relatively simple system can be used for the periodic measurement of actual expenses (see Exhibit 1). In this system, short-term contribution margin is measured as price (or revenues) less the cost of resources acquired as needed: materials, energy, and short-term labor (and overtime). By assumption, the remaining operating expenses represent resources that have been acquired prior to actual usage. The costs of these resources should be unaffected by actual activity levels during the period. The periodic income statement can report, for each activity, the costs of resources used for outputs and the costs of resources unused during the period.

For management purposes, flexible budgets and variance analysis become unnecessary for these expense accounts. A simple comparison of actual to budgeted expenses, account by account, will suffice to provide feedback.[16] Basically, the authorized expenses have been determined either by prior commitments (acquiring plant, property, and equipment; signing take-or-pay contracts) or during the annual budgeting process. One manufacturing manager expressed this point quite forcefully:

> Cost variances are useless to me. I don't want to ever have to look at a cost variance, monthly or weekly. Once you've decided to run a product, you don't have many choices left. Resources are already committed regardless of how the cost system computes costs among alternative processes.
>
> Monthly, I do look at the financial reports.... I look closely at my fixed expenses and compare these to the budgets, especially on discretionary items like travel and maintenance. I also watch head count. But the financial systems still don't tell me where I am wasting money. I expect that if I make operating improvements, costs should go down, but I don't worry about the linkage too much. The organizational dynamics make it difficult to link cause and effect precisely.[17]

Managers may be encouraged to modify their use of resources in the short-run based on information on unused capacity For example, when excess setup capacity exists, they can temporarily decrease batch sizes. Alternatively, managers may be expected to adjust downward the quantity of resources supplied when substantial amounts of unused capacity persist for several periods.

Several organizations, however, not understanding the important distinction between measuring the costs of resources supplied (and expensed) and the costs of resources used, have attempted to use their activity-based systems to budget monthly expenses. A good example of the problems arising from using an activity-based system for monthly performance measurement was documented in the Hewlett Packard: Queensferry Telecommunications Division case.

Hewlett Packard: QTD Case[18]

QTD had recently installed a new activity-based cost system. The system accumulated expenses at each process and assigned these expenses to products with a cost driver defined for each process (e.g., number of axial insertions). The system was developed primarily to provide process cost information to product engineers to help them design products that would be less expensive to manufacture. The system, however, was also used to monitor production performance. The two functions soon came into conflict when production volume dropped due to the postponement of a major contract. The lower production volume led to large monthly volume variances because operating expenses could not be reduced proportionately to the decline in volume. The controller commented:

> In a perfect world, spending would drop to offset lower production volumes. However, in environments like ours, where we retain our employees, it is almost impossible for spending to be cut back when volume drops in a period.

Higher cost driver rates were calculated, based on the lower production volumes, so that the accounts would "clear" each period without large volume variances. This change, however, negated the primary purpose of the newly designed system. With unused capacity expenses now loaded on to cost driver rates, the system no longer provided product designers with accurate information on the expenses of activities performed to manufacture their products.

Companies like QTD, that attempt to budget expenses each month from their activity-based resource usage model, will end up, each month, with a variance representing the unused capacity for every activity and resource for which usage and availability are not perfectly correlated. The unused capacity variance signals only that managers did not adjust the resource availability level to the amount actually required for the volume and mix of outputs produced that period. It is not helpful, however, to predict spending or expense changes.

Once decisions get made on resource availability levels in the organization, typically in the annual budgeting and authorization process, the expenses of supplying most resources will be determined for the year (unless managers deliberately act to eliminate or add to the resources). For

EXHIBIT 1
EXAMPLE OF ABC INCOME STATEMENT

SALES			20,000
Less: EXPENSES OF RESOURCES SUPPLIED AS USED			
Materials	7,600		
Energy	600		
Short-term labor	900		9,100
CONTRIBUTION MARGIN			10,900
Less: ACTIVITY EXPENSES: COMMITTED RESOURCES	Used	Unused	
Permanent direct labor	1,400	200	
Machine run-time	3,200		
Purchasing	700	100	
Receiving/Inventory	450	50	
Production runs	1,000	100	
Customer administration	700	200	
Engineering changes	800	(100)	
Parts administration	750	150	
TOTAL EXPENSES OF COMMITTED RESOURCES	9,000	700	9,700
OPERATING PROFIT			1,200

example, the resources committed to the purchase-order processing activity will be determined annually as a function of the expected number and complexity of purchase orders to be processed. We would *not* expect, however, the size of the purchasing department to fluctuate weekly or monthly depending on how many purchase orders get processed during a week or a month. Therefore, even when usage of a resource drops, the expense associated with that resource continues at its previous level. The difference between the costs of resources supplied and the costs of resources used for producing products equals the cost of **unused capacity** for the period.[19] The difference should not be interpreted as a change in the cost of performing the activity.

VI. RELEVANCE FOR MANAGERIAL DECISIONS: USING ABC TO INCREASE PROFITS

An improved costing system is a means to an end. The goal is to increase profits, not to obtain more accurate costs. How do activity-based cost systems help companies improve their profitability? We attempt to answer this question through the simple profit equation:

$$\text{Profits} = \text{Revenues} - \text{Expenses}$$

Pricing and Product Mix

Some companies use their ABC information to reprice their products, services, or customers so that the revenues (resources) received exceed the costs of resources used to produce products for individual customers. For example, prices are lowered to customers ordering standard products in high volumes, and prices are raised to customers ordering highly customized products in low volumes. Pricing strategies are part of a broader set of actions taken by managers to improve profits through changes in product and customer mix. For example, some companies, experiencing

declining demand for their standard products, proliferated their product line to offer customized, low-volume varieties. This strategy was influenced by their belief that many costs were "fixed" and that the lost volume in standard products needed to be replaced with customized products that could "absorb overhead" and even sell at price premiums. With this traditional view, the labor hours, machine hours, and materials purchases could be approximately the same between the old product and the new product mix. But the new product mix included many customized, low volume products that made many more demands on resources performing batch and product-sustaining activities. Because sufficient unused capacity did not exist to perform these activities, the companies had to increase their spending so that more resources could be supplied to perform batch and product-sustaining activities. After the product proliferation had occurred, and the companies were incurring higher expenses for support resources, ABC models revealed that many of the newly-added products were unprofitable.[20]

Once this situation has been discovered, managers have typically first attempted to raise prices on the unprofitable products. If this action does not generate sufficient revenues to cover all their product-specific costs, managers contemplate eliminating unprofitable products. Or they consider outsourcing products to suppliers whose total cost of acquisition is below the cost of resources required to make the product internally. Of course, before outsourcing or dropping products, managers should verify that they can eliminate the resources no longer needed or can replace the lost volume with more profitable business. Thus before any decision is taken from activity-based product or customer costs, managers must assess the incremental revenue and spending consequences.

Critics of ABC have stated:
Isn't this what we have been teaching (or practicing) as relevant costing or incremental analysis? Students in introduc-

tory cost and managerial accounting classes are already taught that costs unaffected by whether a particular product is retained or eliminated are irrelevant for that decision and should be excluded from the analysis. Why do companies need an ABC system? Why not just calculate the changes in spending that would occur for any contemplated decision, such as dropping or outsourcing a product, and make a decision based on that analysis? What purpose is served by building, maintaining, and attempting to interpret a generalized activity-based cost model?

Perhaps one can understand the demand for a generalized (activity-based) resource usage model from a similar situation that arises in physics. Introductory physics courses teach Newton's laws of motion, such as conservation of angular momentum or gravitational attraction. The principles are illustrated with problems that require calculating the interactions among two or three objects. Students who survive to more advanced physics courses encounter a subject called statistical thermodynamics, which provides predictions of the aggregate behaviors of large numbers of particles. A naive student might ask, "Why do we need to study thermodynamics as a separate subject? Don't Newton's laws of motion still apply to these particles?" The answer is, of course, they do, but to apply Newton's laws to the large numbers of particles being studied would exceed the lifetime and computational power of the universe. Therefore, physicists have devised laws to describe and predict the aggregate behavior of large numbers of interacting particles.

"Relevant costing"or "incremental analysis" situations are illustrated in introductory courses and books by simple examples with two or three products and simple overhead structures. An activity-based resource usage model can be viewed as the thermodynamic equivalent to the three product examples of introductory cost accounting courses. Consider, for example, the analysis that arises in the Bridgeton Industries case.[21] The plant initially produced five product lines. Because of competitive pressures, the plant's profitability had declined. Special studies were performed and eventually two product lines were outsourced. As the case proceeds, students learn that the total spending on resources declined by less than the loss in revenues so that the economics of the plant had deteriorated further. From a "relevant costing" perspective, how many special analyses would have been required to determine which product lines or combinations of product lines should have been dropped. Certainly each product line individually could have been analyzed. But because most resources come in lumpy amounts, perhaps substantial reductions in resource supply (and therefore spending) would occur only if at least two product lines were dropped, as was actually done. But why stop at two? Why not consider dropping all combinations of three, or four, or even all five product lines? In total, 2^5 or 32 combinations would have to be analyzed, with the relevant costs calculated for each of the 32 possible maintain/drop combinations.

The 32 possibilities may not seem insuperable, but for companies with hundreds and thousands of products, cus-

tomers, processes, and facilities, the combinations, while still finite, would, as in thermodynamics, exceed the lifetime and computational power of the universe to enumerate much less evaluate. And retain versus drop is a relatively simple binary decision. What about shifts in product mix, improvements in production processes, and changes in product designs? Managers cannot possibly apply introductory cost accounting relevant cost calculations to all possible product and customer mix decisions. The activity-based cost model, like the thermodynamics model, provides an aggregate view of the economic laws of motion of a complex enterprise, with thousands of individual products, customers, and facilities.[22]

Borrowing another analogy, integral calculus teaches us that the sum total of doing lots of little things can amount to something substantial. An activity-based resource usage model forecasts the changes in aggregate demands for activities from making decisions on many products, services, and customers. In effect, the activity-based cost model performs the integral calculus function of adding up a lot of small effects into something quite substantial. It approximates the changes in resource demands that will occur from implementing new decisions on pricing, product mix, and customer mix. Before actually implementing the proposed decisions, of course, managers must assess the cash flow consequences by forecasting, as well, the increases and decreases in resource supply (including revenues) that they anticipate will occur. An activity-based cost model serves to direct managers' attention to where more detailed analysis will likely yield the highest payoff. The ABC model reduces the dimensionality of decisions to where the cash flow consequences from only a few alternatives need to he examined closely.

Change Resource Usage

In addition to pricing, product and customer mix changes, which affect profits directly through changes in the margins earned between revenues received and resources expended, ABC models can help managers reduce resource usage, while holding revenues constant. When resource usage is reduced, some unused capacity will be created which can then be either managed away (enabling lower spending to occur) or used to process more throughput (enabling more revenues to be earned). Demands on support resources can be reduced by taking two types of actions:

- Reducing the number of times activities are performed, and
- Increasing the efficiency with which activities are performed.[23]

Reducing number of times activities are performed:

Changing from unprofitable to profitable product and customer mixes, as described above, enables companies to earn the same or even higher revenues while performing fewer activities. Managers can take additional actions to reduce the number of times activities are performed, especially activities performed by support resources. Marketing and sales executives in some companies have set *minimum order sizes* to reduce the large number of activities triggered by many small orders. As engineers *improve the design of products,* fewer engineering change notices are required. Other change activities are reduced when engineering managers discourage their employees from excessive tinkering with existing product designs, and marketing managers discourage or *charge premiums for customer-requested changes* in products and delivery schedules. In addition, design engineers, informed about the resource expenses associated with introducing and maintaining a large number of parts in the system, can develop product designs that use *fewer and more common parts.*[24] All these actions, individually and in combination, reduce the number of demands for activities performed by support resources, while maintaining existing (unit-driven) production volume.

Increasing efficiency (lowering the cost) of activities performed:[25]

A complementary set of actions can be taken to increase the efficiency of performing activities. The increased efficiency enables the same *quantity* of activities to be performed with fewer resources. Continuous improvement programs, such as *total quality management* and *cycle time reduction* (just-in-time), reduce the resources required to inspect products, changeover and setup machines, and move and store materials. Successful implementation of continuous improvement programs produces major reductions in the demands for resources to perform batch and product sustaining activities.

Introduction of advanced *information technology* reduces by substantial amounts the expenses of many batch and product-sustaining activities. Computer-Aided-Design and Engineering (CAD/CAE) equipment reduces the expenses of designing products and making changes to existing products. They also standardize the maintenance of routings and bills-of-materials. Flexible Manufacturing Systems (FMS) and Computer Integrated Manufacturing (CIM) essentially eliminate many batch activities through automatic scheduling, materials movement, inspection, and tool positioning, gauging, and maintenance, plus instantaneous changeovers between operations. In the theoretical limit, a CIM system requires the same resources to make 1 unit of 1,000 different products as it does to make 1,000 units of 1 product.[26] Electronic Data Interchange (EDI) and Electronic Funds Transfer (EFT) link companies with suppliers and customers, greatly reducing the expenses associated with purchasing, scheduling, receiving, shipping, invoicing, and paying for materials and products.

Improving Profits

Through a combination of reducing the quantity of activities performed and increasing the efficiency of performing the remaining activities, companies can maintain production throughput and, hence, revenues while reducing their demands for indirect and support resources. Ideally, managers can now obtain additional business, many of whose demands would be handled by resources currently in excess supply. This would enable the company to enjoy substantially higher profits because revenues would increase with only modest spending increases.[27] Alternatively, the unused capacity created can be reduced in the next budgeting cycle.

Budgeting: Changing the Supply of Resources to Match Resource Demands

As managers adjust their product and customer mixes, introduce new products, phase out mature products, improve operating processes, and introduce new technology, they change the demands for activities performed by indirect and support resources. The revised demands for resources to perform support activities can be estimated with an activity-based model. Differences between the demand for and the supply of resources can then be translated into expected changes in future spending on resources. Used in this way, the activity-based model becomes a central tool for management planning and budgeting. The budgets for each resource are determined based on the activities required for the forecasted product volume and mix, and existing production processes. For resources forecasted to be in short supply, the analysis provides a justification for additional spending to increase resource availability. For a resource forecasted to be in excess of predicted demands, managers can be requested to reduce the availability and hence the expenses of that resource. They can reduce the unused capacity by selling or scrapping machinery without replacement, by not replacing employees who retire or leave the organization voluntarily, by redeploying employees from activities where they are no longer needed to activities where capacity shortages exist, or, more drastically, by laying off now redundant employees. These actions enable the company to generate the same revenues with fewer resources, thereby allowing profits to increase.

Alternatively, companies may not exploit the profit opportunities from having created unused capacity. They may keep existing resources in place, even though the demands for the activities performed by the resources have diminished substantially. In this case, and only in this case, will the actions that reduced activity usage not yield any tangible benefits. Profits will remain the same, since revenues have remained constant and the expenses of resources supplied have also remained fixed. But the failure to increase profits is not due to costs being intrinsically "fixed." Rather, the failure is the consequence of managers being unable or unwilling to exploit the unused capacity they have created. The activity-based cost model focuses managers' attention on decisions that affect the resource demands by activities. If the decisions lead to lower demands for some resources, the company can then realize increased profits by either using these resources to generate higher revenues or by reducing spending on these resources. The costs of these resources are only "fixed" if managers cannot or do not exploit the opportunities from the unused capacity they helped to create.

VII. SUMMARY AND CONCLUSIONS

Activity-based cost systems contain two important insights. First, the activities performed by many resources are not demanded in proportion to the total volume of units produced (or sold). The demands arise from the diversity and complexity of the product and customer mix.

Second, activity-based cost systems are not models of how expenses or spending vary in the short-run. ABC systems estimate the costs of resources used to perform activities for various outputs. During any given period, the production of products and services, and their marketing, sale, and delivery to customers, create a demand for organizational activities. The quantity of each activity supplied to outputs is estimated by activity cost drivers such as the number of setup hours, number of purchase orders processed, number of receipts, number of direct labor and machine hours, and number of parts maintained. By summing across the costs of all resources supplied to perform activities for individual outputs, the ABC model estimates the costs of resources used during the period by all the organization's outputs.

Activity-based systems model how activity usage varies with the demands made for these activities. If activity usage exceeds the quantity available from existing resource supply, then higher spending to increase the supply of resources will likely soon occur. If, however, activity usage is below available supply, spending or the expenses of resources will not decrease automatically. Management, to obtain higher profits, must take conscious actions either to use the available capacity to support a higher volume of business (i.e., by increasing revenues) or to reduce spending on resources by eliminating the unused capacity. Costs and profits are fixed only if management takes no action, and leaves the unused capacity undisturbed. Management behavior, not cost behavior, determines whether reductions in resource demands become translated into higher profits.

APPENDIX
Separate Systems for Measuring Resource Expenses and Resource Usage: A Case Study

The Union Pacific case study illustrates well how a service organization developed a system for measuring the costs of resource usage quite different from the system used for operational and expense control.[28] During the 1960s, the company had developed an extensive system for monitoring spending and expenses in its more than 5,000 cost centers around the country. Cost centers included freight and locomotive repair yards, switching yards, transportation crews, and maintenance of track and right of way. Expenses were recorded in up to 1,200 different account codes.[29] Each month, a cost center manager received a report on actual and budgeted expenses for each of these accounts, supplemented with data on Year-to-Date actual expenses compared with budget and with a similar period in the previous year. The 5,000 individual cost center expense control reports

were aggregated into summary data for higher level managers all the way to senior vice-presidents in Omaha who received a one page summary of operations under their control. This extensive system of monthly reports was used to monitor and control cost center expenses and measure efficiency improvements.

In the deregulated environment of the 1980s, the company realized that despite extensive reporting of cost center expenses, it had no information to estimate the costs of resources used to move a carload of freight from one point to another. This gap occurred for two reasons. The railroad environment provides a vivid example of where almost complete separation exists between resource spending and resource usage. The monthly spending to maintain track and right of way and to repair locomotives and freight cars has no relation to the amount of traffic run that month. The monthly spending reflects the millions of gross ton miles hauled in many preceding months, and management's decision to replenish the supply of these resources so that they will be available for the future. The cost of using those resources occurred in the past; the spending to revitalize the depleted resources was occurring today.

Even apart from the temporal separation between resource usage and resource spending, the railroad like many other service organizations did not measure the use of resources by individual products within each cost center. For example, the railroad supplied switching yards and measured the expenses of operating switching yards. But it did not measure the quantity of use of switching yards by individual freight cars as they moved from shipper to customer.

The railroad had to develop entirely new analytic systems to measure the costs of activities performed to supply its customers with products and services. The costs of resources used to move a carload of freight from shipper to destination could not be estimated based on incremental spending since virtually no incremental spending occurred when the company picked up a freight car from a shipper, scheduled it, connected it to a train, switched it to several different trains, and finally delivered it to the customer. Yet the movement of the freight car required an extensive quantity of railroad resources to be supplied and available. And the actual running of the freight car placed incremental demands on several resources that would require additional spending sometime in the future. The company understood that it could not wait until the freight car, locomotive, or track was repaired to send out bills to all the shippers that made use of these resources in the past. It also understood that the amounts spent to supply train crews, scheduling and information systems, and switching yards were justified by the expected volume and mix of traffic to be carried. The company developed a system that estimated, move by move, the quantity and cost of all the resources used by individual carload moves, even though short-run spending was almost completely independent of these moves.

The railroad example provides a vivid example of the difference between resource usage and resource spending (or resource expenses). The power of the case, however, extends beyond railroads or even service companies since most manufacturing companies' resources are also now characterized by large distinctions between the use of the resources and the amount of current expenses to supply the resources.

Notes

1. Early versions of the transactional demand for resources appeared in J. Miller and T. Voliman, "The Hidden Factory," *Harvard Business Review* (September–/October 1985), 142–150, and Robin Cooper and Robert S. Kaplan, "How Cost Accounting Systematically Distorts Product Costs," *Management Accounting* (April 1988), pp. 20–27.A more comprehensive explanation of the impact of diversity and complexity on indirect costs was presented in the series of *Journal of Cost Management* articles by Robin Cooper, "The Rise of Activity-Based Cost Systems: Parts I–IV" (Summer 1988, Fall 1988, Winter 1989, and Spring 1989).

2. See, for example, Robert S. Kaplan, "John Deere Component Works (A) and (B)," HBS Cases #9-187-107 and -108; Robin Cooper and Karen H. Wruck, "Siemens: Electric Motor Works (A)," HBS Case # 9-189-089.

3. We will use the term "outputs" to refer generically to products, services, customers, projects, facilities or any object that creates a demand for or benefits from organizational activities. Activity-based cost systems assign the organization's operating expenses to outputs based on the activities performed for these outputs.

4. We have adopted the terminology of unused capacity, as suggested by Alan Vercio of Texas Instruments, rather than our initial term of "excess capacity." Not all "unused" capacity represents "excess" capacity.

5. This cost includes the costs of fringe benefits, secretarial and administrative support, equipment costs, and space charges associated with each purchasing department employee.

6. Note that this calculation does not use actual activity levels during the period; the denominator represents service capacity not actual usage of this capacity.

7. Later in the paper, we will show how to develop a new format for the periodic income or expense statement that highlights the costs of resources used and unused.

8. More accurately, the spending on (or expenses assigned to) these resources will be independent of the volume and mix of outputs produced during the period.

9. Charles T. Horngren and George Foster, *Cost Accounting: A Managerial Emphasis, Seventh Edition* (Prentice-Hall, 1991), pages 258 and 265.

10. More complex traditional systems that use multiple allocation bases within the same cost center will have multiple volume variances, but each allocation base is still unit-level, driven by the volume of output.

11. The hierarchy of factory expenses was introduced in Robin Cooper, "Cost Classification in Unit-Based and Activity-Based Manufacturing Cost Systems" (Fall 1990), pp. 4–13, and discussed further in Robin Cooper and Robert S. Kaplan, "Profit Priorities from Activity Based Costing," *Harvard Business Review* (May-June 1991), pp. 130-137.

12. Of course, the commitment fee associated with a line of credit is a counter-example, because the cost of supplying the resource (the right to borrow) is incurred whether the resource is used or not.

13. We are using the word "expense" in its traditional accounting sense; e.g., an outflow or other using up of assets or incurrence of liabilities (or a combination of both) during a period from delivering or producing goods, rendering services, or carrying out other activities that constitute an enterprise's ongoing major or central operations (W.W. Cooper and Yuji Ijiri, *Kohler's Dictionary for Accountants, Sixth Edition* (Prentice-Hall: Englewood Cliffs, NJ, 1983; pp. 203–204). To avoid confusion associated with financial accounting inventory valuation procedures that shift some period expenses forward in time to be matched against future revenues generated, we will assume, for purposes of this paper and without loss of generality,

that units produced always equal units sold. This enables all period expenses to be recognized as expenses in the period they are incurred.

14. The actual expenses of providing this capability in a given period can even exceed the cash outlays in that period. This situation arises when cash-payments made in much later periods, such as for vacations, pensions and other post-employment benefits, are attributed to the supply of the resource during the given period.

15. This prior commitment can also be made for strategic reasons; see Pankaj Ghemawat, *Commitment: The Dynamic of Strategy* (Free Press, 1991).

16. This distinction between the financial system required for periodic performance measurement (reporting on actual period expenses) and the activity-based system reporting on the costs of resource usage underlay the arguments in R. S. Kaplan, "One Cost System Isn't Enough," *Harvard Business Review* (January–February 1988). A good example of a company that separated its monthly reporting system from the system used to estimate the cost and profitability of its products is provided by the Union Pacific case study described in the Appendix.

17. Quote taken from Robert S. Kaplan, "Analog Devices: The Half-Life System," HBS # 9-190-061.

18. Robin Cooper and Kiran Verma," Hewlett Packard: Queensferry Telecommunications Division," HBS Case # 9-191-067.

19. During a period when usage exceeds normal capacity, the difference will represent a "favorable" over-utilization of capacity.

20. Unprofitable products are those for which the expenses assigned to maintain, produce, and deliver them exceed the net revenues received from their sale.

21. Robin Cooper, "Bridgeton Industries: Automotive Component and Fabrication Plant," HBS Case #9-190-085.

22. And even the thermodynamic extension is now known to be an approximation that ignores relativistic and quantum mechanical phenomena. Similarly, the activity-based resource usage model, as currently formulated, is likely just a first order, linear approximation to what may require stochastic, nonlinear formulations in certain situations.

23. These actions are iterative, not sequential, as managers continually adjust the volume and mix of their outputs, and manage the efficiency with which their activities are performed.

24. These design activities were the focus of the ABC systems described in the Tektronix and Hewlett Packard cases: Robin Cooper and Peter Turney, "Tektronix (A)," HBS Case # 9-188-143; and "Hewlett-Packard Roseville Networks Division," HBS Case # 9-189-117.

25. Using activity-based information to focus improvement activities was discussed in H. Thomas Johnson, "Activity Based Information: A Blueprint for World-Class Management Accounting," *Management Accounting* (June 1988), pp. 23–30. Using an activity-based cost system for performance improvement was a central focus in the system described in Robert S. Kaplan, "Maxwell Appliance Controls," HBS Case # 9-192-058.

26. In effect, CIM transforms batch and product-sustaining activities into unit-level activities so that product variety costs approach zero.

27. Spending will increase for resources for which availability and usage are tightly coupled (e.g., materials, energy), and for resources where unused capacity does not exist (perhaps direct labor or machine time). Also, it would be preferable for the added volume to generate revenues in excess of the expenses of resources used so that the new business can be sustained in the long run.

28. Robert S. Kaplan, "Union Pacific: Introduction, (A), and (B)," HBS Cases 9-186-176, 177,-I 78.

29. The larger number of account codes arose from regulatory reporting requirements specified by the Interstate Commerce Commission for Railform A.

Source Note
Many helpful and constructive comments on a previous draft were made by our colleagues including Anthony Atkinson, Toshiro Hiromoto, Jean-Francois Manzoni, Falconer Mitchell, Eric Noreen, Krishna Palepu, William Rotch, Keith Williams, and, especially, G. Peter Wilson.

From R. Cooper and R. S. Kaplan, "Activity-Based Systems: Measuring the Costs of Resource Usage," *Accounting Horizons* (September 1992): 1-13. Reprinted with permission.

Question
3.1 What important insights about resource usage come from activity-based costing systems in Cooper and Kaplan's article?

3.2 Cost Classification in Unit-Based and Activity-Based Manufacturing Cost Systems

Robin Cooper[1]

This article discusses the classification of activities in a manufacturing process and the design of activity-based cost systems. Activities are classified in one of four categories: unit-level, batch-level, product-level, and facility-level activities. Indirect costs are assigned to products using bases ("cost drivers") that capture the underlying behavior of the costs that are being assigned. The costs of facility-level activities are treated as period costs or allocated to products in some arbitrary manner.

This article summarizes a five-year study to develop a conceptual framework for the design of cost systems. The study resulted in a series of business-school cases that document the design, implementation, and use of cost systems. (See Exhibit 1.)

Two types of companies were considered. The first category included companies whose cost systems had proved inadequate given the technological and competitive environments in which the companies operated. The second category included companies that had recently changed their cost systems to become more competitive.

THE SAMPLE

The study looked at fifty cost systems in thirty-one companies. At least one facility in each of these firms was visited for at least one day. At each facility, various managers were interviewed so that the structure of the cost system could be determined and documented. Multiple sites in the same firm were visited only if the cost systems had been designed independently.

The companies chosen for the study were never intended to be representative of the overall population; a company was most likely to be chosen if it had recently made major changes to its cost system. Since research shows that companies rarely change their cost systems,[2] it is doubtful that a random sample of a realistic size would have included companies with innovative cost systems. Existing research also offers little guidance for selecting firms that are more likely to have innovative cost systems.[3]

COST SYSTEMS OBSERVED

All fifty of the cost systems in the study used a two-stage procedure for assigning overhead costs to products.[4] In the first stage, indirect costs and support department costs were assigned[5] to production cost centers. In the second stage, the costs accumulated at the production cost centers were then assigned products.

The designs of the first-stage cost assignments varied from simple to complex. The simple systems allocated support department costs by using one or only a few allocation bases (e.g., direct labor, floor space, headcount, departmental expenses, and other such allocation bases). The more complex first-stage systems were designed to capture the consumption of support-department resources more directly and, thus, to reduce arbitrary allocations. Some cost systems had one (or only a few) production cost centers. Other cost systems (particularly the cost systems of the German companies studied) contained several hundred production cost centers.

In contrast with the diversity of practice observed in first-stage allocations (including the number of cost centers used), the designs for second-stage assignments of costs (i.e., from cost centers to products) were often remarkably similar. Most systems used only one second-stage allocation base to assign the expenses accumulated in a cost center to the products that were processed in that cost center. Furthermore, many of the cost systems used the same allocation base for all cost centers.

The most common second-stage allocation base was direct labor, whether it was direct labor hours or direct labor dollars. Some of the companies used machine hours. Others used machine hours to assign the costs of highly automated manufacturing processes but direct labor to assign the costs of less automated operations. Finally, several companies even used a third allocation base—material dollars—to assign material-related support costs to products.

UNIT-BASED COST SYSTEMS

Despite the differences between the various cost systems (whether, for example, they used direct labor, machine hours, or material dollars for second-stage allocations) all resembled each other in one important respect: They all assigned costs in strict proportion to production volume.

In costs systems of this kind (which are pervasive in U.S. companies[6]), if the volume of a certain product increases by 10 percent, the product consumes 10 percent more labor hours, 10 percent more machine hours, and 10 percent more material dollars. Consequently—whether a cost system uses direct labor, machine hours, or material dollars for second-stage allocations (or even some combination of the three)—the cost system will assign 10 percent more overhead to the product. Cost systems that assign overhead in proportion to production volume can be called *unit-based* systems.

ABC SYSTEMS

Eight[7] of the companies in the study had recently replaced their traditional (i.e., unit-based) cost systems with a more complex kind of two-stage cost system that has come to be called an activity-based cost (ABC) system. The ABC approach assumes that not all overhead resources are consumed in proportion to the number of units produced. Thus, ABC systems recognize up to two more types of allocation bases (or cost drivers) than traditional cost systems:

1. *Batch-level* bases, which assume that certain inputs are consumed in direct proportion to the number of batches of each type of product produced; and

2. *Product-level* bases, which assume that certain inputs are consumed to develop or permit production of different products.

The three different types of bases used by an ABC system (i.e., unit-level, batch-level, and product-level bases) are designed to capture the economics of contemporary production processes. The activities performed in these processes can be described as fitting into the following hierarchy:

1. *Unit-level* activities, which are performed each time a unit is produced;
2. *Batch-level* activities, which are performed each time a batch of goods is produced;
3. *Product-level* activities, which are performed as needed to support the production of each different type of product; and
4. *Facility-level* activities, which simply sustain a facility's general manufacturing process.

Three of these categories used by ABC systems contain costs that can he directly attributed to individual products. The fourth category—facility-level activities—contains costs that are common to a variety of products and can only be allocated to products arbitrarily.[8]

Of all the cost systems studied, none used more than four categories of activities. For product costing purposes, one conclusion was that the cost functions of the innovative firms can be adequately described as a linear formula that is the sum of unit-level costs, batch-level costs, product-level costs, and facility-level costs. Interestingly, the most complex ABC formulas for product-related costs contain only two more categories than the simpler unit-based formula, which expresses total costs as simply the sum of fixed costs plus the variable costs multiplied by the number of units produced.

The costs of batch-level activities (such as setting up a machine or ordering a group of parts) vary according to the number of batches made, but are common (or fixed) costs for all the units in the batch. To assign these costs to products, the more complex ABC systems used batch-level bases.

Product-level activities are performed to support different products in a company's product line. Examples of product-level activities include maintaining product specifications (such as the bill of materials and routing information), performing engineering change notices, developing special testing routines, and expediting products. The costs of these activities can be assigned to individual products, but the costs are independent (i.e., fixed) regardless of the number of batches or the number of units of each product produced. To assign these costs to products, the ABC systems used product-level bases. Exhibit 2, which shows a diagram of the cost system at John Deere Component Works (JDCW), illustrates the four categories of cost drivers.

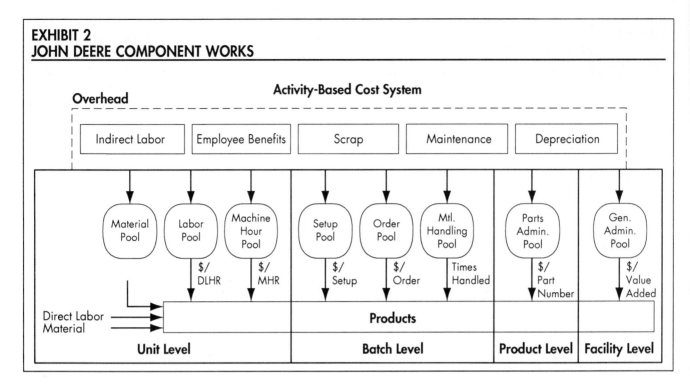

EXHIBIT 2
JOHN DEERE COMPONENT WORKS

Activity-Based Cost System

Overhead

| Indirect Labor | Employee Benefits | Scrap | Maintenance | Depreciation |

| Material Pool | Labor Pool | Machine Hour Pool | Setup Pool | Order Pool | Mtl. Handling Pool | Parts Admin. Pool | Gen. Admin. Pool |

$/DLHR $/MHR $/Setup $/Order Times Handled $/Part Number $/Value Added

Direct Labor → Material →

Products

Unit Level | **Batch Level** | **Product Level** | **Facility Level**

DEFINITION OF ABC SYSTEM

The four-category hierarchy of activities leads to the following definition of an ABC system:

An ABC system identifies and then classifies the major activities of a facility's production process into one of the following four categories: unit-level, batch-level, product-level, and facility-level activities. Costs in the first three categories of activities are assigned to products using bases (i.e., cost drivers) that capture the underlying behavior of the costs that are being assigned. The costs of facility-level activities, however, are treated as period costs or allocated to products in some arbitrary manner.

Note that some cost systems that are loosely described as ABC systems (even in this article) do not meet this strict definition. For example, the bases used in each of the six "ABC systems" in this study are shown in Exhibit 3. All six use unit-level bases. However, only two of the cost systems also use both batch-level and product-level bases; the other four use either batch-level or product-level bases, but not both.

Several possible explanations exist for not using either batch-level or product-level bases.

- First, the designers of the cost systems may not have understood that three different kinds of bases existed (even though, in at least one of the firms that used only two types of bases, the costs associated with the third—and unused—category were significant).
- Second, in some production processes, two of the categories of activities became indistinguishable. At Hewlett-Packard's Roseville Network Division (RND), for example, production batches contained only one unit.

This made the unit-level and batch-level categories identical, so either type of base captured the underlying economics of production.

- Third, the possible benefit of reporting one of the categories of activities separately may have been small. At Siemens' Electric Motor Works (EMW), for example, management believed that improving the company's complex unit-based system by using two batch-level bases would achieve the objective of identifying profitable orders. Management therefore decided that a more complex system was not justified.
- Fourth, even though designers of cost systems may be aware of the existence of all the different types of bases, they may choose, for reasons of simplicity and ease of understanding, to use only two of them. At Tektronix Portable Instruments Division (PID), for example, the cost system was deliberately kept simple so that managers could send a strong message by means of the new bases selected. Management felt that the message would be diluted if additional bases were used to assign indirect manufacturing costs. Consequently, only one base was used for all material-related costs even though doing so oversimplified the underlying cost behaviors. Further research is needed to determine if other good reasons exist for ignoring one of the categories of activities.

Cost systems that use only two types of bases can be considered *partial* ABC systems. According to this classification scheme, cost systems fall somewhere in a continuum that starts with unit-based systems (which use only one type of base) and ends with full-fledged ABC systems (which use all three types of bases).

FIXED AND VARIABLE COSTS IN UNIT-BASED AND ABC SYSTEMS

Unit-based cost systems divide costs into the dichotomy of
fixed and variable costs. Variable costs are those costs that
change in proportion to the number of units produced (i.e.,
unit-level costs), while fixed costs are those that do not vary
in proportion to the number of units produced (i.e., batch-
level, product-level, and facility-level costs). One important
distinction between ABC and traditional cost systems, therefore, is that ABC systems classify overhead cost more precisely. While recognizing that some costs vary in proportion
to production volume, ABC systems go further by identifying
costs that vary in proportion to changes other than production volume. Such changes include, for example, the number
of batches made, or the diversity of products manufactured
(as measured by the total number and type of products).

ABC systems maintain the assumption that the costs of
activities are strictly variable, even though this assumption
rarely holds true in practice. For example, most inputs can
only be acquired in predefined amounts. As a result, the costs
of these inputs do not vary smoothly according to the quantity of activities performed. The product costs reported by
ABC systems are therefore linear approximations to what
(on closer examination) are probably a sequence of step
functions. (Consider, for example, the behavior of costs as
workers, machines, and other resources are added or dropped
in response to changes in activity levels.)

FULL-ABSORPTION COSTING

Unit-based cost systems in the study computed and reported
fully absorbed manufacturing costs at the unit level by allocating fixed costs to units of products and then adding the
fixed costs per unit to the variable costs per unit. (See Exhibit
4.)[9] These full manufacturing costs were used for inventory
valuation. However, many of the product-related decisions in
these facilities were also based on unit product costs that
included an allocation of fixed costs.

Allocations of fixed costs to product units are
inevitably arbitrary, because the activities that cause the costs
are common costs at the unit level. Full absorption is often
criticized for this reason, because it introduces systematic
distortions into reported product costs per unit.[10] For example, a batch of a given product consumes the same amount of
setup resources regardless of the number of units in the
batch. However, unit-based systems allocate more setup
costs to large batches than they allocate small ones simply
because of the greater volume of products that are produced.
Therefore, the unit costs of products in a small batch are too
low because the unit costs do not contain enough setup costs.
Conversely, the reported unit costs of products in a large
batch are too high because the unit costs contain too much
setup costs.

Early identification of the problem. The problems associated with the allocation of fixed costs to product
units have been discussed extensively in the literature. Early
on, several observers noted that overhead resources are not
consumed in proportion to the number of units manufactured. Therefore, they questioned the validity of unit-based
allocations of manufacturing costs to product units.[11] As

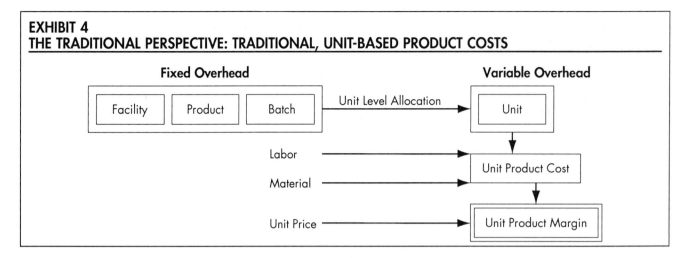

EXHIBIT 4
THE TRADITIONAL PERSPECTIVE: TRADITIONAL, UNIT-BASED PRODUCT COSTS

early as 1923, economist John M. Clark identified possible problems, warning that arbitrary allocations of costs to units of product could lead to "fictitious notions of costs."[12] As W. J. Vatter later observed:

"[Some] costs are of such nature as to remain practically unaffected by changes in the rate of activity over wide ranges. Other costs tend to fall with the rate of activity, perhaps proportionally, perhaps in other ways. Still other costs are of the semi-fixed or semi-variable variety, remaining unchanged over certain narrow ranges but shifting at certain points to higher levels as the rate of activity passes a critical stage. Averaging a mixture of these costs is quite likely to produce a hodge-podge figure."[13]

In 1963, Drucker[14] recognized the difficulties of meeting the financial accounting requirement of assigning cost to product units even when no physical tie existed, the result being allocations in proportion to production volume rather than assignments of costs in proportion to the actual consumption of resources.

"Now the only way the accountant can allocate costs is in a way that is proportionate to volume rather than proportionate to the number of transactions. Thus $1 million in volume produced in one order—or in one product—carries the same cost as $1 million in volume production by 1 million individual orders or by 50 different production runs."

In 1971, Staubus[15] adopted an activity orientation. However, he did not discuss the benefit of using different types of allocation bases to assign costs to products.[16] In his description of an "Activity-Output Costing System," Staubus explicitly traces all costs to the unit level and then reports unit costs. For example, he allocates purchasing costs by using square yardage of material per product as the allocation base. Thus, Staubus allocates the cost of an activity that is not performed every time a unit is produced *as if it were,* which is precisely what a unit-based cost system does.

ABC FULL-ABSORPTION COSTING

All the ABC systems in the study computed full unit product costs. These costs are obtained by:

- Dividing batch-level costs by the number of units in the batch;
- Dividing product and facility costs by the number of product units produced; and
- Adding the results to the unit-level costs.

These full unit costs are not numerically the same as the costs reported by unit-based systems because they rely on different assignment procedures that take advantage of the hierarchical view of activities. The advantage of the different procedures used by ABC systems is that they reduce the distortion of traditionally reported product costs by capturing the fact that many of the supposedly fixed costs actually vary with batch-level and product-level activities.

However, the ABC unit costs do suggest an inappropriate degree of variability. Batch-related costs can only be reduced by decreasing the number of batches (or by making the batch process more efficient), not simply by reducing the number of units produced. The inappropriate suggestion of variability is introduced by the allocations of batch-level, product-level, and facility-level costs to the product units. However, for the batch-level and product-level costs, these allocations do not introduce any numerical distortions, because the total costs associated with the product (as opposed to the product unit) are not changed. From an ABC perspective, only the allocation of facility-level costs to the product units is arbitrary. Facility-level costs should theoretically not be assigned to products in an ABC system. The arbitrary allocation of such costs to products adds no information about the economics of production. However, as previously mentioned, all the ABC systems in this study did report full product costs, which suggests a topic that merits further research.

ABC systems that report unit costs overcome the inappropriate suggestion of variability by reporting product costs separately for unit-level, batch-level, and product-level.

They achieve this by separately reporting the cost assigned by each base. (See Exhibit 5.)

CONDITIONS THAT FAVOR ACTIVITY-BASED COSTING

ABC systems have emerged in companies where managers believe that the costs of the additional measurements required by the ABC systems are more than offset by the benefits the new systems can provide. The managers associate three major benefits of categorizing activities in an ABC system:

- Improved decision making due to more accurate product costs;
- Improved insights into managing the activities that lead to traditional fixed costs; and
- Easier access to relevant costs for a wider range of decisions.

Each of these benefits is discussed below.

IMPROVED DECISIONS

Managers at several of the companies in the study believe that the more accurate product costs reported by ABC systems reduce the risk that poor decisions will be made because of inaccurate product cost information. This is an important consideration, because findings from this study indicate that managers frequently underestimate the distortion of product costs reported by unit-based cost systems.[17] Thus, managers may know even before an ABC system is introduced that their existing cost system understates the unit costs of low-volume products, but they often do not realize how *much* the unit costs are understated. As one division manager at JDCW said, "Parts we suspected we were undercosting have turned out to be even more expensive than we thought." Similarly, the

director of business operations at EMW said, "Without our new cost system, our new strategy would have failed." This failure would have occurred because they would not have been able to identify profitable orders.

The risk of making poor decisions probably increases in proportion to the level of distortion in reported costs. Two characteristics of a company cause unit-based cost systems to report highly distorted product costs. The first is a high cost of non-unit-level activities relative to unit-level activities.[18] At Schrader Bellows, for example, non-unit-level costs accounted for about 50 percent of all overhead; at JDCW, they accounted for about 40 percent of all overhead. The second characteristic is a mix of products that consume unit-level and non-unit-level activities in different ratios. For example, EMW produced some products in batches of one, while similar products were produced in batches of over 100. Even though the total cost of the non-unit-level activities assigned using batch-level bases was only 9 percent of total costs, the reported unit costs of products made in batches of one almost doubled under the ABC system compared with the unit costs reported by the company's former unit-based system.

The risk that a competitor will take advantage of a company's poor decisions that occur because of inaccurate product costs seems to cause firms that face increasing competition to become innovators. For example, PID developed its new cost system when it was suddenly faced with intense Japanese competition; JDCW developed its new cost system when it ceased to be a captive supplier and had to begin competing with other firms; and EMW developed its new cost system when it was facing intense competition from Eastern Bloc companies. Managers at all the companies that had adopted ABC systems identified intense competition as a major reason for developing their new cost systems. The need for a new cost system was particularly apparent when full-line producers faced focused competitors, because the narrow product line of the more focused competitors reduced

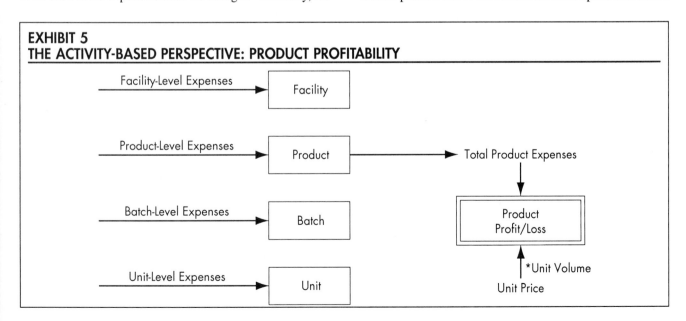

EXHIBIT 5
THE ACTIVITY-BASED PERSPECTIVE: PRODUCT PROFITABILITY

the level of distortion in the product costs reported by their unit-based system.

IMPROVED INSIGHTS INTO MANAGING FIXED COSTS

The companies that considered it important to manage traditional fixed costs designed ABC systems that would direct attention to these costs. At PID, for example, managers designed their new cost system so that it would motivate product designers to reduce the number of low-volume parts used in the next generation of products. To achieve this objective, the designers of the cost system used the product-level base "number of different part numbers" to assign part-related costs to products. Using this base, a product that contains low-volume components has a higher reported overhead cost than a product that contains only high-volume components. PID's management implemented this system in the belief that reducing the number of unique part numbers would decrease the size of some support departments by reducing the demand for product-level activities.

The desire to develop a cost system that creates improved incentives to control non-unit-level activities is driven by problems encountered with the incentives created by traditional unit-based systems. For example, engineers in several of the companies that were studied spent considerable effort reducing the direct labor or machine hours required to produce products. However, they spent relatively little effort reducing overhead. One manager at PID commented on the effects of the firm's original direct labor based system by saying, "Engineering could justify a $10,000 project to remove five minutes (of direct labor) from an instrument, because that five minutes was leveraged by the labor-burdening system. In reality, they were adding to the size of burden and doing little to reduce costs."

The lack of effort directed at controlling fixed costs appear to be driven primarily by two factors. First, unit-based systems average the cost of non-unit-level activities over many (if not all) products. Engineers find it difficult to lower the reported cost of individual products unless they reduce the consumption of the inputs represented by the bases used to assign overhead costs to the products. If all the bases are unit-level, the engineers focus their cost reduction efforts on unit-level activities (typically those related to direct labor). Second, using unit-level bases to allocate non-unit-level costs distorts the relation between the performance of those activities and the production of products. When this distortion is high, management finds measuring and managing these costs difficult. For example, at JDCW and Schrader Bellows, the unit-based cost system failed to highlight the high cost of batch-level activities. As a result, management allowed facilities designed for high-volume production to be used to manufacture an uneconomical production mix that contained many small batches.

EASE OF DETERMINING RELEVANT COSTS

Cost systems report costs that can be modified to give relevant cost information.[19] However, modifications typically require special studies, which usually are expensive. The degree of modification required for a given decision depends on the scope of the decision and the design of the firm's cost system.

The scope of the decision is important because it defines the magnitude of the risk associated with relying on incorrect cost information. The design of the cost system is important because it defines the accuracy of reported product costs and the ease with which they are modified. ABC systems reduce the need to perform special studies by increasing the accuracy of reported product costs and (unlike traditional systems) by reporting the costs of the four different categories of activities separately. For example, if relevant costs require knowledge of the cost of batch-level activities, a unit-based cost system provides little help compared with an ABC system.

ABC systems do not completely remove the need for modifications. Modifications are still required, because the assumption that the cost function of a firm is linear inevitably introduces errors. For example, when products contain common components, adding or dropping products will not necessarily change the number of batches of common components produced. Second, the cost system may not appropriately isolate the relevant costs for a particular decision. For example, a system might treat all costs associated with material movement as a single element, yet some decisions might affect only some of those costs. Third, some of the cost assignments might introduce distortions. This could occur, for example, if "number of setups" is used as a cost driver when setups vary according to products or manufacturing sequence.

CONCLUSIONS

ABC systems represent the production process of a company as a hierarchy of four mutually exclusive and exhaustive categories of activities:

1. Unit-level activities, which are performed each time a unit is produced;
2. Batch-level activities, which are performed each time a batch of goods is produced;
3. Product-level activities, which are performed as needed to support the production of each different type of product; and
4. Facility-level activities, which simply sustain a facility's general manufacturing process.

ABC systems take advantage of this hierarchy by assigning the costs of the first three categories to products by using bases that vary in proportion to the activities in the categories. Thus, a full ABC system contains three different types of bases:

- Unit-level bases, which assume that inputs are consumed in direct proportion to the number of units produced;
- Batch-level bases, which assume that inputs are consumed in direct proportion to the number of batches of each type of product produced; and
- Product-level bases, which assume that inputs are consumed to develop or permit production of individual products.

ABC systems attempt to match the level of a base that is used to assign costs to products to the level of the activity that generates the costs, thus avoiding the distortions inherent in traditional systems that rely entirely on unit-level bases. By reporting the costs of each category of activity separately, moreover, ABC systems provide improved insight into managing supposedly fixed costs, thus providing easier access to relevant costs. In certain companies—typically those that face intense competition, sell a highly diverse mix of products, and have high levels of non-unit-level activities—the benefits of ABC systems outweigh the additional costs caused by their increased complexity. Further research is required to determine the exact conditions that favor using ABC systems instead of traditional, unit-based cost systems.

Notes

1. The author wishes to thank the many people who reviewed earlier versions of this article and provided suggestions for improving it, especially Robert S. Kaplan and Jerry L. Zimmerman.

2. For example, see U.S. Karmarkar, P. J. Lederer, and J. L. Zimmerman, "Choosing Manufacturing Production Control and Cost Accounting Systems," *Measures for Manufacturing Excellence,* ed. R.S. Kaplan (Boston: Harvard Business School Press, 1990).

3. For a discussion of the role of paradigms in guiding the design of experiments, see Thomas S. Kuhn, *The Structure of Scientific Revolutions* (Chicago: University of Chicago Press, 1970).

4. This two-stage procedure is discussed in Robin Cooper, "Two-Stage Procedure in Cost Accounting: Part One," *Journal of Cost Management* (Summer 1987), pp. 43–51, and in Robin Cooper, "The Two-Stage Procedure in Cost Accounting: Part Two," Journal of Cost Management (Fall 1987), pp. 39–45.

5. The cost accounting terminology in this article uses the terms "assign" or "trace" broadly to describe the procedure of associating indirect costs to products. The term "allocate," a more widely used term that means essentially the same thing, has generally been avoided in previous discussions of activity-based cost systems. This shift in terminology occurred because of the negative connotations that "allocate" and "allocation" have acquired over the years. Specifically, for many people an allocation means a largely arbitrary assignment of costs to products (or cost objectives), which is precisely what activity-based cost systems attempt to avoid. For similar reasons, much of the existing literature on activity-based costing has avoided use of the term "allocation base" (which is usually shortened to "base" in this article). Instead, the term "cost driver" has been adopted.

6. H. R. Schwarzbach, "The Impact of Automation on Accounting for Indirect Costs," *Management Accounting* (December 1985), pp. 45–50.

7. Of the eight ABC systems that were studied, two have been ignored because they were in service industries and thus have no place in a discussion of the assignment of manufacturing costs.

8. Facility-level activities can be further broken down by changing the focus of analysis from the product to aggregations of products. For example, facility-level activities can be split into product line-level activities— activities performed to sustain the product line (such as prototype development).

9. For a discussion of why firms allocate fixed costs to products, see J. L. Zimmerman, "The Costs and Benefits of Cost Allocations,"*Accounting Review,* Vol. LIV (1979), pp. 504–521.

10. See, for example, R. Cooper and R. S. Kaplan, "How Cost Accounting Distorts Product Costs," *Management Accounting* (April 1988), pp. 20–27; R. Cooper and R. S. Kaplan, "Measure Costs Right: Make the Right Decisions," *Harvard Business Review,* Vol. 5 (1988), pp. 96–103; A. L. Thomas, "The Allocation Problem in Financial Accounting Theory," *American Accounting Association Studies in Accounting Research,* No. 3 (1969); and A. L. Thomas, "The Allocation Problem, Part Two," *American Accounting Association Studies in Accounting Research,* No. 9 (1974).

11. These procedures have also been called "volume-based allocation procedures. See, for example, P. E. Drucker, "Managing for Effectiveness," *Harvard Business Review* (May–June 1963), pp. 33–60; and J. K. Shank and V. Govindarajan, "Unbundling the Full Product Line: The Perils of Volume-Based Costing" (Working paper, Tuck School, Dartmouth College, 1987).

12. J. M. Clark, *Studies in the Economics of the Overhead Costs,* (Chicago: University of Chicago Press, 1923).

13. W. J. Vatter, *Managerial Accounting* (New York: Prentice Hall, 1950), p. 339.

14. Drucker, "Managing for Business Effectiveness," pp. 55–56.

15. J. S. Staubus, *Activity Costing and Input-Output Accounting* (Homewood: Irwin, 1971).

16. For a more extensive discussion of the history of cost accounting, see H. Thomas Johnson and Robert S. Kaplan, *Relevance Lost* (Boston: Harvard Business School Press, 1987).

17. Since "true" product costs are unobservable, managers still do not know the extent of the distortion in reported product costs. Assuming, however, that activity-based systems are more accurate than unit-based cost systems, the significant shifts in reported costs that result from changing costs systems strongly suggest that unit-based product costs are more distorted than most managers expect.

18. The proportion of non-unit-level costs in many companies has increased as more of the production process is automated and the degree of vertical integration is reduced (see Jeffrey G. Miller and Thomas E. Vollman, "The Hidden Factory," *Harvard Business Review* (September–October 1985), pp. 142–150.

19. The difference between reported and relevant product costs is discussed by R. H. Coase, "Business Organization and the Accountant," *L.S.E. Essays in Cost,* ed. J. M. Buchanan, and G. F. Thirlby (Birkenhead: Willmer Brothers, 1973), p. 98 and Clark, *Economics of the Overhead Costs,* p. 175.

From R. Cooper, "Cost Classification in Unit-Based and Activity-Based Manufacturing Cost Systems," *Journal of Cost Management* (Fall 1990): 4-13. Reprinted with permission.

Question

3.2 What are the important elements of Cooper's definition of an ABC system? What important assumption underlies the ABC approach?

3.3 ABC and Life-Cycle Costing for Environmental Expenditures
The combination gives companies a more accurate snapshot.

By Jerry G. Kreuze, CPA, and Gale E. Newell, CMA

Costs of cleaning up polluted soil, water, buildings, and equipment; related expenditures for equipment record keeping; and monitoring for compliance with government regulations have become significant variables for companies to consider in protecting their financial health. A primary concern is the potential for large losses attributable to environmental problems.

In an earlier article[1] we addressed the role of management accountants in helping their companies deal with hazardous waste problems. We encouraged them to work closely with production personnel in finding cost effective ways to reduce, control, transport, and dispose of hazardous waste. They also should analyze alternative production and disposal methods to reduce the volume or toxicity of hazardous wastes produced and to determine the disposal method(s) that minimizes disposal costs at an acceptable level of risk.

Now we need to determine how environmental expenditures should be allocated to products. Activity-based costing (ABC) and life-cycle costing techniques are the foundation for allocating environmental expenditures to products. By identifying the costs of all activities, a company can attempt to eliminate, or at least minimize, the costs related to those activities that do not add value to the product.

LIFE-CYCLE COSTING FOR ENVIRONMENTAL EXPENDITURES

Life-cycle costing considers the full costs over the product's (system's, operation's) life cycle—from research through disposal, from cradle to grave. Most of the cost of a new product is committed after the design stage, so manufacturing alternatives can influence only a small portion of the total product cost. Life-cycle costing measures the entire 100% of these costs, not just the costs incurred during production, and responsibility for environmental impacts has extended product costs well beyond the life cycle of the product. Responsibility for hazardous waste, for example, lasts forever. Therefore, all costs are discounted to the present to facilitate comparisons with competing products. Life-cycle costing may reveal that a product with low acquisition costs but high operations, maintenance, environmental, or disposal costs may be a less desirable alternative than a competing product with a higher initial cost.

All cost-bearing activities associated with a product throughout its life-cycle time must be identified. The costs of each cost-bearing activity must be accumulated and, in some instances, estimated. In this situation, similar to capital budgeting techniques, future costs are discounted to present-day dollars. Cost estimates, particularly for future environmental expenditures, are unavoidable but are needed for evaluation purposes. All costs throughout a product's life cycle must be considered for a valid comparison of competing products or processes. In light of the potential magnitude of environmental expenditures, it may be better to be vaguely right than precisely wrong.

Paul E. Bailey[2] identified four levels of environmental costs that are important to a full costing analysis: usual capital and operating costs, hidden regulatory costs, contingent liability costs, and less tangible costs.

Usual Costs and Operating Costs. Usual costs are costs associated directly with products, including costs of buildings, equipment, materials, start-up, training, labor, and energy costs. Traditionally these costs have been allocated to products, often using an application rate based on direct labor hours.

Hidden Regulatory Costs. The costs of governmental and regulatory compliance include notification, reporting, permitting, monitoring, testing, training, and inspection expenditures. Proper cost allocation requires these costs to be allocated to those activities causing the expenditures. It is critical because these costs have the potential of being very large. For example, *The Wall Street Journal* reported that the government forms dealing with disposal of dirty cleaning rags at Bernhardt Furniture Company in Lenoir, N.C., created a pile 6' 2" tall. Moreover, Alex Bernhardt, the company's president, says that his company "could easily spend twice as much on (environmental) compliance in the next five years as on R&D and new machinery and equipment" combined.

Contingent Liability Costs. These costs can include both (a) penalties and fines for noncompliance and (b) legal claims, awards, and settlements for remedial actions, personal injuries, and property damage for future routine and accidental environmental concerns. Often these costs must be estimated, and companies must be careful not to underestimate these amounts or the likelihood of their occurring. All companies that generate and release hazardous waste and materials have future contingent liability costs, so when estimating these costs, they must accept that environmental regulations will tend to converge upward, causing contingent liability costs to increase.

Less Tangible Costs. By reducing or eliminating pollution and responding to consumer demands for environmentally friendly products, a company can realize cost savings (less tangible costs) through increased revenues or decreased expenses due to improved consumer satisfaction, employee relations, and corporate image. Given the growing legislative and regulatory pressure and increasing consumer awareness, progressive companies are altering the way they design, make, and market their products so products can be used longer and reused, either in part or whole. If a company makes ecological and economic goals joint objectives, its less tangible costs, at least, partially can offset its contingent liability costs. As Exxon's experience in Alaska demonstrated, however, an accidental release can override many corporate efforts in the area of less tangible costs.

ABC AND ENVIRONMENTAL EXPENDITURES

Activity-based costing techniques can provide the means to identify cost-bearing activities effectively and to allocate costs to individual products. The basic premise of ABC is to cost activities, not products. Costs are allocated to products on the basis of the individual product's demand for those activities. The allocation bases—cost drivers—are the quantification of activities performed.

The merging of life-cycle costing and ABC is not a revolutionary concept. Consideration of all costs, from the introduction phases to product maturity, can allow for the development of better design methods, production methodologies, marketing strategies, and disposal options. Environmental expenditures *must* be a major part of those cost considerations.

Traditionally, ABC allocates activities among unit-level, batch-level, product-sustaining, and facility-sustaining activities. Unit-level activities are performed on individual units, batch-level activities allow batches of units to be processed, product-sustaining activities provide the capacity to produce a particular product, and facility-sustaining activities sustain a manufacturing facility's general manufacturing capacity. Environmental expenditures can occur in any of those levels.

Consequently, the four levels of environmental costs for full costing should be identified and included in the appropriate cost activity level. For example, isopropyl alcohol left over from the production of computer monitor screens would be a unit-level activity cost. That same alcohol can be used as a solvent to clean casts for steel products, making it a batch-level activity cost. Many regulatory and governmental compliance costs would be product-sustaining activity costs, such as the costs associated with the reporting of cleaning rag disposal at Bernhardt Furniture Company. Future contingent cleanup costs at waste sites, product-sustaining activities, also should be estimated for a complete full costing analysis. Finally, air pollution devices installed on manufacturing facilities create significant facility-sustaining activity costs.

ABC AND LIFE-CYCLE COSTING: AN ILLUSTRATION

The use of ABC in a life-cycle costing analysis can be seen in the case of a hypothetical manufacturing company, Ready Manufacturing, with two of its products, Product A and Product B. Product A is a high-volume item that is produced through a single production process that does not generate any

hazardous waste and requires no governmental and regulatory compliance costs. Product B is a low-volume item that generates sufficient quantities of hazardous waste in the production process to qualify Ready Manufacturing as large-quantity producer. As a result, Ready manufacturing is subject to numerous environmental regulations and reporting requirements.

Annual sales of Product A and B are 200,000 and 50,000 units, respectively. Both products require three direct labor hours for completion, causing the company to operate 750,000 direct labor hours per year (250,000 units of product @ three direct labor hours per product). At a rate of $20 per direct labor hour, the cost of direct labor for products A and B is $60 per product. Direct materials costs are $100 for Product A and $80 for Product B.

As presented in Table 1, Ready Manufacturing's overhead costs total $17,250,000. Although the same amount of direct labor hours is required for each product (three hours), Product B requires more machine setups and more quality inspections than Product A because of its design complexity. Moreover, Product B is produced in smaller lots, thus

TABLE 1
READY MANUFACTURING'S OVERHEAD COSTS (CATEGORIZED BY ACTIVITIES)

Activity	Overhead Costs	
Unit-level:		
Machine costs	$2,400,000	
Energy	1,000,000	
Disposal of hazardous waste	400,000	$3,800,000
Batch-level:		
Inspection	1,200,000	
Material movements	1,450,000	
Support services	1,800,000	
Disposal of hazardous waste	300,000	
Environmental reporting requirements	200,000	4,950,000
Product-level:		
R&D and parts maintenance	2,110,000	
Environmental reporting requirements	200,000	
Environmental inspections	500,000	
Waste treatment costs on site	1,000,000	
Landfill disposal costs	800,000	4,610,000
Facility-level:		
Plant maintenance	2,000,000	
Buildings and grounds	1,000,000	
Heating and lighting	600,000	
Environmental standards	290,000	3,890,000
Total Overhead Costs		$17,250,000

TABLE 2
COST DRIVERS AND OVERHEAD RATES FOR READY MANUFACTURING'S OVERHEAD COSTS

Cost Drivers by Activity

Activity	Cost Driver
Unit-level:	
Machine costs	Machine hours used
Energy	Machine hours used
Disposal of hazardous waste	Product B exclusively
Batch-level:	
Inspection	Number of quality inspections
Material movements	Number of production orders
Support services	Number of machine setups
Disposal of hazardous waste	Product B exclusively
Environmental reporting requirements	Product B exclusively
Product-level:	
R&D and parts maintenance	Number of subcomponents
Environmental reporting requirements	Product B exclusively
Environmental inspections	Product B exclusively
Waste treatment costs on site	Product B exclusively
Landfill disposal costs	Product B exclusively
Facility-level:	
Plant maintenance	% value added
Buildings and grounds	% value added
Heating and lighting	% value added
Environmental standards	% value added

Overhead Rates by Activity

Activity	Cost	Number of Events	Rate per Event
Unit-level:			
Machine costs	$2,400,000	20,000	$120/machine hr.
Energy	$2,400,000	20,000	$50/machine hr.
Batch-level:			
Inspection	1,200,000	2,500	$480/inspection
Material movements	1,450,000	500	$2,900/order
Support services	1,800,000	1,500	$1,200/setup
Product-level:			
R&D and parts maintenance	$2,110,000	10	$211,000/ subcomponent

causing it to require a relatively large number of production orders as compared to Product A. The bill of materials indicates that Products A and B are composed of six and four subcomponents, respectively.

Ready Manufacturing has analyzed its operations and determined that activities act as cost drivers in the incurrence of overhead costs as presented in Table 2. The unit-, batch-, and product-level environmental expenditures are related to Product B exclusively and, as such, should be allocated entirely to Product B. That is, no cost driver, other than Product B itself, is appropriate. The facility-level environmental standards expenditures are assumed to relate to pollution control equipment installed on the manufacturing facility's

stacks. The stacks vent the entire factory operation, so they relate equally to Products A and B. Those costs then are allocated to products on the same basis as the remaining facility-level activity costs—on a percent value-added basis.

Table 3 shows the total costs for Products A and B. The allocation of environmental costs, other than facility-level environmental expenditures, partially causes Product B's overhead costs to exceed those of Product A. Environmental costs are allocated to the product(s) causing those expenditures. Given the significance of environmental costs ($3,690,000, or 21% of the total manufacturing overhead costs for Ready Manufacturing), it is imperative that those costs be identified and allocated to products properly.

The importance of using ABC to allocate costs to products is illustrated in Table 4, which presents the product costs for Ready Manufacturing using the traditional direct labor hours method. The manufacturing cost per unit for Products A and B are $229 and $209, respectively. Product A, with direct labor hours as an allocation base, received 68% more overhead cost than under ABC ($69.00 compared to $41.09). Conversely, Product B was allocated 62% fewer overhead costs using direct labor hours as the allocation base ($69.00 compared to $180.65). With direct labor hours, Product A is assigned a greater cost per unit ($229) than is Product B ($209). ABC produces an opposite effect, with the cost/unit for Product A at $201.09 and Product B at $320.65.

Environmental costs related to certain products can cause the traditional direct labor hours cost allocation method to produce faulty product costs. In fact, product-specific environmental costs for many companies may require the use of ABC costing to a greater extent than do differences in volume, machine setups, production orders, quality inspections, and number of subcomponents.

The total manufacturing costs per unit of $201.09 for Product A and $320.65 for Product B were obtained from information contained in the historical-cost-based general ledger system. Life-cycle costing, particularly for environmental expenditures, requires that all costs (past, present, and future) be included in the product's profitability analysis. That is, while the manufacturing costs computed in Table 3 are useful for financial statement preparation and current operating performance measures, a better measure of long-term product performance also should include future environmental expenditures. In particular, the above analysis

TABLE 3
MANUFACTURING COSTS FOR PRODUCTS A AND B (USING ABC COSTING)

| | Product A | | Product B | |
	Events	Amount	Events	Amount
Overhead costs:				
Unit-level:				
Machine costs at, $120/hour	15,000	$1,800,000	5,000	$600,000
Energy at $50/hour	15,000	750,000	5,000	250,000
Disposal of hazardous waste			—	400,000
Batch-level:				
Inspection at $480/inspection	1,000	480,000	1,500	720,000
Material movements at $2,900/order	300	870,000	200	580,000
Support services at $1,200/setup	1,000	1,200,000	500	600,000
Disposal of hazardous waste		—		300,000
Environmental reporting		—		200,000
Product-level:				
R&D and parts maintenance				
at $211,000/subcomponent	6	1,266,000	4	844,000
Environmental reporting		—		200,000
Environmental inspections		—		500,000
Waste treatment costs		—		1,000,000
Landfill disposal costs		—		800,000
Subtotal		$6,366,000		$6,994,000
Facility-level:				
Total costs of $3,890,000,				
% value added				
A – 47.6%		1,851,640		
B – 52.4%				2,038,360
Total overhead cost		$8,217,640		$9,032,360
Number of units produced		200,000		50,000
Overhead cost/unit		$ 41.09		$ 180.65
Direct material cost/unit		100.00		80.00
Direct labor cost/unit		60.00		60.00
Overhead cost/unit		41.09		180.65
Total manufacturing cost/unit		$ 201.09		$ 320.65

TABLE 4		
MANUFACTURING COSTS FOR PRODUCTS A		
AND B (USING DIRECT LABOR HOURS)		
	Product A	Product B
A. Overhead cost/unit		
$17,250,000/750,000 DLH = $23/DLH		
(23 × 3 hours)	$69	$69
B. Direct material cost/unit	100	80
C. Direct labor cost/unit	60	60
Total manufacturing cost/unit	$209	$209

includes only the first two levels of life-cycle costing, namely usual and operating costs and hidden regulatory costs. The remaining levels, contingent liability costs and less tangible costs, have not been considered yet.

Unfortunately, these costs must be estimated because their expenditures occur in the future. But they should not be ignored when determining the long-term profitability of products, especially considering their potential magnitude. For example, cleanup of the United States' known hazardous waste sites now is estimated to cost $752 billion over 30 years under current environmental standards. In all likelihood, those costs have not been allocated to activities/products causing those expenditures. To the extent possible, these future potential environmental costs should be included in a complete life-cycle costing analysis to properly determine the worth of competing products. Environmental consultants, engineers, and lawyers may be required to interpret the facts and evaluate environmental cost exposure.

In estimating contingent liability costs, Ready Manufacturing has identified three environmental activities that may impose some exposure: waste treatment on site, transportation, and disposal in a landfill. Consultations with environmental experts indicate that Ready Manufacturing will be subject to some potential liability from these activities. The annual liability costs attached to those environmental activities, discounted at its cost-of-capital rate, are assumed to be $250,000 per year. Those costs effectively add $5/unit ($250,000/50,000 units of Product B) to the manufacturing cost of Product B. As Ready Manufacturing is operating under the highest environmental standards, no benefits are possible in the less tangible costs area.

These Level 4 environmental costs would be applicable if Ready Manufacturing could use another technology for better waste treatment. The higher costs associated with the better method could be partially offset by potential benefits associated with improved community and labor relations, but these benefits often are uncertain and difficult to quantify. Level 4 environmental costs perhaps can be used best to compare treatment methods and/or products.

IMPLICATIONS

The wave of environmental concerns and regulations sweeping the world have increased costs for many companies. Environmental standards probably will rise. The highest standards today may be marginal tomorrow. Given the current costs associated with environmental concerns and the expected future upward trend in those costs, it is imperative that companies allocate environmental costs to products properly.

Activity-based costing can allocate environmental expenditures to products effectively. Care must be taken to uncover hidden regulatory and compliance costs so that a proper cost allocation can be obtained. By uncovering these costs, management accountants can produce relevant information for their engineers, production personnel, marketing staff, and others. Environmental activities can be highlighted and the magnitude of their costs identified. If those activities do not add value to the product or process, the goal would be to eliminate, or at least minimize, their necessity.

Life-cycle costing extends the ABC analysis to consider future costs, including contingent liability costs and less tangible costs. With environmental matters, current activities can cause costs to be incurred 10, 20, or even 30 years from today. Consequently, potential future environmental liabilities should, at the very least, be considered in a systematic manner when evaluating the long-term profitability of competing products. Care must be taken not to underestimate these potential expenditures. The acceptance of today's highest environmental standards can be good business. Profit enhancement through less tangible costs is possible for companies that are environmentally concerned. Frequently customers, employees, and the general public view a company's environmental record as a proxy for its quality and reliability.

The combination of ABC and life-cycle costing can provide management with accurate product cost information and therefore a realistic understanding of profitability. Relevant product cost information permits management accountants to identify the costs associated with nonvalue-adding activities. Moreover, by identifying potential contingent environmental liabilities, management accountants, along with environmental consultants, engineers, lawyers, and others have relevant information to evaluate the profitability of competing products.

Jerry G. Kreuze, CPA, is professor of accounting at Western Michigan University. He holds a Ph. D. degree in accounting from the University of Missouri-Columbia.

Gale E. Newell, CMA, is professor of accounting at Western Michigan University. He holds a Ph. D. degree in accounting from Michigan State University. Both authors are members of the Kalamazoo Chapter, through which this article was submitted.

Notes

1. G. Newell, J. Kreuze, and S. Newell, "Accounting for Hazardous Waste," MANAGEMENT ACCOUNTING®, May 1990.

2. P. Bailey, "Full Cost Accounting for Life-Cycle Costs—A Guide for Engineers and Financial Analysts," *Environmental Finance,* Spring 1991.

From J. G. Kreuze and G. E. Newell, "ABC and Life-Cycle Costing for Environmental Expenditures," *Management Accounting* (February 1994): 38-42. Reprinted with permission.

Question

3.3 Describe the four levels of environmental costs that are important to a full costing analysis as discussed in the Kreuze and Newell article. Why are all four levels needed in such an analysis?

CHAPTER 4

Cost Behavior

The first article for this section is Reading 4.1, Robin Cooper and Robert Kaplan's *How Cost Accounting Distorts Product Costs*. In this well-known article, Cooper and Kaplan strongly question the relevance of the traditional cost accounting model and its applicability for product costing. The authors discuss problems with traditional cost accounting, including the inadequacy of both variable and full costing methods for accurate product costing, and the failure of both marginal and fixed-cost allocations. Other topics, such as understanding the cost of complexity and transaction costing (an early name for activity-based costing), are introduced. This article helped set the stage for a great deal of research.

The linkages among variations in product and cost standards, cost behavior, and quality costs are highlighted in Harold Roth and Tom Albright's article, *What Are the Costs of Variability*, Reading 4.2. To illustrate the cost of variability, the authors cite a number of examples, including a study that sought to understand the sources of variation in the quality of paperboard output. In that study, data were collected on variables such as the shifts, crews, grades of product, and grade changes, The company under study was operating in a capacity-constrained environment, and the cost accountants developed a product cost analysis that showed how the cost of a product increased due to variations in the manufacturing process. Their model included the variable cost of materials and overhead, a fixed cost allocation, and the lost contribution margin. Using this model, the company was able to determine that the cost of certain grades of paperboard exceeded their selling price. The strategic implications of manufacturing products with high variation in product quality became much more evident as a result of the study.

Ralph Drtina's article, *The Outsourcing Decision*, Reading 4.3, discusses how to determine whether a particular activity should be outsourced. Using a value chain approach, Drtina focuses on outsourcing decisions relating to services. An example used is the decision to outsource fleet maintenance. Three key questions are addressed: (1) Is it possible to purchase the service externally? (2) Does the firm need to control the service activity as would be the case with secret documents or a critical technology? and (3) Is the firm capable of delivering the service at a world-class level of performance? A traditional numerical example that breaks down fixed and variable costs in a make-buy context is provided. Drtina argues that such an analysis ignores qualitative factors and that any outsourcing decision must integrate with the organization's strategy.

4.1 How Cost Accounting Distorts Product Costs
The traditional cost system that defines variable costs as varying in the short term with production will misclassify these costs as fixed.

By Robin Cooper and Robert S. Kaplan

In order to make sensible decisions concerning the products they market, managers need to know what their products cost. Product design, new product introduction decisions, and the amount of effort expended on trying to market a given product or product line will be influenced by the anticipated cost and profitability of the product. Conversely, if product profitability appears to drop, the question of discontinuance will be raised. Product costs also can play an important role in setting prices, particularly for customized products with low sales volumes and without readily available market prices.

The cumulative effect of decisions on product design, introduction, support, discontinuance, and pricing helps define a firm's strategy. If the product cost information is distorted, the firm can follow an inappropriate and unprofitable strategy. For example, the low-cost producer often achieves competitive advantage by servicing a broad range of customers. This strategy will be successful if the economies of scale exceed the additional costs, the diseconomies of scope, caused by producing and servicing a more diverse product line. If the cost system does not correctly attribute the additional costs to the products that cause them, then the firm might end up competing in segments where the scope-related costs exceed the benefits from larger scale production.

Similarly, a differentiated producer achieves competitive advantage by meeting specialized customers' needs with products whose costs of differentiation are lower than the price premiums charged for special features and services. If the cost system fails to measure differentiation costs properly, then the firm might choose to compete in segments that are actually unprofitable.

FULL VS. VARIABLE COST

Despite the importance of cost information, disagreement still exists about whether product costs should be measured by full or by variable cost. In a full-cost system, fixed production costs are allocated to products so that reported product costs measure total manufacturing costs. In a variable cost system, the fixed costs are not allocated and product costs reflect only the marginal cost of manufacturing.

Academic accountants, supported by economists, have argued strongly that variable costs are the relevant ones for product decisions. They have demonstrated, using increasingly complex models, that setting marginal revenues equal to marginal costs will produce the highest profit. In contrast, accountants in practice continue to report full costs in their cost accounting systems.

The definition of variable cost used by academic accountants assumes that product decisions have a short-time horizon, typically a month or a quarter. Costs are variable only if they vary directly with monthly or quarterly changes in production volume. Such a definition is appropriate if the volume of production of all products can be changed at will and there is no way to change simultaneously the level of fixed costs.

In practice, managers reject this short-term perspective because the decision to offer a product creates a long-term commitment to manufacture, market, and support that product. Given this perspective, short-term variable cost is an inadequate measure of product cost.

While full cost is meant to be a surrogate for long-run manufacturing costs, in nearly all of the companies we visited, management was not convinced that their full-cost systems were adequate for its product-related decisions. In particular, management did not believe their systems accurately reflected the costs of resources consumed to manufacture products. But they were also unwilling to adopt a variable-cost approach.

Of the more than 20 firms we visited and documented, Mayers Tap, Rockford, and Schrader Bellows provided particularly useful insights on how product costs were systematically distorted.[1] These companies had several significant common characteristics.

They all produced a large number of distinct products in a single facility. The products formed several distinct product lines and were sold through diverse marketing channels. The range in demand volume for products within a product line was high, with sales of high-volume products between 100 and 1,000 times greater than sales of low-volume products. As a consequence, products were manufactured and shipped in highly varied lot sizes. While our findings are based upon these three companies, the same effects were observed at several other sites.

In all three companies, product costs played an important role in the decisions that surrounded the introduction, pricing, and discontinuance of products. Reported product costs also appeared to play a significant role in determining how much effort should be assigned to marketing and selling products.

Typically, the individual responsible for introducing new products also was responsible for setting prices. Cost-plus pricing to achieve a desired level of gross margin predominantly was used for the special products, though substantial modifications to the resulting estimated prices occurred when direct competition existed. Such competition was common for high-volume products but rarely occurred for the low-volume items. Frequently, no obvious market prices existed for low-volume products because they had been designed to meet a particular customer's needs.

ACCURACY OF PRODUCT COSTS

Managers in all three firms expressed serious concerns about the accuracy of their product-costing systems.

For example, Rockford attempted to obtain much higher margins for its low-volume products to compensate, on an ad hoc basis, for the gross underestimates of costs that it believed the cost system produced for these products. But management was not able to justify its decisions on cutoff points to identify low-volume products or the magnitude of the ad hoc margin increases. Further, Rockford's management believed that its faulty cost system explained the ability of small firms to compete effectively against it for high-volume business. These small firms, with no apparent economic or technological advantage, were winning high-volume business with prices that were at or below Rockford's reported costs. And the small firms seemed to be prospering at these prices.

At Schrader Bellows, production managers believed that certain products were not earning their keep because they were so difficult to produce. But the cost system reported that these products were among the most profitable in the line. The managers also were convinced that they could make certain products as efficiently as anybody else. Yet competitors were consistently pricing comparable products considerably lower. Management suspected that the cost system contributed to this problem.

At Mayers Tap, the financial accounting profits were always much lower than those predicted by the cost system, but no one could explain the discrepancy. Also, the senior managers were concerned by their failure to predict which bids they would win or lose. Mayers Tap often won bids that had been overpriced because it did not really want the business, and lost bids it had deliberately underpriced in order to get the business.

TWO-STAGE COST ALLOCATION SYSTEM

The cost systems of all companies we visited had many common characteristics. Most important was the use of a two-stage cost allocation system: in the first stage, costs were assigned to cost pools (often called cost centers), and in the second stage, costs were allocated from the cost pools to the products.

The companies used many different allocation bases in the first stage to allocate costs from plant overhead accounts to cost centers. Despite the variation in allocation bases in the first stage, however, all companies used direct labor hours in the second stage to allocate overhead from the cost pools to the products. Direct labor hours was used in the second allocation stage even when the production process was highly automated so that burden rates exceeded 1,000%. Figure 1 illustrates a typical two-stage allocation process.

Of the three companies we examined in detail, only one had a cost accounting system capable of reporting variable product costs. Variable cost was identified at the budgeting stage in one other site, but this information was not subsequently used for product costing. The inability of the cost system to report variable cost was a common feature of many of the systems we observed. Reporting variable product costs was the exception, not the rule.

Firms used only one cost system even though costs were collected and allocated for several purposes, including product costing, operational control, and inventory valuation. The cost systems seemed to be designed primarily to perform the inventory valuation function for financial reporting because they had serious deficiencies for operational control (too delayed and too aggregate) and for product costing (too aggregate).

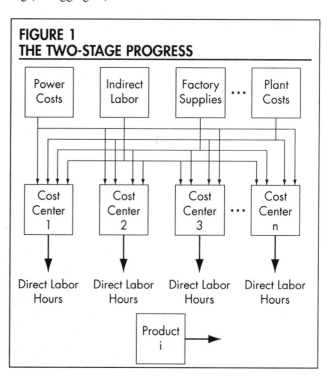

**FIGURE 1
THE TWO-STAGE PROGRESS**

THE FAILURE OF MARGINAL COSTING

The extensive use of fixed-cost allocations in all the companies we investigated contrasts sharply with a 65-year history of academics advocating marginal costing for product decisions. If the marginal-cost concept had been adopted by companies' management, then we would have expected to see product-costing systems that explicitly reported variable-cost information. Instead, we observed cost systems that reported variable as well as full costs in only a small minority of companies.

The traditional academic recommendation for marginal costing may have made sense when variable costs (labor, material, and some overhead) were a relatively high proportion of total manufactured cost and when product diversity was sufficiently small that there was not wide variation in the demands made by different products on the firm's production and marketing resources. But these conditions are no longer typical of many of today's organizations. Increasingly, overhead (most of it considered "fixed") is becoming a larger share of total manufacturing costs. In addition, the plants we examined are being asked to produce an increasing variety of products that make quite different demands on equipment and support departments. Thus, even if direct or marginal costing were once a useful recommendation to management, direct costing, even if correctly implemented, is not likely a solution—and may perhaps be a major problem—for product costing in the contemporary manufacturing environment.

THE FAILURE OF FIXED-COST ALLOCATIONS

While we consistently observed managers avoiding the use of variable or marginal costs for their product-related decisions, we observed also their discomfort with the full-cost allocations produced by their existing cost systems. We believe that we have identified the two major sources for the discomfort.

The first problem arises from the use of direct labor hours in the second allocation stage to assign costs from cost centers to products. This procedure may have been adequate many decades ago when direct labor was the principal value-adding activity in the material conversion process. But as firms introduce more automated machinery, direct labor is increasingly engaged in setup and supervisory functions (rather than actually performing the work on the product) and no longer represents a reasonable surrogate for resource demands by product.

In many of the plants we visited, labor's main tasks are to load the machines and to act as troubleshooters. Labor frequently works on several different products at the same time so that it becomes impossible to assign labor hours intelligently to products. Some of the companies we visited had responded to this situation by beginning experiments using machine hours instead of labor hours to allocate costs from cost pools to products (for the second stage of the allocation process). Other companies, particularly those adopting just-in-time or continuous-flow production processes, were moving to material dollars as the basis for distributing costs from pools to products. Material dollars provide a less expensive method for cost allocation than machine hours because, as with labor hours, material dollars are collected by the existing cost system. A move to a machine-hour basis would require the collection of new data for many of these companies.

Shifting from labor hours to machine hours or material dollars provides some relief from the problem of using unrealistic bases for attributing costs to products. In fact, some companies have been experimenting with using all three allocation bases simultaneously: labor hours for those costs that vary with the number of labor hours worked (e.g., supervision—if the amount of labor in a product is high, the amount of supervision related to that product also is likely to be high), machine hours for those costs that vary with the number of hours the machine is running (e.g., power—the longer the machine is running the more power that is consumed by that product), and material dollars for those costs that vary with the value of material in the product (e.g., material handling—the higher the value of the material in the product, the greater the material-handling costs associated with those products are likely to be).

Using multiple allocation bases allows a finer attribution of costs to the products responsible for the incurrence of those costs. In particular, it allows for product diversity where the direct labor, machine hours, and material dollars consumed in the manufacture of different products are not directly proportional to each other.

For reported product costs to be correct, however, the allocation bases used must be capable of accounting for all aspects of product diversity. Such an accounting is not always possible even using all three volume-related allocation bases we described. As the number of product items manufactured increases, so does the number of direct labor hours, machine hours, and material dollars consumed. The designer of the cost system, in adopting these bases, assumes that all allocated costs have the same behavior; namely that they increase in direct relationship to the volume of product items manufactured. But there are many costs that vary with the diversity and complexity of products, not by the number of units produced.

THE COST OF COMPLEXITY

The complexity costs of a full-line producer can be illustrated as follows. Consider two identical plants. One plant produces 1,000,000 units of product A. The second plant produces 100,000 units of product A and 900,000 units of 199 similar products. (The similar products have sales volumes that vary from 100 to 100,000 units.)

The first plant has a simple production environment and requires limited manufacturing-support facilities. Few setups, expediting, and scheduling activities are required.

The other plant presents a much more complex production-management environment. Its 200 products have to be scheduled through the plant, requiring frequent setups, inventory movements, purchases, receipts, and inspections. To handle this complexity, the support departments must be larger and more sophisticated.

The traditional cost accounting system plays an important role in obfuscating the underlying relationship between the range of products produced and the size of the support departments. First, the costs of most support departments are classified as fixed, making it difficult to realize that these costs are systematically varying. Second, the use of volume-related allocation bases makes it difficult to recognize how these support-department costs vary.

Support-department costs must vary with something because they have been among the fastest growing in the overall cost structure of manufactured products. As the example demonstrates, support-department costs vary not with the volume of product items manufactured, rather they vary with the range of items produced (i.e., the complexity of the production process). The traditional definition of variable cost, with its monthly or quarterly perspective, views such costs as fixed because complexity-related costs do not vary significantly in such a short time frame. Across an extended period of time, however, the increasing complexity of the production process places additional demands on support departments, and their costs eventually and inevitably rise.

The output of a support department consists of the activities its personnel perform. These include such activities as setups, inspections, material handling, and scheduling. The output of the departments can be represented by the number of distinct activities that are performed or the number of transactions handled. Because most of the output of these departments consists of human activities, however, output can increase quite significantly before an immediate deterioration in the quality of service is detected. Eventually, the maximum output of the department is reached and additional personnel are requested. The request typically comes some time after the initial increase in diversity and output. Thus, support departments, while varying with the diversity of the demanded output, grow intermittently. The practice of annually budgeting the size of the departments further hides the underlying relationship between the mix and volume of demand and the size of the department. The support departments often are constrained to grow only when budgeted to do so.

Support-department costs are perhaps best described as "discretionary" because they are budgeted and authorized each year. The questions we must address are: What determines the level of these discretionary fixed costs? Why, if these costs are not affected by the quantity of production, are there eight people in a support department and not one? What generates the work, if not physical quantities of inputs or outputs, that requires large support-department staffs? We believe the answers to these questions on the origins of discretionary overhead costs (i.e., what drives these costs) can be found by analyzing the activities or transactions demanded when producing a full and diverse line of products.

TRANSACTION COSTING

Low-volume products create more transactions per unit manufactured than their high-volume counterparts. The per unit share of these costs should, therefore, be higher for the low-volume products. But when volume-related bases are used exclusively to allocate support-department costs, high-volume and low-volume products receive similar transaction-related costs. When only volume-related bases are used for second-stage allocations, high-volume products receive an excessively high fraction of support-department costs and, therefore, subsidize the low-volume products.

As the range between low-volume and high-volume products increases, the degree of cross-subsidization rises. Support departments expand to cope with the additional complexity of more products, leading to increased overhead charges. The reported product cost of all products consequently increases. The high-volume products appear more expensive to produce than previously, even though they are not responsible for the additional costs. The costs triggered by the introduction of new, low-volume products are systematically shifted to high-volume products that may be placing relatively few demands on the plant's support departments.

Many of the transactions that generate work for production-support departments can be proxied by the number of setups. For example, the movement of material in the plant often occurs at the commencement or completion of a production run. Similarly, the majority of the time spent on parts inspection occurs just after a setup or changeover. Thus, while the support departments are engaged in a broad array of activities, a considerable portion of their costs may be attributed to the number of setups.

Not all of the support-department costs are related (or relatable) to the number of setups. The cost of setup personnel relates more to the quantity of setup hours than to the actual number of setups. The number of inspections of incoming material can be directly related to the number of material receipts, as would be the time spent moving the received material into inventory. The number of outgoing shipments can be used to predict the activity level of the finished-goods and shipping departments. The assignment of all these support costs with a transactions-based approach reinforces the effect of the setup-related costs because the low-sales-volume items tend to trigger more small incoming and outgoing shipments.

Schrader Bellows had recently performed a "strategic cost analysis" that significantly increased the number of bases used to allocate costs to the products; many second-stage allocations used transactions costs to assign support-department costs to products. In particular, the number of setups allocated a sizeable percentage of support-department costs to products.

The effect of changing these second-stage allocations from a direct labor to a transaction basis was dramatic. While the support-department costs accounted for about 50% of overhead (or about 25% of total costs), the change in the reported product costs ranged from about minus 10% to plus 1,000%. The significant change in the reported product costs

TABLE 1
COMPARISON OF REPORTED PRODUCT COSTS AT SCHRADER BELLOWS

Product	Sales Volume	Existing Cost System		Transaction-Based System		Percent of Change	
		Unit Cost[a]	Unit Gross Margin	Unit Cost[a]	Unit Gross Margin	Unit Cost	Unit Gross Margin
1	43,562	7.85	5.51	7.17	6.19	(8.7)	12.3
2	500	8.74	3.76	15.45	(2.95)	76.8	(178.5)
3	53	12.15	10.89	82.49	(59.45)	578.9	(645.9)
4	2,079	13.63	4.91	24.51	(5.97)	79.8	(221.6)
5	5,670	12.40	7.95	19.99	0.36	61.3	(93.4)
6	11,169	8.04	5.49	7.96	5.57	(1.0)	1.5
7	423	8.47	3.74	6.93	5.28	(18.2)	41.2

[a]The sum of total cost (sales volume × unit cost) for all seven products is different under the two systems because the seven products only represent a small fraction of total production.

for the low-volume items was due to the substantial cost of the support departments and the low batch size over which the transaction cost was spread.

Table 1 shows the magnitude of the shift in reported product costs for seven representative products. The existing cost system reported gross margins that varied from 26% to 47%, while the strategic analysis showed gross margin that ranged from −258% to + 46%. The trends in the two sets of reported product profitabilities were clear: the existing direct-labor-based system had identified the low-volume products as the most profitable, while the strategic cost analysis indicated exactly the reverse.

There are three important messages in the table and in the company's findings in general.

- Traditional systems that assign costs to products using a single volume-related base seriously distort product costs.
- The distortion is systematic. Low-volume products are under-costed, and high-volume products are overcosted.
- Accurate product costs cannot, in general, be achieved by cost systems that rely only on volume-related bases (even multiple bases such as machine hours and material quantities) for second-stage allocations. A different type of allocation base must be used for overhead costs that vary with the number of transactions performed, as opposed to the volume of product produced.

The shift to transaction-related allocation bases is a more fundamental change to the philosophy of cost-systems design than is at first realized. In a traditional cost system that uses volume-related bases, the costing element is always the product. It is the product that consumes direct labor hours, machine hours, or material dollars. Therefore, it is the product that gets costed.

In a transaction-related system, costs are assigned to the units that caused the transaction to be originated. For example, if the transaction is a setup, then the costing element will be the production lot because each production lot requires a single setup. The same is true for purchasing activities, inspections, scheduling, and material movements. The costing element is no longer the product but those elements the transaction affects.

In the transaction-related costing system, the unit cost of a product is determined by dividing the cost of a transaction by the number of units in the costing element. For example, when the costing element is a production lot, the unit cost of a product is determined by dividing the production lot cost by the number of units in the production lot.

This change in the costing element is not trivial. In the Schrader Bellows strategic cost analysis (see Table 1), product seven appears to violate the strong inverse relationship between profits and production-lot size for the other six products. A more detailed analysis of the seven products, however, showed that product seven was assembled with components also used to produce two high-volume products (numbers one and six) and that it was the production-lot size of the components that was the dominant cost driver, not the assembly-lot size, or the shipping-lot size.

In a traditional cost system, the value of commonality of parts is hidden. Low-volume components appear to cost only slightly more than their high-volume counterparts. There is no incentive to design products with common parts. The shift to transaction-related costing identifies the much lower costs that derive from designing products with common (or fewer) parts and the much higher costs generated when large numbers of unique parts are specified for low-volume products. In recognition of this phenomenon, more companies are experimenting with assigning material-related overhead on the basis of the total number of different parts used, and not on the physical or dollar volume of materials used.

LONG-TERM VARIABLE COST
The volume-unrelated support-department costs, unlike traditional variable costs, do not vary with short-term changes in activity levels. Traditional variable costs vary in the short run with production fluctuations because they represent cost elements that require no managerial actions to change the level of expenditure.

In contrast, any amount of decrease in overhead costs associated with reducing diversity and complexity in the factory will take many months to realize and will require specific managerial actions. The number of personnel in support departments will have to be reduced, machines may have to be sold off, and some supervisors will become redundant. Actions to accomplish these overhead cost reductions will lag, by months, the complexity-reducing actions in the product line and in the process technology. But this long-term cost response mirrors the way overhead costs were first built up in the factory—as more products with specialized designs were added to the product line, the organization simply muddled through with existing personnel. It was only over time that overworked support departments requested and received additional personnel to handle the increased number of transactions that had been thrust upon them.

The personnel in the support departments are often highly skilled and possess a high degree of firm-specific knowledge. Management is loathe to lay them off when changes in market conditions temporarily reduce the level of production complexity. Consequently, when the workload of these departments drops, surplus capacity exists.

The long-term perspective management had adopted toward its products often made it difficult to use the surplus capacity. When it was used, it was not to make products never to be produced again, but rather to produce inventory of products that were known to disrupt production (typically the very low-volume items) or to produce, under short-term contract, products for other companies. We did not observe or hear about a situation in which this capacity was used to introduce a product that had only a short life expectancy. Some companies justified the acceptance of special orders or incremental business because they "knew" that the income from this business more than covered their variable or incremental costs. They failed to realize that the long-term consequence from accepting such incremental business was a steady rise in the costs of their support departments.

WHEN PRODUCT COSTS ARE NOT KNOWN

The magnitude of the errors in reported product costs and the nature of their bias make it difficult for full-line producers to enact sensible strategies. The existing cost systems clearly identify the low-volume products as the most profitable and the high-volume ones as the least profitable. Focused competitors, on the other hand, will not suffer from the same handicap. Their cost systems, while equally poorly designed, will report more accurate product costs because they are not distorted as much by lot-size diversity.

With access to more accurate product cost data, a focused competitor can sell the high-volume products at a lower price. The full-line producer is then apparently faced with very low margins on these products and is naturally tempted to deemphasize this business and concentrate on apparently higher-profit, low-volume specialty business.

This shift from high-volume to low-volume products, however, does not produce the anticipated higher profitability. The firm, believing in its cost system, chases illusory profits.

The firm has been victimized by diseconomies of scope. In trying to obtain the benefits of economy of scale by expanding its product offerings to better utilize its fixed or capacity resources, the firm does not see the high diseconomies it has introduced by creating a far more complex production environment. The cost accounting system fails to reveal this diseconomy of scope.

A COMPREHENSIVE COST SYSTEM

One message comes through overwhelmingly in our experiences with the three firms, and with the many others we talked and worked with. Almost all product-related decisions—introduction, pricing, and discontinuance—are long-term. Management accounting thinking (and teaching) during the past half-century has concentrated on information for making short-run incremental decisions based on variable, incremental, or relevant costs. It has missed the most important aspect of product decisions. Invariably, the time period for measuring "variable," "incremental," or "relevant" costs has been about a month (the time period corresponding to the cycle of the firm's internal financial reporting system). While academics admonish that notions of fixed and variable are meaningful only with respect to a particular time period, they immediately discard this warning and teach from the perspective of one-month decision horizons.

This short-term focus for product costing has led all the companies we visited to view a large and growing proportion of their total manufacturing costs as "fixed." In fact, however, what they call "fixed" costs have been the most variable and rapidly increasing costs. This paradox has seemingly eluded most accounting practitioners and scholars. Two fundamental changes in our thinking about cost behavior must be introduced.

First, the allocation of costs from the cost pools to the products should be achieved using bases that reflect cost drivers. Because many overhead costs are driven by the complexity of production, not the volume of production, nonvolume-related bases are required. Second, many of these overhead costs are somewhat discretionary. While they vary with changes in the complexity of the production process, these changes are intermittent. A traditional cost system that defines variable costs as varying in the short term with production volume will misclassify these costs as fixed.

The misclassification also arises from an inadequate understanding of the actual cost drivers for most overhead costs. Many overhead costs vary with transactions: transactions to order, schedule, receive, inspect, and pay for shipments; to move, track, and count inventory; to schedule production work; to set up machines; to perform quality assurance; to implement engineering change orders; and to expedite and ship orders. The cost of these transactions is largely independent of the size of the order being handled; the cost does not vary with the amount of inputs or outputs. It does vary, however, with the need for the transaction itself. If the firm introduces more products, if it needs to expedite more orders, or if it needs to inspect more components, then it will need larger overhead departments to perform these additional transactions.

SUMMARY

Product costs are almost all variable costs. Some of the sources of variability relate to physical volume of items produced. These costs will vary with units produced, or in a varied, multiproduct environment, with surrogate measures such as labor hours, machine hours, material dollars and quantities, or elapsed time of production. Other costs, however, particularly those arising from overhead support and marketing departments, vary with the diversity and complexity in the product line. The variability of these costs is best explained by the incidence of transactions to initiate the next stage in the production, logistics, or distribution process.

A comprehensive product cost system, incorporating the long-term variable costs of manufacturing and marketing each product or product line, should provide a much better basis for managerial decisions on pricing, introducing, discontinuing, and reengineering product lines. The cost system may even become strategically important for running the business and creating sustainable competitive advantages for the firm.

Robin Cooper is an associate professor of business administration at the Harvard Business School and a fellow of the Institute of Chartered Accountants in England and Wales. He writes a column, "Cost Management Principles and Concepts," in the Journal of Cost Management *and has produced research on activity-based costing for the CAM-I Cost Management System Project.*

Robert S. Kaplan is the Arthur Lowes Dickinson Professor of Accounting at the Harvard Business School and a professor of industrial administration at Carnegie-Mellon University. Currently, Professor Kaplan serves on the Executive Committee of the CAM-I Cost Management System Project, the Manufacturing Studies Board of the National Research Council, and the Financial Accounting Standards Advisory Committee.

Notes

1. Mayers Tap (disguised name) is described in Harvard Business School, case series 9-185-111. Schrader-Bellows is described in HBS Case Series 9-186-272.

THE IMPORTANCE OF FIELD RESEARCH

The accompanying article, co-authored with Robin Cooper, is excerpted from *Accounting & Management: Field Study Perspectives* (Boston, Mass., Harvard Business School Press, 1987) William J. Bruns, Jr. and Robert S. Kaplan (eds.). The book contains 13 field studies on management accounting innovations presented at a colloquium at the Harvard Business School in June 1986 by leading academic researchers from the U.S. and Western Europe. The colloquium represents the largest single collection of field research studies on management accounting practices in organizations.

The HBS colloquium had two principal objectives. First, the authors were to understand and document the management accounting practices of actual organizations. Some of the organizations would be captured in a process of transition: attempting, and occasionally succeeding to modify their systems to measure, motivate and evaluate operating performance. Other organizations were studied just to understand the system of measurement and control that had evolved in their particular environment.

A second, and even more important, objective of the colloquium was to begin the process by which field research methods in management accounting could be established as a legitimate method of inquiry. Academic researchers in accounting have extensive experience with deductive, model-building, analytic research with the design and analysis of controlled experiments, usually in a laboratory setting; and with the empirical analysis of large data bases. This experience has yielded research guidance and criteria that, while not always explicit, nevertheless are widely shared and permit research to be conducted and evaluated.

At a time when so many organizations are reexamining the adequacy of their management accounting systems it is especially important that university-based researchers spend more time working directly with innovating organizations. We are pleased that MANAGEMENT ACCOUNTING, through publication of this article, is helping to publicize the existence of the field studies performed to date.

The experiences described in the accompanying article, as well as in the other papers in the colloquium volume, indicate a very different role for management accounting systems in organizations than is currently taught in most of our business schools and accounting departments. We believe that present and future field research and case-writing will lead to major changes in management accounting courses. To facilitate the needed changes in curriculum and research, however, requires extensive cooperation between university faculty and practicing management accountants. As noted by observers at the Harvard colloquium:

From R. Cooper and R. S. Kaplan, "How Cost Accounting Distorts Product Costs," *Management Accounting* (April 1988): 20-27. Reprinted with permission.

Question

4.1 What does the term "cost of complexity" mean in Cooper and Kaplan's article? Is this concept used in traditional cost accounting systems?

4.2 What Are the Costs of Variability?
Knowing the answer is key to a company's quest for quality.

By Harold P. Roth, CMA, and Thomas L. Albright, CPA

Certificate of Merit, 1992–93

Zero defects and robust quality are two quality philosophies used to help U.S. companies compete in the global marketplace. An important measure in any quality philosophy is the cost of product variability.

Although variation among products may affect the consumers' perceptions of quality, the importance of consistency to a producer depends on the quality philosophy it follows. For example, with a zero defects philosophy the only cost attributed to variation occurs when products fall outside the specification limits. Thus, the cost of variation depends on whether the product can be reworked, if there are constraints on production, and the distance between product specification limits.

On the other hand, a robust quality program claims that any variation is undesirable and causes costs to be incurred by the manufacturer, consumer, or society. An estimate of these costs is provided by the quality loss function.

TWO PHILOSOPHIES

The term "quality" has many different meanings depending on the context used. When quality is used to describe products, it may mean "conforming to specifications" or "fitness for use." Although these two definitions may mean the same thing to many people, they have different implications for how quality is evaluated and the importance of product variability.

The philosophy underlying the "conformance to specifications" definition generally leads to a zero defects approach to quality while the "fitness for use" philosophy leads to a robust quality approach.[1]

The role of product variability in evaluating quality depends on whether the company has adopted a zero defects or a robust quality philosophy. With a zero defects philosophy, the allowable variation is defined by specification limits, and any variation within those limits is acceptable. According to the robust quality philosophy, any variation from a target value represents a condition that is less than ideal, with potential economic consequences. Thus, robustness is the result of meeting exact targets consistently—not from always staying within tolerances.

In turn, the cost of variation also depends on the philosophy. Generally, companies that adopt a zero defects philosophy will not attribute any cost to variability if the product is within specification limits. But the robust quality proponent will assign a cost to variability whenever a product varies from a target. Companies following a robust quality philosophy believe any variation from target results in a loss. Furthermore, greater losses will occur as the variation from target becomes larger.

VARIABILITY FROM TARGET

A case study at the Sony Corporation supports the idea that a relationship exists between variability and the zero defects and robust quality philosophies.[2] The study involved the color density of television sets produced in two manufacturing facilities—one in San Diego and the other in Tokyo.

The color density distribution associated with the output of each manufacturing site is illustrated in Figure 1. Three reference points: the lower specification limit, target value, and upper specification limit appear on the horizontal axis of the graph.

Generally, Sony considers any television set with color density measurement less than the lower specification limit or greater than the upper specification limit to be defective. However, the approach to quality differs between the two plants.

Sony of Tokyo strives to produce at the target value and does not inspect each unit. Thus, some out-of-spec units are shipped to customers, as evidenced by the tails of the distribution that fall outside the specification limits. In contrast, Sony of San Diego uses 100% inspection to ensure that the televisions fall within the specification limits and to prevent the shipment of defective units to distributors.

After studying the output of the plants, Sony discovered that although the number of defective units was similar in both manufacturing plants, the variation around the target specification was not. As shown in Figure 1, there is less variation in the televisions produced in the Tokyo plant because more sets are near the target value. The distribution of color densities from the San Diego plant (which is shown by the rectangular distribution) indicates greater variability than that of the Tokyo plant because more sets fall farther away from the target value.

Customers who purchased television sets manufactured by Sony of Tokyo reported greater satisfaction and filed fewer warranty claims than those who purchased products manufactured by Sony of San Diego. The lesson to Sony was clear—variation from the target specification of a critical component has implications for customer satisfaction and, therefore, costs.

COST OF VARIABILITY

There are many costs associated with variability in product attributes. For example, raw material costs will be higher if products use more materials than specified by engineering standards (for example, the target value). Likewise, variability in material thickness or weight may result in added wear on downstream machines that cause more maintenance and repair costs.

Also, products that exceed material usage targets may have higher delivery costs because they weigh more than the target weight. However, these costs are not attributed to variability with the zero defects philosophy. Instead, costs of variability are recognized only when a product falls outside the specification limits. When products meet specifications, they are assumed to meet the customers' requirements.

The costs incurred when products fall outside the specification limits depend on three factors: whether the product can be reworked or repaired, production constraints, and where specification limits are set.

When products fall outside the specification limits, it may be less costly to rework or repair them than to discard them. When products are reworked and then sold, there is no loss of the materials and parts that comprise the final product. In addition, disposal costs are reduced or avoided by the producer, so costs are generally lower if rework is possible.

The constraints that exist in the production process also affect the cost. If excess capacity exists and additional units can be produced to replace nonconforming products, the costs incurred because a product fails to meet specifications depend on whether the nonconforming unit is sold or discarded. But if additional units cannot be produced, then the cost of variability includes an opportunity cost for the lost sales. Thus, the economic costs of lost production are higher when there are constraints than if no constraints exist.

A paper manufacturer provides an example of the costs of variability in a capacity-constrained environment.[3] A study was conducted to understand the sources of variation in the quality of paperboard output. The variables studied included crews, shifts, grades of product, rest interval between shifts, and whether a product was produced immediately following a grade change. The variability and cost data that resulted from the study had strategic implications for the company.

Because the company was operating in a capacity-constrained environment, the cost accountants developed a product cost analysis that captured the economic cost of a unit of product that was lost as a result of variability in the

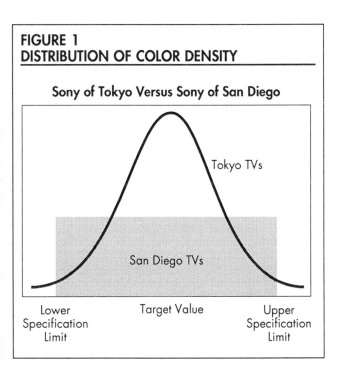

FIGURE 1
DISTRIBUTION OF COLOR DENSITY

Sony of Tokyo Versus Sony of San Diego

Tokyo TVs

San Diego TVs

Lower Specification Limit Target Value Upper Specification Limit manufacturing process. The cost included the variable cost of materials and overhead (less any pulp or chemicals that could be recovered through reworking the product), a fixed cost allocation, and the lost contribution margin (a surrogate for the opportunity cost from producing a defective product in a capacity-constrained environment).

The revised cost numbers had strategic implications for the product mix manufactured by the plant. By analyzing the cost of each grade of product, the company discovered that the cost of certain grades far exceeded the selling price.

For example, the company learned that the production of uncoated paperboard resulted in a much larger proportion of defective units than that of coated paperboard. This knowledge helped the company analyze the strategic implications of manufacturing a product that exhibits extreme variation in the quality of production by attaching a cost to products exhibiting high rates of variability.

CALCULATING THE COSTS

Various costs are incurred when products fall outside the specification limits. These include out-of-pocket costs such as costs of inspection and rework.

If the product can be sold as a first-quality unit after the rework, these out-of-pocket costs are the total costs of variability. If the reworked unit cannot be sold as a first-quality unit, then the cost of variability also may include an opportunity cost. The opportunity cost will be relevant if the second-quality item replaces a sale for a first-quality item. In this case, the opportunity cost of variability is the difference between the contribution margin of the first-quality product and the actual contribution margin.

If a product falls outside the specification limits, cannot be reworked, and must be scrapped, then the cost of variability includes the materials, labor, and other costs incurred in producing the product. In addition, any cost incurred in disposing of the product also is a cost of variability.

To illustrate the computation of costs that are caused by variability, assume a company is producing a product that sells for $50 per unit. The variable production cost is $20, and the unit contribution margin is $30. During the last month, the company manufactured 100,000 units that used all the available machine hours. All units produced are sold.

The weight is a critical dimension for this product. The target value for the weight is 20 kg, and the specification limits are set at plus or minus 2 kg. For the units produced last month, the weights followed a normal distribution with an average of 20 kg and a standard deviation of 0.8 kg. Figure 2 illustrates the distribution of the weights from this production process.

As shown in Figure 2, most of the weights fall between 18 and 22 kg and, therefore, conform to the specifications. However, some of the weights are above the upper specification limit of 22 kg, and some are below the lower specification limits of 18 kg. These units that fall in the tails of the distribution are nonconforming. To determine the number

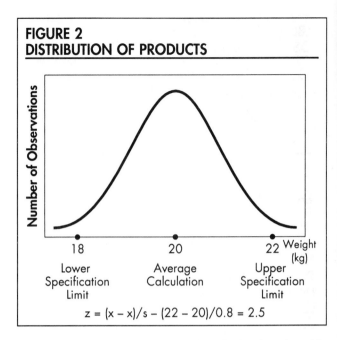

FIGURE 2
DISTRIBUTION OF PRODUCTS

$$z = (x - \bar{x})/s = (22 - 20)/0.8 = 2.5$$

of nonconforming units, a z-value is calculated, and a table for areas under the normal curve is consulted to determine the portion in the tails of the distribution.[4]

For this example, the calculated z-value shows that the specification limit is 2.5 standard normal deviates from the mean (see Figure 2). With z equal to 2.5, a table for the area under the normal curve shows that 0.0062% of the observations exceed 22 kg. Because the distribution is symmetrical, an equal portion falls below the lower specification limit of 18 kg. Thus, the number of nonconforming products manufactured last month was 1,240 [100,000 (2 × 0.0062)].

The cost attributed to the variability of these 1,240 units depends on their disposal. If the units can be reworked[5] for $12 a unit and then sold for the normal sales price of $50, the cost of variability is equal to the rework cost. But if the products only can be sold for $45 a unit, there is also an opportunity cost of $5 per unit, for a total cost of $17. If the product cannot be reworked, then the relevant cost of variability is the variable production cost, the opportunity cost, and any disposal cost.

Table 1 summarizes the cost of variability for various conditions. The total cost of variability for this product can be calculated by multiplying the unit cost by the number of nonconforming units. With 1,240 nonconforming units during the month, the cost of variability could range from a low of $14,880 ($12 × 1,240) if the units are reworked and sold as first-quality units to a high of $68,200 ($55 × 1,240) if the units cannot be reworked and must be disposed of at a cost of $5 per unit.

This example shows how organizations might estimate their costs of variability when they manufacture products that do not conform to specifications. But it ignores any costs incurred because products vary within the specification limits and any costs incurred by consumers because of variability in the products.

TABLE 1
COST OF VARIABILITY

Sales price per first-quality unit			$50	
Sales price per second-quality unit			45	
Variable production cost per unit			20	
Normal contribution margin per unit			30	
Rework cost per unit			12	
Disposal cost per unit			5	

Condition	Variable Production Cost	Rework Cost	Disposal Cost	Lost Contribution Margin	Total Unit Cost
Unit is reworked and sold for $50		$12			$12
Unit is reworked and sold for $45		12		$5	17
Unit cannot be reworked and has no disposal cost	$20			30	50
Unit cannot be reworked and has a $5 disposal cost	20		$5	30	55

Thus, the philosophy of zero defects may understate the total cost of product variability. The quality loss function provides an alternative way to measure the cost of variability that is consistent with the robust quality philosophy.

QUALITY LOSS FUNCTION

The quality loss function (QLF) is a part of the Taguchi quality philosophy.[6] The QLF is based on the idea that any variability from a target value causes a loss to society. Thus, his proponents believe that any variability is costly even if the products still fall within the specification limits.

There are several variations of the quality loss function, and the appropriate one depends on how quality is measured. In the example presented earlier, the quality characteristic (weight) represents a nominal-is-better function. In other words, the target value of 20 kg is the nominal value, and production should strive to manufacture products weighing 20 kg. Any variation from this value results in a loss under the quality loss function.

The quality loss function is a quadratic function where costs increase as the actual product characteristic deviates from the target value. Figure 3 shows the quality loss function for the nominal-is-better case, and Table 2 presents the formula for measuring the quality loss for an individual unit.

To determine the total loss for a period using the quality loss function, an average loss per unit can be calculated and multiplied by the total number of units. When the average and standard deviation are known, the average loss can be estimated using the formula also shown in Table 2.

With 100,000 units, the quality loss is $192,000 [$1.92 x 100,000] which is much larger than the cost of variability estimated using the conformance to specification model. The

reason for the greater cost is that the quality loss function includes a cost for any unit that varies from the target value regardless of whether it falls inside or outside the specification limits.

WHY VARIABILITY IS IMPORTANT

According to research, a lack of product consistency is a major factor in customers' perceptions of poor quality. The relationship between variability and quality is recognized in many quality control techniques such as statistical process control. it is also recognized by companies such as Oregon Cutting Systems where the operational definition of quality is to "reduce variability around the target."[7]

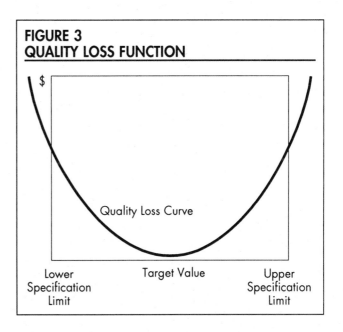

FIGURE 3
QUALITY LOSS FUNCTION

Quality Loss Curve

Lower Specification Limit — Target Value — Upper Specification Limit

TABLE 2
MEASURING QUALITY LOSS

Quality Loss for an Individual Unit:

$$L = k(Y - T)^2$$

where L = unit loss,
  Y = actual value of characteristic,
  T = target value of characteristic, and
  k = proportionality constant.

The value of k is usually computed by dividing the loss for a product which falls at the specification limit by the squared distance form the target value to the specification limit, i.e.:

$$k = \frac{c}{d^2}$$

where c = loss associated with a unit produced at the spec limit, and
  d = distance from target value to spec limit.

In this example, if the loss for a unit at the specification limit is $12, then the proportionality constant is $3:

$$k = \frac{\$12}{(22 - 20)^2} = \frac{\$12}{2^2} = \$3$$

Average Loss per Unit:

$$\text{Average loss} = k\,[s^2 + (Y - T)^2]$$

where s = standard deviation
  Y = average (mean)
  T = target value, and
  k = proportionality constant.

From the data given above, the average loss is $1.92:

$$\text{Average loss} = \$3[0.8^2 + (20 - 20)^2] = \$3 \times 0.64 = \$1.92$$

Measuring variability should provide managers with information that can help them improve operations by identifying opportunities for improving product quality. If specific parts of a product can be identified as the source of variability, then managers know where they should focus their quality improvement efforts.

These efforts may involve educating and retraining employees, redesigning production processes, investing in equipment, and even redesigning products. If a product can be manufactured using a smaller number of components and parts, there is less likelihood that the sum of the individual variations will result in significant quality problems.

Measuring the cost of variability also should help managers in their quest for quality. If managers do not define quality in terms of variability, they may not be aware of the types of costs associated with variability and of the magnitude of the costs. With an estimate of the cost, managers may be more likely to understand the financial implications of variability and the savings that result from their efforts to reduce it. Unless cost savings are measured, the financial impact of the efforts will not be known.

Although all processes and products will show some variation because it is a law of nature, companies need to measure it and strive to reduce it if they want to be competitive. If they do not reduce variation, it is likely their competitors will, and the consistently performing product may be perceived as higher quality by customers.

Harold P. Roth, CMA, CPA, Ph.D., is a professor of accounting at the University of Tennessee, Knoxville. He is past president of IMA's Knoxville Chapter, through which this article was submitted. Dr. Roth can be reached by calling (615) 974-1756.

Thomas L. Albright, CPA, is an assistant professor of accounting in the Culverhouse School of Accountancy at the University of Alabama. He holds a Ph.D. degree from the University of Tennessee. Dr. Albright is a member of IMA's West Alabama Chapter and can be reached at (205) 348-6131.

Notes

1. For a discussion of robust quality see Genichi Taguchi and Don Clausing, "Robust Quality," *Harvard Business Review* January–February 1990, pp. 65–75.

2. This case study is discussed by Taguchi and Clausing, pp. 68–69; and by Ranjit Roy, *A Primer on the Taguchi Method*, Van Nostrand Reinhold, New York, 1990, pp. 12–13.

3. For further details on the study see T. L. Albright and J. M. Reeve, "A Case Study on the Impact of Material Yield-Related Cost Drivers on Economic Improvement," *Journal of Management Accounting Research*, Fall 1992, pp. 20–43.

4. Most statistics books provide tables showing Areas under the Normal Curve. For an example, see Eugene L. Grant and Richard S. Leavenworth, *Statistics Quality Control*, 5th ed., McGraw-Hill Book Company, New York, 1980, pp. 628–629.

5. Because the example states that production uses all available machinery, this example assumes that the reworking is done by laborers using different machines than used for the initial production.

6. Genichi Taguchi is a Japanese engineer who has developed statistical approaches to improving product and process quality. His approaches are discussed in many books dealing with quality engineering and design. Examples include Ranjit Roy, *A Primer on the Taguchi Method,* Van Nostrand Reinhold, New York, 1990; Philip J. Ross, *Taguchi Techniques for Quality Engineering,* McGraw-Hill Book Company, New York, 1988; and Thomas B. Barker, *Engineering Quality by Design,* Marcel Dekker, Inc., New York, and ASQC Quality Press, Milwaukee, 1990.

7. Jack Bailes, Ilene Kleinsorge, and Larry White, "How Support Services Can Use Process Control," MANAGEMENT ACCOUNTING®, October 1992, p. 45.

From H. P. Roth and T. L. Albright, "What Are the Costs of Variability?" *Management Accounting* (June 1994): 51–55. Reprinted with permission.

Questions

4.2a Is the "cost of variability" concept applied consistently under the zero defects and robust quality philosophies? Explain.

4.2b Describe the "quality loss function" in Roth and Albright's article.

4.3 The Outsourcing Decision

Seize the opportunity to focus on activities that give your company the competitive edge.

By Ralph E. Drtina

Each business day the number of management accountants affected by massive restructuring and layoffs increases. In their efforts to streamline operations, managers are dismantling bureaucracies and questioning the benefits of vertical integration.

One alternative is a strategy that focuses internal operations on a small set of critical core activities. Nonessential services are then outsourced to external vendors, who can offer advantages such as cost, flexibility, and access to the latest technology.

Firms in high-technology industries, such as computers and biotechnology, have been pioneers in developing partnered relationships and focused strategies. Consider, for example, the case of Sun Microsystems, a leading maker of computer workstations. Sun concentrates on hardware and software design, where it distinguished itself from competitors, and outsources almost everything else in its value chain. It relies so heavily on external manufacturers and distributors that its own employees never touch one of its top selling products. After a vendor assembles the machine, another contract supplier delivers it to the customer.

Firms like Sun have been referred to as "intellectual holding companies." Numerous other companies—Apple, Honda, and Gallo Winery—also bank their success on a limited number of specific core technologies, although perhaps not to the outsourcing extreme exhibited by Sun Microsystems.

Management accountants can play an important role in deciding which activities should be performed within the firm and which should be bought externally.[1] But what is the correct methodology for helping managers make such strategic make-buy decisions?

Accounting educators, for example, normally frame the make-buy discussion within a manufacturing context. These decisions are presented as short term in duration and

seek to increase corporate earnings by finding ways to reduce costs.

Management strategists, who initiate outsourcing policy, are more concerned with creating shareholder value. Their policies often zero in on eliminating nonmanufacturing service overhead.

ACTIVITIES TO OUTSOURCE

The first step in preparing an outsourcing study is understanding your firm's value chain and the relationships among its service activities. Figure 1 is an example of typical services in a value chain.

Value is added at each stage beginning with product concept and ending with after-sales service. Corporate staff services—such as legal and accounting—provide the secondary support necessary to maintain the organization and its primary value chain activities. Both services provided by corporate staff and in the value chain can qualify for outsourcing.

Each stage of service delivery can be broken down further into its requisite subcomponent activities. Distribution, for example, is subdivided into four specific service activities. Fleet maintenance, an indirect activity that supports the distribution service, is identified in Figure 1 as being a candidate for external outsourcing.

Some activities are eliminated immediately as candidates for outsourcing, either because the service cannot be contracted outside or because the firm must control the activity to maintain its competitive position. For example, a high-technology research facility would not be able to outsource its typing or photocopying due to the highly classified nature of work. Similarly, Hewlett-Packard carefully controls the software for a laser printer it coproduces with Canon Inc. of Japan, thereby preventing its partner from replicating the laserjet technology for its own benefit.

FIGURE 1
KEY SERVICE ACTIVITIES

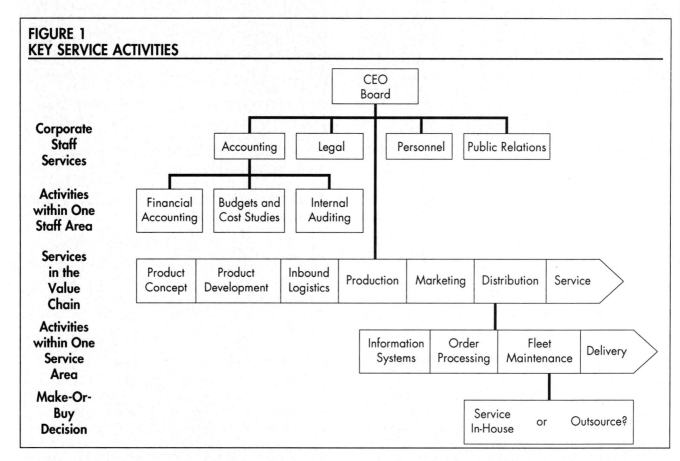

For those activities eligible for outsourcing, the key strategic question to ask is whether the firm can perform a service activity on a level comparable with the best organizations in the world. Productivity measurements should be compiled to capture these critical success factors for the activity: availability, timeliness, flexibility, quality, and cost reduction. Measures are then benchmarked against the results of firms that offer these same services in the marketplace.

Thus, we might find that a firm evaluating its fleet maintenance activity compares performance measures like those listed in Table 1. If the firm's performance does not stand up to the external measures, a determination must be made whether the firm can achieve a world-class level of delivery. If it is not possible to accomplish benchmarked standards of performance, the activity should be outsourced. To reiterate, the firm should concentrate only on those core activities that enhance its unique marketplace advantages.

OUTSOURCING FLEET MAINTENANCE
The service activity in question must pass several hurdles:

- Is it possible to purchase the service externally?
- Does the firm need to control the service activity—as would be the case with secret documents or a critical technology?
- Most important, is the firm capable of delivering the service at a world-class standard of performance?

If the service survives these preliminary cutoffs, the next step is to decide if the service to be outsourced is central to the firm's core strategic activities. Cost analysis plays an important part in the decision to "make" the service activity internally or to "buy" from external sources.

Refer once again to the benchmarks for the fleet maintenance activity in Table 1. Information about the present level of maintenance performance is in Table 2.

TABLE 1
BENCHMARKING THE FLEET MAINTENANCE ACTIVITY

Critical Success Factors	Measures
Availability	Downtime
	Unscheduled repair
	Vehicle breakdowns
Timeliness	Time needed for repair
	On-time vehicle delivery
Flexibility	Turnaround time for unscheduled repairs
Quality	Rework
	Fuel efficiency
	Internal customer satisfaction
	Frequency of unscheduled repairs
Cost reduction	Cost per service operation
	Demonstrated process improvements
Accuracy	Historical record keeping

82

TABLE 2
OUTSOURCE FLEET MAINTENANCE

DIFFERENTIAL COST ANALYSIS

Panel 1. Make option: Service vehicles in-house

	Planning Horizon*					
	Year 1	Year 2	Year 3	Year 4	Year 5	
Vehicles per year	600	625	650	675	700	Total
Variable cost/vehicle supplies, parts	$470	$470	$470	$470	$470	
	$282,000	$293,750	$305,500	$317,250	$329,000	
Fixed costs/per year						
Payroll and training	102,000	102,000	110,500	110,500	119,000	
Facilities-utilities,						
maintenance	15,000	15,000	15,000	15,000	15,000	
Facilities-depreciation						
(cost = $900,000, 30 yr. life)	30,000	30,000	30,000	30,000	30,000	
	147,000	147,000	155,500	155,500	164,000	
Total costs	429,000	440,750	461,000	472,750	493,000	
Less tax effect @ 34%	145,860	149,855	156,740	160,735	167,620	
Net cost of servicing vehicles						
in-house	$283,140	$290,895	$304,260	$312,015	$325,380	$1,515,690
Average cost per vehicle	$472	$465	$468	$462	$465	

Panel 2. Buy option: Outsource vehicle service

	Year 1	Year 2	Year 3	Year 4	Year 5	Total
Vehicles per year	600	625	650	675	700	
Service cost per vehicle	$870	$870	$870	$870	$870	
Total contractual costs	$522,000	$543,750	$565,500	$587,250	$609,000	
Facilities-depreciation	30,000	30,000	30,000	30,000	30,000	
Total operating costs	552,000	573,750	595,500	617,250	639,000	
Less opportunity cost: rental revenue†	135,000	135,000	135,000	135,000	135,000	
Total costs	417,000	438,750	460,500	482,250	504,000	
Less tax effect @ 34%	141,780	149,175	156,570	163,965	171,360	
Net cost of outsourcing vehicle						
maintenance	$275,220	$289,575	$303,930	$318,285	$332,640	$1,519,650
Average cost per vehicle	$459	$463	$468	$472	$475	

	Year 1	Year 2	Year 3	Year 4	Year 5	
Panel 3. Differential cost to outsource†	$7,920	$1,320	$330	($6,270)	($7,260)	($3,960)

*This model is based on a 5-year planning horizon, which represents management's time frame of outsourcing commitment at this stage of strategy formulation.

†In order to focus the illustration on the outsourcing decision process, it is assumed that the maintenance facility will be retained regardless of the decision outcome. If a decision to outsource is accompanied by plant disposal, additional complications arise concerning the amount and timing of disposal proceeds and differences between the planning horizon and the economic life at the facility.

‡Differential costs increase in years 4 and 5 as the in-house service option enjoys scale efficiencies due to increases in the volume of vehicles serviced.

Assume that the accountants conducted a benchmarking comparison that revealed performance measures for fleet maintenance fell slightly short in several areas. After careful study, however, the accountants expect that maintenance can be brought up to a world-class standard by spending an average of $20 more per year for supplies and parts per vehicle and by investing an additional $6,000 per year in training. Hence, to achieve the benchmarked performance standard, supplies and parts will cost $470 per vehicle, and the combined cost of payroll and training is increased to $102,000 for the year.

The top panel of Table 2 presents the "make" option of servicing vehicles internally. Total costs to attain best-in-the-world maintenance performance are projected for each of the next five years.

Management has chosen a five-year planning horizon to allow for a long-term partnering arrangement with the supplying vendor. Also built into the cost schedule is a projection for the expected number of vehicles the firm expects to maintain. The firm's strategic plan calls for an annual increase of 25 fleet vehicles. No adjustments have been made to cost estimates for inflation. That is, all reported numbers are measured in constant year 1 dollars. The only fixed costs expected to change with increased volume are payroll and training, which are adjusted for an addition of a one-half position in year 3 and another one-half position in year 5. Total costs for in-house fleet maintenance are reduced by 34%, the firm's marginal tax rate. Total net-of-tax costs per year and average costs per vehicle per year are reported at the bottom of the panel. Costs per vehicle range from a high of $472 in year 1 to a low of $462 in year 4.

The second panel of Table 2 presents information for the outsourcing buy option. Based on preliminary negotiations, the firm expects to contract out its fleet maintenance service at a cost of $870 per vehicle per year. While the contract calls for annual inflation adjustments to this fee, all costs in the analysis are expected to be affected equally by inflation and thus are ignored.

If the firm chooses to outsource maintenance, it will downsize by eliminating all its current department employees. The only cost it will continue to incur is annual depreciation of $30,000 on the maintenance facility that will be rented for $135,000 per year. Rental revenues represent the opportunity costs of the idled facility and are a deduction to the cost of outsourcing. The tenants will assume all utilities and maintenance fees on the facility as part of the leasing agreement. After adjusting for tax effects, the average annual cost per vehicle ranges from a high of $475 in year 5 to a low of $459 in year 1.

The bottom panel of Table 2 reports the differential cost of servicing in-house versus outsourcing. While there is a cost advantage to outsource of $7,920 in year 1, the total cost effect for the five-year period is ($3,960).

In other words, the firm would show a cumulative decrease to net income of $3,960 if the outsourcing option is chosen. Thus, a conventional make-buy analysis that focuses on income effects for one year would favor the buy option. But a cumulative five-year income analysis supports in-house servicing. Unfortunately, neither of these approaches addresses the time value of invested capital.

The analysis presented in Table 2 concludes with those costs that will change if the firm outsources its fleet maintenance activity as opposed to servicing in-house. Included in the calculation is the opportunity cost of facilities idled by a decision to buy outside.

This format follows the approach normally recommended by accounting educators, who stress the importance of differential costs and opportunity costs in a make-buy calculation. It differs, however, in that it makes explicit the long-term cost effects of a decision to buy outside.

As seen in virtually all cost and management accounting textbooks, the make-buy decision is limited to differential *income effects in the current operating time period alone.* Typically a caveat follows the numeric calculation.

The analyst is encouraged to consider qualitative factors—such as quality of parts, possibility for supply interruptions, and technological innovation—but no examples are given where long-term effects actually become part of the calculation.

Two implicit assumptions seem to explain the short-term emphasis in the accountant's conventional approach to make-buy analysis. First, the underlying decision objective is focused on maximizing the use of available capacity.[2]

This is stated explicitly by authors of two texts: by Horngren and Foster and by Moscove and Wright. This perspective emphasizes alternative ways to use idled facilities, yet it implies that changes in facility use are easily reversible and without cost.

Second, discussions on make-buy are concerned almost exclusively with purchasing parts or subassemblies, with infrequent attention given to decisions on buying services. The modeling implication is that a firm has no particular loyalties to any one vendor, and, as with idled facilities, changes between vendors are accomplished easily in the short term.

Both these short-term assumptions can be challenged in today's global business environment. Efficient use of facilities is an important factor in building market advantage, but use of facilities should be part of an integrated firm-wide plan on the development of its core competencies.

Similarly, moving from vendor to vendor can minimize short-term costs, but long-term advantages can be surrendered as a result. One of the advantages of outsourcing is that firms have the opportunity to develop alliances with established repeat vendors, whose success becomes tied to that of its customers. Both parties can gain from established linkages.

Consider, for example, a medical supplies vendor who receives information directly from a hospital's information system on daily supplies needs for scheduled surgeries. By shifting inventory control responsibilities to its vendor, the hospital saves inventory carrying costs, and the vendor has guaranteed sales. Conversely, firms that insulate themselves through vertical integration run the risk of being bypassed by technological advancements from vendors. (See sidebar.)

CREATING SHAREHOLDER WEALTH

Little will be gained in the long term if management seizes short-term cost savings while losing its broader strategic focus. Unlike assumptions about decision reversibility that underlie conventional make-buy analysis, outsourcing analysis must take into account long-term effects.

As with any long-term investment decision, the criterion for acceptance shifts from an income perspective to one that seeks to optimize shareholder wealth. Thus, the foundation for strategic outsourcing analysis is the use of discounted cash flow to measure changes to a firm's value.

One impediment is the difficulty of identifying, estimating, and measuring the effects of relationships. Following my suggested decision path, however, avoids the need to measure these uncertain potential benefits because of the benchmarking process. Management is convinced that the service activity in question will be performed at a world-class standard if it is performed in-house. By establishing that equal benefit will be gained regardless of whether an activity is performed internal or external to the firm, management can ignore differences in value creation—at least for the first round of investigation. Consequently, the outsourcing analysis can focus on a differential cost comparison similar to the one presented earlier for fleet maintenance service.

To illustrate this point, Table 2 also considers the time-value effects of the outsourcing investment decision. The net costs for servicing vehicles in-house and for outsourcing are converted to cash flows by adding back depreciation, a non-cash expense.

The difference between the cash outflow to service internally and the cash requirement to outsource is shown on the table as the annual cash difference if outsourced. These annual amounts are the same as the differential costs to outsource. The net cash stream is discounted at an uninflated after-tax rate, assumed as 16%, which is in keeping with the use of uninflated dollars in the illustration.

The result of this analysis—a positive net present value of $1,010—suggests the firm will increase shareholder value if the fleet maintenance service is outsourced. This conclusion conflicts with the five-year cumulative effect to income, ($3,960), which would have supported the in-house service option.

STRATEGIC CONCERNS

Before making a final decision, however, management must consider the less tangible, more uncertain benefits and costs that can accrue from global outsourcing.[3] These qualitative factors may prove significant and may take precedence over results favored in the discounted-cash-flow analysis. The following are among the most important strategic considerations.

Technical supremacy. By outsourcing noncritical activities, a firm can gain by sharing in the vendor's expertise and economies of scale. A world-class service provider would be expected to employ the latest innovations and service delivery systems available. The cost of these state-of-the-art processes then can be shared, thus providing customers with technology they otherwise may not have been able to afford.

Flexibility. Firms that outsource services have the advantage of not being tied to past investments. Particularly in fast-changing industries, a firm's survival may depend on its achieving the best in components and service necessary to compete. If a vendor fails to maintain its position of service supremacy, the buyer has the option to look for a competing source.

Opportunities to coproduce innovation. One of the benefits of developing coalitions with external partners is the potential for the emergence of innovative opportunities. For example, a vendor may find ways to improve the very

TABLE 3
DISCOUNTED CASH FLOW (UNINFLATED, AFTER-TAX COST OF CAPITAL 16%)

	Year 1	Year 2	Year 3	Year 4	Year 5
Net cost of outsourcing vehicle maintenance*	($275,220)	($289,575)	($303,930)	($318,285)	($332,640)
Add back depreciation	30,000	30,000	30,000	30,000	30,000
Net cash outflow to outsource	(245,220)	(259,575)	(273,930)	(288,285)	(302,640)
Less net cost of servicing vehicles in-house†	(283,140)	(290,895)	(304,260)	(312,015)	(325,380)
Add back depreciation	30,000	30,000	30,000	30,000	30,000
Net cost to service in-house	(253,140)	(260,895)	(274,260)	(282,015)	(295,380)
Annual cash differential if outsourced	7,920	1,320	330	(6,270)	(7,260)
Discount factor	0.862	0.743	0.641	0.552	0.476
Discounted cash flows	$6,828	$981	$211	($3,463)	($3,457)
Net Present Value‡	$1,101				

*From Table 2, panel 2.

†From Table 2, panel 1.

‡Net present value (NPV) should be recalculated to find its sensitivity to changes in the discount rate. Interestingly, in this case a higher discount rate results in a higher NPV advantage for outsourcing. For example, the NPV at 12% is $254 and at 20%, $1,766. Higher rates reduce the negative differential cash effects in later years.

nature of the activity or its delivery mechanism. In addition, dealings with a specialized vendor may create new market opportunities or partnered ventures.

It is unlikely the analyst can place a reliable dollar number on any of these potential benefits, but their effects should not be overlooked. Bromich and Bhimani suggested a format for scoring intangible benefits related to investments in advanced manufacturing technology.[4] At a minimum, making these benefits explicit, even if not quantified, draws attention to their existence.

Additional intangible costs also might be introduced by outsourcing. One of the greatest potential costs is the damage incurred by a firm that becomes overly dependent on its outsourcing partner. Taken to the extreme, a firm could become so dependent on vendor services that it loses its competitive advantage if the vendor withdraws its service or decides to compete in the same market.

Managers can manage their dependency on vendors by retaining alternative outsourcing options. Further, if a firm's sustainable competitive advantage is threatened by overreliance on the vendor, the service would seem to be an important core activity in the film's value chain. Thus, it may be preferable to perform the service in-house (see Figure 2).

FORMING ALLIANCES

Having completed the computational analysis and considered the qualitative factors, the analyst has laid the foundation for deciding whether to outsource. One critical determination remains: Is this service activity part of the firm's core strategy?

Answering this question will require a strategic analysis on the part of top management—an assignment that calls for a different set of skills than accountants are trained to offer. Understanding the value-added cost impact due to an outsourcing arrangement is, however, a necessary first step toward making these strategic decisions.

Managers embracing a core competency philosophy look to the film's value chain to discover where outsourcing coalitions will offer greatest benefit. Ideally, the firm will capitalize on its own special skills and strengths while forming alliances with other firms to tap into their unique competencies.

This may mean looking outside the firm for such fundamental activities as product design, warehousing, market research, distribution, or after-sale repair and service. The desired result is a leveraging effect in which the firm essentially commands a network of activities that extends its own core competencies into a more sustainable market advantage.

Author's Note: I would like to thank James Targay III, Serge Matulick, and Ted Veit for their helpful comments during my preparation of this article.

Ralph E. Drtina, Ph.D., is professor of accounting and management at the Crummer Graduate School of Business,

FIGURE 2
STEPS IN THE OUTSOURCING DECISION ANALYSIS

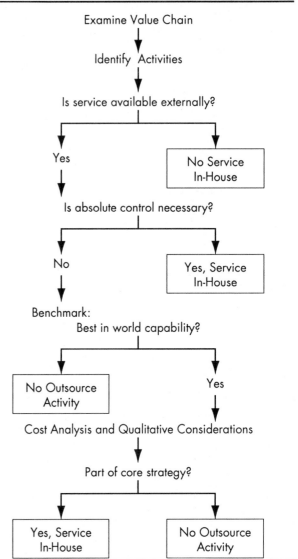

Rollins College, Winger Park, Fla. He is a member of the Mid-Florida Chapter and can be reached at (407) 646-2344.

Notes

1. This article builds on strategy concepts from two articles by James Brian Quinn, Thomas L. Doorley, and Penny C. Pacquette: Beyond Products: Services-Based Strategy," *Harvard Business Review,* March–April 1990, pp. 58–67; "Technology in Services: Rethinking Strategic Focus," *Sloan Management Review,* Winter 1990, pp. 79–87.

2. This is stated explicitly in the writings of Charles Horngren and George Foster and of Stephen A. Moscove and Arnold Wright.

3. For More Information, see Mark L. Fagan, "A Guide To Global Sourcing," *The Journal of Business Strategy,* March/April 1991, pp. 21–25.

4. Michael Bromwich and Al Bhimani, "Strategic Investment Appraisal," *MANAGEMENT ACCOUNTING®,* March 1991, pp. 45–48.

THE CASE OF SEAGATE TECHNOLOGY

Seagate Technology is the world's largest producer of computer hard disk drives and commands about 25% of the world's market Over the past several years, however, it has found itself battling as a "sluggardly giant" in an industry composed of fast-growing, innovative competitors such as Conner Peripherals, Quantum, and Maxtor.

Seagate initially built its market strength by delivering low-cost products that were designed and manufactured internally, while it outsourced its deliveries. Seagate's approach to owning and operating its own plants differs from that of its competitors, who mainly rely on outside suppliers. Quantum, for example, outsources virtually every piece of its disk drives while building its market position on the strength of its software and design.

Seagate has found its position threatened, some say, due to its over-reliance on in-house technologies. The firm's vertically integrated operation, which resulted in cost savings previously, has hampered innovation and the development of new products. Its competitors have been more flexible and have taken advantage of technological advances made in combination with external suppliers. Conner and Quantum, for example, signed rich contracts with computer makers, such as Apple and Compaq, because of their ability to switch faster from 5 1/4-inch to 3 1/2-inch drives.

Seagate also has been hampered during the recent recession by its massive overhead. Its profits fell more than those of its competitors as a result of its high facility fixed costs. The other disk producers proved to be more agile. When demand fell off, they were able to cut costs quickly by simply reducing orders from contractors.

Under the direction of its new CEO, Seagate is making changes. For one, it concedes it may have stuck too long with in-house technologies. It now relies on external vendors to supply 40% of its disks—about twice the percentage of two years ago. The firm also will forego some of its focus on low cost. Current plans are to reduce the time from design to production, even if it means using more expensive materials or a more costly design.

The company still defends its penchant for vertical integration, saying it keeps cost down. Analysts, who do not seem convinced, say the company's long-term outlook depends on its ability to fend off competitors in the high end of the drive market.

Adapted from Ken Yamada, "Once-Battered Seagate Gains in Computer Price War, Wall Street Journal, June 1, 1992, p. B3; and G. Pascal Zachary, "High-Tech Firms Find It's Good to Line Up Outside Contractors," Wall Street Journal, July 29, 1992, pp. A1 and A5.

From R. Drtina, "The Outsourcing Decision," *Management Accounting* (March 1994): 56-62. Reprinted with permission.

Question

4.3 What are the strategic concerns that Drtina contends must be considered before outsourcing occurs? Are these qualitative or quantitative factors? Explain.

CHAPTER 5

Basic Product Costing Systems

Reading 5.1, Robin Cooper's *Does Your Company Need a New Cost System,* poses a critical question for managers: "Do I really know what my products cost?" Answering this question will allow managers to determine whether their costing system is reporting accurate product costs. In order to address this question, Cooper suggests that managers look for symptoms that often point to poor system design. For example, one symptom of a poor system occurs when a firm's customers completely ignore price increases, even though the firm's manufacturing costs haven't changed. In this instance, the cost system may be underestimating product costs, and, thus, the associated markup is still below market. Cooper outlines a number of other design flaws that managers should understand as they attempt to develop more accurate systems.

Consistent with Robin Cooper's article, Norm Raffish argues in *How Much Does That Product Really Co$t* (Reading 5.2) that the business world has changed so much that traditional cost accounting is no longer applicable. For one thing, the relative proportions of what go into product costs have changed significantly with direct labor content dropping to between 5 and 15%, materials content falling between 45% and 55%, and overhead soaring to between 30% and 50%. Raffish builds the case for activity-based costing as a much more accurate method for determining (among other things) more accurate product costs.

William Baker, Timothy Fry and Kirk Karwan's article, Reading 5.3, *The Rise and Fall of Time-Based Manufacturing,* presents a case study of Knussman Corporation's Brice Plant (a fictitious name), an automotive supplier, that established quality and time-based performance measures in order to help it compete more effectively. Unfortunately, the company's managers continued to rely on a traditional cost accounting system that emphasized standard costing and evaluation based on direct labor variances, both of which resulted in manager behavior that obviated the effects of the quality and throughput time measures. The authors suggest alternatives such as just-in-time manufacturing and activity-based costing that the company could have used to be more consistent with its new performance quality measures.

5.1 Cost Management Concepts and Principles
Does your company need a new cost system?

Robin Cooper

Almost a quarter of a century ago, Peter F. Drucker wrote "Managing for Business Effectiveness" for the Harvard Business Review.[1] I don't know how much effect that article had then, but it has little or none today—and, in my opinion, that is a tragedy.

Drucker argued that management's primary responsibility is "to strive for the best possible economic results from the resources currently employed or available." Then he exposed how ineffective cost accounting can obfuscate the route management should take to satisfy this responsibility. Drucker concluded his article with the following advice:

> "And while the job to be done may look different in every individual company, one basic truth will always be present: every product, every operation, and every activity in a business should, therefore, be put on trial for its life every two or three years. Each should be considered the way we consider a proposal to go into a new product, a new operation or activity."

The underlying message is clear. Every product should be reviewed to ensure that the company benefits from its production and distribution. Even if a firm is making an acceptable profit, management should still ensure that every product is making a profit or that there is a strategic reason for selling it at a loss (e.g., razor with blades).

In the past two decades, cost accounting has undergone few innovations. Practitioners have developed an "if it ain't broke, don't fix it" mentality, and academics have paid little attention to cost accounting.[2] The major changes that have occurred—the increased use of machine-hour and material-dollar costing—unfortunately do little to overcome the most serious problems in existing cost system designs.

In most companies, a product profitability analysis offers valuable insights into the sources of profits and losses. Such an analysis requires accurate measurement of each product's production and marketing costs. In most firms, the cost accounting system is expected to perform this task. Unfortunately, considerable evidence suggests that these systems fail to accurately report product costs, for two reasons.

First, they were never designed to report accurate product costs; their primary objective was to report inventory values.[3] Second, they have not been modified as production processes have changed. These systems no longer adequately measure the flow of a firm's costs.[4] In effect, they are obsolete.

THE SYMPTOMS

To determine whether a firm's cost system is reporting accurate product costs and to guard against its obsolescence, management should periodically evaluate it. Managers should ask themselves, "Do I really know what my products cost?" Answering this question requires a detailed analysis of the firm's cost system—an expensive and time-consuming process. Fortunately, management can significantly reduce the risk of undertaking such an analysis unnecessarily by looking for symptoms that usually accompany a poorly designed or obsolete cost system. These are discussed in the following sections.

Products that are very difficult to produce are reported to be very profitable even though they are not premium priced. Not all products are easy to manufacture: some are new, and the work force is still learning how to make them; others are just inherently difficult to make. The second type provides a good test of how well a cost accounting system is operating. If the system is capturing the additional manufacturing costs, these difficult-to-manufacture products should either be selling at a premium or have low margins.

All too often, however, these complex products appear to be highly profitable. They may be sold at a small premium, reflecting the market's willingness to pay more for the product, but their reported product costs do not reflect the difficulty of manufacturing them. In this case, the cost system fails to capture actual costs and instead reports costs that reflect average levels of manufacturing difficulty.

Profit margins cannot be easily explained. Management should usually be able to identify why some products are more profitable than others. Factors that influence profitability include market share, quality differential, production process differences, and economies of scale. If the cost system is accurately reporting product costs, management should be able to explain the overall patterns of product profitability. If management cannot explain the pattern, yet believes it understands the market, the cost accounting system is probably to blame.

Some products that are not sold by competitors have high reported margins. If there is no simple explanation for this situation, the cost system may be at fault. It may be reporting phantom profits; the competitors' systems did not. Obviously, this explanation is invalid if the firm has such competitive advantages as patent protection, high brand recognition, or proprietary production processes.

If the competition purchases the firm's products, repackages them, and then resells them at a higher price, or as part of a larger order at the same price, these products are probably improperly costed and priced. Alternatively, if the competition goes out of its way to identify the firm as the sole source for these products, the competition believes that selling these products at the listed price is detrimental.

The results of bids are difficult to explain. Firms that commonly bid for business can sometimes use the outcomes of their bids to determine how well their cost accounting system is working. If management is unable to accurately predict which bids they are going to win, the cost system may be reporting inaccurate product costs. Management should look for bids that were either priced low to win or priced high and were expected to lose. If the aggressively priced bids are frequently lost and the high-priced bids win, the cost system should be examined.

The competition's high-volume products are priced at apparently unrealistically low levels. When smaller competitors with no apparent economic advantage are pricing high-production-volume products at very low levels and are simultaneously making good returns, the cost system is the prime suspect. Cost systems tend to report averaged costs. High-volume products are inherently less expensive to produce than low-volume products, and most cost systems fail to accurately account for this difference. In fact, high-volume products are usually overcosted and low-volume products are undercosted. Smaller companies that manufacture fewer products, however, often suffer less distortion and therefore have a better understanding of their product costs.

Even if cost-plus pricing is not used, this volume-based distortion of reported product costs can be a very serious problem. Because the low-volume products appear more profitable, the full-line producer is tempted to concentrate on them and leave the high-volume products to the focused competitors. If the cost system is distorting the source of profits, the firm could be chasing imaginary profits and the profitability may be slowly deteriorating. This deterioration may be difficult to explain because no clear competitive disadvantage exists and no changes in the fundamental market structure have been made.

Vendor bids for parts are considerably lower than expected. Parts are often put out to bid because they appear to be too expensive to manufacture in-house. If vendors' bids on these parts are much lower than expected given the estimated production economies involved, the cost system may be at fault.

Cost information plays an important role in make-or-buy decisions. Unfortunately, conventional cost systems cannot provide the appropriate cost data. In particular, these systems fail to accurately specify the amount of overhead that is actually avoided by buying. They overestimate the savings, thus favoring the buy decision. When this bias is coupled with the overestimation of production costs, the buy decision might be adopted too frequently.

Customers ignore price increases, even when there is no corresponding increase in cost. When prices increase, customers usually react negatively. If there is little or no reaction, the cost system may be underestimating product costs. This concern is increased if the competition's prices also increase and the firm is not the price leader.

If customers don't complain, they were probably paying less for the product than its perceived value. If competitors also raise their prices, they may have been aware that the product was underpriced but wanted another firm to take the risk of increasing prices. For cost-plus pricers, the apparent excess profitability is the final clincher. By supplying costs that were too low, the system caused management to underprice the product in the first place. These symptoms can be detected only if the cost system is reporting product costs that are significantly incorrect. This occurs only if the design of the cost system is badly flawed.

THE DESIGN FLAWS

Cost accounting systems can be flawed in several ways. The flaws discussed in this section are very common and can result in a significant distortion in reported product costs.

Only direct labor hours (or dollars) are used to allocate overhead from cost pools (cost centers) to the products. The dependence on direct labor can be traced to the very origins of cost accounting. At the end of the last century, managers installed elaborate direct labor measurement systems to keep the direct labor force productive. The designers of early cost accounting systems took advantage of these systems and adopted direct labor hours for all allocation purposes, even when other bases would have been just as effective. At that time, this simplification was acceptable because manufacturing processes were highly labor-intensive, overhead was a smaller percentage of total cost, and product diversity (i.e., the range of different product cost structures) was lower. Under such conditions, the quantity of direct labor in a product was generally a reliable measure of the total value added.

Today, direct labor costs arc usually less than 10 percent of the total production cost of the product, whereas overhead is more than 30 percent of total cost. No longer are direct labor hours necessarily a good predictor of the value added to a product. Nevertheless, most cost systems still rely heavily on direct labor hours to allocate costs to the products.

Only volume-related allocation bases (e.g., labor hours, machine hours, and material dollars) are used to allocate overhead from cost pools to products. These bases assume that the cost of producing a production lot is directly proportional to the number of items in that lot. This assumption is correct for volume-related activities (e.g., direct labor, production supplies, and parts) but not for such non-volume-related costs as inspection, setup, or scheduling. These costs vary with the number of inspections performed, the number of setups, and the quantity of scheduling, respectively.

Allocating a non-volume-related cost requires the selection of an allocation base that is itself non-volume-related. In manufacturing processes whose percentage of non-volume-related costs is high, cost systems using only volume-related bases produce inaccurate product costs. The error in reported product costs increases significantly if products are manufactured in highly varied lot sizes. Many non-volume-related costs depend on the number of lots being manufactured. Traditional cost systems usually undercost the small-volume production lot products and overcost the high-volume production lot products.

The early designers could ignore this problem for two reasons. First, the percentage of non-volume-related costs was much smaller. Consequently, the error in reported product costs from using only volume-related allocation bases was much lower. Second, a single facility typically manufactured a smaller range of products in less diverse lot sizes. Today, the percentage of non-volume-related costs is high and often accounts for about 25% of total production costs. Therefore, low-production-volume products may be significantly undercosted, whereas high-volume products are slightly overcosted. This distortion in the reported product costs also distorts the strategy selected by the firm. Low-volume products appear to be more profitable than they really are, tempting management to focus incorrectly on low-volume, specialty business.

Cost pools are too large and contain machines that have very different overhead cost structures. This problem is caused by simplifications made by the early designers. First, the production processes that they dealt with were much simpler than today's; although different machines might have been used in the process, within each major step the machines tended to have similar overhead cost structures. This allowed each step to be treated as a cost center without a major distortion in reported product costs. Second, to minimize the number of calculations required to cost products, early designers kept the number of cost centers as low as possible. This constraint reflected the high cost of performing calculations in a precomputer society.

Because of extensive automation, cost centers now contain a mixture of conventional and automated machines. This guarantees the reporting of distorted product costs. Although automated machines generally have higher overhead costs than their conventional counterparts, they require less labor. The cost system charges each product an average overhead charge that is too high for conventional machines and too low for automated machines. Products manufactured on labor-intensive conventional machines are allocated a higher proportion of the overhead costs than they warrant.

The cost of marketing and delivering the product varies dramatically by distribution channel, and yet the cost accounting system effectively ignores marketing costs. Cost accounting principles are applied only to production costs; other costs (e.g., marketing) are ignored and treated as single line items. This omission reflects the domination of the inventory valuation objective in cost accounting. Although production costs can be inventoried under generally accepted accounting principles, marketing costs must be treated as a period cost and written off. Therefore, marketing and distribution costs are not allocated to products by conventional accounting systems.

Many firms currently sell their products through a multitude of distribution channels, and the costs associated with these channels can be as high as 25 percent of total cost. For example, one channel might require a specially trained sales force that frequently calls the customer before the sale is made, whereas in another channel the customer can simply call and place an order. Obviously, the cost of doing business in the two channels is very different, but if the firm is trying to maximize gross margin, this difference is ignored. Cost accounting systems similarly ignore a wide range of selling and administrative expenses because they are period costs. If these costs differ systematically by product or product line, using gross margin to rank products is a dangerous technique.

CONCLUSION

Distorted knowledge of product costs makes it difficult for management to know how to best employ the resources available and, in Drucker's terms, satisfy its primary responsibility. Unfortunately, although it is relatively easy to prove that a cost system is reporting inaccurate product costs, it is extremely difficult to prove that the firm is suffering because of it. No business decision depends solely on product costs; product cost information is commonly used in decisions that rely on a wide range of information.

The symptoms of reliance on distorted costs can be used to determine whether the cost system needs redesigning. This approach is advantageous because it is relatively fast and inexpensive. It is not, however, a perfect test. First, the symptoms are not always easy to detect, and the inability to detect them does not guarantee that the firm is not suffering. Second, there are several competing explanations for each symptom, and it is not always possible to rule them out. The risk of unfairly blaming the cost system can be reduced by determining whether it suffers from one of the more common design flaws.

It is not sufficient just to check for the design flaws. There is no easy way of telling that the distortion in reported product costs is sufficient to cause problems. The level of distortion depends on the production process, the range of products produced, and the distribution channels used. It is the joint occurrence of the symptoms with the flaws that heralds the need for a new cost system.

Robin Cooper is an assistant professor of business administration in the Graduate School of Business Administration at Harvard University.

Notes

1. P. F. Drucker. "Managing for Business Effectiveness." *Harvard Business Review* (May–June 1963): 33–60 (Reprint No 63303).

2. R. S. Kaplan. "The Evolution of Management Accounting," *Accounting Review* (July 1984): 390–418.

3. H. T Johnson and R. S. Kaplan. *Relevance Lost: The Evolution of Management Accounting* (Boston: Harvard Business School Press, 1987); R. Cooper and R. S. Kaplan. "How Cost Accounting Systematically Distorts Product Costs." *Harvard Business School Working Paper.* (1986).

4. R. S. Kaplan. "Yesterday's Accounting Undermines Production." *Harvard Business Review* (July-August 1984): 95–101 (Reprint No 84406).

RECOMMENDED READING

R. G. Eiler, W. K.Goletz, and D. P. Keegan. "Is Your Cost Accounting System Up to Date? *Harvard Business Review* (July–August 1982): 133–139 (Reprint No 82403).

M. J. Sandretto. "What Kind of Cost System Do You Need?" *Harvard Business Review* (January–February 1986): 110–118 (Reprint NO 85113).

From R. Cooper, "Does Your Company Need a New Cost System?" *Journal of Cost Management* (Spring 1987): 45–49. Reprinted with permission.

Question

5.1 What are three of the symptoms that Cooper says accompany a poorly designed or obsolete costing system? Do each of these definitely mean that the existing system needs to be abandoned?

5.2 How Much Does That Product Really Co$t?
Finding out may be as easy as ABC.

By Norm Raffish

It's not that traditional cost accounting doesn't work—it's that the world it was designed for is rapidly disappearing. Product costs used to consist primarily of direct labor and material; today we have a manufacturing environment in which direct labor usually accounts for a ballpark figure of 5% to 15% of the costs and material accounts for 45% to 55%. That leaves us with a whopping 30% to 50% for overhead (see Figure 1). And the overhead is shifting from variable to fixed as a result of our investments in automation. Given this scenario, it's not difficult to imagine that our current cost accounting systems probably don't reflect the true costs of our products.

What clues do we have that this description is true? An article by Professor Robin Cooper of Harvard University in the *Harvard Business Review*, January–February 1989, was titled "You Need a New Cost System When. . . ." The article describes several symptoms of problems with existing cost systems. Cooper says it may be time to redesign your cost system if:

- Functional managers want to drop seemingly profitable lines;
- Hard-to-make products show big profits;
- Departments have their own cost systems;
- You have a high-margin niche all to yourself;
- Competitors' prices are unrealistically low.

We need to recognize that our existing cost systems were meant primarily to value inventory and provide data for the profit and loss statements. They really were never designed to

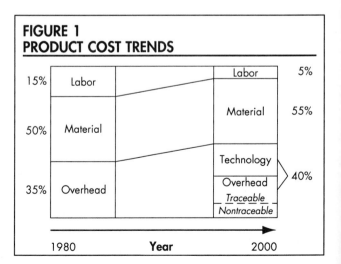

**FIGURE 1
PRODUCT COST TRENDS**

discriminate between product lines or products within those lines. Cost systems were meant to focus on "how much," not "why." It is understanding the "why," however, that permits management to focus on the issues that require action.

INTERORGANIZATIONAL COST PERFORMANCE

Consider the concept of interorganizational cost (intercost) performance. How would your current cost systems deal with the cost of an engineering change or segregating the cost of quality? How would you assign those costs, if you knew them, to a specific product line or product? Just to focus on one example of the intercost problem, let's examine a production schedule change requested by Marketing to meet a customer's needs.

Normally, the various costs of expediting an order are borne by all the orders that pass through the production environment, through the standard technique of absorbing in direct costs into manufacturing overhead. Thus, the expedited order will appear to have a more favorable margin than it should. And, did anyone charge Engineering for total cost of the ECN? How much cost should have been assigned to the particular part or work order? In the long run, Manufacturing's operating results, when compared to budget, will look less favorable, and Marketing's performance actually may improve in the customer satisfaction area (see Figure 2). Do we really know the cost of that order, and did we capture or even understand the intercost effect on performance?

Two other points about traditional costing systems are worth mentioning before we move forward. The first deals with the identification of nonvalue-added activities. Current systems don't have any mechanisms to assist management in this critical area. It's difficult to put a continuous improvement program in place if you can't identify and quantify the nonvalue-added activities.

The second point is more fundamental to costing in general. Our systems today measure that segment of a product's life beginning at the time it enters production. The system is oblivious to the fact that 85% of the cost of a new product is committed after the design phase, and manufacturing can influence only about 10% to 15% or so of the cost (see Figure 3). We are not capturing and allocating research and development costs so that management can determine the true profitability of a product over its life.

Let's consider a different but not necessarily replacement approach. Does this imply two cost systems? Maybe. More on this subject when we discuss strategic versus tactical approaches to costing.

ACTIVITY-BASED COSTING

Activity-based costing (ABC) has been a concept waiting for the computer and a few innovative people. What is it? A good basic definition was developed by the Computer Aided Manufacturing-International (CAM-I) organization of Arlington, Texas, a nonprofit industry-sponsored consortium that works on contemporary industry problems. Its Cost Management System (CMS) project defines ABC as "the collection of financial and operation performance information tracing the significant activities of the firm to product costs."

CAM-I used cost management as an umbrella for many related issues. This broader definition encompasses activity-based costing, life cycle management, performance management, investment management, and cost planning and control. We will focus on ABC and its relationship to the intercost performance issues.

The three key areas of ABC are product cost differentiation, activities and their cost drivers, and identification of nonvalue-added cost improvement opportunities. ABC assigns product costs based on the activities that a product draws upon. An activity may be defined as a particular operation in the production cycle, or it could be defined as the entire material acquisition process. Activities use resources such as support labor, technology cells, or utilities. The agents that cause activities to happen are called cost drivers. An example of a cost driver is an engineering change order (ECO). The issuing of an ECO causes many activities to occur, such as release of the ECO documentation package, changes to the production schedule, acquisition of new material, changes to the process, and new quality instructions.

Figure 4A illustrates the basic ABC Logical Model. The Cost View indicates the general flow of costs. For example, the resources assigned to the inventory control activity will be directly traced or allocated to particular products based on some causal relationship. The Process View indicates the flow of information and transactions. As an example, the receipt of material on the dock triggers the inventory handling activities. In addition, information such as the number of moves, how many times an order was moved, and the cost per move, can be obtained for performance analysis. An expanded example of this model is illustrated in Figure 4B.

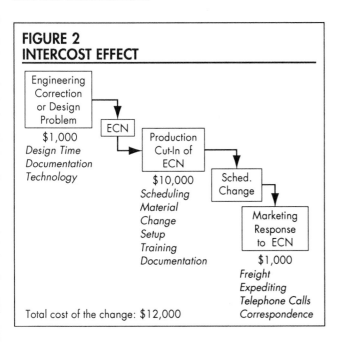

**FIGURE 2
INTERCOST EFFECT**

Engineering Correction or Design Problem

$1,000
*Design Time
Documentation
Technology*

ECN

Production Cut-In of ECN

$10,000
*Scheduling
Material
Change
Setup
Training
Documentation*

Sched. Change

Marketing Response to ECN

$1,000
*Freight
Expediting
Telephone Calls
Correspondence*

Total cost of the change: $12,000

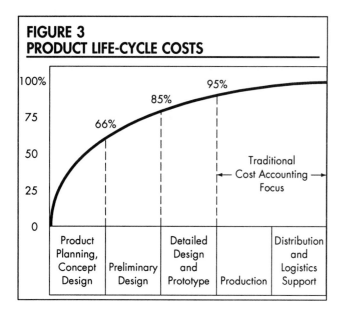

FIGURE 3
PRODUCT LIFE-CYCLE COSTS

The identification, measurement, and control of cost drivers is essential to ABC. Some cost drivers are very inefficient. They may have root causes that have been hidden from management's view for a long time. As an example, one root cause of having too much inventory may be the performance measurement that rewards the buyer for obtaining the lowest unit price of an item. If the buyer is procuring by the truckload to obtain his desired measurement, and the company needs only a few cases, then the result is predictable. One of the more severe and insidious of root causes stems from inappropriate or obsolete policies, procedures, and performance measurements.

Often policies and procedures have been overcome by events but remain in force through inattention to the new reality of the situation. For example, a vendor's goods might be certified as "source inspected," but, when they arrive, they are routinely moved to receiving inspection—because that is the procedure on the dock for all production goods. Then, of course, when the inspector sees the certification, he calls material handling and has the goods moved to Stores. This policy/procedure adds lead time to the process, causes the cost of a secondary material move, and has taken up the time of the inspector who should be inspecting material that needs his attention.

After we analyze and define activities and are able to isolate and measure their cost drivers, then we will be in a position to determine product cost information as it most closely fits the reality of the manufacturing environment.

Let's revisit the intercost issue to gain a better focus on the subject. We can assume that the engineering change referred to in Figure 2 was proposed and approved based on demonstrated need (the actual cost to propose, prepare, and deliver a complete ECO package will usually be far less than the impact of the change). That change, in this example, will affect Manufacturing and Marketing. Manufacturing will absorb the associated costs of the change into its budget and schedule. Marketing will absorb effects relating to changes

in distribution costs and any customer ill will that may have been generated due to possible delays in the shipment. Using the concept of tracing or allocating the cost of activities to products, we can capture and evaluate true product costs as well as understand the intercost impact and its effect on performance measurement. In this case, understanding the root cause of the cost driver may lead us to discover that the product is of poor design and therefore needs constant engineering maintenance. This discovery could lead to redesigning the product or raising the selling price to cover the real product support costs.

How do you capture and allocate costs in an ABC system? It has been said that all you need is lots of cost pools. That statement is somewhat exaggerated, but there is some truth in it. Certainly in order to capture the necessary detail, new activity cost pools would be established. It is the direct cost tracing and allocation schemes that are critical, however. Traditionally we have assigned costs based on three volume-related criteria: direct labor (dollars or hours), material cost, and machine-hours. While these criteria still are valid for certain cost entities, cost assignment bases are needed for many overhead and indirect cost entities. Some of these new bases are number of setups, number of orders, number of times material is handled, and number of part numbers processed. Using such bases as a way to trace or allocate activity costs to a product offers a whole new perspective on product cost assignment.

As an example, the number of purchase orders or line items processed may be a much better way to assign material acquisition costs than the value of the material ordered. A work order may have one purchase order with $100,000 of material assigned to it. Another work order may have 10 purchase orders worth $75,000 assigned to it. Guess which one incurred the most acquisition costs. Under today's methods, guess which one was allocated the most cost.

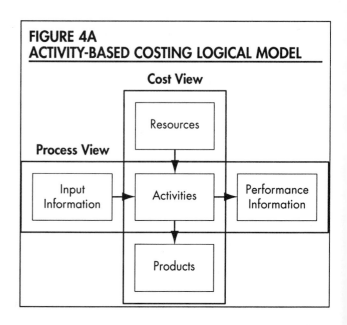

FIGURE 4A
ACTIVITY-BASED COSTING LOGICAL MODEL

FIGURE 4B
EXPANDED ABC LOGICAL MODEL EXAMPLE

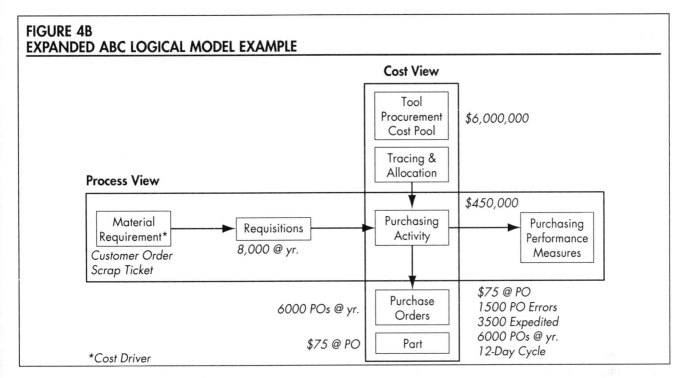

REAL LIFE

Discussing new concepts can be interesting and even exciting, but if they don't work "in the field," they don't work.

A large industrial electronics firm was dissatisfied with the product costing information it was receiving, especially at the printed circuit board level. Management decided to try a new costing approach based on the work that CAM-I had done on ABC and activity-based performance analysis. In order not to disrupt the division or disturb the current financial systems, it chose a single department that fabricated printed circuit boards.

The division finance department coordinated the pilot project with support from Manufacturing Engineering. In its presentation to management, it explained why it felt the experiment was needed. The controller said that the current system did not provide accurate information for make/buy decisions or for investment opportunities and that the current decision-making process was using distorted information. The major deficiencies of the current system were the inability to recognize unnecessary (nonvalue-added) activities and the lack of adequate traceability of costs and of a way to quantify quality, throughput, and flexibility.

Project objectives as stated by management were:

- Provide a breakout of department costs into activity costs,
- Identify cost drivers and their causal relationships,
- Determine actual costs for each product line, and
- Provide a tool for better decision making.

The process began by defining the activities for the PCB shop based on its actual practices. In the main, most of the activities involved either preparation for production or the actual production of various product families. Next, a survey instrument was constructed. The primary purpose of the survey was to develop a database that defined what people really did and for which product line. For example, the survey disclosed that direct labor operators spent a far greater share of their time in material-handling tasks than had been recognized. In light of their pay scale, the delivery of material to the line is being reviewed for possible reorganization. Further, the analysis showed that support costs that had been allocated on a straight-line basis among products did in fact vary significantly by product family, especially as they related to the number of layers on a PC board.

Cost drivers were defined and quantified. Typical of the types of cost drivers were lack of technical supervision, chemical contamination, schedule change, excessive quality verification, time card audits, and Material Review Board activities. In all, more than 50 cost drivers were isolated. Some, of course, were meaningful while others generated little cost and were not tracked. The exercise of developing the activity and cost driver database was invaluable, however, for future and much larger application of ABC in the company.

In the final analysis, the percentage spread of overcosting to undercosting of the PC board product families ranged from a negative 100% to a positive 80%. The division now plans to expand the ABC activity to other departments.

A second example involves a large multidivisional consumer electronics manufacturer. In this case the manufacturer wanted to understand the impact of allocated costs on the two main product lines in one key division. One line (product line L) is older and has a moderately high labor content. The second line (product line A) is newer and uses more automation.

The initial figures indicated that the average base cost of the product line L (high labor) was about $350 a unit and that of product line A (high automation) was $240 a unit. Keep in mind that product line L was manufactured at about a 7:1 rate over product line A. This will explain the impact of shifting a small percentage of L's dollars to A.

The activity cost analysis showed several interesting points for management to consider. First, after cost based on activities was reallocated and the technology costs of product line A were isolated, the costs were restated to show product line L as $300 and product line A as $450. Second, because most of the technology costs were fixed or semi-variable, as production in A was forecasted to increase the base unit cost would be reduced considerably, but in later years.

Third, product line L would have a longer profitable life than originally anticipated, and some price reductions would be in order so that it could remain competitive. Finally, the firm gained some valuable insights on activities and costs drivers with respect to automation. The current allocation schemes had no method for differentiating technology costs, such as the cost of industrial engineering support. The activity analysis revealed that the IE cost allocation for A versus L in actuality ran about 4:1. The current system had indicated that the ratio was about 1:8 because labor had been the basis for the allocation.

WHAT NOW?

Activity-based costing is not a panacea for all the product cost accounting ills or shortcomings in manufacturing. It does not directly address the issues of life cycle costing or performance measurement, for example, although ABC will support those functions with valuable information. ABC is, however, a more relevant method for costing products than some older methods because it forces traceability of costs to products, based on the resources consumed by the activities needed to produce individual products. The key factors are activities and their associated cost drivers. If a product does not use an activity, it should not absorb any of its related costs.

The costing methods commonly used today, for example, may tie allocations of overhead to direct labor so that some products are being charged for resources they never used. Unless we change our allocation methods to recognize the shift in the character of overhead from variable toward fixed, as the use of technology increases, severe product cost distortion will only accelerate.

One final topic—will ABC necessitate another set of accounting records? At this stage of ABC's acceptance and development, many consider it an advanced analytical tool for management as opposed to an official set of records. It certainly may not yet be robust enough to replace our day-to-day systems. Each implementation of ABC at this point probably will be tailored to each user's objectives. There is not yet an "off the shell" solution that has been accepted as the standard. In the last two years we have begun to see the emergence of commercially available software to assist in the implementation process.

Thus, although we currently may view ABC as a significant management tool for issues such as pricing schemes and product abandonment analysis rather than as a tactical accounting system, some firms are evaluating the impact of a conversion to ABC as the accounting system of record. As the ABC "body of knowledge" is expanded and codified, activity-based costing may well eventually replace our current cost accounting systems.

Norm Raffish, CPIM, is a senior manager in the management consulting practice of Ernst & Young. Prior to joining the firm, he spent several years as a consultant and 12 years with the Xerox Corporation's Computer Services Division, engaged in industry and strategic product planning and the design and development of integrated manufacturing systems. He says that in 1991 the CAM-I CMS project will publish a new glossary on activity-based costing. It is hoped that this glossary will be the basis for a future common language in the area of ABC.

From N. Raffish, "How Much Does that Product Really Cost?" *Management Accounting* (March 1991): 36–39. Reprinted with permission.

Question

5.2 In Norm Raffish's paper, what are the five steps involved in product life-cycle costs? How much of a product's cost is committed after the design phase, and why is this number important?

5.3 The Rise and Fall of Time-Based Manufacturing

A stubborn refusal to abandon traditional performance measures put the brakes on an automotive supplier's efforts to compete.

By William M. Baker, CMA, Timothy D. Fry, and Kirk Karwan

In the late 1980s, foreign competition—particularly from the Japanese—forced U.S. automotive suppliers to switch from competition based upon (lowest) cost to competition based upon on-time delivery and high quality. In order to meet these objectives, many companies began to implement programs to minimize throughput time and maximize quality.

Companies also realized that traditional standard costing systems, entrenched in direct labor and variance calculations, should be viewed first as financial accounting mechanisms and then used cautiously for the purpose of controlling costs. Knussmann Corporation's Brice Plant[1] is an example of an automotive supplier that strived to move away from its emphasis on traditional performance measures but failed.

In January 1988, Knussmann's president established time-based and quality-based goals for its plants located throughout the United States. Each plant, according to the president, was to develop a throughput time of one week (work-in-process inventory was to be turned over 52 times per year) and to reduce scrap to 0.5% of cost of goods sold.[2]

When these objectives were established, work-in-process inventory turnovers averaged approximately 10 per year at the Brice plant. Scrap was about 4.5%.

During 1988, no noticeable changes in inventory ratios or scrap levels occurred. Consequently, in December 1988 Knussmann's president called a meeting with his plant managers. Essentially, his message was: "Meet these objectives or I will get someone who can!"

Prior to 1988, the Brice plant used a traditional costing system similar to systems used in most American manufacturing facilities. Product costs at the Brice plant were direct materials, 30%; direct labor, 8%; factory overhead, 62%. The Brice plant used standard costing and applied factory overhead using direct labor costs.

The emphasis placed upon direct labor costs by the standard cost system permeated the entire plant. Production output from each department was measured by "earned standard dollars," which is a standard measure of actual output.

Monthly variance reports were generated and variances calculated for "controllable" costs such as supplies, indirect labor, maintenance, and machining. The variance for "direct labor" was considered so important as to be calculated and supplied to management in a separate report. Primary emphasis was given to minimizing direct labor variances. Departmental managers had to explain all unfavorable variances in weekly meetings. The reliance on these tradi-

tional performance measurements hindered the Brice plant from achieving the two company objectives.

Figure 1 presents the manufacturing performance at the Brice plant. Work-in-process inventory turnover (turns) for the 24-month period are shown. "Inventory turns this year" results from dividing the monthly standard dollars shipped by the monthly ending inventory in standard dollars and multiplying by 12 to obtain turns per year. Corresponding monthly scrap levels are expressed as a percentage of standard dollars shipped. "Earned standard direct labor dollars," as referred to by the Brice cost accounting system, is shown along with the actual dollars spent on direct labor. The difference between the two, representing a favorable or unfavorable variance, also is shown.

BRICE'S FALL

Brice plant managers responded to the ultimatum given by the company president by stressing inventory reductions and quality improvements in all departments. As a result, the amount of money spent on direct and indirect labor was increased from May 1989 to October 1989 (see Figure 1). Additional labor costs resulted from hiring more workers to operate machinery, move materials, and inspect production. In addition, existing workers were paid overtime.

During this same period, the earned direct labor standards did not increase at a comparable rate because the input of work into the shop was not increased beyond demand levels. This factor resulted in a marked decrease in the level of inventory in the plant over the same time period. As indicated by Figure 1, this drop was from $1,122,000 to $806,000. A comparable increase in the dollars shipped and inventory turns resulted, partly due to the decrease in inventory.

Inventory turns (Figure 1) increased from 14 in April 1988 to a high of 28 at one point in September 1989. Inventory levels reached their low point of $806,000 in August 1989. No reduction in inventory occurred in September 1989. Thus, standard dollars shipped fell to a more typical level of $1,435,000. The temporary increase in standard dollars shipped for June, July, and August was due to the reduction of inventory alluded to earlier. When further inventory reductions ceased, output rates leveled off to expected levels.

Due to the increase in actual dollars spent on direct labor and the lack of an increase in earned standard direct labor dollars, unfavorable direct labor variances for the six-month period (May–October 1989) increased dramatically, as shown in Figure 1. In direct response to these unfavorable variances (and standard dollars shipped leveling off), the cor-

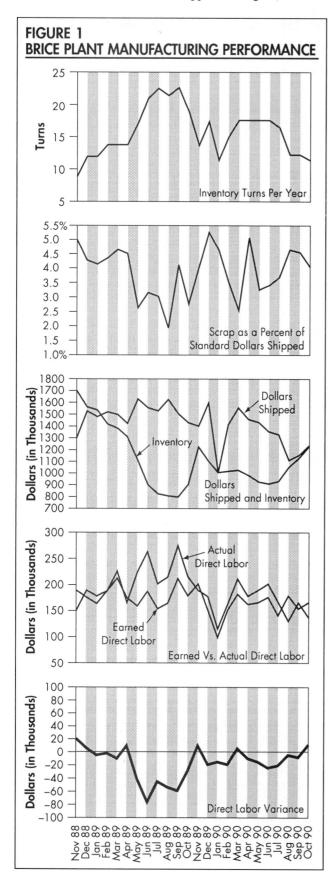

FIGURE 1
BRICE PLANT MANUFACTURING PERFORMANCE

porate vice president for manufacturing sent a memorandum to the Brice plant manager demanding an explanation.

For a while top management at Knussmann "looked the other way." They accepted the unfavorable variances in May, June, July, and August due to the high increase in dollars shipped. But when the standard dollars shipped leveled off in September and October, they were no longer willing to disregard the unfavorable variances. A memo, stressing a need for the control of direct labor costs, was followed by several phone calls from the corporate controller to the Brice plant manager.

Brice management responded by not allowing any overtime in the plant. As a result, the actual dollars spent on direct labor decreased. Also, more material was input into the plant by starting scheduled orders early. This served to increase inventory, which also increased the earned standard direct labor.

As expected, unfavorable direct labor variances decreased, with a comparable decrease in inventory turns. By the end of 1989, inventory turns had decreased to 18 and inventory had increased from the low of $806,000 in August to $1,108,000.

Throughout the next 12 months, no noticeable change was apparent in inventory or scrap. Inventory turns in October 1990 were 12 per year, which was the lowest level since the beginning of the 24-month period.

A comparison of data on "scrap as a percent of standard dollars shipped" to "dollars shipped and inventory" shows that when inventory levels went down, scrap percentages went down. In December 1988 and January 1989, scrap averaged about 4.4%. In August 1989, when inventory was at its lowest level, scrap was at its lowest level, too—1.9%! From August 1989 until October 1990, dramatic fluctuations in scrap levels occurred. But the scrap levels tended to move upward, and by the end of the 24-month period, scrap averaged 4.1%.

While scrap levels decreased when management spent additional labor dollars to control for scrap, it was clear by the end of the 24-month period that no marked improvement in scrap levels had been realized. This had been one of the two major objectives set forth by the corporation.

Thus, reliance on a traditional, yet improper, set of performance measures not only hinders the implementation of time-based or quality-based manufacturing but actually may halt it. Despite the development of time-based and quality-based corporate objectives at Knussmann—a one-week manufacturing lead time thereby turning work-in-process 52 times per year and a quality objective of 0.5% scrap—the use of standard costing and the concentration on direct labor variances prevented the Brice plant from making long-run progress towards meeting these objectives.

Despite noticeable improvements in turnover and scrap levels during a six-month period in 1989 and for a very brief period in 1990, top management at Knussmann was unwilling (or unable) to discard a cost-based performance system that had been used for several decades. No performance measures that related to the new company objectives were developed.

Simply setting the new objectives was not enough. Strategic planning would suggest that plans are necessary to achieve the new objectives. Managers at the Brice plant seemingly implemented such plans. Through direct and indirect labor expenditures, they acquired sufficient capacity to achieve the new objectives. But while corporate objectives were communicated, plans were not.

No new performance measures were designed. Knussmann managers set forth new objectives and attempted to measure achievement using the traditional standard cost system. Managers at Brice developed new measures—simple measures such as turnover and scrap percentages. They seemed appropriate. But Knussmann managers were overwhelmed by direct labor variances and reliance upon cost measures.

CHANGE THE COST SYSTEM

Who is the scapegoat now that Brice failed to meet its objectives? Are managers at Knussmann at fault for not adopting a new performance measurement system? Should Brice managers be blamed for not insisting that measures relating to the objectives be used? Perhaps the cost accounting system itself is to blame. Is the cost system wrong, or is it simply being misused? Are variances at fault, or are there better variances?

Today managers realize that some thing must change if companies are to become effective manufacturers. Many alternatives for change, some which can co-exist, some which cannot, should be considered for the Brice plant.

Turn to JIT. Many companies have adopted some type of just-in-time (JIT) philosophy in order to compete on the basis of time. This is more effective for some companies than for others. Certainly, the idea of eliminating waste would be effective at the Brice plant. And just about any company can benefit from the value-added/nonvalue-added ideas offered by some JIT philosophies.

What if the Brice plant had implemented a JIT philosophy? A vast array of nonvalue-added activities would probably be identified. This might be quite effective. Anything might seem effective to a company that has tried for too long to depend on a standard cost system to identify inefficiencies when the standard cost system is obsolete.

Adopt ABC. Similarly, activity-based costing (ABC) might seem effective to a company such as the Brice plant. ABC does not change the financial process to inventory costing materially, so top management may be more willing to adopt ABC than JIT. JIT and other new production philosophies seem "more radical" than ABC.

The costing mechanism inherent in ABC may not provide immediate benefit, but the activity-based management aspects of ABC could help the Brice plant. By identifying the activities that, when reduced, will accomplish Kussmann's

objectives, Brice can obtain its goals successfully while using ABC. But ABC may be more than what the Brice plant needs.

Modify the existing cost accounting system. ABC and JIT may be important enough to warrant consideration at the Brice plant. But top managers, especially those entrenched in traditional cost accounting systems, often are reluctant to change the cost accounting system. Typically, any modification to existing systems involves only the overhead allocation approach. This might be enough for the Brice plant!

Hiromoto[3] suggests that the allocation base should be determined by the activity that management wants to minimize. The cost accounting systems in Japan, for example, use allocation bases that will *motivate* management decision making toward long-run objectives rather than to pinpoint short-run costs. American accountants often are accused of being good "pinpointers," carrying calculations to extra decimal places while ignoring the long run.

Managers at Knussmann want the Brice plant to become a time-based manufacturer. In that case, the one activity that must be minimized is the time required from the release of raw materials until the shipment of the finished product to customers (throughput time). Using product throughput time as the allocation base encourages operations managers to strive constantly to reduce throughput time and, in turn, reduces product cost.

At the same time, these efforts improve the company's competitive advantage—time. If throughput time is used as the allocation base, direct labor still could be traced to products. Overhead costs would be allocated using throughput time.

Managers who concentrate on minimizing product cost need to reduce the time required to manufacture each product, if product costs are to decrease. This focus encourages both the production of smaller batch sizes and setup time reductions to minimize a product's queue time at each machine.

It also encourages managers to move materials more quickly and thereby improve the process flow. Quality improvements, the second objective set forth by Knussmann management, would be encouraged (and necessary). As quality improves, quality appraisal time (for example, inspection time) can be reduced and throughput time decreased.

Direct labor cost must be reduced to justify purchasing new inspection equipment to allow workers to inspect their own work. Such direct labor cost reductions could not be shown at the Brice plant. Such expenditures were not made. The beauty of throughput time as an allocation base is that time reductions would *require* such investments. And the cost accounting system's effects on net income calculation will not be altered by the use of throughput time.

As with any standard cost system, if throughput time is used, the standards must be kept accurate and up-to-date. We believe that if standards are up-to-date, throughput time should serve the Brice plant well. Before you know it, managers at Brice would do everything they could to reduce throughput time. They would be searching for activities that do not add value, and they would attempt to eliminate them. They would move inventory out quickly, and inventory levels would go down.

Crude as it seems, we think that such actions sound like activity-based management and JIT philosophies. Even if they are not, such actions should still help the Brice plant. If nothing else, managers at Brice would then have a better chance of convincing managers at Knussmann to consider adopting JIT or ABC.

THE PROBLEM: STUBBORN MANAGERS

Top managers were successful in getting managers at the Brice plant to try to compete on the basis of time and quality, not cost. While the Brice plant had some success in achieving those objectives, it was short-lived.

Who's to blame? Knussmann's management? Brice's management? Lack of goal congruence? Failure to plan?

Even the cost accounting system appears as a potential cause for failure. For whatever reason, managers at Knussmann were unwilling to abandon traditional cost accounting performance measures, and this was the plant's downfall.

When managers are unwilling to abandon traditional cost accounting measures, it may be difficult, or impossible, to compete based upon time and quality. This outcome seems to be especially true when the traditional measures revolve around labor in nonlabor-intensive processes.

When traditional cost accounting is that entrenched, the best hope usually is to begin by trying to convince man-agement to try a different allocation base. For the Brice plant, we recommend throughput time as an allocation base. Once a new allocation base is in place, other good things such as JIT and ABC might happen.

William M. Baker, CMA, Ph.D., CCE, CCA, is an assistant accounting professor at Appalachian State University in Boone, N.C. He is a member of the Catawba Valley Chapter, through which this article was submitted. Timothy D. Fry and Kirk Karwan are associate professors in management science at the University of South Carolina in Columbia.

Notes

1. These are not the real names. These names are used to maintain the confidentiality of both the company and the plant.

2. No finished goods inventory is carried by any plant as finished products are either shipped directly to the customer or to a distribution warehouse. Work-in-process is the only inventory that the plant is charged with carrying.

3. Toshiro Hiromoto. "Another Hidden Edge—Japanese Management Accounting," *Harvard Business Review,* July–August 1988, pp. 22–26.

From W. M. Baker, T. D. Fry, and K. Karwan, "The Rise and Fall of Time-Based Manufacturing," *Management Accounting* (June 1994): 56–59. Reprinted with permission.

Question

5.3 In the article *"The Rise and Fall of Time-Based Manufacturing,"* the authors state that one traditional measure was so important that management received a separate report on it. What is this measure, and what is its significance to the problems experienced at the Knussmann company?

CHAPTER 6

Two-Stage Allocations and Activity-Based Costing Systems

Four articles on activity-based costing are included in this section. Taken together, the articles highlight the applications of ABC to many different types of organizations. The first article, T. L. Estrin, J. Kantor, and D. Albers' *Is ABC Suitable for Your Company?* (Reading 6.1), presents a method for determining whether ABC is appropriate for a particular company. The authors develop what they call a contingency grid based on two dimensions: the potential for ABC to provide costing information that is significantly different from what a traditional system would generate, and the propensity for the organization's managers to use the newly generated information. By answering a series of questions, an organization can score and locate itself on the grid. The authors state that while there is subjectivity in how an organization scores itself and that the factors used are not exhaustive, the contingency grid provides some structure that will allow managers to determine whether ABC should even be attempted in their organizations.

While the early applications of ABC were developed in manufacturing settings, more recent applications have surfaced in service organizations. William Rotch's article, Reading 6.2, *Activity-Based Costing in Service Organizations,* addresses two questions relating to whether ABC can be adapted for use in service organizations, and if so, whether there are special considerations that need to be made. Citing examples from a hospital, rail services, and data analysis organizations, Rotch believes that services can quite easily adapt ABC. Services do differ from manufacturing in that output is harder to define, and there are some difficult issues such as joint capacity costs to deal with, but these are not insurmountable problems. In fact the last two articles in the section, David Carlson and Mark Young's *Activity-Based Total Quality Management at American Express* (Reading 6.3), and Lawrence Carr's *Unbundling the Cost of Hospitalization* (Reading 6.4) provide examples of how ABC can be applied in other service settings.

Carlson and Young (Reading 6.3) studied a division of American Express, American Express Integrated Payment Systems (now called First Data Corporation). The article documents the FACT (Functional Administrative Control Technique) approach for combining activity-based costing, strategic cost management and total quality management. Developed by Brian Higgins, director of quality assurance, the system has a feature that distinguishes it from many other systems. Apart from a regular activity hierarchy, Higgins' model incorporates nonfinancial information, such as customer and supplier comments on the level and types of costs, into the data base and ultimately into decision making. Apart from its intuitive appeal, FACT saved Integrated Payments Systems over $1 million dollars during the first year of operation.

Reading 6.4, *Unbundling the Cost of Hospitalization,* by Lawrence Carr, illustrates the implementation of an ABC system at Braintree Hospital in Boston. This application was designed to tease apart (or unbundle) the fixed cost allocation of nursing services. In the past, nursing costs were simply allocated into the cost per day of a hospital room. However, since nurses have different professional qualifications and skills, and patients require different care and have differential lengths of stay, devising a more accurate costing system would be beneficial to patients and the hospital. Certainly a patient would no longer be charged the average cost of nursing, especially if he or she required little nursing care, and the hospital would have a much more diagnostic system for activity and cost control.

6.1 Is ABC Suitable for Your Company?
An impartial analysis of overall operations can tell you yes or no.

By T. L. Estrin, CMA, Jeffrey Kantor, and David Albers

How do you know if activity-based costing (ABC) would be right for your company? There's an objective way to decide before your company takes the plunge. For ABC to be effective, a majority of all costs incurred by a significant unit of a business must be analyzed systematically. These costs include not only most fixed and variable factory burden costs, but also some fixed and variable marketing and administrative costs. Implementation of ABC requires a complex, comprehensive process that is costly and time-consuming, so naturally managers would want to be assured of the advantages before embarking on the implementation of ABC.

The potential benefits of ABC can be analyzed in advance along two separate dimensions. The first is based on the probability that, in a given application, ABC will produce costs or other results that are significantly different from ones that could be generated with more conventional or less costly methods. The ABC-generated costs may or may not be "better" or more accurate, but they are different in amount. The second dimension of the model seeks to establish that, given that cost information generated by ABC is indeed different, management will use it for significant decisions. Managers must regard ABC information as superior, and the nature of the organization and its competitive, legal, and social environments must allow managers to use the information freely.

The factors involved in the first dimension include the number and diversity of products or services produced, the diversity and differential degree of support services used for different products, the extent to which common or joint processes are used, the effectiveness of current cost allocation methods, and the rate of growth of period costs. The factors involved in the second dimension are management's freedom to set prices, the ratio of period costs to total costs, strategic considerations, the climate and culture of cost reduction in the company, and the frequency of analysis that is desirable or necessary.

A CONTINGENCY APPROACH TO IMPLEMENTING ABC

This methodology is based on a company's analysis of itself. It consists of weighting and combining the weights of the above factors and dimensions in order to evaluate the likelihood of success of implementing ABC. The combined weighted scores are plotted as a point on one of the four quadrants of a graph. Meanings are attached to the quadrant and the location of the final score in that quadrant. The methodology is not designed to produce a ratio-scale number indicating the relative benefits of ABC but to structure a systematic analysis by which the managers of a company can discuss the common factors that support or reject implementation.

To start, management must analyze the nature of the company in light of responses to two key questions:

1. For a given organization, is it likely that ABC will produce costs that are significantly different from those that are generated with conventional accounting, and does it seem likely that those costs will be "better"?
2. If information that is considered "better" is generated by the new system, will the new information change the dependent decisions made by the management?

FINDING THE ANSWERS

Ten mediating factors can guide management in determining the answers. The first five address the potential advantages of ABC versus traditional costing methods, and the second five deal with management's need and ability to react to product costing distortions.

Product diversity (PD). Product diversity refers to the quantity or range of distinct products or the variety of product families offered. Minor product variations should not be confused with product diversity. For example, it is unlikely that .20 cm. diameter ball bearings are a different product offering from .21 cm. diameter ball bearings. Differences in the complexity of various products also should be reflected in this analysis. Products that appear relatively homogeneous but that vary greatly in complexity are indicative of high diversity (such as 64K memory chips versus 1024K memory chips). Color variations, if applicable, need to be examined carefully. Does changing the color materially change the product? Is the function color dependent? (For example, contrast red ink versus blue ink pens and red versus blue cars.)

There are numerous considerations in evaluating the extent and degree of product diversity:

- Accounting product classifications. Does the general ledger incorporate different product classifications? Are there internal reports that attempt to split sales, margins, or earnings by product lines?
- Markets served. Are they broken into geographical or industrial groups that purchase different types of products? Is the manufacturing department organized sequentially or in parallel? Sequential organization suggests limited product differentiation; parallel organization can indicate product diversity.
- Stockrooms. Are different stockrooms handling the same inventory classification (for example, raw material, finished goods) for different products?
- Sales. Does the company sell both OEM and manufactured items?
- Advertising. Does the company advertise only its name and/or one product, or does its advertising reflect different products?

Support diversity (SD). Support diversity refers to the range or variation of support overhead given to products. Assumptions can't be based on size. Even if the organization is only a cost center or a production facility, if it has more than one basic product or family of products, diversity in product support requirements probably exists. In this connection, reference to the manufacturing activities required is particularly useful. A superficial look at the organization may indicate little diversity, but a closer examination may reveal that actual activities vary greatly by product.

To determine and evaluate the degree of support diversity, companies should answer the following questions:

- Do departmental titles contain product names, and/or are departmental activities driven by specific products? Are there engineering support departments, and, if so, are their efforts skewed toward specific products?
- Are different manufacturing locations included in the one costing system?
- Are the manufacturing products relatively complex? (As a rule of thumb, complex products require more support, so the likelihood of diversity in support requirements increases.)
- Do different products use different distribution channels, have separate advertising requirements, or go to different markets?
- Is research and development homogeneous or product oriented?

- Is the company organized in (product-focused) modules, or do product task forces exist?
- Do different products require different material handling processes? Do different stockrooms exist?
- Is the organization operating in or moving toward a JIT environment?
- Are there major differences in product volumes or lot sizes?
- Is there a "new product introduction" organization?
- Does the company sell both OEM and manufactured items?

Common process (CP). Common process refers to the degree of commonality of processes among the different product offerings. "Processes" encompass all identifiable activities including manufacturing, engineering, marketing, distribution, accounting, material handling, quality control, research and development, and administration. If there is a high degree of commonality of processes or activities among products, period costs required by each product cannot be separated using conventional management accounting. ABC, by its nature, may be more effective.

Before assigning a common process value, companies should answer the following questions:

- If the organization examines profitability by product, are many expenses captured directly, or are they based on allocation or other arbitrary factors? Direct capture of most expenses may indicate a high degree of process segregation.
- Do different products require different production processes? Do production departments have more than one product to which to charge time?
- Are there distinct material handling processes? Do various products use different stockrooms? Is purchasing organized by product type or by type of material purchased? What degree of commonality exists between suppliers?
- Are engineering or shop support departments organized by product? Do engineers or technicians frequently support different products? Can they charge their time to different products?
- Is more than one distribution channel used?
- Is quality control organized by products?
- Do research and development personnel concentrate on specific products, or is the R&D more general in nature? Are R&D costs captured by product?
- Is administration organized by product?

Period cost allocation (CA). Period cost allocation refers to the existing costing system's conceptual ability to allocate period costs properly. In essence, period cost allocation is an analysis of the allocation methodology to determine if it is capable of mimicking the results of ABC. It is a premise of ABC that, over time, so-called period costs (indirect, variable, and fixed costs) are attributable to the activities required in making various products. Thus, a major focus of ABC analysis is on associating period costs with products. ABC also suggests that many nonmanufacturing costs, such as marketing costs, also are a function of product activity and should be loaded onto the products responsible for their incurrence.

- Is the general ledger set up to capture support expenses by product through the use of product-specific departments, engineering time sheets, indirect labor classifications, and the like?
- To what extent are indirect expenses not identified by product?
- How many concurrent bases of allocation are used?
- Are they consistent with the major cost drivers?
- How many levels are in the allocation hierarchy? If multi-level, are the allocations on a product-specific basis?
- Is the allocation hierarchy riddled with estimates or arbitrary factors?
- How many cost centers exist, and how product-specific are the cost centers?
- If only one allocation basis is used, can it distribute the costs by product accurately despite the probable lack of correlation between output and the consumption of resources? Would the distribution of costs still be accurate if there were significant changes in the nature of the period costs? (Assume that the more allocation bases are used, the more readily changes can be reflected in product costs.)
- Can the allocation bases reflect the impact of product volume fluctuations accurately? (For instance, burden rates are established based upon anticipated product volumes. Will the allocation bases recognize the probable change in support requirements if the product mix changes significantly?)

Rate of growth of period costs (PG). Rate of growth of period costs refers to the growth in period costs as an indicator of the dynamism required by the costing system. One of ABC's strengths is its ability to capture changes in the support requirements of products quickly through its direct measurement of activity levels. If period costs, as a percentage, remain relatively stable over years, management can to some extent adjust implicitly for the distortions produced by a conventional cost system. Also, given period cost stability for several years, a traditional costing system can be structured to provide product costs similar or identical to those calculated by ABC (excluding below-the-line, cost of goods manufactured costs).

HOW DOES MANAGEMENT USE COST INFORMATION IN DECISIONS?

If management agrees that the nature of the products, the productive processes, and the marketing of the products are such that the costs generated by ABC will be significantly different from traditional management accounting costs and that ABC costs reflect true product costs more accurately, it still may not be able to, or may not want to, use this better information. A number of factors will influence management's desire for or ability to use cost information in its deliberations. Among these factors are pricing freedom, period expense ratio, strategic considerations, cost reduction efforts, and analysis frequency.

Pricing freedom (PF). Pricing freedom refers to the company's degree of power and freedom to set prices and therefore establish product profitability. The more freedom a company has, the less important product costs become. Pricing will be set to maximize profits and will depend on market elasticity. Where monopoly conditions apply and demand is inelastic, high prices will be set. Where there are pure competition, many competitors, and good substitute products available, however, prices will be determined entirely by market forces.

Because the vast majority of organizations face situations somewhere between the two extremes, companies should answer the following questions as they evaluate this factor:

- Are all product prices regulated? If so, are the prices based on costs and subject to appeal and revision?
- How competitive is the market? Are price surveys common or available? Does the profitability of the industry appear unusually high or low? Are the competitive aspects based on some factor other than price?
- Are there high barriers to entry?
- Do the company's products occupy a unique position within the market? Can premium prices be justified due to service?
- Where are the products within their life cycle?
- Is the company a price leader or a price follower?
- How dynamic are the products' prices? What are the causes of the changes or lack thereof?

Period expense ratio (FE). Period expense ratio addresses the possible materiality of product cost distortions directly. If possible distortions are so minimal that no management actions would result from their correction, then the distortions become irrelevant. Although the materiality of this factor also should be evaluated from the perspective of percentage change in reported costs, the primary focus should be on the impact upon product profitability. (For example, a reported cost change of 5% may be immaterial to a jeweler operating on 300% markup, but it is extremely significant to a volume-based grocery working with 2%–4% margins).

Although there is no specific formula for quantifying possible product cost distortions and determining the materiality of those distortions, the following questions may help the appraisal process. When answering these questions, companies should consider only period costs that must be allocated; variable costs that can be loaded directly onto products should be ignored.

- What is/would be the plant average or blanket burden rate? Is it a large multiple of labor? How does it compare to various product or cost center rates?
- Are period costs a "significant" proportion of the total cost structure (including direct costs)? What would be the impact upon total profitability if the percentage of period costs increased 10%? 50%? 100%?
- Are cost reduction activities focused upon product costs (such as reduction of supplier prices) or upon period costs? Is it management's belief that focusing upon direct costs offers greater potential benefits? Is this belief appropriate?

Strategic considerations (SC). Strategic considerations refer to the constraints imposed upon management's decisions by its explicit or implicit strategies—in other words, the degree to which strategies override costs in the decision-making process. These strategies are not limited to marketing strategies; they also include secondary strategies and objectives related to technology, manufacturing, quality, and the like.

- Is a "market niche" strategy being employed? Is the strategy dependent upon product profitability/costs?
- Are capital expenditures for new products, manufacturing changes, or capacity expansions frequently justified explicitly on the basis of "strategic reasons" instead of economic returns?
- Are capital expenditures frequently initiated implicitly and driven by strategic considerations, with the financial benefits of the project being used merely to obtain project approval?
- What type of analysis and justification is necessary for approval of R&D expenditures? Is the true rationale more strategic in nature?
- Does the organization establish customer prices based upon costs or market? If the company sells to related entities using prices based upon costs, would changes in the transfer pricing result in changes in volume or in the receiving location's decisions?
- Are make-versus-buy comparisons performed frequently? Does the organization have this option, or do technological or policy restrictions constrain it?
- Are changes in product design or manufacturing processes driven mainly by costs, or are other sources such as market or product requirements critical?
- Are product discontinuation analyses performed regularly in an attempt to (indirectly) reduce costs or for reasons such as fostering specific market perceptions?

Cost reduction (CR). Cost reduction involves the corporate culture as it affects the relationship between internal cost-related decisions and the indirect component of the total cost of products. It involves the nature of internal cost-related decisions and the degree to which the decisions depend upon accurate allocations of period costs. A number of potential internal decisions depend on accurate costs—

manufacturing process changes, product design modifications, make-vs.-buy comparisons, product scrubbing, capacity expansion evaluation, and so on. Analysis of these activities will indicate the likelihood of management action resulting from changes in reported product costs due to the elimination of distortions in the period cost allocation.

- How extensive are cost reduction activities within the organization? Do any engineering groups focus exclusively upon cost reduction? Is there an employee suggestion plan?
- Are there numerous or frequent cost-oriented task forces? Are cost reduction metrics tracked internally? Are there frequent changes in head count unrelated to load?
- Are the above cost reduction activities general in nature and not related to specific products? Are cost reduction targets established in total only, or by function/activity, or by product?
- Do the cost reduction activities focus upon nonperiod targets? Are there material or labor variance targets?
- Are make-versus-buy comparisons applicable? If so, how frequent are the analyses? How close are the decisions?
- Are product scrubbing decisions both frequent and dependent upon costs? Are period costs a major factor in the decision?
- Are process modifications focused upon the manufacturing organization? Are period costs relevant?
- Are capacity changes dependent upon costs? Are allocated period costs incorporated into—or even relevant to—the decisions?

Analysis frequency (AF). Analysis frequency refers to the frequency, either routine or special, of product cost analyses and incorporates both the current and the desired frequencies. A measure of dynamism, it also embodies the other management action factors. A discrepancy between the existing and desired frequencies of analysis indicates dissatisfaction with the existing costing system.

- Are product profitability reports issued routinely from the existing costing system? Are they believed, or are "adjustments" made? If believed, are they used fruitfully?
- How frequently are special studies or ad hoc analyses of product costs performed or requested? Is there a lack of credibility in the existing data, or are the existing data insufficient? If studies/analyses are infrequent, why? Is it due to a low requirement or to the difficulty of obtaining "accurate" data.
- What prompts special cost study requests, volume fluctuations, pricing requests, and the like? Do these changes occur often?
- Would management like more frequent or more detailed product cost analyses? For what purpose?

PLOTTING THE ANSWERS

Now let's assign values to the factors listed above and plot them on a chart to provide a focus for a discussion among managers and give them a mechanism for highlighting their differences in order to reach a consensus in a more effective manner.

Figure 1 shows a grid that may be used to plot the situational factors in an evaluation of the potential of ABC for a particular situation. Each of the 10 factors is scored on a −5 to +5 scale, and the scores of each of the two sets of five factors are weighted and combined into the two scores, which are plotted on the grid. A weighted aggregate score of the five factors affecting "product cost distortion," which indicates the potential benefits of ABC for the company, is plotted on the "Y" axis of the grid. A weighted composite score of all the factors affecting management's need and ability to act on better cost information in making decisions is plotted on the "X" axis.

In order to show the scores from the two sets of factors on the two-dimensional contingency grid, we must combine the scores of each set into a single score on that characteristic. It is necessary to weigh each of the five factors in both classifications to recognize that differences exist in the relative importance of each factor in a given company.

Each of the five factors on each dimension of the grid can be assigned a score depending on management's analysis of its situation. The weighting process begins with the presumption of equal ranking (i.e., weighting of 20%). Then managers examine each factor to determine if the weighting should be changed. This end can be achieved in a "Delphi" process where managers from all pertinent areas submit scores and their reasoning for all factors by mail. Then they receive the high, low, and average scores with rationales and revise their estimates. The first rounds of this process can be on an area-by-area basis (such as accounting or production), and the last rounds of this process can be done with broadly representative members of management meeting to determine the scores.

The examination is based on three main criteria:

1. If this factor had the extreme value of + or -5, to what extent is the main characteristic impacted? For example, without product diversity, will product cost distortions occur? Without material pricing freedom, will management actions occur?
2. If this factor has the extreme value of + or -5, what is the impact upon the other factors?
3. Is this factor extremely subjective or difficult to measure, and should weighting be structured to ameliorate its impact?

INTERPRETING THE RESULTS

Quadrant I. Results that are plotted in Quadrant I (both "X" and "Y" are positive) initially suggest because product cost distortions are likely and management is free to act upon

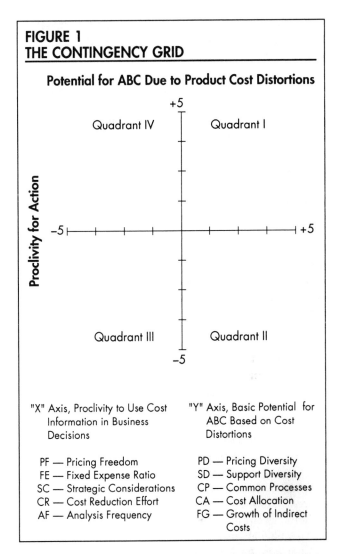

**FIGURE 1
THE CONTINGENCY GRID**

Potential for ABC Due to Product Cost Distortions

Proclivity for Action

Quadrant IV   Quadrant I

Quadrant III   Quadrant II

"X" Axis, Proclivity to Use Cost Information in Business Decisions

PF — Pricing Freedom
FE — Fixed Expense Ratio
SC — Strategic Considerations
CR — Cost Reduction Effort
AF — Analysis Frequency

"Y" Axis, Basic Potential for ABC Based on Cost Distortions

PD — Pricing Diversity
SD — Support Diversity
CP — Common Processes
CA — Cost Allocation
FG — Growth of Indirect Costs

corrected product costs, an ABC system should be implemented. It is possible, and even likely, however, that the source of the cost distortions is included in the category of "below-the-line" (selling and administrative) expenses and that the current traditional allocation technique is providing adequate overhead cost information. Because recommendations differ depending on the source of the distortions (traditional "overhead" or the "below-the-line" category), managers must perform the "potential for ABC due to product cost distortions" section of the analysis again, omitting any consideration of nonoverhead, organizations, activities, or similar expenses.

If the revised composite score remains Quadrant I, it is an indication that the source of the distortions is within the category defined as traditional overhead. In this case, companies should consider implementing a full ABC system or a costing system that incorporates ABC concepts. Product cost distortions probably are occurring, and because those costs are being used extensively within the organization, it is likely that less than optimal decisions are being made.

If the revised composite score shifts to Quadrant II, the source of the distortions is within the category known as "below-the-line" (selling and marketing, administration, and research and development). In this case, implementation of a full ABC system is not warranted—the existing traditional allocation technique is providing adequate cost information for the overhead component of the product costs, and there is no reason to incur the implementation and maintenance costs of a full-blown ABC system. If "below-the-line" expenses for total product cost purposes are the main culprits in reporting incorrect products costs, however, managers should scrutinize the allocation methodology of those analyses for possible errors. A standalone system using ABC concepts and addressing only "below-the-line" costs may be appropriate.

Quadrant II. If the results of the analysis are plotted in this quadrant, it indicates that although management is free to utilize product cost information, it is unlikely that those costs contain material distortions. Because there are no direct benefits, implementing ABC at this time is not recommended. The situation should be monitored for changes over time, however, particularly if the "'Y" value is relatively small.

Quadrant III. Results plotted in this quadrant clearly indicate that ABC is not recommended. It is unlikely that material product cost distortions are present, and management has limited ability to utilize or react to modified costs.

Quadrant IV. Results occurring in this quadrant suggest that although product cost distortions are likely, management has little ability to modify its decisions that are cost dependent. Management should re-examine its use of product cost information and its freedom to react to changes, including performing the "management action" section of the model analysis again. Although management may be constrained from acting on cost information in the short run, many valuable long-term uses for this information may appear. Only when management is satisfied that it would *not* use corrected product cost information should it reject possible implementation of an ABC system.

THE FINAL DECISION

After reading about ABC, attending ABC seminars, or being approached by ABC consultants, many managers still may be in a quandary as to whether the implementation of this technique will improve the competitiveness of their particular companies. These executives need some method of evaluating whether the potential claimed benefits of ABC will outweigh the certain and substantial costs of its implementation. Our contingency analysis model should help them by matching the characteristics of their company, its products, and the costing system used with the factors that make ABC most effective.

The factors we presented are neither mutually exclusive nor collectively exhaustive. While the scoring system is subjective, it is grounded on factors cited in the ABC literature as being causal in determining the superiority of ABC over traditional costing. Most important, it presents a structure for managers to use in their deliberations and encourages them to arrive at some consensus with regard to the degree to which the factors are present in their company and ultimately to convince themselves as to either the uselessness, the desirability, or the critical necessity for the implementation of ABC.

T. L. Estrin, CMA, Ph.D., is an associate professor of business administration at the University of Windsor, Windsor, Canada, and a director of the Cost Management Group there. He is a member of the Society of Management Accountants of Canada and the Institute of Management Accountants. He may be reached at (519) 253-4232, ext. 3457.

Jeffrey Kantor, Ph.D., CA., is a professor of business administration at the University of Windsor and a director of the Cost Management Group.

David C. Albers is the regional support international manager for Multimedia Communication Systems and has done process analysis with Northern Telecom Inc. for several years.

From T. L. Estrin, J. Kantor, and D. Albers, "Is ABC Suitable for Your Company?" *Management Accounting* (April 1994): 40–45. Reprinted with permission.

Question

6.1 Using Estrin, Kantor and Albers' contingency grid, if an organization's score puts it in Quadrant III, is ABC implementation recommended? Explain. Is their method "foolproof?"

6.2 Activity-Based Costing in Service Industries

By William Rotch

ABC has mainly been applied to manufacturing companies, but it can also prove useful to service enterprises. This article identifies how ABC is applied in manufacturing settings, then discusses any special challenges that service companies encounter in trying to use ABC systems.

A number of articles and cases recently have described and analyzed activity-based costing (ABC). Since ABC has mainly been applied to manufacturing companies, however, the question arises whether ABC can also be used in service businesses. To answer this question, this article first considers how ABC works in manufacturing settings to identify key characteristics of both the manufacturing setting and of the cost systems. This background provides a point of departure for considering the suitability of ABC to service businesses and also any special challenges that arise in using ABC in those businesses.

ABC SYSTEMS IN MANUFACTURING

As a number of recent articles and cases explain,[1] ABC deals with indirect costs, which are costs that are not easily traceable to outputs (output being defined as all tangible and intangible benefits provided for customers). In the short run, many indirect costs are fixed. ABC, however, implicitly takes a longer-term view by recognizing that, over time, these indirect costs can be changed and hence are relevant to management choices.

The following two sections explain the two primary benefits derived from using ABC.

More accurate costs for output. More accurate costs are possible when support costs (e.g., setup and inspection) that are not driven by volume are allocated to products by using a volume-related base (traditionally, direct labor hours or dollars). By shifting the allocation base to an activity that is related to output or output characteristics, the link between the use of resources and product output becomes more accurate. An activity such as "product runs," for example, could be used to capture all the setup, inspection, and material-handling costs caused by production runs. Then, if a company has product diversity in terms of run length, short-run products will not be undercosted and long-run products will not be overcosted. How much the accuracy of costs improves depends on how different the products are in their use of the activities.

Behavioral influence. Besides more accurate output costs, ABC can provide benefits by influencing the behavior of design engineers, production managers, or marketing strategies. Identifying and costing activities provide potentially powerful information such as the following:

- Knowing the high cost of parts handling (a defined activity) can encourage design engineers to simplify production design;
- Recognizing that volume-based overhead allocations can give false signals (e.g., knowing that automation-related support costs will not go down by reducing direct labor) helps production managers determine the optimum level of production technology); and
- Knowing even the approximate cost of various customer services can guide marketing strategists toward a profitable mix of service and volume.

Relationship between activities and strategy. Activities and strategies are closely linked in ABC because strategic choices drive activities. ABC deals with activities and costs that can be changed only gradually, which reflects the long-term perspective taken by ABC and its concern with strategic issues. Support costs ordinarily cannot be changed much in one week. Over time, however, changes that occur in a company's production methods, product design, and marketing strategy ultimately affect the company's indirect support costs. This important linkage is illustrated by Exhibit 1, which shows the relationship between strategy and activities (which, together, comprise the firm's operations).

Strategy. A company's strategy can be seen as a plan to provide certain outputs to attract and serve customers. Those outputs, whether manufactured products or units of service, have characteristics that cause certain activities to take place, and those activities cost money. When a company's strategy changes—say, toward greater customer service and shorter production runs—certain activities (e.g., setups and product design) occur more often or are used more. The costs of these activities, therefore, increase. Unless they can measure the link between output characteristics (e.g., better customer service) and activities (e.g., improved product design because of an expanded product design department), managers cannot compute the cost of strategic choices. If they use traditional systems based on direct labor hours or machine hours, these managers may well have misleading information.

Several examples of how strategic choices can influence or drive activities are given in the following cases.

The Schrader Bellows case. In the Schrader Bellows case,[2] the company's strategy was to offer a broad line of valves and to respond favorably to customer requests for rush orders and specially designed products. The result was many short runs and interruptions of longer runs. All support activities that were driven by the frequency of production

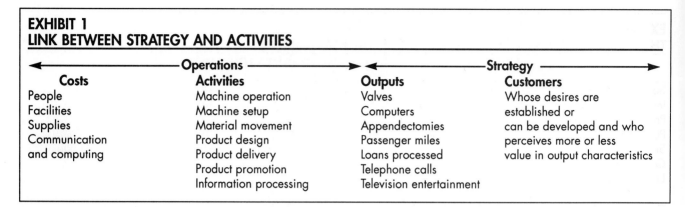

EXHIBIT 1
LINK BETWEEN STRATEGY AND ACTIVITIES

← Operations →		← Strategy →	
Costs	**Activities**	**Outputs**	**Customers**
People	Machine operation	Valves	Whose desires are
Facilities	Machine setup	Computers	established or
Supplies	Material movement	Appendectomies	can be developed and who
Communication	Product design	Passenger miles	perceives more or less
and computing	Product delivery	Loans processed	value in output characteristics
	Product promotion	Telephone calls	
	Information processing	Television entertainment	

runs were heavily used (the application of ABC to Schrader Bellows is discussed next).

Siemens Electric Motor Works. The Siemens Electric Motor Works case[3] found that 40 percent of its support-related manufacturing costs (or 10 percent of total costs) were driven by two kinds of activities: order processing and the handling of special components. The company's strategy had led it toward producing custom motors and away from long-run, commodity-type motors. As a result, 90 percent of all orders were for custom motors. The average order was for less than ten units although almost half the motors sold were on orders for 100 or more units. The company's strategy clearly made both order processing and component handling into large and costly activities, especially for small production runs.

A hospital. A Pennsylvania hospital decided in 1986 to become certified as a trauma center. That strategic decision set in motion a number of activities and affected some existing ones. The hospital recruited four doctors to staff the trauma center so that it could be covered twenty-four hours a day. Each of these doctors received compensation guarantees. Other incremental one-time and continuing expenses were incurred for facilities, equipment, training, and support staff. Although a few activities and staff members were unique to the trauma center, many were used by other hospital services. A continuing review of the strategy of maintaining a trauma center benefited from knowing the link between the new trauma center's work and related support activities.

ABC PROCESS

There are three essential steps in establishing an ABC system:

1. Defining the activities that support output (which often requires defining output—or characteristics of output—in a way that describes how the output drives activities). In the Schrader Bellows case, for example, the traditional output definition would be "a valve" with certain specifications. With ABC, the output is defined as "a valve with a particular average number of units per run." This output definition highlights the activity "making runs," which is different from making

units. Note also that the activity "making runs" is chosen to capture output diversity because runs in Schrader Bellows varied greatly in length.

2. Defining the links between activities and outputs. Again using the Schrader Bellows example, the link between the activity "runs" and the output would be "cost per run" and the "average units per run" (or runs per unit) for each valve produced.

3. Developing the cost of activities (often costs are customarily gathered by function or organizational unit, so special allocation methods have to be used to relate costs to activities). In the Schrader Bellows case, the activity "making runs" was supported by a number of functions (such as setup, inspection, material handling, and labor reporting). The costs of those functions combined to become the cost of the activity "making runs."

Schrader Bellows. While each of these steps is essential, the difficulties that they present vary from company to company. Exhibit 2, for example, portrays these steps for the Schrader Bellows case. The exhibit shows how both the traditional and the new cost systems looked, using the same framework.

Under the "old way," the activities are the work done in manufacturing departments, and the link is overhead cost per direct labor hour. The "new way," by contrast, uses a number of activities (e.g., purchasing and shipping), each with its own appropriate link to output. (Exhibit 2 focuses on only one activity: setting up and making a run.)

The Schrader Bellows ABC system was not easy to set up. All three steps required some ingenuity. Activities had to be defined so that they reflected what people in the support groups actually did and also in a way that could be linked to product output. Relating costs to activities required data gathering on how people spent their time, which was not information that was readily available.

Structure of ABC systems. At this point, one might ask whether ABC is just a traditional two-stage overhead allocation system that uses more overhead cost pools and a variety of appropriate allocation bases. Technically, ABC is just that, but companies using it seem to have obtained some important benefits that are not obvious when viewing cost systems from an overhead cost pool perspective.

EXHIBIT 2
THE SCHRADER BELLOWS CASE: AN ABC CASE STUDY

The Old Way

Support Costs	Links	Activities	Links	Products
Inventory management Production control Purchasing Setup Quality control Engineering	Mostly based on direct labor; setup on estimates of time	Manufacturing departments (machining, assembly, etc.)	Overhead rate labor hour	Valves with specified amount of direct labor

The New Way (ABC Costing)

Costs	Links	Activities	Links	Products
Same as above	Percentage of time spent in support of specified activities	A *run* Setting up and making a run of a component or finished product	Cost per run	Run cost of products with specified number of units and runs
		(*Other activities* Purchasing Shipping Handling customer orders Direct labor etc.)	Other appropriate-links	Cost of purchasing Cost of shipping Cost of handling order Overhead related to labor Total cost per item

One benefit is that learning about the links between output characteristics and activities helps managers make product decisions directly, even without dollar figures. A circuit board manufacturer discovered, for example, that certain board designs require more hand work. The manufacturer also recognized that the hand work was expensive and prone to quality problems. Therefore, the manufacturer concluded that changes in board design could eliminate the manual operation. Alternatively, if changes were not feasible for particular applications, the price of the boards might be raised. Defining the linkages between board designs and product costs, therefore, helped the manufacturer identify where improvements could be made.

Another benefit seems to arise from defining activities according to how they relate to output characteristics rather than in relation to organizational units, which are more oriented toward input characteristics. It is obvious, for example, that the cost of a setup is the time that setup people spend in setting up for a new run. But if the activity is defined more broadly as a production run, many other costs are also caused by setups, including the following:

- Material movement;
- Inspection; and
- Labor reporting.

Although the activity "setups" is indeed an overhead pool, notice that the pool is defined by an *output-related activity* (runs) rather than by an organizational unit (the setup department).

ABC may also make it easier to include activities outside the factory walls (e.g., marketing and distribution) in product costs. Reorienting and broadening the definition of activities in this way makes the allocation of overhead cost pools more useful in making strategic choices that depend on product costs.

Another benefit of ABC comes from its untraditional way of looking at the relationship between outputs and activities. ABC rejects any clear split between fixed and variable costs and accepts the notion that many costs that are usually considered fixed in fact change over time largely because of changes in strategy. Therefore, not only are these "fixed" costs relevant for strategic decisions, but also the most effective way to control them may be through changes in output strategies.

When management simplifies a product, as IBM did with its ProPrinter, the need for many activities is reduced, so costs can be cut. IBM achieved significantly lower product cost by designing the ProPrinter with fewer parts, thus reducing the costs of parts manufacturing, storage, and handling. By highlighting non-value-adding activities (such as labor reporting) and high-cost activities (such as managing part numbers), ABC systems direct management attention to likely areas for improvement.

The structure of an ABC system (with its use of activity cost pools), therefore, resembles the structure of a traditional overhead cost pool system. The benefits of an ABC system lie in choosing activities that are oriented toward output characteristics and that capture output diversity. The analytical process of defining activities and of establishing their linkages to output helps managers to evaluate the cost of strategic choices and to discover ways to reduce costs.

ABC SYSTEMS IN SERVICE ENTERPRISES

Given that ABC systems work in a manufacturing setting, can they also work in service enterprises? If so, what would an ABC system for a service company look like, and would the service setting present any special challenges?

Although differences between manufacturing and service enterprises tend to get blurred because of an emphasis on service in the strategies of many manufacturing enterprises, service enterprises do have several distinctive characteristics:

- Output is often harder to define;
- Activity in response to service requests may be less predictable; and
- Joint capacity cost represents a high proportion of total cost and is difficult to link to output-related activities.

Output in a service enterprise. Output in a service enterprise is sometimes described as a "package of service benefits,"[4] many of which are intangible: for example, speed of service, quality of information, or satisfaction provided. But—just as in a manufacturing environment—these benefits drive activities that cost money. Viewed in this way, service enterprises have characteristics similar to manufacturing although the intangible nature of service output makes costing more difficult.

Despite these difficulties, service businesses are beginning to develop systems that look very much like ABC even though that term is usually not used. Here are some examples, including discussions of any particular difficulties that these service enterprises encountered in implementing an ABC system.

ALEXANDRIA HOSPITAL

Consider another hospital, Alexandria Hospital, for example. A hospital's "product" can be defined as a patient's stay and treatment. The total charge for each stay includes charges for many different services (e.g., tests, medications, treatments, supplies, and a daily rate). The daily rate usually covers three kinds of costs:

- "Hotel" cost for the room;
- Meal costs; and
- Costs of nursing services.

In most hospitals, a different daily rate is charged for different types of care. The private room charge for stays in the intensive care unit, for example, is higher than the private room charge for stays in the obstetrics unit. Within each unit, however, all patients are charged the same daily rate for the same type of room.

The Alexandria hospital recognized that patients in the same unit require and receive different amounts of nursing care and that overall nursing care accounted for about half the total daily rate. There was diversity in service provided, and the amount of money involved was significant.

In a recently installed system[5] designed to measure more accurately how much nursing care each patient requires, each unit's head nurse rates each patient and arrives at a level of "acuity" on a 5-point scale. Level 5 patients in the cardiac care unit, for example, need more than ten times as much nursing care as level 1 patients (twenty-four hours versus two hours). The hospital's financial office uses projected costs and patient mix to compute a nursing service charge per day for each level of acuity, and the patient's bill shows nursing service as a separate line from the daily rate. The result is that each patient's charges more accurately reflect the actual service received. In addition, the acuity ratings are used to prepare a flexible budget for nursing in each unit.

The hospital's new system is actually an ABC system (although the hospital does not call it that). Under the previous system, the activity was "patient care and feeding" (see "Old Way" under Exhibit 3), and the hotel, feeding, and nursing costs were bundled into one cost per day.

The new system redefines the hospital's "product" by specifying characteristics that related to separable activities: "nursing care" and "occupancy and feeding" (see "New Way" under Exhibit 3). The nursing activity is driven by acuity levels. "Occupancy and feeding" was considered a daily cost that was the same for all acuity levels.

UNION PACIFIC[6]

In any given hour, the Union Pacific Railroad operates up to 200 trains, covers over 21,500 route miles (using 2,400 locomotives), and moves some 80,000 freight cars. Thousands of shipments are processed every day, each different from the others. To cost this traffic, Union Pacific uses a form of ABC that is sufficiently real time to recognize that the cost of a particular shipment is influenced by the other shipments that ride with it. Exhibit 4 depicts this system.

If Union Pacific were to use a costing system with one all-encompassing activity, that activity would be "moving freight," and the link to output would be cost per ton mile. But since ton miles of freight are not all alike, Union Pacific devised a system that relates characteristics of freight shipments to activities and the costs of those activities.

Essentially none of the railroad's operating costs relates directly to a shipment; all are support costs. The costs are collected by function and organizational unit. In that form, however, they cannot easily be linked to the distinctive characteristics of shipments. To accomplish this goal, Union Pacific has defined a series of activities that can be linked to shipments and developed a mechanism for collecting the costs of those activities. For example, each shipment will be on a freight car that will be handled one or more times in one or more switching yards (an activity). The route and train specifications determine how many switching minutes will be needed. The cost of that switching activity is an accumulation of several functional

EXHIBIT 3
ALEXANDRIA HOSPITAL: EXAMPLE OF AN ABC IN A HOSPITAL

The Old Way

Costs	Links	Activities	Links	Service Output
Nurses Nursing supervision and support supplies Facilities Dietary Overhead	Costs related to patient nursing, occupancy, and feeding	Patient care, including nursing, occupancy, and feeding	Cost per day (about $500)	A patient day's stay in the hospital

The New Way

Costs	Links	Activities	Links	Service Output
Nurses Nursing supervision and support	Costs related to nursing and acuity level	Nursing care that varies with acuity	Cost per day for each acuity level ($50 to $600)	Nursing service for specified acuity level
Supplies Facilities Dietary Overhead	Costs related to hotel and dietary functions	Occupancy and feeding	Cost per day ($335)	Occupancy per day Total cost per day

EXHIBIT 4
UNION PACIFIC: EXAMPLE OF ABC FOR A RAILROAD

Support Costs[a]	Link	Activity	Link	Service Output or Output Characteristic
Maintenance of ways and structures	Groups of support costs allocated to activities in appropriate ways	Moving freight trains	Cost per gross ton mile	Gross ton miles per shipment
Equipment maintenance and depreciation		Switching freight trains	Cost per yard/train switching minute	Yard/train switching minutes per shipment
Transportation, including switching costs and fuel station platform labor		Handling and depreciation of freight cars	Cost per freight car mile	Freight car miles per shipment
		Handling freight in and out of freight cars	Cost per ton of freight	Tons of freight per shipment Total cost of a specific shipment

[a]Each of these groups of costs corresponded to a function of railroad operation as well as the organization structure, and each group of costs supported three or four of the activities.

Source: Adapted from teaching notes prepared by Professor Robert S. Kaplan for three cases he wrote about Union Pacific in the *Harvard Business School Case Series* (cases 186–176, 186–177, and 186–178).

support costs, such as maintenance of track in the yards, depreciation and maintenance of switching equipment, and labor costs in the yards.

Union Pacific's system enables it to develop the actual cost of each shipment, gathering data each day from many locations on movements of trains and shipments. Furthermore, by using the same activity cost information, Union Pacific can estimate the cost of future shipments, which helps the marketing department identify profitable business.

EXHIBIT 5
ADDITIONAL AMTRAK: EXAMPLE OF ABC FOR A RAILROAD

Costs and Activities	Percent	Link	Service Output
Train and engine crews[a]	18%	Direct charge	Trip-specified consist
Fuel	11	Estimate based on route specs	Trip-specified consist
Yard and mainline operations; other transp.	6	Cost per train trip	Trip
Locomotive maintenance	6	Locomotive miles	Trip-specified locomotive(s)
Car maintenance	18	Cost per car miles (80%) and trips (20%)	Trip-specified consist
Maintenance of way	3	Rate per train unit per track mile	Trip
Onboard service	10	Direct charge	Trip-specified consist
Station services	3	Cost per route and per train	Trip-specified route
			Total trip cost
Depreciation, administration, etc.	18	Percentage of total cost	Route-specified frequency
Sales, marketing, reservations	7	Percentage of projected sales	Sales
	100%		Cost of route with a given frequency and consist

[a]Approximate percentage of total cost.

AMTRAK[7]

Although many of Amtrak's costs are similar to Union Pacific's, the unit of service output is different. For Union Pacific, the output is a shipment. For Amtrak, the output is service on a specific route with a defined frequency of trips and a specified makeup of cars and engine (the "consist"). Whereas Union Pacific's diversity of output precluded use of ton miles as the definition of output, Amtrak's diversity meant that the single definition "route miles" would not produce accurate costs. Exhibit 5 depicts Amtrak's costing system.

Cost categories are the same as activities in this instance. Of all the costs listed, only train and engine crews and on-board service are directly related to a train on a route. All the others costs are indirect. Most of them, however, represent activities that are closely related to departments and functions for which costs can be computed without extensive allocation.

For Amtrak, the problem is in defining the links between activities and output. The links between some are easy-fuel, for example. Even though fuel is not metered by train, engineered consumption standards can be reliably used to estimate fuel consumption by route. Maintenance is more difficult, partly because locomotives and cars are shifted around from route to route. Output diversity is also problematical. For example, does a 400-mile trip cause 4 times as much locomotive maintenance as a 100-mile trip? Probably not although Amtrak has used a straight mileage measure (that particular type of diversity was evidently not considered material).

Defining the links between activity usage and product definition may also involve deciding which activity costs should be considered variable. If a strategic, longer-range perspective is taken, all (or almost all) costs are variable. Amtrak has called variable costs "short-term avoidable," a concept that was developed in the political context of decisions about dropping specific routes. Specific costs (or percentages of costs) are defined as short-term avoidable.

For other decisions (about frequency or consist, for example) different definitions of relevant costs are used. A particularly thorny issue has been how to handle costs that follow a step function. A certain station and its staff might be able to handle ten trains a day. Additions in frequency from six to ten trains would, therefore, cause no increase in cost, but adding an eleventh train would increase costs significantly. Should the linkage between activity and "product" assume average activity cost or somehow recognize the actual costs? In the expectation that a series of decisions are likely to come along, average costs probably make more sense.

With Amtrak, defining service output and support activities has been fairly clear: Establishing the links between the two, however, has proven difficult.

DATA SERVICES, INC.[8]

Data Services, Inc., a subsidiary of Armistead Insurance Company, was set up to market Armistead's unused third shift of computer time. By the end of two years, Data Services had established a service that provided data analysis for about forty fast-food franchisors, each with varying numbers of units. The data analysis was performed on each unit. The number of units per franchise ranged from under five to several hundred. Data Services charged an installation fee and a monthly service fee per unit. Unfortunately, the operation taken as a whole was not profitable. Armistead Insurance Company wanted to know what the trouble was.

This case requires defining the service output in a way that will suggest useful links to the support activities. Data Services was not just selling computer time. The company was providing an information system that required four types of support activities:

• Selling the system;
• Installing the system;

- Maintaining relations with each franchisor: and
- Processing data from each unit.

There were costs associated with each of these activities although Data Services charged only for installation and data processing.

Exhibit 6 depicts Data Services' old and new ways of costing its service output. Under the new system, the costs that were previously collected by function were allocated to the three distinct activities shown in the center column of Exhibit 6. This allocation made it possible for Data Services to compute the cost of acquiring a customer (including the installation costs) and the cost of servicing a customer (including the cost of monthly visits to each franchisor's headquarters plus the cost of servicing each of the franchisor's units). The issues involved in determining pricing and market strategy for Data Services focused on the different sizes of franchisors. Specifically, what was the relative profitability of franchisors of different sizes, and how should that information influence Data Services' marketing and pricing? Only by separating out customer acquisition costs and linking service costs to different sizes of customers could Data Services see the strategic reorientation needed to become profitable. The result was that Data Services charged higher per-unit fees for small franchisors and paid special attention to streamlining the customer-acquisition process.

ABC FOR SERVICE INDUSTRIES

The two questions stated at the beginning of this article were whether ABC could be used in service enterprises and, if so, whether doing so presented any special challenges. To answer the first question, it appears that ABC can indeed be useful to service enterprises, at least in some instances. Robin Cooper and Robert S. Kaplan have pointed out the conditions that make manufacturing enterprises good candidates for ABC (e.g., diversity of resource consumption; products and resource consumption not correlated with traditional, volume-based allocation measures).[9] The implication is that while ABC is useful in some manufacturing enterprises, it may not be useful in others.

The Cooper-Kaplan conditions also apply to service enterprises. All the examples described in this article show diversity of resource consumption. Traditional allocation bases fail to capture that diversity:

- In the Alexandria hospital example, patients require different levels of nursing care. Although this diversity is significant, it was missed altogether by the all-in-one rate that the hospital had formerly used in charging patients.
- In the Union Pacific example, the cost differences between shipments was not captured by a gross-ton-mile measure.
- In the Amtrak example, the cost of a route could not be computed accurately using a single measure such as route miles.
- In the Data Services example, the varying size of customers in terms of units served per franchisor created output diversity. The all-inclusive monthly expense for servicing franchisors did not reflect that diversity.

Identifying and costing activities. Identifying and costing activities may reveal opportunities for more effi-

---

EXHIBIT 6
DATA SERVICES, INC.: ACTIVITY-BASED PRODUCT COSTING IN A SERVICE INDUSTRY

The Old Way

Costs	Links	Activities	Links	Services
Data entry		Running Data	Cost per month or	Data analysis service
Service agents		services (the total	year	for customers
SG&A		enterprise)		
Computer				
Travel, etc.				

The New Way

Costs	Links	Activities	Links	Services
Data entry	Cost of specific	Customer acquisi-	Cost per succesful	Customer under
Service agents	visits	tion and installation	customer acquisition	contract
SG&A	Travel, analysis			Total customer
Computer	Setup			acquisition cost
Travel, etc.				
	Cost of specific	Servicing cus-	Cost per month per	Customer
	visits	tomers	customer company	satisfaction
	Travel			
	Cost of data	Servicing units	Cost per unit or	Data reports to the
	analysis		shift served	units
				Total customer
				service cost

cient operations. The Data Services case provides an example because Data Services chose to isolate and cost out customer acquisition activities. This decision made it possible to focus on opportunities to streamline the selling process. These opportunities might not have been discovered if the company had not learned how high the selling costs really were.

Special challenges. The differences between service enterprises are at least as great as the differences between service and manufacturing enterprises as a whole. However, service companies and manufacturing companies can present similar problems. Schrader Bellows and Data Services, for example, have much in common: both have product setup costs and other costs that vary with volume. Both must also grapple with strategic issues about selling and pricing products with varying unit volumes.

However, service enterprises can present special difficulties in allocating costs to activities. Consider, for example, the hospital trauma center. Certain personnel and facilities costs are directly attributable to the center. But the center also draws on other resources, such as helicopter transportation, laboratory work, and regular nurses, physicians, and staff. Specifying resource use by the trauma center is difficult, so it is not easy to define the links between the trauma center as an element in the hospital's strategy and the activities that support it. The need to be responsive to unpredictable external demands adds another element of uncertainty. Service cannot be inventoried, so unused capacity is often an unavoidable cost.

Output diversity. Service enterprises also present difficulties in defining output diversity. In manufacturing, parts are specified, and it is clear when one product uses many parts and another uses only a few. But in service settings, diversity that draws on support activities in different ways may be hard to pin down. For example, a bank's checking account customers do not all use the same services or provide the same revenue. To try to control this tendency, some banks have begun to segment customers and offer varying service packages. Each package drives a known mix of activities that the bank hopes will please the customer and that will have a predictable cost. Such a strategy does not eliminate diversity, but it does make the diversity somewhat more measurable.

Some service enterprises have quite clearly definable measures of output diversity and clear links between relevant output characteristics and support activities. The four cases described in this article are examples. Other service enterprises are far more difficult to analyze. For such companies, implementing an ABC system would be expensive and the benefits of doing so would be questionable: The information produced is likely to have a wide range of uncertainty.[10] In such situations the basic framework used in Exhibits 2–6 can still be followed but without the efforts to quantify the links. Certain kinds of service may be known as "hard to execute." As a result, they may draw excessively on support activities. In a printing plant, for example, certain jobs with tight schedules may require more attention than jobs with more relaxed timetables. The jobs with tight schedules interrupt the smooth flow of work and place extra burdens on setup activity.

Other support activities may be identified as not being essential to the service strategy. Although this framework fails to quantify costs and relationships, the conclusion that can be drawn from it can still prove helpful.

ABC can be successfully applied in some service enterprises. It provides an analytical framework that can be useful even in settings where it would be impractical actually to quantify costs and relationships.

Notes

1. A number of articles have described and analyzed ABC systems in the past few years. At the center of these is Robin Cooper's four-part series called "The Rise of Activity-Based Costing" in the *Journal of Cost Management:* "Part One: What Is an Activity-Based Cost System?" (Summer 1988): 45–53; "Part Two: When Do I Need an Activity-Based Cost System?" (Fall 1988): 41–48; "Part Three: How Many Cost Drivers Do You Need, and How Do You Select Them?" (Winter 1989): 34–54; "Part Four: What Do Activity-Based Cost Systems Look Like?" (Spring 1989): 38–49.

Note also these other important articles on ABC systems: H. Thomas Johnson, "Activity-Based Information: Blueprint for World-Class Management,." *Management Accounting* (June 1988): 23–30; Robin Cooper and Robert S. Kaplan, "Measure Costs Right: Make the Right Decisions," *Harvard Business Review* (September–October 1988): 986.

An application of ABC is described in the following articles: Gary B. Frank, Steven A. Fisher. and Allen R. Wilkie, "Linking Cost to Price and Profit," *Management Accounting* (June 1989): 22.

Among the cases that deal with ABC systems are the following: Robin Cooper, "Schrader Bellows," *Harvard Business School Case Series, 186–272;* Robert S. Kaplan, "John Deere Component Works (A) and (B)," *Harvard Business School Case Series 187–107/108;* Robin Cooper and Peter B. B. Turney, "Tektronix: Portable Instruments Division (A), (B), and (C)," *Harvard Business School Case Series 188–142/143/144;* Robin Cooper and K. H. Wruck, "Siemens Electric Motor Works (A) and (B)," *Harvard Business School Case Series 189–089/90.*

2. See Cooper, "Schrader Bellows."

3. See Cooper and Wruck, "Siemens Electric Motor Works."

4. See, e.g., W. E. Sasser, R. P. Olsen, and D. D. Wyckoff, *Management of Service Operations* (Boston: Allyn and Bacon, 1978).

5. This system is described in William Rotch and W. Schell, "Alexandria Hospital." *University of Virginia Darden Graduate Business School Case No. UVA-C-2007* (1987).

6. This system is described in Robert S. Kaplan, "Union Pacific Introduction, (A) and (B)," *Harvard Business School Case Series 186–176/177/178.*

7. This system is described in William Rotch and S. Allen, "Amtrack Auto-Ferry Service," *University of Virginia Darden Graduate Business School Case No. UVA-C-988.*

8. The names of these entities have been disguised. This cost system is described in J. L. Colley. Jr., R. A. Gary IV, J. C. Reid, and R. C. Simpson III, "Data Services, Inc. (B)," *University of Virginia Darden Graduate Business School Case No. UVA-OM-582.*

9. See Cooper and Kaplan, "Measure Costs Right: Make the Right Decisions."

10. See "The Rise of Activity-Based Costing—Part Two: When Do I Need an Activity-Based Cost System?" Cooper discusses the cost/benefit balance. If applied to many service enterprises, the cost curve will rise steeply with increasing accuracy requirements, and the benefit curve, shown as the cost of errors, will be uncertain. See also Robin Cooper, "You Need a New Cost System When. . . ," *Harvard Business Review,* (January–February 1989): 77–82, in which he uses the same cost/benefit curves.

William Rotch is the Johnson and Higgins Professor of Business Administration at Darden Graduate School of Business Administration at the University of Virginia in Charlottesville.

From W. Rotch, "Activity-Based Costing in Service Industries," *Journal of Cost Management* (Summer 1990): 4–14. Reprinted with permission.

Question

6.2 Rotch cites examples of outputs in service organizations. List three of these. Do you think that they are different from outputs in manufacturing organizations? Why?

6.3 Activity-Based Total Quality Management at American Express

By David A. Carlson and S. Mark Young

Product costing and a quality strategy are related in the sense that both seek answers to the difficult questions of how and where information workers spend their time. This article illustrates how activity-based costing contributes not only to the achievement of accurate product costs, but also to improved quality at American Express Integrated Payment Systems (IPS). Activity costs at IPS were determined by asking each manager to estimate the time that his department spends on each activity, then splitting those activity estimates across each product line. To achieve the objectives of total quality management (TQM), these activity costs were augmented with perceptual data that various stakeholders expressed about the activities. The article suggests how similar approaches to TQM can benefit other service organizations or the service functions of manufacturing companies.

At American Express, a commitment to total quality management (TQM) comes from the top. The Chairman, CEO, and Chief Quality Officer at American Express is James D. Robinson III, who stresses that quality must be integrated with business strategy. As a result, business unit heads must present their strategy for quality improvements as part of their annual budget and business plans.

As of 1992, each American Express business unit must undergo a self-assessment based on the criteria specified in the guidelines for the Malcolm Baldrige National Quality Award. American Express wants to ensure that its investments in training and technology are paying off.

Will the changes at the American Express business units improve the bottom line? The activity-based costing (ABC) method used at American Express Integrated Payment Systems (IPS) in Denver can help answer this question.[1]

TQM AND ABC AT AMERICAN EXPRESS

IPS manages one of the oldest financial services American Express has: American Express Money Orders. Introduced in 1882, customers use money orders to pay bills and make mail-order purchases. Money orders provide a stable source of income that has helped support IPS's entry into markets for similar financial services, including:

- American Express MoneyGram, which is a relatively new and rapidly growing service that lets consumers transfer funds around the world, usually within minutes;
- American Express Official Checks, which are negotiable instruments that financial institutions use as substitutes for their own disbursement items (e.g., teller checks and loan checks); and
- Cash Management Services, a service that works as an electronic clearinghouse to collect, concentrate, and disburse funds and data for corporations and financial institutions.

Early in 1990, IPS instituted a TQM philosophy that would involve all 1,000 employees in the Denver metro area. Charlie Fote, the president of IPS, hired Brian Higgins as director of quality assurance to lead this initiative.

Fote and other IPS executives were unaware of any particularly troublesome quality problems; in fact, IPS was (and remains) a service leader in the markets it serves. Instead, the reason for pursuing TQM was to expand IPS's competitive advantages by improving service and to increase income without increasing costs.

Defining continuous improvement. Defining continuous improvement in a service organization is a difficult task. In defining and measuring quality, the quality assurance staff at IPS tried to answer the following questions:

- In the spirit of TQM, how do our customers and suppliers feel about the reliability of the activities we perform or about the contribution that those activities make toward their requirements?

- What do our employees do that contributes value to our services or that advances our company's mission?
- Conversely, what do our employees do that does not contribute value?

THE RESTRUCTURING IMPERATIVE

In an article in the *Harvard Business Review,* Stephen S. Roach states:

> Services need an accounting framework that can identify which activities add the most value . . . . Activity-based managerial accounting is a step in the right direction, but much more work in this area remains to be done . . . . It should go without saying that a metric for quality is equally important. Admittedly, quality in the service sector is hard to define.2

As this quotation suggests, the improvement of white-collar productivity has not been embraced by business leaders, probably because of the nature of knowledge work. Poor productivity is difficult (if not impossible) to remedy. Many people consider knowledge work unstructured, self-directed, and intangible. It is often difficult to relate activity costs to the value provided. Nonetheless, improving white-collar productivity is not a hopeless task. Many managers simply do not understand the difficulties associated with assessing and improving the productivity of knowledge workers; they also lack the tools needed to adequately address the problem. IPS appears to have made important progress, however.

ACTIVITY-BASED TQM

The TQM initiative at IPS began by getting all employees involved in continuous improvement efforts. Customer satisfaction, vendor satisfaction, and employee satisfaction were processes that were assessed regularly, and efforts were made to gain a better understanding of the activities and performance measures at IPS.

Activity analysis began in the customer service department and telephone operations and quickly became interwoven with concerns about product costing. In particular, senior management wanted to manage growth better by gaining a better understanding of the fixed versus variable costs for each product line. Product costing was connected with the quality strategy because both efforts tried to answer the difficult questions of how and where information workers spent their time.

ABC is central to recent efforts to redesign cost accounting systems to account for a wide variety of changes that have occurred in high-technology manufacturing and service firms. These changes require accountants and all other employees to alter their mindsets away from cost accounting toward "cost management." Cost management emphasizes an active approach to planning and managing an organization's costs, whereas cost accounting usually focuses on the historical reporting of costs.[3]

Cost management integrates consideration of corporate strategy, which leads to the notion of strategic cost management (SCM),[4] which is closely related to the functional administrative control technique (FACT) approach used at IPS (see Exhibit 1). Managers at IPS have explicitly tied the

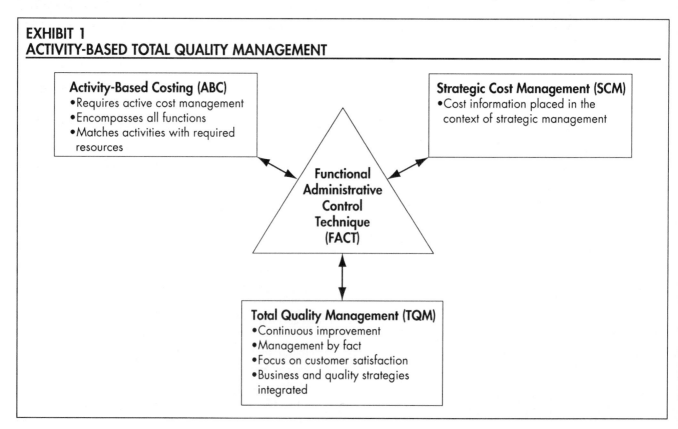

EXHIBIT 1
ACTIVITY-BASED TOTAL QUALITY MANAGEMENT

Activity-Based Costing (ABC)
- Requires active cost management
- Encompasses all functions
- Matches activities with required resources

Strategic Cost Management (SCM)
- Cost information placed in the context of strategic management

Functional Administrative Control Technique (FACT)

Total Quality Management (TQM)
- Continuous improvement
- Management by fact
- Focus on customer satisfaction
- Business and quality strategies integrated

results of FACT studies to achievement of the company's TQM strategy and its product strategies.

VALUE ENGINEERING

The FACT approach has its roots not in accounting but in value engineering, which is a technique for increasing the value of a product or organization rather than simply decreasing its cost. A product-oriented value engineering study, for example, would first create a functional description of a physical product, then map the product's parts onto the functions that those parts perform. Thus, a costed functional description is produced. Customers' requirements are balanced with the costs of the functions in assessing value.

Cross-functional analysis. During the 1960s, General Electric refined some of the value engineering disciplines developed during the 1940s, which had proved useful in reducing material costs. GE's refinement, which is called *cross-functional analysis,* was designed to examine cross-functional effort applied to organizational activities.

Using cross-functional analysis, a business model is constructed that contains the activities performed throughout an entity. Typically, 150-200 such activities are defined and grouped into major business processes. Effort and cost are then recast into this business model. The contribution of each functional organization is examined to identify specific activities that are unique or that contain duplication, redundancy, or overlap. An organization's resources are then redeployed—added to some activities or reduced in others—to increase the value of the business to employees and to customers. Brian Higgins worked as a value engineer when he began designing FACT in 1972; his efforts began with no knowledge of GE's cross-functional analysis.[5]

PHASES OF A FACT PROJECT PLAN

As Exhibit 2 shows, FACT uses a five-phase project plan for analyzing and improving organizational performance. Although the duration of a complete FACT project varies according to the scope and complexity of the organization, a project can usually be completed within sixteen weeks.

Project planning phase. The first phase—the project planning phase—is guided by the FACT project leader, who carefully selects a small team to conduct the study. Depending on the scope of the project, from two to ten people may be required, either part or full time. The project leader typically introduces the objectives and plan for the FACT study in a meeting of all managers involved.

Data collections phase. In the data collection phase, FACT project team members gather information by using standardized data collection forms. They conduct interviews with three questions in mind:

1. What does the organization do?
2. What does it cost to do what it does?

3. What is the acceptance or worth of what it does?

Interviewers use questions that provoke managers, customers, and vendors to identify problem areas and possible opportunities for change. Interviewees are asked to imagine how the organization would look if everything worked perfectly, then to respond to the questions accordingly.

For each primary activity that affects the interviewee, three questions are asked:

1. If the organization worked in the most efficient and effective manner, how would things be organized, and how would the activity be performed?
2. What inhibits the organization from working in the most efficient and effective manner?
3. How else can the activity be provided?

Final three phases. The last three phases of a FACT project plan are crucial for building consensus among the team members and management. Specialized corrective action teams are established at the start of the data analysis phase. These teams champion changes through the collaborative participation of all affected individuals, departments, customers, and suppliers. A corrective action team retains control of the project until final recommendations are presented to management, and often until final implementation is completed.

As Higgins points out, crucial assumptions are made when (as in many traditional accounting systems) a large proportion of product costs are allocated from pools of overhead expense. One half of IPS's expenses, for example, were allocated overhead, but the accountants at IPS admitted that they were comfortable with only 15 percent of the allocations.

EXHIBIT 2
FACT PROJECT PLAN

☐ **Project Planning**
  • Understand the scope and structure of the organization to be studied
  • Establish the hierarchy of activities
  • Plan the duration of the project and identify critical milestones

☐ **Data Collection**
  • Interview all managers, and selected customers and vendors
  • Document interviews
  • Enter data into FACT database

☐ **Synthesis**
  • Run reports from FACT database
  • Identify major issues

☐ **Data Analysis**
  • Select opportunities for change
  • Perform analyses using FACT data
  • Identify preliminary recommendations

☐ **Recommendations**
  • Prepare final report
  • Present recommendations to executive management

For example, data processing expenses were allocated to products based on the volume of transactions. Since IPS processes hundreds of thousands of money order transactions per day, money orders received the lion's share of data processing allocations, even though everyone admitted that MoneyGram's on-line systems were more CPU-intensive per transaction. Higgins concludes, "You have to question the assumptions people made when their decisions are based on allocating huge overhead pools to products. Such assumptions are often wrong!" By directly allocating expenses to activities and to products, a more accurate picture can be obtained.

DEFINING ACTIVITIES

The foundation of the FACT model lies in the concept of an activity—i.e., a response to the question "What does the organization do?"

An activity can best be stated as a brief verb-noun description of a process: for example, "resolve customer problems" or "coordinate corrective action." Unlike GE's cross-functional analysis and many applications of ABC, FACT derives significant benefits from using a hierarchical structure of activities (see Exhibit 3). Thus, a response to the question "How is an activity performed?" leads from left to right in Exhibit 3 from the general to the more specific activities in the hierarchy.

Conversely, a response to the question "Why is an activity performed?" leads from specific to more general activities (i.e., from right to left in Exhibit 3). This structure permits both macro- and micro-level analyses of an organization. The level of detail expressed by these activities depends on the purpose for which the FACT model will be used.

FACT has been applied to individual work groups as small as five people as well as to organizations having 1,000 employees and overhead expenses exceeding $60 million. In small departments, for example, the activities may address such, processes as "document customer problem" or

"reconcile invoices," whereas in large organizations the activities are conceptualized at a higher level (e.g., "research market," "establish pricing," or "identify inventory variation"). Exhibit 3 shows the top levels of an activity hierarchy for IPS.

LINKING ACTIVITIES TO BUSINESS AND QUALITY STRATEGIES

FACT begins by defining the costed hierarchy of activities, but it does not end there. An activity structure provides the basis for assembling information that can later be used in creating and evaluating solutions to problems and in linking activities to business and quality strategies (see Exhibit 4).

Managers follow an incremental process for constructing an organizational model that begins with the definition of a costed activity set. Each activity's cost is determined by assigning a fraction of each person's time (and therefore salary) or a fraction of a departmental expense item to a particular activity. Thus, all the organization's costs are allocated to the activity hierarchy. The fractions are determined by a variety of methods (e.g., time sampling or interviews with managers), depending on the scope of the organization. Once costs are allocated, additional information is collected and related to the model.

NONFINANCIAL INFORMATION

The principal nonfinancial information used consists of attitudes of customers and suppliers—those who receive the outputs of the organization and those who supply its inputs. This attitudinal information includes both quantified variables and statements of perceptions (see the box "Customer and Supplier Comments" in Exhibit 4).

Quantified data consists of rating each activity for its contribution and reliability on ten-point scales. Perceptual

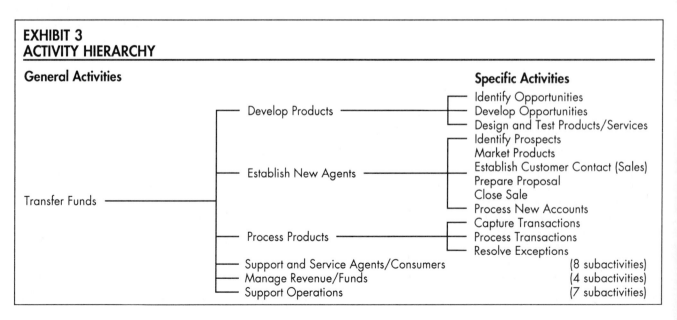

EXHIBIT 3
ACTIVITY HIERARCHY

General Activities		Specific Activities

Transfer Funds
- Develop Products
  - Identify Opportunities
  - Develop Opportunities
  - Design and Test Products/Services
- Establish New Agents
  - Identify Prospects
  - Market Products
  - Establish Customer Contact (Sales)
  - Prepare Proposal
  - Close Sale
  - Process New Accounts
- Process Products
  - Capture Transactions
  - Process Transactions
  - Resolve Exceptions
- Support and Service Agents/Consumers — (8 subactivities)
- Manage Revenue/Funds — (4 subactivities)
- Support Operations — (7 subactivities)

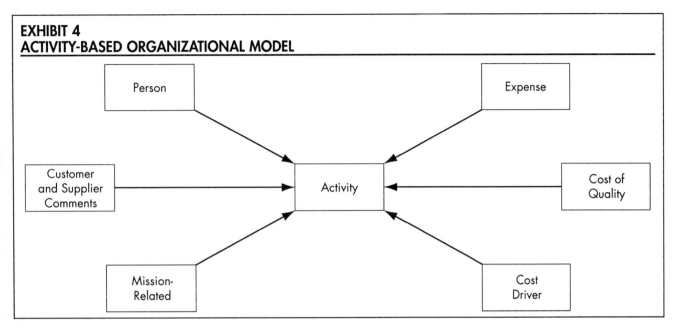

EXHIBIT 4
ACTIVITY-BASED ORGANIZATIONAL MODEL

data includes verbal comments that provide either favorable or unfavorable opinions about one or more activities. This data is crucial for satisfying the objectives of TQM. The Malcolm Baldridge criteria place 30 percent of their emphasis on customer satisfaction; the activity hierarchy provides a framework for comprehensive assessment of satisfaction across the total business.

CLASSIFYING ACTIVITIES AS MISSION-RELATED OR NOT

Each activity is also classified as being either mission-related or not (see Exhibit 4). Information about cost drivers—i.e., those events or environmental situations that cause costs to be incurred—may also be associated with each activity. These two information sources work in tandem to tell managers which activities contribute to accomplishing business strategies and how costs are generated.

COST OF QUALITY

Activities may be associated with one of the four "cost of quality" categories (i.e., prevention, appraisal, internal failure, and external failure) or with the "cost of business" (e.g., advertising or production).

Many companies have spent years developing an accounting system that can estimate the cost of quality (though few service organizations attempt such analyses). Using FACT, however, an accurate estimate can be produced in a matter of hours. Although many people express disbelief that the cost of quality can be computed so quickly, with an activity and cost database as extensive as the one developed for a FACT study, the assignment becomes straightforward. The activities are so detailed that each one is simply assigned to a cost of quality category or split between two categories. (The activity "train agents," for example, is a cost of prevention,

while "resolve customer problems" is a cost of external failure.) Computing cost of quality thus becomes trivial; all that has to be done is to sum the activity costs in each category.

A FACT study is a relatively short—but intensive—process. After data is collected, the information is entered into a proprietary software program, which produces summary reports for analysis. The study of all 1,000 employees at IPS took about two months to gather all the data, then another two months to analyze the data and to develop initial recommendations. Since the FACT team consisted of twelve part-time members, it was possible to conduct the study without disrupting ongoing organizational processes.

RESTRUCTURING THROUGH FACT ANALYSIS

In discussions of advanced manufacturing technologies, it is often stated that implementation of just-in-time processes uncovers a "hidden factory" of overhead expenses for logistical, balancing, quality, and change transactions, all of which account for a large portion of the effort expended in production.[6] Similarly, service organizations may discover overhead expenses that were previously obscure by identifying "hidden service providers." This point is clearly illustrated by a situation uncovered through the FACT study at IPS. The following example provides a fictionalized example of this situation.

Example of MIS manager. John, the vice-president of management information systems at IPS, spends several thousands of dollars each year traveling to customer sites. Under the conventional accounting system, these expenses were charged to the travel accounting in his department. Meanwhile, directors of customer service departments for each product line reviewed their respective budgets and believed they were managing all costs of customer service. As FACT revealed, however, customer service costs were higher than the costs indicated by the conventional cost system. Since 100 percent of John's travel was related to supporting customers and resolving their problems, all his travel costs were allocated to the subactivities "support and service agents and consumers." As this example shows, IPS discovered that John was a hidden service provider; the true cost of customer service was higher than had been thought.

Example of controller. The controller at IPS also discovered hidden service providers. Costs related to the activity "administer financials" range far beyond the Accounting Department's budget as it exists in typical cost accounting systems. At first glance, the controller believed that the FACT data were wrong, because the reported costs were twice what he expected. After reviewing the details, however, he agreed that the numbers were right. Managers throughout the company "help" the controller with such activities as "budget/forecast operations" or "document employee travel and entertainment expenses (T&E)." Similarly, in the Human Resources Department, all managers contribute to the activities "hire exempt employees" or "review employee performance." In each of the three examples, the actual cost incurred to provide these activities far exceeds the apparent cost shown in the respective department's budget.

The realization that actual activity costs often significantly exceed or fall short of presumed costs is of central importance in promoting and guiding restructuring. Restructuring is promoted by creating disenchantment with the status quo; it is guided by providing a sound basis for restructuring decisions.

PROMOTING EFFORTS TO RESTRUCTURE

Managers resist change[7]—or, at least, they resist unfounded or unjustified change. Once a foundation has been laid and changes justified, however, resistance quickly breaks down and may even turn into enthusiasm.

The examples of hidden service providers given previously illustrate one way that resistance to change was overcome at IPS. Other means were used that were also based on the data collected during the initial phases of FACT. Pareto analysis, which is commonly taught as an analytical technique in quality circles, involves sorting a set of items into descending order and focusing quality improvements on the top of the list—i.e., on the largest items.

A Pareto analysis of activity costs is illuminating; managers are often surprised to discover how large a fraction of total cost occurs because of only a few activities. It is also surprising to note *which* activities show up at the top of the list. Managers often have an intuition that the cost of some activity is too high, but intuition alone cannot justify significant investments. The relative positions of activity costs, however, can provide information that was previously unavailable for justifying corrective investments. A similar list of activity costs can be produced for each category of

the cost of quality. Having this list allows managers to focus on the top offenders in each area.

Focusing attention on the top of a sorted list, however, tells only one half of the story. When Higgins gave one IPS executive an eight-page list of activity costs for the Money-Gram product, the executive was prepared to throw away the last seven pages and focus on reducing the largest activity costs on page one. Higgins, however, pointed out that the activities at the bottom of the list are also candidates for attention, because important activities may not be receiving enough resources. For example, a costly activity at the top of the list may represent an internal or external failure cost, while an ignored activity at the bottom of the list may represent a preventive item that, with a small investment, could dramatically reduce the failure-related activity. This example illustrates the difference between value analysis and cost reduction.

Cross-functional and cross-product summaries of activity costs. Perhaps the most powerful analyses enabled by the FACT process are cross-functional and cross-product summaries of activity costs. A matrix is constructed with an indented list of the activity hierarchy on the left side and either the major functional areas or the product families across the top. As the fictionalized example in Exhibit 5 shows, the percentage of cost allocated to the activity "support and service agents" has a wide variance across products. Exhibit 3 shows that the total cost of this activity is divided among eight subactivities. By itself, this observation is interesting, but of limited value. The obvious next question is "Why?" Fortunately, the FACT model provides a response.

A FACT study includes a record of how each person's time (and therefore salary) is allocated to activities. A department's expense items (other than personnel) are also allocated to the activity. (Note that a department does not allocate its personnel costs as one cost pool.) Thus, if an activity's total cost is out of line or if the cost is oddly split between product lines, the supporting data is easily available for explaining these anomalies. In general, this audit trail of detailed data is crucial for investigating activity costs.

EXHIBIT 5
CROSS-PRODUCT ANALYSIS

Activity	Product A	Product B	Product C
1 Develop Products etc.			
4 Support and Service Agents	3%	7%	5%
41 Receive and Document Inq.	1.5%	2%	2%
42 Handle Agent Problems	0.5%	3.5%	0.7%
43 Supply Agents etc.	1.0%	2.5%	2.3%
Totals	**100%**	**100%**	**100%**

Comparing ratios of activities. If the old cliché "numbers speak louder than words" applies anywhere, it applies here. The numbers are arrived at through a logical estimation process that is validated through a structured interview with each manager.

Although the numbers may be only estimates, the ratios of activity costs provide powerful information. Suppose, for example, that the ratio between the activities "resolve agent problems" and "train agents" is 20:1. Even if the respective costs are off by 10 percent or even by 25 percent, the size of the ratio still suggests a potential problem and a way to solve it—namely, to reduce agent problems by increasing training. A similar conclusion may be drawn from an analysis of the cost of quality. Agent problems (a cost of external failure) may be reduced by investing in agent training (a cost of prevention). The data provided by FACT support either of these analyses.

Cost of quality has been faulted by the quality expert W. Edwards Deming, who asserts that if you focus on process improvement, the cost of quality will take care of itself. The ease of computing cost of quality within the FACT framework, however, can motivate efforts to change the status quo and to restructure.

GUIDING FIRMS IN RESTRUCTURING

To avoid the slash-and-burn mentality of most cost-cutting efforts, a better basis must be provided for decision making. Stephen Roach warns that "cost cutting must be judicious" if service organizations are to avoid the problem that occurred when the manufacturing sector sold its future short by trading long-term capacity requirements for the sake of near-term financial gain.

One of the most useful mechanisms for guiding restructuring is cost driver analysis. Cost drivers cause activities to be performed. They may be positive (customer orders) or negative (customer complaints). By eliminating negative cost drivers, the associated activity costs are also reduced.

During the data collection phase of FACT, each activity is identified as being either mission-related or not (see Exhibit 4). Employees may spend disproportionate time on activities that are not directly related to the mission of their work group. Efforts to restructure the organization should focus on shifting effort toward mission-related activities. For example, are members of the sales department performing the activity "close sales," or are they instead "resolving agent problems" or "preparing department reports"? Only the first activity contributes to the department's mission.

Major work activities are often diffused across the organization. Many different individuals may be involved in an activity that represents only a few full-time-equivalent employees. When activities are highly fragmented, they should automatically be subjected to further analysis. Though some activities should remain distributed among managers, consolidating activities may improve performance. (Budgeting, personnel reviews, and similar tasks are examples of normally fragmented activities that contribute to effective management.)

EMPOWERMENT VS. ENFORCEMENT

The way that FACT information is used can have an important impact. This warning is especially true in promoting a successful TQM strategy, which must have the support and involvement of every employee. If a company uses data about misallocations of resources as a stick that is used to beat people, employees are unlikely to give their heartfelt commitment to creating and implementing improvements or to producing accurate estimates of activity costs.

Downsizings. There are exceptional situations when an activity-based analysis is the best means for quickly downsizing an organization that is having severe profitability problems. Unless FACT is carefully managed, however, it is likely to be viewed as an axe for paring organizational fat. While this approach is superior to the slash-and-burn mentality that cuts necessary activities along with the fat, the benefits are unlikely to become long-term, strategic changes.

The approach IPS uses seeks to empower corrective action teams to develop and implement changes. These teams are armed with copious data for guiding their efforts in the most fruitful directions. FACT process facilitators serve as consultants to the corrective action teams by helping them interpret their data and teaching them additional data analysis techniques to restructure their respective organizations, to refocus their efforts, and to refine their processes. This approach is consistent with TQM objectives (e.g., instilling attitudes to promote continuous improvement and establishing quantitative performance measures to assess quality level and monitor improvement).

IMPLICATIONS FOR SERVICE ORGANIZATIONS

At IPS, FACT has provided valuable insight into operations and yielded substantial savings in several operational areas. Not surprisingly, FACT uncovered information that could result from a similar study conducted in a manufacturing organization, including:

• High cost areas;
• Costs for systems changes; and
• A more accurate estimation of overhead costs.

At IPS, however, the study went further to identify less tangible—but no less valuable—opportunities for quality improvement.

"The study was helpful in creating a fact base for potential organizational improvements," said Eula Adams, an executive vice-president at IPS who has twenty years of audit experience at a large accounting firm. "In the past, these kinds of changes at service firms were driven largely by opinion—by what people thought would work. Our study

123

provides a solid fact base and, consequently, justification for changing the organization."

Support for organizational improvements. According to Adams, the study garnered support for organizational improvements by identifying areas of overlap and duplication and by focusing attention on non-value-added activities. "Overlap and noncontributing areas are usually fairly evident in manufacturing environments, but that wasn't necessarily the case in the service sector, until now. This study was helpful in identifying those opportunities and indicating how we might address them."

Bob Kuhnemund, the chief financial officer at IPS, agrees with Adams's assessment. He believes that the study is helping to link customer satisfaction to specific organizational activities. "In addition to hard numbers, it helped us develop an understanding for mission-related activities—what's hot and what's not. That's extremely helpful from an organizational perspective and can have a dramatic impact on overhead costs—reducing in some areas and increasing in others."

Documented savings. Just two months after the FACT study was completed and results tabulated, IPS documented savings in several areas totaling more than $1 million. While creating considerable savings, the changes also created some equally dramatic customer service improvements.

Dan Carrington, vice-president of MoneyGram Operations at IPS, stated that information from FACT led to new ways of streamlining the operating processes of some very important customer functions for MoneyGram. "Normally," he said, "improvements like these are associated with large one-time expenses. But we realized savings of $350,000 and improved the speed of providing these services. These are the kinds of changes we have to make because we're competing in what many people perceive to be a commodity service area. Also, we have a competitor with more experience; we have to set ourselves apart from their way of doing business."

ABC results. In spite of the rather unlikely emergence of ABC within the Quality Assurance Department at IPS, these testimonials point to the fact that ownership and backing of the FACT approach to cost management transcends the quality function. As Higgins concludes, "The FACT results have now become Accounting's numbers. They own it. But we're also finding out that other areas can own it too—areas like customer service and operations." IPS is currently considering ways of supplementing its existing cost accounting systems with an activity-based approach based on the initial FACT study.

TYING TQM TO THE BOTTOM LINE

The FACT project plan provides a structure and methodology for assessing the current situation: where effort is being expended and what value those efforts have from a customer's viewpoint. An activity-based model is used for this assessment, and a number of approaches have been described for guiding a firm's restructuring decisions. But an answer has not been supplied to the CEO's concern about whether the investment that American Express has made in TQM can be tied to improvements in the bottom line.

Using ABC to quantify expected benefits. The results of TQM efforts in a service organization—changes to processes that affect an activity's performance—can be measured by using activity costs to quantify the expected benefits of the change and by computing a return on investment. For finer resolution, activity costs may be separated by department, product, employee classification (e.g., manager, individual contributor, or clerical), or all of the above to better estimate the benefits of a proposed change.

In relatively small-scale FACT studies, activity costs can be traced according to the percentage of time devoted by individual employees. These cost savings can then be accumulated by activity for an accurate estimate of the benefits derived from TQM. These analyses are often performed within corrective action teams at IPS as they progress through the phases of the FACT project plan.

SUMMARY

In the same article mentioned near the beginning of this article, Stephen Roach concludes by saying: "Only with the proper measurement tools in hand can services assess restructuring options." FACT provides such a tool. Roach suggests that an activity-based value analysis can assist banks in reallocating information technology away from low-value-added activities (e.g., transaction processing and administration) toward more analytical applications (e.g., interest-rate swaps).

To more directly address Roach's concern about redeploying information technology in a firm, FACT might be extended to allocating capital investments to the activity hierarchy. A cross-functional analysis could then yield summaries of information technology investment by functional area for each activity. In a similar manner, both expenses and capital investments could be summarized for those activities related to two or more competitive strategies (or for non-mission-related activities) to analyze the relative cost consumed by each one. If costs of strategies are dramatically out of line with strategic priorities, some form of restructuring would be indicated.

David A. Carlson is assistant professor of information systems at the University of Colorado in Boulder, Colorado. S. Mark Young is associate professor of accounting at the University of Southern California in Los Angeles.

Notes

1. Subsequent to implementing activity-based costing, IPS and a related group of companies within American Express were spun off into First Data Corporation, an independent corporation which is 54 percent owned by American Express. This article continues to refer to the relationship that IPS had with American Express at the time that this study was conducted.

2. See S. S. Roach, "Service Under Siege—The Restructuring Imperative," *Harvard Business Review* (Sept.–Oct. 1991): 82-91.

3. See H. T. Johnson and R. S. Kaplan, *Relevance Lost: The Rise and Fall of Management Accounting* (Boston: Harvard Business School Press, 1987).

4. Strategic cost management, as described by John Shank ("Strategic Cost Management: New Wine, or Just New Bottles?" *Journal of Management Accounting Research* (Fall 1989): 47), calls for integrating strategic considerations into activity-based costing.

5. See T. C. Fowler and B. Higgins, "Organization Analysis Made Easy," *Society of American Value Engineers Conference Proceedings* (Southfield, Mich.: Society of American Value Engineers, 1974): 3.1–3.7; and B. Higgins and C. M. Dice, "Quantifying White-Collar Functions," *National Productivity Review* (Summer 1984): 288–302.

6. See J. G. Miller and T. E. Vollmann, "The Hidden Factory," *Harvard Business Review* (Sept.–Oct. 1985): 142–150.

7. See M. D. Shields and S. M. Young, "A Behavioral Model for Implementing Cost Management Systems," *Journal of Cost Management* (Winter 1989): 17–27, for a summary of the factors that contribute to the resistance of an organization and its employees to change.

From D. Carlson, and S. M. Young, "Activity-Based Total Quality Management at American Express," *Journal of Cost Management* (Spring 1993): 48–58. Reprinted with permission.

Question

6.3 The FACT approach to cost management described in Carlson and Young's article uses nonfinancial information that often is not used in ABC. Why does FACT use this nonfinancial information?

6.4 Unbundling the Cost of Hospitalization
ABC can keep health care providers off the critical list.

By Lawrence P. Carr

In the health care industry, the insurance companies leverage their considerable power by scrutinizing the billing practices of the health care providers. A serious concern of insurers is the cost of hospital nursing care and related services.

Traditionally, the cost of nursing is factored into the daily room charge for a hospital stay. For example, a rate of $500 to $800 per day covers the 24-hour nursing availability for the patient. Nursing expenses, primarily labor costs, are part of the overhead rate comprising the daily $500 to $800 billing to the patient. Charges are aggregate in nature with the same average fixed fee applied to all patients.

The problem with this typical convention is that not all patients use nursing services in equal amounts. Patient utilization of nursing services is individualistic. Fixed charges are not always related to the services rendered. Further, nursing services are available "on call" to handle possible patient emergencies where the value may not be readily quantifiable.

Braintree Hospital is a private rehabilitation hospital providing in-patient and out-patient treatment. It is one of the largest rehabilitation network care providers in the country with 168 beds on site and management contracts covering 200 more beds. Generally patients are referred to Braintree by other hospitals or private physicians.

The patient's average stay is approximately 21 days, during which time the individual progresses through a comprehensive program aimed at restoring and maintaining functional abilities (basic living skills). Patients enter with physical disabilities due to neurological and orthopedic diseases or injury and normally are diagnosed as one of the following: stroke, spinal cord injury, congenital deformity, amputation,

major multiple trauma, fracture of femur, brain injury, polyarthritis & joint replacement, neurological disorders, burns and neoplasms.

An activity-based costing system enabled Boston's Braintree Hospital to satisfy, in the near term, the insurance industry's changing approach to reimbursement. In the medium term, it positioned the hospital to enter the 1990s with the shifting payment paradigm of managed care. Knowing the cost of nursing care provided to each individual patient by diagnosis gave management reliable data to negotiate per diem rates.

NURSING SERVICES PROVIDED

Typically, nursing services in the hospital consist of a varied skill mix: professional registered nurses (RNs), licensed practical nurses (LPNs), and ancillary nursing assistants (NAs). These professionals have different levels of education, training, and hospital experience.

For example, the north wing of the second floor of Braintree Hospital has 43 beds. The nursing staff consists of a nurse manager, RNs, LPNs, and NAs who work varying shifts to cover the unit 24 hours, seven days a week. The staff is reduced for the 11 p.m. to 7:30 a.m. shift due to workload distribution.

Teams of nurses perform many different functions. They administer medication, maintain daily patient records, assist the physicians with medical care, monitor medical devices, conduct routine tests, and so on. They are responsible for the routine jobs of feeding the patients, administering to their bodily needs, bathing, ensuring patient safety,

FIGURE 1 ??? SERVICE CLASSIFICATION FORM

PRIMARY DIAGNOSIS_____

CLASSIFIER'S NAME_____

DATE_____

ADDRESSOGRAPH

PILOT CLASSIFICATION TOOL   DRAFT 3

In each of the following sections, place a check mark in the most appropriate box corresponding to the most complex level of case documented in the past 24 hours.

FEEDING
- A1 ☐ Setup
- A2 ☐ Enteral Feed
- A3 ☐ Distant Supervision
- A4 ☐ 1:1 Supervision
- A5 ☐ Dependent P.O. Feed

MOBILITY
- B1 ☐ Contact Guard, Walker, Independent, Stand Pivot Min-Mod of 1, Sliding Board Independent or Assist Min-Mod of 1
- B2 ☐ Hoyer Lift/Transaid
- B3 ☐ Max of 1, Mod-Max of 2, Stand Pivot, Squat, Sliding Board Max 1

ADL
- C1 ☐ Setup or Min Assist
- C2 ☐ Min-Mod Assist
- C3 ☐ Mod Assist
- C4 ☐ Mod-Max Assist
- C5 ☐ Total Dependence
- C6 ☐ Dependent Shave
- C7 ☐ Dependent Bed Shampoo

MEDICAL
- D1 ☐ Routine Medical Supervision
- D2 ☐ VS Q VShift
- D3 ☐ Assist with M.D. Procedure
- D4 ☐ # of Procedures Performed in 24 Hours
- D5 ☐ Frequent Vital Signs (Q 1-2 hrs over 24 hrs)
- D6 ☐ Precautions, Respiratory
- D7 ☐ Precautions, Wound/Skin, Enteric

MEDICATIONS
- E1 ☐ Routine Meds, P.O.
- E2 ☐ Meds IM, SC
- E3 ☐ Meds PR, Enteral, or Topical
- E4 ☐ Meds PRN (any route)
- E5 ☐ Receiving Meds and/or Hydration IV

ELIMINATION
- F1 ☐ Continent Bowel/Bladder or Continent of Bowel with Foley Catheter
- F2 ☐ Incontinent Bowel and/or Bladder
- F3 ☐ Assist-Dependent Ostomy Care
- F4 ☐ Texas Cath
- F5 ☐ Straight Cath

SAFETY/BEHAVIOR/PSYCH-SOC/TEACHING
- G1 ☐ Teaching, Psych/Soc Support, Safety Interventions (Non-Aggitated Patient)
- G2 ☐ Q 15 Minute Safety Checks by M.D. Order
- G3 ☐ 1:1 Observation
- G4 ☐ # Shifts
- G5 ☐ Skill (RN, LPN, RT, NA)
- G6 ☐ Frequent Aggressive or Aggitated Behavior Requiring Intervention of Only 1 Staff Member
- G7 ☐ Frequent Aggressive or Aggitated Behavior Requiring Intervention More Than 1 Staff Member

SKIN CARE
- H1 ☐ Routine Skin Care, Includes Topical Treatments
- H2 ☐ Wound Care
- H3 ☐ # Treatments in 24 Hrs.
- H4 ☐ Central Line

RESPIRATORY
- I1 ☐ Routine TCDB, 02 Equipment
- I2 ☐ Routine Tracheostomy Care (include up to one additional suctioning per shift)
- I3 ☐ Requires Suctioning Two or More Times Per Shift
- I4 ☐ Manage Meds by Nebulizer Incentive Spirometry, Humidification

and evaluating the care provided. Perhaps most important, they provide personal comfort and care for the patient.

The professional RN is licensed and can perform all of the many nursing functions in the hospital. But he or she concentrates primarily on the more intense and demanding patients and functions. At the same time, RNs are responsible for the delivery of care to a specific group of patients on a floor or ward.

The other nursing team members normally work with the RNs to deliver care to their group of patients. Thus, the array of services is delivered by a team with varying skill levels. There is a hierarchy of nursing from the RN to the NA with the top level capable of doing all of the functions of the levels be low. Pay scales vary from $26 per hour to $8 per hour, depending on the personal skill/educational level and specific position.

As you might imagine, there is a wide variation in the amount of nursing services consumed by patients, just as there is a wide variety of patient ailments that require differing degrees of nursing attention. The health care industry has recognized this phenomenon, and third-party payers are pushing very hard to pay only for services used by the patient and at the lowest price.

Patients are becoming more aware of and interested in the distribution of care and the inherent costs, probably due to the economy and media attention focused on health care costs. Such comments as, "Mrs. Smith is getting all of the nursing attention. She needs it and, thankfully, I don't, but I have to pay for it. This doesn't seem fair," are quite common.

NO HARD DATA

Mary-Jean Crockett, the progressive-thinking vice president of nursing, recognized that nursing services delivery needed to be understood better. She felt the growing pressure from the insurance companies that pay for most of Braintree's patient care and heard the "buzz" at national professional conferences. She was determined to find an easy, reliable, and fair method to ascertain the amount, mix, and resulting cost of nursing services consumed by individual patients. She also wanted a more accurate approach to forecasting the skill mix associated with care of the different diagnostic groups. She remained cognizant that she also needed to monitor the high level of quality, comfort, and safety that leads to positive patient outcomes.

Two years ago, Mary-Jean initiated the nursing services analysis project by chairing a project team of nurses and administrators. Team members included the staff development instructor, nursing MIS project manager, and the nursing supervisor/coordinator of quality assurance. All the team members worked as staff members on the nursing care units and were familiar with the actual work flow at Braintree.

After the first organizational meeting and the sharing of the concerns for the nursing service issues, the team realized it had no hard data upon which to make its assessment. Everyone had anecdotal stories with the constant theme of the imbalance between the actual delivered nursing and the fixed single billing rate. Additionally, Mary-Jean was very interested in the efficiency as well as the effectiveness of the current nursing staffing levels and delivery of care system.

THE PILOT STUDY

A literature review and discussion with "experts" in the field did not provide insight into assessing the work flow in the Braintree environment. Then a process analysis was conducted that produced time, motion, and frequency studies of the routine and special medical events on all of the nursing units.

The routine events such as vital sign test, medication, and bed changing were easy to predict and consistent across all units. The percentage of baseline routine nursing time could vary from 5% to 70%, depending on the medical problem and length of hospital stay. For example, a new brain injury patient requires constant care, and routine nursing may comprise just 5% of the total daily nursing services consumed. On the other hand, a burn patient about to be discharged may be quite self-sufficient, and the routine care would consist of 70% of the total daily nursing care. The team concluded that it needed more data to predict the nonroutine, variable, or special events that consumed considerable nursing time. It believed the nonroutine events were the driving forces behind the varying levels of services needed and provided.

The team, after many additional meetings, developed a simple but quite reliable data gathering instrument to capture variable and unpredictable events and build a database. Figure 1 shows the nursing service classification data form. The established procedure provided that the nurses from each shift simply checked the appropriate boxes for the service rendered for each individual patient. The sheets were collected daily for the previous 24 hours and entered into the database system created for the study. The nursing staff openly accepted the study and, with very few exceptions, completed the form accurately and in a timely manner.

This cooperation reflects the strength of employee empowerment because the nursing staff assisted with the system implementation. The project manager reviewed the input daily and followed up quickly to correct any data collection problems. Currently this system is automated with touch-screen data entry at the locations and automatic download to the database.

The staff became very proficient at completing the form, and the project team members monitored the process. They were very pleased with the data integrity. Table 1 shows a daily summary of the data. Panel A shows the distribution of nursing care by types of activities. The unit in this case is the floor and wing of the hospital (2N—2nd floor North Wing). Panel B shows the distribution of nursing by diagnosis (illness for which the patient was admitted to the hospital). Panels C and D organize the data around the hospital unit.

Table 2 shows an individual patient classification summary of the data over a 44-day period. Using a database system, the team was able to organize the fields of data in an appropriate configuration. Mary-Jean immediately saw how she could use this information for nurse staffing and operational planning. Team members were pleased with the process insight provided by the amassed data, but they were not clear how to use the information in the managed care environment. The missing element was the assignment of the percentage of nursing time used for each skill level.

MODEL OF ACTIVITIES

The pilot team met with a consultant, who explained how to assign the skill mix information by activity. The consultant, using activity-based costing principles, revealed to team members how they had captured the nursing resources consumed by the various patients' diagnosis.

A further analysis of these data also demonstrated that the nursing resource consumption changed with the length of stay of the patient. Most patients have a large

TABLE 1
PATIENT CLASSIFICATION SUMMARY (PANELS A AND B)

PANEL A — DISTRIBUTION OF CARE ACTIVITIES — CLASSIFICATION DATE — 11/05/92

UNIT	CENSUS	NUTR	MOBIL	ADL	MEDICAL	MEDS	ELIM	SAFETY	SKIN	RESP	INDIR	OTHER	HOURS	AVERAGE
2N	41	7.0%	8.0%	10.0%	1.0%	5.0%	10.0%	5.0%	3.0%	0.0%	45.0%	5.21%	208.4	5.1
2S	30	11.0%	10.0%	13.0%	1.0%	5.0%	9.0%	4.0%	1.0%	1.0%	40.0%	5.21%	170.4	5.7
3N	40	6.0%	7.0%	10.0%	1.0%	5.0%	8.0%	6.0%	1.0%	0.0%	49.0%	5.21%	187.9	4.7
3S	41	5.0%	5.0%	12.0%	3.0%	5.0%	6.0%	5.0%	2.0%	1.0%	49.0%	5.21%	191.0	4.7
	152	7.2%	7.5%	11.2%	1.7%	5.1%	8.2%	5.3%	2.0%	0.4%	46.1%	5.2%	757.7	5.0

PANEL B — BY DIAGNOSIS

CASE MIX	DX	CENSUS	NUTR	MOBIL	ADL	MEDICAL	MEDS	ELIM	SAFETY	SKIN	RESP	INDIR	OTHER	HOURS	AVERAGE
32%	1	49	25.1	23.8	30.8	2.6	12.3	23.4	12.3	3.4	0.0	112.7	13.5	259.9	5.3
16%	6	24	3.1	8.3	11.0	1.2	6.0	10.4	6.0	2.9	0.0	55.2	5.7	109.9	4.6
15%	12	23	6.7	6.8	12.6	4.6	5.8	7.8	7.8	3.3	1.5	52.9	6.0	115.7	5.0
11%	8	17	0.9	3.7	7.4	0.9	4.3	3.4	4.3	1.8	0.0	39.1	3.6	69.1	4.1
9%	7	13	9.8	6.3	9.0	0.8	4.0	6.6	3.3	0.9	1.5	29.9	4.0	75.9	5.8
7%	9	11	3.9	3.2	5.3	0.6	2.8	3.8	2.8	0.7	0.0	25.3	2.6	50.8	4.6
4%	4	6	0.3	1.8	2.7	0.3	1.5	2.0	1.5	1.4	0.0	13.8	1.4	26.7	4.4
3%	11	5	3.0	2.5	3.4	1.7	1.3	3.4	1.3	0.8	0.0	11.5	1.6	30.3	6.1
1%	5	2	0.1	0.3	0.8	0.1	0.5	0.4	0.5	0.0	0.0	4.6	0.4	7.8	3.9
1%	2	2	1.8	0.3	1.8	0.1	0.5	1.2	0.5	0.3	0.0	4.6	0.6	11.7	5.8
0%													0.0	0.0	0.0
		152													

consumption of nursing services during the initial period of their stay, and, over time, the consumption declines. Thus, the consumption of nursing services is a function of both the mix of patient diagnosis and the length of hospital stay.

The team reviewed each activity and assigned a percentage of time spent for each skill level of nursing (RN, LPN, and NA). In this manner, a matrix was built where all the activities performed by the various skill levels were determined for each category of patient illness. This relationship was tracked over the length of hospital stay by patient category.

The data were reconfigured to provide the nursing skill level needed to deliver care (based on their activities) for each type of patient. In addition, the total amount of the time each skill level spent in each activity was readily available. The team now had a model of the activities consumed by each patient by classification based on the patient's use of all skill levels as well as the amount of nursing services. The team had developed the nursing resource consumption model for the hospital.

For example, a patient entered the hospital on 12/24 with a traumatic head injury and was released on 2/22 for a total stay of 60 days. As shown in Table 3, the total nonroutine nursing services used on 12/29 were 7.68 hours with RN 2.54 (33%), LPN 1.68 (22%), and NA 3.47 (45%) hours. On 2/22, 57 days later, the total nonroutine nursing is 3.90 hours, 50% less than the initial consumption. The distribution also has changed with RN 1.79 (45%), LPN .82 (21%), and NA 1.30 (34%). This trend over time and composition mix change has economic and staffing implications for the hospital.

As demonstrated, nursing costs by skill level were applied to the data, producing a predictable and reliable cost of nursing service by diagnosis over the length of the patient stay model. This information is invaluable when the hospital contracts with the insurance companies for a fixed daily hospital fee for specific rehabilitation diagnosis.

IT WORKS

The system unbundled a previously fixed cost allocation for nursing. The consumption of nursing services based on patient diagnosis and length of stay, coupled with the other cost ele-

TABLE 1
PATIENT CLASSIFICATION SUMMARY (PANEL C)

UNIT	CLASSIFIED HOURS		HOURS WORKED	PRODUCTIVITY CLASSIFIED HAVE	APPROPRIATE STAFFING HAVE CLASSIFIED
2N	208.398		186	112%	89%
	93.779	DAY	85.225	110%	91%
	73.9812	EVE	62	119%	84%
	40.6375	NOC	38.75	105%	95%
2S	170.418		186	92%	109%
	76.688	DAY	77.5	99%	101%
	60.4983	EVE	62	96%	102%
	33.2314	NOC	46.5	71%	140%
3N	187.931		201.5	93%	107%
	84.5688	DAY	85.25	99%	101%
	66.7154	EVE	69.75	98%	105%
	36.6465	NOC	46.5	79%	127%
3S	190.955		178.25	107%	93%
	85.9298	DAY	77.5	111%	90%
	67.789	EVE	69.75	97%	103%
	37.2362	NOC	31	120%	83%
TOTAL	757.701		751.75	101%	99%
	340.965	DAY	325.5	105%	95%
	268.984	EVE	263.5	102%	98%
	147.752	NOC	162.75	91%	110%

WORKLOAD DISTRIBUTION

DAY	45.0%	EVE	35.5%	NOC	19.5%

TABLE 1
PATIENT CLASSIFICATION SUMMARY (PANEL D)

Panel D						DIAGNOSTIC DISTRIBUTION BY UNIT						
UNIT	Dx 1	Dx 2	Dx 3	Dx 4	Dx 5	Dx 6	Dx 7	Dx 8	Dx 9	Dx 10	Dx 11	Dx 12
CENSUS	49	2	0	6	2	24	13	17	11	0	5	23
2N	31%	0%	0%	100%	50%	25%	0%	24%	9%	0%	0%	35%
2S	31%	0%	0%	0%	0%	0%	100%	0%	9%	0%	20%	0%
3N	18%	0%	0%	0%	0%	38%	0%	41%	36%	0%	20%	43%
3S	20%	100%	0%	0%	50%	38%	0%	35%	45%	0%	60%	22%

ments of a hospital stay, enabled the hospital to contract knowledgeably with the third-party payers. Prior to this information, the hospital cost management called for full bed occupancy and hoped for the right mix of patients to allow the hospital to cover its costs. Or, it operated with a more costly, inefficient mix. The new system produced the costs for those nursing services actually used by the patient. This information changes the management economic focus from filling all beds to looking at the nursing skill level and seeking those patients who have a consumption level compatible with the available nursing services. Or, adjust the nursing mix for the forecasted consumption level.

The team was elated with the model and its potential use. To confirm the model's accuracy, extensive validity and reliability tests were performed. These tests showed a 99% accuracy as correlated to actual staffing patterns and standards of practice as established by the nursing department. The model works!

At present the hospital uses these data to structure its contract negotiations with insurance carriers and for

TABLE 2
PATIENT CLASSIFICATION SUMMARY

Sample patient listing of a single patient throughout hospitalization

CLASSIFIER	DENUM, M	LAURENCE, J	DENUM, M	BRODERICK, K	GILMORE, J
PATIENT			MYPATHY		
REC #			092131		
UNIT			2S		
ROOM #			217A		
SEX			M		
DATE	12/29/92	01/13/93	01/29/93	02/10/93	02/22/93
ADM	12/24/92	12/24/92	12/24/92	12/24/92	12/24/92
NUTR	1.70	0.33	0.05	0.33	0.05
MOBIL	1.00	0.17	0.17	0.17	0.17
ADL	0.72	0.58	0.72	0.58	0.42
MEDICAL	0.05	0.05	0.05	0.05	0.05
MEDS	0.25	0.25	0.25	0.25	0.25
ELIM	1.00	1.00	1.00	1.00	0.20
SAFETY	0.25	0.25	0.25	0.25	0.25
SKIN	0.02	0.02	0.22	0.02	0.02
RESP	0.00	0.00	0.00	0.00	0.00
INDIR	2.30	2.30	2.30	2.30	2.30
OTHER	0.40	0.27	0.28	0.27	0.20
UNIT	2S	2S	2S	2S	2S
DX	1	1	1	1	1
HOURS	7.68	5.22	5.28	5.22	3.90
DAY	5	21	36	48	60
RN	2.54	2.18	2.32	2.18	1.79
LPN	1.68	1.13	1.19	1.13	0.82
NA RT	3.47	1.91	1.77	1.91	1.30

management decisions concerning nursing work flow trends and stalling. Mary-Jean Crockett uses the database to aid in the management of the delivery and quality of nursing services. She points out that "the purpose of our patient classification system is to provide quality nursing care by providing a sufficient number and skill mix of staff necessary to do so, based upon actual patient care requirements." She can match the necessary total staff by skill mix with the actual staff by skill mix and make the necessary adjustments to ensure both quality of care and cost effectiveness.

The new data permit the hospital to unbundle the previously fixed single nursing services charge. The effect of patient mix and length of stay by diagnosis on the economic structure of the hospital becomes apparent. In an environment of reduced third-party payments and increased competition, the hospital can use this new information. Jeffrey Goode, vice president-finance, said, "Rates are negotiable depending on circumstance. The third-party payers are very sophisticated today. I use the new information to help negotiate per diem rates with the insurance companies. Rate

TABLE 3 PATIENT CARE SUMMARY						
MYPATHY	12/29	5	7.68	33%	22%	45%
	1/14	21	5.22	42%	22%	36%
	1/29	36	5.28	44%	22%	34%
	2/10	48	5.22	42%	22%	36%
	2/22	60	3.9	45%	21%	34%

negotiation is one of the keys to our success. Having this information is critical in today's health care environment."

Financially, the hospital matches the daily revenues with the daily expenses to arrive at a hospital profit. Normally the daily patient stay is 40% of the revenue, with inpatient ancillary services representing 60% of the daily revenue. Wherever possible, ancillary services such as physical therapy, medication, and so on are billed directly. The costs of the ancillary services are captured directly, while the costs of a patient's daily stay are rolled into the fixed daily charge. Nursing services costs are approximately 50% of the total fixed daily charge. With the new activity-based system, 50% of the fixed patient overhead—nursing services—can be allocated based on the direct consumption by the patient.

Armed with this new information, financial forecasting is more reliable. The patient load and mix projections can be translated into a cost behavior model based on resource consumption. More important, the hospital armed with new cost data can negotiate rates and fees more intelligently with the third-party payers.

KEY SUCCESS FACTORS

The ability to understand the nursing services delivery process and to unbundle the nursing tasks was critical to the success of the project. The project team members were nurses with many years of practice. Even the designer and manager of the database was an RN. The project leader, Mary-Jean, understood the balance of delivering quality nursing care in the changing economic structure of our health care delivery system. She was determined to maintain and value appropriately the quality and caring of nursing services.

The hospital senior management fully supported the project. Team members worked well together and they communicated their progress and findings regularly. The output was nonthreatening. The nursing staff viewed this information as an enabler, which permitted better staffing.

The enthusiasm and seriousness of the team sent a clear and convincing message to the hospital staff. The data collection was made simple and easy, first the paper form and later the electronic form. It was part of the nursing deliv-

ery process. The Braintree nurses shared Mary-Jean's concerns and knew that the data somehow would benefit them and make their job better understood. The high validity of the pilot test was very convincing.

The accounting and finance departments became involved after the consultant showed the team how to add cost data to the operational data. They saw which operational factors drove the costs and arrived at an activity-based costing and management system. This linkage is invaluable for doing business and managing in the new managed care economic health care environment.

HEALTHY RESULTS

The success at Braintree Hospital was communicated to the 32 other rehabilitation facilities throughout the parent company. The model has been replicated successfully at many of the network facilities. In fact, the parent company's Big 6 auditing and consulting firm has incorporated the model into the financial program of all of company facilities. Now the activity-based cost model is a key part of the entire company's cost accounting system.

Using basic process analysis and sensible data collection, they developed an activity-based cost management system (ABC-MS). It provided valuable operational information for managing nursing services delivery and the cost consumption data to meet the changing health care reimbursement practices. This information changed the way Braintree Hospital conducts business. By understanding the delivery process, the hospital is compensated for the actual services delivered, and the third-party payers have a feeling of equity. The ideal health care system is where we pay for what we use and we use only what we need. The activity-based cost management system moves us toward this goal.

Lawrence P. Carr, Ph.D., is the Trivisonno term chair and assistant professor, Babson College. He can be reached at (617) 239-5138.

Note:

This work was made possible by the openness and cooperation of the Braintree Hospital staff. A special thanks is extended to the members of the CMS project team (M. DiBlasi, P. Flaherty and K. Sampson) and Mary-Jean Crockett, vice president of nursing.

From L. P. Carr, "Unbundling the Cost of Hospitalization," *Management Accounting* (November 1993): 43–48. Reprinted with permission.

Question

6.4 In Lawrence Carr's article on the cost of health care, the consumption of nursing services is a function of what factors? Did the system work?

131

CHAPTER 7

Pricing and Product Mix Decisions

Reading 7.1, *How Manufacturers Price Products,* by Eunsup Shim and Ephraim Sudit presents the results of a survey on pricing practice. The authors report data from 141 surveys across major U.S. industries. Typically, the respondents were from top management such as CFOs, controllers and vice-presidents. Survey results show that full-cost pricing was the dominant pricing strategy (69.5%) with variable costing second (17.7%) and market-based costing third (12.1%). Further, for those companies using full cost pricing, 49 percent determine prices based on a percentage of manufacturing costs with 51 percent using a percentage of all costs. Forty-seven percent of companies using variable costing report using a percent of variable manufacturing costs to determine prices while 53 percent use a percentage of all variable costs. The authors suggest that the continued use of full-costing, consistent with another survey conducted in 1983, may be the result of companies adopting ABC. ABC enables companies to trace traditional fixed costs more directly to products.

In *Pricing Strategies for Manufacturers* (Reading 7.2) Thomas Dudick suggests close scrutiny of each company's pricing strategy to ensure that it is being implemented appropriately and offers sound prescriptive advice on a variety of pricing topics. For example, Dudick argues that companies following a premium pricing strategy often simply add a fixed dollar amount for their deluxe models rather than a predetermined profit percentage. In many cases, the fixed dollar amount results in a lower percentage return than on standard models, thereby shortchanging the bottom line. Other topics discussed include marginal pricing as an appropriate strategy when a firm has developed a cost advantage over its competitors, pricing new products, pricing replacement parts, and cost-based pricing.

Ronald Lewis' piece, *Activity-Based Costing for Marketing* (Reading 7.3), focuses on the problem of how to account for marketing costs, and in particular, distribution costs. Since marketing costs constitute more than 50% of the total costs in many product lines, not considering them appropriately can result in inaccurate product costing and pricing. Using data from the Atlanta Company, Lewis develops an activity-based costing approach to handling marketing costs. Cost drivers for activities such as selling, advertising, warehousing, packing and shipping, and general office are developed, and costs are assigned accordingly. Analyses can then be undertaken by product, sales territory and product line.

Reading 7.4, is Kenneth Manning's article *Distribution Channel Profitability.* Many companies still do not scrutinize their sales, general and administrative costs (SG&A) to the same extent that they do their manufacturing costs. Without such detailed scrutiny, revenue and cost trade-offs related to the various distribution channels through which companies deliver products cannot be made. This article discusses three approaches to distribution channel profitability — a standard approach, an ABC approach, and a strategic cost management approach. Manning develops a four-step process to developing accurate channel and customer costs, which is applied to two companies facing different competitive issues.

132

7.1 How Manufacturers Price Products

Companies continue to practice full-cost pricing, but there is a shift toward target costing.

By Eunsup Shim CMA, and Ephraim F. Sudit

Certificate of Merit, 1993–94

In 1983, V. Govindarajan and R. N. Anthony (G & A) surveyed Fortune 1,000 companies, finding that most large companies price their products based on full cost rather than variable cost.[1] Full-cost pricing is based on variable costs plus allocated fixed costs.

In 1993, Eunsup Shim conducted a similar survey of pricing practices in U.S. manufacturing companies.[2] These results are compared with the 1983 survey by G &A and are used to assess the relationship between ABC implementation by U.S. manufacturers and their pricing practices. In addition, the rationale for choosing certain product pricing methods is discussed.

Why are pricing practices important? In a new manufacturing environment, managers are faced with global competition and increased productivity. Companies have become customer driven, focusing on delivering quality products at competitive prices. In many areas of manufacturing, domestic and foreign competition demand well-defined pricing strategies. Comprehensive product-cost systems should provide increased accuracy for managerial decisions concerning new products, pricing, and discontinuing and/or reengineering existing products.[3] Some evidence suggests that the distortion in reported product costs and, in turn, product pricing could be reduced by using activity-based costing (ABC).[4]

The use of costing information for pricing decisions has generated considerable debate over the years among economists, accounting researchers, and practitioners. Economists argue that, in order to maximize profits, prices should be set at the level of production where marginal cost intersects marginal revenue. In other words, pricing is based on marginal cost and marginal revenue; fixed charges for associated services are not used. The "profit maximization model" advocates the use of variable-cost pricing.

G & A drew on Herbert Simon's "satisficing" model, which states that the primary objective for companies is to seek a satisfactory return, as opposed to the "profit maximization" model. The "satisficing" model leads companies

to use full-cost pricing and provides a possible rationale for the prevalent use of this method. Practitioners cite savings in gathering cost information as well as its simplicity.

1993 PRICING PRACTICES

In the Shim survey, data were gathered across U.S. industries garnering 141 usable responses, a response rate of 23.5%. The majority of the respondents (81.5%) were in top management including controllers, vice presidents, general managers, or chief financial officers. Most of the responding companies (91%) were in the multi-products environment, averaging 75 products. The reported high product diversification is a phenomenon consistent with companies being more flexible in response to the new manufacturing environment.

The survey showed that full-cost pricing dominated pricing practices (69.5%), with slightly more than 10% (12.1%) of the respondents using a variable cost method (see Table 1). Full-cost pricing determines the selling prices based on full cost plus a certain percentage of profit. The full-cost pricing method is further broken into "percentage of manufacturing costs" and "percentage of all costs." Of the 98 full-cost pricing companies, 48 (49%) are reported to determine the prices based on percentage of manufacturing costs, and 50 (51%) used percentage of all costs in deriving product prices.

Variable-cost pricing follows similar procedures in arriving at product prices except for the use of "percentage of *variable* manufacturing costs" and "percentage of *all variable* costs."

Full-cost pricing, the predominant method, is used especially in the chemicals (80%) and electronics (72%) industries (see Table 2A). The prevalence of full-cost pricing, which requires considerable overhead cost allocation, underscores the importance of rational cost allocation. ABC tends to offer a better allocation scheme with activity analysis.

TABLE 1
COMPARISON OF PRODUCT PRICING METHODS

Pricing Method		Shim (1993)		G & A (1983)	
		Frequency	Percent	Frequency	Percent
Full-Cost Pricing	Percent of Manufacturing Costs	48	34.0	209	41.0
	Percent of All Costs	50	35.5	208	41.0
	Subtotal	50	59.5	417	82.0
Variable-Cost Pricing	Percent of Variable Manufacturing Costs	8	5.7	54	11.0
	Percent of All Variable Costs	9	6.4	30	6.0
	Subtotal	17	12.1	84	17.0
Market-based Pricing (Competitive Pricing)		25	17.7	Not Surveyed	Not Surveyed
Other		1	0.7	4	1.0
Total Respondents		141	100	505	100

TABLE 2
PRODUCT PRICING METHODS BY:

A/INDUSTRY	Full-Cost Pricing	Variable-Cost Pricing	Market-Based Pricing	Total (%)
Chemicals	4	0	1	5 (3%)
Machining	17	4	6	27 (19%)
Electronics	27	4	6	37 (26%)
Transportation	2	0	1	3 (2%)
Medical	34	7	9	50 (36%)
Others	14	2	3	19 (14%)
Total (%)	98 (70%)	17 (12%)	26 (18%)	141 (100%)

B/SIZE (ANNUAL SALES) OF COMPANY				
Under $10 Million	11	0	3	14 (10%)
$11–100 Million	59	11	19	89 (63%)
$101–500 Million	25	6	4	35 (25%)
$501 Million–1 Billion	1	0	0	1 (0.7%)
1–5 Billion	2	0	0	2 (1.3%)
Total (%)	98 (70%)	17 (12%)	26 (18%)	141 (100%)

C/ABC IMPLEMENTATION				
Fully or Partially Implemented	26	6	6	38 (26.9%)
Plan to Implement	33	7	13	53 (37.6%)
Not Plan to Implement	39	4	7	50 (35.5%)
Total (%)	98 (70%)	17 (12%)	26 (18%)	141 (100%)

The 1993 survey reported that almost 20% of the respondents' companies use market-based (competitive) pricing. This result seems to indicate a movement to market or "target cost" pricing from cost-based pricing. Target costing is the long-run cost that a customer will bear or a market-based cost that is calculated using a sales price necessary to capture a predetermined market share.[5]

Full-cost pricing is the most popular method in companies of all sizes. Of the 14 small companies (sales under $10 million), 11 use full-cost pricing. For mid-sized

134

companies ($11 million-$500 million in sales) there was a higher incidence of variable-cost pricing and competitive pricing (Table 2B).

The relationship between pricing method and stages of ABC implementation is highlighted in Table 2C. Companies that do not plan to implement ABC show the highest use of full-cost pricing (78%). Companies that have implemented or plan to implement ABC systems exhibit a slightly higher percentage of variable-cost pricing or market-based pricing methods (32% and 39%) than companies that do not plan to implement ABC systems (22%). The majority of companies, however, adhere to full-cost pricing.

The 1983 G & A survey showed similar results to the 1993 Shim survey, with 82% of the responding companies using full-cost pricing and 17% using variable-cost pricing. Thus, both surveys reveal the continuously prevailing use of full-cost pricing from 1983 to 1993. The consistent practice of full-cost pricing underscores the importance of proper cost allocation and product costing.

An interesting result of the 1993 survey is that 25 companies (18%) reported using market-based (competitive) pricing, which was not reported in the 1983 survey. This result indicates an important change in arriving at prices, one that is based on competitive market conditions rather than cost structures.

RATIONALE FOR FULL COST

There are a number of plausible reasons for the continuing use of full-cost pricing. First, increased implementation of ABC systems is likely to rationalize the allocation of fixed costs and makes more seemingly fixed costs variable or semi-variable. ABC systems enhance ways of tracing fixed costs to a specific product and lead to a better allocation of these costs. ABC systems provide more accurate product cost estimates that serve as a basis of determining full-cost price. The rapid implementation of ABC systems, therefore, tends to supply a support for the prevalent use of full-cost pricing practice.

Second, full-cost pricing provides a motivation to control fixed costs. For example, allocation of fixed costs to profit centers affects the performance of those centers. Accordingly, the profit center managers, whose performance varies with the amount of allocated fixed costs, can raise questions about the amount of corporate over-head (that is, fixed costs) and, as a result, may reduce the "empire building" phenomenon.[6] The use of fully allocated fixed costs in determining price could provide an alternative risk-sharing arrangement between profit center managers and top managers.

Finally, the difficulty in estimating marginal cost and marginal revenue for various products may prevent companies from using the marginal-cost approach. With manufacturing companies producing an average of 75 products, estimating marginal cost and marginal revenue may not be feasible or economical.

The majority of companies in the new manufacturing environment continue to practice full-cost pricing. The possible reasons for this practice are: "satisficing" behavior, availability of finer product costing information with implementation of ABC systems, possibility of controlling fixed costs, and difficulty in estimating marginal cost and marginal revenue in a multiproduct environment.

THE FUTURE?

Full-cost pricing continues to be the most popular product pricing method, but there is a shift toward variable-cost pricing or market-based (competitive) pricing. The 1993 survey exhibits only a very slow trend in this direction. The fierce domestic and foreign competition in the new manufacturing environment may bolster the use of some form of competitive pricing in the future.

Eunsup Shim, CMA, CPA, Ph.D, is assistant professor of accounting at Saint Joseph's University, Philadelphia, Pa. He is a member of the Philadelphia Chapter, through which this article was submitted, and can be reached at (610) 660-1660.

Ephraim F. Sudit, Ph.D., is a professor of accounting and Information systems at the Graduate School of Management, Rutgers University, Newark, N. J. He is a member of the IMA and can be reached at (201) 648-5241.

Notes

1. V. Govindarajan and R. N. Anthony, "How Firms Use Cost Data in Pricing Decisions," MANAGEMENT ACCOUNTING®, July 1983, p. 30–37.

2. Eunsup Shim, "Cost Management and Activity based Cost Allocation in a New Manufacturing Environment," Unpublished Dissertation, Rutgers University, Newark, N.J., January 1993.

3. R. Cooper and R. S. Kaplan, "How Cost Accounting Systematically Distorts Product Costs." *Accounting and Management: Field Study Perspective,* Harvard Business School Press, Boston, Mass., 1987, p. 226.

4. R. Cooper, "Implementing an Activity-Based Cost System," *Emerging Practices in Cost Management,* Warren, Gorham & Lamont, Inc., Boston, Mass., 1990, p. 69.

5. C. Berliner, and J. A. Brimson, *Cost Management for Today's Advanced Manufacturing: The CAM-I Conceptual Design,* Harvard Business School Press, Boston, Mass., 1988.

6. Anthony Dearden, and Govindarajan, *Management Control Systems, 7th ed.,* Irwin, Homewood, Ill., 1992, p. 184.

From E. Shim and E. F. Sudit, "How Manufacturers Price Products," *Management Accounting* (February 1995): 37–39. Reprinted with permission.

Question

7.1 Based on Table 1 of Shim and Sudit's article, what are the biggest differences between the 1983 and 1993 survey? Are these differences significant? Explain.

7.2 Pricing Strategies for Manufacturers
Pricing decisions should not be based on intuition alone.

By Thomas S. Dudick

Certificate of Merit, 1988–89.

Increasing market share is a popular battle cry heard in many companies. Unfortunately, the marketing department's strategy to achieve higher volume includes price cutting.

Corporate management is often unaware of this tactic until it's too late—profits decline sharply and an industry shakeout occurs. Then each company affected by the resulting profit squeeze points an accusing finger at their price-cutting competitors.

The solution is for companies to focus on being profitable rather than on increasing the volume of sales dollars. Instead of price cutting, employee compensation should be adjusted so that a greater portion of the paycheck is based on the profitability of orders rather than dollar sales volume.

PRICING STRATEGIES

Companies should also examine whether their pricing strategies are being used properly. Some of the most common pricing strategies and guidelines for their use are analyzed here.

Premium Pricing. When setting a premium price for a deluxe model, don't merely add a flat dollar amount. The premium price should result in a higher percentage return than the return on the standard model.

Recently, a manufacturer of mixers, blenders, skillets, and oven broilers made a decision to add a new model to the mixer line. This model had a stainless steel bowl with a nylon button on the bottom of the beater to avoid scarring. The factory selling price of the standard version model was $49.54, while the price established for the deluxe model was $53.50. When the two prices were compared to the cost, the gross profit for the standard model was 35% of the selling price while the gross profit for the deluxe model was only 33%.

The same kind of inconsistency was found with the company's standard and deluxe blenders. The deluxe model had a chrome motor cover and solid state features. The selling price of the standard model was $34.50 and the deluxe model was priced at $36.95. In this case, the comparison of percentage gross profit for the two showed 37% for the standard and 34% for the deluxe model. Thus, selling prices for the deluxe models must go beyond increasing absolute dollars—percentage of profit should determine price.

Premium pricing is not always dependent upon a product's features. In some cases, the customers perception that a higher price means higher quality influences pricing—even when products are exactly the same. For example, a vodka made by one U.S. firm doesn't vary that much from another U.S. company's vodka. Production costs are about the same regardless of the vodka's brand name, but if the company is aware of consumer psychology the prices can be quite different.

Making a good product at a high premium price can be highly profitable. Maytag's reputation for quality has been known for years. The premium prices charged by Maytag have yielded the company the highest return on investment in the industry.

Two factors, however, have weakened Maytag's position. First, Maytag doesn't sell to the large catalog chains, and, therefore, it lacks the aggressive marketing support of a company like Sears. Second, real estate contractors usually don't look for the longest lasting product on the market when they make purchases for acres of tract housing—they consider price. To strengthen its market position, Maytag should consider introducing a lower-priced private brand to broaden its market appeal.

Marginal Pricing. This pricing strategy is appropriate when a company has an advantage over its competitors, for example, if a company's use of new manufacturing technology reduces cost materially or if it adds a private brand in addition to its existing name brand product. The fixed cost content of the private brand's selling price can be reduced but the brand name should continue to carry its full measure of fixed costs.

In marginal pricing, which is an adaptation of variable costing, the fixed cost content in the selling price is reduced to make the price more attractive, thus increasing volume. It is more often applicable in the growth stage when new technology provides an innovative company with an advantage over competitors.

Henry Ford used this tactic when he developed the moving assembly line. This competitive advantage enabled him to increase his share of market. Costs per car were greatly reduced, and he was able to increase wages to a then unheard of sum of five dollars per day.

Marginal pricing is also appropriate in the maturity stage when a company making a brand name product decides to add a private brand at reduced prices. An exception would be if the company is not innovative.

The controller of a large candy manufacturer proposed the adoption of marginal pricing. The company had purchased automatic chocolate molding equipment for Easter Bunnies, Santa Clauses, and other molded figures in order to reduce the large labor costs incurred because of the labor intensive nature of the operations. The controller, a proponent of variable costing, demonstrated that the labor savings would decrease total variable costs by more than a third. Because this reduction would increase the contribution to fixed costs and profit to about 50% of sales, he recommended that prices be dropped 5% below the prices of competitors.

What the controller overlooked was that the company had been losing money on its molded chocolate products. The decision to automate its production required a capital equipment investment in excess of $500,000 to purchase equipment similar to that already in use by competitors. Another factor that was overlooked by the controller was an allowance for a costly debugging period that could last as long as six months.

BREAKEVEN TEST

When a new product is introduced, common practice in many companies is to calculate the total cost of making a specific quantity and then to apply a percentage markup in obtaining a selling price. If the price at this specific level appears to be too high in relation to competitors' prices, arbitrary adjustments are frequently made to the markup factor and/or manufacturing cost to arrive at a price that will be more competitive.

This pricing method has a major weakness because it is based on figures that relate to only one volume level. It does not take into account the fact that the price leader who "sets" the market price may be basing the price at a different volume level.

The breakeven test, illustrated in Table 1, was used to calculate the breakeven cost per fan for five production levels within the normal operating range. A markup was added to these levels to arrive at the selling prices. The figures for columns A through E are explained:

- *Column A:* This column shows the number of fans produced at five different levels of production within the normal operating range.
- *Column B:* The total nonvariable dollars ($226,560) is the total of all costs that remain constant within the nor-

mal operating range. These include such items as equipment depreciation building depreciation, real estate taxes, insurance, and supervision.
- *Column C:* This column shows the nonvariable cost on a per fan basis for each of the five production levels. These figures were calculated by dividing the $226,560 dollars by each of the five production levels shown in Column A.
- *Column D:* The variable cost, which remains constant per fan, is made up of the following variable costs:

Material/fan	$4.76
Direct labor/fan	1.39
Variable overhead/fan	3.77
Total variable cost/fan	$9.92

- *Column E:* Because this column shows the total cost per fan with no markup for profit, it represents the breakeven cost for each of the five levels of production.

Once the markup has been applied to the five levels, the logical question is: "Should we set the selling price higher to recover our product development costs sooner or should we set it low to discourage competitors?" The decision initially was made to introduce a deluxe model at a higher price and then to follow it up with a standard model. As volume increased, prices were progressively reduced to make competition less inviting.

A NEW ADDITION

When a new product fits into a family of similar products don't reinvent the wheel. A company should fit the newcomer into its proper position within the family to ensure a consistent relationship to the other members of the family.

Electrical connectors are an example of a family of products. The manufacturing process and the materials used are similar. The differences are in the number of electrical contacts, contact arrangement, and alternate insert positions. When new products are added to a family it is important that

TABLE 1
BREAKEVEN TEST

Number of Fans in Normal Range of Operations	Nonvariable Costs		Variable	
	Dollars	Per Fan	Cost Per Fan	Breakdown Cost Per Fan
12,000	226,560	$18.88	$9.92	$28.80
14,000	226,560	16.18	9.92	26.10
16,000	226,560	14.16	9.92	24.08
18,000	226,560	12.59	9.92	22.51
20,000	226,560	11.33	9.92	21.25
(A)	(B)	(C)	(D)	(E)
				Col C + D = E

there be a consistency in costing and pricing of all family members.

Table 2 shows how new products that are added to an existing line of products can be positioned so that comparisons can be made of the variations in costs and prices. This will ensure a reasonable degree of consistency in establishing selling prices.

Table 2 shows the costs of seven electrical connectors, three of which are new products. Four of the types have been in the line for some time, but three types, 43-2424, 43-2425, and 45-2507 are new types for which selling prices have to be established.

All costs are based on reasonably attainable standards that are competitive. To arrive at selling prices for the three new types, the percentage of cost to selling price was first calculated for the existing types. The percentages show that product 42-2511 has a cost to selling price ratio of 79%; this ratio for 42-2440 is 80%, and 76% for both 44-2467 and 44-2447. The selling prices for these items are based on known competitive prices.

In the case of 43-2424 and 43-2425, it was felt that the 76% ratio that applies to the 44-2467 and 42-2447 should also apply to these because of similarity in volume and manufacturing. The 76% was then divided into the manufacturing cost of $18.15 to arrive at a selling price of $24. For the 45-2507, the industry volume was anticipated to be somewhat lower than the rest of the line because the number of applications of this item is small.

TABLE 2
COMPARISON OF COST WITH SELLING PRICE

Electrical Connectors

Material Top Plate	2 Contacts		3 Contacts		4 Contacts		5 Contacts
	42-2511	42-2440	43-2424	43-2425	44-2467	44-2447	45-2507
12-2524 1/32 XP	3.60						
12-2466 1/16 XP		3.74					
12-2448 1/32 XP			5.62				
12-2460 1/32 XP				5.62			
12-2440 1/32 XP					7.50		
12-2423 1/32 XP						7.50	
12-2412 1/32 XP							9.37
Bottom Plate							
13-2524 1/16 XP	4.00						
13-2466 3/64 XP		4.24					
13-2448 3/64 XP			6.37				
13-2460 3/64 XP				6.37			
13-2440 3/64 XP					8.50		
13-2423 3/64 XP						8.50	
13-2412 3/64 XP							10.62
Contacts							
10-431	2.00	2.00					
10-562			3.00				
10-567				3.00			
10-632					4.00	4.00	
10-636							5.00
Eyelets							
46	.60	.60	.60	.60			
48					.70	.70	.70
Total component cost	$10.20	$10.58	$15.59	$15.59	$20.70	$20.70	$25.69
Assembly labor and overhead	2.00	2.00	2.20	2.20	2.40	2.40	2.40
Spoilage allowance	.24	.25	.36	.36	.46	.46	.56
Total Cost	$12.44	$12.83	$18.15	$18.15	$23.56	$23.56	$28.65
Selling Price	15.75	16.00	24.00*	24.00*	31.00	31.00	38.75*
% cost to selling price	79%	80%	76%*	76%*	76%	76%	74%*

Note: Selling prices rounded off to nearest $0.25

*New types

While a 72% or 73% ratio would have been desirable for this new five-contact unit, it would have resulted in a selling price that would have exceeded the price of a two-contact plus a three-contact unit. Therefore, a 74% ratio was used.

This method of pricing products within a family rather than using a "standalone" approach when new items are added has the advantage of ensuring that there will be a consistency within the family for both costing and pricing.

UNDERPRICED REPLACEMENT PARTS

Too many companies underprice replacement parts even if they are not proponents of marginal pricing. Underpricing, in many cases, is due to failure to take into account the cost of maintaining an inventory of such parts for 10 or more years after production of a product or model has been discontinued.

Doral Electronics (not its real name) is a case in point. Although Doral does not use marginal pricing consciously, the net effect of the method it does use is the same. The sales price for replacement parts was set to yield an 18% profit, which the company felt was quite adequate.

A study showed that the inventory carrying costs alone amounted to 23.8% of inventory value. The items considered as inventory carrying costs include:

- Rent equivalent costs: Building depreciation and/or rent, Building maintenance, Electricity, Heat, Real Estate Taxes and/or rent.
- Taxes and insurance: Personal property taxes, Liability and fire insurance.
- Stockhandlers' payroll and benefits.
- Breakage.
- Cost of money.

Cost of money is the largest item in the 23.8% inventory carrying cost. It, as well as other costs, can vary depending on economic conditions, inventory carrying costs must be monitored closely to ensure that costs affected by higher interest rates and inflation are taken into account.

SUBSTITUTE MATERIAL

Contrary to popular belief, the substitution of one material for another does not always reduce costs. Companies should consider increasing prices when the advantages of more expensive materials outweigh the increased price.

For example, consider the use of substitute materials in the construction of residential homes. Many tract housing developers, in the interest of lowering costs, have shifted away from wood siding to aluminum. Aluminum siding has baked-on finish that eliminates the cost of exterior painting. Not to be outdone, the plastics industry introduced vinyl siding, which also eliminates the need for painting and is available with an embossed grain similar to that of wood.

Use of substitute materials does not always result in reduced costs. On the contrary, the substitute material may be more costly.

In the manufacture of metal garbage cans, for example, the sheet metal accounts for 21.4% of the manufacturer's selling price. The plastic material used in making the plastic version accounts for 41.2% of the manufacturer's selling price.

The higher price for the plastic item does not necessarily mean that buyers will favor the lower-priced product. Plastic garbage containers have certain advantages over their metal counterparts. These include resistance to denting, reduction in noise, less weight, and freedom from rusting.

COST-BASED PRICING

When companies add new products to a line, there is a tendency to treat them the same as existing products. If exist-standard costing procedures are followed, the costing for any new version of the same product is likely to be the same. Commercial pricing strategies are also likely to be followed.

This is precisely what happened when nuclear power plants in the 1970s ordered nuclear components. The Atomic Energy Commission (AEC) required all manufacturers of such nuclear components as valves, pumps, pressure vessels, reactor vessels, safety valves, and piping to adhere to engineered specifications. There were companies, however, that continued to cost and price the nuclear components as if they were to be used for the less restrictive applications. As the percentage of nuclear business increased and profitable companies started to show reduced profits—and even losses—only then did many managers begin to question the selling prices received for the nuclear part of the business.

A study of several companies producing both the commercial and nuclear components revealed that costs such as engineering, drafting, quality, rework, factory supplies, and shipping costs were substantially greater for the nuclear components. However, the companies' standard cost systems allocated these costs through an overhead rate(s) based on production hours.

In view of the highly engineered, and customized nature of the nuclear components, the following costs should have been charged directly to individual jobs on a "direct charge basis".

Engineering Costs. Nuclear components require double or triple the amount of engineering effort that is allocated to commercial components.

Quality Assurance Costs: Quality assurance must relate to the total controlled manufacturing system. This includes:

- Audit and control of internal departments and suppliers to ensure conformance to code and contract requirements.
- Internal training of inspection personnel.

- Development and monitoring of programs for calibration of measuring equipment.
- Control of internal quality standards and quality documentation.

Inspection Costs: The cost of inspection for nuclear components (in this case, nuclear valves) is more than double that required for the commercial types. There can be more than 900 inspection, hold, witness, approval, and verification points by the manufacturer, Atomic Energy Commission, and the utility company.

Rework Costs: These costs are relatively small for commercial valves because the presence of sand holes in the casting is not as serious a defect as it might be in a casting used in a nuclear component. In the event that a defect is found in such a casting, the following corrective operations are required:

- Gouging out the defect,
- Welding the hole(s),
- Grinding the weld,
- Hand dressing,
- X-ray,
- Heat treat, and
- Remachine and inspect.

The cost of supplies, shipping expenses, tools, and fixtures are substantially greater for the nuclear components than for the commercial types. There is no doubt that selling prices for the nuclear components should be cost-based. In preparing the cost estimates, it is necessary to correctly identify the costs applicable to nuclear components as a basis for establishing the selling price. This is no different than what is being done on many defense contracts and for many products that are unique to one customer.

When implementing the required job costing system, proper reporting of labor according to individual customers can be troublesome. Many salaried professionals resist accounting for their time. Frequently, they will wait until the end of an accounting period, at which time they will "guesstimate" how their time was used during the period. Management must therefore explain the significance of reporting by job and emphasize the importance of accurate and timely reporting.

PRICE INFORMATION REQUESTS

The goal of pricing strategy is to maximize profits. Thus, management should regularly monitor the effectiveness of its price quotations.

Checking the bottom line on the income statement is too broad a measure. The company should review the number of quotation requests received during the period, the number that resulted in firm orders (success ratio), and the breakdown of these orders by gross profit percentages (See Table 3).

Note that of a total of 843 requests for price information received during the period, 81, or 9.61%, resulted in firm orders. This result raises the question as to whether a 9.61% success ratio is adequate. Unfortunately, there are no industry figures available as a comparison. But, each period's success ratio percentage can be compared with subsequent periods.

Monitoring the success ratio percentages by the five individual profit percent ranges also can be quite useful. Note that the percentage success ratio for the first three lines averages less than 3%, while the last two average 13.33%. It's clear that the success ratio is skewed too heavily toward the least profitable orders.

Does this mean that the markup many companies factor applied is excessive—resulting in prices that are too high? An evaluation of the products in question revealed almost half the items on the list contained molded parts that were being purchased on the outside. Thus, the company should consider purchasing the necessary equipment to expand its own molding capacity, rather than having the work done on the outside.

TABLE 3
PRICE INFORMATION REQUESTS

Gross Profit Percentage	Number of Requests for Price Information	Breakdown of Firm Orders	% Success Ratio by Profit Category
40% and higher	63	-0-	-0-
35 to 39%	114	3	2.63
30 to 34%	126	6	4.76
25 to 29%	288	30	10.42
5 to 24%	252	42	16.66
Total	843	81	9.61
30% to over 40%	303	9	2.97
5% to 29%	540	72	13.33
Total	843	81	9.61

INTUITIVE PRICING

Is there a place for managers who make pricing decisions based on intuition or "feel of the market." Yes, but only after the appropriate pricing strategy is applied and the results evaluated carefully.

Thomas S. Dudick is consultant to Ernst & Young in cost systems, product costing, pricing, manufacturing cost, and operating controls. He has served as budget director at Allen B. DuMont Laboratories, plant controller for GTE-Sylvania, and internal consultant for Raytheon Company. He is a member of NAA's New York Chapter through which this article was submitted.

From T. S. Dudick, "Pricing Strategies for Manufacturers," *Management Accounting* (November 1989): 30–35. Reprinted with permission.

Question

7.2 According to Dudick, what is marginal pricing and under what conditions is it appropriate to use it?

7.3 Activity-Based Costing for Marketing

By Ronald J. Lewis

Certificate of Merit, 1990–91.

Manufacturing costs and traditional cost accounting systems are not the only cause of America's problems in the world-class Competitiveness arena. Marketing functions, particularly physical distribution. are a significant cost factor, yet marketing costs are being ignored in the mainstream discussions today. Also, activity-based costing (ABC) techniques and total cost management (TCM) concepts have been recommended and used by some companies for marketing activities since the late 1960s. How can they be merged with the concepts being promoted today?

THE PROBLEM'S HIDDEN CAUSE

Critics of traditional cost control systems who concentrate on production costs alone are overlooking a significant portion of the total costs of many manufactured products.

A major cause of the higher cost of these products is the cost of physical distribution activities and other marketing functions. Marketing costs make up more than 50% of the total costs in many product lines and approximately 20% of the U.S. Gross National Product.

Physical distribution is a major cost factor in the United States. It may not be a major cost factor in geographically small countries, such as Japan or Great Britain, within their own domestic markets. Nevertheless, when foreign companies establish factories in the United States, they face the same logistics problems that U.S. companies encounter.

The theoretical advantages of just-in-time JIT methods may not work in all real-life situations, even in Japanese transplants. In addition, the familiarity that U.S. companies have had with physical distribution problems may be an advantage for them over their foreign competitors. For example, a Japanese-American joint venture established a plant in Michigan to provide parts to a Japanese assembly plant in Ohio. In the Michigan plant, observers found that boxes of parts were stacked to the ceiling in all available floor space of the factory. When asked about JIT and other inventory reduction methods, the plant manager explained that parts were shipped from Japan by freighter to the West Coast, then by rail to Chicago, and finally by truck to Michigan. Therefore, it was more economical to ship in large quantities and store the extra supplies on the factory floor.

The joint-venture supplier in this example is majority owned by the Japanese company, which supplies another Japanese company, an automobile manufacturer, with these particular parts. Competition is not a factor because the two Japanese companies have prearranged agreements, so these physical distribution costs are considered unavoidable under the circumstances.

Although this example illustrates the fallacy of assuming that the Japanese have some magic formula for manufacturing efficiency, it also indicates that marketing costs, particularly the costs of physical distribution, are a major factor in worldwide competition and should not be ignored in discussions of performance measurements and integrated cost systems.

ABC TECHNIQUES FOR MARKETING

The objective of marketing cost analysis is to provide relevant quantitative data that will assist marketing managers in making in-formed decisions regarding such important areas as profitability, pricing, and adding or dropping the product lines or territories. in achieving this objective it is necessary to be able to trace costs directly to product lines or to territories where possible and to establish a rational system of allocating nontraceable costs to the cost objective. The accounting profession has not pursued this challenge!

ABC principles can be applied in attempting to trace marketing costs to product lines and territories in order to measure profitability. I'll show you how. All you have to do is follow the procedure outlined next.

1. Establish activities performed as advertising, selling, order filling, shipping, and warehousing.
2. Accumulate direct costs for each activity, and separate into variable and fixed categories.
3. Determine cost drivers for each activity. For *selling,* the cost driver is gross sales, or orders received, or number of sales calls. For the activity of *order filling, shipping,* and *warehousing,* the cost driver would be number, weight, or size of units shipped. For the activities of *credit and collection* and *general office,* the cost driver is number of customer orders or number of invoice lines.
4. Calculate unit costs for each activity. The unit cost of each activity is determined by dividing the total activity cost by the cost driver selected. Where conditions justify the practice, the unit cost can be used as the basis for budgeting and for the establishment of standards in a standard cost system.
5. Apply contribution cost analysis. The accumulation of direct costs and the allocation of indirect costs to marketing activities enables management to assign total cost responsibility to each marketing activity although the identification of total costs does not always provide relevant information for specific decisions. Only by applying contribution analysis will the company be able to determine profit contribution by product line or by territory.

Tables 1–5 were prepared by the controller of Atlanta Company to provide information about marketing profitability. Table 1 shows selling prices, unit manufacturing costs, units sold, and other bases of variability. Table 2 shows total variable and fixed costs for each activity and develops unit rates for variable and fixed costs of each major marketing activity: selling, ware housing, packing and shipping, and general office.

Selling. The selling function is represented by the dollar value of sales. There may be justification for basing variability of selling cost on other factors, such as the number of sales calls or orders obtained, and the controller must select the basis that has the main causal effect on cost variability. Atlanta Company uses the basis of dollar value of sales.

Advertising. Advertising is a promotional activity, similar to selling, which possibly could be attributed to the cost factors. Atlanta selected units of product sold. Note that advertising may or may not have variable cost characteristics. Some companies increase their advertising when sales are down, so the cost may bear an inverse relationship with sales. Atlanta found that a portion of advertising varies with sales and that a larger portion is fixed.

Warehousing. Warehousing is the general distribution function of storage terminating. The factor of variability selected by Atlanta is weight of product sold.

Packing and Shipping. Another physical distribution function, packaging and shipping, usually has a greater proportion of variable expenses and is related to the quantity of units of product shipped. Atlanta assumes units shipped are equal to units sold.

General Office. Atlanta needs clerical accounting, credit and collection, and other activities to service the overall marketing function. Each service has its own variability, but Atlanta assumes that number of orders affects all.

Table 3 provides additional product and territory transactions data. For example, the quantity of product C sold in the West territory during the period was 14,000 units. Customers' orders for product A in the South total 50. These data form the basis for the determination of the cost calculations in subsequent tables.

The profitability analysis by territory (shown in Table 4) reveals that both territories show a profit from operations. Table 5 shows the total company profitability by product line. The profitability statement by product line provides additional information for marketing managers. Product lines A and B are profitable, whereas product line C shows an operating loss of $16,000. This statement has revealed that although the overall company shows a profit and that both territories are profitable, one product line requires further analysis. Additional tables could be presented with data

TABLE 1 ATLANTA COMPANY PRODUCT LINE DATA YEAR 19X1			
Product Line Information	Product Line		
	A	B	C
Selling price	$10.00	$8.00	$12.00
Unit manufacturing cost	$ 8.00	$5.00	$11.00
Quantity of units sold and shipped	50,000	30,000	20,000
Average weight of units sold	2.0 lbs.	3.0 lbs.	4.0 lbs.
Number of customers' orders	100	200	200
Variable portion of manufacturing cost	60%	60%	60%

TABLE 2
ATLANTA COMPANY CALCULATION FOR PER UNIT COST RATES

TOTAL COSTS

Marketing Activity	Cost Driver	Total Volume	Cost of Marketing Activity	
			Total	Unit Rate
Selling	Dollar value of sales	$980,000	$49,000	5.0%
Advertising	Quantity of units sold	100,000	$40,000	$ .40
Warehousing	Weight of shipped	270,000 lb.	$27,000	$ .10
Packing and shipping	Quantity of shipped	100,000	$20,000	$ .20
General office	Number of customers' orders	500	$10,000	$20.00

VARIABLE AND FIXED COST RATES

Marketing Activity	Variable Cost	Unit Rate	Fixed Cost	Unit Rate
Selling	$29,400	3.0%	$19,600	2.0%
Advertising	$10,000	$ .10	$30,000	$ .30
Warehousing	$13,500	$ .05	$13,500	$ .05
Packing and shipping	$12,000	$ .12	$ 8,000	$ .08
General Office	$ 2,000	$4.00	$ 8,000	$16.00

TABLE 3
ATLANTA COMPANY SALES AND ORDERS BY TERRITORY (IN UNITS) YEAR 19X1

Transaction by Territory	Total	Products		
		A	B	C
Products sold:				
West	60,000	26,000	20,000	14,000
South	40,000	24,000	10,000	6,000
Total	100,000	50,000	30,000	20,000
Customers' Orders:				
West	280	50	80	150
South	220	50	120	50
Total	500	100	200	200

by product line for each territory separately to further isolate the operating loss of product C.

As you can see, "Charging costs direct eliminates the need to allocate or assign costs. Costs that cannot be charged directly should be assigned to the product through activity-based costing."[1]

This modern advice dovetails with my illustration, which demonstrates that the techniques recommended for marketing cost analysis at least 20 years ago are conceptually equal to those now being recommended for production costs by Robert Kaplan, William Ferrara, Michael Ostrenga, and others contributing to the deluge of activity-based costing literature.[2] The only differences are that only marketing costs were involved, the state of technology was less developed, and the accounting profession did

TABLE 4
ATLANTA COMPANY PROFITABILITY STATEMENT BY TERRITORY (ALL PRODUCTS) YEAR 19X1

	Total Company	Territory		Allocation Basis
		West	South	
Sales revenue	$980,000	$588,000	$392,000	
Less: cost of sales	770,000	462,000	$308,000	
Gross margin	$210,000	$126,000	$ 84,000	
Less: Expenses				
Selling	$ 49,000	$ 29,400	$ 19,600	5% of sales
Advertising	40,000	24,000	16,600	$.40/unit sold
Warehousing	27,000	16,800	10,200	$.10/lb. shipped
Packing and shipping	20,000	12,000	8,000	$.20/unit sold
General office	10,000	5,600	4,400	$20/order
Total expense	$146,000	$ 87,800	$ 58,200	
Operating income (Loss)	$ 64,000	$ 38,200	$ 25,800	

TABLE 5
ATLANTA COMPANY PROFITABILITY STATEMENT BY PRODUCT LINE (ALL TERRITORIES) YEAR 19X1

	Total Company	A	Product Line B	C	Allocation Basis
Sales revenue	$980,000	$500,000	$240,000	$240,000	
Cost of sales	770,000	400,000	150,000	220,000	
Gross margin	$210,000	$100,000	$ 90,000	$ 20,000	
Less: Expenses					
Selling	$ 49,000	$ 25,000	$ 12,000	$ 12,000	5% of sales
Advertising	40,000	20,000	12,000	8,000	$ .40/unit sold
Warehousing	27,000	10,000	9,000	8,000	$ .10/lb. shipped
Packing and shipping	20,000	10,000	6,000	4,000	$ .20/unit sold
General office	10,000	2,000	4,000	4,000	$20/order
Total expense	$146,000	$ 67,000	$ 43,000	$ 36,000	
Operating income (Loss)	$ 64,000	$ 33,000	$ 47,000	$ (16,000)	

not recognize the importance of marketing costs and the methods being recommended.

WE MUST EMPHASIZE MARKETING COSTS

The main theme of management accounting journal articles in recent years has been worldclass competition, emphasizing the gradual slipping of U.S. manufacturers, particularly in comparison with Japanese manufacturers. Production costs have been the center of attention, while marketing costs have been ignored. We must focus on marketing costs as an important component of the total cost of a product.

The use of activity-based costing techniques for marketing functions arose during the years 1968 through 1973 when marketing executives urged members of the accounting profession to develop a better system of identifying, classifying, and allocating physical distribution costs. At that time, several articles (including one of mine[3]) isolated the activities in the major marketing functions. Cost drivers, a modern euphemism for activity bases, were identified for each activity within the marketing functions.

Techniques that resemble the recently discovered activity-based costing system and the total cost concept which is the forerunner of total cost management were discussed thoroughly and recommended for physical distribution costs at the request of the marketing managers of several hundred U.S. corporations. The accounting profession largely ignored the recommendations of the practitioners and overlooked the fact that physical distribution activities have cost characteristics similar to those of production activities. Now, 20 years later, accountants are attaching new names to these same techniques. Activity-based costing techniques have been and should continue to be applied to marketing costs to assist companies in management decision making.

Ronald J. Lewis is Professor of accounting at Central Michigan University in Mt. Pleasant, Mich., and a member of the Saginaw Valley Chapter of the IMA, through which this article was submitted. He holds A.B. and A.M. degrees from Wayne State University and a Ph.D. degree from Michigan State University. Formerly he was the vice-president of academic affairs at Tri-State University, Angola, Ind. He may be reached at (517) 774-3796.

Notes

1. Michael R. Ostrenga, "Activities: The Focal Point of Total Cost Management." MANAGEMENT ACCOUNTING®, February 1990, pp. 42–49.

2. Robert S. Kaplan, "The Four-Step Model of Coat Systems Design." MANAGEMENT ACCOUNTING®, February 1990, pp. 22–26. Also, William L. Ferrara, "The New Cost/Management Accounting: More Questions than answers," MANAGEMENT ACCOUNTING®, October 1990, pp. 48–52.

3. Ronald J. Lewis, "Strengthening Control of Physical Distribution Costs," *Management Services* (AICPA), January–February 1968. Also, J. L. Heskett, R. M. Ivie, and N. A. Glaskowsky, Jr., *Business Logistics Management of Physical Supply and Distribution,* The Ronald Press Company, New York, N. Y., 1964.

From R. J. Lewis, "Activity-Based Costing for Marketing," *Management Accounting* (November 1991): 33–36. Reprinted with permission.

Question

7.3 In Lewis' article, what are the appropriate cost drivers for selling, advertising, warehousing, packing and shipping, and general office activities? Is there any flexibility in the choice of cost drivers for these categories? Explain.

7.4 Distribution Channel Profitability
ABC concepts can help companies make strategic decisions.

By Kenneth H. Manning

Which of your distribution channels is most profitable? If you analyze them using an approach built on activity-based costing (ABC) concepts, you may find an unexpected answer.

Distribution costs are a fact of life for almost every manufacturer, distributor, and supplier. As major retailers, wholesalers, distributors, and manufacturers reconfigure their supply chains, all participants in the supply chain need to understand the revenue and cost tradeoffs associated with the various channels through which they deliver products and services.

To evaluate strategic issues within the distribution system, formulate potential responses to those issues, and estimate the impact of improvements on the overall business, you need reliable and accurate information. One approach to gaining the necessary data is constructed around activity-based costing (ABC) concepts that many companies have adopted over the last several years.[1] ABC provides a more accurate view of a company's cost structure than a standard cost approach, particularly for companies that produce a broad range of products and volumes. The benefits of ABC have been discussed in great detail in other publications and will not be presented here.[2] Building on these ABC concepts, the methodology presented here allows practitioners to determine the relative profitability of their distribution channels and customer groups. The methodology assumes that the practitioners have at least a conceptual view of an ABC approach, although a working knowledge of ABC techniques is highly recommended.

COMPARISON OF THREE APPROACHES

The typical approach to developing knowledge of channel profitability, using standard product costing, is shown in Figure 1. This approach creates two cost pools: product costs and sales, general, and administrative (SG&A) costs. The product costs are transferred to the channels based on standard unit costs and the product mix sold through that channel. The SG&A expenses typically are allocated to the channels based on net revenue or sales volume by channel.

If the organization is aligned by channel or customer group, this approach may yield accurate profitability figures. But most often, companies are aligned by region, product line, or facility location, which makes the translation to channel or customer difficult using conventional approaches.

This approach may help answer some questions related to distribution costs, but there are numerous issues that it cannot address. In addition, it has all the drawbacks associated with traditional standard product costing, which have been shown to distort costs in many situations. Because this

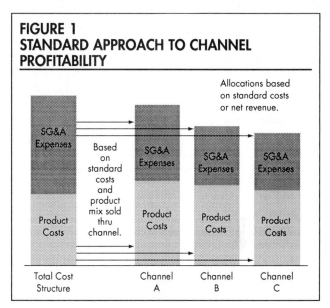

FIGURE 1
STANDARD APPROACH TO CHANNEL PROFITABILITY

approach makes no attempt to adjust product costs, the analysis related to product costs can be misleading.

A more refined approach to channel profitability is to use an ABC methodology. Figure 2 illustrates the more accurate ABC approach to this problem. The ABC approach has one large advantage over the conventional approach: It costs products more accurately. Overhead costs are allocated to product lines in a more logically related fashion than under the conventional approach. The result is improved accuracy over the typical standard costing approach.

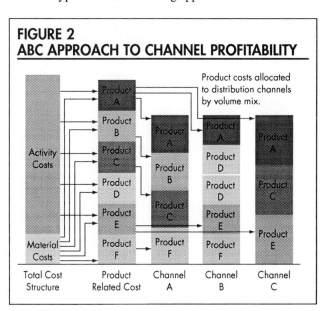

FIGURE 2
ABC APPROACH TO CHANNEL PROFITABILITY

The drawback to this approach is that while we are allocating cost in a much more logical and rigorous manner, the analysis is based on one major assumption that is probably not true: that all costs are product-driven costs and therefore must be traced or allocated to products. For most companies, organizational costs are driven by more than just the products they produce.

The strategic cost management approach outlined below recognizes that cost is not driven solely by the products produced but also by the customers served and the channels through which the product is offered. Removing the restriction that all costs must be related to products allows the development of a more accurate view of cost consumption. Under the traditional ABC methodology, it was not possible to detect if product costs were high due to certain customer groups or to certain channels. However, this approach gives us additional insight into the reasons for the product line cost position by creating three different types of costs: product-related costs, channel-related costs, and customer-related costs. Examining the cost structure from this perspective allows management to understand cost differences related to any one of these categories or related to interactions between these categories. (See Figure 3.)

DEVELOPING ACCURATE CHANNEL AND CUSTOMER COSTS

The approach used to develop this view of costs relies on several guidelines:

- Include all costs (direct, indirect, overhead, implicit).
- Focus on relevance over precision.
- Use issues to drive analysis.

The methodology follows a four-step process, which is outlined below.

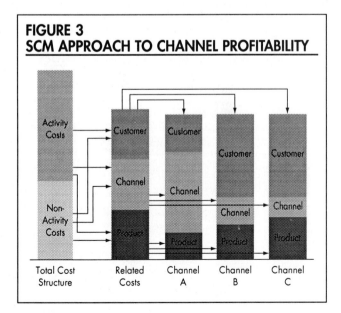

FIGURE 3
SCM APPROACH TO CHANNEL PROFITABILITY

1. *Separate the organization's cost structure into activity costs and nonactivity costs.* The cost structure of the organization should be translated into activity and non-activity components that reflect the operations of the enterprise. The number and detail of these components should be determined by the issues the study is addressing. Table 1 lists several activity and nonactivity components one would expect to see in a manufacturing company. Through the use of traditional ABC concepts, the cost associated with each of these components should be estimated. The sum of these component costs should equal the organization's total cost structure.

2. *Identify the cost behavior of all activity and nonactivity costs.* The activity and nonactivity components are organized into three categories of cost behavior: product-related, customer-related, and channel-related (see Table 1). Each cost component should be related to only one category. If a cost component cannot be related to just one category, either further decompose the activity or nonactivity definition, or, if it is judged immaterial, assign the component to the primary behavior category.

3. *Trace these costs to the individual products, channels, and customers.* Once the different cost components are classified as product-related, channel-related, or customer related, it is necessary to identify the tracing factor that relates those costs back to the appropriate products, channels, or customers. *Tracing factors are quantifiable, repeatable measures that closely approximate the level of effort associated with an activity.* They are used to trace the activity cost to the individual component groups, e.g., product line A, product line B, channel A, and so on.

For example, the activity cost of "non-EDI order processing" was determined to be $432,500 for the one-year period. The number of order lines filled was identified as the tracing factor, as shown in Table 2.

This same procedure is performed for all cost components to develop a total cost view for the three types of cost categories. Nonactivity costs are treated in a similar manner, except direct cost linkages are easier to find for these items. In most cases it will be possible to allocate those costs directly to the product, customer, or channel that created them.

4. *Translate the product, channel, and customer cost elements into a total cost view for the business.* The final step requires that two matrices be constructed for the purpose of linking these three views. The first matrix links the product and customer view by capturing the customer purchases by product. The second matrix links the customer and channel view by capturing the customer purchases by distribution channel. These two matrices then are used to translate the costs driven by each channel into a total cost view for product, customer, or channel.

TABLE 1
COST BEHAVIOR OF ACTIVITY COSTS AND NONACTIVITY COSTS

	Product Related	Channel Related	Customer Related
Activity Costs	• Schedule Production • Setup and Changeover for Machine A • Test Quality Parameters • Maintain Equipment	• Attend Trade Shows • Order/Invoice Processing • Sales Force • Telemarketing • Advertising Brand A • Arrange for Shipping	• EDI and Computer Interfaces to Customer • Special Shipping and Handling Requests • Collect Bad Debt • Technical Support for Customer A • Prepare/Deliver Annual Sales Bid
Nonactivity Costs	• Material Costs • Royalties	• Trade Discounts • Freight	• Bad Debt Expense • Customer Rebates

TABLE 2
ACTIVITY COST OF NON-EDI ORDER PROCESSING

	Activity: Non-EDI Order Processing	Tracing Factor: Number of Order Lines
Channel A	$ 78,140	$123,045
Channel B	208,358	328,095
Channel C	146,002	229,903
Total	$432,500	$681,043

Following this methodology will provide any necessary cost view of the organization. Obviously, it is also necessary to capture revenue information for the same products, channels, and customers for which costs were calculated.

PRODUCT VIEW VS. CHANNEL/CUSTOMER VIEW

The traditional ABC approach is probably most consistent with the way corporate planners think about business strategy and planning: by product area. The majority of businesses are formed around product lines and product groups, a fact that obviously influences the way we think about them. But alternative views certainly are becoming more important as products are served through increasingly varied channels—distributors, catalogs, mega-stores, direct mail, and so on. As companies develop future business plans, understanding the cost and profitability of serving different channel and customer groups will become critical to making good business decisions.

In essence, we have recast the entire company's costs and created a database of costing information around several new views: activity, nonactivity, product, channel, and customer. Attempting to perform these manipulations without the assistance of a powerful PC would be impossible, but with the introduction of the PC and numerous software applications, it is now relatively easy. The data are organized in a way that encourages analysis of number of different issues.

The best results have been obtained when this methodology was used in an issues-driven approach—the type and nature of the decision being made should drive the level of detail and direction of the analysis. The effort to arrive at good, accurate channel and customer costs is worth making only if you need to address business issues. The key issues should be identified, documented, and articulated in advance of any analysis. For instance, the sections below describe how two companies facing different competitive issues could use the approach to develop their strategic responses.

FOCUSED COMPETITOR ENTERING MARKET

A specialty chemical manufacturer supplied products to a broad range of customers in the food, consumer products, and manufacturing industries. The products were made primarily in-house although some were purchased and repackaged and then sold through a network of representatives, a direct sales force, and a telemarketing customer service center. Customers could opt for several delivery and pricing options including customer pick-up, bulk delivery, or less-than-truckload (LTL) delivery.

It recently had become known that a new competitor was planning to enter a key segment of the company's market. The management team knew that the impact would be negative but did not know to what extent. The vice president of sales & marketing particularly was concerned. He believed that the targeting segment provided a significant portion of the division's profit although the financial report indicated that it was not very profitable due to above average discounts. The head of sales and marketing decided to sponsor a study to understand the "true" profitability of the various delivery options and customer groups (or market segments).

The study team uncovered several significant findings:

• The large customers did provide a disproportionate percentage of the division's profits, despite their much lower gross margin, due primarily to less customer service, lower bad credit expenses, and reduced handling charges on large orders.

- Cost differentials within the large customer grouping depended on the use of the product. Customers in the food industry consumed more technical marketing, demanded more research support, and required a finer-grade product, which slowed process run rates.
- The "true" cost difference among the different delivery options was surprising. The conventional cost approach assumed that the only difference between these options was the freight costs. The study revealed that the customer pick-up option after adjustment for freight charges actually cost less than the other delivery options due to much lower damage claim losses and reduced freight scheduling costs.
- The gross sales generated by small customers did not cover even the cost of selling and servicing these accounts. It turned out that smaller customers often had limited resources with which to solve technical problems and relied on the company's assistance in this area. Because there was no rationing mechanism or internal R&D tracking system, these costs went undetected for the most part.
- Several of the large-volume outsourced products did not provide sufficient margin to cover their full distribution costs. While they appeared profitable under the standard cost and profit reporting system, the study indicated they were unprofitable once the inbound logistics cost and purchasing cost were taken into account.

Given this information, the head of sales & marketing worked with the vice presidents of operations, R&D, and finance to develop the following set of responses:

1. Technical resources were shifted away from smaller customers and assigned to work exclusively on the large consumer product and manufacturing accounts. The sales force then attempted to discover customer problems that could be solved by making these valuable resources available to the customers. The R&D department also created a simple time reporting system to track these "soft" costs better.
2. The customer pick-up delivery price was lowered to attract more volume through this channel. This move was intended to attract the largest-volume users of the product—consumer product and manufacturing. It also had the advantage of encouraging the competitor to take away our lowest-margin business, food processors, because these companies did not use sufficient volume to take advantage of the new price discounts.
3. The company began to look actively for other suppliers for the products they outsourced so as to improve the profitability of this operation. In addition, they decided to redesign the vendor relations group and reengineer the purchasing process with the goal of reducing the overall handling cost by 50% for purchased goods.

Using the cost and revenue information in the model, management was able to estimate the impact of these changes on the overall results under several different scenarios. While the impact of the new competitor definitely would be negative, the overall effect would be mitigated substantially by these responses.

SALES FORCE RESTRUCTURING

An industrial equipment supplier had one of the oldest and most capable sales forces of all the suppliers in its field. As a result, several competitors recently had started to shift their focus to other distribution channels. While competitors moved away from dedicated sales forces, the management team chose not to pursue these alternative methods because they still considered the in-house sales force a source of real advantage in the marketplace. Due to several periods of unsatisfactory results and the continued growth of alternative distribution and sales channels, however, the company's management decided to undertake a distribution profitability study focused on understanding the strategic value of the sales force.

The primary issues management wanted to address was sales force effectiveness, so the analysis was structured to focus on this aspect of the cost structure. The detailed log of sales-force activity was tracked to customers or channels, depending on the activity. By creating a very detailed cost picture of the various channels, the company could see the relative profitability of the various channel configurations and the source of cost differentials. By building this detail, management was able to see the sales force costs consumed by different customer and product groups.

With this cost baseline, management estimated the impact of several changes to the structure. In addition, the cost differential between the company and its competitors was estimated from knowledge of how its competitors' activities and sales volumes differed across their sales forces. Combining these cost and profitability views with an understanding of the customer buying factors provided insight into several issues.

A FRAMEWORK
FOR DISTRIBUTION ISSUES

After performing the analysis, management became aware of several points that had not been clear before:

- Some high-margin product lines that were thought to be profitable were, in fact, unprofitable due to the channel-related costs.
- Sales volume did not correlate with restated customer profitability.
- The cost of selling product differed dramatically depending on the customer application.
- One product line that was low margin and thought to be a loss leader was, in fact, relatively profitable.

Based on these findings, management formulated several changes in response to this new information:

- The loss leader was priced lower to attract additional volume from existing customers.
- Another product line was dropped because the primary customer base for it was extremely unlikely to buy any of the other products, and the revenue from these single-product customers would never justify the cost to serve them through a sales force.
- In addition, several representatives were taken on to serve those customers who were small- to medium-volume purchasers and did not require technical expertise from the sales force. These reps were offered a margin that encouraged them to deal exclusively with this company. The cost savings from shifting the sales force more than compensated for the margin passed on to the distributors.

The sales force then was refocused on those customers who valued their technical expertise and would be likely to buy additional product lines from this supplier in the future.

By assessing the cost and profit differentials among customers and channels, this company was able to shift its sales resources to those opportunities that provided better long-term growth and profitabilitiy.

The analysis described above forms the basis for multiple types of decisions including: pricing levels, warehouse investments, cost reduction targets, make/buy decisions, new channel options, channel rationalization, and selection of target markets and key customers.

This approach is not presented as the complete solution to the distribution issues of the 1990s, but it is a very important analytical framework that should accompany most distribution strategy developments. It forms the basis for developing a solid quantitative understanding of the current distribution and customer situation. The findings and models developed in this phase can be used to evaluate current performance, estimate future impacts, and track improvements from new distribution strategies.

Kenneth H. Manning is with Deloitte & Touche in Atlanta, Ga. He can be reached at (404) 220-1147.

Notes

1. Robin Cooper and Robert S.Kaplan, "Measure Cost Right Make the Right Decision," *Harvard Business Review,* September/October 1988, pp. 96–103.
2. Philip Rhodes, "Activity-Based Costing: What Will It Do for You?," *APICS,* August 1992, pp. 29–31.

From K. H. Manning, "Distribution Channel Profitability," *Management Accounting* (January 1995): 44–48. Reprinted with permission.

Questions

7.4a Discuss the four-step process that Manning uses for developing accurate channel and customer costs.

7.4b In developing the four-step process, Manning discusses both activity and nonactivity costs. What are two examples of two nonactivity customer related costs? Why are these labeled as "nonactivity costs?"

CHAPTER 8

Process and Activity Decisions

The readings in this section all relate to various aspects of process and activity decisions. A. Faye Borthick and Harold Roth's *Accounting for Time: Reengineering Business Processes to Improve Responsiveness* (Reading 8.1) discusses how the concept of time must be considered in all process decisions. Many companies compete now on time-based variables, such as speed to market and cycle time. A goal of many of these firms is to significantly reduce "noncontributing time" (or non-value added time), or the amount of time in the total product or service life cycle that can be eliminated without diminishing the value of products or services. Techniques for reducing noncontributing time include: eliminating redundant activities, decreasing the time it takes to perform activities, and coordinating deliveries in order to ensure that all parts of an order arrive simultaneously. Activity-based costing is recommended for identifying activities and developing costs for each activity.

D. Dhavale's *Activity-Based Costing in Cellular Manufacturing Systems* (Reading 8.2) is an in depth discussion of how an activity-based costing model can be developed contingent on process characteristics of cellular manufacturing systems. The article describes the typical job shop environment and contrasts this with cellular manufacturing. Dhavale then develops his model which is a mixed cellular environment consisting of both manufacturing cells and a job shop. Through a series of detailed diagrams, the author illustrates how resources flow in a cellular manufacturing environment and how resource drivers, cost pools, and activity drivers relate to the resource flow. The model is then applied to a Fortune 500 company, and the author discusses how managers adapted the model to their operating environment.

Another process that is critical for many firms is reducing costs without adversely affecting the mission and objectives of the organization. In *Effective Long-Term Cost Reduction: A Strategic Perspective* (Reading 8.3) authors Michael D. Shields and S. Mark Young caution against the most expedient, short-term, traditional method for reducing costs — firing employees. This traditional approach has a number of significant ramifications such as reducing employee morale and motivation and losing valuable work-related knowledge as each employee is fired. Both morale and motivation can decline as remaining employees experience greater stress given their greater work load and their constant worry that they will be next. In turn, coordination problems - such as production delays, missed schedules, and decreases in quality and delivery time, - can occur. Shields and Young argue for a much more strategic approach to cost reduction and develop a set of guidelines that firms can use to avoid the "slash and burn" traditional approach. These guidelines focus on reducing costs by improving organizational activities and processes and viewing employees as resources rather than as costs.

READINGS
CHAPTER 8

8.1 Accounting for Time: Reengineering Business Processes to Improve Responsiveness

By A. Faye Borthick and Harold P. Roth

As competition intensifies, companies must become more responsive to customers. The most effective strategy for improving responsiveness is to eliminate noncontributing time by reengineering business processes. Noncontributing time is any time in the total product or service life cycle that could be eliminated without diminishing the product's or service's value. Time is a competitive element; companies can manage time better if accounting and financial analyses support the goal of reducing and eliminating non-contributing time. Methods for eliminating noncontributing time include consolidating redundant activities, compressing the supply chain cycle, and synchronizing lead times and capacities. This article shows how financial data can be used to support these methods, but the analyses must often be expanded to include cost savings that accountants and managers sometimes ignore. If companies do not manage time in their product cycle, their competitiveness and profitability will be jeopardized by competitors that do.

The current competitive environment has forced many companies to reconsider their goals and strategic plans. Instead of trying to compete solely on the basis of cost, many companies now consider quality and responsiveness key components of competitiveness. Although quality and responsiveness have typically been approached separately, improving one usually has an effect on the other. Fortunately, the effects are often complementary. For example, being more responsive to customers requires higher-quality products delivered closer to when customers want them. In contrast, producing lower-quality products increases inspection and rework time, which delays responding to customers. Thus, quality and responsiveness are positively correlated, and both are related to the management of time. Hence, managing time is essential to being competitive.

This article discusses techniques that can be used to help manage time. The article illustrates how accounting data can be analyzed to support investments for improving time management. To show why accounting for time is important, the article first discusses the importance of time in the current competitive environment, and considers how noncontributing time can be identified and eliminated. Subse-

quently, it illustrates how accounting can support the elimination of noncontributing time. The techniques illustrated include:

- Implementing electronic data interchange (EDI);
- Modifying capital investment evaluations; and
- Improving communications with suppliers.

The article concludes by summarizing the reasons why noncontributing time exists. By becoming aware of noncontributing time and its effects on responsiveness, companies should learn how to manage time better to improve their competitiveness.

TIME—THE NEW COMPETITIVE ELEMENT

Time has become a critical competitive element as companies try to compete in the global marketplace. Many current management philosophies, such as just-in-time (JIT), are based on the effective management of time. As companies adapt these philosophies to their specific products, manager's and accountants need to recognize the implications of time-based competition. All companies are likely to be affected because of the implications these philosophies have for relationships between suppliers and customers. Relationships will now be based as much on responsiveness as on cost; time management will be critical to a company's success.

Management and accounting writers have recently begun to recognize the importance of time management. For example, Stalk and Houk note that "Time is a more useful management tool than cost."[1] They support the importance of time as follows:

Managing time . . . opens up the company for analysis. Time is an objectively measurable current flow, not a calculation shaped by accounting conventions. A manager can measure and quantify the flow of activities directly and ask with respect to each whether it is adding real value. For example, inventories are idle materials, just as in-baskets contain idle information. Reworking is doing something twice. Holding up a decision because the necessary data is late in arriving is response time lost. Time is a common, direct measure.[2]

Blackburn also notes the importance of time and how time-based competition affects companies:

A growing body of evidence suggests that time will be an increasingly important strategic weapon. Companies are learning what it takes to become a time-based competitor, and it is not something that can be purchased from a supplier or uncrated and installed. Time-based competition requires a fundamental reconstruction of the processes by which goods are manufactured and services delivered. More than that, it may require rethinking how those processes are managed.[3]

JIT. The JIT philosophy is one way of rethinking how processes are managed. As Dodd notes, time is one of the critical elements of JIT:

JIT constantly focuses on cycle time. It stresses the need to reduce setup time, eliminate wait time. reduce or eliminate buffer stocks, and decrease move time and distance. All these practices constantly increase inventory velocity and throughput as JIT identifies process bottlenecks and emphasizes continuous process improvement. These practices all contribute to enhanced delivery capability.[4]

Performance measurement. Time is also one performance measure that is identified with the balanced scorecard approach for evaluating companies. Maisel notes as follows:

Since the creation of value begins with the customer, it is natural that performance measurement should start by viewing products or services through the eyes of the customer. To that end, customer measures can often be broken down into five attributes: time, quality, service, cost, and market share. Companies are now establishing measures to track these attributes.[5]

Examples of specific time measures identified include product development cycle, order to delivery cycle, and service cycle.

Time an element of competitive advantage. As these writers observe, time is an important competitive element that applies to both manufacturers and retailers. When companies begin competing on the basis of time, however, their behavior changes. These changes affect all companies in the supply chain, including suppliers, manufacturers, distributors, and retailers.

For example, when retailers recognize the importance of time, they delay sending orders to their suppliers, wait to confirm orders until just before shipment, and demand that manufacturers fill orders immediately. Unless they can become more time competitive, manufacturers are caught in the middle. They are desperate to get orders to continue production, but they are forced to maintain higher inventories to be more responsive. Of course, the higher inventories lead to higher inventory carrying costs (e.g., because of longer storage times and increased obsolescence and spoilage).

Unless all parties in the supply chain adopt time-based competition, customer behaviors shift the risk of higher inventories and service capacities to suppliers. To avoid the increased risk, the suppliers need to reengineer their processes to manufacture and deliver to order. If companies do not, they are likely to incur the penalties for being slow to respond to customers. Those penalties include loss of customers, decline in profits, and possibly bankruptcy of the company.

Financial data can play a critical role in helping companies reengineer their processes. Rather than focusing exclusively on costs, however, the analyses should include other factors, such as quality and responsiveness. Although most accountants and financial personnel have not been trained to measure quality or evaluate responsiveness, companies need information to manage these competitive elements better. In a time-based competitive environment, one of the major purposes of financial information should be to support the reengineering[6] of business processes to manage time better to make companies more responsive to customers.

IDENTIFYING NONCONTRIBUTING TIME

To manage time effectively, companies need to distinguish between contributing time and noncontributing time. Contributing time adds value to a product. For example, the functions of order entry, material transformation, part assembly, product packaging, and product delivery are all essential to a product's value

Noncontributing time is any time in the total product life cycle that could be eliminated without diminishing the product's value. It includes time the product waits for the next value-adding process to be applied. Examples include waiting in inventory, in buffers between machines, and on loading docks. Noncontributing time also includes any time in a value-adding process that could be eliminated by more effective processes. By this definition, all rework and much inspection generate noncontributing time. For services, noncontributing time is analogous—it is any time the service is waiting for action (e.g., approvals by higher-ups or excessive time spent performing the service).

Reducing or eliminating noncontributing time. Several methods are available for reducing or eliminating noncontributing time.[7] These methods include:

1. *Using the information in the supply chain to avoid redundancies.* In any process that involves sequential activities, the possibility exists that some activities are redundant and could be eliminated. For example, rekeying order information from a paper purchase order produced by a customer's computer ordering system is redundant if EDI could be used. With EDI, the customer could avoid the time for sorting, printing, stuffing, and delivering the paper order, and the sup-

plier could avoid the time for opening, handling, rekeying, storing, and disposing of the paper order. Thus, the electronic exchange of information benefits both the supplier and the customer.

2. *Compressing the supply chain cycle, internally and externally.* This method involves reducing the time required to perform an activity within a chain of activities. For example, modest investments in equipment may make substantially shorter setup times possible, which makes producing smaller batches feasible. Producing in smaller batches lets a manufacturer be more responsive to its customers while decreasing its finished goods inventory. An example of how the supply cycle can be reduced through external means is to coordinate buffer stock levels with one's suppliers and customers to reduce cycle times and inventories.

3. *Synchronizing lead times and capacities in the supply chain.* What customers want is for all parts of an order (e.g., a computer system) to arrive together ready to be used. If components arrive at different times, waiting for the last component is a source of noncontributing time. To eliminate this source of noncontributing time, suppliers need to adjust lead times and capacities so that all components of a system arrive together.

These prescriptions for reducing noncontributing time seem intuitive, as indeed they should be. The challenge, however, is to identify where noncontributing time exists and justify how it can be reduced or eliminated. Problems may occur in trying to justify the elimination of noncontributing time if traditional accounting and management methods are used. These methods may need to be expanded or modified if companies want to use financial data to justify investing in projects to improve responsiveness.

USING FINANCIAL DATA TO IMPROVE RESPONSIVENESS

If a company wants to use financial data to help evaluate how noncontributing time can be reduced or eliminated, it needs accurate information about the activities that cause the noncontributing time and the cost of those activities. Thus, a company needs to use activity-based costing (ABC) for identifying activities and costing products or services. Without ABC, any analysis of the cost of reducing or eliminating activities will be limited because of the cost distortions inherent in traditional cost systems.[8] It is also crucial to construct and use a value chain to specify the linked set of value-creating activities that the company relies on to turn raw materials into products.[9] Constructing a value chain makes it easier to determine cost drivers, link consecutive activities, value intermediate products, and calculate supplier and customer margins.

ILLUSTRATION

After a company implements ABC, it can use the information about activities and their costs to help justify projects that will improve responsiveness. To illustrate how financial data can be used, assume that a company produces two products, A and B, using two raw materials, X and Y. Exhibit 1 shows production data and raw materials usage for the past period. The average daily raw materials usage is based on a 250 working-day year. The following analysis shows how financial data can be used to support the three methods discussed previously for reducing and eliminating noncontributing time.

USE THE INFORMATION IN THE SUPPLY CHAIN TO AVOID REDUNDANCIES.

Purchasing provides a good example of how EDI can be used to avoid redundancies in a process involving sequential activities. In addition to the data about purchases in Exhibit 1, the company collected the following information relating to purchasing activities:

1. *Cycle time for purchase orders.* The cycle time for purchase orders is 25 days, including:

   • 4 days preparation: Whenever the inventory count in the automated inventory system drops below the reorder point, the system produces a paper report that is delivered to the inventory manager, who approves the order. The system prepares the purchase order. A purchasing clerk verifies that the managers request and the purchase order agree and stuffs the mailing envelope.
   • 3 days mail: The supplier receives the order in the mail.
   • 4 days receipt: The supplier opens the mail, delivers the order to order entry, and keys in the order.
   • 5 days in process: The supplier produces a purchase order report, verifies the customer's credit status, and mails a confirming memo to the company.
   • 5 days supplier confirmation: The supplier confirms a ship date with the company, prepares shipping documents, and delivers them to the warehouse.
   • 4 days delivery: The supplier loads the truck, dispatches the truck, and delivers the material to the company inventory dock.

2. *Inventory reorder point for raw material.* The inventory reorder point for each raw material is 16,000 units, which is determined by multiplying the approximate usage of 400 units per day by the 40 days of minimum inventory needed (25 days cycle time for purchase orders plus a 15-day safety stock).

One source of noncontributing time in the purchasing process is the supplier's rekeying of the order information from the company's paper purchase order. Even if the company has

EXHIBIT 1
ACTIVITY AND COST DATA

Cost Component	Product A	Product B	Both Products	Cost
Units produced	10,000	10,000	20,000	
Raw materials used (units)				
X	50,000	50,000	100,000	$800,000
Y		100,000	100,000	$1,200,000
Daily usage of materials				
X			400	
Y			400	
Labor hours used				
Department 1				$681,000
Direct labor	20,000	5,000	25,000	
Indirect labor				
Inspection	2,500	2,500	5,000	
Machine operations	5,000	10,000	15,000	
Setups	200	200	400	
Department 2				$462,000
Direct labor	5,000	5,000	10,000	
Indirect labor				
Inspection	2,500	5,000	7,500	
Machine operations	1,000	4,000	5,000	
Setups	200	400	600	
Purchasing				$100,000
Number of purchase orders				
Material X			200	
Material Y			300	

automated its ordering system and the supplier has automated its order-filling system, neither is helping itself (or the other) to avoid redundant efforts. If they used EDI[10] for sending or receiving purchase orders and related information, the company's preparation, mail transit, supplier receipt, supplier process, and supplier confirmation functions could all be performed in electronic time (i.e., almost instantaneously rather than in days for each physical move).[11]

EDI is the computer-to-computer exchange of formatted business and technical data such as:

- Quotations;
- Purchase orders;
- Acknowledgments;
- Transportation plans;
- Invoices; and
- Remittance advices.

The exchange can be directly between a company and its supplier or indirectly through a third-party service provider. EDI can be accomplished with computers of any size. Regardless of how EDI is implemented, companies need communications equipment and translation software to interface with their own accounting systems. They can write their own software, buy it, lease it, or pay a third-party service provider for using its software. With all these options, EDI can be used by companies of all sizes.

If this company and its major supplier implement EDI for ordering and filling orders, both can benefit from the decrease in processing times. As Exhibit 2 shows, if the time for each activity in the purchasing process could be reduced to 0.1 days, for example, the purchasing cycle time would be only 4.5 days. On the basis of the times achieved through EDI as shown in Exhibit 2, the company's inventory level can be reduced by the amount of raw materials needed for the 20.5 (25.0-4.5) days removed from the order process. This 20.5-day reduction permits a 51 percent (i.e., 20.5 days/40 days) decrease in raw materials inventory. At an average usage of 400 units per day for each material, inventory can thus decrease by 8,200 units (20.5 days × 400 units/day) for each raw material. This means a decrease of $65,600 for raw material X (8,200 units × $800,000/100,000 units) and a decrease of $98,400 for raw material Y (8,200 units × $1,200,000/100,000 units), for a total inventory reduction of $164,000. If the carrying cost of raw materials is 10 percent, this reduction results in annual savings of $16,400.

Other cost reductions. In addition to the savings in inventory, there are other cost reductions. Purchasing would need less space because less paper would have to be kept and for shorter periods. This should reduce purchasing's occupancy costs. Purchasing should also be able to reduce its direct costs. Since all of the company's preparation tasks for orders would be automated, less labor and supplies would be needed for the purchasing function.

EXHIBIT 2
PURCHASING CYCLE TIMES

Order or Order-Filling Function	Number of Days Without EDI	Number of Days with EDI
Company preparation	4.0	.1
Order in mail transit	3.0	.1
Supplier receipt	4.0	.1
Supplier process	5.0	.1
Supplier confirmation	5.0	.1
Supplier delivery	4.0	4.0
Total for order process	25.0	4.5

To justify the EDI implementation, these cost savings can be compared with the cost of implementing and maintaining the system. Thus, for example, if the cost of implementing the EDI system was $80,000, the continuing yearly cost was $20,000, and purchasing costs are reduced by $40,000 a year because of the use of EDI, the EDI system would pay for itself in approximately 2.2 years [$80,000/($40,000 + $16,400-$20,000)]. Note, however, that if the cost savings from the decrease in purchasing activities were not included in the analysis, the system would not be acceptable from a financial viewpoint because the annual costs of $20,000 exceed the $16,400 of annual savings in inventory carrying costs. Thus, it is critical that all costs identified with noncontributing activities be analyzed and evaluated if financial data are to be used to justify investments in projects such as this.

Compress the supply chain cycle, internally and externally. Another way for companies to eliminate or reduce noncontributing time is by reducing the supply chain cycle time. The supply chain refers to all processes involved in purchasing materials, manufacturing, and selling a product or service.

Cycle compression can result from internal or external activities. For example, an internal activity might be investing in automated equipment that permits shorter setup times. An external activity might include getting suppliers to provide higher-quality raw materials that require less inspection time.

Internal changes. To show how financial data can be used to justify an investment for compressing the supply chain cycle time, assume that the same company is considering a $60,000 investment in new equipment to reduce the time required for setup activities shown in Exhibit 1. Getting approval for this investment may be difficult if the cost savings are not great enough to justify the project when it is evaluated using traditional capital budgeting models.

Two possible causes of this problem are as follows:

1. Some measurable cost savings may be omitted from the analysis; or
2. Some cost savings may not be measurable.

An initial evaluation of this investment might be based on the cost savings from the reduced setup times. Setup times per batch with and without the investment in automated equipment are shown below:

SETUP TIME IN HOURS PER BATCH

Department	Product	Without Investment	With Investment
1	A	5	1
1	B	5	1
2	A	5	1
2	B	10	2

Exhibit 3 shows the cost savings resulting from these reduced setup times. Since setup costs without the investment are $18,000 per year and the costs with the new equipment are $3,600 per year, the annual savings amount to $14,400. If the equipment has an expected life of 5 years and no salvage value, it would have an internal rate of return of 6.4 percent and a payback period of 4.2 years. With these cost savings, it is unlikely that the project would be acceptable.

Omitted cost savings. One problem with the analysis in Exhibit 3 is that some cost savings have been omitted. These savings are possible because the average batch size and the related inventory can be reduced if the setup times

EXHIBIT 3
ANALYSIS OF SETUP COSTS

	Without Investment				With Investment			
	Department 1		Department 2		Department 1		Department 2	
	Product A	Product B	Product A	Product B	Product A	Product B	Product A	Product B
Units produced	10,000	10,000	10,000	10,000	10,000	10,000	10,000	10,000
Batch size	250	250	250	250	250	250	250	250
Number of setups	40	40	40	40	40	40	40	40
Batch setup time	5	5	5	10	1	1	1	2
Setup hours	200	200	200	400	40	40	40	80
Setup hour cost	$ 15	$ 15	$ 20	$ 20	$ 15	$ 15	$ 20	$20
Setup costs	$3,000	$3,000	$4,000	$ 8,000	$600	$600	$800	$ 1,600
Total setup costs				$18,000				$ 3,600
Cost savings								$14,400

155

are shorter. Thus, the cost savings analysis should be expanded to include the reduced carrying costs resulting from lower inventories. Exhibit 4 shows the cost savings when the average inventory is one-half of the batch size. Note in Exhibit 4 that the annual cost savings are higher than they are in Exhibit 3, even though the setup costs are higher with smaller batches. With annual cost savings of $31,500, the internal rate of return is 44 percent and the payback period is less than 2 years. As this example shows, excluding the savings that result from reducing inventory when the company is more responsive penalizes the project by ignoring over 50 percent of the cost savings.

Survival investments. If there are savings that the company cannot or does not want to estimate, another approach to justifying the project might be to consider it a survival investment. Just as a company may have to invest in pollution control equipment if it is going to stay in business regardless of the equipment's payback or internal rate of return, the company may also have to invest in projects to reduce noncontributing time if it wants to survive. This approach clearly identifies such investments as critical so that they can receive high priority in the capital expenditure process.

External changes. Companies should also consider external changes to decrease the internal noncontributing time. For example, higher-quality raw materials may result in significant reductions in inspection times. These savings can also be calculated.

As the inspection line items in Exhibit 1 show, the company spent 5,000 hours in Department 1 and 7,500 hours in Department 2 on inspecting activities. By obtaining higher-quality raw materials, the company may be able to reduce these hours by 50 percent, resulting in savings of $112,500 [(2,500 × $15) + (3,750 × $20)] a year. The company will benefit from the savings to the extent that the sup-

plier does not charge a higher price for higher-quality raw materials. In addition, the company will obtain any other benefits that accrue from higher-quality materials.

SYNCHRONIZE LEAD TIMES AND CAPACITIES IN THE SUPPLY CHAIN

Another approach to reducing noncontributing time is to synchronize activities in the supply chain. For example, if a supplier cannot anticipate the quantity variation in the orders it receives, it cannot smooth day-to-day production activities.

A better approach would be for the supplier to get frequent and complete data about materials usage from the customer, which could be accomplished via EDI. In exchange for the data, the supplier may offer to guarantee maximum delivery times. Having this guarantee would allow the customer to reduce its safety-stock level since it could rely on the supplier's deliveries. This reduction in safety stock leads to cost savings that can be calculated and analyzed in a manner similar to that illustrated for the EDI purchasing activity.

Other lead time and capacity synchronizations are also possible. For example, a company could work with its equipment supplier to plan for, and even influence, the supplier's designs of machine upgrades. Influencing machine design might be especially desirable if the company is thinking about adding a companion product C that would be sold with products A and B but would be dissimilar enough to have a markedly different cycle time from products A and B. If the machine supplier could incorporate features that permitted the company to make product C with a cycle time equal to that of products A and B, it would be much easier for the company to balance its production schedule to ensure that all parts of an order were always ready to be shipped together. Balancing production in this manner should mean lower inventories, which would result in additional cost savings.

EXHIBIT 4
ANALYSIS OF SETUP AND CARRYING COSTS

| | Without Investment | | | | With Investment | | | |
| | Department 1 | | Department 2 | | Department 1 | | Department 2 | |
	Product A	Product B	Product A	Product B	Product A	Product B	Product A	Product B
Units produced	10,000	10,000	10,000	10,000	10,000	10,000	10,000	10,000
Batch size	250	250	250	250	100	100	100	100
Number of setups	40	40	40	40	100	100	100	100
Batch setup time	5	5	5	10	1	1	1	2
Setup hours	200	200	200	400	100	100	100	200
Setup hour cost	$ 15	$ 15	$ 20	$ 20	$ 15	$ 15	$ 20	$ 20
Average inventory in units	125	125	125	125	50	50	50	50
Average unit carrying cost	$ 50	$ 100	$ 50	$ 100	$ 50	$ 100	$ 50	$ 100
Setup costs	$3,000	$ 3,000	$ 4,000	$ 8,000	$1,500	$1,500	$2,000	$ 4,000
Carrying costs	6,250	12,500	6,250	12,500	2,500	5,000	2,500	5,000
	$9,250	$15,500	$10,250	$20,500	$4,000	$6,500	$4,500	$ 9,000
Total costs				$55,500				$24,000
Cost savings								$31,500

156

REASONS FOR NONCONTRIBUTING TIME

If noncontributing time is as obvious as it is in the company illustrated here, why is there so much of it? The chief reasons are given in the following paragraphs.

1. *The need to be more responsive has only recently become critical.* When the only competitors were neighbors or companies in other parts of one's own country and the dominant strategy was low-cost production, there was no demand for responsiveness. Every company had its customers who may not have liked the lack of responsiveness, but there were no better alternatives. The very idea of time-based competition is a recent phenomenon.[12]

2. *The tradition of thinking about cost alone is so entrenched that thinking more broadly is difficult.* Every accountant practicing today grew up thinking mainly about minimizing cost. Until recently (with the adoption of ABC), most allocation procedures focused primarily on direct labor costs. Since traditional product cost is just an accumulation of manufacturing costs incurred, no distinction was made between costs that were necessary for production and those that were incurred because of inefficiencies. Under traditional costing, these are all lumped together. As a result, it is impossible to discern the costs of non-contributing time, which includes (for example) machine downtime, rework of defectives, production of scrap, and waiting due to lack of process coordination.

Another problem with traditional cost accounting is that often it is not connected to the rest of the company. In many cases, traditional costing cannot measure the impact of changes in processes where investments are needed. For example, traditional product costing systems may not answer the question of whether or not it would be better to invest in new automated equipment that would decrease setup times. As Peter Drucker said, "traditional cost accounting can hardly justify a product *improvement,* let alone a product or process *innovation.* Automation, for instance, shows up as a cost but almost never as a benefit."[13]

3. *Product costing focuses on manufacturing costs.* Traditional cost accounting concepts do not include many support and administrative function costs in product costs. Since many companies focus their efforts on reporting and controlling product costs, many nonmanufacturing activities have never been analyzed critically to determine if they are necessary or if they are being performed efficiently. Examples of these include order processing, materials receiving, product development, and general and administrative functions. Since the costs of these activities are not classified as manufacturing costs, many companies fail to recognize how inefficiencies in these activities affect the responsiveness of the company.

4. *Cooperation is required among people who have not traditionally worked together.* For the internal supply chain, people in different functional areas in the company must cooperate. For example, finance personnel must interact with engineers, production employees, and marketing personnel. For the external supply chain, people in different companies all along the supply chain must work together. In some industries, the largest blocks of noncontributing time can be eliminated only through the cooperation of companies all along the supply chain. Companies with a history of treating fellow members of their supply chains as adversaries will have a hard time cooperating with them to eliminate noncontributing time from the chain.

5. *Expensive, time-consuming changes are needed in information systems.* Although the acknowledged backlog in information system development is about two years, an even longer undocumented development queue exists. As in the case of other innovations, a major difficulty is the lack of a means for evaluating the potential contribution of a new or revised information system.

Complicating this need for rapid system development is the need to make many system changes at once. When many changes need to occur simultaneously, it is difficult to know where to begin. It is generally infeasible to change everything at once, but that may be what is needed. For example, decreasing the inspection time by ordering raw materials from suppliers that can ensure the quality of their raw materials may require more coordination with the suppliers. Decreasing raw material inventory levels may require the use of EDI to facilitate smaller, more frequent orders. Fortunately, the changes are generally complementary. For example, using EDI makes it easier for a company and its suppliers to keep each other informed about quality matters and product demand.

Another impediment to the development of responsive information systems is the widely accepted assumption that access to information should be limited to only the few people that have a need to know. Cooperation requires sharing information, among people in the company and with others in the company's supply chain.[14] To compete successfully in a time-based environment, more people need access to more information than is now customary.

6. *The implied changes in working relationships, procedures, and expectations threaten people.* In any company, change causes uncertainty that may result in dysfunctional behavior. For example, if machine operators are accustomed to maximizing throughput on a machine and producing to inventory, they may resist a production strategy of frequent changeovers to produce to order. To encourage new behavior, the company will need to train operators in new procedures, explain what the changes accomplish and how, and modify performance metrics

to make them consistent with producing to order. If the performance metrics are not changed, the operators will never embrace the new strategy wholeheartedly because they will still be maximizing throughput to meet performance objectives. It may be even harder to influence middle managers that have staked their careers on accustomed ways of operating.

SUMMARY

Time-based competition is becoming more important. A time-based competitor can more easily change its processes in response to changes in customers' requirements, thus keeping or increasing its market share. In industries that already have time-based competitors, the shift in processes is underway.

In other industries, time-based competition will come. Time-based competitors in many industries are likely to come from other countries because some of them already feel the need to enlarge their customer base to support their fixed costs. Companies that fail to incorporate time-based competition into their strategies will lose customers, market share, and profits.

Noncontributing time can be identified and eliminated by using information in the supply chain to avoid redundancies, compress the supply chain cycle, and synchronize lead times and capacities in the supply chain. The impediments to eliminating noncontributing time are formidable but not insurmountable. The biggest impediments are the lack of vision to see the need for it and the lack of will to do it.

Also contributing to the problem are performance measures that emphasize short-term financial results instead of long-term improvements in quality and responsiveness. Companies must make progress in managing time, however; the enabling tools (including inter- and intra-firm information systems) can be created with existing information and communications technology. The enabling spirit—cooperation with insiders and with outsiders — can be motivated by thinking through what needs to be done cooperatively. The greatest limitations to reengineering business processes to improve a company's responsiveness result from its managers' lack of commitment and creativeness.

A. Faye Borthick is an associate professor of accounting and Harold P. Roth is a professor of accounting, both at the University of Tennessee in Knoxville, Tennessee.

Notes

1. George Stalk, Jr. and Thomas M. Hout, *Competing Against Time: How Time-Based Competition Is Reshaping Global Markets* (New York: The Free Press. 1990): 192.

2. *Id.*

3. Joseph D. Blackburn, "Trends in Manufacturing and Time-Based Competition," in Barry J. Brinker, ed., *Handbook of Cost Management* (Boston: Warren Gorham Lamont, 1992): A2–A21.

4. Andrew Dodd, "The Just-in-Time Environment," in Barry J. Brinker, ed., *Handbook of Cost Management* (Boston: Warren Gorham Lamont, 1992): A3–A7.

5. Lawrence S. Maisel, "Performance Measurement: The Balanced Scorecard Approach," *Journal of Cost Management* (Summer 1992): 50.

6. Michael Hammer, "Reengineering Work: Don't Automate, Obliterate." *Harvard Business Review* July–August 1990): 104–112.

7. For case histories and more detailed development of these ideas, see Stalk and Hout, *Competing Against Time.*

8. Harold P. Roth and A. Faye Borthick, "Are You Distorting Costs by Violating ABC Assumptions?" *Management Accounting* (November 1991): 39–42.

9. John K. Shank and Vijay Govindarajan, "Strategic Cost Management and the Value Chain," Journal of Cost Management (Winter 1992): 5–21.

10. For an introduction to EDI, see Margaret A. Emmelhainz, *Electronic Data Interchange: A Total Management Guide* (New York: Van Nostrand Reinhold, 1990). Evidence, record-keeping, and control implications of using EDI are discussed in Benjamin Wright. *The Law of Electronic Commerce* (Boston: Little, Brown, and Co., 1991).

11. Examples of companies using EDI are described in Margaret A. Emmelhainz, "Electronic Data Interchange: Does It Change the Purchasing Process?" *Journal of Purchasing and Materials Management* (Winter 1987): 2–8; Arjan T. Sadhwani and M. H. Sarhan, "Electronic Systems Enhance JIT Operations," *Management Accounting* (December 1987): 25–30; Bor-Yi Tsay, "Speeding Up Securities Transactions with EDI." *Management Accounting* (August 1989): 43–47; Martha M. Heidkamp, "Reaping the Benefits of Financial EDI," *Management Accounting* (May 1991): 39–43.

12. Although not specifically labeled time-based competition, aspects of it (such as shorter product delivery lead times, shorter product life cycles, and greater responsiveness to changing requirements) were incorporated in James A. Brimson, "How Advanced Manufacturing Technologies Are Reshaping Cost Management," *Management Accounting* (March 1986): 25–29, and C. J. McNair, William Mosconi, and Thomas Norris, *Meeting the Technology Challenge: Cost Accounting in a JIT Environment,* (Montvale, New Jersey: National Association of Accountants, 1988). John K. Shank discussed the concepts in terms of strategic cost management in "Strategic Cost Management: New Wine, or Just New Bottles?" *Journal of Management Accounting Research* (Fall 1989): 47–65. The earliest comprehensive treatment of time-based competition in wide circulation was George Stalk, Jr., "Time—The Next Source of Competitive Advantage." *Harvard Business Review* (July–August 1988): 41–51, which won the 1989 McKinsey Award for the best *Harvard Business Review* article of the year. Examples of companies implementing time-based strategies are beginning to appear (e.g.. Lawrence Klein and Randy M. Jacques, "'Pillow Talk' for Productivity," *Management Accounting* (February 1991): 47–49, and Mark E. Beischel and K. Richard Smith, "Linking the Shop Floor to the Top Floor," *Management Accounting* (October 1991): 25–29).

13. Peter Drucker, "The Emerging Theory of Manufacturing," *Harvard Business Review* (May–June, 1990): 97.

14. The practices of two companies whose policy is to permit access to information are explained in T. J. Rodgers. "No Excuses Management," *Harvard Business Review* (July–August 1990): 84–98, and Ikujiro Nonaka. "The Knowledge-Creating Company," *Harvard Business Review* (November–December 1991): 96–104.

From A. Faye Borthick and H. P. Roth, "Accounting for Time: Reengineering Business Processes to Improve Responsiveness," *Journal of Cost Management* (Fall 1993): 4–14. Reprinted with permission.

Question

8.1 What are the definitions of contributing and noncontributing time? What are the reasons for so much noncontributing time in many organizations?

8.2 Activity-Based Costing in Cellular Manufacturing Systems

By Dileep G. Dhavale

This article presents an activity-based costing model based on process characteristics of cellular manufacturing systems. The model reflects typical relationships between parameters of a cellular manufacturing system. The article provides rationales behind different components of the model so that users can modify the model to represent any cellular manufacturing environment. Finally, the article discusses an actual application of the model at a Fortune 200 company.

To receive the most benefits from new manufacturing, engineering, and management concepts, users must adopt the philosophy of, *group technology.* Simply stated, group technology entails solving problems by:

1. Identifying differentiating characteristics in a set of elements;
2. Forming subsets of the elements that exhibit similar characteristics; and
3. Exploiting similarities within a subset to obtain a solution.

Even though this idea of concentrating on commonality within a group may appear unsophisticated, impressive results have been obtained.[1]

Group technology has many different facets, much of which is beyond the scope of this article.[2] Nonetheless, one facet of group technology—the grouping of products or parts with similar processing requirements-forms the basis for developing cells in cellular manufacturing systems. After a brief description of cellular manufacturing, this article investigates activity-based costing (ABC) in such a system.

CELLULAR MANUFACTURING

Cellular manufacturing is an innovative production method that can help solve the problems caused by the inherent inefficiencies of batch production. These inefficiencies result from the operational characteristics of the type of factories that are used to manufacture products in batches—job shops. The following sections explain job shops and then define cellular manufacturing.

Job shops. A job shop makes many different products whose mix and demands are, for the most part, unknown until orders are actually received. A job shop must thus maintain a variety of general-purpose machines, which are usually physically segregated into departments, according to their functions. But this mode of operation creates enormous scheduling difficulties, because process planners must first determine the least-cost method for processing a given batch, then the appropriate machine routing, based on machine capacities and prior loading.

Sometimes costly substitute machines may have to be used at bottlenecks. These scheduling problems create delays. Indeed, it is estimated that some 90 percent of throughput time is spent waiting in queues for machines to become available.[3] As each machine completes a batch, it must be prepared for the next batch by (for example) changing tooling, fixtures, and dies. Such setups are time consuming and costly, and they reduce productive time. Job shops also expend considerable effort in transporting batches between departments according to machine routings. Cellular manufacturing overcomes these problems and provides many other benefits that result in enhanced efficiency and cost savings.

Definition of cellular manufacturing. Application of the group technology principle to a job shop environment suggests that parts with similar machining requirements should be grouped together and manufactured together. Such groupings are known as *part families.*

Since products in a part family have similar machining requirements, they can be manufactured sequentially without much setup change, and their flow is generally unidirectional. When machines required to manufacture a part family are physically laid out in the appropriate sequence as a production line, a *cell* is formed. A *cellular manufacturing* system consists of several such cells that manufacture a range of part families.

Classifying manufactured parts. Several steps are necessary to transform a job shop operation into a cellular manufacturing operation. The first step involves application of a classification scheme to all manufactured parts.

A classification scheme consists of assigning an alphanumeric code for each part. The character values in the code are determined by properties of a part. These properties may include such factors as:

* Material used;
* Shape;
* Size;
* Finish; and
* Tolerance.

Commercially marketed schemes are available, and others have been developed by universities and professional associations.[4]

Many benefits accrue immediately from the classification and coding of parts. Some of these benefits include:

* Improved design retrieval;
* Elimination of duplicate design;
* Standardization of parts;

- Identification of inconsistent manufacturing processes;
- Lower estimating costs;
- Standardization of process for a family of parts;
- Analysis of the capacity of existing machine tools;
- Improved product mix; and
- Better knowledge of the requirements of new machines.[5]

These benefits are made possible by a computer's ability to retrieve, manipulate, sort, group, identify, and organize the part codes in any fashion desired.

Process planning. The next step in transforming a job shop operation into a cellular manufacturing operation is process planning, which involves analyzing the processing requirements of each part to determine which machines should perform the job.[6]

Once the processing requirements are known, each part can be grouped into families based on similarities. Several methods, which differ in terms of the criteria and assumptions used to detect similarities, have been devised to group parts into families.[7]

Identifying machines needed. The last step involved in transforming a job shop into cellular manufacturing is identifying the machines needed to process part families and determining their optimal configurations. Production lines can then be formed such that each line (i.e., a cell) manufactures a part family.

Since only similar parts are manufactured in a cell, setup times are dramatically reduced by designing tooling and fixtures appropriate for the whole part family. The setup efficiency and production efficiency can be further enhanced by purchasing special-purpose machine tools. The insignificant time required to change production from one part to the other makes efficient manufacturing of very small batches economical.

Reduction in setup effort. This reduction in setup effort is the crucial requirement of the new manufacturing concepts, such as flexible manufacturing system, computer-aided manufacturing, and the just-in-time philosophy.[8] Products can thus be manufactured only in the quantities needed and when they are needed, one result of which is the virtual elimination of work-in-process and finished goods inventories. In other words, the full benefits of computer-aided manufacturing systems cannot be achieved without implementing the group technology philosophy to create manufacturing cells.

Other benefits of cellular manufacturing include the following:

- Sizable reductions in transportation costs of parts within the shop because the parts no longer have to be taken from a machine in one department to a machine in some other department for processing;
- Improved quality and reduction in scrap because of the expertise developed by workers who produce similar parts;
- Drastically reduced throughput times, which lead to superior on-time performance; and
- Uncomplicated scheduling of parts.

SCOPE OF THE MODEL

The model that this article develops determines manufacturing costs incurred in the production of parts in cellular manufacturing using ABC and generally accepted accounting principles (GAAP). Thus, the inventory and cost of goods sold valuations from this model are acceptable for external reporting purposes. Adherence to GAAP makes users far more likely to accept this method.

It should be noted, however, that this model may not always provide the best decision-making tool possible in all circumstances because it ignores opportunity costs, which are useful in portraying decision alternatives and their impact. Opportunity costs of unused capacity, idle machines, defective parts, and suboptimal routings due to bottlenecks have all been used in operations research models for cellular manufacturing.[9] Including opportunity costs in product costs would violate GAAP, because opportunity costs are not based on actual transactions.

Types of cellular manufacturing systems. Cellular manufacturing systems differ considerably in practice, depending on such factors as:

- Types of products manufactured;
- Degree of automation achieved in cells;
- Degree of adherence to the group technology philosophy;
- Deviations from preferred processes due to lack of machine capacity; and
- Mix of cellular manufacturing and job shop routing.

Modifications to the model developed here will probably be necessary before it can be applied. These modifications could be in the form of eliminating, adding, or combining resource or activity drivers, cost pools, or activity centers. Other modifications could include changing some cost flows to represent the operating conditions at the site in question.

The complexity of an ABC system depends on such factors as the number of resource or activity drivers and cost pools. The complexity increases in direct proportion to product and process diversity of a manufacturing operation. In cellular manufacturing, however, similarities in products processed in a cell and the operational simplicity of the system make it easier to form homogeneous cost pools, which help reduce the complexity of an ABC system.

AN ABC CELLULAR MANUFACTURING MODEL

The model developed here does not assume that the factory converts completely to cells (i.e., a pure cellular manufacturing environment) but allows for the coexistence of cells and a job shop (i.e., a mixed cellular manufacturing environment).

Most companies that have converted from a job shop toward cellular manufacturing indicate that the change is gradual. Product families are switched over as cells are formed either by relocating or dedicating the required machines. Even after the conversion is complete, many companies continue to maintain a job shop (albeit on a much smaller scale), because some parts cannot be categorized into families and thus must continue being made the old-fashioned way. A job shop also maintains flexibility by providing alternate routings for bottleneck machines in the cells. Consequently, the model given here assumes several cells and a job shop.

Unidirectional routing. The preferred routing of batches in a cell is unidirectional, but the model presented in this article does not restrict routing to one sequence. Many companies operate following the principle of cellular manufacturing, but without physically rearranging machines into separate cells. This avoids the cost of a new layout of machines, but transportation costs, supervisory costs, and the like are higher than they would be if the layout were improved. The model allows for these variations.

Exhibit 1 shows a schematic diagram of a mixed cellular manufacturing system that includes many cells (three of which are shown) and a job shop. Even though the exhibit shows physically separated cells with unidirectional parts flow, the model (as just described) represents a more general situation.

EXHIBIT 1
SCHEMATIC DIAGRAM OF A MIXED CELLULAR MANUFACTURING SYSTEM

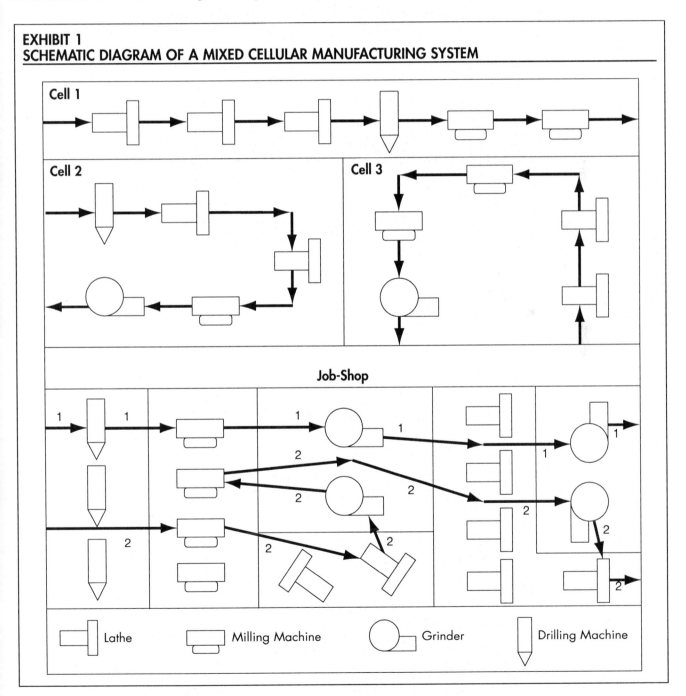

Exhibit 2 shows a schematic diagram of the proposed ABC model for a mixed cellular manufacturing. The first column shows fifteen different manufacturing overhead resources used in the production of parts. As the resources are used, their costs are allocated to the units (the last column) through intermediate resource and activity drivers and pools. These resource and activity drivers and pools were identified after a thorough study of the operational aspects of group technology and cellular manufacturing, and based on visits to companies that use these techniques. The objective of this study was to develop a detailed yet general model that can be modified or simplified to fit any cellular manufacturing site.

Capital outlays vs. recurring expenses. The resources shown in Exhibit 2 are identified as either *capital* (C) outlays or *recurring* (R) expenses. Of the two resource drivers shown, both are used for creating cost pools for machines. Capital outlay costs are allocated by either resource or activity drivers based on expected activity levels over the economic life of an asset. To allocate recurring expenses, on the other hand, expected activity levels for one-

EXHIBIT 2
SCHEMATIC DIAGRAM OF ACTIVITY-BASED COSTING IN A MIXED CELLULAR MANUFACTURING SYSTEM

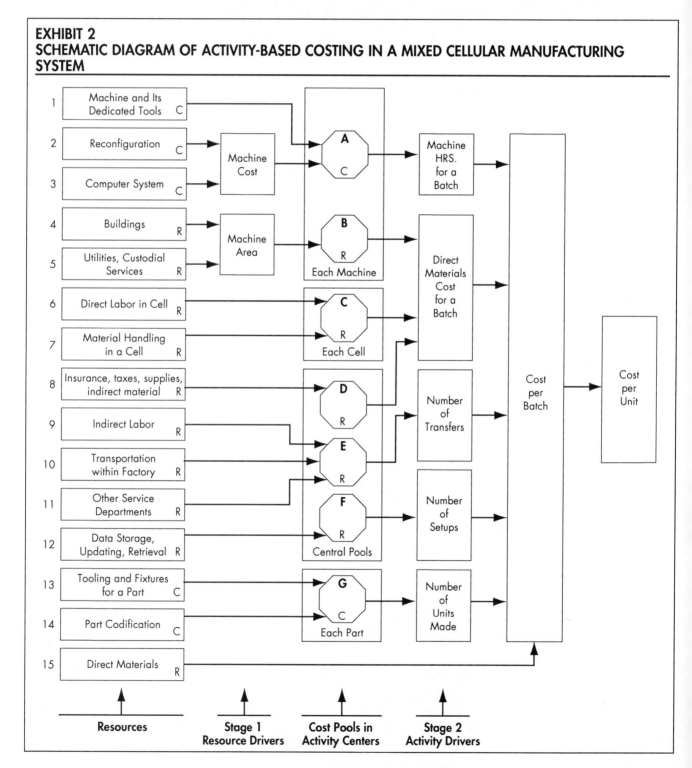

year periods are used. By keeping these costs separate, a clearer causal relationship is shown between the activities and the drivers, and the model is simpler to understand and operate. This is analogous to not mixing cost of an asset and its routine maintenance expense.

Activity centers. Activity centers play an important role in cost control, because resources costs are first pooled at each activity center. This pooling of costs gives managers data for planning and controlling activities and for measuring the performance of the activity centers.

An activity center may have one or more cost pools. For example, the activity center "each machine" has two cost pools: one collects capital outlays and the other recurring expenses. "Each cell" and "each part" are activity centers with one cost pool each. The cost pool "each cell" collects recurring expenses, whereas the cost pool "each part" collects only capital outlays.

Three cost pools are called *central pools.* In a pure cellular manufacturing environment in which machines have been reconfigured into cells, the central pools will not exist; instead, the activity center "each cell" will have additional cost pools. For the purpose of applying the model, the job shop is viewed as an additional cell. Thus, if a site has four cells and a job shop, computations will be based on five cells.

Activity drivers. Activity drivers are used to allocate costs from cost pools to a batch of parts based on the consumption of resources by that batch at each activity center. Each cost pool has exactly one activity driver associated with it. Seven cost pools are shown in Exhibit 2 but only five activity drivers, because the activity driver "direct materials cost for a batch" is shared by three pools. Once the manufacturing cost per batch is known, the calculation of unit costs is straight-forward.

In the following sections, rationales and relationships between the model components and costs flows are explained, so that users may determine any modifications needed for particular cellular manufacturing operations.

RESOURCES

This section explains the fifteen resources listed in the left-hand column of Exhibit 2.

1. Machine and its dedicated tools. This cost includes the purchase cost of a machine and all other costs necessary to get the machine ready for production (e.g., cost of tools and fixtures developed for that machine). In other words, this is the historical cost of the asset as shown on the balance sheet. Each machine is treated as an activity center, and a cost pool A (see Exhibit 2) is created for that machine, and to which this amount is added. As explained earlier, the small letters C and R that characterize each resource and cost pool stand for capital outlay or recurring expenditure, respectively. Cost pools contain only pure capital outlays or only recurring expenditure, never a mixture of the two.

2. Reconfiguration. Reconfiguration costs are incurred when existing machines are moved to form cells; included

are all costs incurred in getting a machine ready for production at the new location. New machines purchased to be put directly into cells would not incur this cost.

If the cost of moving each machine can be determined, that cost can be directly added to cost pool A. In the absence of such information, the total reconfiguration cost may be allocated to cost pool A in proportion to the historical cost of the machines that were moved. Since this cost can be substantial, some companies opt for a system in which machines are dedicated to a part family but are left scattered throughout the factory instead of being reconfigured into a physical cell. Any savings obtained by such "reconfigurations," however, are nullified by the substantially higher transportation costs incurred, and by the decrease in manufacturing efficiency because of the lack of automation and the higher demands made on labor and supervision.

A reconfigured cell works like a miniassembly line (i.e., a part starts at one end and is completed when it leaves the last machine in the cell). An automatic material handling system may be used to transfer parts efficiently from one machine to the next in the cell. The capital outlays for automatic material handling equipment should be included in reconfiguration cost. Resource 7, Automatic Material Handling in a Cell, is the recurring cost of that system, which is discussed later.

3. Computer system. To obtain the maximum advantage from group technology, a computer system is needed to store and manipulate information about part families. This information is useful in design as well as manufacturing phases of the operation.

Computer costs are assigned to cost pool A in proportion to the costs of machines used in a cellular manufacturing. The rationale behind this allocation method is that the computer is an essential part of the machines. Hence (just as in the case of dedicated tools and fixtures of the machines) computer cost should be borne by the machines in proportion to their costs.

4. Buildings. Building rent or depreciation expense is allocated to each machine based on its floor work area and is added to cost pool "B," which is also formed for each machine. Hence, each machine has two cost pools, A and B.

5. Utilities, custodial services. Costs of utilities and custodial services are also allocated to each machine (based on its floor work area) and added to cost pool B. Although this allocation basis is quite logical for heating and cooling expenses and for custodial services, electrical power consumption may not be exactly proportional to machine areas. Ideally, a meter is used to measure the energy consumption of each machine; the actual expense can then be added directly to the cost pool rather than allocated using a resource driver. if meters are not used, and if none of the machines are intensive energy consumers (e.g., a furnace for heat treatment), the area of a machine is probably a good surrogate for its consumption of energy.

6. Direct labor in a cell. Direct labor used to play a dominant role in manufacturing. With increased automation, however, manufacturing has become far less labor intensive. In electronics manufacturing, direct labor costs are reportedly as low as 3 percent.[10] For fully automated flexible manufacturing systems, the range is from 5 percent to 10 percent.[11]

Because of automation, an operator can often look after several machines in a cell that may be working on different batches. This makes it difficult for the operator to allocate his time to batches with any objectivity. Consequently, since direct labor is no longer a prime cost, it becomes difficult to trace direct labor to batches.

Since direct labor constitutes a small percentage of total cost and is difficult to allocate properly, it has been suggested that direct labor cost often should no longer be considered a major component of manufacturing costs. Consequently, its use as an activity driver should be limited to situations where it can be measured accurately and its costs can be allocated in proportion to production volume.[12]

The model explained in this article does not treat direct labor as a major cost category: It is not separately pooled, and it is not directly traced to batches. Instead, the direct labor cost in a cell is collected in cost pool C, which is later allocated to batches. If a user finds it necessary to trace direct labor costs to batches, it can be done simply by bypassing the pool C and adding the cost directly to a batch, as is done in the case of resource 15, direct material cost.

7. Material handling in a cell. As described earlier, the capital outlays of material handling equipment are added to reconfiguration cost; only recurring expenses are dealt with here. Recurring expenses are added to cost pool C, which is formed at each cell as an activity center along with direct labor cost in that cell.

8. Insurance, property taxes, supplies, indirect materials. Insurance and property taxes are based on the value of the assets. Consequently, the related costs can easily be traced to those assets and hence to the cells where the assets reside. The other resources, supplies and indirect materials, are also used within cells. Thus, in a pure cellular manufacturing system, all costs in this pool are traceable to individual cells. In a mixed system, however, supplies and indirect materials are difficult to trace to products in a job shop, so a separate cost pool becomes necessary to correctly allocate these costs.

Insurance, property taxes, supplies, and indirect materials are pooled together because these cost components, even though characteristically different, are homogeneous as far as their proportional consumption by various products is concerned. If a manager wants more details about any of the cost components, additional cost pools may have to be formed.

9. Indirect labor. Indirect labor is used all over the factory, in the cells as well as in the job shop. Its use is not uniform. Usually, a job shop consumes more indirect labor compared to a cell. The indirect labor is accumulated in a pool E.

10. Transportation within the factory. The transportation costs discussed here are not the automatic transportation costs within a cell, which were discussed earlier. Rather, the transportation costs within the factory include the costs of transporting raw materials to, and finished goods from, the cells and the job shop, as well as transportation of parts within the job shop.

One of the incentives for switching to cellular manufacturing from a job shop operation is the reduction of these transportation costs. The job shop section of the mixed cellular manufacturing will tend to consume a great deal of this resource compared to all the cells put together. This cost is accumulated in a central cost pool E.

11. Other service departments. The support of several service departments in cellular manufacturing is essential to the smooth functioning of the manufacturing system. These departments include:

- Maintenance;
- Process Planning;
- Manufacturing and Industrial Engineering; and
- Plant Accounting and Administration.

While computer systems, utilities, custodial services, material handling, and transportation are handled separately, all other service departments are grouped together here. The cost of these departments, which can be substantial, is accumulated in cost pool E, along with the costs of the two previous resources.

12. Data storage, updating, retrieval. A computer system is an important component of cellular manufacturing; without a computer system, data retrieval, manipulation, storage, sorting, grouping, and organizing cannot be done. This data handling capability is necessary for:

- Designing new parts;
- Modifying old parts;
- Scheduling parts in proper cells;
- Avoiding duplication of design efforts; and
- Standardizing manufacturing.

The recurring cost of storing, maintaining, and updating these data sets and software is accumulated in a separate cost pool F.

13. Tooling and fixtures for a part. There are two types of tooling and fixtures. The first type, the machine dedicated, is attached to a machine as long as the machine continues to be a member of a cell. These attachments are designed for the part family. The other type of tooling and fixtures is designed specifically for a part and is attached to the machine when that part is being made. This cost is added to cost pool G at activity center "each part."

14. Part codification. Parts must be represented in alphanumeric code which forms the database that is used in grouping parts into families, in computer-aided manufacturing and design (CAD and CAM), and in computer-aided process planning. The cost incurred in analyzing a part so that it can be coded is added to the cost pool G.

Instead of actually measuring the cost for each part that was coded, the total coding cost may be divided by the number of parts coded to obtain this figure.

15. Direct materials cost. The cost of direct materials for each batch is determined from requisitions from inventories and supplies. Since this cost is directly available for each batch, no intermediate cost pools or activity drivers are necessary. Since direct material cost can be measured with great accuracy (i.e., with no allocations or measurement errors), it has a desirable property of a good activity driver, so it is used as such.

ACTIVITY DRIVERS

Activity drivers play a crucial role in allocating pooled costs to batches of parts. Ideally, an activity driver should reflect the actual use of a resource by the batches. In practice, however, it is not always possible to identify an appropriate activity driver because the relationship between it and resource use may be indirect, spurious, or nonlinear. Moreover, an activity driver should be easily and accurately measurable. Errors in measurement are serious and will be magnified when allocations are performed.

Five activity drivers are identified in Exhibit 2 based on an analysis of manufacturing operations in cellular manufacturing systems. Each is discussed below.

1. Machine hours for a batch. The activity driver "machine hours for a batch" is used to allocate cost pool *A,* which contains capital outlay costs associated mainly with machines. In a traditional setting, capital costs of this kind are depreciated using the straight-line method. Since machine usage is not uniform over the life of a machine, the straight-line method does not provide accurate product costing data. A machine that is new is used more often because of its newer technology, higher productivity, lower breakdown rates, and higher-quality output. Therefore, the units produced early in a machine's life are subsidized by those produced later. But if depreciation is based on actual use of a machine—e.g., based on machine hours used in manufacturing a batch—more accurate costing is achieved.

2. Direct materials cost for a batch. The activity driver "direct materials cost for a batch" is the only activity driver that is partly based on the volume of production; it is used to allocate the costs in cost pools *B, C,* and *D* to the batches.

The parts manufactured in a cell require similar processing and are made from the same, or similar, raw materials. Hence, the higher the weight of a part, the more demand placed on resources required to complete the processing. Consequently, the weight of a part can be used as an activity driver.

If the raw material used for all parts in a family is the same, the cost of the raw material (which would be proportional to the weight of a part) could be used as an activity driver. Under certain conditions, direct materials cost can be the single most important volume-related activity driver in cellular manufacturing and can appropriately be used as a base to develop a flexible budgeting system.[13] When one automotive parts factory switched its operation to cellular manufacturing, the weight of parts was used as an activity driver.[14] The weight of a part or the cost of raw materials can thus be appropriate activity drivers for cellular manufacturing.

3. Number of transfers. The cost pool *E* consists of cost accumulations from three resources. Each resource is examined separately in the following to explain its use with "number of transfers" as the activity driver. Almost all indirect labor (resource 9) can be traced in cellular manufacturing environments to cells, because it is used within one of the cells. Indirect labor for a cell can thus be included with the direct labor of that cell, because no clear distinction exists between the two. In other words, in a pure cellular manufacturing environment, all labor (i.e., both direct and indirect labor) could be used instead of direct labor as resource 6. In the mixed model shown in Exhibit 2, however, indirect labor continues to be separately identified.

Transportation within the factory (resource 10), which occurs predominantly in the job shop, does not include material handling within a cell. In a pure cellular manufacturing operation, this resource would not be distinguishable from material handling in a cell (resource 7) and would be added to it. Other service department costs (resource 11) in a traditional facility are indirect costs, but in a mixed cellular manufacturing environment, many of the costs become direct costs with respect to the activity centers where the cost pools are formed. For example, utilities and custodial service costs are accumulated for each machine. In a mixed cellular manufacturing environment, costs of process planning and scheduling, plant accounting, and plant engineering departments continue to be indirect. In a pure model, on the other hand, most of these costs are direct to cells and are thus accumulated there (see Exhibit 3).

The three resources discussed previously—indirect labor (resource 9), transportation within the factory, (resource 10), and other service departments (resource 11)— are consumed at a greater rate in a job shop than in a cell, because they are consumed every time a job moves from one machine to the next machine in its routing sequence. In a cell, only when a job is started and removed from the cell does the resource consumption take place.

The activity driver "number of transfers" correctly reflects the consumption of these resources. It is defined as the number of times a job is transferred from one machine to the next until completion. These transfers include the transfer of raw material to the first machine in a sequence and the transfer of finished goods from the last machine to a warehouse. Thus, the number of transfers equals the number of machines used in the processing plus one. For a cell, this number is always two because a cell is considered one machine for this purpose.

4. Number of setups. Every time a part is produced in a cell or in the job shop, information about it (e.g., raw materials needed and the processing sequence) must be provided before the setup can be performed. Consequently, the number of setups is used as an activity driver for allocating costs of data storage, updating data, and retrieving data—i.e., the operating costs of the computer system. Note, however, that

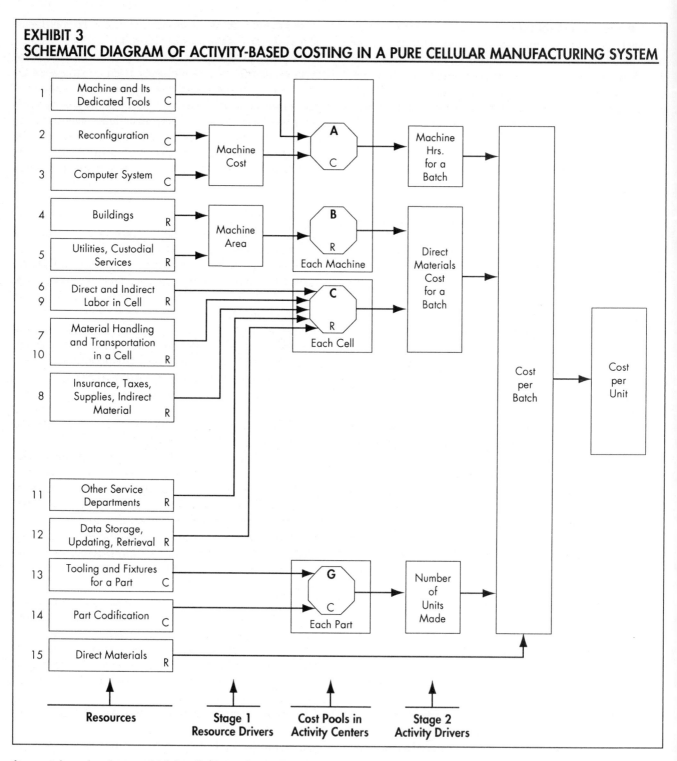

EXHIBIT 3
SCHEMATIC DIAGRAM OF ACTIVITY-BASED COSTING IN A PURE CELLULAR MANUFACTURING SYSTEM

1	Machine and Its Dedicated Tools C	
2	Reconfiguration C	
3	Computer System C	Machine Cost
4	Buildings R	
5	Utilities, Custodial Services R	Machine Area
6 9	Direct and Indirect Labor in Cell R	
7 10	Material Handling and Transportation in a Cell R	
8	Insurance, Taxes, Supplies, Indirect Material R	
11	Other Service Departments R	
12	Data Storage, Updating, Retrieval R	
13	Tooling and Fixtures for a Part C	
14	Part Codification C	
15	Direct Materials R	

A C — Machine Hrs. for a Batch

B R — Each Machine — Direct Materials Cost for a Batch

C R — Each Cell

G C — Each Part — Number of Units Made

Cost per Batch → Cost per Unit

Resources — **Stage 1 Resource Drivers** — **Cost Pools in Activity Centers** — **Stage 2 Activity Drivers**

the capacity-related cost, which is a fixed cost, is accumulated in cost pool A.

The number of setups for a batch in a job shop equals the number of machines needed to process the job, since each machine in the routing sequence must be set up with appropriate tools, dies, and fixtures. The number of setups for a part manufactured in a cell, however, is always one, because machines in the cell are always set up to manufacture that part family (although additional minor setups may be required for some parts).

The two activity drivers "number of setups" and "number of transfers" as they are defined here, are perfectly correlated, since

Number of transfers = Number of setups + 1.

Either one of the activity drivers can be substituted for the other; thus, one fewer activity driver may be used. The activity driver that is easier to track or measure accurately should be selected.

166

5. Number of units made. Cost pool *G*, which is created for each part, accumulates costs incurred specifically for each particular part. These costs include the cost of tooling and fixtures (resource 13) needed to manufacture each part, and also the part codification costs (resource 14). These costs are allocated based on the number of units of each part expected to be manufactured over its life span.

COST PER BATCH AND UNIT COST

Activity drivers provide the cost per batch based on the actual values of the five activity drivers for each batch. Cost per unit is obtained by simply dividing the cost per batch by the number of units in that batch.

   Simplifying the model. Considerable simplicity in the model could be achieved if there were no job shop. The three central cost pools (i.e., cost pools *D*, *E*, and *F*) that were created to account for operational differences between a job shop and the cells would no longer be needed. Resource 8 could thus be traced directly to each cell and accumulated in cost pool *C* instead of cost pool *D*. Exhibit 3 provides a schematic diagram of such a cellular manufacturing system.

   As mentioned, indirect labor (resource 9) can be traced to each cell; since the distinction between direct and indirect labor disappears, both are accumulated in cost pool *C*. Transportation within the factory (resource 10), which is movement of batches in the job shop, also disappears. The transportation of raw material to the cells and finished goods from the cell is thus included with resource 7, material handling in a cell.

   Most other service department costs (resource 11) can be directly traced to the cells once the job shop is removed. Those that cannot be traced can be allocated to cells equally if the cells have about equal activity. If not, the costs can be allocated in proportion to the number of different parts manufactured in a cell, because demand for services (e.g., accounting and process planning) is based on the number of different parts made in each cell. The same reasoning described also applies to resource 12, data storage, updating, and retrieval; its cost is added to cost pool *C*.

   To summarize, in a pure cellular manufacturing operation, resource 9 is not considered separately. Cost pools *D*, *E*, and *F* are added to cost pool *C*. Moreover, two activity drivers, "number of transfers" and "number of setups," are no longer used. As Exhibit 3 shows, four cost pools and three activity drivers remain. With the removal of central pools, cost pools are now formed at the cells or on lower levels—namely, at machines and parts. This kind of detailed tracing provides a manager with accurate data for product costing.

   In a pure cellular manufacturing environment, the direct materials cost for a batch becomes the dominant activity driver. As Exhibit 3 shows, it is used for nine out of fourteen resources. Direct materials cost is a volume-related activity driver for production within each cell. Further simplification is possible if parts in a family are similar in terms of design or shape as well as manufacturing process. In that case, a high correlation exists between the weight of the part (hence its cost) and the amount of machining required. Under such circumstances, the activity driver "machine hours for a batch" can be replaced by the activity driver "direct materials cost for a batch." The only other non-volume-related activity driver under these circumstances would be the number of units made in a batch.

APPLICATION OF THE MODEL

The model developed in this article must be modified to reflect local operating conditions. To exemplify this procedure, a firm that uses a cellular manufacturing system was chosen—EG&G, Inc., a Fortune 200 company with sales of over $2.5 billion.

   EG&G has several business segments that specialize in different types of manufacturing. The division that was contacted, EG&G Sealol, is in Warwick, Rhode Island, and is well known for its early adoption of cellular manufacturing (in 1980). At that time, the machines were not reconfigured into physical cells. The reconfiguration, which took place in 1990, has greatly improved overall efficiency and also created additional working space.

   EG&G Sealol has five major product lines. Each product line is treated as a separate department. Each product line has between four and six product families, which thus determines the number of cells. A job shop and tool room are considered together as a cell. The flow of jobs in the cells is not unidirectional. Although, EG&G Sealol currently does not use an explicit ABC system, many elements of its costing system are based on a careful analysis of activity drivers.

   The managers most closely associated with EG&G Sealol's cost accounting system were provided detailed information about the model explained in this article. After presentation and discussion of the model, the managers were asked to modify the model to reflect their operating environment. After further discussion, the managers arrived at the modified version of the model shown in Exhibit 4. Their reasons for changes are discussed in the following.

   Operating conditions that affect how ABC is applied. As mentioned earlier, each plant or firm has unique operating conditions that affect how the general ABC model explained so far would be modified.

   EG&G Sealol is a defense contractor. It manufactures military and civilian products in the same departments and often in the same cell. The Department of Defense requires that product costing procedures be described in detail, submitted for review, and approved before they are used. The model described next is modified to fit within currently approved procedures. Any deviation from an approved procedure would necessitate EG&G Sealol's performing a cumbersome cost impact study to indicate how the product costs under the new method differ from the product costs under the old method.

The two main requirements of the existing approved costing method dictated how the normative ABC model explained earlier would be modified. First, the department-wide cost pools that are currently being used must continue. The advantage of this is that it avoids having to allocate costs to the departments, because many support department costs are either direct as far as the department is concerned (i.e., because the support department employees are assigned to the departments), or they can be traced to the departments based on actual usage. The direct cost to the departments obviates the need for first-stage allocation procedures, which must be approved by the Department of Defense. The modified ABC model therefore uses cost pools at the department levels. Second, the approved procedures require that direct labor be used as the allocation base. Use of a different activity driver would require a lengthy and time-consuming cost impact analysis statement; moreover, use of a different activity driver would probably be forbidden in any case. The modified ABC model shown in Exhibit 4 therefore uses direct labor dollars as the activity driver.

These requirements make the modified ABC model less accurate than what could be achieved with data currently available to the company. Nonetheless, this provides a good example of how exogenous considerations often play an important role in the selection of activity drivers and cost pools. Given a choice, a company probably would use a cost pool at the level of each cell, rather than at the level of each department.

Each department has one product line. The definition of a product line is based on marketing considerations, rather than considerations about manufacturing similarities. As a result, product families within a product line may have significantly different processing requirements. Having cost pools at each cell would avoid the product diversity within departments and related costing problems. The disadvantage of cost pools at each cell is that there would be fewer direct costs to cells and that additional resource drivers would be needed to allocate costs to cells from the resources. A more serious problem is the use of direct labor cost (which constitutes only about 14 percent of the total manufacturing costs) as the activity driver for each department. The problems associated with using direct labor as an activity driver also appear to exist at the company. EG&G Sealol's managers were aware of these problems and expressed a willingness to change from direct labor dollars to other activity drivers.

Other possible modifications. Some other interesting modifications to the model are as follows. The job shop and the tool room at EG&G Sealol were small enough to have an insignificant impact on costs in other cells. For

practical purposes, therefore, EG&G Sealol has a pure cellular manufacturing.

Reconfiguration costs. A portion of the cost of reconfiguration was treated as an R&D expense and was charged to income in the period when the reconfiguration occurred. The capitalization of reconfiguration cost (as suggested in the normative model) would have increased the cost of the items manufactured after the reconfiguration. The remaining portion of the reconfiguration cost was charged to the parent corporation, which had agreed to this charge-back in order to support this attempt of EG&G Sealol to improve its manufacturing efficiency.

Depreciation, tooling, and fixtures. The depreciation expense of the computer system is not differentiated from its recurring expenses and is charged to the other departments based on usage.

The cost of tooling and fixtures for a part (resource 13) also receives an interesting treatment. Specifically, the cost of tooling, and fixtures of a routinely manufactured part is charged to the department in which the part is made, but a one-time-only order is charged for its tooling and fixture expenses.

Part codification costs are not separately tracked. Instead, the costs are included with other service department costs and are allocated when the supporting department costs are allocated (i.e., they are included with resource 11).

In a sense, EG&G Sealol is not a run-of-the mill manufacturer. It specializes in various types of high-precision seals for submarines and aircraft pumps. Many simplifications obtained in its modified costing system (compare Exhibits 2 and 4) are a result of the basic similarities between its products and the requirement that direct labor be used as the activity driver. In a more diversified product environment, the modified model would probably not be as simple.

CONCLUSION

The normative ABC model presented in this article should be viewed as a prototype model and a framework from which to start developing a company's own model. Each cellular manufacturing shop will have its own unique operating environment in terms (for example) of:

• Processes involved;
• Product mix and changes;
• Output volumes;
• Externally enforced requirements (e.g., government regulations); and
• Internally enforced requirements (e.g., availability of data, budget restrictions on reconfigurations, and buying new equipment to form cells).

Users must modify the normative model explained here to reflect their own operating environments.

EXHIBIT 4
SCHEMATIC DIAGRAM OF A MODIFIED ACTIVITY-BASED COSTING SYSTEM FOR CELLULAR MANUFACTURING AT EG&G SEALOL

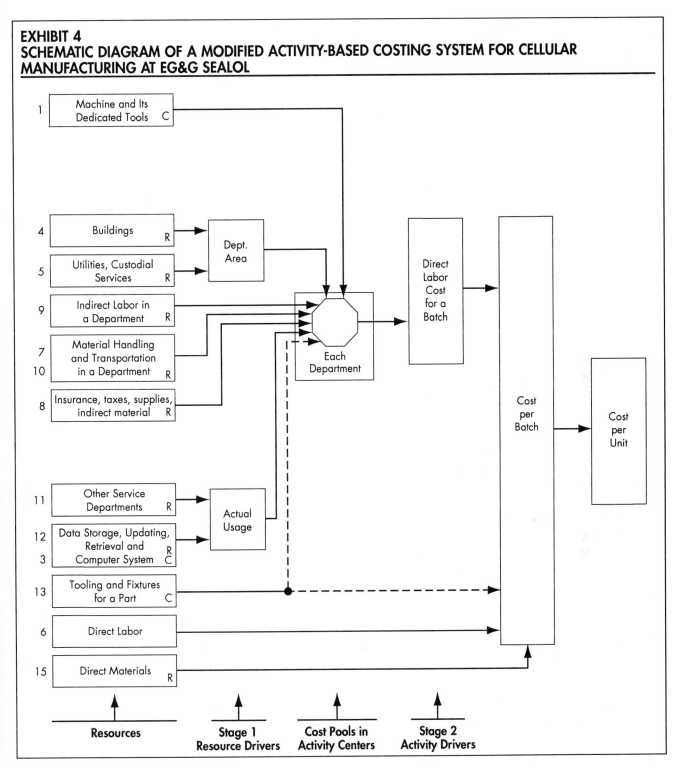

Resources	**Stage 1 Resource Drivers**	**Cost Pools in Activity Centers**	**Stage 2 Activity Drivers**

Dileep G. Dhavale is a professor of accounting at Clark University in Worcester, Massachusetts.

Notes

1. N. L. Hyer and U. Wemmerlov, "Group Technology and Productivity," *Harv. Bus. Rev.* (July–Aug. 1984)140–149.

2. For more information about group technology, see C. C. Gallagher, and W. A. Knight, *Group Technology* (London, U. K.: Butterworths, 1973); see also M. P. Groover, *Automation, Production Systems and Computer-Integrated Manufacturing* (Englewood Cliffs, N. J.: Prentice Hall, 1987).

3. J.B. Young, "Understanding Shop Lead Times," *Proceedings of the 22nd Annual Conference of the American Production and Inventory Control Society* (1979): 177–179.

4. See, for example, H. Opitz and H. P. Wiendahl, "Group Technology and Manufacturing Systems for Small and Medium Quantity Production," *International Journal of Production Research* (Vol. 9, No. 1,1971): 181–203; see also Robert N. Stauffer, "The Rewards of Classification and Coding," *Manufacturing Engineering* (May 1979): 48–52.

5. D. T. Desai, "How One Firm Put a Group Technology Parts Classification System into Operation," *Industrial Engineering* (Nov. 1981): 78–81.

6. For further information on computer-aided process planning, see L. Alting and H. Zhang, "Computer Aided Process Planning: The State-of-the-Art Survey," *International Journal of Production Research* (Vol. 27, No. 4, 1989): 553–585.

7. R. G. Askin and S. P. Subramanian, "A Cost-Based Heuristic for Group Technology Configuration," *International Journal of Production Research* (Vol. 25, No. 1, 1987): 101–113; see also A. J. Vakharia, "Methods of Cell Formation in Group Technology: A Framework for Evaluation," *Journal of Operations Management* (Vol. 6, No. 3, May 1986): 257–271.

8. D. G. Dhavale, "A Manufacturing Cost Model for Computer-Integrated Manufacturing Systems," *International Journal of Operations and Production Management* (Vol. 10, No. 8. 1990): 5–18.

9. Askin and Subramanian, "A Cost-Based Heuristic for Group Technology Configuration," 101–113.

10. Rick Hunt, Linda Garrett, and Mike G. Merz, "Direct Labor Costs Not Always Relevant at H-P," *Management Accounting* (USA) (Feb. 1985): 58–62.

11. D. G. Dhavale, "Product Costing in Flexible Manufacturing Systems," *Journal of Management Accounting Research* (Vol. 1, No. 1, 1989): 66–88.

12. George Foster and Charles T. Horngren, "Flexible Manufacturing Systems: Cost Management and Cost Accounting Implications," *Journal of Cost Management* (Fall 1988): 16–24; see also "Product Costing in Flexible Manufacturing Systems," 66–88.

13. D. G. Dhavale, J. Sounderpandian, "Flexible Budgets for Cellular Manufacturing Systems," Forthcoming in *Abacus* (Vol. 29, No. 1, 1993): 75–89.

14. A. Phillips and D. E. Collins, "How Borg-Warner Made the Transition from Pile Accounting to JIT," *Management Accounting* (USA) (Oct. 1990): 32–35.

From D. Dhavale, "Activity-Based Costing in Cellular Manufacturing Systems," *Journal of Cost Management* (Spring 1993): 13-27. Reprinted with permission.

Question

8.2 What are three factors that distinguish the different types of cellular manufacturing systems? What are the implications of these factors on the ABC model developed in the article?

8.3 Effective Long-Term Cost Reduction: A Strategic Perspective

By Michael D. Shields and S. Mark Young

Effective long-term cost reduction is a continuous activity that must be a strategic and cultural priority. In contrast to traditional cost reduction, with its emphasis on expedient and quick reductions in short-term costs because of immediate crises, strategic cost reduction must be part of a competitive strategy that integrates technological and human resource management strategies to provide a coordinated, broad-based, and long-term approach to reducing costs. Long-term competitive cost advantage depends on establishing a culture of continuous improvement of quality, time, and cost through innovation. Long-term cost reduction is most effectively accomplished by continuously learning about target core competencies faster than competitors can and by establishing long-term employment relationships with innovative, multiskilled employees who are paid above-average compensation.

Between the recessions of the late 1970s and early 1990s, several million managers and workers received significant pay cuts or were laid off because of cost reduction programs.[1] These programs were intended primarily to increase cost competitiveness. The business press described these cost reduction programs in phrases such as "slash and burn," "retrenching," "meat axing," "cutting and slicing," "repositioning," "restructing," "demassing," and "downsizing." In an attempt to justify the overall approach to cost reduction, the term "rightsizing" was coined. It is still unclear whether firms that engaged in these cost reduction programs will experience long-term success, since little systematic empirical evidence exists. Nonetheless, as articles in the business press show, cost reduction programs aimed at reducing the work force are still being implemented.[2]

This article first describes and evaluates the cost reduction programs employed in the late 1970s and throughout the 1980s, then sets forth a more viable basis for effective long-term cost reduction. The ultimate conclusion is that long-term controllable costs are caused (i.e., both increased and decreased) by employees, individually and in groupings, that range from small teams to entire organizations. As a consequence, the key to successful long-term cost reduction is to make cost reduction part of organizational culture—i.e., part of a competitive strategy based on the integration of human resources and technological strategies.

TRADITIONAL COST REDUCTION PROGRAMS

Starting in the late 1970s and throughout the 1980s, most firms relied on traditional cost reduction, which means a collection of crash programs that focus on cutting costs by reducing payrolls and eliminating jobs.[3] The key features of traditional cost reduction are identified in Exhibit 1.

A traditional cost reduction program is typically a distress tactic targeted at all employees. It is triggered in reaction to an immediate threat, such as poor performance, loss of contracts, or price reductions. Some of these programs (especially offshore retreat and diversification, both of which are explained below) are employed in the hope of escaping to places where labor and facilities costs are cheaper. While

EXHIBIT 1
DIFFERENCES BETWEEN TRADITIONAL AND STRATEGIC COST REDUCTION

Attribute	Traditional	Strategic
Goals	Specific	Competitive advantage
Scope	Narrow	Broad
Time frame	Short-term	Long-term
Frequency	Periodic	Continuous
Trigger	Reaction	Proaction
Target	Labor	Entire value chain

these traditional approaches often reduce costs immediately, the associated reduction in the value of human assets sets the stage for potential long-term failure. Five frequently used traditional cost reduction programs are described in the sections below; their effectiveness is also analyzed.[4]

THE TECHNOLOGY APPROACH

The technology approach focuses on replacing direct labor with technology to increase operating efficiency and to reduce the influence of unions. This approach is usually adopted or intensified after performance measures indicate poor performance. But the successful implementation of this approach requires money, time, an effective innovation process, and highly skilled employees-all of which, in firms that are performing poorly, are in short supply.

It is doubtful whether this labor-focused cost reduction—with its emphasis on immediate improvements in direct labor efficiency—can provide sustainable competitive advantage.[5] Its effectiveness is questionable because, in many manufacturing settings, a products cost of direct labor is typically no more than 10 percent of its sales price. This means, for example, that a 100 percent increase in direct labor efficiency can only reduce a product's total cost as a percentage of its sales by 5 percent. Alternatively, the complete elimination of direct labor can only reduce the product's total cost as a percent of its sales by 10 percent (*assuming* that the substitute for this labor is costless).

Thus, attempts to gain or sustain competitive advantage by reducing labor cost would appear to be weak foundations for a successful cost reduction program. As Hamel and Prahalad[6] point out, the *cost* of labor is rarely a source of sustainable competitive advantage. First, labor is a small percentage of total cost. Second, when the labor force is the key to a firm's competitive advantage, that advantage stems from labor's ability to be innovative through work methods (e.g., through total quality management) and flexibility. Moreover, many firms adopt technology-intensive strategies (e.g., computer-integrated manufacturing, or CIM) when they reduce their work force. Importantly, the success of these strategies requires having highly skilled employees who can design, implement, operate, and service these advanced technologies. Unfortunately, these critical human resource issues are ignored or receive only lip service

because of short-term cost considerations. Ironically, however, long-term success with technology is determined by how employees work with the technology.

Another important consideration in achieving good performance from a technology-intensive strategy is knowing when and how much should be spent on technological innovation. Evidence indicates that the relationship follows an elongated S shape, with spending related to technology on the x-axis and technological performance on the y-axis.[7] This elongated S relationship indicates that initial spending on technology results in little, if any, increase in performance. At some point, as spending continues to increase, there are dramatic increases in the performance of the technology. Finally, a point is reached at which further increases in spending result in only small (or no) increases in performance as the limits of the technology are hit (e.g., conventional washing machines can get clothes only so clean).

The implication for cost management is that a firm will achieve a better payoff from its spending on technology if it knows where it is on the S curve. For example, when a new technology is first introduced, a firm may decide to stop spending for the new technology when only a negligible increase in performance is obtained. At the other extreme, a firm at the far end of its S curve may fail to realize that it has moved beyond the point at which increased spending will lead to worth-while increases in performance. The result could be wasted spending as the technology hits its performance limit.

"LEAN AND MEAN"

The "lean and mean" approach has been a popular cost reduction program since the 1980s. Firms that follow this approach apply tough policies and controls to reduce the number of employees. A common approach is to employ across-the-board cost cuts through layoffs and reductions in pay and benefits.[8]

An appropriate depiction of the effects of a lean and mean program is a roller coaster traveling through time. The end of the ride can be—and frequently is—a long-term failure, despite short-term thrills and success. Exhibit 2 illustrates the interaction of lean and mean cost reduction efforts and the state of the economy. As shown in Exhibit 2, a firm's costs—total and unit—rise when the economy is "good" and fall when the economy is "bad." We define a good (or bad) economy as one in which there is low (high) unemployment and a growing (shrinking) gross national product.

When the economy is good, the lean and mean approach is not employed; as a result, costs creep up as inefficiency increases and new programs are initiated or expanded. As costs rise across firms, the economy begins to soften as prices become inflated. In response, firms begin to implement lean and mean programs to cut costs by reducing and eliminating discretionary programs and employees. While there is an immediate cost decrease, adverse effects become noticeable shortly thereafter.[9] The morale, motivation, and commitment of remaining employees begins to

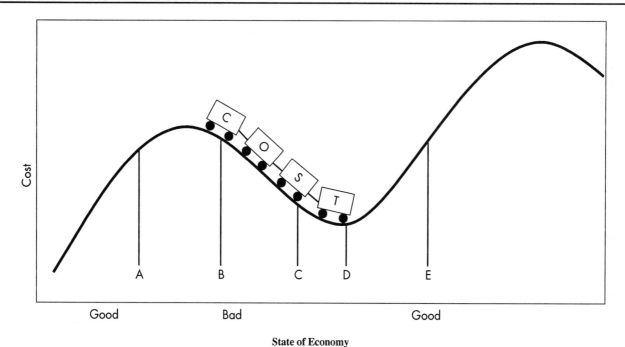

EXHIBIT 2
COST REDUCTION ROLLER COASTER

Cost

C O S T

Good   Bad   Good

A   B   C   D   E

State of Economy

A: As costs rise. the economy goes soft.
B: To reduce costs, cut discretionary programs, reduce work force, etc.
C: Problems develop: morale, motivation, conflict, shortages, delays.
D: To reduce problems and to react to the expanding economy, hire new employees.
E: Incur extra costs to train new employees and to cover learning curve effects.

decrease. Their stress increases because they worry about being the next ones who will be laid off, and also because they are overworked because of the layoffs.[10] Having fewer employees also leads to coordination problems (e.g., production delays and missed schedules), which can cause decreases in quality and increases in delivery time. Another bad consequence is that the creative and motivated employees leave for better employment opportunities.

In time, the economy begins to expand again as firms' products regain their competitiveness as a result of their cost reduction program. In response, firms abandon their lean and mean programs: they begin to hire employees again and to reestablish or expand programs to reduce the adverse effects of the previous cost reduction programs. As the economy expands, firms continue to hire new employees and to incur associated training and learning-cure costs.[11] The net result is that costs begin to increase again. This cycle keeps repeating, but as time goes on, each new cost peak becomes higher than the previous cost peaks.

Lean and mean is not effective in the tong term, because it attempts to reduce costs by reducing workers, but it does *not* reduce the work that needs to be done to make and sell products. While cutting workers, but not work, is a popular approach to traditional cost reduction, it causes an immediate decrease in costs that is usually followed by an increase because the work still needs to be done.[12] The long-

term effects of lean and mean programs are like the roller coaster ride shown in Exhibit 2.

OFFSHORE RETREAT
Many firms have tried to reduce costs by escaping to places (e.g., Asia) that offer the promise of lower labor costs. Many of these firms have found, however, that start-up costs of off-shore retreats are higher than expected, while quality and delivery performance are lower.[13] The success of this cost reduction approach often depends on how employees at home are treated and on the vagaries of exchange rates and currency fluctuations. Employee morale at home can be hurt if domestic or local employees are laid off when the firm moves jobs offshore.

MERGERS
Mergers purport to create economies of scale by eliminating overlapping employees, products, plants, and overhead. The idea is to build on the strengths of each merging entity, but the result is often that the worst aspects of each firm survive.[14] Problems often occur in assimilating diverse or incompatible management styles, corporate cultures, product lines, and technologies. Frequently, these mergers result in layoffs and compensation reductions, with the result that

172

morale and motivation decrease. Ultimately, the hoped-for economies of scale from the merger are not realized as hidden or unexpected costs arise.

DIVERSIFICATION

Diversification into new industries is an approach that firms often use when they are searching for cheaper operating environments. if a firm expands beyond its core competency, however, it is likely to experience difficulties in developing and implementing new products, technologies, or distribution systems, with the result that costs are higher than expected.[15] The increasing diversity also increases the cost of complexity, which in many cases exceeds the incremental revenue.

WHEN CAN TRADITIONAL COST REDUCTION APPROACHES SUCCEED?

Given these five approaches to traditional cost reduction, the question arises: "Are there situations when traditional cost reduction can be effective?" (See accompanying box, "How Effective Are Traditional Cost Reduction Programs?") Some managers have found that traditional cost reduction is effective in only the following three situations:

1. When "dressing up" a business for divestiture;
2. When implementing a harvest strategy; and
3. When reducing operating costs—but only when a firm's overall strategic position is good.[16]

While traditional approaches to cost reduction may be effective in these special situations, in general, traditional approaches do not appear to provide a basis for long-term competitive success.

STRATEGIC COST REDUCTION

In contrast to the traditional approach, this article advocates strategic cost reduction as an approach that can provide companies with better opportunities for creating and sustaining long-term competitive advantage. Strategic cost reduction is a long-term approach that integrates competitive strategy, technological strategies, human resource management strategies, and organizational design considerations to provide a focused and coordinated basis for sustaining competitive advantage. Exhibit 1 compares traditional and strategic cost reduction strategies.

The importance of viewing cost reduction as part of a long-term competitive strategy is reinforced by evidence that Ferdows and DeMeyer provide.[17] Their analysis of 187 European manufacturers indicates that cost reduction is the result of having achieved success with other manufacturing strategies. Specifically, they argue and empirically show that long-term cost improvement is the result of having first achieved improvement in quality, then dependability, and finally speed. There is a cumulative effect by which prior gains influence current gains, a process that can he illustrated as a pile of sand with four layers: quality at the bottom and cost at the top (see Exhibit 3). Increases in quality help increase dependability; then gains in both quality and dependability spur gains in speed. Finally, the cumulative effects of these prior gains result in cost efficiency gains.

Ferdows and DeMeyer also point out that, due to the shape of the pile of sand, achieving a small gain in cost requires successively larger gains for these other aspects of performance (e.g., a 10 percent cost gain may require a 15 percent gain in speed, a 25 percent gain in dependability, and a 40 percent gain in quality). The implication is that

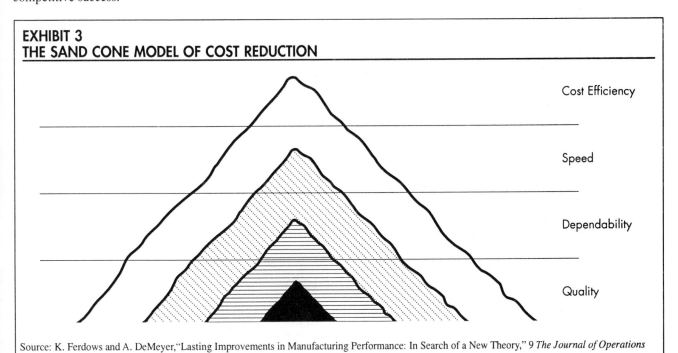

EXHIBIT 3
THE SAND CONE MODEL OF COST REDUCTION

Cost Efficiency

Speed

Dependability

Quality

Source: K. Ferdows and A. DeMeyer, "Lasting Improvements in Manufacturing Performance: In Search of a New Theory," 9 *The Journal of Operations Management* 168-184 (No. 2, 1991).

long-term successful cost reduction is achieved indirectly—through gains made in other strategically important areas. Thus, the cost reduction strategy should be deeply embedded in the firms competitive strategy.

Strategic cost reduction occurs continuously and is intertwined with competitive strategy.[18] Ideally, competitive strategies and also cost reduction strategies are derived from analyses of a firm's own value chains and of the value chains of its competitors to identify key activities that offer the best competitive alternatives. Strategic cost reduction is part of a competitive strategy that is focused on improving the performance of key activities and their cost drivers in a firm's value chain.

FOCUS

Two critical aspects of developing a strategic cost reduction program involve deciding where to focus the program and the mix of methods to use to reduce strategically important costs. Many manufacturing firms achieve competitive advantage from activities that occur before (e.g., R&D) or after (e.g., distribution) manufacturing, rather than in manufacturing itself. For many manufacturers, the most effective strategy to reduce a product's total life cycle cost is to focus cost reduction efforts on those activities that occur before manufacturing begins.[19] For instance. many Japanese manufacturing firms focus their cost reduction efforts on activities that occur before manufacturing begins, because they have found that this gives them the most and the quickest reductions in costs.[20] Quickly reducing costs significantly is crucial to maximize market share and achieving target cost strategies.[21] Thus, for most firms, initial efforts at cost reduction should be focused on those activities that occur before manufacturing ever begins—i.e., conception, development, and design.

SET OF METHODS

While manufacturing firms use many methods to reduce costs, there is only limited evidence that they are used in coordinated ways to achieve synergistic gains.[22] Thus, an important aspect of developing an effective cost reduction strategy is to identify a set of cost reduction methods that can be used in concert to continuously reduce strategically important costs. The methods selected should be compatible with—and should reinforce—a firms competitive strategy, culture, and human resource management strategy.[23]

For instance, the implementation of a cost reduction strategy may coincide with the adoption of a competitive strategy and a corporate culture of continuous improvement. A set of methods can be employed to achieve continuous improvement, including activity based management (ABM), value analysis and engineering, just-in-time (JIT) manufacturing methods, total quality management (TQM), cross-functional teamwork, employee involvement, and employee skill enhancement.[24] Rappaport[25] provides a list of coordinated ways by which a firm can reduce its long-term costs if it

is pursuing a cost leadership strategy, or a differentiation competitive strategy. Hayes, Wheelwright, and Clark[26] provide examples of how manufacturing firms can use a set of cost reduction methods to achieve synergistic gains in performance.

TRADE-OFFS

In some cases, the strategically important issue is to *increase* cost to achieve other competitive gains. For example, a study by McKinsey and Company found that being six months late to market but meeting the developmental cost budget resulted in actual profits that were one-third lower than budgeted profits.[27] In contrast, bringing a product to market on time but 50 percent over the developmental budget resulted in a profit loss of only 4 percent. The important point of this example is that sometimes it is strategically advantageous to increase costs if doing so can help achieve other competitive gains.

EMPLOYEES ARE THE ULTIMATE LONG-TERM COST DRIVER.

Effective cost reduction (especially in the long term) requires changing employees' behavior. In the long-term, the decisions and actions of employees cause costs; only employees can make decisions and take actions to reduce costs. Thus, the key to effective long-term cost reduction is employees—their beliefs, values, and goals. This means that successful cost reduction depends on establishing and nurturing an appropriate organizational culture, such as one based on continuous improvement are cost consciousness.[28] In the long term, successful cost reduction depends on establishing and nurturing an appropriate organizational culture, such as one based on continuous improvement and cost consciousness.[28] In the long term, successful cost reduction depends on how well a cost reduction strategy fits with a firm's competitive strategy, culture, and human resource management strategy.

The major reason that traditional cost reduction fails to have a positive long-term strategic impact is that is excludes the value of having employees who are broadly and deeply skilled—employees who work together and are committed to the long-term success of a firm. This human resource management approach is one of the most important reasons for the comparative success of Japanese firms. For example, one key to the success of Japanese firms has been their treatment of human resource management as long-term and strategic; human resource management is an important, if not *the* most important, part of their competitive strategy.[29]

The importance of employees as long-term cost drivers can be illustrated based on a discussion of quality improvement. Many firms have adopted the approach of trying to improve quality and reduce the cost of quality by substituting technology for people. But, behind all this technology are employees who design, operate, and service it. Technology can produce products that are only as good as the employees who develop and operate the technology—software programmers, machine technologists, design engineers, and others.

In the long term, the way to improve product quality and reduce the cost of quality through technology is to use technology to supplement high-quality employees. Technology will work better if it is complemented by employers who are highly educated, highly skilled, highly motivated, and committed to continuous improvement. All the innovation that is necessary for technology to be effective comes from humans. Having creative employees is important because, when trying to sustain competitive advantage through technology, technology does not stand still. Technology-intensive firms must continuously innovate to improve existing technology or to introduce new technology; otherwise, they will fall behind their technology-intensive competitors.

Three prerequisites to realizing the maximum benefits to be derived from long-term cost reduction efforts of employees are: having good top management, having a cost culture, and offering long-term employment. Each provides an important and necessary contribution to the establishment of an organizational setting in which employees are willing and able to make strategic cost reductions. The next sections discuss how top management, cost culture, and long-term employment affect long-term costs. Later sections explain how organizational cost drivers affect strategic cost reduction.

TOP MANAGEMENT

Top management must take the initiative in decision making and action to demonstrate to other employees and stakeholders that they are serious about improving the competitive position of the firm.[30] Top management should be prepared to set examples by taking tough action (e.g., taking a bigger reduction in pay than do the workers, laying off senior executives before laying off line workers, and eliminating executive perks) and getting involved with all employees. Top managers should take these actions to show that they are aware of the problems other employees face and that top management cares about employees and their fate during tough times.

One important determinant of success is the ability of top management to establish *strategic intent,* which means that they must provide *leadership* to achieve a *vision* by exploiting *core competencies.*[31] Top management must provide the leadership that makes all employees committed to achieving this strategic intent.[32] Top management must discuss strategic problems, challenges, and opportunities with employees. Finally, top management must set a steady course of action, set clear targets, and establish review mechanisms.

Top management must establish strategic goals for cost reduction. These goals should be based on supporting or reinforcing the firm's core competencies and competitive strategy. For example, top management may decide that the best way to reduce cost and to increase both quality and flexibility in the long-term is by exploiting the firm's competence in mechanical, manufacturing, and software engineering by implementing CIM. Accompanying this introduction would be a change in the human resource management strategy to increase employees' knowledge of how to use the new technology. For example, direct labor employees could be retrained to become machine technologists and monitors.

COST CULTURE

Top management must also develop a cost-conscious culture. The goal of a cost-conscious culture is continuous improvement of quality, time, and cost through innovation. Achieving this goal can be aided by redesigning the organization to focus attention on factors that have to do with sustaining continuous improvement strategies. The acid test of a cost-conscious culture is whether employees are motivated to take actions that reduce long-term costs but expose them to short-term risk. An example is a culture in which workers are willing to be innovative enough to eliminate their own jobs because they believe that they will then be assigned to more challenging and rewarding jobs.

Eight ways to develop a cost culture. Eight ways to develop a cost culture are as follows:[33]

1. Have top management demonstrate daily to employees the importance of reducing costs to the firm's success.
2. Hire the best-qualified employees. These employees can then develop high-quality activities and products, because long-term total cost with high quality is less than long-term total cost with low quality.
3. Empower employees through participation, involvement, and autonomous, cross-functional work teams.
4. Increase the levels of education, training. retraining, and cross-training provided to employees to increase and broaden their skills, commitment, and innovation.
5. Motivate employees to break existing paradigms (e.g., eliminating existing constraints rather than optimizing within them).
6. Communicate horizontally more than vertically; eliminate conflicting bureaucratic messages; focus all employees' communication on two or three keys to success; reduce the number of rules, policies, and standard operating procedures; and provide scoreboards for continuous feedback.
7. Link compensation to cost reduction (such as gains in productivity and efficiency, achievement of target costs, and improvement over the previous period's costs).
8. Provide all employees with continuous feedback about competitors' costs, their own performance, and the performance of other teams.

Train[34] provides an interesting description of a firm with cost problems that is struggling—philosophically and politically—with whether to implement a traditional cost reduction program (i.e., deep across-the-board cuts). Analysis of this case by senior executives and consultants illustrates why and how such situations should be a strategic cultural priority that is dealt with by methods like the eight outlined above.

LONG-TERM EMPLOYMENT

Many firms have found that the best way to realize the maximum potential from all employees to reduce long-term costs is to establish a long-term employment relationship in which both employees and the employer can adjust to changing circumstances.

For example, a human resource strategy that is based on long-term employment, cross-training of employees, continuous education, job rotation, and work teams creates an organizational skill set that provides a firm with the flexibility to adapt quickly to changes, opportunities, and threats. Having broadly skilled employees also increases flexibility when product and activity volume decrease and it becomes necessary to rearrange employee work assignments, The bottom line is that if firms want employees to be committed to long-term cost reduction, they must make long-term commitments to their employees. An employee's commitment will extend only as far into the future as his expected employment benefit horizon (e.g., including pension benefits).

Avoiding layoffs. Many firms have found that it is in their best interest not to lay off workers as a means of cutting costs.[35] Over a period of time, it is cheaper to keep excess employees. For example, the employees can be put to work on projects that will improve efficiency or eliminate non-value-added activities; alternatively, they can be provided with additional training. Some firms have used excess workers to lay the groundwork for an expected expansion in business by having them prepare the firm to use new technologies. This proactive approach can help a firm adapt faster when the business environment improves.

Laying off employees causes motivational problems for the remaining employees and, when business improves, the firm must incur the cost of hiring and training new employees who will probably not be as effective and efficient as were the employees who were laid off. Thus, while laying off employees may bring about an immediate reduction in cost, over a period of several years, it could become the more costly alternative because of the roller coaster effect.

When a company must lay off employees, a program should be implemented to maintain (if not increase) the morale of the remaining employees. Imberman[36] suggests a three-step program:

1. *Define the sources of the firm's competitive problems.* In many cases, this requires changing the corporate culture to accept the problems for what they really are. Changing the culture will help the survivors establish a shared vision of what is required for success, which usually requires communication and innovation.
2. *Initiate action to solve the problem.* This requires realistic challenges and experiments. It is critical that employees believe that to solve these problems they must work smarter, not harder or longer.
3. *Increase employees' skills.* This is accomplished through education, training, retraining, and cross-training.

ORGANIZATIONAL COST DRIVERS

An organization is a collection of people. Based on the view that employees are the ultimate long-term cost driver, it is a natural extension to see an organization as an important long-term cost driver. If an employee causes and reduces costs, then groups of employees will also cause and reduce costs.

Organizations group employees into teams, departments, divisions, and similar groupings to efficiently and effectively accomplish activities. The way in which employees are organized affects the long-term cost structure. The diversity of operating units and their boundaries (e.g.. functional or geographical boundaries) affect a firm's complexity (e.g., its number of parts and their interrelationships), which, in turn, affects long-term costs. Some have offered ABM as a solution to reducing the cost of complexity, because ABM focuses on eliminating non-value-added activities and reducing the number and frequency of cost drivers.[37] Gingrich and Metz[38] provide examples of how to reduce the cost of organizationally induced complexity by making changes in organizational structures and processes.

Organizational cost drivers include organizational structure, organizational process, and organizational learning. Examples of organizational cost drivers include vertical structure, horizontal structure, work units (e.g., individuals versus teams), educational programs, process sequence (e.g., linear versus concurrent), and culture and management style (e.g., decentralization, a vertical chain of command, or entrepreneurial): see Exhibit 4.

Firms adapt their organizational structure and processes over time in response to various challenges and opportunities. Many of the contemporary changes to these organizational cost drivers are intended to increase a firm's speed, flexibility, quality, and innovation. Organizational structure and process significantly affect what and how fast an organization learns.

Organizational cost drivers determine a significant percentage of a firm's long-costs. Thus, organizational cost drivers should be the focus of a cost reduction strategy.

A specific example of how these cost drivers affect long-term costs can be seen in the case of a large aerospace firm whose cost structure was analyzed by a well-known strategic consulting firm. This consulting study predicted that unit operating costs could be reduced by 47 percent if the aerospace firm changed its cost drivers as follows:

- A 17 percent reduction could be achieved if the firm adopted a focused manufacturing strategy and flattened the organizational structure;
- A 6 percent reduction could be achieved if the firm implemented efficient cross-functional communication; and
- A 24 percent reduction could be achieved if the firm switched product design structures (e.g., by implementing concurrent engineering) and emphasized throughput time (e.g., by adopting JIT and cycle time management).

176

A more general example is based on Skinner's argument[39] that a manufacturing firm's cost reduction efforts are most effective when they focus on structure and process. Skinner advances the view that cost reduction and improvements in productivity are based on a "40-40-20" rule concerning the sources of competitive advantage: That is, about 40 percent of the possible advantage stems from long-term manufacturing structure (e.g., number, size, location, and capacity of facilities) and basic approaches to materials and work force management. Another 40 percent comes from equipment and process technology (e.g., JIT, TQM, and flexible manufacturing systems). Only about 20 percent is derived from traditional approaches to productivity improvement (e.g., those that focus on labor). The implication of this argument is that the key to successful long-term manufacturing cost reduction is to focus on improving organizational cost drivers.

ORGANIZATIONAL STRUCTURE

Organizational structure is how responsibility for activities is differentiated horizontally and vertically. These structures evolve over time in response to changing opportunities and challenges.

For example, throughout the 1970s, most firms were structured like a pyramid with many vertical layers (see the left-hand side of Exhibit 5). This structure was used to transmit information vertically between the top and the bottom layers of the firm. Humans were the key communicators, and an extensive vertical hierarchy was needed to increase the probability that effective and efficient communication occurred. The limiting factor was the horizontal span of control within a vertical layer. For example, assuming a horizontal span of control of ten, if there are 1,000 workers at the bottom level of a pyramid, the firm's vertical structure would consist of at least three additional vertical levels with 100 first-level supervisors, ten second-level supervisors, and one third-level supervisor (e.g., the CEO). Extrapolating this analysis to firms with 100,000 workers indicates that they will have at least six vertical layers with at least 11,110 employees between the top and bottom vertical layers. An important detrimental consequence of these pyramidal structures was slow and distorted vertical communication, which reduced the quality of outputs and increased their time-to-market and cost.

A significant change began in the 1980s. The introduction of new information processing and communication technologies (e.g., personal computers, facsimile machines, and local area networks) allowed the tops and bottoms of pyramids to communicate more directly. This greatly reduced the need for middle managers. Firms therefore began to transition their vertical structures from the pyramid form to the hourglass form (see the middle figure in Exhibit 5). This change is continuing in the 1990s. Now it is predicted that in the future companies will be organized like flat networks, as the figure on the right-hand side of Exhibit 5 illustrates.[40]

While these flatter vertical structures reduce costs because fewer managers are needed, that is not their primary strategic benefit. These flatter structures speed up and increase the quality of information exchange, which (in turn) results in getting products of higher quality and lower cost more quickly to customers.

Horizontal structure. A significant portion of the cost of complexity arises from how firms are horizontally structured. Many firms are organized horizontally by product, geography, or function. This creates a firm that is fragmented and has a series of narrow goals or visions (e.g., one for each horizontal unit). One result is myopic, short-term management. This fragmentation also reduces a firm's speed and flexibility.

The most common organizational structures consist of many horizontal layers. These can create functional barriers, especially if information is intended to flow vertically rather than horizontally. One way to reduce the cost of this horizontally induced complexity and rigidity is to design the firm so that the primary organizational structure is horizontal. The intention of this organizational approach is to break down the functional barriers that impede the horizontal flow of information.

EXHIBIT 5
TEMPORAL CHANGES IN VERTICAL ORGANIZATIONAL STRUCTURES

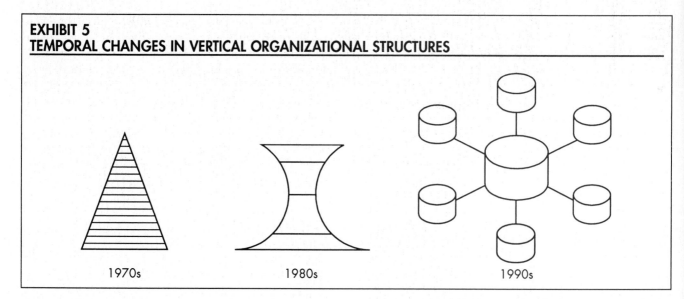

1970s	1980s	1990s

It is important that information flow horizontally at the lowest level possible (i.e., rather than up to a high level in the organization, where senior managers make decisions that are then channeled back down to the function areas). The importance of keeping the information down at the local level is highlighted by the fact that it is employees in the field or on the shop floor who are most aware of problems, and how to resolve them. Thus, firms should consider organizing so that the various functional employees can regularly meet to exchange information, quickly solve problems, and coordinate action.

Another way to reduce costs of horizontal complexity is to tear down the functional lines and horizontally reorganize the firm into cross-functional teams that have broad responsibility for all aspects of a product.[41] These local employees are better able to deal with product diversity and process complexity. A firm is better off not transmitting this complexity upward to senior managers, who are often not as intimately familiar with the details as local employees. Besides, transmitting information vertically increases time, and hence cost. The goal is to reduce the cost of horizontal communication, which could also increase quality, speed, learning, and flexibility by breaking down functional barriers (e.g., through concurrent engineering). The result of this change in horizontal structure is an expected decrease in long-term costs.

Firms can also reduce their long-term costs by organizing horizontally based on groups of activities.[42] For example, Prahalad and Hamel[43] argue that to achieve global competitive advantage, an effective basis for horizontal structuring is to organize based on core competencies. Core competencies are activities or knowledge that a firm has that make it a world-class performer.

Appropriate groupings of activities into horizontal units can reduce the costs of coordinating across diverse functions; they can also focus each grouping of activities on a customer (whether the customer is internal or external). An example of this is a Navy supply center that, after intro-

ducing ABC, found that its previous functional structure resulted in processes that were cost inefficient.[44] In response, the supply center changed its organizational structure so that it was based on groupings of activities that were required to deliver completed services to customers. The supply center also increased employees' training in team building and statistical quality control. Within two years, the supply center found that its operating costs had decreased, that delivery performance had increased, and that no layoffs were necessary. Using an ABM approach to organizational design also allows a firm to analyze how expected long-term costs vary depending on how the various activities are aggregated and linked together to form linear and parallel processes. A further advantage of an ABM approach to organizational design is that the activity representation of a firm fits nicely with value chain analysis.[45]

Some Japanese firms are now designing their organizational structures and management accounting systems based on horizontal relationships. Accounting systems are being designed primarily by product line rather than by functional areas.[46] The basic unit of design is a product line, with functional areas nested within each product line. These firms have decentralized responsibility for costs and defined cost centers based on product lines. The advantage of this horizontal organization is that it clearly divides responsibility for products, activities, and costs. Since the organization and its accounting system are designed based on products rather than functional areas, most costs are direct to products, which significantly reduces the amount of costs that are allocated to products. To reduce costs, these Japanese firms have a continuous improvement strategy for each product line

ORGANIZATIONAL PROCESSES

Organizational design also includes developing processes to accomplish and coordinate activities. In the strategic consulting literature, executional cost drivers are thought to affect the ability of a firm to implement action successfully.[47]

These cost drivers include work force involvement (which means participation, culture, and commitment to continuous improvement), total quality management, capacity utilization, plant layout efficiency, product configuration, and exploiting linkages with suppliers and customers (e.g., through JIT and electronic data interchange). As discussed above, how activities and employees are linked determines the basic processes within an organization and, hence, how—and how much—they drive organizational costs.

ORGANIZATIONAL LEARNING

Exhibit 6 provides a general example of how organizational cost drivers affect long-term costs. The idea behind this example is that the rate of organizational learning determines whether a firm can sustain a competitive cost advantage. To do so requires that the firm learn about a core competency (e.g., new product technology or manufacturing process technology) faster than its competitors.[48] Important sources of organizational learning are educational programs, R&D, information systems, budgeting and performance evaluation systems, and cross-functional teams.

Organizational learning occurs when a firm learns about its environment and how to make it better. Organizational learning also deals with how this learning is stored in organizational memory for future use.[49] Much of management accounting can be interpreted as strategies for organizational learning. For example, budgeting is a process that organizations use to solve problems (i.e., to learn better ways to manufacture and market products to achieve desirable financial outcomes), to share this information across vertical and horizontal levels, and to serve as an organizational memory for storing this information.

Organizational cost drivers (e.g., vertical and horizontal structures and processes, culture, and education pro-grams) determine the type and rate of organizational learning because they affect the type and extent of communications and problem solving by various parts of a firm (Exhibit 6). For instance, a firm learns faster about product and process interactions when it is structured according to concurrent engineering guidelines rather than function (e.g., according to design, engineering, and manufacturing). Organizational learning affects the rate of managerial innovation (e.g., learning about total quality management), which then seems to promote process and product innovation (e.g., product designs with no quality defects and manufacturing processes (that minimize the occurrence of errors).[50] The result is a sustainable source of competitive advantage that derives from learning faster and better than competitors can about core competencies and about process and product innovation. Thus, an important source of long-term cost reduction is organizational learning, which (in turn) is determined by how an organization is structured and the processes that occur within the structure.

CONCLUSION

The central idea that this article develops is that effective long-term cost reduction is a continuous activity that is a strategic and cultural priority. In contrast to traditional cost reduction, with its emphasis on expedient and quick reductions in short-term costs in response to immediate crises, strategic cost reduction is part of a competitive strategy that integrates technology and human resource management strategies to provide a coordinated, broad-based, and long-term approach to reducing costs.

Firms will be better long-term performers if they can get off the short-term cost reduction roller coaster. Long-term competitive cost advantage depends on establishing a culture of continuous improvement of quality, time, and cost

EXHIBIT 6
AN EXAMPLE OF ROW ORGANIZATIONAL COST DRIVERS CAN REDUCE LONG-TERM COSTS

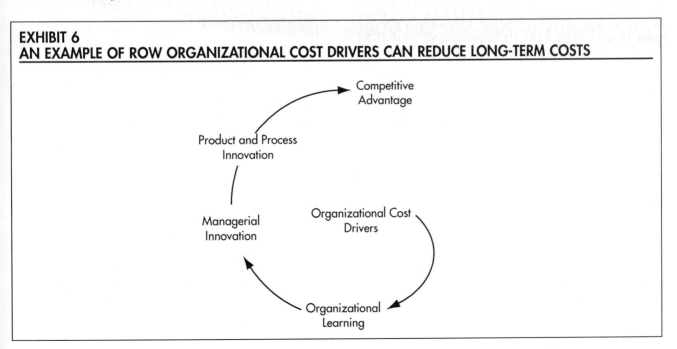

through innovation. Long-term cost reduction is most effectively accomplished by continuously learning about target core competencies faster than competitors can and by establishing long-term employment relationships with innovative, multiskilled employees who are paid above-average compensation.

Michael D. Shields is professor of accounting at San Diego State University in San Diego, California. S. Mark Young is KPMG Peat Marwick Faculty Fellow at the University of Colorado-Boulder, in Boulder, Colorado.

Notes

1. R. M. Tomasko, *Downsizing—Reshaping the Corporation for the Future* (New York: AMACOM 1987).

2. "The New Executive Unemployed," *Fortune,* Apr. 8, 1991, at 36–48.

3. P. Richardson, *Cost Containment: The Ultimate Advantage* (New York: The Free Press 1988).

4. *Id.*

5. W. Skinner, *Manufacturing: The Formidable Competitive Weapon* (New York John Wiley & Sons 1985); also G. Hamel & C. Prahalad, "Strategic Intent," *Harv. Bus. Rev.* 63–76 (May–June 1989).

6. Hamel & Prahalad, "Strategic Intent." *supra* note 5.

7. R. Foster, *Innovation—The Attacker's Advantage* (New York: Summit Books 1986).

8. R. Henkoff, "Cost Cutting: How To Do it Right," *Fortune,* Apr. 9. 1990, at 40–49.

9. Business international Research Report, *Strategic Cost Reduction: How International Companies Achieve Cost Leadership* (Geneva: Business International S. A. 1987); Henkoff, "Cost Cutting," *supra* note 8.

10. T. Jick, "The Stressful Effects of Budget Cuts in Organizations," in L. Rosen, *Topics in Managerial Accounting* 267–280 (New York: 3d ed., McGraw-Hill Ryerson Limited 1984).

11. B. C. Ames & J. D. Hlavacek, "Vital Truths About Managing Your Costs," *Harv. Bus. Rev.* 140–147 (Jan.–Feb. 1990).

12. Henkoff, "Cost Cutting," *supra* note 8.

13. Richardson, *Cost Containment: The Ultimate Advantage, supra* note 3.

14. *Id.*

15. C. Prahalad & G. Hamel, "The Core Competence of the Corporation," *Harv. Bus. Rev.* 79–91 (May–June 1990).

16. Business International Research Report, *Strategic Cost Reduction, supra* note 9.

17. K. Ferdow's & A. DeMeyer, "Lasting Improvements in Manufacturing Performance: In Search of a New Theory," *9 The Journal of Operations Management* 168–184 (No. 2 1991).

18. Business International Research Report, *Strategic Cost Reduction, supra* note 9.

19. M. D. Shields & S. M. Young, "Managing Product Life Cycle Costs: An Organizational Model," *Journal of Cost Management* 39–52 (Fall 1991).

20. T. Makido, "Recent Trends in Japan's Cost Management Practices," in *Japanese Management Accounting,* Y. Monden & M. Sakurai, eds. (Cambridge, Mass.: Productivity Press 1989); M. Tanaka, "Cost Planning and Control Systems in The Design Phase of a New Product," in *Japanese Management Accounting.*

21. C. Berliner & J. Brimson, *Cost Management for Today's Advanced Manufacturing: The CAM-I Conceptual Design* (Boston: Harvard Business School Press 1988); Makido, "Recent Trends," *supra* note 20; R. Cooper & M. Sakurai, "How the Japanese Manage Overhead" (unpublished paper, Harvard Business School, 1990); Toshiro Hiromoto, "Another Hidden Edge—Japanese Management Accounting," *Harv. Bus. Rev.* 22–27 July–Aug. 1988); M. Sakurai, "Target Costing and How to Use It," *Journal of Cost Management 39–50* (Summer 1989); Tanaka, "Cost Planning," *supra* note 20; F. Worthy, "Japan's Smart Secret Weapon," *Fortune,* Aug. 12, 1991, at 72–75.

22. Shields & Young, "Managing Product Life Cycle Costs," *supra note* 19.

23. A. Majchrzak & M. Ranimi, "Transitioning to CIM Systems: Effects of Human Factors and Resources Management," in *Success Factors for Implementing Change: A Manufacturing Viewpoint,* K. Blanche, ed. (Dearborn, Mich.: Society of Manufacturing Engineers 1988); D. Opalka & J. Williams, "Employee Obsolescence and Retraining: An Approach to Human Resource Restructuring," *The Journal of Business Strategy 90–96* (Spring 1987); H. Thompson & R. Scalpone, "Managing the Human Resource in the Factory of the Future." *5 Human Systems Management* 221–230 (1985): R. Hayes, S. Wheelwright, & K. Clark, *Dynamic Manufacturing* (New York: The Free Press 1988); R. Schuler & I. MacMillan. "Gaining Competitive Advantage Through Human Resource Management Practices," *Human Resource Management* 244–255 (Fall 1984).

24. Shields & Young, Managing Product Life Cycle Costs," *supra note* 19.

25. A. Rappaport, *Creating Shareholder Value* Chap. 4 (New York: The Free Press 1986).

26. Hayes, Wheelwright, & Clark, *Dynamic Manufacturing, supra* note 23.

27. "A Smarter Way to Manufacture," *Business Week,* Apr. 30, 1990, at 110–117.

28. M. D. Shields & S. M. Young, "A Behavioral Model for Implementing Cost Management Systems," *Journal of Cost Management* 17–27 (Winter 1989): Shields & Young, "Managing Product Life Cycle Costs, *supra* note 19.

29. V. Pucik & N. Hatvany, "Management Practices in Japan and Their Impact on Business Strategy," in *Advances in Strategic Management* Vol. 1, 103–131 (Greenwich, Conn.: Jai Press 1983).

30. Business International Research Report, *Strategic Cost Reduction," supra* note 9: Richardson, *Cost Containment, supra* note 3.

31. Hamel and Prahalad "Strategic Intent," *supra* note 5; Prahalad & Hamel, "The Core Competence," *supra* note 15.

32. R. Walton & G. Susman, "People Policies for the New Machines," *Harv. Bus Rev.* 98–106 (Mar.–Apr. 1987); Shields & Young, "Managing Product Life Cycle Costs," *supra* note 19.

33. Richardson, *Cost Containment," supra* note 3; Shields & Young. "A Behavioral Model," *supra* note 28; Henkoff, "Cost Cutting," *supra* note 8; E. Lawler, G. Ledford, & S. Mohrman, *Employee Involvement in America: A Study of Contemporary Practice* (Houston, American Productivity & Quality Center 1989); E. Lawler, *High-Involvement Management: Participative Strategies for Improving Organizational Performance* (San Francisco: Jossey-Bass Publishers 1986).

34. A. Train, "The Case of the Downsizing Decision," *Harv. Bus. Rev.* 14–30 (Mar.–Apr. 1991).

35. B. Saporito, "Cutting Costs Without Cutting People," *Fortune,* May 25, 1987, at 26–32; Schuler & MacMillan, "Gaining Competitive Advantage," *supra* note 23.

36. W. Imberman, "Managers and Downsizing," *Business Horizons* 28–33 (Sept.–Oct 1989).

37. Berliner & Brimson, *Cost Management for Today's Advanced Manufacturing, supra* note 21: P. Turney, "How Activity-Based Costing Helps Reduce Cost," *Journal of Cost Management* 29–35 (Winter 1991).

38. J. Gingrich & H. Metz, "Conquering the Costs of Complexity," *Business Horizons* 64–71 (May–June 1990).

39. W. Skinner. "The Productivity Paradox," *Harv. Bus. Rev.* 55–59 (July–Aug. 1986).

40. P. Drucker, "The Coming of the New Organization," *Harv. Bus. Rev.* 4–53 (Jan.–Feb. 1988); R. Miles & C. Snow, "Organizations: Concepts for

New Forms," *California Management Review* 62–73 (Spring 1986): J. B. Quinn, T. Doorley. & P. Paquette, "Beyond Products: Services-Based Strategy," *Harv. Bus. Rev.* 58–67 (Mar.–Apr. 1990); H. Thorelli, "Networks: Between Markets and Hierarchies," 7 *Strategic Management Journal* 37–51 (1986).

41. Shields & Young, "Managing Product Life Cycle Costs," *supra* note 19.

42. C. J. McNair "Interdependence and Control: Traditional vs. Activity-Based Responsibility Accounting." *Journal of Cost Management* 15–24 (Summer 1990): M. Hammer, "Reengineering Work: Don't Automate. Obliterate." *Harv. Bus. Rev.* 104–112 (July–Aug. 1990).

43. Prahalad & Hamel. "The Core Competence." *supra* note 15.

44. D. Harr, "How Activity Accounting Works in Government," *Management Accounting* 36–40 (Sept. 1990).

45. J. Shank & V. Govindarajan, *Strategic Cast Analysis* (Homewood, Ill.: Richard D. Irwin 1989); M. Hergert & D., Morris "Accounting Data for

Value Chain Analysis," 10 *Strategic Management Journal* 175–188 (1989).

46. Cooper & Sakurai, "How the Japanese Manage Overhead," *supra* note 21.

47. D. Riley, "Competitive Cost-Based Investment Strategies for Industrial Companies," *Manufacturing Issues* (New York: Booz, Allen & Hamilton Inc. 1987).

48. R. Stata, "Organizational Learning—The Key to Management Innovation." *Sloan Management Review* 63–74 (Spring 1989); P. Senge, "The Leader's New Work: Building Learning Organizations," *Sloan Management Review* 7–23 (Fall 1990).

49. C. Fiol & M. Lyles, "Organizational Learning," *Academy of Management Review* 803–813 (1985); B. Levitt & J. March, "Organizational Learning," 10 *Annual Review of Sociology* 319–340 (No. 4 1988).

50. C. Fine, "Quality Improvement and Learning in Productive Systems," *Management Science* 1301–1315 (Oct. 1986).

HOW EFFECTIVE ARE TRADITIONAL COST REDUCTION PROGRAMS?

Recent surveys suggest that traditional cost reduction programs do not meet their objectives.* One survey found that—out of 350 senior managers in 275 companies that, together, make up 26 percent of the U.S. gross national product—half responded that the cost-cutting or restructuring programs at their companies had failed to achieve what had been hoped. Results of the other survey (this one of managers from 1,005 corporations) found as follows:

- Less than one half of the companies had met their cost reduction targets;
- Only 32 percent had raised profits to an acceptable level;
- Only 21 percent had improved return on investment appreciably;
- 55 percent reported that employee morale was battered;

- 37 percent were having trouble persuading the survivors to remain; and
- 87 percent reported that early retirement programs led to decision by star employees to leave.

*Surveys by the Cresap division of the consulting firm Towers Perrin and by consultant: Wyatt Co. cited in Anne Fisher, "Morale Crisis," *Fortune*, Nov. 18, 1991, at 71–72.

From M. D. Shields and S. M. Young, "Effective Long-Term Cost Reduction: A Strategic Perspective," *Journal of Cost Management* (Spring 1992): 16–30. Reprinted with permission.

Question

8.3 What are five of the most frequently used traditional cost reduction programs, and how effective is each one?

CHAPTER 9

Budgeting: Resource Allocation to Achieve Organizational Objectives

Reading 9.1, *Continuous Budgeting at the HON Company,* by Drtina, Hoeger and Schaub illustrates this large furniture maker's approach to staying competitive with the help of its budgeting process. Unlike many companies, HON uses a continuous, quarterly, budgeting system. For each quarter a budget is prepared, which includes plans not only for that particular quarter but also for the next three quarters. As each new quarter arrives, the budgeting process is repeated. HON employees believe that the information generated is timely and comprehensive and provides them with information to respond quickly to their volatile environment. The article provides a detailed step-by-step approach to illustrate HON's method.

Reading 9.2, Christopher Bart's *Budgeting Gamesmanship,* describes the games that managers play with their budgets. Bart defines budgeting gamesmanship as "the deliberate and premeditated manipulation of current year sales, cost and profit forecasts by product managers to project an overly conservative image into their product budgets." Using interview and company data from eight large diversified companies, Bart documents how, and why, managers pad their budgets. Two key factors for why such padding occurs are the fear that senior management will arbitrarily slash their submitted budgets, and the managers' own concerns about uncertainty in the competitive environment in which they work.

In *Why Budgets Are Bad For Business,* Thomas Stewart (Reading 9.3) continues with the theme developed by Bart and adds more cautionary notes when trying to understand the budgeting process. Stewart argues that while necessary, budgets focus attention and control on the line items shown on the budget and often ignore the key underlying concepts, such as quality and customer service and satisfaction, that make a business successful. Consistent with Bart's article, managers can become extremely preoccupied with playing budgeting games. If managers are intent on "making budget" as their key goal and organizational rewards are contingent on this goal, then they may never be able to be forward looking and innovative.

9.1 Continuous Budgeting at the HON Company
This furniture manufacturer builds a solid competitive strategy with progressive quarterly budgets.

By Ralph Drtina, CPA; Steve Hoeger, CMA; and John Schaub, CMA

Survival in today's competitive environment means that businesses must be flexible and innovative, largely through development of new products and services, while simultaneously improving productivity and customer service. But building the effects of innovation into the annual budget can be difficult because actions and outcomes often are evolutionary and only become known as the year progresses. Under these conditions it is understandable that the annual budget is not an effective control tool because revenue and spending targets are based on operating conditions different from those actually encountered.

Standard cost accounting systems are not helpful either when budgeting for continuous change because of built-in contradictions. One shortcoming of standard costs for companies seeking continuous improvement, for example, is that they presuppose the goal is to optimize efficiency within a given state of operating conditions rather than to strive for ongoing improvement. Consequently, when production processes undergo continuous change, standards developed annually for static conditions no longer offer meaningful targets for gauging their success.

The HON Company, the largest maker of mid-priced office furniture in the United States and Canada, has overcome these obstacles through use of a continuous three-month budget cycle. The budget has become the integral planning and control device for achieving two strategic objectives: ongoing new product and service development and rapid continuous improvement. The budget also serves as an important vehicle for ensuring that the corporate culture is unified in its understanding of—and commitment to—strategic objectives.

VOLATILE FURNITURE INDUSTRY
The largest of nine operating companies that compose HON Industries, The HON Company operates exclusively as a manufacturer of office furniture and accessories. Organized along functional lines, it has 14 production plants located throughout the United States and operates as an independently run profit center with its operations tied to its parent through its strategic plan and budget.

Highly dependent on the overall economy's health, the office furniture industry is characterized by cyclical demand and uncertainties that make planning difficult, even in the short term. Furniture buyers often postpone purchases until their own business operations are profitable, and demand is normally seasonal with sales much higher in the second half of the calendar year.

Dominated by larger but fewer customers, the office furniture industry is faced with an increasing level of industry competition. As these customers continue to consolidate and grow, they put tremendous price pressure on their suppliers. Manufacturers that do win contracts often expand capacity to meet increased volume. As time passes, the large customers pressure suppliers to maintain or even lower prices, thereby disallowing cost increases incurred by suppliers to be passed on. Suppliers often find they are victims of their own success-their revenues increase, but profits are squeezed by rising costs. Yet they become captive suppliers to the large customers whose volume is needed to absorb the cost of expanded capacity. Given these highly uncertain industry conditions, considerable planning and coordination is needed to ensure that production capacity is used fully and unit costs are maintained or reduced.

DOVETAILING STRATEGY AND BUDGET
Managers at The HON Company communicate and coordinate operating plans through a process called continuous quarterly budgeting. All departments work together to produce an updated four-quarter budget at the beginning of each quarter. Thus, as shown in Figure 1, a budget prepared for the third quarter 1996 includes plans for the third and fourth quarters of 1996 and the first and second quarters of 1997. Each quarterly budget requires the next four quarters to be completely re-budgeted. By having a detailed quarterly budget that is up-to-date and comprehensive, managers and employees in all areas are prepared to deal with rapid change.

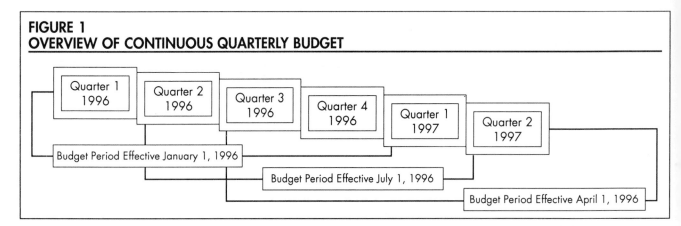

FIGURE 1
OVERVIEW OF CONTINUOUS QUARTERLY BUDGET

In The HON Company's aggressive but realistic budget philosophy, senior management expects each quarter's performance to exceed the previous one. New products and services drive company growth, and research to define and meet emerging customer demand is ongoing. In 1996, for example, the company expects to launch dozens of new product series in addition to introducing hundreds of variations to the size, shape, and features of existing models. Recognizing that service is critical, too, HON offers two- and three-week delivery for orders of any product size and combination. Competitors typically require four- to five-week lead time for single product orders.

Budget targets must be supported by action plans that coordinate operational improvements throughout the organization. For example, when the strategic plan calls for a specified increase in productivity (8% in 1995), all departments are expected to work together to bring about needed change. In manufacturing, production processes repeatedly are challenged and bottlenecks removed. Sales and marketing are expected to generate increased sales volume to make full use of capacity gained through manufacturing improvements. Distribution then must develop plans to handle increased deliveries while reducing the cost of delivery per sales dollar.

PREPARING THE BUDGET

The typical quarterly budget process is done in five basic steps over a six-week period. (See Figure 2.)

Step 1—Develop sales budget. Preparation of the sales budget begins with the territory sales managers when they submit quarterly sales budgets to the sales department for consolidation. Then the sales budget is summarized by geographic territory and by distribution channel. At the same time the sales department is preparing territory budgets, the marketing department independently prepares a sales budget based on general product types and distribution channels. These two sales budget submissions typically differ, largely due to divergent perspectives and sources of information. While the sales department bases its estimates on historical patterns of existing products, marketing has more detailed information about new products and their introduction dates and about special promotion programs.

After the marketing and sales departments have made their separate sales forecasts, the two groups compare forecasts, analyze differences, and reach agreement on the final sales targets. If the two sales targets differ by a substantial amount, more detail about sales derivation and rationale is shared and discussed. Negotiations over acceptable targets continue until the two parties reach a consensus.

Once sales and marketing reach agreement, their sales targets are compared to the strategic plan at a top-level meeting attended by the president and senior staff. The purpose of the meeting is to identify major product group sales levels that appear too low or too high. As a result of discussions on the issues causing these discrepancies, changes are made to reconcile budgeted sales and market share with the strategic plan. Upon final approval, sales dollar targets are sent to production scheduling for conversion to production units and shipping volume.

Step 2—Convert the sales budget to a plant production and shipping schedule. The scheduling group allocates production targets to the company's 14 plants to gain greatest production and distribution efficiencies. This group has one week to convert the sales budgets derived in Step 1 into unit production targets for each plant. Scheduling makes this conversion by analyzing the history of each product category and including such factors as product destination, delivery distance, and plant capabilities. It also takes into account current product inventories and adjusts for planned increases or decreases. After unit production targets are assigned, production managers begin budgeting their quarterly costs.

Step 3—Prepare cost/expense budgets. All The HON Company's functional areas are organized as either cost or expense centers. Separate budgets are prepared for research and development, SG&A, customer service, production, and distribution. In this step, area managers submit expense budgets that determine spending and efficiency targets for the upcoming quarter and year. Each area is expected to provide for improvements designated in the strategic plan. Managers have five working days to complete their expense budgets.

Preparation of a production plant's budget within one week requires widespread participation of department managers and employees and the full commitment of the plant

184

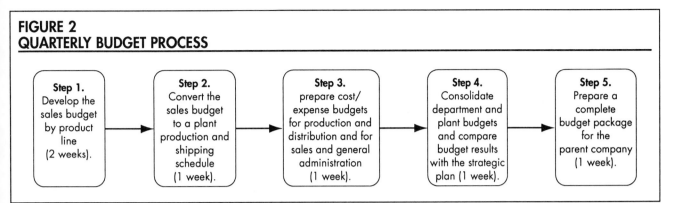

FIGURE 2
QUARTERLY BUDGET PROCESS

| **Step 1.** Develop the sales budget by product line (2 weeks). | **Step 2.** Convert the sales budget to a plant production and shipping schedule (1 week). | **Step 3.** prepare cost/ expense budgets for production and distribution and for sales and general administration (1 week). | **Step 4.** Consolidate department and plant budgets and compare budget results with the strategic plan (1 week). | **Step 5.** Prepare a complete budget package for the parent company (1 week). |

accountant. The budget process pushes responsibility down to the lowest departmental levels within each plant. Department managers are expected to base their budgets on action plans that detail how improvements will be made. The plant accountant must prepare the direct and indirect salary budgets, consolidate department budgets into an overall plant budget, and prepare productivity performance measures. The plant manager helps to guide improvement efforts between departments and makes sure that overall outcomes agree with goals set forth in the strategic plan.

Company-wide productivity improvements begin with the production and distribution processes. Every department in these two areas is expected to initiate changes that allow more units to be processed without incurring added cost. For example, as unit sales increase, it is presumed that production plants will keep inventory levels constant by striving for a one-piece production flow through which products are processed, without interruption, from the time they are started to the point of being loaded on delivery trucks. Similarly distribution is expected to reduce average costs by increasing use of freight container capacity.

The strategic plan specifies an allowable sales percentage for R&D, for SG&A expenses broken down by functional area (general administration, marketing, selling), and for customer service. At the beginning of the budget process, area managers are given general expense guidelines based on past history. Here, as in production, budget responsibilities are pushed down to department levels where guideline targets are refined to take into account the effects of improvements and new programs.

As improvement projects are implemented, SG&A areas are expected to trade spending authority among themselves. For example, if marketing were to find that a new product was to be delayed for one quarter, it could push back its planned expense for printing new literature and for new product training. SG&A managers then would prioritize needs to find where these funds might best be used while still meeting the allowable spending targets for all of SG&A. They may agree, for instance, that MIS can best use the free resources to bring in temporary workers to help speed up completion of a current high-priority project, such as putting customers on electronic data interchange.

Step 4—Consolidate budgets and compare with strategic plan. After individual budgets are completed by functional areas, they are forwarded to The HON Company headquarters. At this point, the company accounting group has one week to review the budget for obvious errors and assemble the final budget package. The budget is analyzed to ensure that strategic plans are being accomplished and that the plants and the SG&A departments are focused on the correct efforts. For example, the budget for the first two quarters of the year— when seasonal activity is low—should include adequate provision for periodic maintenance. If budgeted maintenance expenditures are low, a production plant may have under-budgeted preventive maintenance or neglected special overhaul projects which would require further budget revision.

Step 5—Prepare a budget package for parent company. The company's controller department has one week to prepare a complete set of financial statements plus a host of comparative data: budgeted return on assets employed, productivity measures, budgeted sales attributable to new product introductions, major tooling expenditures, and an analysis of list prices to net sales. These data first are analyzed to ensure that The HON Company's performance trends satisfy the targets set forth in the strategic plan. Normally, any shortfalls already would have been identified and corrected prior to this point in the process. If additional deficiencies are identified, however, the company controller first must correct problem areas before proceeding further.

Then the completed budget is sent to the parent company, HON Industries, for approval. If the parent does not approve the budget, The HON Company controller must investigate needed changes, such as additional cost cuts. In these cases, The HON Company president normally has one additional week to assure the parent company that the budget is the best that is attainable, or, if such arguments fail, the budget is trimmed further. This type of approach has proven effective because The HON Company's philosophy is that a change in the budget is not simply a change in numbers, but rather it means that the company's action plans also must be changed.

BUDGETING FOR COMMITMENT AND ACTION

The HON Company's continuous budgeting system enables senior managers to inspire and motivate the achievement of corporate strategies. Employees at all levels and in all departments are kept informed of new product and process developments, and they in turn update their own performance targets accordingly. By planning in three-month time frames, managers and front-line employees can make a fair assessment of their work improvements and thus can set realistic targets. This interactive approach pushes decisions down to the production floor, and, as a result, helps to gain employee commitment and faster adoption of productivity improvements. It also ensures that standard costs and variance reports are meaningful, an important consideration for helping employees gain the satisfaction of short-term victories in their work.

Does quarterly budget preparation consume a disproportionate amount of company time? Experience has shown that managers improve their budgeting skills over time and need no more time to do quarterly budgets than would be needed for one annual budget. Information technology advances also have shortened budget preparation time. A highly integrated computer budgeting system supplies each department manager with four-quarter histories and four-quarter projections of budget line items. Driver codes for revenue and cost targets are set by default, and, thus, managers need only change budgets for line items on an exception basis. The budget system speeds up information flows to higher levels, too, because proposed targets are rolled up to the next level immediately where they can be reviewed and revised quickly by senior management.

Most important, The HON Company's process of continuous quarterly budgeting unites senior-level strategy with a committed corporate culture. Corporate management best understands where energies need to be focused to enhance the firm's competitive edge, but attaining strategic goals depends on a workforce that can translate corporate strategies into a well-coordinated action plan. Continuous budgeting is the vehicle for ensuring both understanding and ownership by front-line workers by communicating a corporate vision, empowering employees to act on the vision, and targeting and tracking short-term wins.

The result is an attitude among employees that ongoing improvement is a way of life.[1]

Ralph Drtina, CPA, is professor of accounting and management, Crummer Graduate School of Business, Rollins College, Winter Park, Fla. He is a member of Mid-Florida Chapter, through which this article was submitted.

Steve Hoeger, CMA, CPA, is manager of financial analysis, Speed Queen, a Raytheon Company, Ripon, Wis. He is a member of Illowa (Wis.) Chapter.

John Schaub, CMA, is assistant controller, The HON Company, Muscatine, Iowa. He is a member of Illowa Chapter.

Notes

1. For more on this perspective, see John P Kotter, "Why Transformation Efforts Fail," *Harvard Business Review,* March–April 1995, pp. 59–67.

From Drtina, R., S. Hoeger, and J. Schaub, "Continuous Budgeting at the Hon Company," *Management Accounting* (January 1996): 20–24. Reprinted with permission.

Questions

9.1a Is HON's budgeting philosophy an aggressive one? Is there a downside to this philosophy? Explain.
9.1b How are HON managers able to develop their budgets without the process taking all of their time? Explain.

9.2 Budgeting Gamesmanship

By Christopher K. Bart, Faculty of Business, McMaster University Canada

While most managers dislike having to deal with them, budgets are nevertheless essential to the management and control of an organization. Indeed, budgets are one of the most important tools management has for leading an organization toward its goals. As viewed in the literature, budgets are required to "institutionalize" a firm's goals, monitor the performance and progress of both the business and individual products, and measure the performance of managers.[1] While not all firms have five- or ten-year financial forecasts, practically all firms (beyond a certain maturity and size) have budgets.[2]

Given their unique role and importance in the overall planning process, it may seem superfluous to state that budgets need to be rooted in reality. In fact, one of budgeting's main principles is that the budget numbers be challenging (yet realistic), honest, and accurate—given the best information available.[3] Otherwise, both the purpose of strategic planning in general and manager motivation in particular is destroyed.

The translation of strategic plans into measurable financial standards and goals for an organization, however, is not a precise science.[4] In the first place, there is always uncertainty in the business environment. Consequently, making precise predictions as to a firm's performance and position vis-a'-vis the competition can be problematic. Second, it is generally assumed that lower-level managers are wont to "play games" in preparing their budget forecasts - resulting in distorted and even falsified information for those to whom it is reported.[5] Consequently, this "budgeting gamesmanship" is generally considered a form of dysfunctional behavior in that it frustrates both the planning process and the accuracy of business and manager evaluations. It is, therefore, typically recommended that senior managers actively strive to discourage and eliminate budgeting gamesmanship.[6]

PRIOR RESEARCH AND THEORY

The games that managers play with their budgets is a topic that has received only limited attention from business writers and academics. In addition, budgeting gamesmanship activities have been reported largely by way of anecdotal reference in qualitative and very limited studies.[7] What research there has been has tended to confirm the general notion that when budgets are used to evaluate managerial performance, they influence the attitude of managers toward accounting information. Some of the budget-related variables that researchers have investigated to determine their impact on managerial behavior include the degree of budget participation, the level of budget difficulty, and the frequency of budget feedback.[8]

Despite these efforts, the topic of budgeting games has generally remained an area of speculation among budgeting researchers and academics.[9] The nature and extent of budget games are still relatively unknown; most managers, therefore, do not know how widespread budgeting gamesmanship is within their organization. Unfortunately, some previous studies have also tended to confuse faulty accounting systems with the way that managers use the information provided by those systems.[10] Thus, while budgeting gamesmanship is of interest, it remains understudied and misunderstood.[11]

Relatively little is known about how budgeting activities operate at the product level within large, multiproduct firms. The business policy literature on the strategy formulation process and its associated budgeting activities has generally confined itself to the corporate level.[12] Fortunately, research at the product level is becoming more common.[13] However, given the diversification trend among firms generally and the widespread use of product managers by firms to manage their multiproduct circumstances,[14] it is important that "strategic processes and their related practices at the product level" be further explored.[15]

This article presents findings from some recently conducted clinical research that investigated budgeting gamesmanship at the product level in several large. diversified companies.

RESEARCH FINDING'S

Budgeting gamesmanship was found to be a widespread practice in six of the eight firms we examined—specifically, at the companies we will call Alpha, Beta, Delta. Kappa, Omega, and Phi. The types of games that product managers play in these firms; the size of the games; and the factors motivating, facilitating, and constraining the playing of games are examined in the following sections. Thereafter, the two firms where budgeting games were not found to exist (which we will call Gamma and Sigma) are discussed.

THE FIRMS WITH GAMES: THE CASES OF ALPHA, BETA, DELTA, KAPPA, OMEGA, AND PHI

The Games that Product Managers Play

Although they never referred to them as "games" per se, the product managers interviewed were not wanting for a rather extensive lexicon to describe their budgeting manipulations. "Cushion," "slush fund," "hedge," "flexibility," "cookie jar," "hip/back pocket," "pad," "kitty," "secret reserve," "war chest," and "contingency" were just some of the colorful terms used to label the games that managers played with their financial forecasts and budgets. For the most part, however, all of these terms could be used interchangeably.

We asked the product managers to expand on the specific types of games that were played with their budgets. A list of these games and their frequency of mention is provided in Exhibit 1. The responses show that the potential for budget games exists wherever a product manager is asked to make an estimate of his or her plans—in other words, practically anywhere. Their responses also suggest that some games are played more often than others (see rankings in Exhibit 1).

The Size of the Games

Product managers were asked to state the exact amount of "cushions and hedges" that they had built into their plans. The relevant statistics are displayed in Exhibit 2. As the exhibit

---

EXHIBIT 1
PRODUCT MANAGERS' BUDGET GAMES

Type of Game	Frequency of Mention	Rank
Understating volume estimates	48.5%	1
Undeclared/understated price increases	39.4%	3
Undeclared/understated cost reduction programs	36.4%	4
Overstated expenses		
— Advertising	48.5%	1
— Consumer promotions	45.5%	2
— Trade-related	33.3%	5
— Market research	27.3%	6
Undeclared line extensions	33.3%	5

EXHIBIT 2
THE SIZE OF THE BUDGET GAMES ($ IN 000)[a]

Company	Mean ($)	Range ($)	Mean (% of sales)	Range (% of sales)
Alpha	$83.2	$11-210	0.3%	0.2-1.5%
Beta	175.0	50-500	1.5	0.5-3.0
Gamma	0.0	0-0	0.0	0.0-0.0
Delta	93.3	80-100	1.2	1.0-1.7
Kappa	640.0	100-1,400	1.9	0.4-3.2
Omega	298.8	44-750	0.8	0.6-1.5
Phi	940.0	100-2,460	2.1	0.5-5.0
Sigma	0.0	0-0	0.0	0.0-0.0
Average[b]	$364.3	n.a.	1.4%	n.a.

[a]Calculations are per product manager or per product assignment.
[b]Overall average calculations exclude Gamma and Sigma because product managers in these firms did not have any cushions in their budgets.

shows, the size of the games can be quite substantial in absolute dollar terms and in relative terms as a percentage of sales. In some cases, the games could be said to have a material impact on overall company profitability. The overall average also appeared to be fairly large.

Facilitating Factors in Budgeting Gamesmanship
Product managers were quick to identify how certain situations facilitated—even encouraged—budgeting games in their strategic plans. The consensus was that the bigger the promotional budget, the greater the opportunity.

Product history was another factor identified as facilitating cushions. New products, in particular, seemed to provide greater latitude in negotiating volume estimates as the firm had no prior experience with the product.

Other managers claimed, however, that even among products with fairly long histories, the opportunity for budget games was there—though greater for some products than for others. Opportunity seemed to vary with the *strategic posture* of the product. For example, in the case of "growth" postured products, managers stated that the amount of competitive activity was higher than normal and that prices tended to be unstable. Senior management was seen as being committed in terms of spending money. It was, therefore, deemed easier to convince top management of the need for "spending even more."

Products with a "harvest" strategic posture, on the other hand, were said to be characterized by less environmental uncertainty and usually smaller promotional budgets. The "cushionability" of these products was consequently seen to be reduced considerably.

Another condition identified as facilitating budgeting games was the time constraints imposed on senior managers during the product plan review period. As one manager put it:

"Senior management just doesn't have the time for checking every number you put into your plans. . . . So one strategy is to 'pad' everything. If you're lucky, you'll still have 50% of your cushions after the plan reviews."

Finally, product managers claimed that the less knowledgeable a group manager was about a product and the less experience he or she had, the less able he or she was at finding where the cushions were. One product manager was particularly candid in describing how his group manager's lack of experience was capitalized on:

"We've got this new group manager this year who came to us from a consumer promotion house. This just means that I'll have to be especially careful in estimating the costs for my brands' consumer promotions. But I know that I'll be able to 'get him' when it comes to my advertising and trade promotion forecasts."

Factors That Constrain Budget Games
Several factors appeared to aid senior managers in the detection of budget games. One was the historical promotional spending pattern of the products. If current promotional expenses—calculated as a percentage of sales—were significantly out of line with earlier figures, they would be closely examined by senior management. Surprisingly, not all firms required these calculations and, where they did, a few product managers actually admitted to manipulating them to avoid calling attention to their current budget numbers. Some also stated that they would take advantage of "rounding out effects" in their calculations to accomplish the same purpose.

Interestingly, while all the product managers recognized that glaring, obvious, or ridiculous cushions invited their detection, many claimed that their selective use sometimes served a purpose. As one manager pointed out:

"It doesn't hurt to have a few things that 'stick out.' Management thinks that you're hiding something, so it's good if you give them some things to find. Sometimes they're happy with it. Other times, they come back and ask you for still more [profit]."

Another factor contributing to the discovery—and often the elimination—of product managers' budgeting games was the practice among senior managers of telling product managers what their total assignment profit target had to be. In such circumstances, if a product manager were unlucky, his or her cushions would be wiped out instantly. A variation of this practice was for the group product manager simply to demand that he or she be informed of where the hedges were. Few of the product managers who had experienced this latter situation, however, admitted to "telling all."

Most product managers expressed the view that the greater the profit pressures on the company, the more the marketing vice-president and group product managers would be driven to "ferret out the cushions." And, as previously mentioned, many managers said that for products with a harvest strategic posture, it was much more difficult to play budgeting games. Several remarked, however, that because the environment for harvest-postured products was relatively stable, there was less need for cushions to begin with.

Why Product Managers Play Games with Their Budgets

There were a number of factors motivating product managers to play games with their budgets. The first involved the objective setting process itself. One product manager described the problem as follows:

"When a product manager puts together his plans, he usually has a fairly good idea of what he thinks his business can do next year in both volume and profit terms. However, most managers here know that when their forecasts and budgets are submitted, invariably they will be changed by senior management—often with the simple 'stroke of a pen.' Consequently, if a manager were to give a realistic 'call' on his numbers, he could wind up with an even higher volume target and also [fewer] promotional dollars to achieve it. In the end, the product manager would have a profit target that everyone tells him 'he set' but that he would be hard pressed to deliver. So, you have to learn how to play the game.

Along similar lines, many managers commented that arbitrary budget cuts by senior management during the year also prompted the necessity of hedges. And several product managers blamed the budgeting gamesmanship within their firms on senior management's request for forecasts so early in the planning process.

A second major factor motivating managers to put hedges into their plans was market uncertainty. if "unanticipated competitive activities" threatened a product's volume forecast—and if additional funds were not available to counter the attack—a product manager would use his or her hedge (for example, cancel some "approved" but "not intended to be used" marketing program) in order to meet his original profit commitments.

The main reason motivating product managers to play games with their plans, however, was the drive to achieve their product's profit targets. This drive was, in turn, nurtured by one of two factors:

1. *formal company systems* that specified the performance evaluation criteria for product manager salary adjustments and/or bonus payments; and
2. *informal company* practices that led product managers to perceive what the real performance evaluation criteria were within the organization.

At Beta, for example, product managers were rewarded with a bonus payment that was determined, in part, on their products' profit performance compared with the "original plan." Cushions were, therefore, considered a form of insurance for product managers in meeting their profit targets—and thus earning their bonus. As one product manager put it:

"Some of the more successful managers here last year were the ones that really got their profit targets as low as possible and then 'exceeded plans' in terms of results. Unfortunately, last year I called my numbers realistically and am now being penalized in terms of my bonus. You might say, though, that last year I was young and innocent. This year, I'm older and wiser!"

In two of the other firms, Alpha and Delta, either the product manager's formal job description or his or her formally contracted salary performance evaluation criteria was used to reinforce the notion of profit responsibility. Consequently, product managers in both these firms placed a very high premium on achieving their products' profit objectives.

There were other firms, however, where such formal mechanisms were not used (Kappa, Omega, and Phi) and still product managers were strongly motivated to achieve their profit targets. in other words, product managers somehow perceived that it was incumbent on them to deliver their products' budgeted profit targets. As one of them expressed it:

"Sure, I don't have anyone telling me that I have to meet my targets but I know that it's the first thing that the boss looks at before he considers my performance appraisal. After all, that's what I'm really being paid to do. He may not even bring up the fact that I missed my targets in some areas but I just know he takes that fact into account when he tells me my salary increase—or worse!"

Interestingly, the method by which reward criteria was conveyed (formal/explicit or informal/implicit) did not appear to have any influence on the degree of product manager gamesmanship as shown in Exhibit 3. Consequently, it does not seem to follow that the more explicitly rewards (such as pay, promotion, and incentives) are tied to goal achievement, the more product managers will try to pad their budgets.

Senior Management Attitudes

Senior managers in the firms where product managers played budget games acknowledged that they were aware of such practices among their subordinates. But there were important differences in terms of their acceptance of it. Two dominant attitudes seemed to prevail.

EXHIBIT 3
EXPLICITNESS OF REWARD CRITERIA AND BUDGETING GAMESMANSHIP ACTIVITIES

Company	Reward Criteria Explicitness	Budget Games (mean % of sales)	Return on sales (%)	Return on assets (%)
Alpha	Job Description	0.3%	3.4%	8.8%
Beta	Bonus criteria	1.5	3.5	5.7
Delta	Merit criteria	1.2	8.2	12.2
Kappa	Perceived/implicit	1.9	5.1	7.2
Omega	Perceived/implicit	0.8	3.9	9.5
Phi	Perceived/implicit	2.1	2.4	7.0

The situation at Alpha, Delta, and Omega. For the most part, the senior executives in these firms did not seem to be overly concerned that game playing at lower levels existed. The attitude frequently expressed was: "I like to know that my product managers have some flexibility built into their plans." Their reasoning seemed to parallel that of their subordinates—that is, senior executives want to feel assured that if a product manager's market environment does not turn out as forecasted, he or she will be able to cancel certain programs and still be able to deliver the "bottom line." This tacit acceptance, in turn, enabled senior executives to feel more confident about meeting their more macro targets.

There was much more concern expressed, however, about knowing the actual size of the product managers cushions. In fact, this was a traditional area of debate and negotiation among the various levels as senior managers tried to pinpoint just how much flexibility existed one level down. Top management's rationale in wanting to know was quite simple: "We've got to know so we can judge whether those guys down below have gone too wild—and in the process screwed up our inventory and capacity planning—or whether there is not enough slack built in." Given their profit responsibilities, however, it did not seem unusual that product managers were reluctant to disclose the scope of their game playing activities. After all, disclosure of the cushions could mean their reduction or removal.

The situation at Beta, Kappa, and Phi. The senior managers in these firms, however, were not so relaxed about allowing their product managers to build cushions into their plans. The attitude in these firms was that senior management should be the custodian of the company's cushions, not lower-level managers; that it was top management's job to balance the portfolio of products, not individual product managers and that it was senior management's prerogative to decide which—if any—product managers were to be excused for not meeting their profit targets. The view was frequently expressed that giving lower-level managers "tight numbers" enabled senior managers to "see what stuff [the product managers] were made of"; and that holding all cushions at the corporate level put pressure on product managers which produced higher creativity and energy than would oth-

erwise be achievable. The role of product managers at these firms, in turn, was to present their best profit forecasts and then "work like hell" to achieve them since they knew (as in the case of Beta) or strongly suspected (as in the case of Kappa and Phi) that they were going to be held responsible for their product assignment's profit target.

Attitudes, Cushion Size, and Performance

Unfortunately. results did not match expectations in the cases of those firms where senior managers opposed product manager game playing. In fact, their opposition seemed to have the opposite effect as product managers at these firms appeared to be more determined than managers elsewhere to have cushions. As Exhibit 4 shows, Beta, Kappa, and Phi have much higher cushioning levels, on average, than firms where product manager game playing is not so actively discouraged (Alpha, Delta, and Omega).

Senior management attitude also seemed to be related to company performance in a number of ways. For example, Exhibit 4 shows that firms where senior managers tolerate the reasonable use of cushions by lower-level managers (Alpha, Delta, and Omega), outperform the companies where game playing is discouraged—both in terms of profits as a percentage of sales and profits as a percentage of assets. It is also our impression that in the firms where senior managers were at odds with their subordinates on the use of cushions, there were both more morale problems and higher turnaround than in the companies where senior management and product managers were more of one mind on the issue.

FIRMS WITHOUT GAMES: THE CASES OF GAMMA AND SIGMA

In two of the firms examined (Gamma and Sigma), product managers were found not to use cushions in their budgets. There were a number of factors to explain this occurrence.

First, senior managers at these companies did not encourage product managers to pursue budgeting activities. But unlike their counterparts at Beta, Kappa, and Phi (who were prodded into disobeying their superiors because of the reward criteria), product managers at Gamma and Sigma were not formally or informally held responsible for their

Company	Senior Management Attitudes	Budget Games (mean % of sales)	Return on sales (%)	Return on assets (%)
Alpha	Tolerate games	0.3%	3.4%	8.8%
Delta	Tolerate games	1.2	8.2	12.2
Omega	Tolerate games	0.8	3.9	9.5
Beta	Discourage games	1.5	3.5	5.7
Kappa	Discourage games	1.9	5.1	7.2
Phi	Discourage games	2.1	2.4	7.0

products' profit performance, nor did they perceive such responsibility. Instead, product managers in these firms stated that their performance evaluations tended to focus on three-areas: (1) personal development, (2) training of assistants, and (3) overall management of their products. Thus, there appeared to be no formal or informal signals prompting product managers to play games with their budgets. This does not mean, however, that the product managers at Gamma and Sigma did not strive to achieve their products' profit targets, because they did. The difference—as the product managers themselves explained—as that of being "profit conscious" as opposed to being "profit responsible":

"You have to ask yourself: Why is the product manager here? He is the person responsible for formulating and executing the objectives and strategies of the brands in his assignment. It's expected, then, that he's going to work toward—strive— to achieve the financial targets in his plans. You don't have to tell him what his job is—he already knows. The key point is that the product manager has to take his assignment and job personally. If he does then, naturally, he'll have high commitment to seeing his brands' financial objectives realized."

But profit consciousness without game playing also depended on one critical assumption. This product manager put it most succinctly:

"You have to believe that your boss isn't going to hurt you at performance evaluation time when you did everything humanly possible to hit your targets but still you missed them."

Thus it appeared that in the firms without budgeting gamesmanship, there was a good deal of trust between senior management and product managers. Senior managers trusted their subordinates to report honestly and to work ambitiously. Product managers, on the other hand, relied on their superiors to treat and judge them with fairness and understanding.

But how does this climate of trust maintain its balance? Why should product managers trust their bosses? Why shouldn't product managers in these firms try to put cushions into their plans and succeed? And why should they rely on

their bosses not to betray them at performance evaluation time?

Essentially, the relationship of trust seemed to be sustained largely as a result of senior management effort. Senior managers at both Gamma and Sigma stated that they worked hard to maintain the climate of trust; that trust smoothed the relationship between superiors and subordinates; and that betraying the trust of lower-level managers had serious implications for both the prosperity of the firm and their own career paths. As one group product manager put it:

"The moment I betray my product manager, I've had it in this company. My bosses will be angry with me for being unfair. And my subordinates will never take my word at face value again. They'll start to play games with me and I'll have to try and catch them. . . and that sure can waste a lot of time!"

ATTITUDES, REWARD CRITERIA, AND PERFORMANCE

Throughout our study, the attitude of senior managers in conjunction with the product managers' reward criteria seemed to be related to both the scope of the games product managers played and the performance of the firm as a whole. Referring to Exhibit 5, the firms with the highest amount of game playing and the lowest performance were those firms in which the senior managers actively opposed budgeting games at lower levels and where the product managers felt that they had "profit responsibility" (at Beta, Kappa, and Phi). Lower levels of budgeting gamesmanship and higher company performance, on the other hand, were associated with two different situations. In one situation (Gamma and Sigma), senior managers opposed budgeting games at lower levels but also took the steps necessary to ensure that product managers did not feel they had to play them for rewards. In the other situation (Alpha, Delta, and Omega), senior managers did not discourage game playing—they even tacitly encouraged it—but product managers were either formally or informally held responsible for their products' profits. It appears, therefore, that where budgeting games are concerned, as long as that attitudes of senior managers are consistent with the product managers'

EXHIBIT 5
SENIOR MANAGEMENT ATTITUDES, PRODUCT MANAGER SALES/PROFIT RESPONSIBILITY, BUDGETING GAMESMANSHIP, AND PERFORMANCE

Company	Senior Management Attitudes	Sales/Profit Responsibility	Budget Games (mean % of sales)	Return on sales/assets (%)
Beta	Discourage games	Yes	1.5%	3.5/5.7%
Kappa	Discourage games	Yes	1.9	5.1/7.2
Phi	Discourage games	Yes	2.1	2.4/7.0
Gamma	Discourage games	No	0.0	9.5/44.3
Sigma	Discourage games	No	0.0	9.3/9.4
Alpha	Tolerate games	Yes	0.3	3.4/8.8
Delta	Tolerate games	Yes	1.2	8.2/12.2
Omega	Tolerate games	Yes	0.8	3.9/9.5

reward system, superior performance may result. And because game playing was found to occur in both high- and low-performing firms, it cannot be automatically, regarded as dysfunctional behavior among product managers.

SUMMARY AND CONCLUSIONS

The findings presented in this article attempt to shed light into the games that product managers play in the course of preparing their products' budgets. Our study has shown that product managers do indeed play games in their budgets, that the games are many and varied, that some games are preferred to others, and that the actual size of the budgeting games appears to be quite large on average. The study has also identified the factors that contribute to and facilitate the playing of budgeting games and those that frustrate and constrain their occurrence.

Four of the findings, however, deserve highlighting. First, the data suggest that formal and explicit performance evaluation criteria are no more likely to result in higher levels of budgeting gamesmanship than less formal and more implicit reward criteria. Second, the firm's reward system seems to have a greater influence over the behavior of product managers (insofar as budgeting games are concerned) than the verbal dictates of senior managers. In other words, lower-level managers will ignore the orders of superiors not to play budgeting games if they perceive that their performance evaluation will be based on whether they achieve their budget target. Third, the attitudes of senior managers in conjunction with the product managers' reward systems seem to be related to both the scope of the games that product managers play and the performance of the firm as a whole. Finally, the findings suggest that budgetary game playing by product managers does not necessarily constitute dysfunctional behavior as it is conventionally viewed in the management literature. Instead, budgeting games may simply be a form of tactical maneuver that product managers deploy to survive in what they consider to be a hostile environment.

Endnotes

The author wishes to express his appreciation to the Social Sciences and Humanities Research Council of Canada for funding this research study. The author is also indebted to Professors Robert Cooper, Peter Banting, Julie Desjardins, Wayne Taylor, and Frank Tyaack of McMaster University for their comments and suggestions on earlier versions of this article.

Notes

1. J. Bower, *Maintaining the Resource Allocation Process: A Study of Corporate Investment Planning,* Boston: Graduate School of Business, Harvard University, 1970; W. J. Bruns and D. T. DeCoster, *Accounting and Its Behavioral Implications,* New York: McGraw-Hill, 1969; A. Hopwood, *Accounting and Human Behavior,* Englewood Cliffs, NJ: Prentice-Hall, 1977; H. Koontz and C. O'Donnell, *Principles of Management: An Analysis of Managerial Functions,* New York: McGraw-Hill, 1964; P. Lorange and R. F. Vancil, *Strategic Planning Systems,* Englewood Cliffs, NJ: Prentice-Hall, 1977; G. A. Steiner, *Strategic Planning: What Every Manager Must Know,* New York: The Free Press, 1979; and G. A. Welsch, *Budgeting: Profit Planning and Control,* Englewood Cliffs, NJ: Prentice-Hall, 1976.

2. See Bruns and DeCoster. Endnote 1.

3. See Bruns and DeCoster, Koontz and O'Donnell, Steiner, and Welsch, Endnote 1.

4. See Hopwood. Endnote 1.

5. C. Argyris, *Impact of Budgets on People,* New York: Controllership Foundation, 1952; J. Cherrington and D. J. Cherrington, "Budget Games for Fun and Frustration," *Management Accounting,* January 1976, 28–32; F. Collins, "The Interaction of Budget Characteristics and Personality Variables with Budgetary Response Attitudes," *Accounting Review,* April 1978, 324–335; and H. Simon, H. Guetzkow, G. Kozmetsky, and C. Lyndall, *Centralization vs. Decentralization of the Controller's Department,* New York: Controllership Foundation, 1954.

6. See G. H. Hofstede's *The Games of Budget Control,* London: Tavistock Publications, 1968: Hopwood, Steiner, and Welsch, Endnote 1.

7. See Argyris. Cherrington et al., Collins, and Simon et al., Endnote 5; and P. Munter, F. Collins, and D. Finn, *Gameplay in Budgeting,* Oxford, OH: Planning Executives Institute, 1983.

8. S. Becker and D. Green, "Budgeting and Employee Behavior," *Journal of Business,* Vol. 35, October 1962, 392–402; Bruns and DeCoster, and Hopwood, Endnote 1; Collins, Endnote 5; D. Searfoss and R. Monczka, "Perceived Participation in the Budget Process," *Academy of Management Journal,* December 1973: and R. Sapp and R. Seiler, "Accounting for Performance: Stressful But Satisfying," *Management Accounting,* August 1980, 29–35.

9. Munter et al., Endnote 7.

10. A. Hopwood. "An Empirical Study of the Role of Accounting Data in Performance Evaluation," *Empirical Research in Accounting: Selected Studies,* 1972, supplement to the *Journal of Accounting Research,* Vol. 10, 156–182; R. Dew and K. Gee, *Management Control and Information,* New York: Macmillan, 1973.

11. Munter et al., Endnote 7.

12. D. E. Schendel and C. W. Hofer, *Strategic Management: A New View of Business Policy and Planning,* Boston: Little, Brown, 1979.

13. C. K. Bart, "Product Strategy and Formal Structure," *Strategic Management Journal,* 7, 1986, 293–312; J. Bower, Endnote 1.

14. *Current Advertising Practices: Opinions as to Future Trends,* New York: Association of National Advertisers, 1974.

15. T. J. Peters and R. H. Waterman, *In Search of Excellence: Lessons from America's Best Run Companies,* New York: Harper & Row, 1982.

Dr. Christopher K. Bart is a recognized expert in the areas of corporate strategic planning for turnaround situations, planning for performance, strategy implementation, and new venture management. He has a unique expertise in helping firms organize their internal structure better to achieve their goals. Dr. Bart has been involved in examining the issues and problems associated with managing multibusiness firms in the consumer products industry. Currently, he is investigating the organizational practices that large, diversified firms use to manage and control product innovation.

Dr. Bart is an associate professor of business policy at the Faculty of Business, McMaster University, in Hamilton, Ontario, Canada. He has also recently been a Research Fellow at the newly created National Centre for Management Research and Development in London, Ontario, Canada. Professor Bart holds degrees in business administration from York University (MBA, 1975) and the University of Western Ontario (Ph.D., 1982). A highly regarded lecturer, he has been named both "Outstanding Undergraduate Business Professor" and "MBA Professor of the Year," He has also received many academic awards and honors.

Among his other qualifications, Dr. Bart is a chartered accountant. He is a past director of the Planning Executives Institute and a member of numerous boards of directors and professional organizations.

RESEARCH METHODOLOGY

Budgeting Gamesmanship

This term is defined as the deliberate and premeditated manipulation of current year sales, cost, and profit forecasts by product managers to project an overly conservative image into their product budgets. To measure this variable, product managers in the study were simply asked whether they "played games" in their budgets. While most managers initially expressed reluctance to discuss such a sensitive matter, all eventually spoke candidly—on the understanding that individual identities would be kept strictly confidential.

Sample Selection and Size

The study was based on in-depth interviews with product managers in eight large diversified firms. Firms engaged in diverse activities were selected to ensure a wide variety of situations and circumstances. Six of the firms (Alpha, Beta, Gamma, Delta, Kappa, and Omega) were wholly owned subsidiary divisions of major U.S.-based firms. The remaining two firms (Phi and Sigma) were single-division, stand-alone companies. A summary of key financial and operating performance statistics for the units is presented in the accompanying exhibit.

The unit of analysis was the individual product manager. The budgeting system in each firm was also mature.

Research Instrument.

The following list of questions constituted the research instrument for the study on which this article is based:

- Do product-level managers play games with their budgets? If yes, why?
- How widespread are budgeting games among product managers?
- What exactly are the types and scope of budget games that product managers play?
- Are there preferred games?
- Is there a relationship between budgeting gamesmanship and different product strategies?
- What factors contribute to the detection of product managers' budget games by senior managers and what factors allow them to go undetected?
- How does the product managers' performance evaluation system influence budgetary game playing?
- Do senior managers encourage or discourage budget gamesmanship by their product managers?
- Do product manager budgeting games represent a form of dysfunctional behavior?

Data Collection

The point of entry into each company was the president or a divisional general manager. Data on the management of products were gathered by on-site interviews with product, product group, and corporate-level managers and by physical inspection of company documents (such as individual product plans). In total, 113 managers (including 41 of the firms' 57 product managers) were interviewed over a period of 151 hours.

Limitations

The research method restricted the sample size. The sample selection method (judgmental) and the sample size also limited the generalizability of the findings. The high response rate by company managers, however, gives the results high validity in spite of the small number of firms sampled. It should also be noted that the exploratory nature of this study precluded the testing of all possible variables.

PERFORMANCE AND OPERATING STATISTICS FOR THE EIGHT RESEARCH FIRMS[a] (IN MILLIONS OF DOLLARS)

	Alpha	Beta	Gamma	Delta	Kappa	Omega	Phi	Sigma	Avg.
Sales	$110	$267	$94	$87	$201	$300	$1,900	$2,100	$632
Profit									
Percentage of sales	3.4%	3.5%	9.5%	8.2%	5.1%	3.9%	2.4%	9.3%	5.8%
Percentage of assets	8.8%	5.7%	44.3%	12.2%	7.2%	9.5%	7.0%	9.4%	8.9%
Total number of products	23	24	16	33	25	40	12	24	24.6
Number of "growth" products	9	9	8	11	10	22	4	8	10.1
Number of "harvest" products	14	15	8	22	15	18	8	16	14.5
Number of product managers/product assignments	5	9	4	9	7	9	10	4	7.1
Average product assignment size									
Number of products	4.6	2.7	4.0	3.7	3.6	4.4	1.2	6.0	3.5
Sales volume	$21.6	$15.9	$5.4	$5.1	$25.7	$30.0	$106.0	$375.0	$58.4
Product concentration	Food	Food	Health & Beauty Aids	Home & Beauty Aids	Food	Food	Beverages	Commodity Metals	

[a]Adapted from company data. Absolute numbers have been disguised. Key ratios, however, have been preserved.

From C. Bart, "Budgeting Gamesmanship," *Academy of Management Executive* (1988): 285–294. Reprinted with permission.

Question

9.2 What are some of the factors that constrain the budget games discussed by Christopher Bart? Explain.

9.3 Why Budgets Are Bad for Business
They encourage dumb moves and discourage smart ones, like investing for growth. But some companies are breaking away from this crazy numbers game.

By Thomas A. Stewart

You have an inspiration—a microdemagnetizing digital doodad, say, or a new way to organize the business, like making the technical support guys report to the sales director. You sound out a couple of colleagues and customers, estimate costs, and take it to your boss. "I like it," he says. Then he utters the most dismal sentence in corporate life: "But it's not in the budget."

Those words signal problems far bigger than frustration. Budgets, say experts, control the wrong things, like head count, and miss the right ones, such as quality, customer service—and even profits. Worse, they erect walls between the various parts of a company and between a company and its customers. A. T. Kearney consultant Robert Gunn says, "When you're controlled by a budget, you're not controlling the business."

Donald A. Curtis, a senior partner at Deloitte & Touche, goes further. Reliance on budgets, he says, is "the fundamental flaw in American management." That's because they assume that everything important can be translated into this quarter's or this year's dollars, and that you can manage the business by managing the money. Wrong, he argues: "Just because a budget was not overspent doesn't mean it was well spent."

Budgets, forecasts, plans—whatever you call them, you cannot escape the annual ritual. For tracking where the money goes, budgets are dandy. They become iniquitous when they are made to do more—when the budget becomes management's main tool to gauge performance, or when it distorts long-term planning or blocks managers from shifting resources when they need to. Then the budget becomes an end in itself. Managers lock their radar onto the signals it sends out. "Making the numbers" becomes their overriding goal.

The result can be madcap or maddening, depending. Managers, says A. T. Kearney's James Morehouse. "do incredibly stupid things" to make budget, especially if incentive pay is at stake. They woo marginal customers. They cut prices too deeply. They overload distributors with goods—then take them back or shell out for costly promotions to sell them. Riding that merry-go-round, RJR Nabisco overstated profits by some $250 million before it stopped last fall (FORTUNE, December 4). Says David Nadler, president of Delta Consulting Group: "We once found a guy who made his sales budget by selling stuff to a dummy company. He put it in his basement and returned it the next year." And who hasn't endured a fourth-quarter spending freeze that cost more than it saved?

Then there's the manager whose problem is running *under* budget. Consultants swap tales of late autumn spending sprees as executives realize that a penny saved is a penny lost from next year's budget. Nadler had a client whose managers used to pay in December for consulting time that they did not want until the next year. Use-it-or-lose-it is still a fact of life at many companies. "My phone rings off the hook in November and December," says Columbia business professor Kathryn Rudie Harrigan, a sought-after consultant.

Expensive or silly budget games end sooner or later. Not so the pressures that engender them, whose damage is subtle but greater. Over time, says Morehouse, "cost center managers may do what's in the best interest of their budgets, even if it is to the detriment of other cost centers or the rest of the company." Manufacturing, which benefits from economies of scale, resists tooling up for new products or demands long production runs before the size of the market is clear. Marketing, by contrast, wants new stuff, the more the merrier, and phooey on the cost in the labor factory In these turf wars, managers may spend more time arguing over who pays for what than trying to serve customers.

The result ends up in the warehouse: Big stacks of slow-moving inventory are often a tip-off that each department has its own agenda. Ironically, when the finance department notices that too many assets are tied up in inventory, it makes matters worse by putting *its* priorities above all others. Explains Morehouse: "Out goes a memo telling all unit managers to cut inventory 25% in six months. But only the hot items move out fast. The rest sits there. When it's all over, inventories are down 10%, the CFO declares victory—and the only items left are the ones nobody wants, so customer service goes to pot. You wouldn't believe the alligators that slither up on the newly exposed rocks."

The great budget game is the result of trying to control negative behavior, like spending too much, while largely ignoring positive behavior, like building the business. "The problem with that," says Donald Curtis, "is that it works, and it works for a long time if the business is in decent shape when you get it. Anyone can manipulate the figures to make, say, $6 a share this year. The question is what *else* you should

be doing so that it's easier to make $6 next year." Adds Pillsbury chief operating officer Paul Walsh: "It's easy to extrapolate a trend. Management's job is to damn well change the trend."

The worst failure of budgets is what they don't measure. Budgets show what you spend on customer service, but not what value customers put on it. They count noses, but not brains: In the arithmetic of the budget, Curtis points out, the day Seymour Cray left Control Data to go out on his own, nothing happened.

In many companies, budgets actually discourage spending to protect market share or improve products. "It takes a real hero to invest in off-the-balance-sheet assets," says Curtis, "especially when the guy can sit at his kitchen table and calculate exactly what it'll cost him in his bonus."

Think of a budget as being like a detailed golf scorecard: It can tell you what clubs you used, how far you hit each drive, whether you made par on the ninth hole, and whether you shot a 72 or an 84. But it cannot tell you if your backswing is lousy or your grip is wrong—knowledge you require to help you play better next Saturday.

For that information you need other measures. They exist, of course—financial measures like returns on invested capital, and nonfinancial data on quality, market share, and customer satisfaction. The trick is to base the control system on *them,* not on budgets. Companies as diverse in style as 3M, Emerson Electric, and Digital Equipment Corp. have done just that. Here's how:

Measure output, not input. The worst budgets set cost targets only, leading managers to control how much their operation spends and to ignore how much it earns. Says Jason S. Schweizer; a professor at the American Graduate School of International Management (Thunderbird): "It's easier to control the money going in than to control something like P&L." But the simplicity is costly. It turns an organization inward, values rules above initiative, and may lead controllers to query every little variance in a department's budget.

Not at Emerson. Profit, not spending, is the key measure, and it is tallied in operations as far down on the organization chart as possible. As a result, says President Al Suter; "if a division president has an opportunity to gain market share, he can go out and buy all the steel he needs. No one has to ask."

What about operations like R&D, billing, or personnel, which have *only* expenses and no revenues? They need other relevant measures of achievement-like percentage of company sales that come from new products, age of receivables, and employee turnover. Well designed, such measures not only forestall capricious liposuction, they also motivate staff units to support operating units rather than obstruct them.

"Plan first, budget later." So says Ronald Mitsch, a 3M vice president. Without a plan, you are doing last year's budget, not next year's.

Some traditional budget items are better handled in the long-term planning process. At Emerson, for example, cost reduction is part of the five-year planning cycle, not the annual budget. Why? Because real savings come from investment in new processes or equipment. Quick fixes don't so much cut costs as defer them. And, says vice chairman Robert Staley, "because cost reduction is important in good years too."

Budget for managers, not accountants. Sure, FASB and the SEC tell you which figures to report, and how, but who says management reports have to be the same? "Those numbers are irrelevant internally," says Bruce J. Ryan, controller at Digital Equipment Corp. DEC has a dazzling new information system that can slice and dice the company more ways than a Cuisinart. Designed to cut paperwork—quarterly closings had become an Augean mess of over 1,700 pages of documents—the system allows DEC to customize a business plan for each division. One might shoot for return on sales, another return on assets, a third market share. The choice is part of strategic planning and depends on factors like the maturity of the business and the state of competition.

Making sure the shoe fits is especially important when business is tough, as it is now for DEC. Says Ryan: "It would be easy for me to tell everyone, 'Cut your numbers by 10%.' We are working the cost issue, but at the same time we've got a planning process going on. If you do that right, you've got a list of all the possible investments—and that's how you pull it back to reality, as opposed to saying, 'Everybody's got to cut.'"

Design against turf wars. Divisions intent on making budget are always trying to foist work and costs onto each other. That's an excellent formula for enraging customers. Says Curtis: "An excuse like 'It's not my fault, it's the credit department's fault' is a non-answer to a customer." To make it a non-answer to a manager, too, look for ways to link budgets together horizontally, not vertically. Xerox has restructured field operations to combine sales, service, and order-entering in geographical units rather than run them up through parallel hierarchies that might fight over funds. At Emerson there are good reasons for all operations in a division to pull together because it is held to account for its profits, not its costs, and because incentive pay is based on the unit's performance as a whole.

By contrast, 3M's 46 divisions are neatly stacked in 16 groups within four sectors. The orderly pyramid is deceptive. The group that makes tape for disposable diapers also makes reflective material for stop signs. ("Damned if I know why," says Mitsch, the group's former head.) At 3M, people, tech-

nology, and money cross more borders than a Cook's tour. Salesmen who sell Scotch tape, for example, report to the Commercial Office Supply Division but sell the wares of eight others.

That matrix like structure could easily breed Pyrrhic budget warfare. But creative financial management and ingrained cultural habits keep squabbling to a minimum. When a sales force sells for a division other than its home unit, the income shows up on the internal report cards of both. To sweeten the deal, says group VP Robert Hershock, "I might throw in marketing money, or some people-support off the books"—a flexibility 3M encourages. Managers who need extra cash usually find it in their own pyramid, but they can dip into bags of money that are cached all over the company. Last year a unit making industrial filters had a chance to expand its international business, but the effort would have consumed virtually all of its budgeted resources. It got extra money from the company's area management for Europe, which serves all 46 divisions.

Build budget busting into the system. The value of an annualized budget depreciates fast. Simply revising it every few months may tighten the budgetary coils instead of releasing managers to act strategically.

Contingency plans and even some purposefully fuzzy thinking can help. 3M CFO Roger Roberts asks operating managers to include in their strategic forecasts a line labeled NIGOs—"nonincremental growth opportunities." These are products that might pop out of the lab in the coming year, or potential entries into new markets—items whose costs and revenues are hard to predict. Emerson executives budget for bad news by writing three different plans for varying contingencies.

Ultimately, says consultant David Nadler, "people can figure a way around any control system." Budgets can tell you who runs a tight ship, but a good admiral demands more: captains who know the difference between a reef and a tail wind, for example. 3M CEO Allen Jacobson told his division general managers in November, "I never want to hear anyone put down a project because it isn't in the budget." Fine words like those have been uttered as often as the dismal ones with which this story began. But opportunities to toss out the budget won't work unless managers feel safe to act on the knowledge that the world is not on a fiscal year. Says Hershock, who was promoted to his group vice presidency four months after he heard the boss speak: "I've overrun budgets—overrun them pretty good sometimes. I was never criticized if I could justify it."

THE CEO WHO SEES BEYOND BUDGETS

Many U.S. managers are ripping up confining, old-fashioned budgets, but few of the budget bashers have gone further faster than Europe's Jean-Marie Descarpentries. A portly Frenchman with a Rabelaisian taste for ribald jokes and country cooking, he runs the Franco-British CMB Packaging (1989 sales: $4.6 billion) as a federation of entrepreneurs who strive to multiply sales, profits, and productivity as fast as they can. For Descarpentries, 54, following a formal budget would mean curbing his epic ambitions. "If the budget is the basis of your plan, you content yourself with an extrapolation of the past," he says. "How can you budget the 26%-a-year compound growth we've achieved?"

By reaching for the sky; Descarpentries has turned in one of the best corporate performances of the 1980s. When he took over a debt-laden French tin-can maker called Carnaud in 1982, its market value was $19 million. Now, after a 1989 acquisition, the rechristened CMB is worth $3 billion.

In lieu of binding budgets, Descarpentries sets dramatic targets designed to make managers stretch for the seemingly unreachable. Each year he asks the heads of 94 profit centers to project their best possible performance if everything, including product demand, goes just right. Those estimates become the budget. "Then we promptly forget about them," he says. "The purpose is to get managers to dream the impossible dream."

Unlike most companies, CMB doesn't measure managers against the budget. Descarpentries says that removes budgeting's biggest evil, aiming too low: "Normally, managers try to negotiate easy targets so they can surpass them and earn big bonuses. The guy who sets an ambitious goal and just misses is penalized."

Instead, CMB rates its managers mainly on how they did this year vs. last year, and how they stack up against the best managers in the industry Besides growth in sales and operating profits, the main criteria are productivity, debt levels, and hours spent on training. Each month the division heads get a chart comparing their performance on each criterion. "It's management by pride," says Descarpentries. "They all want to be first."

Money is also at stake. Each year CMB rates the 94 profit-center heads on a scale ranging from a low of -5 to a maximum of 15. Poor performers often get no bonus at all, while the stars receive bonuses equal to 30% of their salary, plus lucrative stock options. How does Descarpentries fit in? "My job is offering consulting advice—not orders—and choosing people," he says. If a manager posts consistently low ratings for 18 months, Descarpentries replaces him.

Last year during a 10-day company outing in the Jordanian desert, he exploited the surrealistic setting to unveil his new goal: a monumental $17 billion in sales by 2000. Reaching it will require huge effort. But for Descarpentries—and the managers he taught to substitute dreams for budgets—nothing seems impossible.

-Shawn Tully

From T. A. Stewart, "Why Budgets Are Bad For Business," *Fortune* (June 4, 1990): 179–190. Reprinted with permission.

Question

9.3 In Stewart's article, what does Ronald Mitsch, a 3M vice president mean when he says, "Plan first, budget later"

CHAPTER 10

Capital Budgeting

Reading 10.1, John Shank and Vijay Govindarajan's *Strategic Cost Analysis of Technological Investment,* suggests that a strategic cost management approach to investing in new technology is the most effective method. Arguing that all previous approaches are lacking in one way or another, Shank and Govindarajan incorporate the ideas of value chain, cost driver, and competitive advantage into an expanded financial analysis framework. Combining these three ideas and analyses overcomes a central limitation of other proposed frameworks which is the failure to incorporate a firm's strategy clearly into technological investment decisions. The article provides several illustrations of how the framework can be successfully applied.

Kalagnanam and Schmidt's *Analyzing Capital Investments in New Products* (Reading 10.2) presents a case study of a biotechnology firm, Cyto Technologies. The company manufactures hundreds of products such as enzymes and biochemical reagents, and its R&D scientists also are involved in developing scientific techniques to aid others in conducting experiments. Historically, Cyto used rough financial methods to determine whether a new product or technique should be developed. Due to external competition and the high cost of capital, Cyto has developed a much more rigorous four-phase process to determine whether a project should be funded. The article discusses the four phases as well as the reactions of R&D scientists to this new form of project evaluation.

Reading 10.3 is Hamner and Stinson's article *Managerial Accounting and Environmental Compliance Costs.* This article discusses the pressure on organizations to change their traditional cost accounting systems in light of new state and federal regulations requiring the proper allocation of environmental compliance costs. Historically, environmental compliance costs were part of general overhead and were allocated in some arbitrary fashion to production processes. This approach was deemed acceptable given the relatively low level of such costs. However, as state and federal regulations have become more stringent, environmental compliance costs have increased dramatically. Companies are now required to determine cost drivers related to environmental costs and to allocate these costs in a much more direct manner to specific production processes. The article provides a good overview of state and federal regulations and examples of new allocation systems.

10.1 Strategic Cost Analysis of Technological Investments

By John K. Shank and Vijay Govindarajan

The decision to invest in new manufacturing technologies is often hampered by using conventional methods of capital investment analysis. The authors discuss the limitations of four current approaches and show how their own framework—Strategic Cost Management—applies to a large forest products company that is making a decision on a major technological innovation.

A frequent charge in recent years has been that many firms fall behind in global markets because they are too slow in implementing the new manufacturing technologies—CIM (Computer Integrated Manufacturing), FMS (Flexible Manufacturing Systems), AMT (Advanced Manufacturing Technology), or the more familiar CAD, CAE, and CAM.[1] A popular argument is that conventional methods of capital investment analysis do not capture the full impact of the technology change decision. A project-level net present value (NPV) framework, it is argued, places such a premium on short-term financial results, and so little emphasis on difficult-to-quantify issues, such as quality enhancement or manufacturing flexibility, that major manufacturing breakthroughs do not pass the NPV test.[2]

Current literature suggests four approaches to evaluating investments in technological change; each of these approaches has significant shortcomings. One approach suggests that we discard all formal financial analysis (such as NPV analysis) and simply "bet" on new technologies. We believe that we can do better than this. A second approach, proposed by Kaplan, calls for a refined NPV model;[3] a major shortcoming of this framework is that it does not give explicit attention to strategic issues and concerns. Porter's approach links technology decisions to strategic analysis;[4] however, Porter's framework does not give explicit attention to financial analysis. The fourth method, suggested by Bromwich and Bhimani, argues for an integrated "strategic-financial" analysis framework;[5] however, these authors have not pushed their ideas far enough to give meaningful guidance to managers in evaluating technology change investments.

After summarizing these four approaches and indicating their strengths and limitations, we then offer an approach—Strategic Cost Management (SCM)—that addresses those limitations (see the sidebar for a brief description of the SCM methodology). We illustrate the strategic power of our framework and the drawbacks of the previous approaches by presenting an example of a large forest products company that must make a decision on a major technological innovation.

THE MINIMALIST RESPONSE

Some argue that we should deemphasize, or even eliminate, formal investment analysis techniques when considering major manufacturing technology issues. Studies have shown that as many as 40 percent of firms used no formal evaluation at all for AMT projects.[6] This approach, however, is conceptually troubling because it reduces some of the most important choices a firm faces to "technology roulette"—place your bet, spin the wheel, and hope! This process is not without its own risks. There have been many well-known failures in recent years from poorly conceived technology experiments:

- General Motors pushed the concept of robotics in its factories very hard in the early 1980s, and Westinghouse made an investment in excess of $1 billion in robotics manufacturing in 1983. Yet the projected improvements proved difficult to achieve. Many of the robots purchased were never used, and Westinghouse closed down its robotics subsidiary in 1989.
- General Electric's spectacularly abortive venture in new condenser technology for refrigerators cost the firm hundreds of millions of dollars and irreplaceable momentum in product leadership.
- Sky Channel, the widely heralded $2 billion experiment in satellite distribution of TV signals ("wireless cable") by RCA, News Corp., and CableVision, was quietly disbanded in the late 1980s in the face of mounting costs and implementation problems.

The point of these examples is certainly not that technological experimentation is always a mistake, nor that conventional NPV analysis techniques must be used despite their limitations. We also do not mean to imply that these firms made some simplistic mistake that they could have readily avoided. Deciding when and how to implement change in product or process technologies is a very difficult and, at the same time, critically important task that demands the best thinking senior managers can muster. But to argue that no formal analysis is a plausible alternative to overly restrictive financial analysis seems to us to be just as misguided. The idea is to find an appropriate analytic framework.

EXPANDED FINANCIAL ANALYSIS FRAMEWORK

Kaplan's attempt at an appropriate framework has been widely hailed for its insight in getting beyond the narrow perspective often imposed in NPV analysis.[7] In summary, Kaplan argues that conventional financial analysis has four major weaknesses when applied to major investments in technological change. The first is misassessment of the appropriate discount rate. It has been fairly common to see companies use *real* hurdle rates in the range of 15 percent to 20 percent. Kaplan presents persuasive arguments based on the weighted average cost of capital concept, actual returns over the past sixty years, and comparative risk assessments to show that *real* hurdle rates closer to 8 percent to 10 percent are more appropriate. Using significantly lower hurdle rates can dramatically improve the attractiveness of new investments.

A second major factor he cites is undue optimism in projecting continuing stable returns under the "no Investment" alternative. If one recognizes that failure to adopt technological advances can often lead to rapid deterioration of the "base case," then the attractiveness of projected modest growth or even stable profits from new investments is cast in a much different light. Combining these first two points may suggest that rejecting new technological advances is often more risky than adopting them.

A third area Kaplan highlights is concern about "intangible" versus "tangible" benefits. He challenges the belief that it is not practical to quantify the benefits from better product quality, enhanced manufacturing flexibility, or shorter factory cycle times. Quantifying such benefits is often possible, he argues. This can dramatically improve projected returns from so-called "soft benefit" investments. Reductions in work-in-process inventory from FMS conversions, for example, can often offset the cost of much of the equipment required by the new system. Finally, he notes the importance of giving explicit attention to often overlooked spin-off benefits of technology investments. Early investment, for example, in computer-aided manufacturing in one area of a factory can yield dramatic improvements later when the new technology is extended to other areas of the factory.

Kaplan illustrates his thesis very effectively in his study of a tap and die manufacturing subsidiary of TRW.[8] The company had an excellent history of market leadership and strong financial returns throughout the 1950s, 1960s, and early 1970s. By the late 1970s, numerically controlled technology was beginning to alter competitive relationships in the industry. The subsidiary's management was exploring options to convert significant manufacturing operations from electromechanical to electronic technologies. Since corporate management emphasized financial control systems very heavily, the subsidiary submitted a conventional capital expenditure proposal for new machines that was fraught with the problems Kaplan has identified. The conventional financial justification for the project did not even come close to meeting corporate financial targets.

From a conventional financial perspective, the proposal was marginal at best. However, because of line management's strong belief in the new technology, the subsidiary went ahead with the investment in spite of the inability to present a compelling financial rationale. its decision resulted in dramatic success for the firm, but the opportunity might well have been missed. Several of TRW's competitors in this market did not change quickly enough and did not survive the next ten years. For example, one major consumer of taps and dies, Caterpillar, cut its list of drill bit suppliers from twenty-four to three between 1981 and 1986. The TRW subsidiary was one of the three to survive.

Using Kaplan's *extended* financial analysis framework shows much more clearly the justification for the new manufacturing technology in this industry segment. There is no question in our minds that Kaplan is right.

The limitations he cites are very real impediments to effective use of the NPV framework. There is also no question that expanding the model in the ways he recommends will significantly enhance its usefulness in the CIM context.

While we appreciate Kaplan's pioneering effort, we believe we can go beyond just expanding the NPV model. In our view, strategic issues need to be given much more explicit attention than a project evaluation model permits, no matter how carefully the project model is carried through.

COMPETITIVE ADVANTAGE FRAMEWORK

Another approach, proposed originally by Porter, explicitly addresses the strategic dimensions of the problem using the competitive advantage perspective on strategic management.[9] This approach sees the relationship between technological change and competition as more complex than it first appears. Technological change is often viewed as valuable for its own sake. Any technological modification a firm can pioneer is believed to be good because it represents progress. But, from a business perspective, technological progress is not always a good thing. For example, the sailboard and snow ski industries today are suffering from continuing technological evolution that just does not translate into profits. The products are overengineered for the average customer. From a business perspective, technological change is important only to the extent that it affects competitive advantage or industry structure.

Technology, however, does pervade a firm's value chain. It extends far beyond those technologies associated directly with the product. There is no such thing as a low-technology industry if one takes a broader view. Viewing any industry as technologically mature can well lead to strategic disaster. For example, magazine publishing is in turmoil today because of the emergence of desktop publishing in an industry deemed technologically mature just ten years ago. The belief in the old technology for page layout, color separations, or typesetting is preventing many large firms from competing effectively. Moreover, many important innovations for competitive advantage are mundane and involve no scientific breakthroughs, such as Federal Express's overnight delivery. Of course, the erosion of overnight delivery market share by fax technology is a counter-example. But innovation can have important implications for low-tech as well as high-tech companies.

Technology and Competition

Everything a firm does involves technology of some sort, even though one or more technologies may appear to dominate the product or production process. For example, imaging technology may dominate the copier business, but paper feed technology is also an issue. Any particular technology is important for competition if it significantly affects a firm's competitive advantage or industry structure.

Technology and the Value Chain. The basic tool for understanding the role of technology in competitive advantage is the value chain. A firm, as a collection of activities, is a collection of technologies. Technology is embodied in every value activity of the firm, and technological change can affect competition through its impact on virtually any activity. Every value activity uses some technology to combine materials and machinery with human resources to produce some output. This technology may involve several scientific disciplines or subtechnologies. The existing technology of a value activity represents one combination of these subtechnologies.

The technologies in different value activities can be related. This linkage is a major source of competitive advantage within the value chain. For example, product technology can be linked to the technology for servicing a product (such as self-diagnosing computer systems that relay maintenance information directly to the manufacturer). Or component technologies can be linked to end-product technology. Desktop layout of advertising pages, for example, makes possible a lower-cost magazine. Thus a technology choice in one part of the value chain can have implications for other parts of the chain. In extreme cases, changing technology in one activity can require a major reconfiguration of the value chain. When the basic oxygen furnace replaced the open hearth furnace in steel making, scale became much less important. This resulted in the emergence of the mini-mill, which has fundamentally changed the structure of the steel industry.

A firm's technologies are also clearly interdependent with its buyer's technologies. The points of contact between a firm's value chain and its customers' or suppliers' chains define another area of potential interdependence of technologies. For example, Union Camp put PCs linked to its warehouses into paper distributors' offices and increased sales by offering immediate product availability and order status information. A firm's product technology influences the product and process technology of the customer and vice versa.

Technology and Competitive Advantage. Technology affects competitive advantage if it has a significant role in determining relative cost or differentiation. Since technology is embodied in every value activity and is involved in achieving linkages among activities, it can have a powerful effect on both cost and differentiation. Computer airline reservations systems represent an excellent example of technology impacting differentiation (such as American Airlines and the Saber system). Technology affecting relative cost is illustrated by the rise of continuous casting in steel making; continuous casters significantly reduce manufacturing cost.

In addition to affecting cost or differentiation in its own right, technology affects competitive advantage through changing or influencing the other drivers of cost or uniqueness. For example, the development of the interstate highway system dramatically changed the basis of competition between trucking and railroads in many basic ways. The successful railroads today (Burlington Northern, for example) are the ones that have adapted to those changes.

Tests of a Desirable Technological Change. The link between technological change and competitive advantage suggests a number of tests for a desirable direction of technological change. According to Porter, a firm's technological change will lead to sustainable competitive advantage under any of the four following circumstances:[10]

1. *The technological change itself lowers cost or enhances differentiation and the firm's technological lead is sustainable.* Procter & Gamble's patented dry fluffing technology for tissue papers provides softer paper at no increase in drying cost.
2. *The technological change shifts cost or uniqueness drivers in favor of a firm.* A new assembly process that is more scale sensitive than the previous will benefit a large-share firm that pioneers it even if competitors eventually adopt the process.
3. *Pioneering the technological change translates into first-mover advantages besides those inherent in the technology itself.* A firm that moves first may establish a reputation as the pioneer or leader, a reputation that emulators will have difficulty overcoming (e.g., Kodak in film or Coca-Cola in beverages). A first mover also may be first to serve buyers and thus to establish loyal relationships.

It is interesting how many firms that were first movers have remained leaders for decades. In consumer goods, for example, such current leading brands as Crisco, Ivory soap, Life Savers, Coca-Cola, Campbell Soup, Wrigley gum, Kodak film, Lipton tea, and Goodyear tires were already leaders by the 1920s. Of course, early leaders do not always persist, evidenced by Singer sewing machines, Bowmar calculators, Bulova watches, and RCA television sets.

A first mover may be at a disadvantage if early investments are specific to the current technology and cannot be easily modified for later generations. In semiconductors, for example, Philco moved early for leadership with a large automated plant. It enjoyed a period of success, but the later development of a different manufacturing process for semiconductor chips made its earlier investment obsolete. Similarly, the early mover will be disadvantaged if its product or process reflects factor costs or factor quality levels that have changed.

Technological discontinuities can also work against the first mover by making its investments in the established technology obsolete. Technological discontinuities are major shifts in technology to which a first mover may be ill prepared to respond, given its investment in the old technology. Weyerhaeuser, for example, pioneered the introduction of the technology for "oriented strand board" (a plywood substitute). But later innovations cut the cost of a new plant in half, leaving Weyco at a competitive disadvantage in its early plants. Discontinuity favors the fast follower who does not bear the high cost of pioneering.

4. *The technological change improves overall industry structure.* For example, the jet engine improved the competitive position of all airlines versus substitute forms of transportation.

Although Porter's approach to understanding technological change investments is clearly very insightful at a conceptual level, it suffers from a significant drawback: Porter does not explicitly link his strategic framework to financial analysis. Without such a linkage, it is difficult to decide on specific technological investments. It is not surprising that we find no examples in the literature using Porter's framework to resolve technological choices in the seven years since it was introduced. This is in strong contrast to the extensive literature applying and testing other aspects of Porter's model.

STRATEGICALLY AUGMENTED FINANCIAL ANALYSIS FRAMEWORK

A fourth approach, proposed by Bromwich and Bhimani, addresses the lack of explicit attention to strategic issues in conjunction with project evaluation models.[11] They envision a formal financial analysis, broadly based and carefully executed, but augmented by explicit consideration of strategic issues that do not lend themselves to quantification in project

terms. As Bromwich and Bhimani note, "Many of the effects of AMT may be plant or division or even corporatewide, . . . while also frequently flowing from the interaction with other systems. . . .The full benefits of AMT investments are unlikely to be captured by investment appraisal techniques which rely solely on financial data input. The long and wide-ranging discussions which are used in Japanese decision making allow these benefits to be considered without precise quantification and to be tested against a wide range of managerial experiences."

Bromwich and Bhimani propose a framework that explicitly considers strategic benefits which can be derived from AMT investments, both within the firm and externally in its market positioning:

Internal Strategies
    Cost advantages
    More control of production systems
    Improved organization
    Beneficial interactions
Market Strategies
    Diversification
    Expanded product portfolio
    New products with new skills
    New skills in new areas
Enhancement of existing products
    Enhanced corporate image
    Response to fluctuating demand
    Lower cost of meeting demand
    Improved quality
Risk reduction
    Stronger skill base
    Better control
    Better planning
    Reduced working capital
    More flexible responses

Figure 1 is an example of a strategic investment appraisal matrix designed to reflect the blending of financial quantification and qualitative strategic analysis that Bromwich and Bhimani recommend.

Bromwich and Bhimani are correct in their assessment that an explicit blending of financial analysis and nonfinancial strategic considerations deserves careful consideration. Neither approach alone is as strong as a blending of the two. However, they have not pushed these ideas far enough to explain *how* to structure the strategic assessment phase. More can be applied across all firms to focus the strategic evaluation of technology change investments. Since the previously described approaches for evaluating investments in technological change are inadequate in important ways, we suggest here a different method that addresses those limitations.

THE STRATEGIC COST MANAGEMENT FRAMEWORK

The SCM perspective, suggested by Shank, involves three key themes that are taken from the strategic management literature:[12]

FIGURE 1
STRATEGIC PLANNING MATRIX

Strategies/Benefits	Improved Revenue	Lower Costs	Higher Reliability	Better Supply Response	Meeting Customer Requirements	Fit with Other Products	Enhanced Image	New Skills	Better Information	Risks of Not Investing	Costs of Investment	Costs of Operation	Organizational Pains	Totals
Product Enhancement	X*						X**							
New Products	X*			X*			X**	X**						
Risk Reduction				X**										
Cost Advantages		X*		X										
Improved Organization Structure														
Companywide Impact														
Monetary Items														
Items which can be expressed in monetary terms*														
Scored Items**														
TOTALS														

*Items which can be converted into monetary terms.

**Items which can be expressed in monetary terms scored on a single 'points' scale (1 to 10).

Source: M. Bromwich and A. Bhimani, "Strategic Investment Appraisal," *Management Accounting*, March 1991, p. 48. Reprinted by permission of the publisher.

1. Value Chain Analysis
2. Cost Driver Analysis
3. Competitive Advantage Analysis

Each of the three represents a stream of research and analysis about strategy in which cost information is viewed differently from the way it is viewed in conventional management accounting. Blending the three themes represents the most powerful way to focus cost analysis for strategic choices—Strategic Cost Management. Each is a *necessary* component of the SCM analysis, but a *sufficient* analysis must involve all three.

We illustrate the application of the SCM framework in analyzing technology investments by using a disguised example of a large forest products company that is evaluating a proposal for a major technological innovation.

The SCM Perspective on Technology Costing
Yakima-Olympia Corporation, a multibillion-dollar, highly vertically integrated forest products company, must choose

equipment for logging operations in its Virginia timberlands. The prevailing technology for logging is clear cutting by using "feller-bunchers," which are similar to large farm tractors and have heavy-duty scissors attached at the front to shear off standing trees at ground level. These tractors also have large clamps that can hold several tree trunks upright at one time so that the tractor can shear them off before stopping to dump the load on the ground. The machine literally fells trees in bunches. After felling, the bunches of trees are dragged (skidded) to a roadside staging area (the deck) by another variety of tractor called a skidder. The feller-bunchers and skidders leave no trees standing as they move through a wood lot. At the deck, workers use hand-held chain saws to delimb the trees as best they can, usually leaving many short limbs on the log. Cranes then load the logs onto flatbed trucks for transport to wood yards, where the logs are sorted and cut into segments for sawmills, plywood mills, or pulp mills, depending on the quality and species of the trees.

The tempo and pace of this process can best be described as pandemonium. There is no sophistication involved, only brute force applied in an environment that is hot, insect-ridden, snake-infested, and alternately thick with dust or deep in mud. This process represents the latest technological stage in the evolution of a process geared to cut down and move as many trees as possible in as short a time as possible. The methods achieve high-volume throughput but also seriously damage the trees and the land and cause great discomfort and danger for the workers.

The alternative technology, widely used in northern Europe but, in 1990, virtually unknown in the United States, involves sophisticated computerized machines that resemble *Star Wars* robots. A worker in a harvester, a closed-cab tractor that uses computer programs, moves carefully through the woods, selecting individual trees for cutting based on current needs in the processing mills. The machine fells each tree with a smooth saw cut (as opposed to scissors cut), precisely delimbs each log flush to the stem, cuts the stem into sections of predetermined lengths, and gently drops the sections in neat piles. A forwarder then picks up the logs according to computer-programmed sequences and carries them gently to the roadside. Later the forwarder will load the cut logs onto trucks destined directly for specific processing mills, bypassing the wood yard step altogether. In this system, the wood lot is not clear-cut. Only the fully mature trees whose size and species meet current processing mills' needs are harvested.

In terms of tempo and pace, the harvester-forwarder system resembles ballet dancers performing an elegant pas de deux in the woods. It represents the latest technological stage in the evolution of a process in which the logger sees each individual tree as a precious object and takes full responsibility to deliver clean, undamaged, sorted, and cut logs to specific processing mills, based on their current needs, while doing minimal damage to the land. The work is performed safely and cleanly from air-conditioned cabs.

How these two approaches to logging developed in such dramatically different ways in Northern Europe and the United States is beyond the scope of this paper. In 1990, the issue for Virginia loggers was whether to stay with feller-buncher/skidder technology or switch to harvester/forwarder (H/F) technology for Yakima-Olympia's 450,000 acres of timberland in the tidewater region.

Yakima-Olympia (Y-O), like many major forest products companies, was vertically integrated from research-intensive farms that developed and planted genetically improved seedlings to wholesale and retail distribution of paper and solid wood products. The only step in this chain in which Y-O did not participate was logging. Primarily for cost reasons (nonunion wages and work practices), most of the forest products firms had long ago exited the business of cutting their own trees. Y-O hired private logging contractors to cut the mature trees from its lands and transport them to Y-O's processing mills. How Y-O should evaluate a proposal to switch logging technologies is the subject of our field study.

Three Components of the SCM Perspective
We will consider in turn each of the three components of the SCM perspective as it applies to the choice of logging technology, starting with the value chain component.

Value Chain Analysis. In the SCM framework, managing costs effectively requires a broad focus, external to the firm. Porter has termed this perspective the value chain.[13] The value chain for any firm in any business is the linked set of value-creating activities from basic raw materials (starting ultimately with the periodic table of the elements) through to component suppliers, to the ultimate end-use product delivered to the consumers, and perhaps through recycling to the beginning of a new value chain cycle. The external focus sees each firm in the context of the overall chain of value-creating activities of which it is only a part. We are aware of no firms that span the entire value chain in which they participate. Value chain analysis is contrasted with value-added analysis, which starts with payments to suppliers (purchases) and stops with charges to customers (sales), while focusing on maximizing the difference, the value added (sales minus purchases) for the firm.

Value-added analysis is far too narrow a view because it misses the importance of linkages upstream and downstream in the value chain.[14] In the CIM context, the principal benefits of new investment may well fall elsewhere in the value chain than where the investment itself takes place, as the logging example illustrates.

The power of the value chain perspective for this situation is highlighted by its contrast with a conventional, project level, value-added analysis. Table 1 shows the conventional analysis for a logging contractor comparing the two alternative logging systems. From the logger's perspective, the return is virtually identical for the two options. Given the comparable economic returns, the logger currently using feller-buncher technology is not inclined to switch. The new technology involves a significantly larger investment for a

TABLE 1
NPV COMPARISON OF FELLER-BUNCHER/SKIDDER TECHNOLOGY VERSUS HARVESTER/FORWARDER TECHNOLOGY FOR VIRGINIA LOGGING*

Capital Cost

A   One harvester/forwarder pair = $608,000. Can work two shifts with lights on the equipment.

B   One feller-buncher with two skidders and one crane = $370,000. Can work only one shift.

Running two shifts, A processes 17,600 cunits of wood in one year, which is equal to what B can process working one shift.

Financial summary

	A	B
Capital cost	$608,000	$370,000
Cash operating costs		
Labor	94,000	105,000
Fuel	15,000	75,000
Supplies, repair, and maintenance	91,000	91,000
Insurance and taxes	3,000	3,000
Supervision	50,000	35,000
Total	253,000	309,000
Depreciation (five years)	122,000	74,000
Salvage value (after year five)	60,000	18,000
Assume 36% combined tax rate		
Processing revenue (for 17,600 cunits)	407,000	407,000
Five-year NPV (at 12%)	(70,000)	(42,000)
Five-year internal rate of return	7.4%	7.3%

*For purposes of this example, the comparison is framed in internal rate of return (IRR) terms rather than net present value (NPV) to avoid the issue of risk-class comparability between two options. The well-known caveats about ranking projects in IRR terms are acknowledged, but are not a concern in this context.

small business, a much heavier reliance on highly skilled labor (versus low-wage, day-rate laborers for conventional logging), much more complex maintenance issues, and a much more complex job task than the old technology.

Y-O experimented with the new technology at test sites. Senior management at Y-O knows that the logger does not really stand to gain directly from any of the potential benefits. From this perspective, there is really no way to encourage the logger's technological innovation. Table 2 summarizes the anticipated financial returns from the new technology, broken down by where in the value chain they are realized. As shown, although the switch to harvester/forwarder logging technology could save Y-O an estimated $33.6 million per year in just one of its several timberland regions, none of the gains are realized at the stage of the value chain where the investment must be made. Applying a value-added perspective in a project evaluation mode at the logging stage will never lead to the change. Applying a value

chain perspective in a business unit evaluation mode reveals the tremendous potential benefits from the change.

Cost Driver Analysis. In conventional management accounting, cost behavior is seen largely as a function of volume. Examples of management accounting concepts that hinge on volume as the cost driver include fixed versus variable cost, average versus marginal cost, cost-volume-profit analysis, break-even analysis, flexible budgets, and contribution margin, to name a few. In SCM, output volume per se is seen to capture very little of the richness of cost "behavior." In this regard, SCM draws much less on the simple models of basic microeconomics and much more on the richer models of industrial organization economics.

There are structural cost drivers that relate to the firm's explicit strategic choices regarding economic structure such as scale, product-line complexity, scope of operations (vertical integration), or experience.[15] Technology investments also represent structural choices about how to compete.

There are also executional cost drivers that are major determinants of a firm's cost position and hinge on its ability to execute successfully within the economic structure it chooses.[16] Whereas structural cost drivers are not monotonically scaled with performance, executional cost drivers typically are. That is, for each of the structural drivers, more is not always better. There are potential diseconomies of scale and vertical scope, as well as potential economies. A more complex product line is not necessarily better or worse than a less complex line. Too much experience can be as bad as too little in a dynamic environment. For example, Texas Instruments emphasized the learning curve and became the world's lowest-cost producer of obsolete 8K microchips! Technological leadership versus followership is a legitimate choice for most firms.

In contrast, for each of the executional drivers, more is almost always better. The list of potentially important executional drivers includes at least these:

- Workforce involvement (participative management).
- Workforce commitment to continuous improvement (*kaizen*).
- Adherence to Total Quality Management concepts.
- Utilization of effective capacity (given the scale choices on plant construction).
- Efficiency of production flow layout.
- Effectiveness of product design or formulation.
- Exploiting linkages with suppliers and customers all along the value chain.

While it may not always be true that a higher level for these executional factors improves cost position, the examples of diseconomies are much less frequent.

The value chain perspective can reveal the critical importance of the logging step in the chain, but value chain importance alone is not a sufficient test of the desirability of changing the logging technology. A second necessary component is that technology choice is an important cost driver at the logging stage. That is, what factors are driving success or failure at the logging stage, and how important is the technology factor compared to other cost drivers? Of the structural drivers, scale does not prove to be very important in this context. Minimum efficient scale for logging is quite small. One or two sets of equipment are adequate to spread the supervision cost element, which is the only cost element with any scale effects. Vertical scope also yields no economies in this context. In fact, because the private logger avoids the union wage rates and work practices in the large forest products firm, there are actually diseconomies of vertical scope. Learning is also not a major cost driver with conventional equipment. Workers learn the job quickly and high labor turnover does not generate a significant cost disadvantage. Learning is a more important issue with H/F equipment because high labor turnover can destroy many of the benefits. However, learning is still not, in itself, a dramatic cost driver—workers with only average intelligence and diligence can learn the job in about twelve months.

Product line complexity is also not an important cost driver since the mix of tree species and sizes is very narrow in the Tidewater region. The area was logged once near the turn of the century and again in the 1950s. Since all the land has already been harvested once or twice in the past seventy-five years, the homogeneity of the forest is enhanced.

As summarized in Table 2, technology choice *is* a critical cost driver in this situation. In fact, our brief overview indicates that of all the structural cost drivers, technology choice is the single most important factor. The next step is to consider the executional drivers to see if they offset or reinforce the structural impact of the technology factor.

Layout of the production process is a neutral factor in this study. It is important because the proximity of the mills to the trees is critical, but it is not a variable in the current context. Similarly, product formulation is also neutral. Developing genetically improved seedlings is an important issue, but it is not a variable in the current context. Capacity utilization is also not a factor since the small scale of operations for any one logger means they are always busy. Chronic oversupply is not nearly as big an issue here as it is for the pulp and paper operations of Y-O.

Participative management, continuous improvement philosophy (*kaizen*), and Total Quality Management are important here, as they almost always are, and they all reinforce the technology factor. The H/F technology is much more amenable to a high-quality/high-commitment workforce management program than is the clear-cutting technology that seems to almost assume and guarantee an alienated workforce.

This leaves the linkages issue, which is of equal importance to the technology issue itself. Unless the contract logger can be induced to see and value the overall benefits across the value chain from the high-tech logging option, there is little hope of achieving the benefits. The linkages between the logger and the landowner and between the log-

TABLE 2
A VALUE CHAIN PERSPECTIVE

Annual returns from switching to harvester/forwarders from feller-buncher/skidders for Y-O's 450,000 acres (about 15,000 acres harvested each year).

Returns to the landowner

Improved product mix selection	$ 2.6 million
Saved stem damage waste (saw cut is better than shear cut)	.3 million
Saved cost for site repair (H/F does much less damage to the residual land)	.2 million
	$ 3.1 million

Returns to the logger

Virtually none!	$ 0.0

Returns to the processing mills

For pulp mill wood supply:	
Saved processing cost from precise sorting classification	$26.0 million
For solid wood supply (sawmills and plywood mills):	
At the wood yard:	
Saved cost of sawing trees to logs in the wood yard	$ .5 million
Saved trim loss in the wood yards	1.6 million
Saved cost from logs misapplied by the saw operators in the wood yard	.5 million
Saved wood loss from wood yard saw spacing	.3 million
	$ 2.9 million
At the processing mills:	
Kiln drying savings from more precise sorting	.2 million
Savings by using lighter duty debarkers	.1 million
Savings from double handling of off-grade logs in the plywood mills and sawmills	1.3 million
	$ 1.6 million

ger and the processing mill are dramatically underexploited. Unless Y-O decides to do the logging itself, thus eliminating the need to deal with loggers as independent businesses, some form of gain sharing to induce a tighter linkage along the value chain must be developed. The diseconomies of vertical integration here make Y-O very reluctant to participate in the logging business. In order to make the technology change investment attractive to loggers, it must address the linkage problem by sharing the potential benefits that are likely to accrue ahead of and behind the logger.

An interesting dilemma is how much sharing of potential gains will be necessary to get loggers to switch. Risk avoidance attitudes and overcoming inertia may require more profit sharing than might seem rational in purely financial terms. If Y-O cannot induce the technology change without giving away what it sees as a proportionate share of the benefits, it may see the diseconomies of vertical scope as less significant after all and reenter the logging business. How overall returns are shared along a value chain is a very complex issue. How enhancements to the overall value created by one player reach an equilibrium distribution across all the players is an equally complex issue.

We will turn now to a consideration of the third component from the SCM framework for technology costing—competitive positioning analysis. Even if technology choice is an important cost driver for logging and logging is potentially an important step in the value chain, a sufficient test for investing in the new logging technology requires that the benefits achievable are consistent with the competitive positioning strategy adopted by the firm. That is, in more general logical terms, each of the three components is necessary in the analysis, but all three are required for sufficiency.

Competitive Advantage Analysis. In the SCM perspective, understanding the implications of how the firm chooses to compete is fully as important for cost analysis as understanding the value chain and understanding the key strategic cost drivers at critical steps in the chain. As discussed by Porter, the basic choice on how to compete is between cost leadership and differentiation.[17]

1. **Low Cost.** The primary focus of this strategy is to achieve low cost relative to competitors. Cost leadership can be achieved through approaches such as economies of scale in production, learning curve effects, tight cost control, and cost minimization in areas such as R&D, service, sales force, or advertising. Examples of firms following this strategy include: Texas Instruments in consumer electronics, Emerson Electric in electric motors, Hyundai in automobiles, Briggs & Stratton in gasoline engines, Black & Decker in machine tools, and Commodore in business machines.

2. **Differentiation.** The primary focus of this strategy is to differentiate the product offering of the business unit, creating something that is perceived by customers as being unique. Approaches to product differentiation include: brand loyalty (Coca-Cola in soft drinks), superior customer service (IBM in computers), dealer network (Caterpillar in construction equipment), product design and product features (Hewlett-Packard in electronics), and product technology (Coleman in camping equipment).

How this choice affects cost management for a firm is discussed by Shank.[18] The relevance for technology costing is illustrated by the logging industry field study.

Y-O has embarked on a differentiation strategy in its solid wood operations for more than twenty years. Its strategy is built around plantation forestry to plant and grow genetically improved trees that will yield a wood mix with a much higher than average value at maturity. With an approximate thirty-five-year growing cycle in the Virginia Tidewater region, the strategy still has about fifteen years to go before it can be fully implemented.

By the year 2000, if conventional logging is used, each year Y-O timberlands will be yielding about 80 percent of the high-grade logs that its expanded set of sawmills and plywood mills will require, up from the 67 percent supplied internally in 1985, but still well below total requirements. The remaining 20 percent will have to be met by outside purchases, as shown here:

Estimated Wood Supply and Demand

Year	Pulp Mills	Sawmills/ Plywood Mills
1985		
Demand	1,500,000 units	300,000 units
Supply from Y-O timberlands	600,000 (40%)	200,000 (67%)
2000		
Demand	1,500,000 units	500,000 units
Supply from Y-O timberlands:		
Using conventional technology	500,000 (33%)	400,000 (80%)
Using H/F technology	500,000 (33%)	450,000 (90%)

If the H/F technology were to be used, the net supply of high-grade logs from the same acreage would increase by 50,000 units each year. This would save the sawmills and plywood mills more than $5 million each year in purchased logs. Thus, adopting the new logging technology moves Y-O substantially closer to self-sufficiency in supplying the high-grade log needs of the expanded set of sawmills and plywood mills it has built as part of its high-value extraction strategy. These savings are in addition to the quality savings shown in Table 2 from stem damage, sorting losses, kiln drying losses, and double handling.

The situation for one of Y-O's major competitors, Marathon Paper Company (disguised), which also owns substantial timberlands in the coastal Southeast, highlights the relevance of the competitive positioning choice to the technology choice. Whereas Y-O's strategy emphasizes "grade extraction" (logs for sawmills and plywood mills) and distribution in global markets, Marathon's strategy emphasizes "fiber extraction" (pulp mill logs) and concentrates primarily on domestic markets. Because Marathon sees its timberlands primarily as a source of low-value pulp logs to supply its pulp mills, it has a much smaller commitment in sawmills and plywood mills and is not nearly as concerned about the problems of conventional logging. Marathon uses a much shorter growing cycle (twenty-two years) and does not spend money each year in its forests (fertilizing, burning, pruning, and thinning) to achieve a high-value wood mix.

It is not necessarily obvious, but growing better trees is only justifiable if there is a strategy for subsequently extracting that extra value in end-product markets.

Furthermore, whether a high-value timber strategy is superior to a low-value strategy depends on a complex set of assumptions that play out over a twenty-five- to thirty-five-year growth cycle. Various forest products firms have made different choices on this issue.

Conventional logging technology with its emphasis on high-volume (but lower-value) throughput is fully consistent with Marathon's strategy of lower value/low cost. At the same time, Y-O is moving ahead aggressively to find gain-sharing mechanisms to induce its logging contractors to switch to the H/F technology, which represents a much better fit with its strategy of a longer growth cycle with higher cost, but higher value.

To summarize, Yakima-Olympia faced a significant problem in the logging operation stage of the value chain. The prevailing technology for logging was cost effective for firms pursuing a strategy of high-volume/low-value-added wood products. But it was not cost effective for firms pursuing a strategy of differentiation/high-value-added wood products. But, since independent contractors did the logging, there was no direct way for Y-O to control the loggers' choice of technology.

Conventional project-level financial analysis does not suggest to the logger that a change of technology is a good business decision. An expanded financial analysis framework, as recommended by Kaplan, also does not catch the significance of the change. Even from the expanded viewpoint, the benefits from the new technology fall ahead of and behind the logger in the value chain, but the logger must incur the cost and assume the risks. A competitive strategy perspective is required, but the conceptual framework proposed by Porter not explicit enough on financial analysis to be very helpful. An augmented cost analysis framework, as recommended by Bromwich and Bhimani, also does not capture the significance of the change because they have not pushed strategy and financial analysis ideas far enough. Explicitly considering the strategic issues involved in the technology change from the loggers' perspective does enrich the decision metric. But, again, one will never see the power of the change by focusing solely on the logger, even when using an expanded and augmented cost analysis framework.

Y-O tried to convince the contract loggers it hired to move from feller-buncher technology to harvester/forwarder technology using conventional project-level financial analysis. Its efforts failed to persuade any loggers to change. Even careful attention to intangible factors, coupled with hurdle rate subsidies (investment guarantees) and appeal to long-run declines under current logging methods did not induce contractors to switch. Subsequent attempts to couch the decision in strategic terms, for the loggers, gained somewhat more receptivity to change, but still nowhere near the groundswell Y-O felt it needed.

No real progress was made until Y-O adopted an SCM framework. First, viewing the problem from a value chain perspective clearly reveals the paradox that, although the change involves major financial benefits, the stage in the chain where the investment must be made earns none of the resulting benefits under current pricing regimes. Second, the cost driver perspective shows that technology choice in this situation is indeed a key structural cost factor that is further reinforced by executional cost factors. Third, the com-

petitive positioning perspective reveals that, although this technology change is not compelling under all conceivable strategic postures, it is compelling under the positioning strategy to which Y-O has committed, virtually irrevocably, over the next ten to fifteen years. Each of these three components of the SCM analysis is necessary to establish the rationale for the new investment.

Whether Y-O can effect a voluntary changeover to H/F logging among its contractors is still not clear. It will certainly be necessary to explicitly consider gain-sharing mechanisms across the supplier-customer linkages to encourage a change in the logging system Y-O believes to be optimal. If the loggers decide that Y-O's incentives are still inadequate, Y-O may be forced to reconsider its decision to exclude the logging step from its vertical integration chain. In SCM terms, Y-O might realize that, given its strategic position, the potential economies from technological change are large enough to offset the diseconomies from vertically integrating at this value chain step if gain-sharing inducements for more explicit customer-supplier linkages are not successful.

CONCLUSION

The Y-O study represents the limitations of all four of the current approaches for evaluating technology investment opportunities—conventional financial analysis, expanded financial analysis,[19] competitive advantage analysis,[20] and strategically augmented financial analysis.[21] The study is also an excellent example of how the Strategic Cost Management framework provides a more useful way to apply the power of cost analysis concepts to technology investment opportunities within a fully articulated strategic analysis context.

Clearly, one essential step in the effective management of technology change is effective analysis of the investment opportunities. We believe that Strategic Cost Management is a useful way to structure the analysis of such opportunities and thus represents an important component of technology management.

John K. Shank and Vijay Govindarajan are professors at the Amos Tuck School of Business Administration, Dartmouth College.

References

A modified version of this article will appear in the authors' forthcoming book, Strategic Cost Management *(New York: Free Press).*

1. R. Jaikumar, "Postindustrial Manufacturing," *Harvard Business Review,* November–December 1986, pp. 69–79.

2. R. Hayes and W. Abernathy, "Managing Our Way to Economic Decline," *Harvard Business Review,* July–August 1980, pp. 67–77.

3. R. Kaplan, "Must CIM Be Justified on Faith Alone?" *Harvard Business Review,* March–April 1986, pp. 87–95.

4. M. Porter, "Technology and Competitive Advantage," *Journal of Business Strategy,* Winter 1985, pp. 60–78.

5. M. Bromwich and A. Bhimani, "Strategic Investment Appraisal," *Management Accounting,* March 1991, pp. 45–48.

6. M. Wood, M. Polorny, V. Lintner, and M. Blinkhorn, "Investment Appraisal in the Mechanical Engineering Industry," *Management Accounting* (UK), October 1984, pp. 36–37.

7. Kaplan (1986).

8. R. Kaplan, "Wilmington Tap and Die," 9-185-124 (Boston Harvard Business School, 1987).

9. Porter (1985).

10. Ibid.

11. Bromwich and Bhimani (1991).

12. J. K Shank, "Strategic Cost Management: New Wines or Just New Bottles?," *Journal of Management Accountings Research,* Fall 1989, pp. 47–65.

13. M. Porter, *Competitive Strategy* (New York: Free Press) 1980.

14. J. K Shank and V. Govindarajan, "Strategic Cost Management: The Value Chain Concept," in *Handbook of Cost Management,* ed. Barry J. Brinker (New York: Warren, Gorham & Lamont, 1991), chapter 2.

15. D. Riley, "Competitive Cost Based Investment Strategies for Industrial Companies, *Manufacturing Issues* (New York: Booz, Allen & Hamilton, 1987).

16. Ibid.

17. Porter (1980).

18. Shank (1989).

19. Kaplan (1986).

20. Porter (1985).

21. Bromwich and Bhimani (1991).

A STRATEGIC COST MANAGEMENT APPROACH TO TECHNOLOGICAL INVESTMENT

Blending these three themes represents the most powerful way to focus cost analysis for technological change-Strategic Cost Management:

1. **Value Chain Analysis.** The value chain in any business is the linked set of value-creating activities all the way from basic raw materials through to component suppliers, to the ultimate end-use product delivered into the final consumers' hands. Even though a firm may participate in only a part of the value chain, the firm should analyze its technological investments from the standpoint of their impact throughout the chain—the impact on its suppliers, the impact on the firm itself, and the impact on its customers. "Value chain" analysis can be contrasted with "value-added" analysis, which is typically used in conventional, NPV framework. Value-added analysis starts with payments to suppliers (purchases) and stops with charges to customers (sales) while focusing on maximizing the difference, the value added (sales minus purchases) for the firm. Value-added analysis is far too narrow a view because it misses the importance of linkages up-stream and down-stream in the value chain.

2. **Cost Driver Analysis.** Value chain analysis alone is not a sufficient test of the desirability of changing technology. A second necessary component is that technology choice must be an important cost driver. Costs are a function of "structural" drivers (such as scale, product line complexity, scope of operations, experience and technology) and "executional" drivers (such as Total Quality Management, capacity utilization, and workforce participation). In short, there are multiple drivers of cost. Technology must be an important driver of cost at critical steps in the chain.

3. **Competitive Advantage Analysis.** Technological choices cannot be justified by just understanding the value chain and understanding the key cost drivers. A final component in the analysis involves analyzing whether technological change enhances the way the firm has chosen to compete—either on the basis of cost or on the basis of differentiation.

Question

10.1 What are the four approaches to evaluating technological investments that Shank and Govindarajan critique? What are the problems with each approach?

10.2 Analyzing Capital Investments in New Products

By Suresh Kalagnanam and Suzanne K. Schmidt

To succeed in the rapidly growing, highly competitive biotechnology industry, companies will have to develop innovative products, processes, or technologies that can be realized within reasonably short time periods. Playing an important part is the high cost of capital. Because capital has to be used wisely to generate sufficient returns, companies investing large sums of money in research and development (R&D) are compelled to conduct rigorous *a priori* financial analyses to evaluate their new projects.

To see the effect of this development, we followed the experiences of a biotechnology company that placed increased emphasis on the financial performance of its new projects. In particular, we addressed the issues of the accuracy of the financial numbers and the behavioral implications of this recent financial emphasis. We collected information through discussions and interviews with several employees in the marketing, R&D, and accounting departments and from documentary evidence.

THE PROJECT DEVELOPMENT AND EVALUATION PROCESS

Cyto Technologies[1], which started approximately 15 years ago, is a rapidly growing biotechnology company with manufacturing operations in the United States and sales operations there and abroad. Cyto manufactures and sells hundreds of products in seven major product areas: enzymes, nucleic acid, molecular biology, cellular regulation, eukaryotic transcription, protein translation, and biochemical reagents. Two typical uses for the company's products are providing life science researchers with materials and techniques for their experiments and providing private and government-supported testing laboratories with materials and techniques for use in DNA and food testing.

In the past, the project selection process at Cyto lacked a structured approach. Projects were selected with just sketchy ideas about financial numbers and rough ideas of payback periods. Increasing competition and the higher cost of capital have forced Cyto to change its approach. A project approval team (PAT) was set up three years ago to provide structure for the project development and evaluation process. The PAT consists of five constant members (the heads of manufacturing, quality assurance, finance and accounting, research and development, and marketing) and two rotating members (one each from marketing and R&D). This team oversees the allocation of resources to new projects in alignment with the company's objectives.

The current project development and evaluation process consists of four phases: idea-initial screening, product design, product development, and launch.[2] See Figure 1 for an example.

Phase 1, idea, consists of two stages: idea generation and investigation. In the generation stage, any R&D scientist with an idea for a new product or technique is granted a certain (small) sum of money to conduct a literature search or preliminary laboratory research. The idea, which is documented in an idea evaluation report, is screened by the marketing and R&D (or manufacturing) co-chairs. If the idea appears promising, it enters the investigation stage. An additional sum (usually three times the initial amount) is allocated to the project, an identification number is assigned to it, and all time is charged to that number. The investigation stage results in a report that contains a proposal for a feasibility study or product development, and that report is reviewed by members of the project approval team.

Phase 2, product design, consists of a feasibility study. The study results in a report on the final definition of the product—image, specifications, marketing potential, and initial return on investment (ROI) or internal rate of return (IRR) estimates. Once again this report is reviewed by the project approval team. A favorable review moves the project into the next phase.

Phase 3, product development, consists of two stages: specifications and final optimization. The specifications

FIGURE 1
PROJECT DEVELOPMENT PROCESS AT CYTO

Phase 1			Phase 2			Phase 3			Phase 4
Idea	Initial screening by marketing and Research & Development co-chairs	Investigation	PAT Review	Review Technological and Marketing Feasibility	PAT Review	Specifications (including financial analysis)	PAT Review	Final Optimization	Launch

stage establishes product definitions (in terms of the components), packaging and fitness testing, and hazard and stability evaluation. Production cost estimates also are figured, and marketing personnel determine the final sales forecasts. Then the final estimate of IRR is computed, and test marketing is conducted. At this point, the PAT once again reviews the project, which, if approved, enters the next stage. In the final optimization stage, the first batch is made, documentation is completed, quality assurance specifications are detailed, regulatory compliances are met, and the final design is demonstrated. The marketing personnel are involved in planning product promotion and advertising campaigns. Finally, in Phase 4, the product is launched.

PROJECT SELECTION CRITERIA

The project approval team uses nine criteria to evaluate projects (see sidebar). Financial performance is only one of the nine, so a project may be approved even if it performs relatively poorly on that test. For example, the first criterion, potential for proprietary position (patent and technical strength), is very important in this industry. Once a company has a patent, it can gain market advantage by forcing competitors to stop pursuing that line of products. Also, patents enhance the reputation of the company and of its scientists. In such situations, Cyto may be willing to accept short-term losses in exchange for future benefits, but it will not accept projects that are totally without financial promise.

In recent years, Cyto has decided to increase the importance of financial returns for three reasons. First, the company has been growing rapidly, so total costs have multiplied. It has a larger workforce, more sophisticated equipment, greater work space, and bigger and more expensive buildings (costlier infrastructure). Cyto must invest wisely to maintain this infrastructure.

Second, there are more ideas than funds available. One product team that brainstormed on new project ideas two years ago came up with almost 25. Unfortunately, only five could be selected for further research because the allocation of funds among multiple project ideas necessitates capital rationing. Thus, financial analysis can help in the earlier stages of the evaluation process.

Third, increased competition and a higher cost of capital also have compelled Cyto to be wise about its investments.

CURRENT FINANCIAL ANALYSIS

Cyto conducts a capital investment analysis (which it calls ROI analysis) during the product development phase. The analysis involves computing the payback period (PBP), net present value (NPV), and the internal rate of return of a project. R&D scientists track their time for conducting literature searches, preliminary laboratory testing, and so on, on time sheets, by project numbers as soon as a project receives a number. This result represents the direct labor cost of the R&D department. All of the other costs incurred by R&D,

and costs allocated to R&D from three service departments,[3] are classified as overhead costs. The total R&D cost is divided by the number of direct R&D labor hours in order to determine a burden rate for allocating the R&D costs to various projects on the basis of the direct labor hours consumed.

The above R&D cost allocated to each project, plus any initial marketing costs, represent the investment in the project (cash flow at time zero). Cyto uses a three-year time horizon in its investment analysis, and the cash flows for periods one to three are the estimated after-tax earnings adjusted for accruals. The computer model allows the project team to conduct a sensitivity analysis by varying some of its parameters. Although payback period, net present value, and internal rate of return are computed, IRR appears to be the most easily understood number and forms the basis of analysis.

PROBLEMS WITH THE NEW EMPHASIS

Cyto's employees had five major concerns about the increased emphasis on financial performance: (1) cost accuracy, (2) cost specification, (3) timing, (4) evaluation criteria, and (5) behavioral implications. They also had suggestions for dealing with the problems.

Cost accuracy. Any financial analysis can be only as good as the data used. In our interviews, employees raised two important concerns regarding the accuracy of the numbers used in the analysis—the allocation of R&D overhead costs and costs that differ for different products.

Overhead costs account for more than 58% of the total R&D costs. Currently they are assigned to projects on the basis of direct R&D labor, even though many overhead items are unrelated to direct labor. Activity-based costing (ABC), however, suggests that the sole use of direct labor allocation can lead to potentially inaccurate costs. Further analysis would be required to determine if the use of ABC or any other allocation method would be better than the current setup.

The management at Cyto also wants a clearer picture of R&D cost behavior (fixed versus variable cost). The single, predetermined overhead rate does not allow a separation of these costs.

The suggestion from the employees concerning this situation is to use multiple drivers to increase accuracy. For example, the current allocation procedure could be modified by computing separate rates for the fixed and variable portions of the total overhead.

Further analysis would be required to determine the extent of modification that would be cost beneficial.

The use of one overhead cost driver implies that all products use resources in the same proportions. Our discussions with several Cyto employees revealed two separate types of products, innovative and "me-too," that use resources in different quantities. An innovative product is defined as one that offers new features or is produced in a totally new way. A "me-too" product does not offer any new features compared to competing products. On the average, Cyto produces approximately 50% innovative and 50% "me-too" products.

It can be argued that the two product types have different cost structures. The R&D and marketing costs associated with each type of product can be quite different. Innovative products require more time because new markets have to be developed, and the marketing personnel have little idea of the characteristics of these new markets and so must do more market research. R&D personnel may need to do more extensive reading and laboratory work. The outlay costs for innovative products are likely to be higher than those for "me-too" products. Employees have suggested that more in-depth analysis of the differences in the resource consumption of the two types of products is required.

Cost specification. Cyto does not distinguish between pre-launch and post-launch costs. For example, although marketing, quality assurance, and process development personnel are involved in pre-launch activities, their times are not captured in the initial investment amount. The costs associated with their activities typically are classified as post-launch costs; they are a part of the cost of goods sold—COGS.

With respect to marketing, the directors spend considerable time on new products, conducting market research and competitor analysis—both pre-launch activities. The costs of these activities are included in the marketing and administration costs and are allocated to the COGS using a formula based on historical data. It is clear that this allocation to COGS is partially incorrect. Some of the marketing and administration costs should be classified as pre-launch costs.

Although Cyto's system could result in some distortion in the capital investment analysis, the company uses it with the idea that more accuracy may not be cost beneficial. Additional resources would be required to track the time spent by non-R&D personnel on new projects.

Employees suggested including a few additional steps to capture more accurate time allocation in the marketing department. In order to capture the more routine (post-launch) activities, the relevant personnel could maintain log books to record activities and times. The times for the non-standard (pre-launch) activities performed by more senior employees, however, are relatively difficult to capture. These activities can be measured ". . . by asking these employees to estimate the percentages of their time available to spend on each defined activity."[4]

A logical approach would be to develop a survey to gather information such as: (1) the factors that influence the amount of time marketing personnel spend on the activities listed in Table 2, (2) an estimate of the time spent on these activities based on past experience, and (3) the proportion of time spent on pre-launch activities versus post-launch activities. This information, if possible, should be obtained based on project categories ranked on a scale from innovative to "me-too" (see Table 1 for the characteristics of the possible product categories).

Timing. Cyto evaluates projects over a three-year period, yet the typical life cycle of a product is five to seven years. Omitting the cash flow data for the additional years may result in misleading NPV and IRR estimates, especially for products that do well in the later years. On the other hand, one can argue that any cash flow data (especially sales revenues) pertaining to years five and beyond are just fuzzy estimates (especially for products selling in new markets).

Scientists at Cyto say that using a three-year time horizon may be inappropriate. Cyto could consider conducting analyses using more than one time horizon. Additional suggestions include investigating the life spans of innovative and "me-too" products and examining the life spans of previous similar products. This information would allow Cyto to develop norms for time horizons to be used in the financial analyses of different products.

TABLE 1
POSSIBLE PRODUCT CATEGORIES

Application	Technology	Market	Competition	Category	Category Rank
New	New	New	No	Highly innovative	1
New	New	Existing	No		2
New	Existing	New	No		3
New	Existing	Existing	No		4
Existing	New	New	No		5
Existing	New	New	Yes		6
Existing	New	Existing	No		7
Existing	New	Existing	Yes		8
Existing	Existing	New	No		9
Existing	Existing	New	Yes		10
Existing	Existing	Existing	No		11
Existing	Existing	Existing	Yes	Me-too	12

Note; An innovative product is defined as one that is revolutionary in that it offers new features to the customer or is produced in a totally new way. A "me-too" product does not offer any new features compared to the competing products that are available.

Financial analysis is performed only during phase three of the development process. Several Cyto employees expressed concern that the analysis is conducted too late in the process. Although it would be ideal to conduct a financial analysis sooner, it is not possible because sales estimates are finalized only in phase three, and more accurate COGS numbers also are available only in this phase (after the first batch has been made). This means that projects must be evaluated more carefully during phases one and two, based on market research, product design, and technological development.

Additional concerns were raised about the likelihood of terminating financially unsatisfactory projects at such a late step in the evaluation process. At this point in the process, a significant amount of money (as much as $100,000) already has been invested. Employees and management were concerned that such a decision would come too late, creating a potential for significant losses. Because this amount is a sunk cost, the crucial decision would be whether to proceed with minimum additional investment and recover the money if the project comes in or to abort and accept the loss. This decision involves evaluating a trade-off between possible future returns from the current project and the cost of starting a new project.

Evaluation criteria. Cyto has not established an *a priori* cut-off internal rate of return. One PAT member noted, ". . . . I don't think we have . . . a cut-off, that . . . [below a certain IRR] we are not going to consider [a project]. . . ." This lack of an appropriate hurdle rate sometimes is beneficial but at other times poses a problem. On one hand, members of a PAT will not reject projects outright because they do not meet "acceptable" financial criteria, but, on the other hand, they also do not have objective financial criteria upon which to make project approval decisions.

Possible changes that have been suggested to correct this problem include the use of a minimum acceptable IRR based on historical returns and the use of different cut-off rates for the innovative and "me-too" products. Higher cut-off rates of return could be used for innovative products especially "when . . . new [markets are] being created, [because] the investment requirements and the corresponding risks are . . . large."[5]

Behavioral implications. The scientists at Cyto may resist the changes caused by the increased importance of financial performance because it may impact the way their performance is measured, and there could be problems of de-skilling (a reduction in the number and kind of tasks performed), alienation (from new work that employees may find unsuitable), and sabotage (tampering with the new system).[6]

Currently, the R&D scientists are not evaluated on the basis of strict, objective guidelines. With more emphasis on the financial performance of projects, however, these scientists may perceive that increasingly they are being evaluated on how well their projects do financially. This belief could have both positive and negative repercussions. Some scientists probably will be more careful about designing and developing their products and consciously will work toward developing products that add value to the company. Others

may attempt to get around the problem by fudging the numbers so that pet projects show favorable results. Two obvious tactics to get around the numbers would be to log fewer hours or to change the time horizon.

A change in the evaluation criteria for new projects may cause scientists emotional conflict. The creativity and reputation of a scientist in the biotechnology industry is important for his or her career survival. Management must provide some flexibility in how these scientists function. Overemphasis on financial performance could stifle their creativity, and they may be encouraged to develop more "me-too" rather than innovative products. As a result, the challenges of the tasks that the scientists perform may diminish, resulting in de-skilling.

The overemphasis on financial performance also has the potential to create an atmosphere of fear. One scientist remarked that he would hardly be able to sleep the night before his presentation to the PAT because of the possible rejection of his project. These consequences can demoralize the scientists, leading to acts of sabotage such as logging fewer hours, not including certain costs, and so on. Emphasis on both financial and nonfinancial criteria, however, should alleviate a scientist's fear about the consequences of a project's poor financial performance. Thus the scientist will be confident that his or her project will not be rejected strictly on poor financial performance.

Increased emphasis on financial performance also can lead to decreased motivation and eventually alienation if the change is not handled appropriately Cyto scientists felt they would be less motivated because their opinions on projects would be less valued. The danger is that unhappy employees could lead a migration out of Cyto over to a competitor. This point is very relevant to the biotechnology industry because losing creative scientists, who are key resources, can be very damaging.

What could Cyto do to reduce the negative impact of change? The controller, with the leader of the R&D team, could educate the scientists about the level of competition Cyto is facing, providing the rationale for emphasizing financial performance. The company could stress the fact that IRR is only one of the nine project evaluation criteria and that financially marginal projects could still be accepted based on the other criteria. In addition, Cyto could involve more of its employees (scientists, marketing personnel, production personnel) in the development and continual revising of the guidelines for the project development and evaluation process.

CHANGES HAVE OCCURRED

Several important changes affecting the project development and evaluation process have taken place at Cyto since we concluded our data collection in October 1993.

Four important system changes now allow communication regarding individual projects to be online rather than on paper. First, each project's status is monitored on the computer, and project progress reports are readily available, so any changes to the project are relayed quickly. Second, R&D personnel maintain their time sheets online, so data are available for analysis. Third, Cyto has installed its new cost accounting System (called BPICS). The system allows more accurate tracking of product manufacturing costs. As a result, more accurate COGS numbers are available to perform capital investment analyses. In addition, costs of product and sales support are available online. Fourth, the initial project identification numbers, assigned during phase one, are tied to the final catalog numbers so that actual sales information can be compared to the forecasts made before the product was launched. This before-and-after comparison of returns lets Cyto identify which projects did or did not generate the expected returns and why.

With the increased emphasis on financial performance, Cyto saw the need for more training for R&D scientists in product cost terminology and the costing issues involved. The controller and his staff made several presentations to the R&D staff regarding the importance of a detailed financial analysis along with other criteria. The R&D scientists also were taught the basics of the BPICS system so they could understand the variables of the system.

Now Cyto is addressing the issue of the effectiveness of the project development and evaluation process under the project approval team. The company has developed a brief survey designed to obtain employees' opinions regarding the PAT process. It also seeks insight into what can be done to improve the process, so Cyto is involving its employees in a redesign. The vice president of R&D says that R&D personnel and other employees are more amenable to the idea of PAT today than even a year ago. She also feels that the increased emphasis on financial performance has resulted in cost consciousness among the R&D scientists.

The core issue in dealing with the PAT process involves a cost-benefit trade-off. Cyto is expending greater effort, and significant sums of money to track activities and costs more accurately. More accurate cost information will allow Cyto to make more informed decisions and to maintain a competitive edge. Moreover, Cyto is finding ways to deal with possible dysfunctional behavior among the scientists. Management firmly believes that an increased emphasis on financial performance will result in the scientists' developing more cost-effective products that will enhance the future performance of the company.

Suresh S. Kalagnanam is an associate professor at accounting at the University of Saskatchewan, Sasketoon, Canada. He is a member of IMA's Madison (Wis.) Chapter and can be reached at (306) 966-8453. He holds M.S. and MBA degrees from the University of Saskatchewan and is completing his doctorate studies at the University of Wisconsin-Madison.

Suzanne K. Schmidt is a bookkeeper at Kohl's Food Stores. She has an MACC degree from the University of Wisconsin-Madison and can he reached at (608) 244-7596.

Notes:

This project was conducted under the guidance of Prof. Ella Mae Matsumura; we thank her for her contribution to this project. We also thank Marilyn Sagrillo for her comments, and the individuals of the case study firm for contributing their time to this research project.

1. The company name has been changed at the request of management.

2. We conducted this study between February and October 1993. The details in this Section are taken from Cyto's following document: "Idea to New Product Guidelines," dated September 1992. The project development process used at Cyto resembles the Stage-Gate model for moving a new product from idea to launch. See R. G. Cooper. "Stage-Gate Systems: A New Tool for Managing New Products," *Business Horizons,* May–June 1990, pp. 44–54, for details.

3. The three service departments are immunological services, scientific support, and purchasing.

4. R. Cooper and R. S. Kaplan, *The Design of Cost Management Systems,* Prentice-Hall, Inc., Englewood Cliffs. N. J., 1991, p. 468.

5. G. S. Day, *Market Driven Strategy: Processes for Creating Value,* The Free Press, New York. N. Y. p. 31.

6. M. D. Shields and S. M. Young, "A Behavioral Model for Implementing Cost Management Systems," *Journal of Cost Management,* Winter 1989. pp. 17–27.

PROJECT EVALUATION CRITERIA

1. Potential for proprietary position.
2. Balance between short-term and long-term projects and payoffs.
3. Potential for collaborations and outside funding.
4. Return on investment.
5. Need to establish competency in an area.
6. Potential for spin-off products.
7. Strategic fit with the corporations planned and existing technology, manufacturing capabilities, marketing and distribution systems.
8. Impact on long-term corporate positioning.
9. Probability of technical success.

From S. Kalagnanam and S. K. Schmidt, "Analyzing Capital Investments in New Products," *Management Accounting* (January 1996): 31–36. Reprinted with permission.

Question

10.2 What are some of the negative behavioral implications of evaluating the work of R&D scientists with Cyto's new method? Can these be overcome? Is so, how?

10.3 Managerial Accounting and Environmental Compliance Costs

By Burt Hamner and Christopher H. Stinson

Executive Summary

- Many firms are reexamining their traditional cost accounting systems due to new state and federal regulations requiring the proper allocation of environmental compliance costs. They hope to improve finance and investment decisions based on developing and maintaining a successful environmental accounting system.

- Traditionally, environmental costs had been assigned to general overhead, since they were relatively low and the cost of tracking them relatively high. These allocation methods are becoming inappropriate due to decreased reporting and compliance costs and soaring environmental compliance regulations.

- Adopting proper environmental compliance practices can decrease pollutant levels and save money. Penalties and law suits can be more costly for those not complying with federal and state regulations.

- Correctly tracing and allocating environmental costs involves properly identifying cost drivers, which imply cause-and-effect relationships between assigned costs and allocation bases, and identifying nonlinear cost relationships to avoid distorted cost estimates.

- Strategies for managing environmental costs involve giving managers appropriate incentives for environmental compliance costs, because successful financing, sound investment decisions, and competitive advantage primarily rely on the accuracy of the data supplied by management.

As companies experience increasing environmental regulation, higher environmental compliance costs, and huge penalties for noncompliance, managers need to reconsider how their cost accounting systems assign environmental compliance costs, which were usually assigned to general overhead rather than being traced directly to the operations where they originated.

This article reviews market and regulatory pressures for accurate assignment of environmental compliance costs, identifies various environmental compliance costs, and discusses typical cost drivers for some of these costs, which primarily are nonlinear functions of the cost drivers. Finally, the article gives a brief discussion of practices that can facilitate developing and maintaining a successful environmental accounting system.

COMPETITIVE PRESSURES FOR IMPROVED MANAGEMENT ACCOUNTING

Because of pressures to maintain profits and keep product costs low, companies regularly compare the costs of current production processes with the costs of alternative processes. These process costs include significant expenses of complying with environmental regulations, including the following:

- Permit fees;
- Costs of filling out compliance forms;
- Training costs; and
- Other environmental costs.

Traditionally, environmental costs were not traced to specific production processes; instead, they were assigned to general overhead[1] and then allocated to all production processes. This was an acceptable way to account for environmental costs because they were relatively low and the cost of tracking them relatively high, so production costs were not grossly distorted.

Today, these traditional cost allocation methods are often inappropriate due to declining information systems costs and soaring environmental compliance costs. As compliance costs increase relative to other costs, accurate assignment of compliance costs becomes much more important.

For example, if a company has one production process that generates hazardous waste, aggregating the associated waste-disposal fees into general overhead that is allocated over all the Company's production processes leads to understating costs for some products and overstating costs for others. Consequently, some leading companies now include environmental compliance costs in project analyses[2] and trace waste-management costs to the departments where they originate. In these companies, accounting for environmental costs is an intrinsic part of corporate decision making.

IDENTIFYING COSTS THAT CAN BE AVOIDED

One of the most important issues in accounting for environmental costs is to correctly distinguish preventable costs from unavoidable costs. Traditionally, cost accounting systems have tended to underestimate avoidable costs (e.g., by using pollution-preventing alternatives). Failure to estimate avoidable costs can have serious social and economic consequences, because companies may fail to adopt measures that would reduce pollutant levels and also save money.

For example, researchers at the Tellus Institute,[3] compared the traditional cost analysis (which did not trace all environmental compliance costs to specific processes) used by two pulp and paper producers with the total cost analysis[4] (which did trace all environmental costs). For one pulp mill's project, the net present value of the $1.7 million pollution-prevention expenditure shifted from $600,000 under the traditional analysis to $1.8 million under a total-cost analysis; the internal rate of return (IRR) increased from 6 percent to 36 percent; and the payback period dropped from 11.4 years to 2.0 years. For a second company's project, the net present value of the $600,000 pollution-prevention expenditure shifted from $100,000 to $1,200,000 under a total-cost analysis; IRR increased from 16 percent to 27 percent; and the payback period dropped from 5.3 years to 3.0 years.[5]

Most companies will not find it practical to trace all costs because, for some small costs, the marginal cost of tracing the costs can be greater than the marginal benefit of slightly increased accuracy in cost estimates. Nevertheless, research indicates that many existing cost accounting systems treat environmental costs in a way that leads to inaccurate production and investment decisions.

LEGAL REQUIREMENTS

In addition to competitive pressures, recent state and federal regulations have required increased accuracy of accounting for environmental costs. Several federal regulations set management accounting standards for regulatory reports from certain companies.

Draft Environmental Protection Agency (FPA)[6] guidelines on waste minimization programs required for all hazardous-waste generators propose a cost allocation system under which departments and managers are charged "fully loaded" waste management costs (i.e., costs that factor in liability, compliance, and oversight costs) for generated waste.

Many states also require businesses to prepare plans that compare the total costs of current waste- and pollution-generating processes with the total costs of pollution-reducing alternative processes. For example, the State of Washington's Hazardous Waste Reduction Act requires industrial companies to describe the accounting systems they use to record costs associated with hazardous-substance use and hazardous-waste generation.

ENVIRONMENTAL COSTS IN BUSINESS

Most environmental costs that businesses incur involve state and federal regulation compliance costs. For example, the Occupational Safety and Health Act regulates the exposure of employees to hazardous chemicals and requires worker right-to-know training on handling the chemicals. The Superfund Amendments and Reauthorization Act (SARA) of 1986 and the Emergency Planning and Community Right-to-Know Act of 1986 also regulate the use and storage of hazardous substances. Federal legislation regulating the monitoring, handling, and treatment of hazardous waste includes the Resource Conservation and Recovery Act (RCRA) of 1976, the Hazardous and Solid Waste Amendments of 1984, and the Comprehensive Environmental Response, Compensation and Liability Act (CERCLA) of 1980. The Clean Air Act, the Clean Water Act, and SARA provide the basis for

most federal regulation of air and water emissions. In addition to costs imposed by regulations, businesses must pay for insurance to protect against liabilities arising from hazardous substance use or pollution.

Exhibit 1 lists a number of costs and activities that may be relevant when comparing the costs of different production processes. The first column lists costs that traditionally are traced to specific processes. The second column (compliance costs) lists costs directly imposed by regulations, including pollution-control equipment costs, disposal fees, mandated safety supplies, and required worker training. The third column lists oversight costs that arise indirectly from satisfying various compliance requirements, including compliance-report generation, waste collection, and other related management activities.

Both compliance and oversight costs have usually been assigned to general overhead rather than traced to particular manufacturing processes. Issues to consider in the correct treatment of environmental compliance costs are the focus of the next section.

TRACING VERSUS ALLOCATING ENVIRONMENTAL COSTS

Traditional accounting systems commonly trace costs such as direct labor and direct materials to specific manufacturing processes. Other expenses are aggregated into overhead accounts, which are usually allocated to processes on the basis of allocation bases such as direct labor or direct machine hours.[7] (The term *cost driver* is often used instead of the term *allocation base* to imply a cause-and-effect relationship between the costs being assigned and the allocation base; i.e., the cost driver is what causes the cost to be incurred.)

Exhibit 2 lists common production costs of complying with environmental regulations. Companies with these costs either trace them to their source or allocate them as part of overhead to various production processes.

If the allocation rules are reliable (i.e., if the allocation bases/cost drivers correlate well with the incurrence of compliance costs), allocating overhead can yield results similar to those obtained by tracing. However, nonlinear cost relationships can distort cost estimates based on allocated compliance costs. For example, compliance costs typically arise from hazardous substance use, hazardous waste generation, and production of other pollutants. The allocation bases commonly used to allocate overhead costs, such as direct labor and machine hours, usually do not correlate well with the actual factors that generate compliance costs (see Exhibit 2). In addition, environmental compliance costs do not increase proportionately to the increased use of hazardous substances or the increased generation of hazardous waste and other pollutants (see Exhibit 2).

NONLINEAR COST FUNCTIONS

Exhibit 3A describes a cost relationship where the cost (hazardous waste disposal) varies in proportion to its cost driver

EXHIBIT 1
BUSINESS ACTIVITIES CREATING ENVIRONMENTAL COMPLIANCE COSTS, COMPLIANCE OVERSIGHT COSTS, AND NONENVIRONMENTAL COSTS

The costs of activities in the left-hand column have traditionally been traced to specific processes; environmental compliance and oversight costs have usually been allocated to overhead.

Costs Traditionally Traced

Depreciable Capital Costs
engineering
procurement
equipment
materials
utility connections
site preparation
facilities
installation

Operating Expenses
start-up
training
initial raw material
working capital
raw materials
supplies
direct labor
utilities
maintenance
salvage value

Environmental Compliance Costs

Receiving Area
spill response equipment
emergency response plan

Raw Materials Storage
storage facilities
secondary containment
right-to-know training
reporting and record-keeping
safety training
safety equipment
container labels

Process Area
safety equipment
right-to-know training
waste collection equipment
emission control equipment
sampling and testing
reporting and record-keeping

Solid and Hazardous Wastes
sampling and testing
containers
labels and labelling
storage areas
transportation fees
disposal fees

Air and Water Emission Controls
permit preparation
permit fees
capital costs
operating expenses
recovered materials
inspection and monitoring
record-keeping and reporting
sampling and testing
emergency planning

Related Oversight Costs

Purchasing
product/vendor research
regulatory impact analysis
inventory control

Engineering
hazard analysis
sampling and testing

Production
employee training
emergency planning
medical monitoring
rework
waste collection
disposal management
inspections and audits

Marketing
public relations

Management
regulatory research
legal fees
information systems
penalties and fines
insurance

Finance
credit costs
tied-up capital

Accounting
accounting system
development
accounting system
maintenance

(volume of hazardous waste produced). By contrast, Exhibits 4A and 4B illustrate costs that typically do not vary linearly with their cost drivers (see Exhibit 4). Ignoring nonlinear relationships between overhead costs and their allocation bases can lead to distorted cost estimates and inappropriate production decisions.[8]

Compliance costs have nonlinear cost drivers for reasons such as the following:

- The costs may vary with the number of hazardous substances used in a production process (Exhibits 3B and 4A);
- The costs may vary with the number and amount of hazardous waste generated by a production process (Exhibits 3A and 4B); or
- The costs may vary with the amount of regulated effluent produced by a production process.

EXHIBIT 2
ENVIRONMENTAL-COMPLIANCE COSTS CLASSIFIED ACCORDING TO THEIR COST DRIVERS

Cost Driver	Compliance Requirement	Expected Relationship of Compliance Cost to Cost Driver(s)
Hazardous substances (HS) used	Permit preparation and fees	per HS per plant
	Inspection and monitoring	per HS per plant
	Worker right-to-know training	per HS per plant
		per new worker per process
	Filing and record-keeping	per HS per plant
		per new worker per process
	Regular (periodic) training	per number of workers per plant
	Process safety equipment	per process
	Process emission controls	per process
	Emergency response planning	per HS-generating process per plant
Hazardous wastes (HW) produced	Permit preparation and fees	volume-related step function per HW*
	Inspection and monitoring	per HW per plant
	RCRA reporting costs	volume-related step function per HW*
	Filing and record-keeping	volume-related step function per HW*
	Worker training requirements	per worker
	Pre-disposal storage costs	volume-related step function per HW*
	Hazardous waste transportation and disposal fees]	per volume of HW
	Minimization planning	per HW-generating process**
	Emergency response planning	per HW-generating process**
Regulated effluents (RE) produced	Permit preparation and fees	per RE volume per process
• Air and water emissions	Inspection and monitoring	per RE per plant
	Record-keeping and reporting	per RE volume per process
	Emergency response planning	per RE-generating process
	Annual (and other) discharge fees	per volume of RE
• Nonhazardous solid wastes	In-house temporary storage costs	per volume of RE
	Nonhazardous waste transportation and disposal fees	per volume of RE

*See text for discussion
**Minimization plans are required if firms either manifest HW under RCRA or report HW under other regulations.

EXHIBIT 3
EXAMPLES OF LINEAR COST DRIVERS

A. The cost of hazardous waste (HW) transportation and disposal probably varies in proportion to the volume of HW produced at a plant.

B. The compliance reporting costs for HW production typically increase in proportion to the number of different hazardous wastes generated at a plant. Eliminating an HW from one process can have no effect on reporting costs if a volume threshold is not crossed but can have a substantial effect if that elimination causes the plant's output to drop to a new reporting level.

As regulations increase the relative size of environmental compliance costs and inaccurate allocations, assigning environmental costs to general overhead or assuming a proportionate cost variance to a regulated substance volume can lead to distorted decisions about competitive production and pricing. The following sections discuss the relationship between various compliance and oversight costs, and their cost drivers.

HAZARDOUS SUBSTANCES USED IN PRODUCTION

When hazardous substances are used in a manufacturing process, a number of costly compliance requirements must be met. When comparing the costs of current processes versus pollution-preventing alternatives, decision makers must determine:

- The functional relationship between the hazardous substances used and their associated cost (Exhibit 2); and
- Whether these costs can be avoided by pollution-preventing alternative processes.

Some costs (e.g., permit preparation and fees) and some filing and record-keeping requirements (e.g., material safety data sheet requirements) are incurred if hazardous substances are used at any level; otherwise, they are not incurred (Exhibit 4A). These costs are unlikely to decline unless hazardous chemicals are eliminated from all plant processes.

Yet costs such as inspection and monitoring, worker right-to-know training, and process safety equipment (Exhibit 4B) usually decline if a hazardous chemical is eliminated from at least one out of several plant processes.

Hazardous waste produced. When a plant generates hazardous waste, another set of compliance requirements becomes effective. A step function based on the volume of hazardous waste produced triggers different levels of RCRA compliance:

- "Small-quantity generators" (i.e., plants that produce less than 100 kilograms (kg) of hazardous waste per month) are exempt from RCRA reporting requirements;
- "Regulated generators" (100-1,000 kg of hazardous waste per month) and "large quantity generators" (more than 1,000 kg of hazardous waste per month) face increased reporting requirements; and
- "Treatment, storage, and disposal (TSD) facilities" face the most extreme reporting requirements.

Some costs of hazardous waste production decline based on reducing waste volume (e.g., transportation and disposal fees; see Exhibit 3A). However, other costs (e.g., permit preparation and fees) will decline only if the hazardous waste volume declines sufficiently to decrease the plant's regulated status. Conversely, increased hazardous waste volume produced or processed can drastically increase compliance costs by moving the plant to a new compliance category (Exhibit 3B illustrates this for RCRA reporting costs.)

Similarly, many cement companies in the Pacific Northwest accept shipyard sandblast waste as a component of their cement. However, many of these companies avoid using materials classified as hazardous waste even if the materials could be safely incorporated into cement, because the companies would be reclassified as TSD facilities.

Regulated effluents produced. Regulated effluents include many air and water pollutants. As with hazardous chemical use and hazardous waste production, the costs associated with regulated effluents vary according to the volume produced. Although some costs (e.g., annual discharge fees) can be reduced by decreasing the amount of regulated effluents produced by each process, other costs (e.g., emergency response planning costs and emission-control equipment) will decline only if the regulated effluent is eliminated from all plant processes.

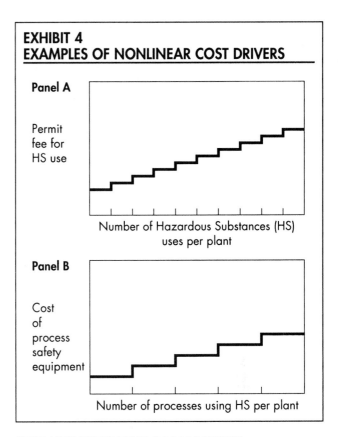

EXHIBIT 4
EXAMPLES OF NONLINEAR COST DRIVERS

Panel A

Permit fee for HS use

Number of Hazardous Substances (HS) uses per plant

Panel B

Cost of process safety equipment

Number of processes using HS per plant

STRATEGIES FOR MANAGING ENVIRONMENTAL COSTS

When decision making is centralized, managers can focus their efforts primarily on collecting appropriate cost information. However, as decision making becomes more decentralized, senior managers must be certain that incentives for middle managers are aligned with the goals of senior management. This section addresses issues that arise when decision making is decentralized.

A central requirement for success in any business undertaking is obtaining the commitment of top management. Many progressive companies have established an across-department environmental committee to oversee corporate environmental affairs (e.g., determining specific responsibilities for the management accounting team, planning for periodic audits of environmental costs and activities, and forecasting regulatory requirements and trends for planning and budgeting purposes).

As with any company goal, it is important to align managers compensation and incentives with achievement of goals. Environmental compliance goals require careful consideration when incorporated into compensation plans. For example, although it might be desirable for some accounting purposes to trace cleanup costs for past activities to specific segments, it could well be counterproductive to incorporate these costs into compensation plans. If cleanup of prior-period waste reduces current-period compensation, line managers may be tempted to underinvest in cleanup activities.

Another example of accounting decision making occurred when a manufacturing company in the Seattle area planned to start tracing waste-disposal fees to the specific processes that generate the waste instead of continuing to aggregate the fees into general overhead. The company's financial managers became concerned that this new system would create a perverse incentive for the production staff to report only a portion of the generated waste and to dispose of it illegally. Thus, it is important to reevaluate the performance evaluation system when allocation rules are changed to ensure that local managers are given appropriate incentives for environmental compliance costs.

The U.S. Sentencing Commission recently proposed guidelines for sentences imposed on officers of corporations convicted of federal environmental offenses.[9] These sentences may be reduced if an environmental compliance program is currently in place; no reduction is permitted if the corporation has not instituted explicit incentives for environmental compliance.

CONCLUSION

Modifying cost accounting systems so that they trace environmental compliance costs to the processes where they originate can lead to better financing and investment decisions. companies should use cost drivers that accurately match the compliance cost component of overhead to the events that generate those costs. Improved cost accounting practices can help companies improve their competitive position, prepare more accurate cost data, and document their commitment to improving their stake-holders' environment.

Burt Hamner is pollution prevention manager for Shapiro & Associates in Seattle, Washington. Christopher H. Stinson is assistant professor of accounting at the University of Texas in Austin, Texas.

Notes

1. U.S. General Accounting Office. *Waste Minimization: Major Problems of Data Reliability and Validity Identified* (Washington, D. C.: U.S. General Accounting Office, 1992): PMED-92–16.

2. General Electric Corporation, *Financial Analysis of Waste Management Alternatives* (Fairfield, CT: General Electric Corporation Corporate Environmental Programs, 1987); U.S. Environmental Protection Agency, *Pollution Prevention Benefits Manual, Volume II: Appendices* (Washington, D. C.: Office of Pollution Prevention and Toxics, 1989).

3. U.S. Environmental Protection Agency, *Total Cost Assessment: Accelerating Industrial Pollution Prevention Through Innovative Project Financial Analysis With Applications to the Pulp and Paper Industry* (Washington, D. C.: Office of Pollution Prevention and Toxics, U.S. Environmental Protection Agency, 1992): EPA/741/R-92/002.

4. Raftelis, G. A., "Financial and Accounting Measures as Part of Pollution Prevention Assessment," *Environmental Finance* (Summer 1991): 129–149.

5. See note 3.

6. U.S. Environmental Protection Agency, "Draft Guidance to Hazardous Waste Generators on the Elements of a Waste Minimization Program," *Federal Register 54*: 25056–25057.

7. *Foster, G., and M. Gupta, "Manufacturing Overhead Cost Driver Analysis," Journal of Accounting and Economics* (1990 Vol. 12): 309–337.

8. Noreen, E., and N. Soderstrom, "Are Overhead Costs Strictly Proportional to Activity? Evidence from Hospital Service Departments," *Journal of Accounting and Economics* (1994 Vol. 17): 255–278.

9. Anderson, U. L., "The New Federal Sentencing Guidelines: Implications for the Internal Audit Function," *Internal Auditing* (1992 Volume 8, No. 2): 71–77.

From B. Hamner and C. H. Stinson, "Managerial Accounting and Environmental Compliance Costs," *Journal of Cost Management* (Summer 1995): 4–10. Reprinted with permission.

Questions

10.3a What is a nonlinear cost function and what causes compliance costs to have nonlinear cost drivers?

10.3b What are the implications of ignoring nonlinear relationships between overhead costs and their allocation bases within the context of environmental compliance costs? Explain

CHAPTER 11

Planning and Control

Robert Kaplan and David Norton's article, *Using the Balanced Scorecard as a Strategic Management System* (Reading 11.1), extends the authors earlier development of the balanced scorecard as described in the text. In this article, four new processes designed to link more effectively long-term strategic objectives with short-term actions are presented. The four processes are: (1) translating the vision, which aids managers in building consensus around the organization's vision and strategy; (2) communicating and linking, which helps managers communicate their strategy throughout the organization and to link it to department and individual objectives; (3) business planning, which allows companies to integrate business and financial plans; and (4) feedback and learning, which provides managers with information about how well their departments and employees have done in meeting their budgeted financial goals. The article presents examples within each category of recent company experiences in applying these processes.

Kenneth Merchant's *The Control Function of Management* (Reading 11.2) presents a framework for determining the appropriate use of management controls. Merchant discusses specific action controls, those designed to make sure that individuals take the most appropriate actions; controls over results, those related to meeting targets such as budgets; and personnel controls, those based on hiring people who will do what is best for the organization. Using this framework, Merchant discusses a number of topics including how to choose among the various forms of control and the kinds of financial and behavioral costs that are incurred in using each form of control.

Gerald Ross writes in *Revolution in Management Control* (Reading 11.3) that management control systems are in a state of revolution due to two major factors: changes in technology and changes in the marketplace. The technological changes that Ross refers to relate to the shift from standardized repetitive manufacturing to much more flexible operations, while marketplace changes pertain to the shift from mass market to mass customization. These changes also signal a need for the redesign of management accounting and control systems. New designs should incorporate real time controls, rather than after the fact controls, and peer pressure and social controls should supplant traditional top down control.

11.1 Using the Balanced Scorecard as a Strategic Management System
Building a scorecard can help managers link today's actions with tomorrow's goals.

by Robert S. Kaplan and David P. Norton

As companies around the world transform themselves for competition that is based on information, their ability to exploit intangible assets has become far more decisive than their ability to invest in and manage physical assets. Several years ago, in recognition of this change, we introduced a concept we called the *balanced scorecard.* The balanced scorecard supplemented traditional financial measures with criteria that measured performance from three additional perspectives—those of customers, internal business processes, and learning and growth. (See the chart "Translating Vision and Strategy: Four Perspectives.") It therefore enabled companies to track financial results while simultaneously monitoring progress in building the capabilities and acquiring the intangible assets they would need for future growth. The scorecard wasn't a replacement for financial measures; it was their complement.

Recently, we have seen some companies move beyond our early vision for the scorecard to discover its value as the cornerstone of a new strategic management system. Used this way, the scorecard addresses a serious deficiency in traditional management systems: their inability to link a company's long-term strategy with its short-term actions.

Most companies' operational and management control systems are built around financial measures and targets, which bear little relation to the company's progress in achieving long-term strategic objectives. Thus the emphasis most companies place on short-term financial measures leaves a gap between the development of a strategy and its implementation.

Managers using the balanced scorecard do not have to rely on short-term financial measures as the sole indicators of the company's performance. The scorecard lets them introduce four new management processes that, separately and in combination, contribute to linking long-term strategic objectives with short-term actions. (See the chart "Managing Strategy: Four Processes.")

The first new process—*translating the vision*—helps managers build a consensus around the organization's vision and strategy. Despite the best intentions of those at the top, lofty statements about becoming "best in class," "the number one supplier," or an "empowered organization" don't translate easily into operational terms that provide useful guides to action at the local level. For people to act on the words in vision and strategy statements, those statements must be expressed as an integrated set of objectives and measures, agreed upon by all senior executives, that describe the long-term drivers of success.

The second process—*communicating and linking*—lets managers communicate their strategy up and down the organization and link it to departmental and individual objectives. Traditionally, departments are evaluated by their financial performance, and individual incentives are tied to short-term financial goals. The scorecard gives managers a way of ensuring that all levels of the organization understand the long-term strategy and that both departmental and individual objectives are aligned with it.

The third process—*business planning*—enables companies to integrate their business and financial plans. Almost all organizations today are implementing a variety of change programs, each with its own champions, gurus, and consultants, and each competing for senior executives' time, energy, and resources. Managers find it difficult to integrate those diverse initiatives to achieve their strategic goals—a situation that leads to frequent disappointments with the programs' results. But when managers use the ambitious goals set for balanced scorecard measures as the basis for allocating resources and setting priorities, they can undertake and coordinate only those initiatives that move them toward their long-term strategic objectives.

The fourth process—*feedback and learning*—gives companies the capacity for what we call strategic learning. Existing feedback and review processes focus on whether the company, its departments, or its individual employees have met their budgeted financial goals. With the balanced scorecard at the center of its management systems, a company can monitor short-term results from the three additional perspectives—customers, internal business processes, and learning and growth—and evaluate strategy in the light of recent performance. The scorecard thus enables companies to modify strategies to reflect real-time learning.

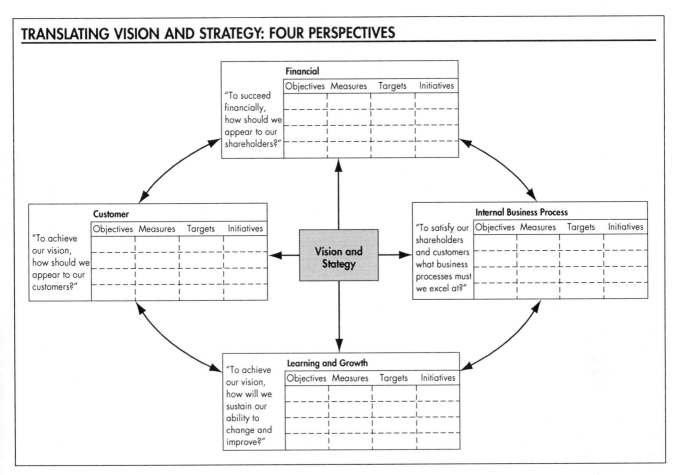

None of the more than 100 organizations that we have studied or with which we have worked implemented their first balanced scorecard with the intention of developing a new strategic management system. But in each one, the senior executives discovered that the scorecard supplied a framework and thus a focus for many critical management processes: departmental and individual goal setting, business planning, capital allocations, strategic initiatives, and feedback and learning. Previously, those processes were uncoordinated and often directed at short-term operational goals. By building the scorecard, the senior executives started a process of change that has gone well beyond the original idea of simply broadening the company's performance measures.

For example, one insurance company—let's call it National Insurance—developed its first balanced scorecard to create a new vision for itself as an underwriting specialist. But once National started to use it, the scorecard allowed the CEO and the senior management team not only to introduce a new strategy for the organization but also to overhaul the company's management system. The CEO subsequently told employees in a letter addressed to the whole organization that National would thenceforth use the balanced scorecard and the philosophy that it represented to manage the business.

National built its new strategic management system step-by-step over 30 months, with each step representing an incremental improvement. (See the chart "How One Com-

pany Built a Strategic Management System.") The iterative sequence of actions enabled the company to reconsider each of the four new management processes two or three times

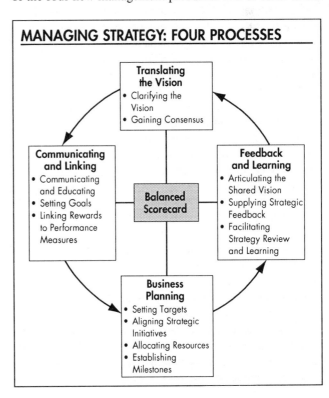

MANAGING STRATEGY: FOUR PROCESSES

Translating the Vision
- Clarifying the Vision
- Gaining Consensus

Communicating and Linking
- Communicating and Educating
- Setting Goals
- Linking Rewards to Performance Measures

Balanced Scorecard

Feedback and Learning
- Articulating the Shared Vision
- Supplying Strategic Feedback
- Facilitating Strategy Review and Learning

Business Planning
- Setting Targets
- Aligning Strategic Initiatives
- Allocating Resources
- Establishing Milestones

HOW ONE COMPANY BUILT A STRATEGIC MANAGEMENT SYSTEM

2A *Communicate to Middle Managers:* The top three layers of management (100 people) are brought together to learn about and discuss the new strategy. The balanced scorecard is the communication vehicle. *(months 4–5)*

2B *Develop Business Unit Scorecards:* Using the corporate scorecard as a template, each business unit translates its strategy into its own scorecard. *(months 6–9)*

5 *Refine the Vision:* The review of business unit scorecards identifies several cross-business issues not initially included in the corporate strategy. The corporate scorecard is updated. *(month 12)*

Time Frame *(in months)*

0	1	2	3	4	5	6	7	8	9	10	11	12

Actions:

1 *Clarify the Vision:* Ten members of a newly formed executive team work together for three months. A balanced scorecard is developed to translate a generic vision into a strategy that is understood and can be communicated. The process helps build consensus and committment to the strategy.

3A *Eliminate Nonstrategic Investments:* The corporate scorecard, by clarifying strategic priorities, identifies many active programs that are not contributing to the strategy. *(month 6)*

3B *Launch Corporate Change Programs:* The corporate scorecard identifies the need for cross-business change programs. They are launched while the business units prepare their scorecards. *(month 6)*

4 *Review Business Unit Scorecards:* The CEO and the executive team review the individual business units' scorecards. The review permits the CEO to participate knowledgeably in shaping business unit strategy. *(months 9–11)*

---

before the system stabilized and became an established part of National's overall management system. Thus the CEO was able to transform the company so that everyone could focus on achieving long-term strategic objectives—something that no purely financial framework could do.

TRANSLATING THE VISION

The CEO of an engineering construction company, after working with his senior management team for several months to develop a mission statement, got a phone call from a project manager in the field. "I want you to know," the distraught manager said, "that I believe in the mission statement. I want to act in accordance with the mission statement. I'm here with my customer. What am I supposed to do?"

The mission statement, like those of many other organizations, had declared an intention to "use high-quality employees to provide services that surpass customers' needs." But the project manager in the field with his employees and his customer did not know how to translate those words into the appropriate actions. The phone call convinced the CEO that a large gap existed between the mission statement and employees' knowledge of how their day-to-day actions could contribute to realizing the company's vision.

Metro Bank (not its real name), the result of a merger of two competitors, encountered a similar gap while building its balanced scorecard. The senior executive group thought it had reached agreement on the new organization's overall strategy: "to provide superior service to targeted customers." Research had revealed five basic market segments among existing and potential customers, each with different needs. While formulating the measures for the customer-perspective portion of their balanced scorecard, however, it became apparent that although the 25 senior executives agreed on the words of the strategy, each one had a different definition of *superior service* and a different image of the *targeted customers.*

The exercise of developing operational measures for the four perspectives on the bank's scorecard forced the 25 executives to clarify the meaning of the strategy statement. Ultimately, they agreed to stimulate revenue growth through new products and services and also agreed on the three most desirable customer segments. They developed scorecard measures for the specific products and services that should be delivered to customers in the targeted segments as well as for the relationship the bank should build with customers in each segment. The scorecard also highlighted gaps in employees' skills and in information systems that the bank

224

7 *Update Long-Range Plan and Budget:* Five-year goals are established for each measure. The investments required to meet those goals are identified and funded. The first year of the five-year plan becomes the annual budget. *(months 15–17)*

9 *Conduct Annual Strategy Review:* At the start of the third year, the initial strategy has been achieved and the corporate strategy requires updating. The executive committee lists ten strategic issues. Each business unit is asked to develop a position on each issue as a prelude to updating its strategy and scorecard. *(months 25–26)*

13	14	15	16	17	18	19	20	21	22	23	24	25	26

6A *Communicate the Balance Scorecard to the Entire Company:* At the end of one year, when the management teams are comfortable with the strategic approach, the scorecard is disseminated to the entire organization. *(month 12–ongoing)*

6B *Establish Individual Performance Objectives:* The top three layers of management link their individual objectives and incentive compensation to their scorecards. *(months 13–14)*

8 *Conduct Monthly and Quarterly Reviews:* After corporate approval of the business unit scorecards, a monthly review process, supplemented by quarterly reviews that focus more heavily on strategic issues, begins. *(month 18–ongoing)*

10 *Link Everyone's Performance to the Balanced Scorecard:* All employees are asked to link their individual objectives to the balanced scorecard. The entire organization's incentive compensation is linked to the scorecard. *(months 25–26)*

Note: Steps 7, 8, 9, and 10 are performed on a regular schedule. The balanced scorecard is now a routine part of the management process.

---

would have to close in order to deliver the selected value propositions to the targeted customers. Thus, creating a balanced scorecard forced the bank's senior managers to arrive at a consensus and then to translate their vision into terms that had meaning to the people who would realize the vision.

COMMUNICATING AND LINKING

"The top ten people in the business now understand the strategy better than ever before. It's too bad," a senior executive of a major oil company complained, "that we can't put this in a bottle so that everyone could share it." With the balanced scorecard, he can.

One company we have worked with deliberately involved three layers of management in the creation of its balanced scorecard. The senior executive group formulated the financial and customer objectives. It then mobilized the talent and information in the next two levels of managers by having them formulate the internal-business-process and learning-and-growth objectives that would drive the achievement of the financial and customer goals. For example, knowing the importance of satisfying customers' expectations of on-time delivery, the broader group identified several internal business processes—such as order processing,

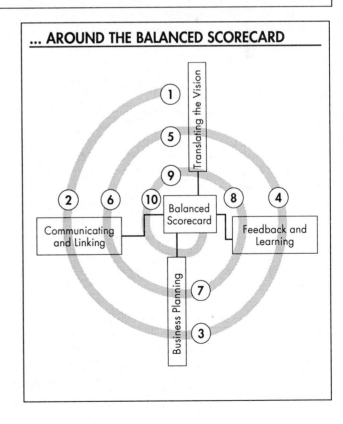

... AROUND THE BALANCED SCORECARD

225

scheduling, and fulfillment-in which the company had to excel. To do so, the company would have to retrain frontline employees and improve the information systems available to them. The group developed performance measures for those critical processes and for staff and systems capabilities.

Broad participation in creating a scorecard takes longer, but it offers several advantages: Information from a larger number of managers is incorporated into the internal objectives; the managers gain a better understanding of the company's long-term strategic goals; and such broad participation builds a stronger commitment to achieving those goals. But getting managers to buy into the scorecard is only a first step in linking individual actions to corporate goals.

The balanced scorecard signals to everyone what the organization is trying to achieve for shareholders and customers alike. But to align employees' individual performances with the overall strategy, scorecard users generally engage in three activities: communicating and educating, setting goals, and linking rewards to performance measures.

Communicating and Educating. Implementing a strategy begins with educating those who have to execute it. Whereas some organizations opt to hold their strategy close to the vest, most believe that they should disseminate it from top to bottom. A broad-based communication program shares with all employees the strategy and the critical objectives they have to meet if the strategy is to succeed.

Onetime events such as the distribution of brochures or newsletters and the holding of "town meetings" might kick off the program. Some organizations post bulletin boards that illustrate and explain the balanced scorecard measures, then update them with monthly results. Others use group-ware and electronic bulletin boards to distribute the scorecard to the desktops of all employees and to encourage dialogue about the measures. The same media allow employees to make suggestions for achieving or exceeding the targets.

The balanced scorecard, as the embodiment of business unit strategy, should also be communicated upward in the organization—to corporate headquarters and to the corporate board of directors. With the scorecard, business units can quantify and communicate their long-term strategies to senior executives using a comprehensive set of linked financial and nonfinancial measures. Such communication informs the executives and the board in specific terms that long-term strategies designed for competitive success are in place. The measures also provide the basis for feedback and accountability. Meeting short-term financial targets should not constitute satisfactory performance when other measures indicate that the long-term strategy is either not working or not being implemented well.

Should the balanced scorecard be communicated beyond the boardroom to external shareholders? We believe that as senior executives gain confidence in the ability of the scorecard measures to monitor strategic performance and predict future financial performance, they will find ways to inform outside investors about those measures without disclosing competitively sensitive information.

Skandia, an insurance and financial services company based in Sweden, issues a supplement to its annual report called "The Business Navigator"—an instrument to help us navigate into the future and thereby stimulate renewal and development." The supplement describes Skandia's strategy and the strategic measures the company uses to communicate and evaluate the strategy. It also provides a report on the company's performance along those measures during the year. The measures are customized for each operating unit and include, for example, market share, customer satisfaction and retention, employee competence, employee empowerment, and technology deployment.

Communicating the balanced scorecard promotes commitment and accountability to the business's long-term strategy. As one executive at Metro Bank declared, "The balanced scorecard is both motivating and obligating."

Setting Goals. Mere awareness of corporate goals, however, is not enough to change many people's behavior. Somehow, the organization's high-level strategic objectives and measures must be translated into objectives and measures for operating units and individuals.

The exploration group of a large oil company developed a technique to enable and encourage individuals to set goals for themselves that were consistent with the organization's. It created a small, fold-up personal scorecard that people could carry in their shirt pockets or wallets. (See the exhibit "The Personal Scorecard.") The scorecard contains three levels of information. The first describes corporate objectives, measures, and targets. The second leaves room for translating corporate targets into targets for each business unit. For the third level, the company asks both individuals and teams to articulate which of their own objectives would be consistent with the business unit and corporate objectives, as well as what initiatives they would take to achieve their objectives. It also asks them to define up to five performance measures for their objectives and to set targets for each measure. The personal scorecard helps to communicate corporate and business unit objectives to the people and teams performing the work, enabling them to translate the objectives into meaningful tasks and targets for themselves. It also lets them keep that information close at hand-in their pockets.

Linking Rewards to Performance Measures. Should compensation systems be linked to balanced scorecard measures? Some companies, believing that tying financial compensation to performance is a powerful lever, have moved quickly to establish such a linkage. For example, an oil company that we'll call Pioneer Petroleum uses its scorecard as the sole basis for computing incentive compensation. The company ties 60% of its executives' bonuses to their achievement of ambitious targets for a weighted average of four financial indicators: return on capital, profitability, cash flow, and operating cost. It bases the remaining 40% on indicators of customer satisfaction, dealer satisfaction, employee satisfaction, and environmental responsibility (such as a percentage change in the level of emissions to water and air). Pioneer's CEO says that linking compensation to the scorecard has helped to

THE PERSONAL SCORECARD

Corporate Objectives
☐ Double our corporate value in seven years.
☐ Increase our earnings by an average of 20% per year.
☐ Achieve an internal rate of return 2% above the cost of capital.
☐ Increase both production and reserves by 20% in the next decade.

Corporate Targets					Scorecard Measures	Business Unit Targets					Team/Individual Objectives and Initiatives
1995	1996	1997	1998	1999		1995	1996	1997	1998	1999	1.
					Financial						
100	120	160	180	250	Earnings (in millions of dollars)						
100	450	200	210	225	Net cash flow						
100	85	80	75	70	Overhead and operating expenses						2.
					Operating						
100	75	73	70	64	Earnings (in millions of dollars)						
100	97	93	90	82	Net cash flow						
100	105	108	108	110	Overhead and operating expenses						3.
Team/Individual Measures						**Targets**					
1.											
2.											
3.											4.
4.											
5.											
Name:											5.
Location:											

align the company with its strategy. "I know of no competitor," he says, "who has this degree of alignment. It is producing results for us."

As attractive and as powerful as such linkage is, it nonetheless carries risks. For instance, does the company have the right measures on the scorecard? Does it have valid and reliable data for the selected measures? Could unintended or unexpected consequences arise from the way the targets for the measures are achieved? Those are questions that companies should ask.

Furthermore, companies traditionally handle multiple objectives in a compensation formula by assigning weights to each objective and calculating incentive compensation by the extent to which each weighted objective was achieved. This practice permits substantial incentive compensation to be paid if the business unit overachieves on a few objectives even if it falls far short on others. A better approach would be to establish minimum threshold levels for a critical subset of the strategic measures. Individuals would earn no incentive compensation if performance in a given period fell short of any threshold. This requirement should motivate people to achieve a more balanced performance across short- and long-term objectives.

Some organizations, however, have reduced their emphasis on short-term, formula-based incentive systems as a result of introducing the balanced scorecard. They have discovered that dialogue among executives and managers about the scorecard—both the formulation of the measures and objectives and the explanation of actual versus targeted results—provides a better opportunity to observe managers' performance and abilities. Increased knowledge of their managers' abilities makes it easier for executives to set incentive rewards subjectively and to defend those subjective evaluations—a process that is less susceptible to the game playing and distortions associated with explicit, formula-based rules.

One company we have studied takes an intermediate position. It bases bonuses for business unit managers on two equally weighted criteria: their achievement of a financial objective—economic value added—over a three-year period and a subjective assessment of their performance on measures drawn from the customer, internal-business-process, and learning-and-growth perspectives of the balanced scorecard.

That the balanced scorecard has a role to play in the determination of incentive compensation is not in doubt. Precisely what that role should be will become clearer as more companies experiment with linking rewards to scorecard measures.

BUSINESS PLANNING

"Where the rubber meets the sky": That's how one senior executive describes his company's long-range-planning process. He might have said the same of many other companies because their financially based management systems fail to link change programs and resource allocation to long-term strategic priorities.

The problem is that most organizations have separate procedures and organizational units for strategic planning and for resource allocation and budgeting. To formulate their strategic plans, senior executives go off-site annually and engage for several days in active discussions facilitated by senior planning and development managers or external consultants. The outcome of this exercise is a strategic plan articulating where the company expects (or hopes or prays) to be in three, five, and ten years. Typically, such plans then sit on executives' bookshelves for the next 12 months.

Meanwhile, a separate resource-allocation and budgeting process run by the finance staff sets financial targets for revenues, expenses, profits, and investments for the next fiscal year. The budget it produces consists almost entirely of financial numbers that generally bear little relation to the targets in the strategic plan.

Which document do corporate managers discuss in their monthly and quarterly meetings during the following year? Usually only the budget, because the periodic reviews focus on a comparison of actual and budgeted results for every line item. When is the strategic plan next discussed? Probably during the next annual off-site meeting, when the senior managers draw up a new set of three-, five-, and ten-year plans.

The very exercise of creating a balanced scorecard forces companies to integrate their strategic planning and budgeting processes and therefore helps to ensure that their budgets support their strategies. Scorecard users select measures of progress from all four scorecard perspectives and set targets for each of them. Then they determine which actions will drive them toward their targets, identify the measures they will apply to those drivers from the four perspectives, and establish the short-term milestones that will mark their progress along the strategic paths they have selected. Building a scorecard thus enables a company to link its financial budgets with its strategic goals.

For example, one division of the Style Company (not its real name) committed to achieving a seemingly impossible goal articulated by the CEO: to double revenues in five years. The forecasts built into the organization's existing strategic plan fell $1 billion short of this objective. The division's managers, after considering various scenarios, agreed to specific increases in five different performance drivers: the number of new stores opened, the number of new customers attracted into new and existing stores, the percentage of shoppers in each store converted into actual purchasers, the portion of existing customers retained, and average sales per customer.

By helping to define the key drivers of revenue growth and by committing to targets for each of them, the division's managers eventually grew comfortable with the CEO's ambitious goal.

The process of building a balanced scorecard— clarifying the strategic objectives and then identifying the few critical drivers—also creates a framework for managing an organization's various change programs. These initiatives—reengineering, employee empowerment, time-based management, and total quality management, among others—promise to deliver results but also compete with one another for scarce resources, including the scarcest resource of all: senior managers' time and attention.

Shortly after the merger that created it, Metro Bank, for example, launched more than 70 different initiatives. The initiatives were intended to produce a more competitive and successful institution, but they were inadequately integrated into the overall strategy. After building their balanced scorecard, Metro Bank's managers dropped many of those programs—such as a marketing effort directed at individuals with very high net worth—and consolidated others into initiatives that were better aligned with the company's strategic objectives. For example, the managers replaced a program aimed at enhancing existing low-level selling skills with a major initiative aimed at retraining salespersons to become trusted financial advisers, capable of selling a broad range of newly introduced products to the three selected customer segments. The bank made both changes because the scorecard enabled it to gain a better understanding of the programs required to achieve its strategic objectives.

Once the strategy is defined and the drivers are identified, the scorecard influences managers to concentrate on improving or reengineering those processes most critical to the organization's strategic success. That is how the scorecard most clearly links and aligns action with strategy.

The final step in linking strategy to actions is to establish specific short-term targets, or milestones, for the balanced scorecard measures. Milestones are tangible expressions of managers' beliefs about when and to what degree their current programs will affect those measures.

In establishing milestones, managers are expanding the traditional budgeting process to incorporate strategic as well as financial goals. Detailed financial planning remains important, but financial goals taken by themselves ignore the three other balanced scorecard perspectives. In an integrated planning and budgeting process, executives continue to budget for short-term financial performance, but they also introduce short-term targets for measures in the customer, internal-business-process, and learning-and-growth perspectives. With those milestones established, managers can continually test both the theory underlying the strategy and the strategy's implementation.

At the end of the business planning process, managers should have set targets for the long-term objectives they would like to achieve in all four scorecard perspectives; they should have identified the strategic initiatives required and allocated the necessary resources to those initiatives; and they should have established milestones for the measures that mark progress toward achieving their strategic goals.

FEEDBACK AND LEARNING

"With the balanced scorecard," a CEO of an engineering company told us, "I can continually test my strategy. It's

228

like performing real-time research." That is exactly the capability that the scorecard should give senior managers: the ability to know at any point in its implementation whether the strategy they have formulated is, in fact, working, and if not, why.

The first three management processes—translating the vision, communicating and linking, and business planning—are vital for implementing strategy, but they are not sufficient in an unpredictable world. Together they form an important single-loop-learning process—single-loop in the sense that the objective remains constant, and any departure from the planned trajectory is seen as a defect to be remedied. This single-loop process does not require or even facilitate reexamination of either the strategy or the techniques used to implement it in light of current conditions.

Most companies today operate in a turbulent environment with complex strategies that, though valid when they were launched, may lose their validity as business conditions change. In this kind of environment, where new threats and opportunities arise constantly, companies must become capable of what Chris Argyris calls *double-loop learning*—learning that produces a change in people's assumptions and theories about cause-and-effect relationships. (See "Teaching Smart People How to Learn," HBR May–June 1991.)

Budget reviews and other financially based management tools cannot engage senior executives in double-loop learning—first, because these tools address performance from only one perspective, and second, because they don't involve strategic learning. Strategic learning consists of gathering feedback, testing the hypotheses on which strategy was based, and making the necessary adjustments.

The balanced scorecard supplies three elements that are essential to strategic learning. First, it articulates the company's shared vision, defining in clear and operational terms the results that the company, as a team, is trying to achieve. The scorecard communicates a holistic model that links individual efforts and accomplishments to business unit objectives.

Second, the scorecard supplies the essential strategic feedback system. A business strategy can be viewed as a set of hypotheses about cause-and-effect relationships. A strategic feedback system should be able to test, validate, and modify the hypotheses embedded in a business unit's strategy. By establishing short-term goals, or milestones, within the business planning process, executives are forecasting the relationship between changes in performance drivers and the associated changes in one or more specified goals. For example, executives at Metro Bank estimated the amount of time it would take for improvements in training and in the availability of information systems before employees could sell multiple financial products effectively to existing and new customers. They also estimated how great the effect of that selling capability would be.

Another organization attempted to validate its hypothesized cause-and-effect relationships in the balanced scorecard by measuring the strength of the linkages among measures in the different perspectives. (See the chart "How One Company Linked Measures from the Four Perspectives.") The company found significant correlations between employees' morale, a measure in the learning-and-growth perspective, and customer satisfaction, an important customer perspective measure. Customer satisfaction, in turn, was correlated with faster payment of invoices—a relationship that led to a substantial reduction in accounts receivable and hence a higher return on capital employed. The company also found correlations between employees' morale and the number of suggestions made by employees (two learning-and-growth measures) as well as between an increased number of suggestions and lower rework (an internal-business-process measure). Evidence of such strong correlations help to confirm the organization's business strategy. If, however, the expected correlations are not found over time, it should be an indication to executives that the theory underlying the unit's strategy may not be working as they had anticipated.

Especially in large organizations, accumulating sufficient data to document significant correlations and causation among balanced scorecard measures can take a long time—months or years. Over the short term, managers' assessment of strategic impact may have to rest on subjective and qualitative judgments. Eventually, however, as more evidence accumulates, organizations may be able to provide more objectively grounded estimates of cause-and-effect relationships. But just getting managers to think systematically about the assumptions underlying their strategy is an improvement over the current practice of making decisions based on short-term operational results.

Third, the scorecard facilitates the strategy review that is essential to strategic learning. Traditionally, companies use the monthly or quarterly meetings between corporate and division executives to analyze the most recent period's financial results. Discussions focus on past performance and on explanations of why financial objectives were not achieved. The balanced scorecard, with its specification of the causal relationships between performance drivers and objectives, allows corporate and business unit executives to use their periodic review sessions to evaluate the validity of the unit's strategy and the quality of its execution. If the unit's employees and managers have delivered on the performance drivers (retraining of employees, availability of information systems, and new financial products and services, for instance), then their failure to achieve the expected outcomes (higher sales to targeted customers, for example) signals that the theory underlying the strategy may not be valid. The disappointing sales figures are an early warning.

Managers should take such disconfirming evidence seriously and reconsider their shared conclusions about market conditions, customer value propositions, competitors' behavior, and internal capabilities. The result of such a review may be a decision to reaffirm their belief in the current strategy but to adjust the quantitative relationship among the strategic measures on the balanced scorecard. But they also might conclude that the unit needs a different strategy

HOW ONE COMPANY LINKED MEASURES FROM THE FOUR PERSPECTIVES

Financial

(+)
Accounts Receivable → Return on Capital Employed
Operating Expense → (-)

(-)

Customer

Customer Satisfaction

(+)

Internal Business Process

Rework

(+)   (-)

Learning and Growth

Employees' Suggestions

Employees' Morale   (+)

(an example of double-loop learning) in light of new knowledge about market conditions and internal capabilities. In any case, the scorecard will have stimulated key executives to learn about the viability of their strategy. This capacity for enabling organizational learning at the executive level—strategic learning—is what distinguishes the balanced scorecard, making it invaluable for those who wish to create a strategic management system.

TOWARD A NEW STRATEGIC MANAGEMENT SYSTEM

Many companies adopted early balanced-scorecard concepts to improve their performance measurement systems. They achieved tangible but narrow results. Adopting those concepts provided clarification, consensus, and focus on the desired improvements in performance. More recently, we have seen companies expand their use of the balanced scorecard, employing it as the foundation of an integrated and iterative strategic management system. Companies are using the scorecard to

- clarify and update strategy,
- communicate strategy throughout the company,
- align unit and individual goals with the strategy,
- link strategic objectives to long-term targets and annual budgets,
- identify and align strategic initiatives, and
- conduct periodic performance reviews to learn about and improve strategy.

The balanced scorecard enables a company to align its management processes and focuses the entire organization on implementing long-term strategy. At National Insurance, the scorecard provided the CEO and his managers with a central framework around which they could redesign each piece of the company's management system. And because of the cause-and-effect linkages inherent in the scorecard framework, changes in one component of the system reinforced earlier changes made elsewhere. Therefore, every change made over the 30-month period added to the momentum that kept the organization moving forward in the agreed-upon direction.

Without a balanced scorecard, most organizations are unable to achieve a similar consistency of vision and action as they attempt to change direction and introduce new strategies and processes. The balanced scorecard provides a framework for managing the implementation of strategy while also allowing the strategy itself to evolve in response to changes in the company's competitive, market, and technological environments.

Robert S. Kaplan is the Arthur Lowes Dickenson Professor of Accounting at the Harvard Business School in Boston, Massachusetts. David P. Norton is the founder and president of Renaissance Solutions, a consulting firm in Lincoln, Massachusetts. They are the authors of "The Balanced Scorecard—Measures That Drive Performance" (HBR January–February 1992) and "Putting the Balanced Scorecard to Work" (HBR September–October 1993). Kaplan and Norton have also written a book on the balanced scorecard to be published in September 1996 by the Harvard Business School Press.

Question

11.1 According to Kaplan and Norton, one organization's members created personal scorecard. What are the elements of this personal scorecard? Is this an effective tool for managers?

11.2 The Control Function of Management

By Kenneth A. Merchant, Harvard University

After strategies are set and plans are made, management's primary task is to take steps to ensure that these plans are carried out, or, if conditions warrant, that the plans are modified. This is the critical control function of management. And since management involves directing the activities of others, a major part of the control function is making sure other people do what should be done.

The management literature is filled with advice on how to achieve better control. This advice usually includes a description of some type of measurement and feedback process:

> *The basic control process, wherever it is found and whatever it controls, involves three steps: (1) establishing standards, (2) measuring performance against these standards, and (3) correcting deviations from standards and plans.[1]*
>
> *A good management control system stimulates action by spotting the significant variations from the original plan and highlighting them for the people who can set things right.[2]*
>
> *Controls need to focus on results[3]*

This focus on measurement and feedback, however, can be seriously misleading. In many circumstances, a control system built around measurement and feedback is not feasible. And even when feasibility is not a limitation, use of a feedback-oriented control system is often an inferior solution. Yet, good controls can be established and maintained using other techniques.

What is needed is a broader perspective on control as a management function: this article addresses such a perspective. The first part summarizes the general control problem by discussing the underlying reasons for implementing controls and by describing what can realistically be achieved. In the second part, the various types of controls available are identified. The last part discusses why the appropriate choice of controls is and should be different in different settings.

WHY ARE CONTROLS NEEDED?

If all personnel always did what was best for the organization, control—and even management—would not be needed. But, obviously individuals are sometimes unable or unwilling to act in the organization's best interest, and a set of controls must be implemented to guard against undesirable behavior and to encourage desirable actions.

One important class of problems against which control systems guard may be called *personal limitations*. People do not always understand what is expected of them nor how they can best perform their jobs, as they may lack some requisite ability, training, or information. In addition, human beings have a number of innate perceptual and cognitive biases, such as an inability to process new information optimally or to make consistent decisions, and these biases can reduce organizational effectiveness.[4] Some of these personal limitations are correctable or avoidable, but for others, controls are required to guard against their deleterious effects.

Even if employees are properly equipped to perform a job well, some choose not to do so, because individual goals and organizational goals may not coincide perfectly. In other words, there is a *lack of goal congruence*. Steps must often be taken either to increase goal congruence or to prevent employees from acting in their own interest where goal incongruence exists.

If nothing is done to protect the organization against the possible occurrence of undesirable behavior or the omission of desirable behavior caused by these personal limitations and motivational problems, severe repercussions may result. At a minimum, inadequate control can result in lower performance or higher risk of poor performance. At the extreme, if performance is not controlled on one or more critical performance dimensions, the outcome could be organizational failure.

WHAT IS GOOD CONTROL?

Perfect control, meaning complete assurance that actual accomplishment will proceed according to plan, is never possible because of the likely occurrence of unforeseen events. However, good control should mean that an informed person could be reasonably confident that no major unpleasant surprises will occur. A high probability of forthcoming poor performance, despite a reasonable operating plan, sometimes is given the label "out of control."

Some important characteristics of this desirable state of good control should be highlighted. First, control is future-oriented: the goal is to have no unpleasant surprises in the future. The past is not relevant except as a guide to the future. Second, control is multidimensional, and good control cannot be established over an activity with multiple objectives unless performance on all significant dimensions has been considered. Thus, for example, control of a production department cannot be considered good unless all the major performance dimensions, including quality, efficiency, and asset management, are well controlled. Third, the assessment of whether good performance assurance has been achieved is difficult and subjective. An informed expert might judge that the control system in place is adequate because no major bad surprises are likely, but this judgment is subject to error because adequacy must be measured against a future that can be very difficult to assess. Fourth, better control is not always economically desirable. Like any other economic good, the control tools are costly and should be implemented only if the expected benefits exceed the costs.

HOW CAN GOOD CONTROL BE ACHIEVED?

Good control can be achieved by avoiding some behavioral problems and/or by implementing one or more types of control to protect against the remaining problems. The following sections discuss the major control options.

Control-Problem Avoidance

In most situations, managers can avoid some control problems by allowing no opportunities for improper behavior. One possibility is automation. Computers and other means of automation reduce the organization's exposure to control problems because they can be set to perform appropriately (that is, as the organization desires), and they will perform more consistently than do human beings. Consequently, control is improved.

Another avoidance possibility is *centralization,* such as that which takes place with very critical decisions at most organization levels. If a manager makes all the decisions in certain areas, those areas cease to be control problems in a managerial sense because no other persons are involved.

A third avoidance possibility is *risk-sharing* with an outside body, such as an insurance company. Many companies bond employees in sensitive positions, and in so doing, they reduce the probability that the employees' behavior will cause significant harm to the firm.

Finally, some control problems can and should be avoided by *elimination* of a business or an operation entirely. Managers without the means to control certain activities, perhaps because they do not understand the processes well, can eliminate the associated control problems by turning over their potential profits and the associated risk to a third party, for example, by subcontracting or divesting.

If management cannot, or chooses not to, avoid the control problems caused by relying on other individuals, they must address the problems by implementing one or more control tactics. The large number of tactics that are available to help achieve good control can be classified usefully into three main categories, according to the *object* of control; that is, whether control is exercised over *specific actions, results,* or *personnel.* Table 1 shows many common controls classified according to their control object; these controls are described in the following sections.

Control of Specific Actions

One type of control, specific-action control, attempts to ensure that individuals perform (or do not perform) certain actions that are known to be desirable (or undesirable). Management can limit the incidence of some types of obviously undesirable activity by using *behavioral constraints* that render the occurrence impossible, or at least unlikely. These constraints include physical devices, such as locks and key-personnel identification systems, and administrative constraints, such as segregation of duties, which make it very difficult for one person to carry out an improper act.

A second type of specific-action control is *action accountability*—a type of feedback control system by which employees are held accountable for their actions. The implementation of action-accountability control systems requires: (1) defining the limits of acceptable behavior, as is done in procedures manuals; (2) tracking the behaviors that employees are actually engaged in; and (3) rewarding or punishing deviations from the defined limits. Although action-accountability systems involve the tracking and reporting of actual behaviors, their objective is to motivate employees to behave appropriately in the future. These systems are effective only if employees understand what is required of them, and they feel that their individual actions will be noticed and rewarded or punished in some significant way.

A third type of specific-action control is *preaction review.* This involves observing the work of others before the activity is complete, for example, through direct supervision, formal planning reviews, and approvals on proposals for expenditures. Reviews can provide effective control in several ways by: correcting potentially harmful behavior before the full damaging effects are felt; or influencing behavior just by the threat of an impending review, such as causing extra care in the preparation of an expenditure proposal. One advantage of reviews is that they can be used even when it is not possible to define exactly what is expected prior to the review.

Control of Results

Control can also be accomplished by focusing on results: this type of control comes in only one basic form, results accountability, which involves holding employees responsible for certain results. Use of results-accountability control systems requires: (1) defining the dimensions along which results are desired, such as efficiency, quality, and service; (2) measuring performance on these dimensions; and (3) providing rewards (punishments) to encourage (discourage) behavior that will lead (not lead) to those results. As with action-accountability systems, results-accountability systems are future-oriented; they attempt to motivate people to behave appropriately. But they are effective only if employees feel that their individual efforts will be noticed and rewarded in some significant way.

Control of Personnel

A third type of control can be called *personnel control* because it emphasizes a reliance on the personnel involved to do what is best for the organization, and it provides assistance for them as necessary. Personnel controls can be very effective by themselves in some situations, such as in a small family business or in a professional partnership, because the

TABLE 1
A CONTROL TOOL CLASSIFICATION FRAMEWORK

Object of Control

Specific Actions	Results	Personnel
Behavioral Constraint: —Physical (e.g., locks, security guards) —Administrative (e.g., separation of duties)	Results Accountability: —Standards —Budgets —Management by Objective (MBO)	Upgrade Capabilities: —Selection —Training —Assignment
Action Accountability: —Work Rules —Policies and Procedures —Codes of Conduct		Improve Communication: —Clarify Expectations —Provide Information for coordination
Preaction Review: —Direct Supervision —Approval Limits —Budget Reviews		Encourage Peer Control: —Work Groups —Shared Goals

underlying causes of the needs for controls (personal limitations and lack of goal congruence) are minimal. However, even when control problems are present, they can be reduced to some extent by: (1) upgrading the capabilities of personnel in key positions, such as tightening hiring policies, implementing training programs, or improving job assignments; (2) improving communications to help individuals know and understand their roles better and how they can best coordinate their efforts with those of other groups in the organization; and (3) encouraging peer (or subordinate) control by establishing cohesive work groups with shared goals.

FEASIBILITY CONSTRAINTS ON THE CHOICE OF CONTROLS

The design of a control system often depends partly on the feasibility of the various types of controls: not all of these tools can be used in every situation. Personnel controls are the most adaptable to a broad range of situations.

To some extent, all organizations rely on their employees to guide and motivate themselves, and this self-control can be increased with some care in hiring, screening, and training. Even in a prison, where administrators are faced with a sharp lack of goal congruence and where few control options are available other than physical constraints, inmates are screened so that dangerous ones are not assigned to high-risk positions, such as in a machine shop.

Most situations, however, require reinforcing personnel controls by placing controls over specific actions, results, or a combination of the two. This is where feasibility becomes a limiting factor.

For control over specific actions, management must have some knowledge of which actions are desirable. While it may be easy to define precisely the required behavior on a production line, the definition of preferred behavior for a research engineer cannot be as precise. Being able to keep track of specific actions is also necessary to enforce actions accountability; however, this is usually not a limiting factor, except in rare situations such as a remote outpost, because actions can be observed directly or assessed indirectly through action reports, such as hours worked, sales calls made, or procedural violations.

For control over results, the most serious constraint is the ability to measure the desired results effectively. (Management usually knows what results are desirable.) Ideally, measurements should: (1) assess the *correct* performance areas—the ones for which results are truly desired; (2) be *precise*—not determined by only crude estimations; (3) be *timely* and (4) be *objective*—not subject to manipulation. While perfect measures are rarely available, reasonable surrogates can often be found or developed. For example, "complaints received" might be a good (negative) indicator of the performance of hotel staff personnel along the customer-service dimension. Significant difficulty in achieving any of these four measurement qualities, however, can lead to failure of a results-oriented control system

Figure 1 shows how the two factors most limiting control feasibility knowledge of desirable actions and the ability to measure results on the important performance dimensions—can influence the choice of controls used.[5] The most difficult control situation, shown in box 4 of Figure 1, is one in which the desirable actions are not known and the important result areas cannot be measured well. Only personnel controls (or problem avoidance) are available options. In a research laboratory, for example, success might be difficult to assess for years, yet prescription of specific actions could be counter-productive. Fortunately, in this specific setting, control is not a serious problem because research scientists tend to be professional—well trained and responsible to the standards of their profession. They tend to

FIGURE 1
KEY CONTROL OBJECT FEASIBILITY DETERMINANTS

		Ability to Measure Results on Important Performance Dimensions	
		High	Low
Knowledge of Which Specific Actions are Desirable	Excellent	1. Specific-Action and/or Results Control	2. Specific-Action Control (e.g., real-estate venture)
	Poor	3. Results Control (e.g., movie director)	4. Personal control (e.g., research laboratory)

control themselves, and consequently, control of research laboratories tend to be dominated by controls over personnel.

In box 3 of Figure 1, where knowledge of desirable specific actions is poor but good results measurements are available, control is best accomplished by controlling results. Movie production is a good example. It is probably impossible to dictate what a movie director should do or even to observe his or her behavior and predict whether the finished product will be good. It is, however, a relatively easy task to measure the economic performance of the movie and the artistic merit, if that is a concern. In this situation, the best control system would seem to be a results-accountability system that defines to the director the results expected, holds him or her responsible for achieving them, and provides some reinforcement in the form of compensation and/or recognition.

For similar reasons, results controls tend to be dominant at most upper-management levels. It is usually not possible to prescribe and keep track of the specific actions each manager should be performing, but it is relatively easy to define the results desired, in terms similar to those desired by shareholders.

Specific-action controls should dominate where there is knowledge about which actions are desirable but where results measurement is impossible or difficult, as indicated in box 2 of Figure 1. Consider, for example, control over a real-estate development business where large capital investment decisions are made frequently. Results of these decisions are difficult to measure in a timely, accurate fashion because of their long-term nature; they tend to be inseparable from the results of other actions and are confounded by changes in the environment. However, the techniques of investment analysis are well developed (e.g., net present value analysis with tests of the sensitivity of assumptions), and control may be accomplished by formally reviewing the techniques used and the assumptions made.

HOW TO CHOOSE AMONG THE FEASIBLE OPTIONS

Often managers cannot rely completely on the people involved in a given area and cannot employ one or more of the avoidance strategies mentioned earlier. When this is the case, the best situation is one in which either specific-action or results controls, or both, can be chosen, as is shown in box 1 of Figure 1. In general, the choice of one or more tools should involve consideration of: (1) the total need for control; (2) the amount of control that can be designed into each of the control devices; and (3) the costs of each, both in terms of money spent and unintended behavioral effects, if any. These decision parameters will be described more fully.

Need for Controls

The need for controls over any particular behavior or operation within an organization depends very simply on the impact of that area on overall organizational performance. Thus, more control should be exercised over a strategically important behavior rather than over a minor one, regardless of how easy it is to control each. For example, controlling the new-product-development activity is far more important in many companies than making sure that the production of existing products is accomplished as efficiently as possible. Consequently, more resources should be devoted to controlling the new-product activity, even though it is a far more difficult area to control.

Amount of Control Provided by Feasible Options

The amount of control provided by each of the control tools depends both on their design and on how well they fit the situation in which they are used. Personnel controls should usually provide some degree of control. But although they may be totally effective in some situations, such as in a small business, they provide little or no warning of failure. They can break down very quickly if demands, opportunities, or needs change.

Specific-action and results controls can provide widely varying amounts of control. In general, reasonably certain (or tight) control requires: (1) detailed specification of what is expected of *each individual*; (2) prevention of undesired actions, or effective and frequent monitoring of actions or results; and (3) administration of penalties or rewards that are significant to the individuals involved.

For example, with specific-action-accountability systems, the amount of control can be affected by changing one or more of the elements of the system. First, tighter control can be effected by making the definitions of acceptability more specific. This might take the form of work rules (e.g., no smoking) or specific policies (e.g., a purchasing policy to secure three competing bids before releasing the purchase order), as opposed to general guidelines or vague codes of conduct (e.g., act professionally). Second, control can be made tighter by improving the effectiveness of the action-tracking system. Personnel who are certain that their actions

234

will be noticed relatively quickly will be affected more strongly by an action-accountability system than will those who feel that the chance of their being observed is small. Thus, constant direct supervision should provide tighter control than would an audit sampling of a small number of action reports some time later. Third, control can be made tighter by making the rewards or punishments more significant to the individuals involved. In general, this impact should vary directly with the size of the reward (or the severity of the punishment), although different individuals may react differently to identical rewards or punishments.

Results-accountability systems can be varied along similar lines. Expected performance can be defined broadly, for instance, with a goal for annual net income. Alternatively, expected performance can be defined in more detailed form by prescribing goals for specific result areas (for example, sales growth, efficiency, quality) and by using line items with short time horizons (e.g., month or quarter). Control is tighter when the performance dimensions for which results are desired are defined explicitly and, of course, correctly: this type of control is particularly effective if well-established results standards are available, perhaps in the form of output from an engineering study, industry survey, or historical analysis. Results-accountability control can also be tightened by improving the measurement of results. This can be accomplished by making the measures more precise, more timely, and/or less subject to manipulation.

In addition, reviews can be used to provide either tight or loose assurance. Tight assurance is more likely if the reviews are detailed, comprehensive, and frequent.

Of course, managers do not have to rely exclusively on a single type of control in a control system. Use of more than one type of control—in effect, overlapping controls—will often provide reinforcement. For example, most organizations rely on selecting good people, establishing some set procedures, implementing some accountability for results, and reviewing some key decisions before they are made.

Costs: Outlay and Behavioral

The cost of a control depends on two factors: the incremental dollar cost of the tool and the cost of any unintended behavioral effects. The actual dollar cost of a control might be considerably less than it first appears because some devices that provide control may already be in place for other reasons. For example, a budgeting process for a small firm does not have to justify its cost on the basis of control reasons alone. Creditors probably already require *pro forma* financial statements, so the incremental cost might involve only additional detail (e.g., down to the operations level) and involvement of a greater number of participants.

The costs of any unintended negative effects must also be considered, and these can be very significant. It is beyond the scope of this article to provide an exhaustive enumeration of the many negative side effects possible. Indeed, they come in many different forms, but it is nevertheless useful to mention a few examples.

A common problem with specific-action controls is that they cause operating delays. These can be relatively minor, such as delays caused by limiting access to a stockroom, but they can also be major. For example, after the executives of Harley-Davidson Motor Company bought the firm from AMF, Inc., they were able to implement a rebate program in ten days, rather than the six to eight weeks it would have taken with all the reviews required in the multilayered AMF organization.[6] Obviously, where timely action is important, delays caused by control processes can be very harmful.

Another problem with specific-action controls is that they can cause rigid, bureaucratic behavior. Individuals who become accustomed to following a set routine are not as apt to sense a changing environment, nor are they likely to search for better ways of doing the tasks at hand in a stable environment.

Results controls can create severe, unintended negative effects when all the measurement criteria are not met satisfactorily. Perhaps the most serious common problem is a failure to define the results areas correctly. This causes goal displacement," a situation where individuals are encouraged to generate the wrong results—in response to the goals defined in the control system—rather than those results truly needed by the organization. For example, a department store introduced an incentive compensation plan to pay employees on the basis of sales volume. The immediate impact was indeed an increase in sales volume, but the increase was accomplished in ways that were inconsistent with long-term organizational goals. The employees competed among themselves for customers and neglected important but unmeasured and unrewarded activities such as stocking and merchandising.[7] Another common example of goal displacement is caused by the practice of rewarding managers on the oft criticized return-on-investment criterion.[8]

Data distortion is another dangerous potential side effect of results controls. If the measurement methods are not objective, then the employees whose performances are being measured might falsify the data or change the measurement methods, and, in so doing, undermine the whole organization's information system.

Many of the ramifications of these unintended effects of control systems are not well understood, and their costs are very difficult to quantify. However, consideration of these effects is an important control-system design factor: they cannot be ignored.

WHERE DOES FEEDBACK FIT IN?

Because feedback does not appear prominently in the preceding discussion, it is useful for clarification purposes to consider where feedback fits in. Control is necessarily future-oriented, as past performance cannot be changed, but analysis of results and feedback of variances can often provide a particularly strong addition to a control system. A prerequisite, of course, is the ability to measure results, so feedback can only be useful in the situations presented in boxes 1 and 3 of Figure 1.

There are three reasons why feedback of past results is an important part of many control systems. First, feedback is necessary as reinforcement for a results-accountability system. Even if the feedback is not used to make input adjustments. it signals that results arc being monitored. This can heighten employee awareness of what is expected of them and should help stimulate better performance.

Second, in repetitive situations, measurement of results can provide indications of failure in time to make useful interventions. This is shown in the simple feedback control model presented in Figure 2. When the results achieved are not satisfactory, the inputs, which include the specific actions and types of persons involved, can be changed to provide different results. Obviously, these input adjustments are more likely to improve results when there is a good understanding of how inputs relate to results; otherwise, the interventions are essentially experiments.

Third, analysis of how the results vary with different combinations of inputs might improve understanding of how the inputs relate to results. This process is depicted in loop A of Figure 3, a slightly more complicated feedback control model. As this input/ results understanding improves, it provides the opportunity to shift the control system from a results-oriented to a specific-action-oriented focus. If managers discover that certain specific actions produce consistently superior results, then it might be beneficial to inform employees of the specific actions that are expected of them, for example, by publishing these desired actions in a procedures manual. The greater the knowledge about how actions bring about results, the greater the possibilities of using a tight, specific-action-oriented control system

Note that these latter two reasons for analyzing feedback—for making interventions and for learning—are only useful in situations that at least partially repeat themselves. If a situation is truly a one-time occurrence, such as a major divestiture or a unique capital investment, management has

FIGURE 3
A FEEDBACK CONTROL MODEL WITH LEARNING

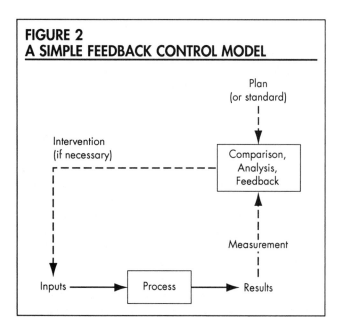

little use for feedback information. In these cases, by the time the results are available, it is too late to intervene, and a greater understanding of how results are related to inputs is not immediately useful.

There are other circumstances where feedback need not, and perhaps should not, be a part of a good control system. In many cases, although feedback control systems are not really feasible, they are used anyway. This occurs because of the consistent tendency "to concentrate an matters that are concrete and quantifiable, rather than intangible concepts," which may be equally or more important.[9] Invariably, this will lead to dysfunctional effects, as will all other failures to satisfy the measurement criteria or to define results appropriately.

Cost considerations also commonly lead to decisions not to include feedback in a control system. The design, implementation, and maintenance of results-tracking information systems can often be very expensive. Thus, it is not feasible to have feedback as part of every control system, nor is it necessarily desirable even when feasibility constraints are not present.

THE DESIGN PROCESS

As discussed at the beginning of this article, management control is a problem of human behavior. The challenge is to have each individual acting properly as often as possible. Thus, it seems logical to start the control-system design process by considering the personnel component of the organization by itself. In some situations, well-trained, highly motivated personnel can be expected, with a high degree of certainty, to perform their jobs satisfactorily without any additional control steps being taken. A confident reliance on personnel controls is a very desirable situation because additional controls cost money and may have undesirable side effects.

FIGURE 2
A SIMPLE FEEDBACK CONTROL MODEL

If, however, management determines that personnel controls should be supplemented, the first step should be to examine the feasibility of the various control options. To do this, management must assess two factors: how much is known about which specific actions are desirable, and how well measurement can be accomplished in the important performance areas. This feasibility test might immediately determine whether the controls that can be added should be oriented toward specific actions or results. Control can be made tighter by strengthening the controls in place, along the lines discussed earlier, or by implementing overlapping controls, such as controls over results and specific actions.

In most cases, management has same, but less than complete, knowledge of which specific actions are desirable and some, but not perfect, ability to measure the important result areas. This situation usually calls for implementation of both specific-action and results controls, with feedback loops to improve understanding of the relevant processes.

AN EXAMPLE: CONTROL OF A SALES FORCE

The above observations about control can be illustrated by describing how control of a sales force might work. Generally, personnel controls are some part of every sales force control system. Consider, for example, this statement by a sales and marketing consultant:

I think I can tell a good salesman just by being around him. If the guy is experienced, confident, well prepared, speaks well, maintains control of situations, and seems to have his time planned, I assume I have a good salesman.

If a sales manager feels confident about all of the salespeople employed, he or she might wish to allow personnel controls to dominate the control system. This is likely, for example, in a small business with a sales force comprised solely of relatives and close friends. But most sales managers are not willing to rely exclusively on hiring and training good people.

What controls should be added? The answer, of course, depends on the type of sales involved. In a single-product, high-volume operation, the volume of sales generated is probably a good simple factor on which to base a results-oriented control system. It provides a reasonable, although not perfect, surrogate for long-range profitability, and the measurements are very inexpensive because the data are already gathered as a necessary input to the financial reporting system. The results-accountability system can then be completed by providing reinforcement in the form of sales commissions. This simple solution will also work where multiple products with varying profitabilities are involved, if the commission schedules are varied so that rewards are assigned in proportion to the profitability of the sales generated.

Consider, however, a situation where salespeople sell large-scale construction equipment and where sales come in very large but infrequent chunks. A commission-type, results-accountability system is still feasible. Measurement

of results is not difficult and can be accurate to the penny. The amount of control provided, however, is not high because the measurements fail on the timeliness dimension. Because sales are infrequent, zero sales is not an unusual situation in any given month. Therefore, a salesperson could be drawing advances on hypothetical future commissions for many months without performing any of the desired promotional activities.

Two solutions are possible. One is to augment the commission system with some specific-action controls, such as activity reports. Some activities are probably known to be desirable, such as the number of hours worked and the quantity of calls made. If the product mix and market environment are fairly stable, then requiring and monitoring activity reports is not as costly as it might seem, because it could provide an important side benefit—an activity-oriented data base. The patterns in this data base can be analyzed and compared with results over time to add to knowledge about which activities yield the best results.

An alternate solution is to improve the results-accountability system. It might be possible to define some factors that are strong predictors of sales success, such as customer satisfaction with the salesperson or customer familiarity with the company's products. Measurement of these intangibles, of course, would have to be done by surveying customers. Even though these measures do not directly assess the desired result area (long-range profitability), and measurement is imprecise, they could provide a better focus for a results-oriented control system than a sales-generated measure because of the improvement in timeliness. Over time, it is likely that the choice of measures and measurement methodologies could be improved. The advantage of this results-oriented solution over an action-oriented system is that it is more flexible and less constraining to the salespeople; they can continue to use styles best suited to their personalities.

CONCLUSIONS

This article has taken a new look at the most basic organizational control problem— how to get employees to live up to the plans that have been established. In the course of discussion, the following major points were made:

1. Management control is a behavioral problem. The various control tools are only effective to the extent that they influence behavior in desirable directions.
2. Good control can often be achieved in several different ways. In some circumstances, the control problems can be avoided, for example, by centralizing or automating certain decisions. If problems cannot be avoided, one or more types of controls are usually desirable or necessary. The options can be classified according to the object of control, labeled in this article as specific actions, results, and personnel.
3. Not all types of controls are feasible in all situations. Figure 4 presents the questions to ask when assessing

FIGURE 4
QUESTIONS TO DETERMINE FEASIBILITY OF CONTROL TYPES

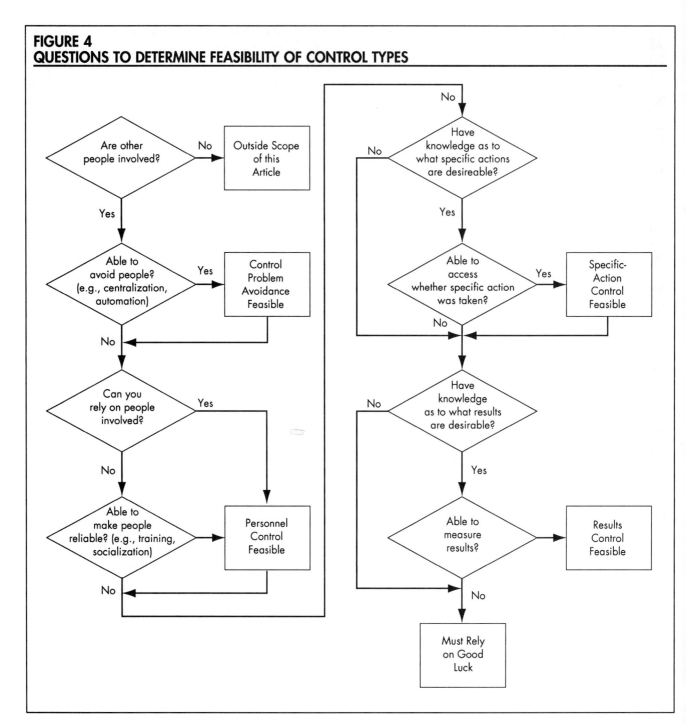

the feasibility of control types. If none of the controls is feasible, the probability of undesirable results occurring is high.

4. Control can be strengthened either by employing a tighter version of a single type of control or by implementing more than one type of control. However, tighter control is not always desirable because of additional system costs and the potential of undesirable side effects, such as destruction of morale, reduction of initiative, or displacement of employee focus toward measurable result areas only.

Some of the qualities, benefits, and costs of each of the major control types are listed in Table 2.

5. The basic management control problems and alternatives are the same in all functional areas and at all levels in the organization, from the lowest supervisory levels to the very top levels of management. The best solutions, however, vary between situations.

An understanding of control can be an important input into many management decisions. For example, control

TABLE 2
QUALITIES OF CONTROL TOOLS

Object of Control:	SPECIFIC ACTIONS			RESULTS	PERSONNEL
	Constraint	Accountability	Review	Accountability	
Amount of Control Provided (tight or loose)	Tight	Tight if Specific; Loose if Vague	Tight if Detailed And Frequent	Tight if Expectations Are Specific And Detailed	Loose
Out-of-Pocket-Cost (relative)	Low	Low	High	High	Varies
Possible Unintended Effects (examples)	Slight Operating Delays	Rigid Bureaucratic Behavior	Operating Delays	Goal Displacement Data Distortion	

problems should be considered in making some types of investments. An investment in an operation in which control is very difficult—such as a highly specialized and technical area where control must depend heavily on personnel controls—is, by definition, risky. Thus, investments in such areas should promise high returns to compensate for this risk.

Similarly, control considerations should affect the design of the other parts of the management system. Consider, for example, the organizational structure. If independent areas of *responsibility* cannot be carved out as part of the organizational structure, results-accountability control systems will not work well because employees will not feel that their individual actions have a noticeable effect on results. (It should be noted that many of the prescriptions calling for "responsibility accounting" only provide the illusion of results independence because of the many allocations of the costs and/or benefits of shared resources.) If independent areas of *authority* are not established, specific-action-accountability control systems cannot work. This principle underlies the internal control principle of "separation of duties." In addition, if tighter reviews of specific actions are necessary for adequate performance assurance, it is likely that the supervisory spans of control will have to be reduced. Similar observations can be made about other management functions, but they are beyond the scope of this article.

This article has attempted to provide a new look at this basic, but often overlooked, management problem. The control area is decidedly complex, and there is much that is not known about how controls work and how employees respond to different types of controls. For example, it would be worthwhile to know more about how controls can be designed to maximize the amount of control provided while minimizing the cost in the form of employee feelings of lost autonomy. However, an increased awareness of the control problem, of what can be accomplished, and of the options available should provide a new perspective that will suggest ways to improve control systems and overall organizational performance.

The author wishes to acknowledge Robert N. Anthony, Peter Brownell, and Martha S. Hayes for their helpful comments.

References

1. See H. Koontz, C. O'Donnell, and H. Weihrich, *Management,* 7th ed. (New York: McGraw-Hill, 1980), p. 722.

2. See W. D. Brinckloe and M. T. Coughlin, *Managing Organizations* (Encino, CA: Glencoe Press, 1977), p. 298.

3. See P. F. Drucker, *Management: Tasks, Responsibilities, Practices* (New York: Harper & Row, 1974), p. 497.

4. A recent summary of many of the findings in this area (illustrating such cognitive limitations as conservative revision of prior subjective probabilities when new information is provided, and the use of simplifying decision-making heuristics when faced with complex problems) is provided by W. F. Wright, "Cognitive Information Processing Biases: Implications for Producers and Users of Financial Information," Decision Sciences (April 1980): 284-298.

5. A similar scheme is presented in W. G. Ouchi, "A Conceptual Framework for the Design of Organizational Control Mechanisms," *Management Science* (September 1979): 833–848.

6. See H. Klein, "At Harley-Davidson, Life without AMF Is Upbeat but Full of Financial Problems," *Wall Street Journal,* 13 April 1982, p. 37.

7. See N. Babchuk and W. J. Goode, "Work Incentives in a Self-Determined Group," *American Sociological Review* (1951): 679–687.

8. For a summary of criticisms of return-on-investment (ROI) measures of performance, see J. Dearden, "The Case against ROI Control," *Harvard Business Review,* May–June 1969, pp. 124–135.

9. See D. Mitchell, Control without Bureaucracy (London: McGraw-Hill Book Company Limited, 1979), p. 6.

The control function of management can be a critical determinant of organizational success. Most authors discuss control only through feedback and adjustment processes. This article takes a broader perspective on control and discusses the following questions: What is good control? Why are controls needed? How can good control be achieved? If multiple control strategies are feasible, how should the choice among them be made? *Ed.*

Question

11.2 Merchant discusses specific action, results, and personnel controls. Provide three examples of each. Can organizations focus on just one major type of control method (e.g. action controls)?

Kenneth A. Merchant is Assistant Professor of Business Administration at Harvard University. Dr. Merchant holds the B.A. degree from Union College, the M.B.A. degree from Colombia University, and the Ph.D. degree from the University of California, Berkeley. His main interests lie in the areas of accounting, information systems, and planning and control. Dr. Merchant has published articles for such journals as *The Accounting Review* and *Accounting, Organizations, and Society.*

11.3 Revolution in Management Control
The JIT world can't be run by layers of supervision and control.

By Gerald H. B. Ross

Management control systems are in a state of revolution. North American companies, responding to global competition, are challenging the fundamentals of the way they do business. They are rewriting the rules of the game—and nothing is sacred!

A total transformation in the economics of business is at the root of this revolution. We are hurrying away from the traditional economies of mass production to the economies of "mass customization," using flexible processes and work forces to provide variety at low cost.

In this new world all the management controls that drive people's behavior are being rethought—accounting, manufacturing process controls, compensation, and related performance measurement systems. The boundaries between these areas are evaporating. The classic example is quality control.

After-the-fact inspection and layers of supervision are being replaced with empowered quality circles that "do it right the first time." These in turn had to be backed up by new information and accounting systems. The results, as some of our foreign competitors have demonstrated, are stunning. Many management accountants, however, are stuck with having to apply the traditional approaches to control—layers of checks and balances, after-the-fact controls, and highly standardized, "one size fits all" rules and procedures, leftovers from the industrial era of mass production.

If management accounting is to be relevant in the future, it must support very different control quality as corporations become transformed.

Two major forces are driving this transformation:

1. Technology—the shift from "hard" automation, based on standardized, repetitive operations, to "smart" technologies that can shift instantly from one task to another with little or no penalty in cost.
2. The marketplace—a shift from the mass market to one that is highly fragmented into myriad niches.

THE SHIFT IN TECHNOLOGY

Technology is a major force driving the transition today as it did in the 19th century. At that time, a new technology, the steam engine, opened up new productive potential.

Although this technology had emerged 50 years earlier, Adam Smith identified a new way of looking at production that ultimately unleashed the potential of the technology. In his now famous treatise on his pin factory, he expressed a very simple idea: the *standardization of the production process,* an approach that Henry Ford later raised to new heights. As the production process moved from job shop to batch processing to continuous process, the unit cost dropped dramatically.

As academic as the idea might have seemed then, the result has been an irrepressible economic driver. The benefits of increasing volume had dramatic effects on costs. This idea, which started in the textile and steel industries, spread across manufacturing to hotels, restaurants, hospitals, retailing, and universities. Although today one still can acquire handmade craft goods, mass production has become the dominant force throughout all sectors of the economy and has generated almost 200 years of economic prosperity.

THE STANDARDIZATION OF MANAGEMENT

The revolution in technology created a parallel revolution in management. The way of managing a cottage industry was hardly adequate for a factory with large capital facilities and hundreds of employees. Management systems had to match the demands of technology. Thus, as the shop floor moved toward standardization, so did management.

A "mom and pop" restaurant, for example, could manage *ad hoc*. If the owners wanted to check their inventory, they simply would go into the back room and look. However, if some one came into the shop to order 2,000 hot dogs for a community picnic, the simple "look and see" management would be overwhelmed.

Instead, the owners would have to order the meat, buns, and mustard in advance, being careful to coordinate delivery to ensure that they arrived at the right time. The owners now would be using *planning* and *scheduling* because they would be producing a *batch* of hot dogs.

If the restaurant were to evolve into a McDonald's, the owners would have to standardize procedures completely, using the principle of *management by exception,* reflecting the nature of the mass production technology. The result of this kind of evolution in many organizations is bureaucracy, with standardized rules and procedures and layers of managers looking over the shoulders of other managers, keeping things "in control."

PRISONERS OF SCALE: THE DILEMMA

Mass production technology has been so successful that virtually everything is now a commodity—with price being the major competitive factor. Automobiles, watches, food, banking services, air travel, hotels, and computers have become commodities. Unfortunately, these very economies of scale make offering variety or customization extremely expensive because of the huge fixed costs required—hence Henry Ford's famous statement that the Model T could be had in any color, as long as it was black.

The dilemma is the "commodity trap" that afflicts many companies. The more they try to differentiate their products and services, the more they add cost, becoming uncompetitive in price and vulnerable to "discounter" competitors. Similarly, as they eliminate the added features or services that make them unique, they end up with "me, too" brands in fiercely cost-competitive markets. Companies can oscillate back and forth between differentiation and low cost, becoming unable to break out of the vicious cycle.

Recently, in a marketing survey, a major dairy identified 24 value-added opportunities for new products. Unfortunately, all were too small to be "economical" given the scale of its operations. These opportunities were lost to smaller, specialized producers.

This predicament results from the fact that customization is the one thing that mass production cannot do easily. By definition, creating "exceptions" adds significant cost.

Because this cost usually is unacceptable, organizations become "prisoners of scale" and can respond only to markets of very large size, leaving the high-margin niche markets to others. They get stuck with the price-sensitive commodities destined for markets that are increasingly fragmented.

STANDARDIZATION: THE DILEMMA OF MASS PRODUCTION

The marketplace is the second major driver of the transformation in the way companies do business. Customers are becoming tired of "one size fits all" products and services and are demanding variety and customization.

Not so long ago, for example, ice cream came in three basic flavors: vanilla, chocolate, and strawberry. Today, every conceivable flavor is available. In retailing, specialized boutiques have displaced department stores. Even in services, customers are demanding exotic wilderness experiences and platinum financial services.

The simple telephone provides another dramatic example. Who would have thought 15 years ago that the market for such a mature product, which came in two styles—desk and wall phone—would explode into a thousand niches: designer phones, portable phones, kids' phones, FAX phones, car phones, and waterproof phones! The market is demanding increasing variety.

Traditional mass production processes, however, demand just the opposite— homogeneity over large production runs. Variety is eliminated because it is the source of cost.

Traditional organizations become overwhelmed with the complexity that variety creates. One manufacturer of computer workstations, for example, has thousands of combinations of features—with virtually every unit being different. The sheer complexity overpowers the manufacturing and logistics systems based on traditional mass production models.

The dilemma: to deliver flexibility and efficiency at the same time. Thus, in systems operating under the principle "management by exception," *everything becomes an exception.*

Organizations become paralyzed with meetings and with the problems of trying to get people to work together across different functions. Senior management becomes increasingly bogged down with these "exceptions," trying to referee decisions, illustrating the adage: "The bottleneck is at the top of the bottle."

THE WAY OUT

A combination of programmable automation and workers empowered to make decisions—"smart" technologies and "smart" people—provides an opportunity to break out of the dilemma of traditional mass production. A new "simple idea" is emerging and displacing the traditional model of economies of scale. It is the "batch of one" or "mass customization"—the ability to produce a customized batch, as small as a lot size of one, at mass production prices.

This idea may seem to be an oxymoron. How could small to medium batch runs be more economical than continuous process?

The "economies of flexibility" are achieved through short cycle times, flexible automation, and the ability to do quick changeovers with little or no production stoppage or cost penalty. People are as important to the production as technology. Pushing down decision making to the line and empowering teams of employees allows the variety to be handled without cumbersome approvals and delays.

The result is variety at low cost. For example, different car models come down the line. The first may be a station wagon bound for Australia. The equipment reads a bar code and then locks into a certain pattern of steps. The next vehicle may be a sports car bound for North America. The bar code is read once again, and the software-driven equipment executes a different pattern. Changeover is instantaneous and virtually costless.

"Batch-of-one" also applies to traditional commodity industries such as dairies. In a yogurt plant, for example, one flavor, such as raspberry, would be run for a week. Then the line would be closed down and washed out for the next flavor, say peach. Meanwhile, the raspberry would be put into storage until there were enough flavors to ship to the store.

The shelf life of yogurt is about 40 days, so 21–25 have been used up in storage waiting for the remaining flavors in the order to be produced. The store would be left with little more than 15 days of shelf life. The return rate, because of off-code, was 5% of sales, several times the actual net profit on the shipment.

With "batch-of-one" technology, the flavors now can be squirted into individual jars at random, like different mixers at a bar, so that each store can order mixed cases exactly reflecting its own buying patterns. The result: A store can get its order in 24 hours, not three weeks, leaving 39 days of code. The consumer gets much fresher yogurt, most of the storage and handling is eliminated, and the return rate of 5% drops to practically zero. All of a sudden, "batch-of-one" is more economical than mass production.

The concept is equally applicable to service industries. An insurance company selling policies to individuals has put the actuarial algorithms in a laptop computer. When the agent visits a customer, he can enter the specific financial objectives and requirements into the computer and write out, on the spot, a policy tailored to that individual—at the same as or lower cost than traditional underwriting.

Similarly, in the publishing industry, a major textbook publisher recently announced customized textbooks. In these books, individual educators can add their own case examples to a diskette or change the vocabulary to be appropriate to their own particular classes—at mass production prices.

EMERGING MANAGEMENT SYSTEMS

The layers of supervision and control in rigid hierarchical organizations are not designed for the world of just-in-time or tailoring to niche markets. If bureaucracy is the creation of mass production, what will management look like in a world of flexible automation?

Through the 1980s, many companies downsized, taking big "bites" out of head office and middle management (Figure 1). Overheads were reduced, but the traditional management processes, accounting, and other measurement systems remained. Often, as with fast-weight-loss diets, the "fat" crept back because the companies cut out the people but not the work. Management became overburdened and restaffed (or used expensive consultants). The old management habits had not changed, so although short-term improvement often was achieved, the basic rigidities in the management process remained.

In the late 1980s, corporations began evolving to a different model that looks more like a molecule—more organic—than a pyramid (see Figure 1). Most organizations are somewhere in the middle of this transition but have introduced initiatives that are part of the transition:

- Reducing layers of management,
- Moving many head-office functions out into the line,
- Using just-in-time relationships with suppliers,
- Introducing employee-empowerment and team-building programs,
- Adopting flexible automation in both production and the office,
- Integrating CAD/CAM,
- Building partnerships with suppliers, including early involvement in design and production,
- Moving from centralized to distributed processing.

The emerging form clusters around specific market niches rather than product lines. Different parts of the business thus define themselves by the customer they serve, not by the product they produce.

Most of the employees in this new "hi-flex" organization are in direct contact with or close to a real customer. In contrast, in traditional bureaucracies, people typically are many layers removed from the market, with little idea as to what the customer really wants. In the emerging form of organization (Figure 2), bright young people want to move out onto the firing line serving the customer, rather than up. Being in the field is much more challenging than getting stuck in a head office that has let go of many of its traditional control functions.

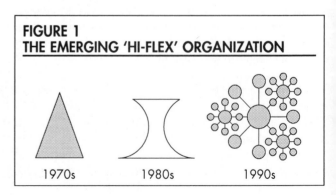

FIGURE 1
THE EMERGING 'HI-FLEX' ORGANIZATION

1970s   1980s   1990s

242

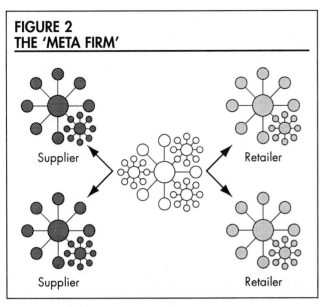
Relationships with suppliers and customers, too, look very different. In place of adversarial relationships, partnerships are formed, involving the sharing of information, managerial expertise, and systems. The result is "families" of suppliers and customers, much like the keiretsu in Japan, that form a larger overall entity—the "meta firm." These clusters are held together by synergy and common self-interest.

Much of the automobile industry is linked together in this way. If Ford, for example, places an order with a supplier such as Magna, the order would be filled and delivered to Ford in 90 minutes, not to the loading dock but to the very place on the line requiring the parts. The order does not go through any accounting department. There are no invoices or receivables. The order goes directly to the robotic stacker in the supplier's loading area arid triggers the loading of a truck. At the same time, the cash is sent over the "wires" by electronic data interchange (EDI).

In retailing, if a major department chain runs out of red sweaters in Des Moines, the store initiates a sequence whereby the red yarn is spun, sent to the manufacturer where it is knitted and packed, and then sent through the store's distribution system. The sweaters reappear on the shelves in Des Moines in six days.

Business is revolutionized. First, the store doesn't have to guess a year in advance what the fashions will be and suffer the consequences. Second, the company can, for example, follow the Rolling Stones around the country and introduce their type of garment or accessories two weeks before a concert in a particular city to capture the market created by the event. This kind of responsiveness is virtually impossible with traditional management processes.

IMPLICATIONS FOR MANAGEMENT ACCOUNTING

To be relevant in the 1990s and beyond, management accounting must be based on a different set of assumptions from the old "people are lazy" and similar theories. Instead, management accounting should be based on these principles: "Work can be challenging at all levels and engage people's interest and commitment"; "People are smarter than we might think and will surprise us with their ability to contribute"; "They also consistently will set higher standards for themselves than would their supervisors."

Trust and mutual self-interest thus replace distrust and inspection as the vehicle for control. Management accounting must support decision making in more decentralized organizations and must facilitate high responsiveness to the customer. In this context "advanced controls" are those that reinforce the combination of high flexibility and low cost to provide the corporation with competitive advantage.

In this world, management accountants are those professionals to whom a corporation turns when it needs to know what control processes will help it be the most fiercely competitive. These processes may involve numerical or human factor controls such as just-in-time supplier relationships.

Paradoxically, some of the most effective controls are based on human factors, such as positive shared norms about performance. The quality circle, for example, relies on the team to solve its own operational problems and provide suggestions for continuously improving production. Workers in quality circles in Japan have been known to commit suicide rather than disappoint or lose face with their team, so peer pressure is probably the most effective means of control. (Suicide is not recommended here, however!)

The British Empire, in its heyday, used much the same principle. For centuries it was run with only six levels of management, including the Queen! The glue that kept it together was the common set of values as inculcated by the infamous British public (our private) school system. At the end of the last century, a young man of 23 was sent out to "run Burma." He could make war, build bridges, or set up banks. Whitehall (head office) didn't have to keep checking up on him or evaluate his performance because he was "from the same school"—his behavior was perfectly predictable and reliable.

Similar principles of control are being applied to management. To meet this challenge, management accounting must:

- *Put control where the operation is.* Layers of supervision and checks and balances must disappear and be replaced with self-guided teams.
- *Use "real time" rather than after-the-fact controls.* Issues and problems must be solved at the source by the people doing the actual work. Management becomes a resource to help out the team.
- *Rebuild the assumptions underlying management accounting to build on trust rather than distrust.* The "hi-flex organization is based on empowerment, not obedience. Information must facilitate decision making, not police it.

- *Move to control based on peer norms.* The Japanese are fortunate in that they have a much more homogeneous culture and set of values than we do. In North America, we must build those norms systematically and put much less emphasis on managing by numbers.
- *Rebuild the incentive systems to reinforce responsiveness and teamwork.* Adding value to the customer and team performance must become the dominant raison d'etre of the measurement systems.

These systems of control operate with very little overhead and are extremely effective, as some of our Asian competitors have demonstrated. They would, however, involve reinventing the basic principles underlying management accounting.

POSITIONING MANAGEMENT ACCOUNTING FOR THE '90s

Management accountants do-not have the "right" to fulfill the new control needs of corporations, but if they do not take the initiative, professionals in information systems, management consulting, quality, and other disciplines will pre-empt the field, leaving management accountants in an ever-shrinking market. Figure 3 shows how some of these other professionals are positioned and where management accountants should stake out their territory.

The segmentation involves a mapping of the "customer" or marketplace for professional services and incorporates two axes or dimensions. The first, on the horizontal plane, indicates the extent to which the customer makes use of advanced management control processes such as those discussed above. The second addresses the level or focus of decision making—on operational, tactical, or strategic issues.

Many accountants are in the "bean counter" segment—routinely collecting and producing information (lower left corner of Figure 3). MIS specialists are moving toward the more advanced control environments but retain much of a traditional mainframe culture and are very much at the day-to-day operating level.

The quality experts and engineers are moving rapidly into the new world of advanced control but, again, remain focused on operations. The cost accountants and CPAs are preoccupied with regulatory and legal pressures and risk returning to the traditional "knitting" in the '90s.

Management consultants are heterogeneous, so are all over the map. Some do, however, operate in the advanced management control environment.

The segmentation shows that most competitors are focused on providing advice at a less strategic level and within a context of more traditional control processes. This situation leaves an opportunity for management accountants to stake out a new position in advanced management controls, a field that has not as yet been claimed by any other professional group.

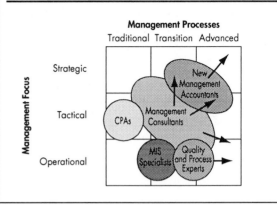

FIGURE 3
SEGMENTING THE 'MARKET' FOR CONTROL PROFESSIONALS

THE NEW TERRITORY

In Canada, certified management accountants have moved aggressively to redefine their territory. The most current statement of the new territory was developed by the Ontario Society. "CMAs, as professionals on the key decision-making team, apply their in-depth understanding of advanced management control processes to set direction of the organization and actively participate in the successful achievement of its goals."

This new focus:

- Positions management accountants to be senior participants on the management team rather than staff accountants,
- Bases their technical expertise on a thorough knowledge of advanced management control processes rather than traditional cost accounting,
- Encompasses control processes outside the purely financial domain, and
- Provides a more strategic business orientation rather than a routine, operational one.

As a result, the Society has redesigned its education and accreditation process to reflect the new positioning in the marketplace. The transition won't happen overnight but will require a clear vision and commitment by management accountants to move ahead.

Management accountants face a choice. They can stay on the traditional turf—generating routine accounting information and reports—and risk being overtaken by computer experts and other professionals, as well as by prepackaged software. (Any "jock" on Lotus can perform incredible gymnastics without management accounting training.) Or they can seize an unparalleled opportunity to bring their companies into the "hi-flex" era. They can become the agents of change!

Gerald H. B. Ross is managing director of Change Lab in Toronto, Ontario, Canada.

Readers who would like to discuss this article with him can reach him at (416) 360-5309.

Editor's note: In view of the significance of this article, the National Association of Accountants and The Society of Management Accountants of Canada are publishing parallel versions in their respective magazines.

From G. H. B. Ross, "Revolution in Management Control," *Management Accounting* (November 1990): 23–27. Reprinted with permission.

Question

11.3 Ross suggests that, to be relevant in the 1990s, management accounting must be based on a different set of principles about human behavior. What are these?

CHAPTER 12

Financial Control

In Reading 12.1, *Linking the Shop Floor to the Top Floor,* Mark Beischel and Richard Smith present a integrative framework for linking manufacturing performance to overall company financial performance. Beischel and Smith state that the first task is to establish critical success factors for the organization that can be clearly measured. Every key aspect of a manufacturing process must be measured and each measure tied to a specific management level. As we go up the corporate hierarchy, the measures are combined into measures at the next level. Ultimately, the entire set of measures in the organization must be linked to the critical success factor at the top of the organization (such as return on assets). The authors argue that, while nonfinancial measures of performance are important, all manufacturing performance measures should be tied, or subject to, some aspect of financial control. The message in this article is important as many units or divisions of organizations develop critical success factors and performance measures for themselves, but often there is a failure to coordinate and integrate measures for the entire organization.

In Reading 12.2, *Financial Managers: Business Advocates or Corporate Cops?,* Steven Jablonsky and Patrick Keating discuss the important issue of how organizations can bring their financial operations and their operations management groups together to integrate financial controls into business operations. The authors argue that traditional financial management has hindered those organizations intent on becoming customer-oriented and team-based. Using a case study conducted at Tektronics Circuit Board Division (CBD), Jablonsky and Keating believe that financial managers can take on one of two roles - Business Advocates or Corporate Cops. The Business Advocate role is characterized by those in the finance organization becoming very involved in their understanding of business operations and creating performance measures and controls that are consistent with operating units goals. The Corporate Cop role is adopted by those who remain distant from business operations and whose task it is to act as a "surveillance unit" and follows corporate rules and regulations in evaluating and controlling operations. The authors state that the Business Advocate role is more consistent with organizations involved with reengineering their operations and presents financial executives with an opportunity to be involved with such important changes.

Robert S. Kaplan discusses the role of flexible budgeting in Reading 12.3, *Flexible Budgeting in an Activity-Based Costing Framework.* In this article, the distinction between the activity-based measurement of the costs of resources used and the conventional financial measurement of the costs of resources supplied is expanded to allow for the possibility that some portion of resources supplied to perform an activity could be committed, while another flexible portion is supplied as needed to meet actual demand for the activity. The paper extends previous thinking by outlining the principles for integrating activity-based costs into a flexible budgeting process and an ex post financial analysis of operating expenses.

12.1 Linking the Shop Floor to the Top Floor
Here's a framework for measuring manufacturing Performance.

By Mark E. Beischel, CMA, and K. Richard Smith, CMA

On the sixth day of the month, Carl, the plant manager, walks apprehensively into the controller's office and asks, "Linda, how did the plant do last month?" Linda replies, "Well, we had an unfavorable purchase price variance of $70,000 and an unfavorable labor efficiency variance of $50,000, but don't worry, the favorable overhead absorption variance of $200,000 more than offset them."

"Wait! Stop! I asked how the plant did last month. I know for a fact that our quality teams improved setup times. I also know that we missed three very important scheduled shipments! I don't want gobbledegook, I want to know how we did!" The plant manager is now pacing hurriedly around the controller's office, waiting for an explanation.

"Oh," replies Linda, "Sorry, I should have also pointed out that our revised LIFO reserve estimate and an increase in our tax provision due to a new IRS ruling adversely affected us last month. We should be able to counter that this month by adjusting our bad debt reserve."

To this response, Carl simply shrugs his shoulders, turns around to go back to his office, and mumbles something about "bean counters."

If the plant manager has a difficult time understanding the plant's performance, imagine how well senior manufacturing management and corporate management understand the plant's performance. Current manufacturing performance measurement systems are inadequate, but what can be done? We offer a framework for measuring manufacturing performance based on two basic premises:

1. Manufacturing performance can and should be linked to company financial performance.
2. All manufacturing measures—at all organizational levels—should be linked to ensure constancy of purpose among organizational levels and to point to cause-and-effect relationships so all employees can attack the problems that cause poor performance and continue practices that cause good performance.

At present, financial measures are introduced at too low an organizational level where they cannot be affected or controlled.

THE FIRST STEP: CRITICAL SUCCESS FACTORS

The first step in establishing a manufacturing performance measurement framework is to establish manufacturing's "Critical Success Factors," items so important to the company that, without any one of them, the company would fail. Critical success factors vary by industry and marketplace. For instance, zero defects may be critical to a defense contractor, and the cost of conversion may be critical to a commodity food producer. Critical factors are universal to all manufacturing companies. Each is critical to the ongoing health of the company. Our five critical success factors and their definitions are:

1. *Quality.* *Product* quality is defined as meeting or exceeding customer needs and achieving customer satisfaction. *Process* quality is defined as "doing it right the first time" or reducing process variation.
2. *Customer Service.* *External* customer service is defined as meeting customer demand for end-products. *Internal* customer service is defined as meeting the demands of internal customers such as other manufacturing departments.
3. *Resource Management.* Resource management is defined as optimizing outputs to inputs in people, inventory, and fixed capital.
4. *Cost.* Cost is defined as the costs that can be managed at the level reported.
5. *Flexibility.* Flexibility is defined as responsiveness to changing market/regulatory/environmental demands.

If these five critical success factors can he measured properly and therefore *managed* better, manufacturing performance will improve at most companies. The problem is that each manufacturing person cannot improve these factors directly. Measuring individual processes with overall gross indicators is analogous to measuring a professional baseball player on his team's overall performance. It isn't fair to say that a player is no good because his team has a losing record. It is fair, however, to measure that player on RBIs, batting average, or on base percentage because he can influence those measures directly. In the manufacturing process it is not fair to measure a line foreman on cost of production as a percentage of sales because he cannot control sales price, sales volume, or many elements of cost. It *is* fair to measure that foreman on utility usage, cycle time, and schedule attainment, which he can control and influence directly and which eventually will contribute to cost as a percentage of sales. As a baseball player's RBIs will contribute to a team's wins, the line foreman's reduced cycle time will contribute to improved plant performance.

LINKAGE IS THE KEY

The only effective way to measure results at the shop floor and concurrently measure overall manufacturing performance through critical success factors is to "link" the measures at each management level. As measures move higher in the organization they become more aggregate and broad in definition. Conversely, as measures move down the organizational ladder, they become very specific and narrow in definition. To be deemed relevant, all measures must meet two criteria:

1. They must be able to be linked to a critical success factor at the top of the organization. If a measure does not relate (or link) to a critical success factor, then it should be discarded. It does not support the strategic direction of the company.
2. They must be able to be linked to the manufacturing process. If a measure does not relate (or link) to the manufacturing process, it should be discarded. It is not controllable by the manufacturer.

Figure 1 shows an example of measures linked at each organizational level. The corporate financial measure "return on assets" is supported by or linked to the manufacturing organization by three key measurements: inventory days, output $/asset $, and output $/square feet occupied.

These three measures link to the critical success factor "resource management." Likewise, as shown in Figure 1, "inventory days" is linked to manufacturing cycle time, which in turn is linked to machine downtime, which ultimately is linked to several manufacturing process drivers.

The power of linking measures at each level of the organization is that it ensures constancy of purpose throughout Each manager at each level can control his measures and knows how they support the measures above him in the organization and where he should look to correct problems that are causing poor performance.

Figure 2 shows a different corporate goal—"quality"—supported in the manufacturing organization by the warranty return rate. This measurement can, in turn, be linked to the processes that drive their success daily. If the department manager in Figure 2 properly manages very specific, controllable items such as the concentricity of the out-

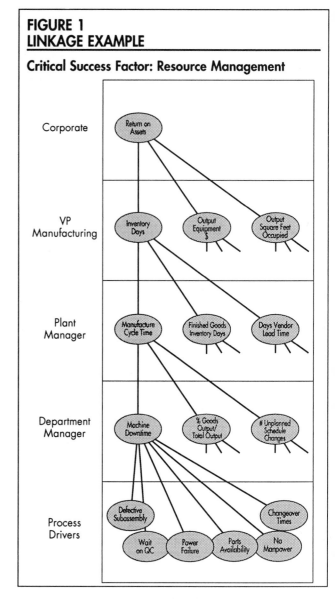

FIGURE 1
LINKAGE EXAMPLE

Critical Success Factor: Resource Management

side diameter of the product, the amount of adhesive applied to the product, and the direct current resistance in the product, he knows that ultimately he is contributing to the overall quality goal of the company.

The measures shown in Figure 2 at the vice president of manufacturing level are defect *prevention* measures. The vice president is measured on his ability to set defect prevention systems in place. Conversely, at the process driver level, root causes are identified so they can be improved upon. The viscosity of the adhesive contributes to the overall product quality, but it is much too specific for the V.P. level. It is very important at the process level, however, and must be monitored closely to ensure quality.

The ability to judge each management level with measures that encourage the entire organization to "pull in the same direction" is rare in manufacturing companies today. A manufacturing company that can motivate each person to strive for common goals will have a clear competitive advantage.

FIGURE 2
LINKAGE EXAMPLE

Critical Success Factor: Quality

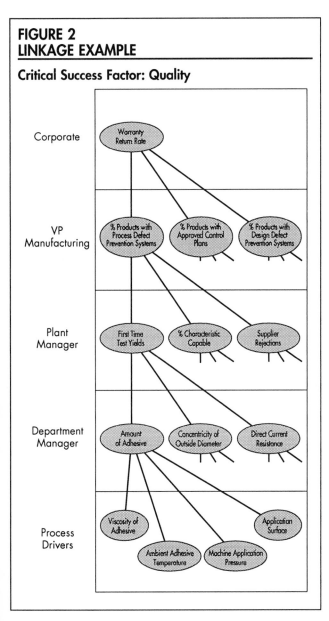

Corporate	Warranty Return Rate
VP Manufacturing	% Products with Process Defect Prevention Systems • % Products with Approved Control Plans • % Products with Design Defect Prevention Systems
Plant Manager	First Time Test Yields • % Characteristic Capable • Supplier Rejections
Department Manager	Amount of Adhesive • Concentricity of Outside Diameter • Direct Current Resistance
Process Drivers	Viscosity of Adhesive • Application Surface • Ambient Adhesive Temperature • Machine Application Pressure

WHY LINK MANUFACTURING MEASURES TO FINANCIAL MEASURES?

All actions taken in any for-profit enterprise ultimately affect the financial health of that company. Companies are measured by the external community (investors, analysts, competitors, and customers) primarily in financial terms. Although some nonfinancial measures are beginning to emerge, such as the Malcolm Baldrige Quality Award, financial measures such as EPS, quarterly profits, and ROA continue to dominate external company measures. Therefore it is very important that the manufacturing organization consider the financial impact of various decisions.

Many companies overemphasize short-term financial gains at the expense of long-term competitive advantage, a fact which has been documented and even popularized as the evil undoing of American manufacturing competitiveness. Although admittedly overplayed in the past, financial measures are very much a reality and provide good aggregate

measures of company health. By linking manufacturing measures to financial measures, we are not subordinating manufacturing measures to short-term profits—we are supporting financial health with sound operating decisions.

The relationship between nonfinancial measures and financial measures is not an "all-or-nothing" proposition but a matter of balance and emphasis. The point is that manufacturing decisions do impact financial results and should be linked.

SCORECARDS FOR SUCCESS

Once the manufacturing measures have been linked throughout the organization, a measurement system or series of "scorecards" can be designed. As shown in Figure 3, scorecards and measures differ at each management level in two very important ways:

1. *Frequency of Measures.* Measures at the top of the organization are more aggregate in quantification, more strategic in content, and are measured infrequently. The measures at this level are overall trends that allow management to make strategic decisions on a quarterly or annual basis. Conversely, measures on the plant floor are performed daily or even continuously to prompt immediate action.
2. *Span of Control.* Measures at the top of the organization make up a very broad span of control. For instance, the senior vice president of manufacturing may be in the position to make a logistical decision that involves several plants and distribution centers. This type of decision requires a broad base of information. The plant line foreman, however, requires specific and narrow information to optimize the functions of his area.

Referring to Figure 3 again, measures at the top such as "output per asset $" are meaningless on a day-to-day basis, but cross-plant comparisons and company logistical strategies depend on this type of information.

Because each manufacturing performance measurement has been linked to one or more measurements at another level, the resulting score cards are linked together also. Remember, if a measure could not be linked to a critical success factor and the manufacturing process simultaneously, it was discarded as irrelevant.

Figure 4 shows a model of linked scorecards. Each measure at each management level is relevant because it at once supports the company goals and can be traced to the process. It is not necessary to attempt to quantify the impact of a change in one measure with the change in another measure.

Although traditional accounting techniques teach us that all numbers must "tie," it is counterproductive to force nonfinancial measures to reconcile.

Certain companies have begun to track and retain the data related to these measures to develop an experience

FIGURE 3
MANUFACTURING SCORECARDS

Critical Success Factor

Quality	Freq.	Customer Service	Freq.	Resource Management	Freq.	Cost	Freq.	Flexibility	Freq.
VP Mfg. Scorecard									
Design Defect Systems	Q	On-Time Shipment %	M	Inventory Days	M	Total Value Chain Cost/Unit	A	Training Days/Employee	A
Process Defect Systems	Q	Order Fill Complete %	M	Output/Equipment $	A			Avg. Cycle Times of Key Products	A
Approved Control Plans	Q			Output/Square Feet	A				
				Output/Total Labor $	Q				
Plant Manager Scoreboard									
First-Time Test Yields	W	Schedule Attainment	W	Manufacturing Cycle Time	M	Variable Cost/Unit	M	Schedule Attainment	W
% Characteristic Capable	M	Schedule vs. Emergency Visits	M	FG Inventory Days	W	Total Plant Cost/Unit	A	Manufacturing Cycle Time	W
Supplier Rejects	W	Number of Crisis Calls	M	Days Vendor Lead Time	M				
Department Manager									
Concentricity of O.D.	D	Daily Schedule Attainment	D	Certified Operations	W	Utility Cost/Unit	W	Changeover Time	W
Amount of Adhesive	D			Machine Downtime	D	Material Usage	W		
Direct Current Resistance	D			% Good Output	D				
				Unplan'd Schedule Changes	D				

A=Annual   Q=Quarterly   M=Monthly   W=Weekly   D=Daily or Continuously

---

database. Eventually they may be able to quantify a causal relationship between certain nonfinancial measures.

NOW WHAT ARE THE RESULTS?
Now that we have a framework for developing linked performance measures, let's revisit the plant manager and the plant controller.

This month, the plant controller is armed with relevant nonfinancial measures that are linked to the process and to the company goals.

"Linda, how did the plant do last month?"

"Manufacturing cycle time is up two days from target. We traced the problem back to parts availability. Our quality team has since solved the problem. This cycle time problem caused us to miss two important shipments, but we made them up yesterday. Our overall variable costs are down $100,000 due primarily to our decision to operate the B line motors at 85 rpms instead of 95.

"Our days of inventory are higher in WIP than plan, again due to the cycle time problem, but we've reduced finished goods inventory by 10%. We received 60 employee suggestions, 40 of which have been acted on by quality teams. The raw material shortage hindered our ability to meet daily schedules as evidenced by our poor 85% schedule attainment this month. We experienced the lowest reject rate in our history and retrained 20 employees on the B line. In all, we met or exceeded six of our 10 key measures."

To this explanation, the plant manager replies "Thanks," As he turns to go, he mumbles something like "Thank God."

250

FIGURE 4
LINKED SCORECARDS

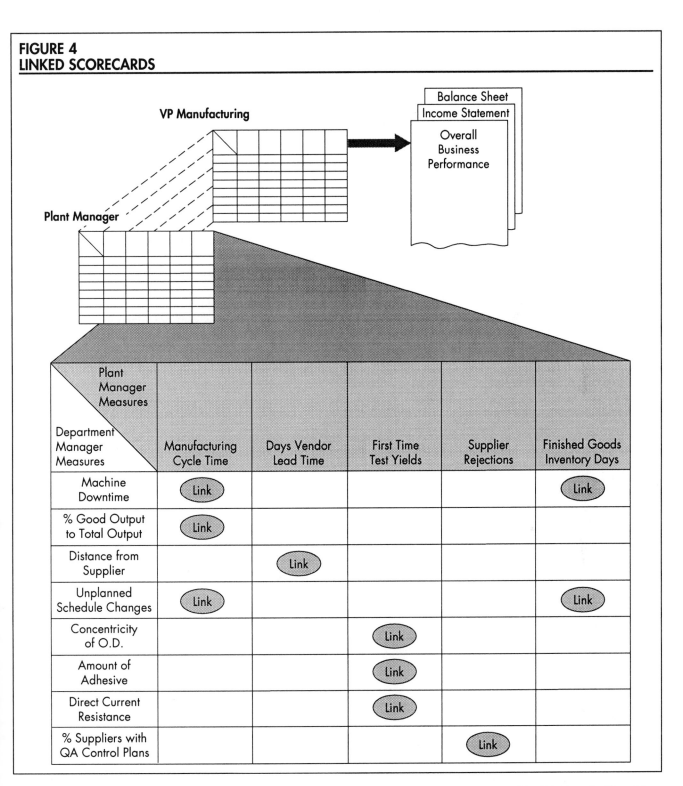

Department Manager Measures	Manufacturing Cycle Time	Days Vendor Lead Time	First Time Test Yields	Supplier Rejections	Finished Goods Inventory Days
Machine Downtime	Link				Link
% Good Output to Total Output	Link				
Distance from Supplier		Link			
Unplanned Schedule Changes	Link				Link
Concentricity of O.D.			Link		
Amount of Adhesive			Link		
Direct Current Resistance			Link		
% Suppliers with QA Control Plans				Link	

Mark E. Beischel, CMA, CPIM, is a senior manager in Ernst & Young's cost management consulting practice in Indianapolis, Ind. He can be reached at (317) 681-7786.

K. Richard Smith, CMA, CPA, CPIM, is controller for Harman-Motive, a division of Harman International, a worldwide manufacturer of audio products. He may be reached at (317) 342-5551. Both authors are members of the Indianapolis Chapter, through which this article was submitted.

From M. Beishcel and K. R. Smith, "Linking the Shop Floor to the Top Floor," *Management Accounting* (October 1991): 25–29. Reprinted with permission.

Question

12.1 According to Beischel and Smith, what are five critical success factors that should be measured, and how are they defined? Does better measurement lead to better management? Explain.

12.2 Financial Managers: Business Advocates or Corporate Cops?

Finance professionals must trade their surveillance mentality for a service mentality

By Stephen F. Jablonsky, CPA, and Patrick J. Keating

The organizing principles of today's high-performance enterprises differ markedly from the command-and-control structures of the past. Companies such as Ford and AT&T have achieved quantum leaps in productivity by reengineering their organizations. They have demonstrated the competitive advantage of employing new forms of integrated work organization with educated workers enabled by advanced information technology.

To realize quantum productivity gains, most companies must break with their past. They must undergo transformation, which requires fundamental changes in an organization's genetic code—the implicit, "tried and true" rules that determine how work is organized and controlled.[1]

Financial professionals must be a part of this transformation. The reengineering of work will not succeed without a corresponding transformation of the company's traditional financial management practices. Financial work must be integrated into the very fabric of business operations. Such integration requires open channels of financial communication supported by a "single stream" management communication and control system that integrates operating and financial data within the same database. This structure is in contrast to traditional modes of financial management characterized by relatively closed, "need to know" channels of communication supported by independent financial systems that must be reconciled to the independent operating systems.

Although the idea of integrating financial work into business operations is fairly noncontroversial, we have found that, for many companies, the rhetoric of change in financial management practices often exceeds the reality of change. The extent of and reasons for this gap vary from company to company. In some cases, senior management's basic operating philosophy is incompatible with efforts to reengineer the basic business processes. A chief executive officer may espouse team organization but adhere to an arm's-length model of financial management. In other cases, the chief financial officer or his or her staff may resist change because of fears about loss of independence. Sometimes change in financial management practices lag other work organization changes because financial managers lack the knowledge or resources to build the capabilities consistent with their commitment to team-based financial work. Whatever the reason, reliance on traditional patterns of financial management appears to inhibit change toward customer-oriented, team-based forms of organization of high-performance enterprises.

Financial executives must develop a plan for transforming their organizations. They must become Business Advocates instead of Corporate Cops if they want to play more than a marginal role in their companies' high performance. For those financial executives who feel their influence and status are taking a turn for the worse, it may be time to reassess the contribution their financial organization makes to the company's overall success.

Two competing management operating philosophies appear to govern how staff organizations such as finance function within a company's overall management communication and control system. Under one philosophy, the financial organization functions as a Business Advocate. Under the other philosophy, it functions as Corporate Cop. Tektronics' Circuit Board Division (CBD) is a good example of a business that has successfully integrated financial management practices into the entire business operation. It clearly is an example of the Business Advocate. B Corp, a major competitor, clearly is a Corporate Cop. Where does your company fit?

TEKTRONICS CIRCUIT BOARD DIVISION (CBD): MANDATED CHANGE AND MARVELOUS TURNAROUND

At Tektronics CBD, operating management and financial management worked together to weave financial controls into the fabric of their business. This integrated operating and financial management system has played a critical role in the renewed profitability of the Division.

As researchers, our involvement with CBD started after the management team had changed the management communication and control system. The general manager graciously allowed us to document the specific changes that had occurred at CBD and also agreed to have members of the management team complete the research questionnaire we developed based on the case studies we had conducted at AT&T, Boeing, Citicorp, Ford, Merck, and 3M. CBD became our living embodiment of the business advocate model of financial management.

Plant management has been quite frank in admitting that a team-oriented operating style is neither complete nor effective without financial information that front-line personnel can use to manage the economics of their operations and that technical sales management can use to make informed choices about product pricing decisions.

CBD is one of more than 3,500 companies worldwide in the $24 billion-dollar printed circuit board market. Domestically, the market is around $6 billion with more than 800 companies competing. In 1990, the industry was just breaking even in North America. The best performers in the United States achieved a 5% pretax profit margin. The best performers worldwide achieved a 12% pretax margin. CBD achieved a 20% pretax margin in 1990, and sustained that margin into 1993. The Division's general manager attributed the group's success to the total revamping of its management communication and control system.

Here's what happened. Between 1983 and 1987, CBD lost money. The greater the volume of business, the greater the losses. The corporate group issued a simple ultimatum to CBD: "Either turn this business around and become profitable, or be sold off or closed down."

In retrospect, the ultimatum was a blessing in disguise. The management team realized it needed to revise its current management communication and control system radically. Basically, the existing culture was characterized by an atmosphere of secrecy and distrust. A "we-they" separation existed between financial managers and operating managers. No one believed the numbers that were being generated on an after-the-fact basis from the full-cost allocation financial system.

Between 1988 and 1990, management "performed radical surgery" on the existing management communication and control system and transformed a dying patient into a healthy world-class competitor. Before 1988, management had begun the process of transforming the operating culture of the plant by instituting total quality management (TQM), continuous improvement, and employee involvement programs. By the plant manager's own admission, however, these programs had not led to a significant turnabout in the plant's financial performance. The turnabout really kicked into high gear with the implementation of the missing link in the plant's management communication and control system—an on-line, real-time activity-based costing system.

CBD's new system is an activity-based *management* system rather than an activity-based *cost* system—for several reasons. First, in the new integrated system, the financial information is never separated from the operating data. Prices (dollars) and quantities (activities) *attach* to a circuit board as the product passes through the manufacturing process. Prices (costs) are not separated and then reallocated to the product on some arbitrary cost allocation basis. Second, the integrated operating and financial information is "owned" by all managers and employees and is shared on a *daily* basis. Managers and employees can "see" the relationship between the numbers that appear on their computer screens (not financial reports) and their day-to-day activities.

The system does so by providing a common ground for monitoring the quality of the manufacturing process and taking corrective action every day. When defects are discovered during the manufacturing process, the cause of the defect quickly is traced to its source—in other words, the activity

station responsible for the defect. Once this information has been entered, the activity management system rolls up the costs of that quality problem by calculating the entire cost of the activities performed on the product up to the point of detection. The system maintains a readout on an on-line real-time basis of the "dollarized" costs of defective products caused by each activity station during the workday.

As part of the plant's program of continuous improvement, station managers and the assistant plant manager meet every morning as a team to resolve quality problems experienced during the preceding day. The two station managers with the highest costs of quality are responsible for reporting to the team how they have addressed the quality problems of the preceding day. Not surprisingly, during each day each station manager continuously monitors the cost of quality produced by the activity-based cost system in order to determine where his or her group stands in the cost-of-quality rankings for the day.

Such experiences at CBD demonstrate the value-creating potential of integrating financial management practices into the fabric of the business operations. CBD has improved its entire management communication and control system while employing substantially fewer (although substantially more sophisticated) financial people.

With respect to the last point, in truly integrated operating and financial systems, capturing data at the source can help eliminate data-entry work performed previously by accounting clerks. Also, the costs of financial management can be reduced even further by embedding the financial controls and analytical tools directly into the integrated systems. At CBD, for instance, the decision support logic for interactive product pricing and profitability has been built into the systems software for technical sales and purchasing managers to use in customer and supplier negotiations. There is no need for a separate accounting "calculation." The result: financial work with substantially fewer financial people.

CHANGING OUR ROLES

The changes that have occurred at Tektronics CBD stand in stark contrast to the reality that exists at other companies with more traditional management communication and control systems. Accounting educators such as ourselves, management consultants, and senior executives charged with transforming their own organizations see CBD as an ideal benchmark for changing the management communication and control system practices at other companies. We have no doubt that businesses will be moving forward with the concepts of instantaneous financial information and financial work with substantially fewer financial people. Some companies will be proactive and realize the benefits—in terms of reduced costs and reduced cycle times—of "going along with flow" made possible by technology. Others will be reactive and always be trying to catch up (Sears chasing Wal-Mart).

From a practical perspective, financial executives must come to grips with the changing role of the finance organization when financial work is integrated with business operations. As a result of our experiences with companies such as CBD, we see an emerging role for financial professionals in the high-performance companies. Financial professionals are likely to become the company's educators and integrators.

As *educators,* financial professionals will be responsible for helping managers focus on the "real economics" (AT&T's term) of the business. Managers and financial professionals will participate in a joint education process. Managers will teach financial professionals to be more knowledgeable about the business operations (becoming more business literate), while financial professionals will teach managers how to analyze business opportunities in financial terms and assess the economic impact of these decisions on the overall organization (become more financially literate).

As *integrators,* financial professionals will focus on bringing all of the diverse functions of the business together through systems that deliver financial information to front-line managers, heads of business units, and senior corporate management—all at the same time. In a world where instantaneous financial information is fast becoming a reality, education and integration skills will be in high demand.

THE COMPETING MODELS

We have found that financial organizations, like people, have personalities. As individuals, we are complex and multidimensional. Psychologists have found that much of our complex individuality can be traced to and understood in terms of fundamental traits or organizing principles. Even though we are unique human beings, our personalities and behaviors can be characterized within a limited number of psychological profiles. For all their apparent idiosyncrasies, financial organizations and financial professionals can be characterized in terms of two competing models of financial management and the four core values that underlie both models.

Using field studies followed up by extensive questionnaire-based research, we identified the operating philosophies that appear to govern how staff organizations function within the overall management communication and control system.[2]

Under the first philosophy, staff functions such as finance are required to adopt a service orientation and be involved in the business. Individual financial professionals must have a high degree of knowledge about the business in order to be acceptable to operating managers within the lines of business. The financial organization functions as a *Business Advocate.*

Under the second management operating philosophy, staff functions such as the financial organization are required to be more removed from the business, serve as a surveillance unit, and follow impersonal procedures in the administration of corporate rules and regulations. Individual financial professionals are expected to make sure that line managers are following the rules. Within this management operating philosophy, the financial organization functions as a *Corporate Cop* (see Figure 1).

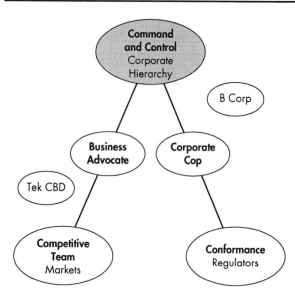

FIGURE 1
MODELS OF FINANCIAL MANAGEMENT AND ORIENTATIONS TO FINANCIAL WORK

As you can see from Figure 1, we have positioned the Tektronics Circuit Board Division (Tek CBD) financial organization as a Business Advocate with a strong market and team orientation. This designation is consistent with our previous description of CBD.

We have positioned the financial organization at B Corp, a competitor of CBD, as a Corporate Cop financial organization. It places a strong emphasis on command and control, and vertical information flows up and down the corporate hierarchy. B Corp has been a highly visible and profitable competitor that has fallen on hard times. Senior corporate management has given the management of B Corp a mandate: "Become profitable, or be divested or shut down."

At present, B Corp is benchmarking its financial organization (and all other staff functions) against CBD. We argue that no significant changes will occur at B Corp until the overall management operating philosophy for staff functions shifts from surveillance to service. If the management operating philosophy changes, the financial organization can become a Business Advocate.

CBD AND B CORP: COMPETING PHILOSOPHIES

In Figure 2, we present a comparison of CBD and B Corp based on an analysis of the management responses to our research questionnaire designed to measure orientations to financial work.[3] We show the numerical scores that underlie the Business Advocate and Corporate Cop designations for CBD and B Corp as well as scores for the four core values of service, role, focus, and responsibility that underlie the profiles.

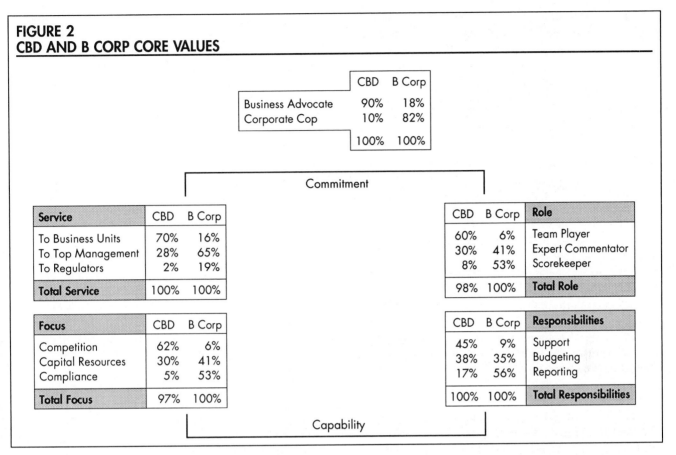

FIGURE 2
CBD AND B CORP CORE VALUES

	CBD	B Corp
Business Advocate	90%	18%
Corporate Cop	10%	82%
	100%	100%

Commitment

Service	CBD	B Corp
To Business Units	70%	16%
To Top Management	28%	65%
To Regulators	2%	19%
Total Service	100%	100%

CBD	B Corp	Role
60%	6%	Team Player
30%	41%	Expert Commentator
8%	53%	Scorekeeper
98%	100%	Total Role

Focus	CBD	B Corp
Competition	62%	6%
Capital Resources	30%	41%
Compliance	5%	53%
Total Focus	97%	100%

CBD	B Corp	Responsibilities
45%	9%	Support
38%	35%	Budgeting
17%	56%	Reporting
100%	100%	Total Responsibilities

Capability

When given an opportunity to assess the function of the financial organization within the overall management communication and control system framework, the managers at each company provide a striking contrast. The financial organization at CBD receives a 90% Business Advocate score and a 10% Corporate Cop score. The financial organization at B Corp is almost the exact opposite (18% Business Advocate and 82% Corporate Cop). We argue that initiatives such as reengineering, total quality management, continuous process improvement, and activity-based management will prove to be fads in the world of the Corporate Cop because the "gap" between the operating managers and financial managers cannot be closed without a drastic change in management operating philosophy. Assessment of core values comes to the fore here.

Directly below the Business Advocate and Corporate Cop scores for CBD and B Corp we present our "four corner" model of core values. The core values of *service* (to customers) and *role* (requirements and expectations) represent the commitments of the financial organization. The core values of *focus* (of the financial systems) and *responsibilities* (of the financial professionals) represent the capabilities of the financial organization.

CBD. We argue that the commitments and capabilities of the Circuit Board Division have been aligned well to help achieve the dramatic turnaround we described. The financial organization is perceived to devote most of its effort to providing service to the business units followed by servic-

ing the needs of top management. The financial professionals are perceived as team players (integrated into the business) who also provide expert commentary on the financial aspects of the business.

As one of many business units within Tektronics, the financial organization at CBD has developed the capability to focus on the competition through the development of integrated operating and financial management systems and by being held responsible for supporting the business unit managers. At the same time, CBD links into the separate corporate-wide financial system tied to the overall corporate governance system, with the financial professionals assuming responsibility for monitoring the operating and capital budgeting process.

Taking CBD's success in changing its organizational "personality" as a guide, the commitment to become a Business Advocate staff function precedes the development of a plan to change the capabilities of the organization.

B Corp. As we mentioned, the situation at B Corp stands in stark contrast to the situation at CBD. In the case of B Corp, senior management received our permission to use our research questionnaire within the business in exchange for completed questionnaires we could analyze for research purposes. At the present time, senior management still has not used the results of our analysis to formulate an action plan.

In terms of commitment, B Corp's financial organization is perceived to serve the needs of top management even though members of the financial organization are on-site at the business unit. Financial professionals are considered scorekeepers first and expert commentators second. Given that scorekeeping gets the highest marks, we suspect that the expert commentary pertains to how to keep score.

In terms of capabilities, the financial systems at B Corp are separate from the business operations and are oriented to meeting the resource-tracking needs of corporate management and the compliance-reporting requirements of external regulators. Financial professionals primarily are responsible for reporting cost data and financial accounting data to superiors at a different level within the corporation.

When we look at the difference in the profiles of the two companies from the perspective of the individual financial professional, the issue of status and legitimacy immediately comes to mind. In the CBD case, the financial professionals are considered to be team players responsible for supporting implementation of the business unit's strategic plan. At B Corp, the financial professionals are perceived to be score-keepers responsible for basic record-keeping and reporting activities.

Given the emphasis on getting the cost out through reengineering efforts, the financial professionals within B Corp seem to be much more at risk than the financial managers that remain at CBD.

WHAT'S THE FUTURE?

Financial executives, along with executives managing other staff functions, are under the same pressure to reengineer their operations as are line management. Financial executives need to "get the cost out" of their operations and become more effective at the same time. The "psychological" profiles we prepared for CBD and B Corp demonstrate that a company's management operating philosophy for staff functions has a significant impact on whether the financial organization (or any other staff group) functions as a Business Advocate or as a Corporate Cop.

The differences between the two financial organizations maybe measured in terms of four core values-service, role, focus, and responsibility. Business Advocates service different customers, play different roles, maintain different types of systems, and perform different responsibilities than Corporate Cops.

We argue that the Business Advocate model of staff work is more in line with the concepts of business reengineering and provides a great opportunity for financial executives to reengineer their own organizations and transform their professional staffs into key integrators and educators within the company. If current financial executives do not take the initiative, a new management team is likely to step in to do the job.

In a recent conversation with a business unit controller at Texas Instruments (TI), we found out that he no longer hires undergraduate accounting and finance majors for the financial organization. Neither will he hire an MBA with an undergraduate degree in accounting or finance. His logic is very simple. TI believes that in order to develop as team-oriented business professionals, finance staff should be rotated regularly between the finance organization and the line functions. Thus, this business unit controller must be able to sell finance staff to the line organizations. Line managers find that individuals trained to be only scorekeepers responsible for cost accounting and financial reporting do not have the background or skills to be effective team players in their organizations. If TI's experience is an isolated case, that is one thing. If TI's experience is an indication of an emerging trend, the implications could be quite traumatic for any number of financial organizations. It's time to become Business Advocates.

Stephen F. Jablonsky, CPA, Ph.D., is associate professor of accounting and management information systems and Kellogg Foundation National Fellow at Penn State University. He has developed the concept of financially based management communication and control systems (MCCS) to teach accounting and finance topics from a management perspective. He can be reached at (814) 865-6473.

Patrick J. Keating, Ph.D., is associate professor of business administration, Dept. of Accounting and Finance, San Jose State University, San Jose, Calif. He is a member of the Palo Alto Chapter, through which this article was submitted, and can be reached at (408) 924-3494.

Notes

1. Michael Hammer and James Champy, *Reengineenug the Corporation,* Harper Business, 1994.

2. Readers interested in looking at the original field research conducted at AT&T, Boeing, Citicorp, Ford, Merck, and 3M are referred to our Financial Executives Research Foundation (FERF) monograph *Changing Roles of Financial Management: Getting Close to the Business* (Keating and Jablonsky, 1990). For more information concerning the development and initial research using the Management Communication and Control Systems Diagnostic Questionnaire (the DQ), readers are referred to our FERF monograph, *Business Advocate or Corporate Policeman: Assessing Your Role as Financial Executive* (Jablonsky, Keating, and Heian, 1993).

3. JK Research Associates has developed the methodology for creating a financial organization "personality" profile based on the analysis of over 2,000 completed research instruments administered at executive development programs, in-house corporate programs, and professional meetings. For more information about developing a personality profile, please contact the authors directly.

From S. F. Jablonsky and P. J. Keating, "Financial Managers: Business Advocates or Corporate Cops?" *Management Accounting* (February 1995): 21–25. Reprinted with permission.

Question

12.2 According to Jablonsky and Keating, what are the four core values on which Business Advocates and Corporate Cops differ? Explain the differences.

12.3 Flexible Budgeting in an Activity-Based Costing Framework
Commentary

By Robert S. Kaplan

Robert S. Kaplan is a Professor at Harvard Business school

A recent article (Cooper and Kaplan, 1992) introduced the distinction between the activity-based measurement of the costs of resources **used** by activities (for products, services and customers) and the traditional financial measurement of the costs of resources **supplied** to enable activities to be performed. The two concepts are related through the unused capacity of the resources supplied, as shown in the following equation:

$$\begin{array}{ccc} \text{Costs of Resources} & = \text{Costs of Resources} & + \text{Cost of Unused} \\ \text{Supplied} & \text{Used} & \text{Capacity} \end{array}$$

Periodic financial statements measure the left-hand-side of the above equation. The activity-based costs assigned to products, services, customers, and other cost objects are aggregated into the first term on the right-hand-side of the equation. The difference between these two amounts represents the cost of unused capacity

Cooper and Kaplan (1992) indicated that some resources, such as energy to operate machines or overtime labor, are supplied only as needed so that no unused capacity can exist for these resources. The costs of supplying such resources are what many people have characterized as "variable costs" since the spending on these resources varies directly with the demands or usage for the resources. The costs of resources contracted for in advance can be considered as "fixed" costs since the spending on these resources will be independent of actual use. The expenses associated with such resources do not vary, within the time period, with variations in the demand for the activities performed by these resources. Cooper and Kaplan (1992) assumed that the resources used for a particular activity were either entirely flexible with demand or entirely committed in advance of demand. They did not explicitly allow for the possibility that some portion of the resources supplied to perform a given activity could be committed, while another, flexible, portion was supplied as needed to meet actual, realized demand for the activity.

The assumption that the costs of resources to perform an activity are either entirely "variable" or "fixed," or **flexible** or **committed,** as they will be referred to in the remainder of this paper, is not an inherent feature of activity-based cost systems. Just as in traditional cost models, some of the resources to perform a given activity can be committed in advance, while other resources may be supplied as needed. In such cases, the activity cost exhibits a mixed behavior, with the total cost of performing the activity representing a combination of committed and flexible supply of resources in response to demand fluctuations. To assign the costs of such activities to cost objects, such as products, services, and customers, within an activity-based framework requires that the cost assignment appropriately incorporate the resource supply/resource use distinction that lies at the heart of ABC systems. When such a distinction is incorporated, the resulting reporting structure enables activity-based cost assignments to be completely integrated with periodic financial performance measurement.

Companies have been urged to start their redesign of cost systems by developing only Stage 3 cost systems (Kaplan 1990) in which the activity-based systems are implemented separately from companies' operational control systems that provide periodic feedback on financial and operating performance. The concepts in Cooper and Kaplan (1992) and this paper begin identifying the design characteristics for Stage 4 cost systems in which activity-based cost and profitability information on products, customers, and services are integrated with periodic reporting on actual activity demands and resource expenses.

The basic principles for integrating activity-based cost assignments with flexible budgeting and *ex post* analysis of actual expenses can be illustrated with a simple numerical example. Let's take a support activity, such as inspection, and assume that the cost driver for this activity is the number of inspections performed. One can think of the demand for this activity coming from set-ups—inspecting the first few items produced after each changeover to verify that the set-up was done appropriately; from receipts— inspecting raw material or purchased parts from non-certified vendors; or from shipments—preventing external failures by verifying that the product meets customer specifications. Table 1 presents the financial and operating assumptions for this activity for a given period, such as a month, as well as the actual results.

I. SIMPLE ABC APPROACH
In a simple ABC approach, a cost driver rate is derived from budgeted figures on expenses and anticipated activity volumes:[1]

$$\frac{\text{Cost per}}{\text{Inspection}} = \frac{\text{Budgeted Inspection Expenses}}{\text{Budgeted Activity Volume}} = \frac{\$280,000}{4,000}$$
$$= \$70/\text{ inspection}$$

TABLE 1
INSPECTION: OPERATING EXPENSES AND ACTIVITY LEVELS

	Expense	Activity Level (# Inspections)
Budgeted	$280,000	4,000
Actual	$250,000	3,500

During the period a $70 charge is assigned to any receipt, batch, or shipment that has an inspection performed; that is, the cost assignment uses a standard cost driver rate applied to actual volumes.[2] Assuming that the operating expense for the inspection activity is considered a committed expense, reconciling the inspection expense charged to products with the inspection expense recognized in the period's financial statement can be accomplished in a straightforward calculation:[3]

Inspection Expense		
Charged to Products:	3,500 @ $70	$245,000
Volume Variance: (Budgeted-Actual Activity Level)		
(4,000—3,500) = 500	@$70	35,000 U
Spending Variance:		
(Actual - Budgeted Expenses)		(30,000) F
Total Actual Expenses		$250,000

The "Simple ABC" approach, however, causes the cost driver rate to fluctuate each period with anticipated activity levels. If anticipated activity levels are falling faster than operating expenses can be reduced, the cost driver rate starts to escalate leading to potential death spirals.[4] More fundamentally, no theoretical reason exists for calculating cost driver rates in this manner. The $70 rate is just a rough surrogate, and perhaps a quite inaccurate one, for the costs of resources used in each inspection. The rate includes not only the costs of resources actually used for the inspection, but also some portion of the unused capacity costs of resources supplied to perform this activity.

II. CAPACITY-BASED ABC APPROACH: COMMITTED EXPENSES

The approach advocated in Cooper and Kaplan (1992) overcomes the limitations in the "Simple ABC Approach" by interpreting the budgeted operating expenses of $280,000 as supplying a **capability** or capacity to perform inspections. With this interpretation, an additional piece of information is required to calculate the cost driver rate for the inspection activity, namely, how much capacity is supplied for this commitment of resources.[5] Assume that contracting to supply $280,000 of resources for inspection provides a practical capacity to perform 5,000 inspections in the period. This assumption leads to a cost driver rate calculation of:

$$\frac{\text{Cost per}}{\text{Inspection}} = \frac{\text{Budgeted Inspection Expenses}}{\text{Capacity Activity Volume}} = \frac{\$280,000}{5,000}$$
$$= \$56/\text{inspection}.$$

In the Capacity-Based ABC approach (referred to as the "Strategic ABC Approach" by Yang and Wu (1993), the cost driver rate is based on the capacity provided by organizational spending, and is not influenced by actual or anticipated levels of actual resource usage. Since, at the anticipated activity level of 4,000 inspections, not all of the capacity provided will be used productively, a cost of unused capacity is anticipated in the budgeting process:

Budgeted cost of unused capacity
= (Practical - Budgeted Capacity) @ $56
= (5,000 – 4,000) @ $56
= $56,000.

Given the actual expenses and use of the inspection activity, reconciling the inspection expense charged to products with the amount recorded in the period's financial statements is now:

Inspection Expense Charged to Products:		
	3,500 @ $56	$196,000
Budgeted Unused Capacity Cost:		
	1,000 @ 56	56,000 U
Capacity Utilization Variance:		
	(4,000 – 3,500) @ 56	28,000 U
Spending Variance: (Actual-Budgeted Expenses)		
		(30,000) F
Total Actual Expenses		$250,000

This capacity-based calculation enables the $84,000 of unused capacity ($56,000 expected, $28,000 unexpected) to be highlighted for management attention. It signals the opportunity for actions such as reducing the supply of this resource or soliciting additional business that could be accommodated within existing resource supply.

The capacity-based calculation continues to assume that all of the expenses associated with supplying resources to perform the inspection activity are incurred independently of the actual demand for this activity during the period. This situation arises when the physical resources for the activity have already been acquired (such as the inspection equipment) and the people performing inspections have an implicit or explicit contract with the organization to continue to come to work and be paid whether or not work is available for them to perform. Also, no alternative activity exists that could productively use these resources when they are not actually performing inspections, their intended activity.[6] Thus, any deviation between actual and budgeted spending is attributed to timing differences or unexpected spending rather than to variations in activity levels.

III. CAPACITY-BASED ABC WITH COMMITTED AND FLEXIBLE RESOURCES

A more general treatment allows some portion of the activity resources to be committed in advance, so that the associated expenses are volume-independent, and a separate portion of resources supplied as needed to meet actual, realized demands. For example, equipment and space may be dedicated to inspections, but people are supplied as needed to perform inspections. In this case, two different cost driver rates are required to assign resource expenses to cost objects. The committed expenses (space and equipment) are assigned, as in case II, based on the capacity or capabilities provided by these resources, while the expenses of the flexible resources (inspectors) are assigned based on the activity volumes actually realized.[7] This procedure resembles what is now a standard textbook recommendation for assigning service department costs to production centers; that is, assign the "fixed" capacity resources based on anticipated usage or demand for the capacity and assign the "variable" portion of service department costs based on actual usage. In the ABC treatment, however, the cost of committed resources is still assigned based on actual usage.

To illustrate this procedure, assume that the numerical example of the $280,000 of budgeted expenses for inspection, $200,000 represents the expenses of committed resources and $80,000 represents the expenses of flexible resources. Table 2 presents a summary of this situation, including calculation of the two different cost driver rates.

Now the amount charged to products can easily be reconciled with the amount of expenses actually recorded:

Inspection Expense Charged to Products:
                  3,500 @ $60 $210,000
Budgeted Unused Capacity Cost:
      (5,000–4,000) = 1,000 @ $60   40,000 U
Capacity Utilization Variance:
      (4,000 – 3,500) = 500 @ 40   20,000 U
Spending Variance: Actual - Budgeted Expenses
        ($250,000 – 270,000[8])   (20,000) F
Total Actual Expenses $250,000

In summary, the assignment of expenses to products (or services, or customers) for both committed and flexible resources associated with performing a particular activity can be easily handled by using two different cost driver rates. One rate assigns the cost of resources that are committed (supplied) in advance of knowing actual demand and the other rate assigns the cost of resources that are supplied in proportion to actual activity demands.[9] This two-tier structure enables product costing to be integrated with expense analysis. Actual spending or expenses can be estimated based on forecasted activity levels. The $250,000 of expenses actually reported during a period can be reconciled with the $210,000 of expenses assigned to products, through expected and unexpected costs of unused capacity and spending variations.

In addition, the analysis reveals which costs assigned to products (or customers or services) represent committed versus flexible resources. Managers can easily see which expenses are expected to vary in the short run and use this information in making short-run incremental pricing and product- and customer-mix decisions.

POSTSCRIPT

Measuring product costs based on a measure of practical capacity is certainly not a new idea. Donaldson Brown, in the 1920s, devised a pricing formula for General Motors that used a standard volume assumption of 80 percent of theoretical capacity (Brown 1924a, 1924b; and General Motors 1960). And even earlier, Gantt (1915) one of the leading figures in the scientific management movement, criticized the apparently already prevailing practice of assigning actual expenses based on actual production volumes and advocated capacity-based costing:

> The only expense logically chargeable to a product is that needed for its production when the factory is running at its full or normal capacity.
>
> In as much as the determination of this fact is primarily an engineering or manufacturing problem, and not primarily an accounting problem, it becomes evident that cost methods must be based on engineering knowledge, and the cost accountant of the future must himself be an engineer or manufacturer, or be guided by one.

Gantt's recommendations to adopt capacity costing, and about the educational and experiential background for cost accountants, were not widely followed by many companies in subsequent decades.[10] General Motors, however, for some 50 years did continue to use two different volume assumptions in its management systems. Donaldson Brown's

---

TABLE 2
OPERATING EXPENSES AND ACTIVITY LEVELS: BUDGET AND ACTUAL

	Expense	Activity Level (# Inspections)	Driver Rate
Budgeted Committed (Supplying Capacity)	$200,000	5,000 (capacity)	$40
Budgeted Flexible (Varying with Volume)	80,000	4,000 (budgeted)	20
Budgeted Total	$280,000		$60
Actual (Realized)	$250,000	3,500 (actual)	

standard volume of 80 percent of theoretical capacity was used for planning and pricing purposes, whereas budgeted volume (called "index volume" in the company) was used for budgeting and control of short-term operating expenses. In the mid-1970s, the apparent confusion from having two different volume assumptions (both standard and index volumes) in the company's management systems caused senior management to eliminate the standard (practical capacity) volume and to use index volume for product costing and pricing purposes. This decision, which led the company to raise prices to cover their higher reported product costs, occurred just as Japanese and European competition combined with a surge in oil prices to cause sales of U.S. domestic automobile companies to plummet. The death spirals induced by assigning committed plant operating expense to a diminished volume base likely led to more than a few plant closings in the General Motors system.

Cooper and Kaplan (1992) applied the Gantt and Donaldson Brown recommendations by advocating that activity-based cost driver rates be calculated using the practical capacity supplied by the resources committed to that activity. The current paper extends that analysis by showing how activity-based analysis can be integrated into a flexible budgeting process and an *ex post* financial analysis of operating expenses. The recommended process allows Donaldson Brown's "standard volume" assumption to be used to assign the costs of using committed resources to products, services and customers. Also, such costing can be integrated with the analysis of expenses of flexible resources whose supply varies with actual activity volumes.

References

Brown, D. 1924a. Pricing Policy in Relation to Financial Control. *Management and Administration* (February): 195–198.

_____. 1924b. Pricing Policy Applied to Financial Control. *Management and Administration* (April): 417–722.

Christensen, L. F., and D. Sharp. 1993. How ABC Can Add Value to Decision Making. *Management Accounting* (May): 38–42.

Cooper, R., and R. S. Kaplan. 1992. Activity-Based Systems: Measuring the Costs of Resource Usage. *Accounting Horizons* (September): 1–13.

_____, and K. Verma. 1991. Hewlett Packard: Queensferry Telecommunications Division. Harvard Business School case #9-191-067.

Gantt, H. L. 1915. The Relation Between Production and Costs. *American Society of Mechanical Engineers Spring Meeting* (June); reprinted in *Journal of Manufacturing and Operations Management* III (1990): 251–267; and in *Journal of Cost Management* (Spring 1994): 4–11.

General Motors Corporation. 1960. Harvard Business School case # 9-160-005.

Kaplan, R. S. 1990. The Four Stage Model of Cost System Design. *Management Accounting* (September): 22–26.

_____, and A. A. Atkinson. 1989. *Advanced Management Accounting*. 2d ed. Englewood Cliffs, NJ: Prentice Hall.

Ostrenga, M. R. 1988. A Methodology for Identifying Your Excess Capacity Costs. *Journal of Cost Management* (Summer): 39–44.

Shillinglaw, G. 1983. *Managerial Cost Accounting*. 5th ed. Homewood, IL: Irwin.

Yang, G. Y., and R. C. Wu. 1993. Strategic Costing & ABC. *Management Accounting* (May): 33–37.

Notes

1. When using an ABC system on an ongoing basis, as exposed to a one-time snapshot of prior period's operations, a **standard** (or **budgeted**) activity cost driver is calculated from budgeted information.

2. Alternatively, a cost driver rate could be determined *ex post* based on actual expenses and actual activity levels ($250,000/S,500 = $71.43 per inspection). This *ex post* calculation has several undesirable aspects, as discussed in standard textbook treatments of service department cost assignments; see, for example, pp. 249–253 in Kaplan and Atkinson (1989).

3. The variances are calculated to reconcile the cost of supplying resources during the period with the cost of resources used for the activities actually performed. These variances can serve as a signal or trigger for managerial action. The appropriate interpretation and use of these reconciling variances are managerial judgments.

4. Cooper and Verma (1991) show how a death spiral can arise in the "simple" use of ABC.

5. Selection of the quantity to use as the capacity or capability of the resource provided is a complex subject, well beyond the scope of this paper. For some resources, such as machines, capacity is acquired in lumpy amounts. A strong argument can be made for using the activity volume anticipated in the acquisition decision—which could be less than the actual capacity acquired—as the "practical capacity" for these resources. For other resources, bottleneck constraints and seasonal and cyclical peak usage demands need to be considered. The particular denominator volume selected does not affect the calculations proposed in this paper, though it may affect interpretation of the results.

6. If, as assumed in the numerical example, resources are not fungible (transferable) across activities, then unused capacity can be measured at the activity level. If resources are fungible across several activities, then the resources but not the activities have the potential for unused capacity. The judgment of when unused capacity exists at the activity level and when at the resource level is not trivial, and should be examined in future research.

7. A multi-tiered structure for cost driver rates to distinguish between capacity-supplying resources and flexibly-supplied resources has been proposed previously (Ostrenga 1988; and Christensen and Sharp 1993). These previous approaches, however, focused only on product costing aspects and did not explore the integration of the approach with flexible budgeting and *ex post* analysis of actual expenses.

8. Flexible Budget for Expenses = $200,000 + $(20 * 3,500) = $270,000.

9. Alternatively as Robin Cooper pointed out to me, we can skip this mixed situation entirely by defining two separate activity pools: one for resources committed in advance to perform the activity, and one for resources provided as needed to perform the activity. The cost of the activity driver for the committed resource activity cost pool would be based on the practical capacity supplied, and the cost of the activity driver for the cost pool containing the flexible resource costs would be based on the actual amount of work performed.

10. Textbooks, however, such as Shillinglaw (1983, 183–185) certainly made this point in connection with assigning service department costs to production departments.

From R. Kaplan, "Flexible Budgeting in an Activity-Based Costing Framework," *Accounting Horizons* (June 1994): 104–109. Reprinted with permission.

Questions

12.3a In Kaplan's article, how are the costs of resources used related to the costs of resources supplied?

12.3b When the resources used/resources supplied distinction is incorporated into an activity-based costing framework, is there still an inconsistency with periodic financial performance measurement?

CHAPTER 13

Contemporary Management Accounting: Methods to Stay Competitive

R. Cooper and W. B. Chew, *Control Tomorrow's Costs Through Today's Designs* (Reading 13.1) discusses the importance of target costing for many of today's manufacturing organizations. In short, target costing is a management process in which companies work backwards to arrive at product costs, after making a detailed assessment of what customers' requirements are for a given product. Once the level of quality and functionality are set and a target price and volume are determined, companies focus on developing manufacturing processes and materials sourcing at a target cost to achieve a target profit. This process is distinct from many traditional Western approaches in which the manufacturing cost plus a desired profit determines selling price. Using examples from Japanese firms such as Olympus Optical Company, one of the world's leaders in single-lens reflex cameras, and Komatsu, manufacturer of earth-moving products, Cooper and Chew detail the process of developing target costs at each firm. The authors also discuss how target costing can be applied in process and service industries.

Reading 13.2 is J. K. Shank and V. Govindarajan's *Measuring the 'Cost of Quality': A Strategic Cost Management Perspective*. This article begins by presenting an even-handed overview and comparison of four of the major schools of quality management thought: Juran, Deming, Crosby and the "Japanese" approaches. The authors argue that traditional views of quality should be abandoned and that organizations should be focusing on total quality management. An impediment for some companies in moving to TQM is the continued use of traditional cost management. Shank and Govindarajan contrast this traditional view with the strategic cost management approach to illustrate that the strategic cost management approach is much more consistent with the TQM philosophy. In the final section of the article, the authors refine their cost analysis framework by introducing the cost of quality (COQ) method as a way of quantifying quality costs. COQ is an integral part of TQM and can help guide companies as they move from traditional thinking about quality to total quality management.

Based on a questionnaire sent to marketing managers and controllers, G. Foster, M. Gupta, L. Sjoblom's *Customer Profitability Analysis: Challenges and New Directions* (Reading 13.3) suggests that customer profitability analysis (CAP) is a significant method of analysis with which management accounting needs to become very familiar. The basic concept behind CAP is that each dollar of revenue does not contribute equally to profits. Historically, methods such as ABC have focused on determining more accurate product costs but have not looked at the cost drivers related to downstream customer costs. For example, each customer of a company may require differential amounts of the company's resources, such as the level and type of service. CAP allows companies to recognize the differences in what it is costing them to serve each customer and to make decisions about altering their customers behavior. Behavioral changes might force customers to increase their business with the company, and thereby increase the company's revenues or reduce the level of service provided, and thus reduce the costs to serve customers. The authors provide numerous examples of how to go about developing a CAP and discuss the many challenges involved in such systems.

13.1 Control Tomorrow's Costs Through Today's Designs

By Robin Cooper and W. Bruce Chew

Over the past 15 years, company after company has learned that quality must be designed into products before they are manufactured—that it is expensive, if not misguided, to attempt to inspect in quality after the product has left the production line. Today the most competitive companies are applying the same logic to determining the price of new products. Before a company launches a product (or family of products), senior managers determine its ideal selling price, establish the feasibility of meeting that price, and then control costs to ensure that the price is met. They are using a management process known as *target costing.*

Target costing drives a product development strategy that focuses the design team on the ultimate customer and on the real opportunity in the market. Leading Japanese electronics and vehicle manufacturers have used target costing to their advantage, and companies are now introducing it in the United States, Germany, and elsewhere. Its rigorous cost-management technique helps prevent senior managers from launching low-margin products that do not generate appropriate returns to the company, but its greater value lies in its ability to bring the challenge of the marketplace back through the chain of production to product designers. Target costing ensures that development teams will bring profitable products to market not only with the right level of quality and functionality but also with appropriate prices for the targeted customer segments. It is a discipline that harmonizes the labor of disparate participants in the development effort, from designers and manufacturing engineers to market researchers and suppliers.

The logic of target costing is simple. Looking at tomorrow's marketplace, the organization maps customer segments and targets the most attractive ones. It determines what level of quality and functionality will succeed within each segment, given a predetermined target price (and volume and launch date). The organization then designs the sourcing, production, and delivery processes that will enable it to achieve its desired profits at this target. In effect, the company reasons backward from customers' needs and willingness to pay instead of following the flawed but common practice of cost-plus pricing. Target costing ensures that success with the customers will yield economic success for the company.

COST DISCIPLINE: WHY NOW?

The logic of target costing is so simple and compelling that one may wonder why it has only recently begun to receive attention. After all, at any time in the past, senior managers could have gained much from becoming involved in the process of pricing and costing a product before it was designed. Their lack of involvement gave engineers and enthusiasts, who were unlikely to see the whole picture, undue influence over the company's competitive position. When senior managers tried to drive costs out of their operations ex post facto by cutting staff, eliminating frills, outsourcing, or reengineering downstream processes, they often discovered that as much as 70% to 80% of a product's costs were effectively immutable after it left the designers' hands. As product and process technologies have become more integrated, a product's cost has become even more strongly tied to its design.

Nevertheless, although a preemptive and disciplined approach to costs has always been reasonable, it has not always been urgent, and companies do not usually undertake difficult tasks if the tasks are avoidable. These days, however, price and cost targeting are no longer avoidable, largely because of the erosion of important first-mover advantages in the new global economy. In the past, many leading companies, especially those that led by technical differentiation, found that they could take a cost-plus approach to releasing new products because they anticipated profiting from serial generations of products. They believed that being first to market was most important; that in preparing to be first, design teams needed to focus only on selecting and executing well the appropriate bundle of product attributes; and that ultimately, over several iterations of the product, the marketplace would allow the company to earn a reasonable return on total capital employed.

By that logic, when the product was first released, it might carry a comparatively high price considered affordable by only a small number of lead users, such as businesses hoping to turn a new technology to their advantage or comparatively wealthy, adventurous technophiles. Lead users would pay a premium for the first-generation product and help create excitement for its new features; they would even help establish the brand. The revenues from lead users would rarely cover the cost of developing the product. Hewlett-Packard Company, for example, did not expect the first releases of its laser printers to recover R&D costs. But first-mover companies have assumed that they would have time to scale up to mass production and introduce serially cheaper versions of products for increasingly broader segments of customers. The mass market would be the source of most profits—as indeed it was for consumer products such as the 35-millimeter camera and the fax, and for components such as ABS brakes and digital TV controls.

Today that strategic assumption would be disastrous for all but the most advanced products, those with highly proprietary technologies. Global markets no longer allow a company time to introduce a product and then scale up. Now imitators—usually lean enterprises—can bring "me too" products to market so rapidly that first-mover companies have no time to inculcate brand loyalty, let alone recover their development costs. Lean competitors, with faster reflexes than old mass-production companies, work on shorter product-development and life cycles, and they manufacture almost anywhere—Korea, Mexico, Israel.

The growing number and increasing ubiquity of lean competitors means that copycat versions of most new products will be available within months, not years. So if market leaders can't recover costs as they used to, they have no choice but to manage costs from the design phase forward and to launch products at prices that will attract broad segments of customers and forestall imitation. How long they can hold on to their market, then, will often depend on how quickly they can offer greater functionality without raising price.

For companies to gain and hold market leadership today, they have to design the cost out of their products when they set initial levels of quality and functionality and they have to calibrate product performance to an identified price niche. In other words, senior managers need to approach new product development controlling for tomorrow's costs, not just today's. And tomorrow comes more quickly than it used to.

OLYMPUS: FROM COST TARGETS TO TARGET COSTING

In Japan, competition among lean companies has become so intense that aggressive cost management is critical to survival in some sectors. It is thus no accident that leading organizations such as Olympus Optical Company and Komatsu developed and adapted target costing early on.

Olympus was a leader in single-lens reflex (SLR) cameras, which had no technological competitor for a generation. But by 1987, "compact" cameras built around a miniaturized electronic shutter had absorbed so many advanced electronic controls—features such as automatic exposure and zoom—that consumers began to view them as a serious alternative to the SLR. Olympus had introduced a compact of its own as early as 1978, but not as a main focus of its product portfo-

lio. In the mid-1980s, Olympus began losing money, and by 1987 its losses were substantial.

Senior managers saw severe problems. Cameras incorporating the new electronic technologies suffered from poor quality and there were no individual product "hits." The managers concluded that the planning and development of product families needed improvement. Externally, Olympus suffered from the sudden shift from SLR cameras to competitors' compact cameras and from a steady appreciation of the yen.

The company reacted first with an effort to regain lost share by introducing a number of new products—for example, SLRs with advanced electronics and compacts with an advanced zoom. A second initiative was aimed at improving quality, which historically had been high at Olympus and which continued to be crucial to its ability to lower the total costs associated with its products.

But most important to Olympus was the third initiative: reconciling production costs to a volatile market. Managers believed that the company's ability to manufacture cameras at a cost that would meet the increasingly stringent expectations of its customers would be central to the success of any new product. Moreover, the company's product development process would have to meet challenging price and profit targets within 18 months of their being set—before the competitive environment could shift again.

This was not the first time that Olympus managers had set cost targets for new products, but earlier targets had been more or less hypothetical. Senior managers had created no imperative to meet them, and missed targets did not prevent products from being launched. Essentially, designers did their best on functionality, manufacturing engineers pursued efficiency, and marketing sold what was produced. All that changed in 1987.

First, Olympus tried to establish a clearer picture of what features future customers would value in new product families. It produced a corporate plan that identified the future mix of businesses by major product line, the desired levels of profitability, and the contribution of each product to the cultivation of the brand. And it performed a technology review to learn how current and future technologies would affect the camera business. The technology review included an audit of Olympus's proprietary technologies that could be turned to the company's advantage. Its market mapping included an analysis of the general business environment to determine how macroeconomic factors, such as changing exchange rates and the further segmentation of income groups, were likely to affect consumer demand. Finally, the marketing research included a survey of information collected from such sources as Olympus questionnaires, group interviews, interviews at fashion centers, and interviews with photographers as well as a competitive analysis that examined areas such as competitors' capabilities, likely price points, and filed patents.

With a clearer sense of what the camera market would bear and what Olympus's profitability goals required, the company identified the price points at which new compact cameras would sell. The U.S. market price for basic compact-camera models in 1991 was about $100. With that price as a baseline, Olympus analyzed consumer trends, competitors' performance, and forward-looking technology to establish what relationship it could anticipate between distinctive camera features, such as magnification capability or smaller size, and higher price points. From each price point, Olympus subtracted the appropriate margins for dealers and its U.S. subsidiary and also subtracted import costs, such as freight and duties, to arrive at the price that would be paid to the factory for any new model. Then, by subtracting its own margin requirement, Olympus finally arrived at a preliminary target cost for each new product.

Now what it needed was a disciplined process for developing products that could be made at those costs. The responsibility for ensuring that the company could produce cameras with the features customers wanted and at costs within the targeted limits fell to a product-development management team at Tatsuno, the site of Olympus's primary manufacturing operations. Only when designers and manufacturing engineers could demonstrate that estimated production costs did not exceed target costs would a camera be submitted for release to production.

OLYMPUS MOVES TO CLOSE THE GAPS

This process may sound straightforward, but it was not: Only about 20% of proposed new models cleared Olympus's hurdle on the first pass. However, the 80% that missed were not abandoned. As at many companies, it was not uncommon at Olympus for product managers to design ''nice-to-have'', but not "need-to-have" features into their products. The product-development management team's job was to ask whether the value those features added really outweighed their costs. Correspondingly, they would ask whether an enhanced product could justifiably be moved to the next higher price point so that its estimated costs would generate acceptable returns.

Soon enough, those reviews ended. If target costs could not be met or price points could not be changed, the team returned the product to research and development for redesign.

In the context of this review, Olympus managers used a life-cycle analysis to reckon the costs of important new technologies incorporated in new product designs. That is, they assessed the value of a technology's contribution to features that could be expected to serve a variety of models over the life cycle of a whole product family; they did not attribute the technology's costs only to the first models introduced. Further, they separated the whole cost of a new technology into its two components: the costs of research and development and the costs of production.

The Olympus product-development team determined that in allocating research and development costs, product designers should consider how long a camera family is likely to be on the market (on the order of three years) or how long a specific feature is likely to find application in other camera families. As for production costs, Olympus managers learned that even after a product family comes to market, the costs associated with new technology often decline quickly and dramatically with the adoption of manufacturing programs that actually increase product quality—for instance, by reducing the number of parts in a subassembly, eliminating labor-intensive mechanical adjustments, or moving from metal or glass to plastic. The number of parts in the shutter unit of one entire class of compact cameras, for example, fell from 105 to 56, a reduction that led to a 58% decrease in production costs for this widely used component. By 1990, Olympus managers had discovered that the company could generally reduce its production costs by approximately 35% across the production lifetime of its new products. The product-development management team incorporated this figure into its target costing of future products.

On the whole, life-cycle analysis helped many potentially profitable products clear the hurdle. The practice may sound vaguely like the old strategy of distributing costs over successive generations of buyers, from lead users to mass markets, but it is different. There is no thought here of introducing the product family at high prices that then fall as volume increases. Cost, not price, is expected to fall.

Cost reductions of this magnitude don't happen without strenuous effort. For existing products and processes, Olympus monitored and managed fixed costs, purchased-parts costs, routine production costs, the costs of defective production, capacity utilization targets, and overhead expenses. And Olympus used its falling production costs in a number of ways. At times, it raised margins; at other times, it selectively dropped price points. On the whole, however, the company used cost savings to improve its products over time. The one thing it did not do was take a short-term profit, which, in the unforgiving environment of lean competition, would have been the most dangerous option. A company that just cashes in its market advantage invites imitation and invests nothing in sustaining its technical differentiation.

KOMATSU'S SUPPLIERS BRING COSTS DOWN

As the Olympus experience illustrates, target costing issues a clear-cut but daunting challenge to product designers. They cannot call a design a success unless they meet the functionality needs of the customer, the price demands of the distribution channel, the manufacturability requirements of the plant, and the financial projections of the corporation.

Komatsu's experience illustrates another way to use target costing—in this case to pressure suppliers to drive their costs down. Komatsu's earth-moving products contain many more components than do Olympus's cameras, and the company relies more heavily on outside suppliers for complete subsystems: hydraulic devices, electrical subassemblies, and the like. In 1993, for example, Komatsu manufactured roughly 30% of the content in its heavy equipment products, designed and subcontracted 50%, and purchased the remaining 20% from outside suppliers.

Moreover, the number of choices Komatsu must make regarding components makes it difficult to control development costs. Which features will the F company offer on which models? Which teams need additional support? Where should the company be refining designs and where should it be rethinking entire design approaches? Komatsu must involve suppliers in product design early in order to make informed decisions in those and other important matters.

Throughout the entire product-development process, Komatsu poses a challenge to its suppliers: to maintain the performance specifications of components and deliver at prices consistent with Komatsu's overall target costs. Komatsu's target costing program provides the parameters that guide its negotiations with suppliers and subassembly makers to ensure a profitable product launch. By linking performance needs and the company's margin requirements back to each major subassembly, Komatsu's design team can track the performance of whole vehicle and keep an eye on the integrated goal: a product launched at a price the end user will find attractive, not simply a subassembly that satisfies product designers.

To develop system and component targets for its suppliers, Komatsu relies on data on historical performance and cost that it has recorded in function and cost tables. Function tables, containing information about the physical characteristics of each component, help designers determine the company's best-performing components. Cost tables, containing information about the costs of components, help designers identify the low-cost components. By, in effect, overlaying one table on the other, Komatsu engineers identify the target cost of the best component for a given project. This target cost becomes the suppliers' target price.

In developing the target cost of an excavator's cooling system, for instance, Komatsu's engineers determined that the most important performance factor was the surface area of the system's radiator. They consulted function tables to calculate the minimum radiator surface area required. They consulted cost tables to calculate the most cost-effective design. Then they calculated the target cost of their radiator to reflect both minimums: least surface area and minimum cost per unit of area. In demanding that the radiator in the excavator's cooling system be both the most efficient at cooling and the most cost-effective, Komatsu forced its suppliers to push the frontiers of their own technology to achieve more efficient designs.

It is important to remember that subsystem target costs must fit within an overall target cost, which has been derived from a projected market price. But if a subsystem's cost exceeds its projected share of the product's target cost, Komatsu does not automatically reject the design or reduce the cost targets for other components. Like Olympus, Komatsu focuses not on some mechanistic algorithm but on the complex relationship between cost and price and the effects of both on value. Komatsu asks whether particular functions need to be continued. It provides engineering support to suppliers that cannot meet targets. It seeks unexploited opportunities to reduce costs even further among components that have already met their targets. Komatsu managers do not measure success one department at a time. They know that the marketplace does not reward an outstanding component, only an outstanding integrated design.

SMOOTHING OUT THE TARGET-COSTING PROCESS

Clearly, target costing involves more than listing dollar targets and projected margins. It is a highly structured product-development discipline, adapted to such specific elements of a company's strategic positioning as industry pricing dynamics, product-complexity and life-cycle analyses, and supplier relations. It requires a company to make a series of decisions that include defining the product that customers want, ascertaining the economics required for profitability, allocating targets to components, and identifying the gap between target costs and initial projections of manufacturing costs. (See the diagram "The Target-Costing Process.")

On the other hand, as the experiences of Olympus and Komatsu suggest, target costing is not an exact science. It depends on credible data and on people who have the courage to make difficult judgments. Target costing is an iterative process that cannot be decoupled from the ordinary push and pull of the design process. The targets evolve as teams seek to balance functionality, price, volumes, capital investment, and costs. Also, because target costing is integrative, responsibility for achieving targets must be shared across functions. Finally, if they are to use target costing, companies must treat their suppliers as partners both during the design process and when they are setting cost targets.

Our description may make target costing sound like a smooth ride, but troublesome roadblocks can show up at different stages.

Defining the Product, Targeting the Marketplace. The choices that drives the entire target-costing process are the customer's. What prices will customers accept? What functionality will they insist on? What will competitors offer them? Because the ultimate goal of target costing is to maximize a product's total profitability, not minimize its cost, companies must do their best to understand how their customers' preferences and their competitors' products will evolve over time. That requires a thorough understanding of the customers' behavior in each market segment.

When the Japanese targeted the luxury car market, for example, they already knew one critical feature of luxury cars: They had to be quiet. For years, manufacturers had tried to lower sound levels in luxury cars and found the task inherently difficult. Sound level not only traded off against acceleration—high-revving engines tended to be loud—but was also an integrative challenge, because sound came from many other design components, including the drive train, tires, and door seals. Japanese researchers discovered, however, that frequency was as important to customers as decibel level; that is, the nature of the sound was as important as its loudness. This discovery pointed to a different design challenge: Instead of minimizing sound, designers could try to "tune" the car in a pleasing fashion—an approach with enormous ramifications for the way companies set their target costs.

The relationship between volume and frequency points to the challenge facing anyone engaged in product positioning. Any approach that asks customers, "Do you like this offering better than that one?" and stops there will not yield much insight. Marketers need an approach that will reveal deeper patterns of customer preference. Fortunately, researchers can use sophisticated surveying techniques such as conjoint analysis to reveal how potential customers cluster around multiple product features and functionalities. These preferences must then be expressed as innovative design options—what we might think of as quality and functionality targets. It is at this point that companies might use such interfunctional design techniques as the House of Quality, which maps the relationship between customers' desired features and specific engineering characteristics.

It is not enough to focus on the customer; competitors are a parallel concern. Most companies define competitors as "companies that make things similar to what we make," which is the producers' view of competition. In target costing, the Japanese companies we have studied tend to define competitors from the customers' perspective: "I am about to make a purchase, so what are my options?" Olympus, for example, benchmarked itself not only against camera manufacturers but also against the makers of CD players and Walkman-type products. The company understood that it was competing for discretionary dollars against makers of all kinds of consumer gadgets, not just against camera makers.

Computing Overall Target Costs. Companies derive overall targets in a number of different ways, but the purpose is always the same: to think rigorously about the company's future profitability. In fact, some Japanese companies classify target costing as a profit-management tool rather than as a cost-control tool. In any case, the task is to compute the costs that must not be exceeded if acceptable margins from specific products at specific price points are to be guaranteed.

For most companies, this order of logic represents a radical shift in thinking. Traditionally, companies perform the financial analysis associated with product development only after much of the development work has been done, and then only to determine whether to continue investment. In contrast, a financial analysis done early in the design process can accomplish much more. In target costing, it can tell design teams and general managers a great deal about what is required to make the product a success. The nature of the analysis may be the same, but shifts in timing and focus make a huge difference.

One U.S. vehicle maker we have worked with performed a financial analysis to estimate a likely return on investment for a redesigned product launched under a single set of hypothetical conditions. The purpose of the analysis was to make senior managers more comfortable with their decision to go ahead. So although the analysis aided the approval process, it provided little guidance to the design team. It displayed no sensitivity to the fact that conditions such as launch date, cost, and volume are variable and that small changes matter. Our analysis of the company's data showed that to miss cost targets would have been catastrophic: A 5% error would have eliminated any return on the company's $200 million investment.

Allocating Target Costs, Identifying the Gap. Once a target cost has been calculated for a new product,

TARGET-COSTING PROCESS

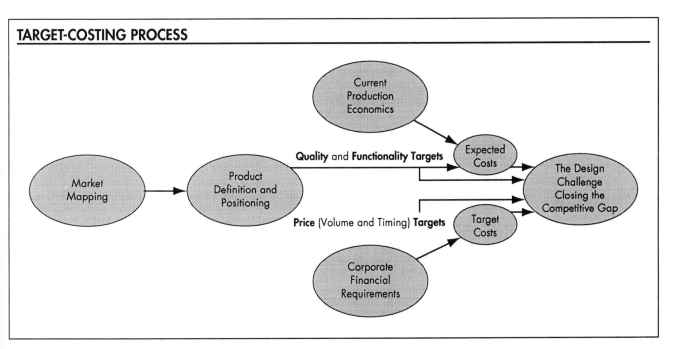

267

the design team has to divide it up among the product's various functions. How much can the team spend on one function as against all the others? The team must first calculate the gap between the target cost and what it estimates it would cost to build the product with today's processes, suppliers, productivity levels, and materials. The difference is a good approximation of the excess cost that must be wrung out of the new product.

It usually makes no sense to apply cost-reduction requirements uniformly across all the components and subsystems of the contemplated product. Rather, the design team can consult customer-value surveys, historical trends, and other data to guide it in determining how much cost it can remove from each component or subassembly. The team will allocate more costs to critical features (allowing for increased engine cost in a car that is intended to have a peppier ride, for example). But every extra dollar it allocates to improving one product feature must come from another function's allocation, because the target cost remains fixed.

Isuzu Motors' target-costing system, like others, aims to keep prices constant while adding as much functionality as possible to each new generation of vehicles. The system therefore attaches great importance to determining what features and level of performance the customer will want most, and it uses those preferences as the basis for allocating costs to major functions and group components. Market researchers ask customers to estimate how much they would pay for a given function. Then they develop ratios of preference by asking customers to estimate the relative importance of each function on a 100-point scale.

Isuzu uses this information to spread a product's target cost among the major specified function improvements. If the target cost for a component is too low to allow a sufficiently attractive or safe version to be produced, the component's target cost is increased and the target cost of other components is decreased. Thus, Isuzu continually uses its best sense of customer value to drive its design team's cost-allocation decisions.

Obeying the Cardinal Rule. All design-team members, whatever their function specialty, must regard the overall final cost target as an unalterable commitment; target commitments outrank design commitments. The idea is that aggressive targets focus the efforts of the design team on creative solutions and press value engineering to its limits.

In other words, to say that target costing is an iterative process is not to say that target costs, once set, are then subject to ongoing debate. They are not. Targets must fall under the protection of what we call the *cardinal rule:* If you cannot meet the targets, you cannot launch the product. That being the case, the process of product definition and target generation continues, but not in the factory.

Some companies have a layered set of targets. The first pass is the simplest, and failure here leads to a more sophisticated life-cycle analysis. But this approach must not become a game with ever lower hurdles, each test becoming less rigorous than the one before. As one manager puts it, "In the past, if a specific project failed the test for funding, we just kept changing the assumptions for the project or revising the test until the project passed. Target costing will not tolerate that."

The cardinal rule applies to the product as a whole. When targets are assigned to individual subassembly teams, some teams will beat their targets, some will meet them, and some will fall short. But success is not determined component by component; it is achieved—or not—by the final product. When components turn out to be more expensive than anticipated, that cost must be offset somewhere else in the design. This requirement demands a degree of cooperation and team spirit that will necessitate change for many organizations.

TARGET COSTING AND THE ORGANIZATION

Any system that cuts across organizational boundaries and communicates so many vital economic and market objectives is bound to have a profound impact on how the organization does business. One of the main benefits of target costing is that it forces companies to delineate their product-development goals very precisely and in a single vernacular.

In many companies, clarity of communication may be sacrificed to a general commitment to decentralization. At one large U.S. industrial company we have worked with, for example, nearly every functional department was using a unit of analysis that it had developed to answer a question of importance to itself only and that varied subtly from every other functional department's unit of analysis. Competitors' specifications were collected by product, existing costs were computed by part, customers' needs were defined in terms of product attribute, manufacturing constraints were determined by installation point, and the capabilities of the supplier were measured by module.

All those measures were related, but none addressed overall cost targets. There was no overall context within which to work. As a result, a product designer assigned to a particular subsystem could not get a clear answer to the question: How much do customers value this subsystem? or What does this subsystem cost?

Target costing requires that such problems be addressed directly. It forces companies to be specific about what customers want and what prices they are prepared to pay. Finally, target costing creates opportunities to demonstrate a commitment to customers. If targets cannot be met, the company cannot simply raise the price and launch the product. Such discipline may be painful to the people who work on a project, but it sends an important message to the organization as a whole: that customers come first and that if the company doesn't create value for them, a competitor will.

MAKING IT WORK

For target costing to succeed, targets must not only be valid, people must also see them as valid. They cannot be the outcome of a "political" process. The market analysis that yields the target prices, the financial analysis that generates the target costs, and the disaggregation procedures that allocate costs among components and subassemblies—all must be trusted. The target-costing process must, therefore, be highly transparent.

Moreover, cost-reduction objectives must be achievable most of the time. Setting the bar too high can be as damaging as having no bar at all; in fact, the Japanese set a series of what they call *tip-toe objectives,* that is, objectives that may be reached by "standing on tiptoes"—a stretch that strains the organization but does not defeat it. Also, the requirements for product functionality must be clearly and publicly articulated so that nobody tries to achieve the target cost by reducing product functionality below acceptable levels. It is no good to reduce costs by shortchanging customers. When target costing works well, quantifiable hurdles are established in a transparent process, and senior managers commit themselves to what the numbers show. Engineers receive goals that are clear and achievable, and everyone adheres to the cardinal rule. A company that meets those requirements is not guaranteed a victory in the markets it enters. It does earn the right to compete.

The authors gratefully acknowledge the assistance of Bernard Avishai in developing and writing this article.

Robin Cooper is a professor at the Claremont Graduate School's Peter F. Drucker Graduate Management Center in Claremont, California, and author of When Lean Enterprises Collide: Competing Through Confrontation *(Harvard Business School Press, 1995), which draws on Cooper's five-year study of the management systems of 20 Japanese companies. W. Bruce Chew is a senior consultant at Monitor Company, a global consulting firm in Cambridge, Massachusetts. He is a former associate professor of technology and operations management at the Harvard Business School in Boston, Massachusetts.*

TARGETING COSTS IN PROCESS AND SERVICE INDUSTRIES

Target costing has made its mark in industries in which products require a good deal of production assembly—cars, cameras, and bulldozers, for example. However, the discipline target costing offers has uses outside the assembly environment.

In processing companies, where the characteristics of the process—time, temperature, and pressure—determine the performance of the product, the focus of target costing shifts from the product to the process. A steel company would tend to focus on the costs associated with routings and processing time; a paper mill, on those associated with speed and breakage. The key issues—understanding market needs, ensuring satisfactory financial performance at a given price, not exceeding the target cost—remain.

Similarly, target costing can be applied to services, for which the focus is the service delivery system. As in process-intensive manufacturing, process is inextricable from product. Think of the issues that are important to the delivery of health care and fast-food functions. Where services and process-intensive manufacturing diverge is in their flexibility. It is enormously expensive to convert a paper machine so that it can produce a grade or weight that was not considered in its initial design. Service delivery systems, however, are a different matter. In people-intensive, customer-responsive service-delivery systems, it is not only possible to add new services, it can be hard not to. Menus are easy to extend. Room services can easily be added. Consulting firms or law firms can always enter a new area of practice. Where is the discipline that ensures that these extensions are profitable?

Because a single service-delivery system may be used to deliver a wide range of services, determining the profitability of individual services becomes an exercise in the arbitrary allocation of costs. In services, particularly those in which waiting time is critical, it is the systemic effects of individual new service—for instance, the extent to which they make the process more complex—that determine whether their revenues and value to customers offset their costs. Target costing can still facilitate a discussion of the appropriateness of a new service, but only if it focuses on the systemic impact of the service extension and questions whether this impact aligns with company strategy and profitability goals. In service industries as in other industries, target costing can help organizations resist the urge to create new market offerings simply because they have the ability.

From "Control Tomorrow's Costs Through Today's Designs," by R. Cooper and W. B. Chew, *Harvard Business Review* (January–February 1996): 88–97. Copyright © 1996 by the President and Fellows of Harvard College; all rights reserved.

Questions

13.1a   Describe the procedure (as characterized by Cooper and Chew) that Isuzu Motors goes through to allocate its target cost among major functional improvements to its vehicles.

13.1b   What are "tip-toe" objectives as discussed in the Cooper and Chew article, and what is their role in target costing?

13.2 Measuring the "Cost of Quality": A Strategic Cost Management Perspective

By John K. Shank and Vijay Govindarajan

Quality has become such an important strategic variable that management accounting can no longer ignore it. This article surveys the authoritative literature on total quality management (TQM) to contrast two paradigms for quality—the traditional view and TQM. Conventional management accounting panders to the traditional views on quality and tends to discourage companies from implementing TQM, which can be characterized as "phase 1" thinking about quality costs. A cost analysis framework that supports TQM ("phase 2" thinking) is explained. This cost analysis framework can be modified for strategic decision making and control to produce a "phase 3" perspective.

Cost is caused, or driven, by many factors that are interrelated in complex ways. Understanding cost behavior means understanding the complex interplay of the set of cost drivers at work in any given situation. Each driver involves choices a company makes (e.g., whether to have a large- or a small-scale operation) that drive unit cost.

To facilitate making the right choices, the relationship of each driver to total cost should be specified. For example, activity-based management (ABM) is a way to emphasize the impact of eliminating non-value-added work on total cost. This article discusses several cost analysis frameworks for one of the "soft" cost drivers: management commitment to total quality. Many firms call this commitment total quality management, or TQM; others believe that quality is best applied without creating yet another formal program with its own three letter acronym.

A SURVEY OF TQM LITERATURE

Quality is now widely acknowledged as a key competitive weapon. Some say it is the key differential advantage in a global marketplace. Such firms as American Express, Ford, General Electric, IBM, and Xerox emphasize quality in their overall strategy. This section presents an overview of the four main "schools" of quality management: Juran, Deming, Crosby, and the "Japanese" approach. While these approaches all have similarities, they differ in subtle, but important, ways. The following short descriptions of the four approaches should help managers focus on the important cost analysis issues.

Joseph Juran. Juran was (with Armand Feigenbaum) a pioneer of quality cost analysis during the 1950s. Juran divided quality costs into four categories:

- Prevention costs;
- Appraisal costs;
- Internal failure costs; and
- External failure costs.[1]

This method of classifying quality costs is still widely used today.

According to Juran, control costs (i.e., prevention and appraisal costs) increase as quality increases, but failure costs (internal and external costs) decrease. Adding these two components together, the result is an overall quality cost curve that is U-shaped, as shown in Exhibit 1. This suggests that the objective of a quality management program should be to find the level of quality (or number of defects) that minimizes the total cost of quality—i.e., to find the bottom of the U-shaped curve.

Conceptually and practically, there is no reason why the minimum total cost position in this model could not be 100 percent quality. That is, there is nothing in the concept that requires optimum quality to be less than 100 percent perfection. Where the optimum point falls is a function of the shape of the various curves. Indeed, it is surprising how many managers in the 1990s still firmly believe in the U-

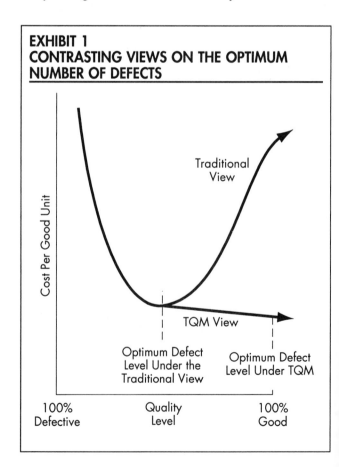

EXHIBIT 1
CONTRASTING VIEWS ON THE OPTIMUM NUMBER OF DEFECTS

Traditional View

Cost Per Good Unit

TQM View

Optimum Defect Level Under the Traditional View

Optimum Defect Level Under TQM

100% Defective

Quality Level

100% Good

shaped quality cost curve—who believe, in other words, that "those last few defects are very expensive to eliminate."

W: Edwards Deming. Deming is perhaps the best-known scholar of quality management. Although Deming is an American, acceptance of his ideas occurred first in Japan. Since 1951, the Japanese have awarded an annual Deming Prize for advancements in the precision and dependability of products. In the United States, recognition of the importance of Deming's ideas did not come until many years later. Not until 1987 was the Deming Prize awarded to a U.S. firm (Texas Instruments). In the same year, the Malcolm Baldrige National Quality Award was established in the United States.

Deming believes that the loss of competitiveness of U.S. industries in the international marketplace has occurred because of a lack of attention to quality.[2] The fundamental tenet of Deming's view of quality is that the costs of nonconformance (and the resulting loss of customer goodwill) are so high that evaluating the costs of quality is unnecessary. For Deming, measuring quality costs and seeking optimum defect levels is evidence of a failure to understand the problem. The proper objective, in his view, is zero defects. Deming's philosophy is summarized in the 14 points shown in Exhibit 2.

Philip Crosby. Like Deming, Crosby believes that the cost of quality is minimized by "making it right the first time."[3] The objective for any operation should therefore be zero defects. Like Juran, however, Crosby does see a need for measuring quality costs.

Crosby divides quality costs into two components:

- The price of conformance; and
- The price of nonconformance.

The price of conformance includes the explicitly quality-related costs incurred in ensuring that things are done right the first time. The price of nonconformance includes all the costs incurred because quality is not right the first time. According to Crosby, the price of conformance for a well-run company is typically 2 percent to 3 percent of sales, while the price of nonconformance of most firms is closer to 20 to 25 percent of sales.[4]

Crosby argues that there is no such thing as a quality problem; there are only engineering, manufacturing, labor, or other problems that cause poor quality. Crosby does not accept Juran's idea of quality cost analysis as a management control tool. As a tool for improving quality, Crosby proposes instead a "quality management maturity grid" (see Exhibit 3) that traces the development of quality thinking from uncertainty through awakening, enlightenment, and wisdom, to certainty. Senior managers achieve certainty when they deem quality management essential to operations.

While Crosby and Juran do not agree on quality costing as a management tool, their views on the elements of quality

cost can be reconciled. Crosby's price of conformance includes Juran's prevention and inspection costs; his price of nonconformance includes Juran's internal and external failure costs. Also, although Crosby rejects the notion of ongoing cost of quality measurement systems, he does believe it is useful for a company to do a quality cost analysis once when

---

EXHIBIT 2
DEMING'S FOURTEEN MANAGEMENT PRINCIPLES

Requirements for a business whose management plans to remain competitive in providing goods and services that will have a market.

1. Create constancy of purpose toward improving products and services, allocating resources to provide for long-range needs rather than short-term profitability.
2. Adopt the new philosophy for economic stability by refusing to allow commonly accepted levels of delays, mistakes, defective materials and detective workmanship.
3. Cease dependence on mass inspection by requiring statistical evidence of built-in quality in both manufacturing and purchasing functions.
4. Reduce the number of suppliers for the same item by eliminating those that do not qualify with statistical evidence of quality: end the practice to awarding business solely on the basis of price.
5. Search continually for problems in the system to constantly improve processes.
6. Institute modern methods of training to make better use of all employees.
7. Focus supervision on helping people do a better job: Ensure that immediate action is taken on reports of defects, maintenance requirements, poor tools, inadequate operating definitions, or other conditions detrimental to quality.
8. Encourage effective, two-way communication and other means to drive out fear throughout the organization and help people work more productively.
9. Break down barriers between departments by encouraging problem solving through teamwork, combining the efforts of people from different areas such as research, design, sales and production.
10. Eliminate use of numerical goals, posters, and slogans for the work force that ask for new levels of productivity without providing methods.
11. Use statistical methods for continuing improvement of quality and productivity, and eliminate work standards that prescribe numerical quotas.
12. Remove all barriers that inhibit the worker's right to pride of workmanship.
13. Institute a vigorous program of education and retraining to keep up with changes in materials, methods, product design, and machinery.
14. Clearly define top management's permanent commitment to quality and productivity and its obligation to implement all of these principles.

EXHIBIT 3
THE QUALITY MANAGEMENT MATURITY GRID

Quality Management Maturity Grid Rater			Unit		
Measurement Category	Stage 1: Uncertainty	Stage II: Awakening	Stage III: Enlightenment	Stage IV: Wisdom	Stage V: Certainty
Management understanding and attitude	No comprehension of quality as a management tool. Tend to blame quality department for "quality problems."	Recognizing that quality management may be of value but not willing to provide money or time to make it all happen.	While going through quality improvement program learn more about quality management becoming supportive and helpful.	Participating. Understand absolution of quality management. Recognize their personal role in continuing emphasis.	Consider quality management an essential part of company system.
Quality organization status	Quality is hidden in manufacturing or engineering departments. Inspection probably not part of organization. Emphasis on appraisal and sorting.	A strong quality leader is appointed but main emphasis is still on appraisal and moving the product. Still part of manufacturing or other.	Quality department reports to top management. All appraisal is incorporated and manager has role in management of company.	Quality manager to an officer of company. Effective status reporting and preventive action. Involved with consumer affairs and special assignments.	Quality manager on board of directors. Prevention is main concern. Quality is a thought leader.
Problem handling	Problems are fought as they occur. No resolution. Inadequate-definition, lots of yelling and accusations.	Teams are set up to attack major problems. Long-range solutions are not solicited.	Corrective action communication established. Problems are faced openly and resolved in an orderly way.	Problems are identified early in their development. All functions are open to suggestion and improvement.	Except in the most unusual cases, problems are prevented.
Cost of quality as percent of sales	Reported unknown. Actual 20%.	Reported 3%. Actual 18%.	Reported 8%. Actual 12%	Reported 6.5%. Actual 8%.	Reported 2.5%. Actual 2.5%.
Quality improvement actions	No organized activities. No understanding of such activities.	Trying obvious "motivational" short-range efforts.	Implementation of the 14-step program with understanding and establishment of each step.	Continuing the 14-step program and starting to make certain.	Quality improvement is a normal and continued activity.
Summation of company quality posture	"We don't know why we have problems with quality."	Is it absolutely necessary to always have problems with quality?	"Through mangement commitment and quality improvement we are identifying and resolving our problems."	"Defect prevention is a routine part of our operation."	"We know why we do not have problems with quality."

SOURCE: Charles Fine, "Managing Quality: A Comparative Assessment." Booz Allen Manufacturing Issues 1985).

it begins a formal quality management program to determine where the company stands on the maturity grid.

The "Japanese" approach. Although no single quality system is followed by all Japanese firms, there are several common themes in the best-known Japanese quality programs. Charles Fine describes the Japanese approach as follows:

Briefly described, the ultimate objective of Japanese quality management is to improve the quality of life for producers, consumers and investors. The Japanese define quality as uniformity around the target, and their goal is continual improvement toward perfection. The Japanese use cost of quality similarly to Crosby—for directing action, not as a goal in itself.

The Japanese allocate responsibility for quality management among all employees. The workers are primarily responsible for maintaining the system, although they have some responsibility for improving it. Higher up the ladder, managers do less maintaining and more improving. At the highest levels, the emphasis is on breakthrough.

There are a number of now-familiar concepts associated with Japanese quality management. These include commitment to improvement and perfection (kaizen), insistence on compliance, correcting one's own errors, and 100 percent quality checks. *Various practices facilitate quality manage-ment in Japanese corporations—small lot sizes, minimal work-in-process inventory, housekeeping, daily machine checking, and quality circles.[5]*

The basic notions of the Japanese approach are that quality is a journey rather than a destination and that quality enhancement is a fundamental way of life, not a business target. Exhibit 4 summarizes the important features of the approaches to quality described so far. While differences exist, the programs suggested by Juran, Deming, Crosby, and others have common themes that can be collectively described using the familiar catch phrase total quality management.

Traditional views—phase 1 thinking about quality and cost. The characteristics of TQM can best be understood by contrasting TQM with traditional views on quality as exemplified by GM cars during the 1970s, the airline industry during the 1980s, or the forest products industry during the 1990s. Exhibit 5 contrasts the key elements of TQM with elements common to traditional approaches to quality.

Traditional responsibility for quality. In the traditional paradigm, quality problems start in "operations"—poor quality is attributable mainly to workers. The best way to control quality, therefore, is to "inspect it in." This requires a large quality control department whose job is to inspect output and certify that it meets customer specifications.

In the traditional paradigm, an adversarial relationship typically develops between the operations personnel (whose objective is to maximize output) and the quality control staff (whose objective is to monitor output quality). Historically, many U.S. companies have placed more emphasis on output than on quality, because customers did not demand defect-free products. But the environment has changed drastically in the last decade. Customers now demand high quality, particularly now that many companies can provide top quality at competitive prices.

Responsibility for quality under TQM. According to TQM, everyone in the organization shares responsibility for quality; in fact, most of the quality problems start long before the operations stage even begins.

Deming argues that a process can be separated into two parts:

- The system, which is under the control of management; and
- The workers, who are under their own control.

Deming's experience indicates that 85 percent of quality problems are attributable to faulty systems and only 15 per-

EXHIBIT 4
SUMMARY OF APPROACHES TO QUALITY

	Deming	Juran	Crosby	Japanese
Definition of quality	Conformance to specs	Conformance to specs	Conformance of specs	Uniformity around target
Why worry about quality	Competitive position	Profits/quality of life	Profits	Quality of life
Goal of program	Improve competitive position	Decrease COQ	Decrease costs	Continual improvement
Quality goal	Zero defects	Minimize COQ	Zero defects	Zero defects
How to select projects	Pareto analysis defects	Coat analysis	Cost analysis	Cost analysis
How to measure improvement	Direct measurement	COQ data	COQ data and direct measurement maturity grid	Direct measurement
Role of QC department	Low	Extensive	Moderate	Low
Role of top management	Leadership	Leadership participation	Must stress participation improvements	Breakthroughs and zero defects
Role of workers	Maintenance and improvement	Moderate	Moderate	Maintenance and improvements
COQ emphasis	None	High	Moderate	Low
Statistical analysis	High use	For lower management	Mixed	High use
Cultural changes required	Great change required Participative management Needed Grave threat	Little change required Fits traditional culture	New quality attitude Fits traditional culture	Great change required Participative management Need Grave threat
Managing the transition state	No guidance much needed	No guidance little needed	Excellent treatment Classic example	No guidance much needed
Decision	Optimize DMOQ zero defects	Minimize COQ	COQ for management Attention DMOQ for implementation zero defects	Optimize DMOQ zero defects

cent to workers. A system can be faulty for such reasons as the following:

- Difficult-to-execute operation;
- Inferior inputs;
- Inadequate equipment maintenance;
- Poor working conditions; and
- Excessive pressure to maximize output.

Since management designs the system, quality is primarily a management responsibility.

Under TQM, the overriding consideration is to "build quality into the output" rather than "inspect quality into the output." Errors should be detected and corrected at the source. Quality at the source implies that the workers should be held responsible for their work and should not pass defective work downstream. Instead of appointing quality inspectors to locate defects, the workers in a TQM operation are their own inspectors. This philosophy also implies a fundamental change in the role of the quality control department, moving away from inspection and toward facilitation. Instead of inspecting in quality at the output stage, the quality control staff should monitor the process and facilitate the workers' ability to do things right the first time.

Linkages with suppliers. The traditional view argues that obtaining inputs from several suppliers gives a firm bargaining leverage: Competition among the suppliers who are pitted against each other leads (at least theoretically) to lower input prices.

The problem with the traditional view is that quality control becomes extremely difficult if there are numerous suppliers. If the firm starts with inputs of inferior quality, it can prove to be very costly even if the process is in control. For example, in 1984, the Ford Motor Company stopped production of the Tempo and Topaz models in four plants because of a faulty engine part purchased from an outside supplier. Each day production was stopped, Ford lost the opportunity to produce about 2,000 cars.

Quality and dependability, not just price. Under TQM, suppliers are selected based on quality and delivery dependability, rather than price alone. The firm certifies a few suppliers who can deliver defect-free inputs on time at a reasonable price. Typically, the firm will procure most of its requirements for each input item from a single supplier out of a list of certified suppliers. Developing long-term relationships with a single supplier pays off both in terms of higher quality and lower price over the long term. Between 1980 and 1985, for example, Caterpillar reduced its suppliers of drill bits from 24 to 3 and cut drill bits cost by 40 percent.

Sourcing from a single supplier results in higher quality for several reasons:

- The company views the supplier as an integral part of its operations. Thus, the company has the time and the motivation to work with the supplier to improve supplier process quality.

- The supplier, for whom the company's business is significant, is motivated to produce and ship small lots with exact specifications, and to work with the buyer to improve process quality.

Single-sourcing can lead to lower costs as well as higher quality, for such reasons as the following:

- If the firm is confident of the supplier's process quality, the inputs can bypass incoming inspection and thus save inspection costs.
- The firm can save the costs of poor quality downstream that are the direct result of processing inferior quality inputs.
- Given the significant purchasing volume from the company, the supplier can enjoy longer runs and the resulting benefits of scale and experience.

Single-sourcing brings with it the risk of a breakdown in supply for such reasons as strikes, machine breakdowns, or natural disasters. However, these concerns are typically overstated for at least two reasons. First, though the company may procure most inputs from a single supplier, typically one or two backup suppliers are qualified to supply and may get an occasional order to keep the channel open. Second, the company faces similar risks every day in its own operations, because downstream stages are 100 percent dependent on upstream stages.

The development stage. Companies that operate under the traditional point of view separate designers from operations personnel. Designers, who are given a charter to conceive new products or services that have high customer appeal, are told not to feel constrained by current operational capabilities. Unfortunately, this approach often leads to elegant designs that are difficult to implement. Indeed, many quality experts insist that 50 percent of quality problems arise at the design stage. It is difficult to produce a product reliably if it has been designed for performance (thus having, e.g., more parts or more features) without due consideration of ease of manufacturing.

According to TQM, the best way to assure quality is to get operations managers and designers closely involved in developing new products and services. If the designers thoroughly understand the operations process, they are more likely to create designs that not only have high customer acceptance but also fit the firm's operations capability.

Overall quality goal. The traditional paradigm argues that mistakes are inevitable and that it is too expensive to rectify all the defects. In contrast, TQM takes the position that zero defects should be the goal. A firm should analyze the causes of all errors and take actions to remedy them.

Exhibit 5 compares the conflicting viewpoints on the optimal number of defects. According to the traditional view, the lowest cost is attained at some nonzero level of defects. Proponents of this view argue that the cost of removing errors increases as more and more errors are detected and fewer errors remain. The last errors are the most expensive to detect and correct. In sharp contrast, TQM maintains that the lowest cost is attained at zero defects. Supporters of this view reason that even though errors are numerous, the cost of rectifying the last error is no higher than the cost of rectifying the first. Hence, the total cost keeps declining until the last error is removed. In this sense, TQM advocates argue that "quality is free."

Contrasting cost management paradigms. More and more companies are convinced that shifting from the traditional quality philosophy to TQM is essential for success. Such a shift requires fundamental changes in the attitudes that managers and workers have about quality. Far from facilitating this change, traditional cost accounting systems can be a great hindrance to implementing TQM.

The serious shortcomings of traditional cost accounting can be best understood by contrasting it with strategic cost management. Such a comparison is presented in Exhibit 6. Several points are noteworthy:

- Standard cost systems usually institutionalize waste (e.g., scrap and rework) by having "normal allowances" for them. In fact, the cost of the defective units are allocated to "good" units based on elaborate cost procedures. This practice of providing a "normal allowance" for waste panders to the traditional views on quality that it is too expensive to rectify all the defects. In TQM, on the other hand, there is no such thing as "allowable waste."
- In a traditional system, overhead variances are used to evaluate performance. Overhead variance analysis encourages managers to maximize production volume — at the expense of quality — as a way to absorb overhead costs and avoid unfavorable variances.
- Traditional systems highlight raw material price variances and penalize managers for unfavorable price variances. This again reflects the traditional view on quality—obtain raw materials from a large number of suppliers and encourage competition among suppliers to obtain lower input prices. This view, as explained earlier, is detrimental to a company's profitability.
- Traditional systems do not directly reward nonfinancial measures of quality, such as parts-per-million defect rates, first-pass yields, on-time delivery, and shorter cycle time.
- Traditional systems emphasize meeting standard costs. (In fact, a regularly exceeded standard is viewed as not tough enough.) Under TQM, the emphasis is on "continual improvement."

The next section describes in more detail a cost analysis framework that should help companies as they shift from traditional views on quality to TQM.

QUALITY COSTING METHODOLOGY— PHASE 2 THINKING

Cost of quality (COQ) analysis aggregates all the costs to the company of doing things wrong by failing to conform to specifications. COQ is a comprehensive financial measure of conformance quality and can be calculated for individual

---

EXHIBIT 5
CONTRASTING QUALITY PARADIGMS: TRADITIONAL VIEWS ON QUALITY VERSUS TOTAL QUALITY MANAGEMENT

Traditional Paradigm	TQM Paradigm
Responsibility for Quality	
Worker is responsible for poor quality	Everyone is responsible for poor quality
Quality problems start in operations	Majority of the quality problems start long before the operations stage
Inspect quality in	Build quality in
After-the-fact inspection	Quality at the source
Quality inspectors are the gatekeepers of quality	Operators are responsible for quality reliability
Quality control department has large staff	Quality control department has small staff
The focus of the quality control department is to reject quality output	The focus of quality control department is to monitor and facilitate the process
Managers and engineers have the expertise workers serve their needs	Workers have the expertise—managers and engineers serve their needs
Linkages With Suppliers	
Procure from multiple suppliers	Procure from a single supplier
Acceptance sampling of inputs at point of receipt	Certify suppliers who can deliver right quantity, right quality, and on time. No incoming inspection
New Product/Service Development	
Separate designers from operations	Use teams with operations, marketing, and designers
Design for performance (with more parts, more features), not to facilitate operations	Design for performance and ease of processing
Overall Quality Goal	
Zero defects is not practical	Zero defects is the goal
Mistakes are inevitable and have to be inspected out	Mistakes are opportunities to learn and become perfect
It costs too much money to make defect-free products	Quality is free
A "reasonable" tradeoff is the key	Perfection is the key; perfection is a journey, not a destination

---

EXHIBIT 6
CONTRASTING COST MANAGEMENT PARADIGMS: TRADITIONAL COST MANAGEMENT VERSUS STRATEGIC COST MANAGEMENT

Traditional Cost Management	Strategic Cost Management
Standard cost system with "normal" allowance for scrap, waste, rework; zero defect is not practical	No allowance for scrap, waste, rework; zero defect is the concept
Overhead variance analysis; maximize production volume (not quality) to absorb overhead	Overhead absorption is not the key; standard costs and variance analysis are de-emphasized, in general
Variance analysis on raw material price; procure from multiple suppliers to avoid unfavorable price variance; low price/low quality raw materials	No control on raw material price; certify vendors who can deliver right quantity, right quality, and on time
No emphasis on nonfinancial performance measures	Heavy use of nonfinancial measures (parts-per-million defects, percentage yields, scrap, unscheduled machine downtimes, first-pass yields, number of employee suggestions)
No tracking of customer acceptance	Systematic tracking of customer acceptance (customer complaints, order lead time, on-time delivery incidence of failures in customers' locations)
No cost of quality analysis	Quality costing as a diagnostic and management control tool
Control Philosophy:	
The goal is to be in the "top tier" of the "reference group"	The goal is kaizen
The annual target is to meet the standards	Industry norms set the floor
Standards are to be met, not exceeded	The annual target is to beat last year's performance
Standards are "tough" but attainable	Strive to beat this year's target ("continual improvements")
A regularly exceeded standard sets is not tough enough	Each achievement level a new floor for future achievement

locations, individual business units, or the entire firm.

This framework attempts to put dollar figures on all the costs that are attributable to a nonconforming operation. As noted earlier, costs that a company incurs for quality can be grouped into the following categories:

- *Prevention costs.* The sum of all the costs associated with actions taken to plan the process to ensure that defects do not occur. Examples:
—Designing a defect-free manufacturing process;
—Stable product design;
—Employee training and development;
—Quality circles; Preventive maintenance;
—Cost of managing supplier relations to increase the quality of raw inputs received.
- *Appraisal costs.* Those costs associated with measuring the level of quality attained by the system (in other words costs associated with inspecting to ensure that customer requirements arc met). Examples:
—Prototype inspection and testing;
—Receiving inspection and testing;
—In-process inspection; and
—Quality audits of finished outputs.
- *Internal failure costs.* Those costs incurred to rectify defective output before it reaches the customer. Examples:
—Scrap;
—Rework;
—Repair;
—Redesign;
—Reinspection of rework;
—Downtime due to defects; and
—Opportunity cost of lost sales caused by having fewer units of product to sell.
- *External failure costs.* Those costs associated with delivering defective output to the customer. Examples:
—Warranty adjustments;
—Investigation of defects;
—Returns;
—Recalls;
—Liability suits; and
—Loss of customer goodwill.

It should be noted that not all quality costs fit neatly into one or another of these categories. For example, the cost of inspecting raw material might be viewed as either an appraisal cost (looking for defects) or a prevention cost (preventing defective raw materials from fouling the production process). In such cases, placing costs in one category or another is somewhat arbitrary. As long as the company classifies the costs consistently, trends over time in the categories can provide powerful insights.

Exhibit 7 presents the quality costs for a disguised manufacturing company, ABC Corporation, over an eight-year period.[6] Based on the experience of ABC Corporation and the quality cost studies completed by other companies, the following two general conclusions emerge.

- Cost of quality is a big opportunity. When bad quality represents such a significant cost item (25 percent of the total cost for ABC Corporation), quality management represents the most significant opportunity for improved profitability.
- Firms spend quality dollars in the wrong place. Companies spend far more on internal and external failure costs than on prevention and appraisal costs, and more on

EXHIBIT 7
AN ILLUSTRATIVE EXAMPLE OF COST OF QUALITY ANALYSIS FOR ABC CORPORATION

Quality cost Category	1982	1984	1986	1988
		(Thousands of Dollars)		
Units produced	10,000	10,000	20,000	
Prevention	$ 200	$ 400	$ 600	$ 800
Appraisal	400	800	800	400
Internal failure	200	$4,800	1,600	600
External failure	4,000	800	400	200
Total	$ 4,800	$4,400	$3,400	$ 2,000
Total manufacturing cost	$20,000			$25,000
Total quality cost as percent of total cost	25%			8%

appraisal than on prevention. This was true for ABC Corporation in 1982. In companies in which total quality cost is in the range of 25 percent of sales, category 4 is usually the largest. When total quality cost is in the 5 percent range, category 1 is usually the largest.

Interaction among the four categories. Spending money on prevention can result in more than offsetting cost savings on the other categories. Thus, it is possible to maintain or improve quality while, at the same time, dramatically lowering quality costs. For ABC Corporation in Exhibit 7, as product quality increased over the eight years, total quality costs declined by 60 percent. The firm achieved this by consciously changing the mix of prevention, appraisal, and failure costs. Prevention and appraisal costs doubled, while internal and external failure costs declined by over 80 percent.

The implication is that improving quality by spending more on upstream activities (prevention costs) is a good investment for any organization. One rule of thumb is that for every dollar a firm spends on prevention, it can eventually save $10 in appraisal and failure costs.

The impact of investing upstream can yield benefits over several years, but there is a time lag between expenditures on prevention and the resulting decrease in failure costs. When ABC Corporation doubled prevention costs in 1984, there was no immediate reduction in downstream costs. This suggests that when changing the mix, management must be prepared to see quality costs increase before they decrease.

Companies that adopt TQM should anticipate interactions among the four categories of quality costs. As ABC Corporation doubled appraisal costs in 1984, the internal failure costs increased dramatically, but the external failure costs decreased even more dramatically. This makes sense: The improved inspection system caused more defects to be detected before they reached the customer. Management should not be surprised to see repair and rework departments exceeding their budgets as a result of increased appraisal spending. Similarly, warranty and customer return costs should show a favorable trend. These trends could be anticipated in setting budgets during a period in which the quality cost mix changes.

Conventional reporting a barrier to TQM. Conventional reporting formats can be a barrier to TQM initiatives, whereas cost of quality reporting can help TQM. Conventional reports often discourage TQM efforts, because any additional costs incurred in prevention appear immediately on a manager's performance report but the resulting benefits (e.g., a reduction in external failure costs) are not fully quantified and are therefore not recognized.

For ABC Corporation, a manager's performance report in the conventional framework would report the total prevention, appraisal, and internal failure costs. These amounted to $800,000 in 1982 and increased dramatically to $3.6 million in 1984. This might imply an adverse performance, whereas COQ reporting tells a very different story. The big gain is in external failure cost, most of which is an opportunity cost that does not show up at all in conventional reports.

One cautionary note should be offered about quality cost reduction. Quality costs, like many other costs, have the frustrating characteristic of being variable on the way up, but fixed on the way down. That is, it is not as easy as one might think to reduce quality costs. We may be able to reduce the level of defective output by 25 percent, but that may not necessarily enable us to reduce the rework department's work force by 25 percent. Reducing that department requires a conscious management decision to scale back or even eliminate the function.

Just as quality costs will not disappear right away, neither will "quality revenues" appear immediately. It is not always the case that customers are anxious to get better quality. Many successful firms have built up, over time, an infrastructure for dealing with the bad quality they receive from suppliers, such as raw material inspection systems or more sophisticated handling equipment. Since much of this infrastructure is a fixed cost, such a customer may find little immediate advantage in a supplier's higher conformance input. In addition, a customer who uses multiple sources of supply may find no advantage—indeed, there may be a disadvantage in the short term—in receiving a higher-quality product from one supplier. It may well be that the industry leaders are those firms that have best learned how to neutralize the bad quality they are receiving. A supplier who begins offering better quality may thus, strangely, be better able to sell it to the less successful firms that have not figured out how to offset bad incoming quality.

COQ reporting. Since investments "upstream" yield benefits over several years, it is often sufficient if quality reporting is done once a year. By preparing a COQ report once a year, a firm can maintain pressure on managers and workers to "continually" improve performance toward the ideal goal of "zero defects."

COQ measurement cannot be the sole basis for facilitating TQM efforts. It should be supplemented with specific and timely feedback on nonfinancial measures of quality as well.[7] Some examples are as follows:

- Suppliers:
—Number and frequency of defective units delivered, by each supplier; and
—Number and frequency of deliveries not on time, by each supplier.
- Product design:
—Number of parts in a product; and
—Percentage of common versus unique parts in a product.
- Production process:
—Percentage yields (good units to total units) (this is a measure of quality at the output stage and does not necessarily measure the firm's efforts on prevention);
—First-pass yields (percentage of units finished without any rework) (this measure reflects the results of the firm's efforts on prevention);
—Scrap;
—Rework;
—Unscheduled machine breakdowns;
—Number and duration of times the production and delivery schedules were not met; and
—Number of employee suggestions. (General Motors averages four suggestions per employee per year, while Toyota averages 61).[8]
- Marketing:
—Number of customer complaints;
—Level of customer satisfaction (which is measured by administering questionnaires to customers);
—Warranty claims;
—Field service expenses; and
—Number and frequency of product returns.

There are two major advantages with these nonfinancial measures:

- Most of them can be reported on almost a real time basis; and
- Corrective actions on these measures can be initiated almost immediately.

Thus, reporting performance on nonfinancial measures is essential to providing continuous feedback to managers and workers in their pursuit of better quality. We view COQ reporting and the related nonfinancial measures as both providing useful information. COQ reporting provides the big picture, whereas the nonfinancial measures give ongoing, actionable feedback about a TQM implementation.

COST OF QUALITY ANALYSIS— PHASE 3 THINKING

This concluding section of the article synthesizes the several schools of thought on measuring quality costs. They range from belief in regular quantification and monitoring of cost of quality to strict attention to zero defects but no attention to cost measurement. There are, nonetheless, several common themes:

- Poor quality costs far more than management usually realizes.
- Most firms' expenditures on quality occur in the wrong places (i.e., they fix things rather than doing them right the first time).
- Spending on prevention reduces the need for inspection and can potentially eliminate internal and external failure costs.
- Large cost savings or revenue opportunities exist in creating customer goodwill by consistently providing conforming products and services.
- For quality programs to succeed, top management must be committed to quality and must accept full responsibility for it.
- Conventional management accounting (i.e., standard costs, overhead variance analysis, analysis of raw material price variances) is a great barrier in implementing TQM.

Supporting TQM. There are three possible approaches to developing and using management accounting systems in support of TQM (see Exhibit 8). These approaches roughly correspond to the approaches of Deming, Crosby, and Juran. A company that adopts TQM for the first time might benefit by starting with Juran's approach, which calls for an explicit quantification of quality costs (as in the third approach in Exhibit 8). The ultimate goal should be to make quality part of a company's culture and way of life so that quality cost measurements ultimately become unnecessary (which is the Deming approach).

Some firms that have experimented with COQ reporting (including Texas Instruments and Florida Power and Light) have decided that formalized reporting requirements are not an aid to enhanced quality. For firms just starting TQM programs, however, the benefits of formal cost reporting are sufficiently important to warrant the risk that the reporting may engender game-playing that would hinder quality enhancement effort; this risk can be managed.

This article has summarized the strategic cost management perspective on quality. As a firm's quality management

EXHIBIT 8
THREE POSSIBLE MANAGEMENT ACCOUNTING RESPONSIBILITIES

Proponent	Approach	Role for Management Accountants
1. Deming	Don't do quality costing analysis. Just spend the money "upstream" to do things "right" the first time.	High
2. Crosby	Do a COQ analysis as a "special" study (to assess the stage of quality management). Do not use this as a management tool on an ongoing basis. Do not prepare periodic COQ reports.	
3. Juran	Prepare qualify costing reports on a periodic basis (say, once a year) as a management control tool.	Low

EXHIBIT 9
THE CONTROLLERSHIP ROLE IN TOTAL QUALITY MANAGEMENT: FOUR POSSIBLE APPROACHES

1. Cost of quality analysis as a regular management reporting and control tool. Examples of this approach include:
   - The companies referenced by Joseph Juran (trade-off between price of conformance and price of nonconformance) in his books;
   - Formosa Plastics; and
   - Ford Motor Company in the 1980s.

   Formal COQ reporting as a regular control tool applied to Ford throughout most of the 1980s and Texas Instruments until about 1990. According to *Management Accounting* in a 1991 article this approach was still being followed then by Formosa Plastics, one of the largest Taiwanese manufacturing firms.

2. Focus on reducing the price of nonconformance, including opportunity losses. Examples of this approach include:

   - Tennant Company;
   - Westinghouse; and
   - Xerox.

   This second approach assumes that "conformance" (i.e., the price of conformance, in Crosby's terminology) will continue at a high level and will be managed by means of budgets and continuous improvement programs for critical nonfinancial performance indicators.
   If spending on conformance remains consistently high, the reporting focus can switch to "nonconformance" costs (i.e., the price nonconformance, in Crosby's terminology), with *specific* inclusion of the opportunity cost of bad quality. The goal becomes a steady reduction in the price of nonconformance toward zero. In 1992, many companies with a strong TQM commitment (e.g., Xerox, Westinghouse, and the Tennant Company) were following this approach.

3. Focus on nonfinancial, "hard science production information to monitor TQM progress with an emphasis on input measures and statistical process control (SPC). Examples of this approach include:
   - Texas Instruments—Materials and Controls Group; and
   - Paper Industry—Daishowa Paper Company (Japan).

   This approach deemphasizes formal COQ cost reporting systems in favor of formal nonfinancial reporting, with a heavy emphasis on continuously improving quality in operations. One name for this is SPC. Notable examples of the success of this approach are Daishowa Paper Company and the Materials and Controls Group in Texas Instruments.

4. Focus on nonfinancial, "hard science" production information to monitor TQM progress with an emphasis on *output* measures of conformance. Examples include:
   - Motorola-ACIS Division;
   - IBM (the MDQ Program); and
   - Analog Devices, Inc.

   This approach also deemphasizes cost reporting in favor of nonfinancial measures, but the focus here is on output measures rather than input measures. Motorola's well-known Six Sigma Program for customer-reported defects in its integrated circuits division is a good example. IBM has announced a similar program for eradicating customer-reported defects, which it calls MDQ for market-determined quality. Analog Devices[10] is another example of a firm whose quality reporting emphasis is on defect-free deliveries rather than on cost reports.

program develops, the approach to COQ reporting can take several different forms. Exhibit 9 summarizes four different approaches in use at various companies today.[9]

Whichever approach a firm chooses, quality is such an important strategic variable that management accounting can no longer ignore it. One way or another, a strategically effective management reporting system must deal explicitly with the issue of quality.

John K. Shank is Noble Foundation Professor of Managerial Accounting and Vijay Govindarajan is Earl C. Daum Professor of Management at the Amos Tuck School of Business, Dartmouth College, Hanover, New Hampshire.

Notes

1. J.M. Juran and Frank M. Gryna, Jr., *Quality Planning and Analysis* (New York: McGraw-Hill, 1970).

2. W. Edwards Deming, Quality, *Productivity and Competitive Position* (Cambridge, Massachusetts: MIT Center for Advanced Engineering Study, 1982).

3. Philip B. Crosby, *Quality is Free* (New York: McGraw-Hill, 1979).

4. Philip B. Crosby, *Quality Without Tears* (New York: McGraw-Hill, 1984): 86.

5. Charles Fine, "Managing Quality: A Comparative Assessment," in *Booz Allen Manufacturing Issues* (New York: Booz Allen, 1985).

6. See James B. Simpson and David L. Muthler, "Quality Costs: Facilitating the Quality Initiative," *Journal of Cost Management* (Spring 1987): 25–34.

7. See Joseph Fisher, "Use of Nonfinancial Performance Measures," *Journal of Cost Management* (Spring 1992): 31–38.

8. Thomas P. Edmonds, Bor-Yi Tsay, and Wen-Wei Lin, "Analyzing Quality Costs," *Management Accounting* (November 1989): 25–29.

9. Lawrence Carr, "Applying Costs of Quality to a Service Business," *Sloan Management Review* (Summer 1992): 72–77.

10. Robert A. Howell et al., Cost Management for Tomorrow: Seeking the Competitive Edge," *Financial Executives Research Foundation Series on Innovative Management* (1992): 127–149.

From J. K. Shank and V. Govindarajan, "Measuring the 'Cost of Quality': A Strategic Cost Management Perspective," *Journal of Cost Management* (Spring 1994): 5-17. Reprinted with permission.

Question

13.2 Does Shank and Govindarajan's view of total quality management depend on only one of the four major schools of quality thought? If so, which one? Explain your answer in detail.

13.3 Customer Profitability Analysis: Challenges and New Directions

By George Foster, Mahendra Gupta, and Leif Sjoblom

Executive Summary
Customer account profitability (CAP) represents an important future direction of management accounting.

- Paradoxically, most management accounting systems focus not on the customer but on products, departments, or geographic regions. Only rarely can a management accounting system produce customer profitability figures.
- The "why?" of customer profitability analysis can be reduced to the simple statement that each dollar of revenue does not contribute equally to profit.
- Profitability depends not only on the unit cost of a product or service, but also on the 'back end' services required, including marketing, distribution, and customer service.
- One challenge in customer profitability analysis is to budget for and track the profitability of customers over extended periods of time.

Many companies claim to be customer-driven. Companies typically emphasize the customer when describing what they mean by a "quality" product or service, as the examples below show:

- *Corning International:* "Providing the requirements of the customer, on time, every time."
- *Federal Express:* "100 percent customer satisfaction, by performing 100 percent to our standards, as perceived by the customer."
- *Procter and Gamble:* "The unyielding and continually improving effort by everyone in an organization to understand, meet, and exceed the expectations of customers.

Paradoxically, most management accounting systems focus not on the customer but on products, departments, or geographic regions. Only rarely can a management accounting system produce customer profitability figures.

There is growing recognition that customer account profitability (CAP) represents an important future direction of management accounting.[1] This article explains challenges in CAP and discusses possible future directions. The field research on which it is based includes:

- A questionnaire that was sent to marketing managers and marketing controllers; and
- Interviews with respondents to the questionnaire.

Much of this article draws on qualitative responses given in these interviews and the questionnaire.

FOCUS OF CUSTOMER ACCOUNT PROFITABILITY

The focus of CAP can vary according to the context. At the lowest level, it focuses on individual customers. At a more aggregate level, it can focus on groupings of customers (e.g., groupings by revenues, size of average transaction, number of transactions, or time since the business association began).

CAP can also focus on different *distribution channels*. In a computer company, for example, a CAP analysis might consider major computer chain customers (e.g., Computerland), large retail stores, independent retail stores, corporate accounts, and direct-mail accounts.

WHY USE CUSTOMER PROFITABILITY ANALYSIS?

The "why?" of customer profitability analysis can be reduced to the simple statement that each dollar of revenue does not contribute equally to net income. Differences in customer profitability can arise from either differences in revenue or differences in cost.

Revenue differences. Revenue differences across customers of a company arise from many sources, including:

- Differences in the prices charged per unit to different customers;
- Differences in the selling volume levels across customers;
- Differences in the products or services delivered to different customers; and
- Differences in the items provided without charge to different customers.

Differences in cost. Differences in cost across the spectrum of company's customers arise from differences in the way different customers use the company's resources. Exhibit 1 shows a value chain of business functions to help illustrate these differences.

For example, companies with manufacturing operations reported that many of their customers differed most in their use of "downstream" functions, such as marketing, distribution, and customer service.

Here are some representative responses to the question about differences in marketing support provided to customers:

- "Some require full support. Others require none. Most are in between. But it does make a difference."
- "Customers with extensive programs versus standard programs require monitoring and communication."

Similarly, pharmaceutical companies that were interviewed reported that doctors differed greatly in the sales time required to promote products to the doctors and in the quantity and range of complimentary products the doctors requested. One respondent stressed that there was not a high correlation between the sales or gross margin for a doctor and the marketing resources consumed by that doctor.

Price discounts and other forms of revenue offsets are a key form of marketing support. Feedback in the interviews indicated that price discounting differs greatly across customers and not always in a way corporate management intends or views as optimal.

Differences in distribution channels. Here are some of the responses on questionnaires about differences in distribution channels:

- "We have the full spectrum of customers, from residential to major industrial customers. Their product use varies widely."
- "Industrial and distribution accounts demand very little beyond a competitive price and quality product. Home centers demand a great deal more service."
- "Customers vary greatly. Ten percent of our business is through organized retailers. Ninety percent is still through mom and pop shelves."

Differences in customer service levels.[2] To illustrate some of the differences between service levels expected by different customers, consider the following responses on questionnaires:

- "Some clients require large teams of people to work around the clock; others like considerable amounts of entertainment."
- "Profitability depends not only on the unit cost of performing work, but also on the 'back end' services required."

When individual customers or groups of customers can influence a company's upstream activities, the customers usually differ markedly in how they use the company's resources. For example, some computer assembly companies permit large customers to order specially configured combinations of hardware and software, which affects many upstream activities. Similarly, some telecommunication assembly companies offer their customers considerable flexibility in how PBX systems are designed and manufactured.

Service companies. Companies in the service sector vary considerably in how customers use their resources. For example, companies with large infrastructures to deliver services (e.g., hotels and transportation providers) often have well defined-options of different levels of service. By contrast, companies with less infrastructure (e.g., law firms and engineering-design firms) can tailor their activities for individual customers in all areas of the value chain.

Illustration of customer profitability analysis. Blue Ridge Company manufactures and sells sport

EXHIBIT 1
VALUE CHAIN OF BUSINESS FUNCTIONS

Research and Development → Product Design → Operations/ Manufacturing → Marketing → Distribution → Customer Service towels, which differ in size, color, logos, embroidery, and dying.[3]

Individual customers of Blue Ridge vary in size as follows:

- *Large customers:* National retail chains.
- *Midsize customers:* Smaller retail chains and licensing agents for sport teams.
- *Small customers:* Customers who purchase towels in response to advertisements, mail-order campaigns, and other forms of marketing.

Exhibit 2 presents summary data about these three customer groupings. Panel A of Exhibit 2 shows actual data, while Panel B presents the same data in percentage form. Note the heterogeneity among the three customer groupings, especially the following:

- *Average number of units sold per order:* large = 100,250/133 = 754; midsize = 58,544/845 = 69; small = 117,406/5,130 = 23.
- *Percentage of units sold that are embroidered:* large = 5,959/100,250 = 5.9 percent; midsize = 6,490/58,544 = 11.0 percent; and small = 29,394/117,406 = 25.0 percent; and
- *Percentage of units sold that are dyed:* large = 20,536/100,250 = 20.5 percent; midsize = 9,935/58,544 = 17.0 percent; small = 12,328/117,406 = 10.5 percent.
- *Average selling price per unit sold:* large = $308,762/100,250 = $3.08; midsize = $183,744/58,544 = $3.14; small = $318,024/117,406 = $2.71.

Blue Ridge faced intense pressure from several large retail chains for price reductions beyond those already provided. To facilitate responding to price reduction requests, Blue Ridge initiated a customer profitability study.

Activity-based Costing. An activity-based costing (ABC) approach was applied to Blue Ridge's marketing, distribution, and customer service areas to better document how each customer differentially used resources. The initial focus of the study was on the three customer groupings rather than on the profitability of individual accounts within those groupings.

For each customer, Blue Ridge traced direct costs such as discounts, commissions, and licensing fees for logos. The activity-based cost pools and the related activity drivers were as follows:

Cost Pools	Cost Driver
Purchase orders	Number of orders
Shipping activities	Number of shipments
Invoices	Number of invoices
Product samples and catalogues	Sales dollars
Marketing by customer type	Sales dollars

PROFITABILITY OF LARGE CUSTOMERS

The key conclusion of the ABC analysis was that the large customer group contributed by far the most toward Blue Ridge's total operating income, as the following table shows:

	Percent of Revenues	Percent of Operating Income
Large customers	38.1%	67.3%
Midsize customers	22.7%	32.8%
Small customers	39.2%	-0.1%

Given the importance of the large customer group, Blue Ridge realized that the large customers were potentially

---

EXHIBIT 2
PROFILE OF CUSTOMER GROUPINGS OF BLUE RIDGE

Panel A	Large	Midsize	Small
Number of customers	8	154	824
Units sold	100,250	58,544	117,406
Sales volume $	$308,762	$183,744	$318,024
Number of orders received	133	845	5,130
Number of shipments	147	923	5,431
Number of units embroidered	5,959	6,490	29,394
Number of units dyed	20,536	9,935	12,328

PANEL B	Large	Midsize	Small
Number of customers	0.8%	15.6%	83.6%
Units sold	36.3	21.2	42.5
Sales volume $	38.1	22.7	39.2
Number of orders received	2.2	13.8	84.0
Number of shipments	2.3	14.2	83.5
Number of units embroidered	14.2	15.5	70.3
Number of units dyed	48.0	23.2	28.8

at risk. Competitors were likely to recognize how profitable the larger customers were and might therefore bid aggressively for these accounts.

Understanding profitability. To understand large customer profitability, an individual customer study was conducted. Exhibit 3 shows individual customer profitability figures for the eight large customers. Panel A of Exhibit 3 ranks the customers based on revenue, while Panel B ranks the customers based on operating income.

Exhibit 4 shows the customer profitability data from Exhibit 3 in graphical form.

- *Revenues:* Panel A of Exhibit 4 ranks customers on revenues with operating income shown as a second column.
- *Operating income:* Panel B of Exhibit 4 ranks customers on operating income.
- *Ratio of operating income to revenues:* Panel C of Exhibit 4 ranks customers on the basis of the ratio of operating income to revenue.

As Panel B of Exhibit 3 shows, three of the eight large customers (B, D, and A) provide 80 percent of the total operating income for large customers. Two of the eight large customers (E and G) cause operating losses.

Options. Blue Ridge has the following options when attempting to improve its profitability:

1. *Reduce setup times:* Reduce embroidery or dying costs by reducing setup times.
2. *Change order interfaces:* Change the order interface with customers to reduce costs and speed the process (e.g., through use of faxes or electronic data exchange).
3. *Change customer Options:* Change options available to customers (e.g., trim the embroidery options).
4. *Charge for all extras:* Fully price out all options so that customers are given economic signals to change their behavior.
5. *Be consistent with revenue offsets:* Maintain consistency when making price discounts and other price offsets. For example, several CAP studies have found little economic rationale to the discounts provided to customers. In one study, an unprofitable customer that was not growing received the largest price discount, in part because of a short-run sales incentive scheme that reinforced revenue increases regardless of profitability.
6. *Identify "preferred" customers:* Identify the key characteristics of a preferred customer and use the resulting profile to guide sales strategy.
7. *Motivate salespeople appropriately:* Reward Blue Ridge salespeople on the basis of customer profitability as computed by an ABC system.
8. *Motivate customers appropriately:* Change the behavior of Blue Ridge customers (e.g., by encouraging them to batch small orders into larger orders).

EXHIBIT 3
CUSTOMER PROFITABILITY ANALYSIS OF LARGE CUSTOMERS OF BLUE RIDGE

PANEL A: Ranked on Revenues

Customer	Revenues	Operating Income Income	Cumulative Revenues	Cumulative Revenue Total Revenues of Large Customers
A	$71,632	$21,662	$71,632	23.2%
B	64,531	37,616	136,163	44.1
C	44,153	15,707	180,316	58.4
D	39,521	23,407	219,837	71.2
E	30,915	-4,209	250,752	81.2
F	25,627	13,654	276,379	89.5
G	18,279	-10,874	294,888	95.4
H	14,104	5,899	308,762	100.0

PANEL B: Ranked on Operating Income

Customer	Operating Income	Cumulative Income	Cumulative % Operating Income of Large Customers
B	$37,616	$37,616	36.6%
D	23,407	61,023	59.4
A	21,662	82,685	80.5
C	15,707	98,392	95.8
D	13,654	112,046	109.1
H	5,699	117,745	114.7
E	-4,209	113,536	110.6
G	-10,874	102,662	100.0

EXHIBIT 4
ALTERNATIVE PRESENTATIONS OF THE PROFITABILITY OF BLUE RIDGE'S LARGEST CUSTOMERS

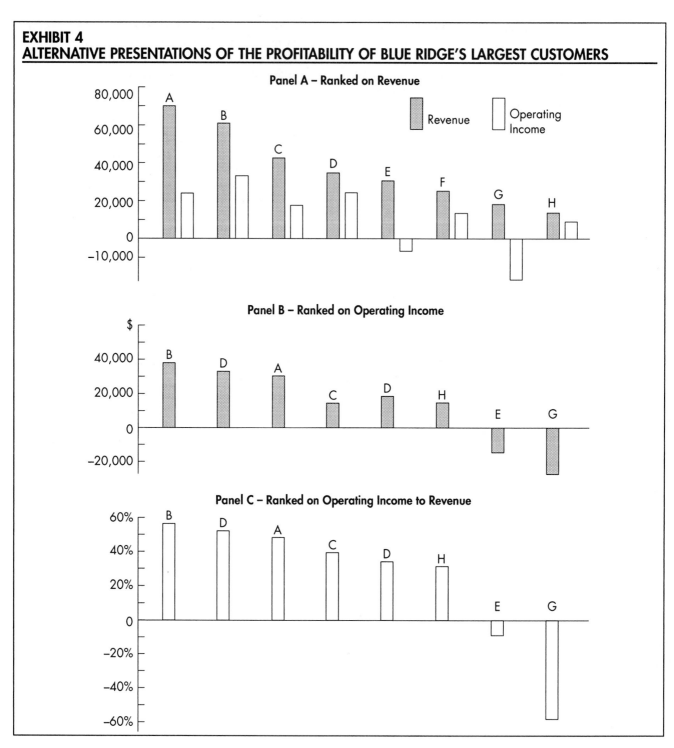

9. *Outsource distribution for some customers:* Outsource the selling and distribution for very small customers to independent distributors.

KEY FEATURES OF ANALYSES OF CUSTOMER ACCOUNT PROFITABILITY
Several features of CAP analysis make it distinctive:[4]

• *Entire value chain:* CAP analysis cuts across costs from potentially all parts of the value chain;

• *Multiple transactions:* CAP analysis focuses on multiple transactions of a customer rather than any single transaction;

• *Multiple products:* CAP analysis focuses on multiple products bought by a single customer rather than a single product bought by multiple customers.

• *Customer-specific costs:* CAP analysis captures costs that are related to a customer but are not specific to a product, service, department, or geographic area; and

• *Aggregate or narrow focus:* CAP analysis can be kept at a highly aggregate level (e.g., different distribution outlets) or brought to the very granular level of individual customers.

These features require major changes in the way most management accounting systems are designed and operated, as the sections below discuss.

CHALLENGES IN DEVELOPING CUSTOMER PROFITABILITY INFORMATION

There are at least four challenges that must be overcome to analyze customer account profitability:

- How to develop reliable customer revenue and customer cost figures.
- How to recognize future downstream costs of customers.
- How to incorporate a multiperiod horizon into the analysis.
- How to recognize different drivers of customer costs.

The sections below discuss each of these challenges in turn.

CHALLENGE NUMBER 1: HOW TO DEVELOP RELIABLE CUSTOMER REVENUE AND CUSTOMER COST FIGURES

Many companies that expressed strong interest in CAP analysis cited problems in reliably estimating customer revenues and customer costs. These problems can be categorized as customer revenue analysis and customer cost analysis.

Customer revenue analysis. Tracking customer revenues involves a variety of challenges, including the following:

- *Different distribution channels or geographic regions:* A customer may make purchases in different distribution channels and in different geographic regions. Many companies cannot readily accumulate revenue data by customer for different distribution channels or geographic regions.
- *Differing decentralization of purchasing:* Customers differ in the degree of decentralization of their purchasing. Consider, for example, a North American tire manufacturing company that sells tires to Ford Canada, Ford USA, and Ford Mexico. If Ford completely decentralizes purchasing decisions to each geographic region, it is reasonable to classify each Ford subsidiary as a separate company. But if Ford centralizes purchasing decisions, it is reasonable to consider Ford North America as the sole customer.
- *Multiple names and codes:* A single customer may have multiple names and codings. Thus, the computer files may have many more customer names than actual customers. (One company reported major problems in this area.)

- *Different credit and payment patterns:* Customers may have different mixes of credit and cash payments. Small companies with a significant percentage of cash receipts may not systematically and reliably track cash receipts to individual customers.
- *Revenue recognition issues:* Many revenue recording issues must be addressed to develop reliable individual customer revenue numbers. Recording issues arise, for example, from barter transactions, possible discounting for extended payment periods, and inconsistent treatment of reductions from list prices. Price discounts should be a major focus in companies where salespeople have discretion over prices charged to ensure that discounts are given only to customers who warrant price reductions.

Customer cost analysis. Tracking customer costs involves one or more of the following challenges:

- *Data not collected by customers:* Accounting systems are usually designed to track costs by product, geographic area, or business function; they do not have customers as the focal point. Many companies noted that their accounting systems failed to track the costs of downstream areas like marketing, distribution, and customer service to individual customers.
- *Lack of source records:* Many of the source records required to track customer usage of company resources do not exist. For example, salespeople may not keep records about how much time they spend with individual customers (though the increasing use of hand-held calculators is reducing this obstacle).
- *Data needed for the entire value chain:* Accumulating costs by individual customers requires the accumulation of costs from many parts of the value chain. Some companies emphasized that their information systems cannot interact with each other. For example, manufacturing and marketing databases are often on separate systems, which makes integration difficult.
- *Allocating costs:* Many costs of interest are common costs — i.e., not specific to individual customers. For example, costs such as research and development and advertising are not customer-specific. These costs must be allocated rather than traced to individual customers. (It may be necessary to develop customer-based costing hierarchies, as described later.)

Systems problems. The most consistently cited problem in developing customer profitability reports is systems. Quotations from the responses to the questionnaire concerning this major challenges include:

- "Systems, systems, systems."
- "Some systems are not integrated. Customer systems are unreliable and difficult to maintain."
- "Computer system software."
- "Resources to manage and maintain information."

Managers who were interviewed stated that system problems loomed larger in analyses of customer profitability than with other management accounting analyses because of the need to accumulate information across business functions and geographic areas.

CHALLENGE NUMBER 2: HOW TO RECOGNIZE FUTURE DOWNSTREAM COSTS OF CUSTOMERS

Traditional costing systems match revenues with costs. The usual emphasis is on costs incurred in the current period or on allocating costs that were capitalized in prior periods. Most systems pay less attention to capturing the future costs of today's actions, though progress has been made with some industries and specialized areas of accounting.

Accounting systems now often recognize as costs of the current period the costs of pensions and medical benefits that will not actually be paid until much later. Similarly, life insurance accounting recognizes as costs of the current period outlays for death benefits that will not be paid until future periods. Moreover, customers with different expected costs in the future (in terms of the timing and magnitude of benefit payments) are priced differently.

Two areas illustrate the challenges of recognizing as current expenses the future costs of today's actions: environment costs and litigation costs.

Environmental costs. Much diversity exists around the world concerning the regulation of environmental costs. In some jurisdictions, for example, customers of automobiles have final responsibility for the disposal of vehicles, while in other jurisdictions, the automobile companies have this responsibility. As a result, customers in different jurisdictions who buy the same product have different life-cycle costs.

Another environmental example relates to the disposal of lead batteries. Increasingly, companies are providing customers return envelopes so that the companies that sell the batteries can recycle or dispose of the batteries. Similarly, companies that sell potentially toxic products may find themselves liable for the cleanup costs faced by individual customers. Those customers that have taken a more responsible attitude toward cleanup of toxic waste will probably have much lower life-cycle costs to the producer.

The challenges these costs pose for accurate customer costing are twofold:

1. To estimate the magnitude of the environmental costs; and
2. To assign the environmental costs to appropriate time periods so that customer profit reports can be calculated. (Some environmental costs occur long after a product is purchased by the customer. A key challenge, therefore, is to assign the costs to the periods in which the costs are caused rather than delay recognition until when the costs are actually incurred.)

Litigation costs. Companies are increasingly being sued by their customers. One high-profile example was breast implants: A settlement of over $4 billion to women with implants has been viewed as inadequate by the plaintiffs. For many years, companies that produced breast implants reported substantially higher profits than they will actually earn given the costs over the entire life cycle of the product. Many customers may receive a settlement amount that exceeds the purchase price they paid for the product. Note, moreover, that different settlement amounts may apply to U.S. versus foreign customers, which will make the U.S. customers more unprofitable than the foreign customers.

This example extends well beyond breast implants. Products that are placed within the human body itself or that later prove hazardous could lead to litigation costs in the future that may exceed the initial purchase price by several orders of magnitude.

There are several dilemmas concerning customer costing:

- *Providing estimates:* Should estimates be made of possible litigation costs? A company's legal advisors may argue against recognizing possible future litigation on the grounds that doing so may be interpreted as admission of a legal liability. Even internal recognition of potential liabilities may be viewed as unacceptable on the grounds the documents could be leaked or uncovered in the course of litigation.
- *Method for estimating:* If an estimate is made, what method should be used?

Conceptually, there is a positive probability that customer-related litigation costs will arise for almost all products. Certain products, however, are clearly more likely to lead to liability than others. The current approach of simply assuming that all future liability costs will be zero can lead to a substantial overstatement of customer profits.

CHALLENGE NUMBER 3: HOW TO INCORPORATE A MULTIPERIOD HORIZON INTO THE ANALYSIS

The importance of having a long-term perspective in business decisions is frequently emphasized. For example, brand managers need a long-term perspective because some brands can persist for many years. Consider, for example, soft drink brands like Coca-Cola and Pepsi, or confectionery brands such as Kit Kat and Mars.

The notion of a product life cycle was created, in part, to emphasize how front-end expenditures are required before product revenues are realized in later periods. The same reasoning can be applied to customer profitability analysis.

The life insurance industry recognizes the multiperiod nature of its policies when pricing policies for individual customers. Each life insurance policy typically has a large front-end cost, which includes:

- The initial marketing and sales effort to obtain an individual customer lead;
- The specific customer-related costs of the sales representative's time, the alternative policy profiles, and any medical visits; and
- The contract-related costs.

The profitability of a written whole-life contract is, in part, a function of how many policy renewals occur before the policyholder either lets the policy lapse or dies. A multi-period approach is explicit in the pricing of the whole-life contract and in the cost conditions imposed on a policyholder who voluntarily lets a policy lapse.

Tracking profitability over time. One challenge in customer profitability analysis is to budget for and track the profitability of customers over extended periods of time. Budgeting for customer profitability over an extended time is critical when making decisions based on reports such as those shown in Exhibits 3 and 4 for the Blue Ridge Company. Consider, for example, the two unprofitable large accounts—Customers E and G. At first, it may seem self-evident that Blue Ridge should drop these two accounts. This could be the wrong decision, however, because a seemingly "unprofitable" customer in the short run may turn out to be profitable in the long run.

Several companies that have experimented with customer profitability reports require sales people to prepare budgeted sales figures for a three-year horizon beyond the current year for each major customer. Having such information for Blue Ridge would provide a basis for determining whether accounts E and G are expected to grow, stay the same, or decline. If this information were supplemented with expected profitability estimates for E and G over a three-year horizon, managers at Blue Ridge would be in a better position for making decisions about which customers to keep. A customer that is unprofitable now and expected to remain unprofitable requires a different set of corrective actions than a customer that is unprofitable now but expected to be profitable in the foreseeable future.

Long-term profitability budgets. Having a profile of the profitability of customers in the past and statistics about the duration of customer relationships facilitates preparation of long-term customer profitability budgets. One proposed measure of the success of a company's new product development is the percentage of total revenues from new products. For example, one U.S. company aims to have at least 50 percent of its sales from products developed in the preceding five years. A comparable statistic can be developed for customer revenues, but interpretation of such a percentage figure requires caution.

Ideally, the aim is to maximize retention of existing profitable customers and to increase the rate at which new profitable customers are added. However, an increase in the percentage of revenues from new customers could be a negative signal if one or more of the following occurs:

- Existing profitable customers are not retained: or
- The new customers attracted are not profitable.

Note the key role customer profitability analysis plays in either scenario when managers interpret changes in the percentage of revenues from new customers.

Exhibit 5 compares the first general customer profitability reports (Panel A) with the extensions outlined in this article:

- Traditional viewpoint with lifetime responsibility (Panel B);
- An extended value chain viewpoint (Panel C); and
- A long-term customer relationship viewpoint (Panel D)

CHALLENGE NUMBER 4: HOW TO RECOGNIZE DIFFERENT DRIVERS OF CUSTOMER COSTS

The first generation of customer profitability reports (as illustrated by the Blue Ridge example) implicitly assumes the following:

- All costs are variable in the long run with respect to the chosen cost drivers; and
- None of the costs are joint (in the sense that two or more products or services are simultaneously produced or delivered to one customer).

Relaxing these assumptions, however, may lead to more accurate customer profitability reports. Consider the first assumption. Several approaches can be taken to relax the assumption that all costs are variable in the long run:

- *Prepare separate analyses for cost drivers and their rates in the short run and the long run.* The reliance of existing customer profitability reports on long-run cost drivers can create the erroneous conclusion that dropping currently unprofitable customers (called *revenue shedding*) will cause the costs assigned to these customers to disappear in the short run. Executives are very reluctant to engage in "revenue shedding," perhaps out of skepticism that costs labeled "customer-driven" will disappear in the short run after severing relations with the customer. Costs are more likely to be variable as output increases than when output decreases.
- *Prepare customer-cost hierarchies that recognize different levels of cost drivers.* First-generation customer profitability reports typically assign all costs to the individual customer level. A customer-cost hierarchy categorizes customer costs into different cost pools on the basis of different classes of cost drivers or of differential difficulty in determining a cause-and-effect or a benefits-received relationship.

Here is a hypothetical example of a customer-cost hierarchy:

EXHIBIT 5
EXTENDING FIRST GENERAL CUSTOMER PROFITABILITY REPORTS

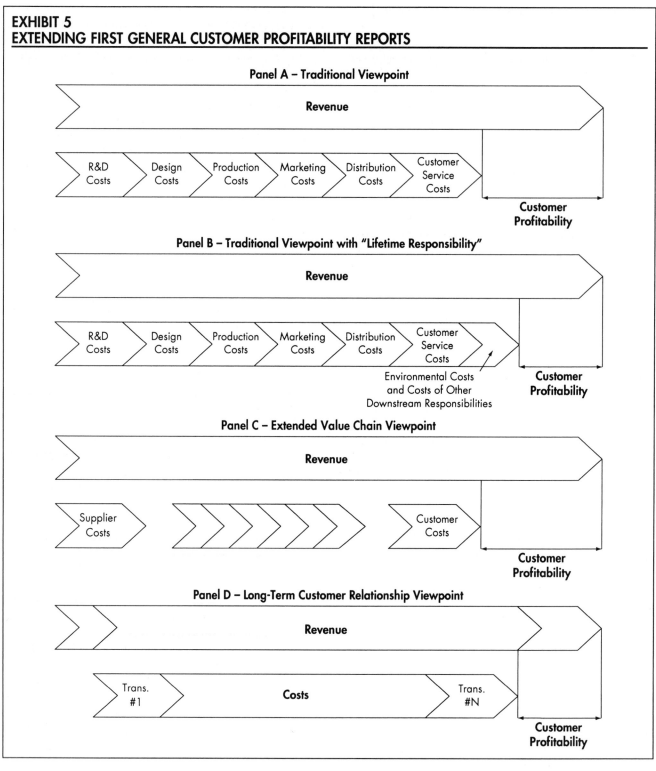

Revenues
—Customer-specific costs
—Customer-specific contribution
—Customer-line costs
—Customer-line contribution
—Company enterprise costs
—Operating income

For cost management purposes, customer-line costs and company enterprise costs need not be assigned to individual customers. Consequently, the company's total operating income will be less than the sum of total customer-specific contributions. The resulting challenge is pricing at the customer level such that customer revenues exceed assigned customer costs *and* make contributions to recovering the costs that are not assigned to customers (i.e., customer-line costs and company enterprise costs).

The management accounting literature has discussed a diverse set of cost hierarchies, including product-cost hierarchies and brand-cost hierarchies. A little-researched area is how alternative cost hierarchies relate to each other. For example, should a customer-based hierarchy be implemented only after a product-based hierarchy is implemented?

NEW DIRECTIONS

The emphasis on adopting a "customer focus" has become pervasive across many areas of management. As a result, research on customer profitability has become central to advances in several high-profile areas of management research, including:

- Supporting strategic decisions;
- Valuing intangible assets; and
- Analyzing customer retention rates.

The following paragraphs illustrate these examples.

Supporting strategic decisions. Customer profitability systems typically assume that the existing business infrastructure will stay relatively constant in the face of various management decisions. This assumption becomes tenuous, however, when significant reengineering occurs.

Consider the Blue Ridge example illustrated in Exhibits 2-4. One of Blue Ridge's strategic options for its small customers would be to use a third-party distributor. Costing out this approach, however, is likely to require adding extra cost pools and cost drivers to the company's ABC system.

Consider also the order interface between suppliers, manufacturers, and customers. By necessity, an ABC system reflects existing activities. If major changes in the company dramatically revamp those activities, supplementary costing analysis will be required. For example, an extensive use of electronic data exchange might make it possible to eliminate many activities modeled in an ABC system.

The more dramatic the reengineering options considered, the less valuable an accounting system based solely on existing activities becomes. The next generation of customer profitability reports may therefore include cost pools and cost drivers for activities that alternative scenarios would require.

This format would increase the usefulness of reports for strategic decision making.

Valuing intangible assets. Most management accounting systems restrict their attention to the valuation of tangible assets (e.g., property, plant, and equipment; computers; and motor vehicles). In many businesses, however, intangible assets (such as brands the company owns) are a significant component of the company's total value. Brand names are pivotal to valuations of consumer products companies such as Anheuser-Busch and Philip Morris. Similarly, a company's customer base is often a valuable intangible asset. Examples include a doctor's patient base and a cellular phone company's subscriber base. Consequently, valuations of service companies for acquisition decisions often recognize customer bases as the single most important asset. Given the importance of customer bases, assessments of management performance should track how the value of customer bases change periodically.

Management decisions can dramatically increase or decrease the value of these intangible assets. For example, consider the effect of implementing a total quality management (TQM) program for a consumer product that has had a low quality ranking for years. If the TQM program causes the company's product to be ranked first in quality, this improvement is likely to have both short-run and long-run effects, yet most accounting systems recognize only the short-run effect (i.e., an increase in income).

By periodically estimating the value of a customer base, the multiperiod effect of increases in customer loyalty can be analyzed systematically. Clearly, the estimates required involve uncertainty, but all management accounting systems involve uncertainty—e.g, in the form of the estimated service life of assets, allowances for bad debt, and estimated warranty costs.

One reason for tracking changes in the value of customer bases is to highlight management actions that focus myopically on the short run. For example, price cuts may well boost short-run profitability for certain key customers, but they may also decrease long-term profitability because customers may begin to expect continued price reductions in the future. The argument for monitoring changes in customer bases, therefore, is analogous to the argument for monitoring changes in brand values.

Models of customer value are in their infancy. Some models take a certainty-based net present value approach. More refined models would recognize uncertainty in the form of likely competitor responses, differences in customer renewal profiles, and alternative ways to compute customer profitability A separate financial statement focused only on intangible assets may increase their visibility.

Analyzing customer retention rates. The importance of retaining profitable customers is widely recognized. Various rules of thumb have been proposed for retaining customers—for example, that it costs five times more to acquire a new customer than it does to keep an existing customer. Such rules of thumb are rarely based on systematic analysis.

Customer profitability databases would facilitate development of more informed decision-making tools in the following ways:

- By tracking the resources required to attract new customers and retain existing customers; and
- By providing more reliable estimates of the operating income derived from new and existing customers.

Alternative approaches to customer retention (e.g., lower prices or better customer service) may yield different customer retention rates. Refinements in tracking customer profitability will permit more extensive testing of the economics of these alternative approaches.

One study, for example, reports the following increase in customer life-time profits from an annual 5 percent reduction in customer defection rates:[5]

- *Branch deposits:* 85 percent;
- *Credit card:* 75 percent;
- *Insurance brokerage:* 50 percent;
- *Software:* 35 percent.

A key input for this study is estimates of customer profitability. Refinements in these estimates can help managers make more informed decisions about alternative investments to improve customer-retention rates.

CONCLUSION

Managers have recently emphasized the importance of attracting and retaining profitable customers. These developments set the stage for management accountants to start and refine their customer profitability systems. Doing so raises many practical problems that have no simple solutions or certain outcomes. Nonetheless, many managers and academics see great promise in resolving these issues, which makes research in this area an intellectually exciting and rewarding challenge.

George Foster is Wattis Professor of Management at the Graduate School of Business, Stanford University, in Stanford, California. Mahendra Gupta is associate professor of accounting at the Olin School of Business at Washington University in St. Louis, Missouri. Leif Sjoblom is professor of accounting at the Institute for Management Development (IMD) in Lausanne, Switzerland.

Notes

1. Examples of recent publications include: A. Anandarajan and M. Christopher, "A Mission Approach to Customer Profitability Analysis," *International Journal of Physical Distribution and Materials Management* (1987): 55–68; R. Bellis-Jones, "Customer Profitability Analysis," *Management Accounting* (UK) (February 1989): 26–28; R. Kaplan, "Kanthal (A)" (Harvard Business School case 9-190-002, 1989); K. Ward, *Strategic Management Accounting* (Oxford: Butterworth-Heinemann, 1992) Chapter 6; and T. Connolly and G. Ashworth. "Managing Customers for Profit," *Management Accounting* (UK) (April 1994): 34–39.

2. Evidence for the importance of post-sales service revenues can be found in T. Kneht, R. Leszinski, and F. Weber, "Making Profits After the Sale," *The McKinsey Quarterly* (1993 Number 4): 79–86.

3. We are indebted to P.E. Juras and P.A. Dierks of Wake Forest University for the Blue Ridge case study. It is described in *Management Accounting* (December 1993): 57–59. We present an adapted version of this case with our own discussion.

4. An example of CAP in the financial services sector is N. Stuchfield and B. Weber, "Modeling the Profitability of Customer Relationships: Development and Impact of Barclays de Zoete Wedd's Beatrice. *Journal of Management Information Systems* (Fall 1992): 53–76.

5. F. Reichheld and W. Sasser, "Zero Defections: Quality Comes to Services," *Harvard Business Review* (September-October 1990): 105–111. See also J. Barsky, *World-Class Customer Satisfaction: Converting Loyalty into Profits* (Chicago: Irwin, 1994).

From G. Foster, M. Gupta, L. Sjoblom, "Customer Profitability Analysis: Challenges and New Directions," *Journal of Cost Management* (Spring 1996): 5–17. Reprinted with permission.

Question

13.3 Describe the four challenges that Foster, Gupta and Sjoblom say must be overcome to analyze customer account profitability.

CHAPTER 14

Compensation Issues

Woodruff Imberman's highly practical article, *Is Gainsharing the Wave of the Future* (Reading 14.1) discusses his experiences in implementing numerous gainsharing plans in organizations. Imberman discusses the three most commonly used gainsharing plans - the Scanlon, Rucker and Improshare plans - but also reveals that there are probably a dozen variations of each of these. Examples of gainsharing experiences are discussed in several types of industries including a box manufacturer, a brushless motor factory, a foundry, and a Volvo GM Heavy Truck Corporation Truck Assembly Plant. The author also offers five guidelines that he has developed to ensure the success of gainsharing plans.

An interesting counterpoint to Reading 14.1 is Bob Nelson's article *Motivating Employees with Informal Rewards* (Reading 14.2). Citing statistics, Nelson argues that traditional financial compensation is becoming less effective in motivating today's employees. What employees really want is some form of recognition or positive reinforcement for their work besides money in the form of pats on the back, company jackets, plaques and employee appreciation day. Nelson presents examples of successful company experiences as well as characteristics of effective, informal rewards and guidelines for implementing an informal reward system. Noting that in the future many companies will begin to move toward fixed compensation systems and that employees will be asked to be more creative and empowered in their work, informal rewards will play an even more important role in motivating employees at all levels of organizations.

Even more strongly articulated than Reading 14.2, Alfie Kohn's *Why Incentive Plans Cannot Work* (Reading 14.3), argues strongly that incentive plans that link rewards to measured performance are fundamentally flawed. Citing research evidence, Kohn believes that employees who expect to receive a reward for their efforts do not perform as well as those who do not expect rewards. What is lacking with current pay-for-performance systems is that they do not foster a work environment in which employees can experience intrinsic rewards. Ultimately, the preoccupation with extrinsic rewards does not lead to organizational commitment, discourages risk taking, and reduces creativity and innovation. Ever controversial, Kohn closes with the following, "Managers who insist that the job won't get done right without rewards have failed to offer a convincing argument for behavioral manipulation. Promising a reward to someone who appears unmotivated is a bit like offering salt water to someone who is thirsty. Bribes in the workplace simply won't work."

READINGS
CHAPTER 14

14.1 Is Gainsharing the Wave of the Future?
Monthly bonus checks can jump-start productivity.

By Woodruff Imberman

A *Wall Street Journal* article reported how a furniture company in Arlington, Va., was able to turn a loss to a profit and increase sales each year since 1991. In that year Rowe Furniture had a net loss of $47,000 on sales of $63.8 million. In 1992, after installing gainsharing, Rowe earned 25 cents a share on sales of $73.5 million.

> *The Wall Street Journal* noted:
> *An important driving force behind the company's performance has been the establishment of its 'gainsharing' program for employees that turned away from the traditional piecework model... Employees are awarded bonuses based on their performance in comparison with a standard cost vs. output measure. For instance, they are encouraged to turn out mistake-free pieces, thus removing the expense of sending pieces through a quality-control step. And employees are encouraged to share ideas for improved productivity with management. 'The program has had a dramatic impact on what we're able to do,' Gerald M. Birnback [president] said, adding that the program has allowed the company to be more competitive and improve productivity. 'Employees are happier and turnover is almost nil.'* [1]

If "gainsharing" can help accomplish such a turnaround for Rowe, can a similar program achieve the same success at other companies? The American Productivity and Quality Center predicts that gainsharing "will become one of the fastest growing strategies in the U.S. in the 1990s and beyond." [2] Let's look at some case studies of the implementation of gain-sharing.

WHAT IS GAINSHARING?

Gainsharing is not an incentive or bonus plan for individuals exceeding a standard or quota. That's the old piecework system. Gainsharing is a group bonus plan. The entire factory work-force is involved in an effort to exceed past performance and achieve target gains. If successful, the gain is translated into cash and shared. Usually the workforce receives 50% of the gain in bonuses, and the company receives an equal share in savings. That's gainsharing in its simplest form.

The concept of gainsharing originated in the 1930s with the Scanlon Plan. This plan involved the ratio of payroll costs to sales (see Figure 1). If, for example, payroll costs were 25% of product sales, and such costs were brought down to, say, 15%, the 10% savings would be translated into dollars and split 75/25 between workforce and company. One possible drawback of the Scanlon Plan is that management must unveil costs and sales data. Many companies are reluctant to reveal such data.

Another variety of gainsharing, the Rucker Plan, was developed in the late 1940s, and it involved the value added by manufacturing (see Figure 1). Value added is calculated as the difference between the selling price of the products and the costs of labor, materials, supplies, and services, so the Rucker Plan provides an incentive to save materials as well as reducing labor costs. The bonus pool resulting from savings under this plan usually is split 50/50 between workforce and company.

ImproShare, developed in 1973, measures only labor costs and uses time standards and past production records to set a production criterion. Its bonus formula is the difference between current labor hours to produce a given output and past labor hours on a similar output (see Figure 1).

Who uses gainsharing? Some major companies with gainsharing plans are Georgia Pacific, Inland Container Mead Paper, Huffy Bicycle, Eaton Corp., TRW and General

---

FIGURE 1
THREE SAMPLE GAINSHARING FORMULAS

Scanlon Plan Base Ratio

$$\frac{\text{Cost of work and nonwork time paid} + \text{pension} + \text{insurance}}{\text{Sales dollars} - \text{returned goods} + \text{inventory changes}}$$

Rucker Plan Base Ratio

$$\frac{\text{Cost of all wages, benefits}}{\text{Sales dollar value of product} - \text{goods returned} - \text{supplies, services, materials}}$$

ImproShare Plan Base Formula

$$\frac{\frac{\text{Standard value hours earned (current period)}}{} \times \frac{\text{Total actual hours worked (base period)}}{\text{Total standard value hours earned (base period)}}}{\text{Total hours worked (current period)}}$$

292

Electric. Virtually every manufacturing industry is represented among gainsharing programs in operation. Yet there are only about 2,200 companies using some variety of gainsharing. Why not more?

GAINSHARING AT A BOX COMPANY

A Missouri company employing about 180 factory workers and manufacturing corrugated boxes, shipping containers, inner packing, and displays illustrates how gainsharing works in practice. Under pressure from an original equipment manufacturer (OEM) customer for lower prices, the box producer was forced to boost his workforce to higher productivity in order to slice unit costs, thereby permitting lower prices.

The gainsharing project began with an examination of the company's production records for the past two years. Such digging found that labor costs (including supervision, plant engineering, scheduling, all indirect labor) hovered around 37% of total cost. That is, for every $1 million of corrugated products, $370,000 went to associated labor expense. The objective was to trim those costs.

With some expert guidance, the company proceeded to design a formula for rewarding the workforce for achieving lower labor costs. The formula involved convincing the workers that if they performed *harder smarter neater and more carefully,* reducing labor costs to (say) $300,000, savings would be $70,000 on the next $1 million production run. The savings (gain) in that period would be shared equally: $35,000 for the workers, as a bonus of $194.44 for each employee, and a $35,000 savings for the company. The employee bonuses were over and above the normal wage rate.

The standard of productivity was set by careful investigation of past experience showing how many hours were required for the average production mix with volume of (good) output. A typical base period was selected to serve as a standard. The fact that past experience involved a mix of corrugated products, containers, and displays that did not duplicate the current run of corrugated products exactly presented no problem. The records showed that the mix held fairly constant. The common element—staff-hours worked or dollars spent on labor—could be distilled out and serve as a standard.

BRUSHLESS MOTORS FACTORY EXPERIENCE

Table 1 summarizes the first year (1990) of the gainsharing plan of a Michigan manufacturer of brushless DC motors with planetary gear reducers for high-power applications. The plan was to cut the number of staff-hours needed to produce a given quantity of output. "Current Hours" is the actual number of hours worked in January 1990 to produce the given output compared with the 1988–89 "Standard Hours" for a similar output. For January 1990, current pro-

TABLE 1
BRUSHLESS MOTOR CASE

Period (1990)	Current Hours (1990)	Standard Hours (1988–1989)	Hours Gained 100%	Gain Share
January	64,216	71,315	7,099	5.52%
February	76,005	90,913	14,908	9.80
March	61,350	72,133	10,783	8.78
April	57,690	62,186	4,496	3.89
May	55,458	51,666	-3,792	-3.41
June	57,474	61,530	4,056	3.52
July	60,370	66,136	5,766	4.77
August	67,496	75,204	7,708	5.70
September	68,106	75,929	7,823	5.74
October	63,241	68,534	5,293	4.18
November	66,660	73,061	6,401	4.80
December	65,327	72,060	6,733	5.15
Total	763,393	840,667	77,274	4.87%

duction required 64,216 staff-hours. The same (or similar) output in the base period, 1988–89, required 71,315 staff-hours. In the month of January 1990, by working harder, smarter, more carefully, the factory workforce gained 7,099 staff-hours.

The typical factory employee was paid $14 an hour for 173 hours during a month (or $2,422 monthly gross). The gain of 7,099 staff-hours was 11% of actual hours worked (64,216 current hours). This gain was divided equally, and each employee received a 5.52% gain for that month, or a bonus of $133.69 for January; the company saved the same amount. The gainsharing pool can be paid out in a lump sum or distributed as a percentage of the employees' wages, which eliminates the question of overtime.

The company chose to pay *level* gainsharing bonuses of 4% every month because the monthly gain shares varied from -3.41% to +9.80%. Those months that showed a bonus return of more than 4% had the surplus *banked* so that 4% could be paid out in the slower months (April, May, June) in order to keep employee involvement high. All surpluses were paid out at Christmas. Since 1990, the first year of its operation, the plan has been successful, with gainsharing percentages increasing.

A FOUNDRY PROFITS

The object of the gainsharing plan in an Ohio gray and ductile iron foundry was to reward employees for a cut in staff-hours per ton of good casting output. In the base period (1990), staff-hours per good ton varied from month to month—30.1 staff-hours in one month to a low of 22.68 in another month. The average for the year was 28.4 staff-hours per ton of good output. That output was the base against which future output (and gains, if any) was to be measured. Table 2 summarizes the results for 1991, 1992, and 1993.

TABLE 2 FOUNDRY CASE	1991	1992	1993
Monthly average tons produced	1,028.58	1,044.00	1,188.89
Monthly average scrap	107.75	129.23	158.19
Monthly average good tons produced	920.00	914.77	1,030.70
Monthly average staff-hours worked	24,505.00	22,574.00	23,275.00
Monthly average staff-hours per ton achieved	26.79	24.68	22.58
Base staff-hours from which improvement is measured	28.40	27.43	25.78
Monthly average tons improved over previous year's base (60% rachet)	0.97	1.65	1.92

Base for 1992 = 28.4 staff-hours (from previous year). Base for 1992 = 28.4−26.79 = 1.16; 1.16 × 60% = .97; 28.4−.97 = 27.43 (base for next year). Base for 1993 = 27.43−24.68 = 2.75; 2.75 × 60% = 1.65; 27.43−1.65 = 25.78.

Today's customers insist on higher-quality standards and lower prices each year. These realities are explained and "rolled down" to employees. Dealing with these issues, the plan called for "ratcheting the base." Ratcheting means that the base, against which improvements are measured, is tightened annually in line with market realities.

Each year, 60% of the improvement was deducted from the base. The measure of "improved performance was a reduction in staff-hours worked per ton of good casting. The ratchet formula, which lowered the base criterion every year, resulted in a gainsharing base for 1993 of 25.78 staff-hours per good ton. That was the level to beat in order to achieve a gain. The result achieved in 1993 was an average of 22.58 staff-hours per ton. After the 60% ratchet, base criterion for the following year, 1994, was 23.82.

This ratchet concept fits quite well philosophically with continuous improvement programs. `The gainsharing motivates employees to give their full support to continuous improvement and TQM programs. Companies often begin gainsharing and TQM programs simultaneously for the synergistic effect. Gainsharing offers a direct, immediate link between performance and employee compensation. All gainsharing plans allow a company to change the base following installation of new production equipment, changes in government regulations, significant changes in processes or materials due to environmental procedures, and so forth. Some companies use a gainsharing formula combining productivity and quality improvement, curtailing ratio of inventory to work in progress, cutting down on gas and electrical use (especially important to foundaries, steel mills, etc.), or reducing lost-time accidents.

GAINSHARING: MANAGEMENT CHALLENGE

There are at least a dozen subvarieties of each gainsharing plan, depending on a company's cost structure, the type of product or service produced, the manufacturing process, kinds of materials, and so forth.[4] The wave of the future in U.S. industry would appear to be pay-for-performance or gainsharing as a way of improving plant performance. In an era of global markets, competitors no longer are located only down the road, in the next town, or even the next state. They are just as likely to be based in Nagoya or Mexico City or Stuttgart. It's a world in which trade barriers never have been lower while the demands of customers and markets never have been higher.

So why aren't more companies using gainsharing? The explanation may be along the lines suggested by noted management authority Peter F. Drucker: "Inertia in management is responsible for more loss of market share, for more loss of competitive position, and for more loss of business growth than any other single factor."[5]

Woodruff Imberman, Ph.D, is president of Imberman & De Forest, a consulting firm in Evanston, Ill. He can be reached by fax at (708) 733-0074.

Notes

1. *The Wall Street Journal*, Dow Jones & Co., October 2, 1992.

2. Cited in "Understanding Gainsharing," *Gainsharing: Plans for Improving Performance,* edited by B. Graham-Moore and T.L. Ross, Washington, D.C., Bureau of National Affairs, 1991, p. IX.

3. A detailed description of how gainsharing formulas are devised in different industries is given by W. Imberman in "Everything You Every Wanted to Know about Gainsharing but Where Afraid to Ask", *Target Magazine,* Association for Manufacturing Excellence, May/June, 1993.

4. Peter Drucker, *Managing for the Future: The 1990s and Beyond,* New York, N.Y., 1992, p. 174.

RULES FOR SUCCESS

Having examined dozens of gainsharing plans and installed a variety of gainsharing programs for various companies, I can suggest five rules to ensure a successful gainsharing program in any plant:

1. The payout formula must be reasonable and doable. A formula that pays out minuscule bonuses or assumes that large improvements will result instantaneously is doomed to failure. Some guidance is helpful in setting the formula.
2. The first six to nine months of a program are vital to long-term success. Key determinants of that success are employee involvement in devising the plan—a delicate process—and employee understanding of the gainsharing program details. Hence a program of employee education must accompany the introduction of the gainsharing bonus formula. Reviewing a gainsharing program carefully with the workforce will produce better results than gainsharing implemented without employee understanding or participation.

Employee participation has a stronger effect in motivating the workforce to improve productivity and quality than bonus share or bonus frequency. If employees have some input on achieving lower costs or high-quality output, they will understand that lowering unit costs or improving quality (or both) will not only add to their take-home pay but also will make their company and their jobs more secure.[1]

3. While some executives like to pay gainsharing bonuses quarterly, that is usually too long an interval to maintain a high level of motivation. Shorter intervals between bonus payments are more effective. In short, monetary rewards should follow performance with minimal delay. Monthly payouts seem to function best in reminding workers of the rewards of gainsharing.
4. Unionism per se is neither a plus nor a minus to gainsharing. What matters is whether the union and management trust each other. Gainsharing provides the opportunity for the workforce and management to concentrate on problem solving and

rewarding improvements, rather than sparring with each other.[2]
5. The greater the degree of expert guidance, the better the resultant gainsharing performance. Unsuccessful gainsharing plans discontinued after a year or so were mainly do-it-yourself plans designed and implemented by a well-meaning company executive. Using another company's gainsharing plan often results in failure, even if both companies are in the same industry and produce similar products. The personnel "chemistry" may differ from company to company and plant to plant. All successful plans are tailor-made for particular plant situations.[3]

[1]W. Imberman, "Employee Participation: What It Is, How It Works:" *Target Magazine*, Association for Manufacturing Excellence. Vol. 9, January/February 1993.

[2]W. Imberman, "Who Strikes and Why?" *Harvard Business Review*, November/October 1983,

[3]W. Imberman and B. Flasch, "Gains and Losses from Gainsharing," *Industry Forum*, December 1989, supplement to *Management Review*, American Management Association, New York, N.Y.

GAINSHARING CREATES AN ENVIRONMENT THAT SUPPORTS TQM

How can we create an environment that encourages employees to take ownership in their jobs? This question is common at most corporations today, and there are hundreds of books on the subject. Based on my experience at six corporations, I would like to answer this question—implement a gainsharing plan.

Why gainsharing? At Volvo GM, we have completed our third year in implementing a total quality management (TQM) culture. A TQM culture requires and expects changes in behavior. A very important principle in TQM is to have a reward and recognition system, which gainsharing can satisfy.

Let's look at some key characteristics of gainsharing and TQM:

- A gainsharing program can be implemented company-wide by individual units or a combination of company-wide and individual units.
- If set up properly, the program will create an environment for earning—not entitlement. That is, until you meet and exceed targets, you are not entitled to any rewards. An attitude of entitlement is a primary reason a TQM culture is difficult to create.

- A properly designed program will use pay to drive results—a win-win situation for the company and the employees.
- The reward system gives validity to TQM—the company is walking the talk.

IMPLEMENTING GAINSHARING AT VOLVO GM

We began with four key principles that are the foundation of our gainsharing program.

Involvement. It is critical that employees participate in making suggestions and decisions. We are fortunate because our company established a successful suggestion program four years ago. Involvement also means cooperation and teamwork.

Identity. We established a mutual understanding between the company and employees so that everyone understands what is expected. The identity principle helps us recognize the need for change and encourages an attitude of *we* rather than *them*—again, cooperation and teamwork are promoted.

Equity. We created a bonus system through gainsharing so employees have a common goal with the company. The equity principle brings the trust necessary to create synergy.

Commitment. Through gainsharing, our company and employees became dedicated to continuous improvement. The principle of commitment brings the recognition for the need to change and the requirement for ongoing education.

A gainsharing program founded and established on these principles must be a starting point. At Volvo GM, our excitement grew the more we learned about the important contribution gainsharing could make in the success of our TQM culture.

Using the four principles as our foundation, we proceeded to design a gainsharing program for our company. The key points for our gainsharing program are that all employees participate, payouts are quarterly, only performance improvement is rewarded, and the program is a natural progression toward total employee involvement.

The foundation of a successful gainsharing program focuses on people and their behavior. Every employee must understand how he or she personally can make a difference. All employees must become business literate, that is, become educated on the key issues in the company and view themselves as stockholders. A properly designed gainsharing program supports TQM, increases recognition, fosters cooperation and teamwork, and provides a feeling of contributing to the organization.

Each company should choose its own measurement to determine the gainsharing payout. Here is our plan at Orrville.

ORRVILLE GAINSHARING PLAN

The multiple cost ratio was the measurement we selected to use. That measurement has direct labor, direct material, and overhead as the numerator with net revenue as the denominator. The financial data for 1992 computed to 92.84%, and for January through September 1993 it was 93.02%. Then, we took the multiple cost ratio and divided it into two measurements: direct material/net revenue; direct labor and overhead/net revenue. Each measurement is worth 50%.

See Table 1, which presumes a goal of a 5% payoff. This measurement is calculated monthly and made known to employees. The payout is quarterly. The logic is that constant awareness is important for focusing on continuous improvement, payout has greater impact when tied closely to a shorter measurement period, and there is a positive psychological effect when participants receive a larger check on a quarterly basis.

The reserve fund gets 50%, and then 50% is divided equally between the company and the employees. The basis of earnings will be a percentage of salary, and the payout will be quarterly based on positive results. For the year-end reserve:

1. Zero-out at year-end—no carryover.
2. Positive balance—pay to employees.
3. Negative balance—company absorbs.

Eligibility is effective immediately for full-time hourly and salaried employees, temporary employees, and new hires. Not eligible are senior management and co-ops (interns). Participants must be employed at the end of the measurement period to receive quarterly payout. To receive the year-end reserve, participants must be employed at 12/31/XX.

Ideas are analyzed, processed, implemented, publicized, and tracked for quick response and implementation using Orrville's existing suggestion program.

We also have a corporate steering committee, made up of two members from each location, and a local committee at each location on which the two local representatives of the steering committee serve.

TABLE 1
THE 5% PAYOFF AT VOLVO GM

	Payroll	$120,000,000
	x	.05
	Payoff	6,000,000
	Company portion	6,000,000
Gainsharing amount needed for 5% payoff		$ 12,000,000

Individual objective		Objective - 5% payoff
	Payroll	
Orrville	$30,000,000	$3,000,000
NRV	40,000,000	4,000,000
Corporate*	24,000,000	2,400,000
Parts and service	10,000,000	1,000,000
Commercial	16,000,000	1,600,000
	$120,000,000	$12,000,000

*Corporate has a specific objective to manage and reduce its $100 million budget.

296

Everyone receives a memo explaining gainsharing, the guidelines, and each individual's role and impact on measurement. Departmental meetings are held as a follow-up on the memo to answer questions.

Gainsharing offers an opportu-nity for employees to earn a meaningful reward for achieving and/or exceeding a goal.—*Lynn McAninch, CMA*

Lynn McAninch, CMA, is controller, Volvo GM Heavy Truck CorporationTruck Assembly Plant, Orrville, Ohio. He is a member of the Canton Chapter, through which this article was submitted, and can be reached at (216) 684-0104.

From W. Imberman, "Is Gainsharing the Wave of the Future?" *Management Accounting* (November 1995): 35–39. Reprinted with permission.

Question

14.1 Describe the five rules that Imberman has developed to "ensure" a successful gainsharing program in a plant?

14.2 Motivating Employees with Informal Awards
Companies substitute jackets and plaques for bonuses—and they work!

By Bob Nelson

The value of informal rewards, that is, spontaneous non-monetary forms of recognition, as employee motivators is increasing today for two reasons. First, traditional rewards such as compensation and promotions—although still important—are becoming less and less effective in motivating today's employees to achieve high performance. Second, informal rewards are effective and highly desired by today's employees.

The use of traditional rewards is declining in U.S. business. Consider these facts:

- 81% of workers say they would not receive any reward for productivity increases.
- 60% of managers feel their compensation will not increase if their performance improves.
- 3% of base salary separates average from outstanding employees.[1]

Clearly our traditional system of rewards in U.S. business is in crisis if it fails to differentiate high performance on such a widespread basis. To make matters worse, rewards that are still in place are losing effectiveness. As Peter Drucker points out:

"Economic incentives are becoming rights rather than rewards. Merit raises are always introduced as rewards for exceptional performance. In no time at all they become a right. To deny a merit raise or to grant only a small one becomes punishment. The increasing demand for material rewards is rapidly destroying their usefulness as incentives and managerial tools."[2]

Material rewards such as cash have in some cases even been found to have a demotivating effect. Explains Cecil

Hill, corporate manager of improvement programs at Hughes Aircraft Company:

"I found certain aspects of the cash awards approach would be counterproductive at Hughes Aircraft. For example, cash awards would reduce teamwork as employees concentrated primarily on individual cash gains. We also found that United Airlines had dropped its longtime cash awards system because of litigation problems. Other companies pointed out a negative boomerang effect whenever ideas were turned down, while many firms reported an ongoing problem with timely response, and others noted disagreements on determining dollar amounts and conflicts regarding what constitutes 'a part of normal job performance.' We have also found instances where 'pay' for certain types of intellectual performance tends to denigrate the performance, and remove it from the intellectual achievement category, which elicits pride and satisfaction, and reduces it to a more mundane 'pay-for-performance' concept. In short, cash awards seemed to have an overall demotivating effect,"[3]

INFORMAL REWARDS ARE EFFECTIVE

Although they are given little or no attention in management literature and practice, informal rewards are effective. In a recent survey of American workers by the Society of Inventive Travel Executives Foundation, 63% of the respondents ranked "a pat on the back" as a meaningful incentive.[4] In another recent study of 65 potential incentives, four out of the top five incentives ranked by employees as most motivating were initiated by their manager, based upon performance, and required little or no money:

1. Manager personally congratulates employees who do a good job.
2. Manager writes personal notes for good performance.
3. Manager publicly recognizes employees for good performance.
4. Manager holds morale-building meetings to celebrate successes.[5]

The effectiveness of such rewards can be traced back to fundamental principles of positive reinforcement. Positive reinforcement is effective for several reasons. First, under conditions of positive reinforcement, the response produces a consequence that results in an increase in the frequency of the response. Second, the adverse emotional responses associated with punishment and extinction are apt to be reduced, and, in fact, favorable emotions may be elicited.

To illustrate the power of positive reinforcement on individual behavior, Daniel Boyle, vice president and treasurer of Diamond Fiber Products, Inc.. describes the impact on an employee when she was presented a nylon and cotton jacket as a special employee recognition reward called "The 100 Club" in his company:

"You might think this is a trivial thing, but it means a lot to the people who earn a jacket. A teller at a local bank told me once that a woman came in and proudly modeled her baby blue 100 Club jacket for bank customers and employees. She said, 'My employer gave me this for doing a good job. It's the first time in the 18 years I've been there they've recognized the things I do every day.'

"During those years she had earned $230,000 in wages, which had paid for cars, a home mortgage, food other essentials, vacations, college educations. In her mind, she had provided a service for her earnings. The money wasn't recognition for her work, but the 100 Club jacket was."[6]

Think of the impact recognition would have had on this employee if it were used on a daily basis instead of once every 18 years! As the example illustrates, many informal rewards cost relatively little or no money so are very cost effective.

Other examples of informal rewards used to acknowledge performance or build morale can be found at many successful companies:

Tektronix, Inc., a Beaverton, Ore., manufacturer of oscilloscopes and other electronic instruments, has the "You Done Good Award" note cards for managers and employees to document and send "thank you's" to others in the company.

ARA Services in Philadelphia, which provides food and leisure services and textile rentals, organizes a day of appreciation for a worthy person. It announces the day in advance (e.g., Bob Jones Day) and the reason for the honor. The honoree enjoys all sorts of frills, such as computer banners and a free lunch.

An executive at NCO Financial Systems in Blue Bell, Pa., buys a new suit for junior salespeople when they first reach their sales goals. Sometimes he also lends his Mercedes to salespeople for the weekends to show them how it feels to be a top salesperson at the company.

Pepsi Co. headquarters in Purchase, N.Y., has a full-time concierge to help its 800 employees with personal errands such as booking restaurant tables and theater seats, arranging events for children, and scheduling household repairs.

When the positive reinforcement is given by colleagues or members of an informal work group, the results can be even more significant. For example, the Office of Personnel Management in Washington, D.C., has the "Wingspread Award." This beautiful engraved plaque was first given to the division's "special performer" by the department head. Later that person passed the award to another person who, he believed, truly deserved it. The award came to take on great value and prestige because it came from one's peers. A recipient can keep it as long as he or she wants or until he or she discovers another "special performer." When the award is to be passed on, a ceremony and lunch are held for the presentation.

CHARACTERISTICS OF INFORMAL REWARDS

What makes informal rewards effective? They are most effective when some simple guidelines are followed. Informal rewards need to be:

Direct reinforcement of desired behavior. The reward needs to be given clearly in response to the desired behavior.

Immediate in their use. Informal rewards need to be given as soon as possible after the desired behavior occurs.

Delivered personally. Part of the power of informal rewards derives from the way they are delivered personally. The fact that a manager is taking time—a limited, precious resource for all of us—to recognize or praise an employee underscores the importance of the activity to the employee. Time taken by a peer to recognize a colleague has an equal or greater effect in that it is both unexpected and not required of the colleague.

Valued by the individual. A final guideline for making informal rewards effective is to be sure they are valued and meaningful to the individuals who receive them.

The rewards that are meaningful to a particular employee, however, depend on personal circumstances and tastes. For example, some employees are interested in increasing their autonomy while others may be more interested in greater visibility, in improving their promotion possibilities, or in merely being thanked for doing a good job for the company. The best way to find out what employees value in terms of rewards and recognition is to ask them.

GUIDELINES FOR IMPLEMENTING AN INFORMAL REWARD SYSTEM

An informal reward system is one or more organizational programs that encourage the use of informal rewards by management or among employees. The informal reward system is part of a broader informal organization that parallels the formal organization in every company. Informal organizations come about as a result of interpersonal interactions among people who come to establish personal relationships that often are independent of their organizational roles.

Individuals tend to be more strongly motivated by the potential to earn rewards than by the fear of punishment, which suggests that management control systems be reward oriented. Here are some guidelines for implementing an informal reward system within an organization:

Link to organizational goals. To be effective, informal rewards need to support behavior that leads to the attainment of organizational goals. Good management is that which leads to the desired behavior by organizational members. Management must see to it that the consequences of employee behavior increase the frequency of desired behavior and decrease the frequency of undesired behaviors.

Individuals respond to many kinds of rewards, tangible and intangible, on the job and off the job. Tying these rewards to controls is not simple. Consequently a careful review of the reward system should be made along with any major redesign of the control system. Insofar as flexibility permits, the granting of rewards should be related clearly and explicitly to desired performance as reflected by the controls.

Define parameters and mechanics. Once the behavior to be reinforced is identified, specifics of a reward system need to be defined. The rules for awarding incentives must be clear and understood by all. This less obvious feature can make an incentive system powerful and make a clear connection between the level of performance and the awarding of the incentive.

Obtain commitment and support. Once the mechanics of an informal reward system are clear, the program needs to be communicated to those you want to use it. Usually this part of the program can be carried out in a group setting by presenting the program as a positive, fun activity that will benefit the employees as well as the company. Better yet is to elicit the help of employees in both planning and implementing the program. Such involvement improves employee understanding of and commitment to the program.

Monitor effectiveness. Any program is only as good as its implementation. Informal reward systems must be monitored to see if they are being used and to see that the desired results are being obtained. Even the best informal reward program will be apt to lose its effectiveness over time because one of the defining characteristics of a reward is that it is special. Old programs often lose their specialness and thus need to be reenergized or discontinued.

Link to formal rewards programs. Management must ensure that informal rewards are in line with the formal reward structure. This outcome can be achieved most easily by making informal rewards a subset of larger, more formal reward programs that are in place. For example, a company award (a formal reward) could be given to the employee who receives the greatest number of praising letters (an informal reward) from customers over the course of a year.

HOW HONEYWELL, BLANCHARD, AND AMERICAN EXPRESS DO IT

Honeywell, Blanchard Training and Development, and American Express epitomize three programs that fit the criteria just described for an informal reward system. At the Honeywell Technology Center of Honeywell, Inc., in Minneapolis, Minn., management implemented a recognition program called "The Winning Edge" for superior performance "above and beyond" his or her job. The program was open to any employee recommended by another employee for the award. A committee reviewed the recommendations, and individuals accepted were awarded $100 cash and a certificate presented at a periodic ceremony. In addition, the names of all award winners were posted in the company's newsletter.

The program was considered a success in getting employees to pay extra attention in helping others with their needs, recognizing those that were committed to excellence, and increasing the general morale and excitement of the work environment. The program ran its course over about a year and was discontinued after it was felt that a majority of the employees had received the award. Although there were some program costs, the benefits of the program exceeded the program costs considerably.

At Blanchard Training and Development, Inc., a management training and consulting company located in San Diego, "The Eagle Award" was established to recognize "legendary service" to customers—one of the organization's strategic objectives. The program, open to any employee, was announced and explained at a company-wide meeting. Employees could submit the name of another employee who had gone out of his or her way to help satisfy a customer request. Typical examples included staying late to ship materials, helping a customer locate a lost order or resolve a billing problem, rearranging trainer schedules to deliver a last-minute training request by a customer, and so forth.

The employees' names were submitted with a brief description of the activity that was considered exceptional. The recommendations were reviewed by a volunteer committee, primarily to screen out items that were considered to be an expected part of someone's job. The Eagle Committee then surprised the winners with a visit and took a picture of the person holding "an eagle award"—one of several eagle trophies that rotated around the company. The photo was displayed on a lobby bulletin board along with a brief description of the activity being recognized. The winner got to keep the eagle trophy on his or her desk until it was needed for a new recipient—typically a week or so. At the end of the year, an "eagle-of-the-year award was selected from a list of multiple eagle award winners. That person was presented an engraved clock at the company's annual celebration program.

One of several such efforts, this program was credited with making "legendary service" become an established part of the company's culture, Once more, it was implemented at virtually no cost. A few employees criticized the program, pointing out that it favored those individuals who dealt with customers on a daily basis, but that was the only brickbat. Management revised the program after about a year to focus more on internal customer service, a new priority for the company.

At Travel Related Services (TRS) of New York-based American Express, a "Great Performer's" program was started to recognize and reward truly exceptional performance. Life-sized posters showing famous people with their greatest performances were displayed throughout the facilities for many weeks. Then the company began to picture American Express employees on posters, with a statement of a major accomplishment by each employee. Afterwards the employee could take the poster home.

Nominations were made by fellow employees, supervisors, and customers. Award winners were eligible to become Grand Award winners, named by the worldwide governing committee. There was no limit on how many people could win, and in a recent year 38 employees captured the award. Prizes for Grand Award winners included an all-expense-paid trip for two to New York, $4,000 in American Express traveler's checks, a platinum "GP" logo pin, and a framed certificate.

The Great Performers' program helped to increase TRS's net income 500% in 11 years, or about an 18% annual compounded rate. The company's return on equity since the program began has been 28%.

IMPLICATIONS FOR THE FUTURE

There are at least three trends favoring the increasing use of informal reward systems today and in the future:

The trend toward fixed compensation. Employee compensation programs today are moving toward fixed compensation systems in which salaries are frozen and merit increases are paid only on a bonus basis. Such changes place pressure on organizations to find other ways to reinforce desired behavior. Informal rewards can help accommodate this need for new reinforcers.

The trend toward empowered employees. Empowered employees have increased responsibility and autonomy to act in the best interests of the company. Management's challenge is thus to build adaptability into the controls of the organization, thus providing employees with more flexibility and freedom to innovate while concurrently directing their activities towards the common purpose of the organization. The use of informal rewards by managers can help influence desired employee behaviors in effective, yet nondirective ways.

The trend toward increased uncertainty. U.S. business is experiencing constant change at a faster and faster rate. Because companies are operating in a dynamic, changing environment, management must use more flexible, less formal coordinating mechanisms that increase the use of informal controls and attempt to reduce reliance upon formal management controls. Informal systems work better during times of uncertainty. In such times, informal systems

can help to stabilize operations better than more formal control systems. As Maciariello and Kirby explain, "The association between the informal and formal changes with the degree of uncertainty. As stability and predictability increase, the use of formal systems increases. In times of major change, the informal system should be the dominant management system. The formal system, that is, the policies and procedures that applied to the past products and customers, may actually be looked upon by management as a potential barrier."[7]

Informal rewards even have increased potential for use with executive management. "In today's business environment, the critical motivational needs of executives and, therefore, the effectiveness of most incentive schemes are undermined. In a climate characterized by debt-laden companies, changing ownership, corporate downsizing, flattening organizational structures, and a $375 million out placement industry, there is less certainty, loyalty, and stability. This environment undermines the needs for belonging, security and control. Most executives have usually satisfied their basic financial needs. While stock options or additional bonus dollars play a role, personal incentives, such as recognition or achievement, become more important."[8]

The challenge is to design management controls that simultaneously encourage continuous improvement and autonomy within current operations and yet are capable of adaptation to major discontinuities in the environment. Informal reward systems can do just that.

Bob Nelson is vice president of Blanchard Training and Development, Inc. in San Diego, Calif.; a doctoral candidate at The Peter F. Drucker Management Center of The Claremont Graduate School in Los Angeles; and author of 1001 Ways to Reward Employees (Workman Publishing, 1994), now in its 11th printing. He can be reached at 1-800-728-6000, ext. 5293.

Notes

1. Craig Eric Schneier, "Capitalizing on Performance Management, Recognition, and Rewards Systems:" *Compensation end Benefits Review,* March–April 1989, p. 23.

2. Peter F. Drucker, *Management: Tasks, Responsibilities, Practices,* Harper and Row, New York, 1974, p. 239.

3. F. Cecil Hill. "Generating Ideas That Lower Costs and Boost Productivity," *National Productivity Review,* Vol. 8, No. 2, Spring 1989, p. 161.

4. Survey conducted by the Society of Incentive Travel Executives Foundation as reported by Christina Lovio-George, "What Motivates Best?" *Sales & Marketing Management* April 1992.

5. Gerald H. Graham and Jeanne Unruh, "The Motivational Impact of Nonfinancial Employee Appreciation Practices on Medical Technologists," *Health Care Supervisor,* 1990, 8(3), pp. 9–17.

6. Daniel C. Boyle, "Ideas for Action—The 100 Club," *Harvard Business Review,* March–April 1987, p. 27.

7. Joseph A. Maciariallo and Calvin J. Kirby, *Management Control Systems: Using Adaptive Systems to Attain Control,* Prentice-Hall, Englewood Cliffs, N.J., 1994.

8. Jeanne Greenberg and Michael Liebman, "Incentives: The Missing Link in Strategic Performance:" *Journal of Business Strategy,* July–August 1990, p. 9.

From B. Nelson, "Motivating Employees with Informal Rewards," *Management Accounting* (November 1995): 30–34. Reprinted with permission.

Question

14.2 What are four characteristics of informal rewards that make them effective? Explain.

14.3 Why Incentive Plans Cannot Work
When reward systems fail, don't blame the program—look at the premise behind it.

By Alfie Kohn

It is difficult to overstate the extent to which most managers and the people who advise them believe in the redemptive power of rewards. Certainly, the vast majority of U.S. corporations use some sort of program intended to motivate employees by tying compensation to one index of performance or another. But more striking is the rarely examined belief that people will do a better job if they have been promised some sort of incentive. This assumption and the practices associated with it are pervasive, but a growing collection of evidence supports an opposing view. According to numerous studies in laboratories, workplaces, classrooms, and other settings, rewards typically undermine the very processes they are intended to enhance. The findings suggest that the failure of any given incentive program is due less to a glitch in that program than to the inadequacy of the psychological assumptions that ground all such plans.

TEMPORARY COMPLIANCE

Behaviorist theory, derived from work with laboratory animals, is indirectly responsible for such programs as piecework pay for factory workers, stock options for top executives, special privileges accorded to employees of the Month, and commissions for salespeople. Indeed, the livelihood of innumerable consultants has long been based on devising fresh formulas for computing bonuses to wave in front of employees. Money, vacations, banquets, plaques—the list of variations on a single, simple behaviorist model of motivation is limitless. And today even many people who are regarded as forward thinking—those promote teamwork, participative management, continuous improvement, and the like—urge the use of rewards to institute and maintain these very reforms. What we use bribes to accomplish may have changed, but the reliance on bribes, on behaviorist doctrine, has not.

Moreover, the few articles that appear to criticize incentive plans are invariably limited to details of implementation. Only fine-tune the calculations and delivery of the incentive—or perhaps hire the author as a consultant—and the problem will be solved, we are told. As Herbert H.

Meyer, professor emeritus in the psychology department at the College of Social and Behavioral Sciences at the University of South Florida, has written, "Anyone reading the literature on this subject published 20 years ago would find that the articles look almost identical to those published today." That assessment, which could have been written this morning, was actually offered in 1975. In nearly forty years, the thinking hasn't changed.

Do rewards work? The answer depends on what we mean by "work." Research suggests that, by and large, rewards succeed at securing one thing only: temporary compliance. When it comes to producing lasting change in attitudes and behavior, however, rewards, like punishment, are strikingly ineffective. Once the rewards run out, people revert to their old behaviors. Studies show that offering incentives for losing weight, quitting smoking, using seat belts, or (in the case of children) acting generously is not only less effective than other strategies but often proves worse than doing nothing at all. Incentives, a version of what psychologists call extrinsic motivators, do not alter the attitudes that underlie our behaviors. They do not create an enduring *commitment* to any value or action. Rather incentives merely—and temporarily—change what we do.

As for productivity, at least two dozen studies over the last three decades have conclusively shown that people who expect to receive a reward for completing a task or for doing that task successfully simply do not perform as well as those who expect no reward at all. These studies examined rewards for children and adults, males and females, and included tasks ranging from memorizing facts to creative problem-solving to designing collages. In general, the more cognitive sophistication and open-ended thinking that was required, the worse people performed when working for a reward. Interestingly enough, the researchers themselves were often taken by surprise. They assumed that rewards would produce better work but discovered otherwise.

The question for managers is whether incentive plans can work when extrinsic motivators more generally do not. Unfortunately, as author C. Douglas Jenkins, Jr., has noted, most organizational studies to date—like the articles published—have tended "to focus on the effects of *variations* in incentive conditions, and not on whether performance-based pay per se raises performance levels."

A number of studies, however, have examined whether or not pay, especially at the executive level, is related to corporate profitability and other measures of organizational performance. Often they have found slight or even *negative* correlations between pay and performance. Typically, the absence of such a relationship is interpreted as evidence of links between compensation and something other than how well people do their jobs. But most of these data could support a different conclusion, one that reverses the causal arrow. Perhaps what these studies reveal is that higher pay does not, produce better performance. In other words, the very idea of trying to reward quality may be a fool's errand.

Consider the findings of Jude T. Rich and John A. Larson, formerly of McKinsey & Company. In 1982, using interviews and proxy statements, they examined compensation programs at 90 major U.S. companies to determine whether return to shareholders was better for corporations that had incentive plans for top executives than it was for those companies that had no such plans. They were unable to find any difference.

Four years later, Jenkins tracked down 28 previously published studies that measured the impact of financial incentives on performance. (Some were conducted in the laboratory and some in the field.) His analysis, "Financial Incentives," published in 1986, revealed that 16, or 57%, of the studies found a positive effect on performance. However, all of the performance measures were quantitative in nature: a good job consisted of producing more of something or doing it faster. Only five of the studies looked at the quality of performance. And none of those five showed any benefits from incentives.

Another analysis took advantage of an unusual situation that affected a group of welders at a Midwestern manufacturing company. At the request of the union, an incentive system that had been in effect for some years was abruptly eliminated. Now, if a financial incentive supplies motivation, its absence should drive down production. And that is exactly what happened, at first. Fortunately, Harold F. Rothe, former personnel manager and corporate staff assistant at the Beloit Corporation, tracked production over a period of months, providing the sort of long-term data rarely collected in this field. After the initial slump, Rothe found that in the absence of incentives the welders' production quickly began to rise and eventually reached a level as high or higher than it had been before.

One of the largest reviews of how intervention programs affect worker productivity, a meta-analysis of some 330 comparisons from 98 studies, was conducted in the mid-1980s by Richard A. Guzzo, associate professor of psychology at the University of Maryland, College Park, and his colleagues at New York University. The raw numbers seemed to suggest a positive relationship between financial incentives and productivity, but because of the huge variations from one study to another, statistical tests indicated that there was no significant effect overall. What's more, financial incentives were virtually unrelated to the number of workers who were absent or who quit their jobs over a period of time. By contrast, training and goal-setting programs had a far greater impact on productivity than did pay-for-performance plans.

WHY REWARDS FAIL

Why do most executives continue to rely on incentive programs? Perhaps it's because few people take the time to examine the connection between incentive programs and problems with workplace productivity and morale. Rewards buy temporary compliance, so it looks like the problems are solved, It's harder to spot the harm they cause over the long term. Moreover, it does not occur to most of us to suspect rewards, given that our own teachers, parents, and managers probably used them. "Do this and you'll get that" is part of the fabric of American life. Finally, by clinging to the belief that motivational problems are due to the particular incentive system in effect at the moment, rather than to the psychological theory behind all incentives, we can remain optimistic that a relatively minor adjustment will repair the damage.

Over the long haul, however, the potential cost to any organization of trying to fine-tune reward-driven compensation systems may be considerable. The fundamental flaws of behaviorism itself doom the prospects of affecting long-term behavior change or performance improvement through the use of rewards. Consider the following six-point framework that examines the true costs of an incentive program.

1. "Pay is not a motivator." W. Edward Deming's declaration may seem surprising, even absurd. Of course, money buys the things people want and need. Moreover, the less people are paid, the more concerned they are likely to be about financial matters. Indeed, several studies over the last few decades have found that when people are asked to guess what matters to their coworkers—or, in the case of managers, to their subordinates—they assume money heads the list. But put the question directly—"what do you care about?"—and pay typically ranks only fifth or sixth.

Even if people were principally concerned with their salaries, this does not prove that money is motivating. There is no firm basis for the assumption that paying people more will encourage them to do better work or even, in the long run, more work. As Frederick Herzberg, Distinguished Professor of Management at the University of Utah's Graduate School of Management, has argued, just because too little money can irritate and demotivate does not mean that more and more money will bring about increased satisfaction, much less increased motivation. It is plausible to assume that if someone's take-home pay was cut in half, his or her morale would suffer enough to undermine performance. But it doesn't necessarily follow that doubling that person's pay would result in better work.

2. Rewards punish. Many managers understand that coercion and fear destroy motivation and create defiance, defensiveness, and rage. They realize that punitive management is a contradiction in terms. As Herzberg wrote in HBR some 25 years ago ("One More Time: How Do You Motivate

Employees?" January–February 1968), a "KITA"—which, he coyly explains, stands for "kick in the pants"—may produce movement but never motivation.

What most executives fail to recognize is the Herzberg's observation is equally true of rewards. Punishment and rewards are two sides of the same coin. Rewards have a punitive effect because they, like out right punishment, are manipulative. "Do this and you'll get that" is not really very different from "Do this or here's what will happen to you." In the case of incentives, the reward itself may be highly desired; but by making that bonus contingent on certain behaviors, managers manipulate their subordinates, and that experience of being controlled is likely to assume a punitive quality over time.

Further, not receiving a reward one had expected to receive is also indistinguishable from being punished. Whether the incentive is withheld or withdrawn deliberately, or simply not received by someone who had hoped to get it, the effect is identical. And the more desirable the reward, the more demoralizing it is to miss out.

The new school, which exhorts us to catch people doing something right and reward them for it, is not very different from the old school, which advised us to catch people doing something wrong and threaten to punish them if they ever do it again. What is essentially taking place in both approaches is that a lot of people are getting caught. Managers are creating a workplace in which people feel controlled, not an environment conducive to exploration, learning, and progress.

3. Rewards rupture relationships.
Relationships among employees are often casualties of the scramble for rewards. As leaders of the Total Quality Management movement have emphasized, incentive programs, and the performance appraisal systems that accompany them, reduce the possibilities for cooperation. Peter R. Scholtes, senior management consultant at Joiner Associates Inc., put it starkly, "Everyone is pressuring the system for individual gain. No one is improving the system for collective gain. The system will inevitably crash." Without teamwork, in other words, can be no quality.

The surest way to destroy cooperation and, therefore, organizational excellence, is to force people to compete for rewards or recognition or to rank them against each other. For each person who wins, there are many others who carry with them the feeling of having lost. And the more these awards are publicized through the use of memos, newsletters, and awards banquets, the more detrimental their impact can be. Furthermore, when employees compete for a limited number of incentives, they will most likely begin to see each other as obstacles to their own success. But the same result can occur with any use of rewards; introducing competition just makes a bad thing worse.

Relationships between supervisors and subordinates can also collapse under the weight of incentives. Of course, the supervisor who punishes is about as welcome to employees as a glimpse of a police car in their rearview mirrors. But even the supervisor who rewards can produce some damaging reactions. For instance, employees may be tempted to conceal any problems they might be having and present themselves as infinitely competent to the manager in control of the money. Rather than ask for help—a prerequisite for optimal performance—they might opt instead for flattery, attempting to convince the manager that they have everything under control. Very few things threaten an organization as much as a hoard of incentive-driven individuals trying to curry favor with the incentive dispenser.

4. Rewards ignore reasons.
In order to solve problems in the workplace, managers must understand what caused them. Are employees inadequately prepared for the demands of their jobs? Is long-term growth being sacrificed to maximize short-term return? Are workers unable to collaborate effectively? Is the rigidly hierarchical that employees are intimidated about making recommendations and feel powerless and burned out? Each of these situations calls for a different response. But relying on incentives to boost productivity does nothing to address possible underlying problems and bring about meaningful change.

Moreover, managers often use incentive systems as a substitute for giving workers what they need to do a good job. Treating workers well—providing useful feedback, social support, and the room for self-determination—is the essence of good management. On the other hand, dangling a bonus in front of employees and waiting for the results requires much less effort. Indeed, some evidence suggests that productive managerial strategies are less likely to be used in organizations that lean on pay-for-performance plans. In his study of welders' performance, Rothe noted that supervisors tended to "demonstrate relatively less leadership" when incentives were in place. Likewise, author Carla O'Dell reports in *People, Performance, and Pay* that a survey of 1,600 organizations by the American Productivity Center discovered little in the way of active employee involvement in organizations that used small-group incentive plans. As Jone L. Pearce, associate professor at the Graduate School of Management, University of California at Irvine, wrote in "Why Merit Pay Doesn't Work: Implications from Organization Theory," pay for performance actually "impedes the ability of managers to manage."

5. Rewards discourage risk-taking.
"People will do precisely what they are asked to do if the reward is significant," enthused Monroe J. Haegele, a proponent of pay-for-performance programs, in "The New Performance Measures." And here is the root of the problem. Whenever people are encouraged to think about what they will get for engaging in a task, they become less inclined to take risks or explore possibilities, to play hunches or to consider incidental stimuli. In a word, the number one casualty of rewards is creativity.

Excellence pulls in one direction; rewards pull in another. Tell people that their income will depend on their productivity or performance rating, and they will focus on the numbers. Sometimes they will manipulate the schedule for completing tasks or even engage in patently unethical and illegal behavior. As Thane S. Pittman, professor and chair of the psychology department at Gettysburg College, and his colleagues point out, when we are motivated by incentives, "features such as predictability and simplicity are desirable, since the primary focus associated with this orientation is to get through the task expediently in order to reach the desired goal." The late Cornell University professor, John Condry, was more succinct: rewards, he said, are the "enemies of exploration."

Consider the findings of organizational psychologist Edwin A. Locke. When Locke paid subjects on a piece-rate basis for their work, he noticed that they tended to choose easier tasks as the payment for success increased. A number of other studies have also found that people working for a reward generally try to minimize challenge. It isn't that human beings are naturally lazy or that it is unwise to give employees a voice in determining the standards to be used. Rather, people tend to lower their sights when they are encouraged to think about what they are going to get for their efforts. "Do this and you'll get that," in other words, focuses attention on the "that" instead of the "this." Emphasizing large bonuses is the last strategy we should use if we care about innovation. Do rewards motivate people? Absolutely. They motivate people to get rewards.

6. Rewards undermine interest. If our goal is excellence, no artificial incentive can ever match the power of intrinsic motivation. People who do exceptional work may be glad to be paid and even more glad to be well paid, but they do not work to collect a paycheck. They work because they love what they do.

Few will be shocked by the news that extrinsic motivators are a poor substitute for genuine interest in one's job. What is far more surprising is that rewards, like punishment, may actually undermine the intrinsic motivation that results in optimal performance. The more a manager stresses what an employee can earn for good work, the less interested that employee will be in the work itself.

The first studies to establish the effect of rewards on intrinsic motivation were conducted in the early 1970s by Edward Deci, professor and chairman of the psychology department at the University of Rochester. By now, scores of experiments across the country have replicated the finding. As Deci and his colleague Richard Ryan, senior vice president of investment and training manager at Robert W. Baird and Co., Inc., wrote in their 1985 book, *Intrinsic Motivation and Self-Determination in Human Behavior,* "the research has consistently shown that any contingent payment system tends to undermine intrinsic motivation." The basic effect is the same for a variety of rewards and tasks, although extrinsic motivators are particularly destructive when tied to interesting or complicated tasks.

Deci and Ryan argue that receiving a reward for a particular behavior sends a certain message about what we have done and controls, or attempts to control, our future behavior. The more we experience being controlled, the more we will tend to lose interest in what we are doing. If we go to

work thinking about the possibility of getting a bonus, we come to feel that our work is not self-directed. Rather, it is the reward that drives our behavior.

Other theorists favor a more simple explanation for the negative effect rewards have on intrinsic motivation: anything presented as a prerequisite for something else—that is, as a means toward another end—comes to be seen as less desirable. The recipient of the reward assumes, "If they have to bribe me to do it, it must be something I wouldn't want to do." In fact, a series of studies, published in 1992 by psychology professor Jonathan L. Freedman and his colleagues at the University of Toronto, confirmed that the larger the incentive we are offered, the more negatively we will view the activity for which the bonus was received. (The activities themselves don't seem to matter; in this study, they ranged from participating in a medical experiment to eating unfamiliar food.) Whatever the reason for the effect, however, any incentive or pay-for-performance system tends to make people less enthusiastic about their work and therefore less likely to approach it with a commitment to excellence.

DANGEROUS ASSUMPTIONS

Outside of psychology departments, few people distinguish between intrinsic and extrinsic motivation. Those who do assume that the two concepts can simply be added together for best effect. Motivation Comes in two flavors, the logic goes, and both together must be better than either alone. But studies show that the real world works differently.

Some managers insist that the only problem with incentive programs is that they don't reward the right things. But these managers fail to understand the psychological factors involved and, consequently, the risks of sticking with the status quo.

Contrary to conventional wisdom, the use of rewards is not a response to the extrinsic orientation exhibited by many workers. Rather, incentives help create this focus on financial considerations. When an organization uses a Skinnerian management or compensation system, people are likely to become less interested in their work, requiring extrinsic incentives before expending effort. Then supervisors shake their heads and say, "You see? If you don't offer them a reward, they won't do anything." It is a classic self-fulfilling prophecy. Swarthmore College psychology professor Barry Schwartz has conceded that behavior theory may seem to provide us with a useful way of describing what goes on in U.S. workplaces. However, "It does this not because work is a natural exemplification of behavior theory principles but because behavior theory principles...had a significant hand in transforming work into an exemplification of behavior theory principles."

Managers who insist that the job won't get done right without rewards have failed to offer a convincing argument for behavioral manipulation. Promising a reward to someone who appears unmotivated is a bit like offering salt water to someone who is thirsty. Bribes in the workplace simply can't work.

Alfie Kohn is the author of four books, including No Contest: The Case Against Competition and the newly published Punished by Rewards: The Trouble with Gold Stars, Incentive *Plans, A's, Praise, and Other Bribes, from which this article is adapted. Kohn lectures widely at universities, conferences, and corporations on education and management.*

ON INCENTIVES

"The Pay-for-Performance Dilemma"
by Herbert H, Meyer
Organizational Dynamics
Winter 1975.

"Financial Incentives"
by G. Douglas Jenkins, Jr.
in *Generalizing from Laboratory to Field Settings*
edited by Edwin A. Locke
Lexington, MA: Lexington Books, 1986,

"Why Some Long-Term Incentives Fail"
by Jude T. Rich and John A. Larson
in *Incentives, Cooperation, and Risk Sharing*
edited by Haig R. Nalbantian
Totowa, NJ: Rowman & Littlefield, 1987.

"Output Rates Among Welders: Productivity and Consistency Following Removal of a Financial Incentive System"
by Harold E Rothe
Journal of Applied Psychology
December 1970.

"The Effects of Psychologically Based Intervention Programs on Worker Productivity: A Meta-Analysis"
by Richard A. Guzzo, Richard D. Jette, and Raymond A. Katzell
Personnel Psychology
Summer 1985.

"One More Time: How Do You Motivate Employees?"
by Frederick Herzberg
Harvard Business Review
January–February 1968.

"An Elaboration on Deming's Teachings on Performance Appraisal"
by Peter R. Scholtes
in *Performance Appraisal: Perspectives on a Quality Management Approach*
edited by Gary N. McLean, et al.
Alexandria, VA: University of Minnesota Training and Development Research Center and American Society for Training and Development, 1990.

People, Performance, and Pay
by Carla O'Dell
Houston: American Productivity Center, 1987.

"Why Merit Pay Doesn't Work: Implications from Organization Theory"
by Jone L. Pearce
in *New Perspectives on Compensation*
edited by David B. Balkan and Luis R. Gomez-Mejia
Englewood Cliffs, NJ: Prentice-Hall, 1987.

"The New Performance Measures"
by Monroe J. Haegele
in *The Compensation Handbook* Third Edition
edited by Milton L. Rock and Lance A. Berger
New York: McGraw-Hill, 1991.

"Intrinsic and Extrinsic Motivational Orientations: Reward Induced Changes in Preference for Complexity"
by Thane S. Pittman, Jolee Emery, and Ann K. Boggiano
Journal of Personality and Social Psychology
March 1982.

"Enemies of Exploration: Self-Initiated Versus Other-initiated Learning"
by John Condry
Journal of Personality and Social Psychology
July 1977.

"Toward a Theory of Task Motivation and Incentives"
by Edwin A. Locke
Organizational Behavior and Human Performance
Volume 3, 1968.

Intrinsic Motivation and Self-Determination in Human Behavior
by Edward L. Deci and Richard M. Ryan
New York: Plenum Press, 1985.

"Inferred Values and the Reverse-Incentive Effect in induced Compliance"
by Jonathan L. Freedman, John A. Cunningham, and Kirsten Krismer
Journal of Personality and Social Psychology
March 1992.

The Battle for Human Nature: Science, Morality and Modern Life
by Barry Schwartz New York: W.W. Norton and Company, 1986.

RECOMMENDED READING

"A Model of Creativity and Innovation in Organizations"
by Teresa M. Amabile in *Research in Organizational Behavior,* Volume 10
edited by Barry M. Staw and L.L. Cummings
Greenwich, CT: JAI Press, Inc., 1988.

Out of the Crisis
by W. Edwards Darning
Cambridge, MA: MIT Center for Advanced Engineering Study, 1986.

"Merit Pay, Performance Targeting, and Productivity"
by Arie Halachmi and Marc Holzer
Review of Public Personnel Administration
Spring 1987.

No Contest: The Case Against Competition,
Revised Edition
by Alfie Kohn
Boston: Houghton Mifflin, 1992.

Punished by Rewards: The Trouble with Gold Stars, Incentive Plans, A's, Praise, and Other Bribes
by Alfie Kohn
Boston: Houghton Mifflin, 1993.

The Market Experience
by Robert B. Lane
Cambridge, England: Cambridge University Press, 1991.

The Hidden Costs of Reward: New Perspectives on the Psychology of Human Motivation
edited by Mark R. Lepper and David Greene
Hillsdale, NJ: L. Erlbaum Associates, 1978.

The Great Jackass Fallacy
by Harry Levinson
Cambridge, MA: Harvard University Press, 1973.

The Human Side of Enterprise
by Douglas McGregor
New York: McGraw-Hill, 1960.

Wealth Addiction
by Philip Slater
New York: Dutton, 1980.

Money and Motivation: An Analysis of Incentives in Industry
by William Foote Whyte and Melville Dalton, et al.
New York: Harper, 1955.

Question
14.3 What are the six reasons that incentive programs fail, according to Alfie Kohn? Explain.

CHAPTER 15

Management Accounting and Control System Design: Behavioral Factors and Change Management

Reading 15.1, Rechtschaffen, G. S., and J. A. Yardley's *Whistleblowing and the Law,* addresses many questions related to what can happen to employees who blow the whistle on their employers. Since many whistleblowers have been demoted or have lost their jobs, the authors' goal is to educate both management accountants and others in their legal rights if they are ever in a position to blow the whistle. The method that Rechtschaffen and Yardley use is to develop a hypothetical whistleblowing scenario involving a management accountant who believes that management has materially misrepresented a company's financial position to the public. The management accountant objects to management and then is fired. Readers are then posed 11 true/false questions to determine their legal knowledge about the nature and extent of their protection against reprisals. The authors discuss each of the answers to the questions and what a reader's score indicates.

In *A Framework for Successful Adoption and Performance of Japanese Manufacturing Practices in the United States* (Reading 15.2), S. Mark Young discusses another topic related to the design of management accounting and control systems. Studying the issue of adopting six factors relating to Japanese manufacturing practices in the United States, Young suggests each factor cannot simply be implemented without consideration of how it will affect the work environment. Young develops a framework for successful implementation and suggests ways that both the practices and the work environment can be modified to accommodate each of the manufacturing methods.

J. Ness and T. Cucuzza's *Tapping the Full Potential of ABC,* Reading 15.3, discusses the authors' consulting experiences with activity based management. By their estimates, only 10% of all companies who have attempted to explore or adopt ABC are still using activity-based management in their operations. Many companies adopting ABC probably did not anticipate how great an organizational upheaval such a change would bring about, and the authors believe that employee resistance to change is the biggest obstacle getting in the way of successful implementation. Both Chrysler Corporation and Safety-Kleen, two very different companies who have been successful in implementing ABC, are discussed. The authors discuss in some detail the reasons why both organizations have succeeded.

Implementing Activity-Based Costing Systems Successfully by M. D. Shields, and M. A. McEwen (Reading 15.4), presents the results of a survey of 143 companies who have had experiences implementing ABC. The survey is quite comprehensive with responding companies varying in size from $1 million to $33 billion dollars in annual sales, representing a wide range of commercial manufacturing, noncommercial manufacturing, and defense and non defense government contractors. Of the critical factors leading to successful ABC implementation, top management support was found to be the most significant. This was followed by the linkage of ABC to competitive strategy (recall Selto and Jasinski's article, Reading 2.2), the linkage of ABC to performance evaluation and compensation, training, nonaccounting ownership of the ABC system, amount of internal resources, and consensus and clarity of ABC objectives.

READINGS
CHAPTER 15

15.1 Whistleblowing and the Law
Are you legally protected if you blow the whistle?

Glenn S. Rechtschaffen, CPA, and James A. Yardley, CPA

Internal or external whistleblowing often results in demotion or discharge for the whistleblower. The threat of demotion or discharge also can deter the impulse to blow the whistle on your employer. Not surprisingly, a recurring theme among whistleblowers is regret for having blown the whistle.

Reprisals against management accountants for whistleblowing could be alleviated if the law would provide protection to management accountants. Although legal consequences may not be the most important factor in the decision to blow the whistle, the possibility of legal protection from retaliation should be known before action is taken.

For legal advice pertaining to a particular whistleblowing situation, readers should consult an attorney. We present the following hypothetical situation establishing a management accountant/whistle-blower scenario. We then ask 11 true/false questions testing the reader's legal knowledge of the nature and extent of protection against reprisals. In attempting to answer these questions, the reader should gain a better appreciation for the legal quagmire surrounding the potential whistleblower. The complexity of the law and the variety of factors that influence the nature and extent of legal protection will be featured.

WHAT IS YOUR LEGAL I.Q.?

In a management accountant's judgment, management materially misrepresents a company's financial condition to the public. The accountant objects and subsequently is dismissed.

Question 1—Suppose that management's misrepresentations violate certain state and federal criminal statutes. *True or false?*—By law, the accountant is required to externally disclose to the appropriate authorities, and this is an allowed exception to the IMA's Standards of Ethical Conduct internal whistle-blowing requirement.

False—Historically, failure to report criminal behavior was considered a crime (known as "misprision"), but it is no longer a crime. Although misprision of a felony in violation of federal law is still a federal offense, and some states follow a similar doctrine, no jurisdiction punishes for mere

knowledge and failure to report. Rather, an additional element such as affirmative concealment always is required. The result is the voluntary reporting of criminal behavior. Thus, because it is not legally required to report an employer's criminal behavior, the exception to the Standards would not be triggered—only internal whistleblowing would be permitted in this case.

Will external disclosing ever be allowed under the Standards? "Yes"—but only if the employee is *compelled* by law to testify. Although some statutes specifically give employees the right to testify against their employers, such testimony is still voluntary and presumably not sanctioned by the Standards. The external whistleblowing exception has limited application.

Question 2—In the hypothetical situation, the accountant is a nonunion employee in the private sector. *True or false?*—Better protection might be available if he or she is unionized or in the public sector.

True—An employer must show "just cause" to fire a union worker covered by a collective bargaining agreement. Furthermore, most public employees (state and federal) are protected against arbitrary dismissals either constitutionally or through statutes or civil service rules. Nonunion employees, as a general rule, are subject to a doctrine known as "employment-at-will" whereby the employer can fire/demote the employee at any time, for any reason, or for no reason at all.

Question 3—True or false?—In order for the accountant to obtain federal protection, a specific federal statute must prohibit employer retaliation for the type of activity engaged in by the employer.

True—For example, the federal Water Pollution Control Act protects employees who internally or externally whistleblow regarding activities covered by the Act. Many analogous statutes exist. Their goals include promoting collective bargaining, outlawing discrimination against minorities, protecting employee health and safety, and outlawing employer violations of environmental or safety standards. Unfortunately, the hypothetical situation does not fall under the protective umbrella of any of these specific statutes, and no federal "all-purpose" whistleblower protection statute exists for private sector employees.

Question 4—In the 1980s, 14 states passed statutes protecting private-industry whistleblowers. *True or false?*— The accountant is protected by such statutes if he or she lives in one of those states.

False—The statutes vary dramatically regarding protection. For example, California only protects external whistleblowing, whereas most of the other states protect internal and external whistleblowing. Some statutes only offer protection for specific issues. Louisiana limits its protection to informants disclosing environmental law violations. Other statutes, such as Michigan's, are broader in nature but restrict available remedies. No statute protects complaints of waste, mismanagement, or violations of professional codes of ethics, unless the activity concurrently violates a law, rule, or regulation promulgated by a branch of government.

Question 5—*True or false?*—To obtain state protection, the accountant's actions in our hypothetical situation must fall under the protective umbrella of a statute.

False—Even if the underlying activity is not covered by a statute, the common ("judge-made") law could provide relief. Most states have created judicial exceptions to the "employment-at-will" doctrine by providing protection for employees who allege their discharge/demotion violated "public policy."

But what violates public policy? One answer was offered by the Illinois Supreme Court in *Palmateer V. International Harvester Co.*, 85 Ill.2d. 124, 421 N.E.2d. 876, 878–9 (1981).

> *When a discharge contravenes public policy in any way, the employer has committed a legal wrong. . . . But what constitutes clearly mandated public policy? (I)t can be said that public policy concerns what is right and just and what affects the citizens of the State collectively. It is to be found in the State's constitution and statutes and, when they are silent, in its judicial decisions. . . . (The) matter must strike at the heart of a citizen's social rights, duties, and responsibilities. . . .*

The courts clearly have some room to maneuver within the "public policy" exception. As a result, the accountant in the hypothetical situation might obtain relief under the common law even if no statute offered protection. For example, if the misrepresentations violated either state or federal law, then a good argument could be made that any dismissal resulting from the reporting of such violation would itself be a violation of "public policy."

Question 6—*True or false?*—Common law has created a protective hierarchy for whistleblowing, ranging from the reporting of criminal violations at one end to ethical violations at the other.

True—For a dismissal to violate "public policy," most jurisdictions insist the whistleblower hold a good faith belief that the underlying activity violated a criminal or civil law. For example, in *Johnson v. World Color Press, Inc.*, 147 Ill.App.3d 746, 498 N.E.2d. 575 (Ill.App. 5th Dist. 1986),

the chief financial officer alleged he was fired for opposing accounting practices that he claimed violated federal securities laws. The court declared that the accountant was entitled to report his good faith belief to his superiors without fear of discharge. Similarly, another accountant was protected for enforcing the accounting requirements of the Foreign Corrupt Practices Act of 1977 (*Thompson v. St. Regis Paper Co.*, 102 Wash.2d 219, 685 P.3d 1081(1984)).

Although some courts have extended the "public policy" doctrine to employees terminated for their refusal to commit acts subject to tort law liability, only a handful cover refusals to violate professional codes of ethics. Most courts point to the fact that such codes, unlike laws, are promulgated by private organizations. Thus, whether the public interest is affected by a particular violation depends on the character of the violation.

The clearest case for considering a code of ethics infraction is where a danger is posed to public safety. One court held that the public interest would encompass an employee questioning the professional qualifications of a fellow emergency technician (*Gould v. Campbell's Ambulance Serv., Inc.*, 130 Ill.App.3d 598, 474 N.E.2d 740 (1984)). This position contrasts sharply with a Michigan case (*Suchodolski v. Michigan Consolidated Gas Co.*, 412 Mich. 692, 316 N.W.2d 710, 712 (1982)) involving a senior internal auditor fired for reporting questionable procedures as required by the Code of Ethics of the Institute of Internal Auditors. The Michigan Supreme Court stated, "This case involves only a corporate management dispute and lacks the kind of violation of a clearly mandated public policy that would support an action for retaliatory discharge. The code of ethics of a private association does not establish public policy."

Question 7—Assume that management's misrepresentations in our hypothetical situation violate certain criminal laws. *True or false?*—No state would deny the accountant whistleblower protection.

False—A few jurisdictions, such as Alabama, Georgia, and the District of Columbia, either by statute or through the public policy exception, have made no inroads into the "at-will" doctrine for private industry employees. Other states have exceptions so narrow that only the most egregious circumstances would entitle the accountant to relief.

New York, for example, has a narrowly drawn whistleblower protection statute. For a whistleblower to be protected, the underlying activity must violate a state, federal, or local statute or regulation and create substantial and specific danger to the public health and safety. No judicial public policy exception has been recognized. In *Sabetay v. Sterling Drug, Inc.* 69 N.Y.2d 329, 506 N.E.2d 919 (N.Y. 1987), New York's highest court denied recovery even though the conduct that caused the whistleblowing was illegal. Plaintiff, a former director of financial projects for defendant Sterling, refused to participate in certain alleged illegal activities (tax evasion schemes and maintenance of slush funds). He disclosed these activities to his supervisor and claimed that he was discharged as a result.

The Court held that because the parties had not expressly agreed to limit the employer's unfettered right to terminate at will, the plaintiff could not state a claim for relief. Any alteration to the "at-will" doctrine would have to come from the legislature, not the courts.

Question 8—True or false?—The extent of common law protection accorded whistleblowers differs between (1) whistleblowers who were asked to participate in the underlying activity but refused and (2) whistleblowers who merely obtained secondhand knowledge.

True—Courts give more protection to whistleblowers who have direct, personal knowledge of the underlying activity. The courts legitimately are concerned about the quality of the information. For example, many organizations are structurally complex or geographically dispersed. In such organizations, employees easily can misperceive the motivations of supervisors.

Question 9—True or false?—Most of the 14 state legislatures protecting private sector whistleblowers—and most state courts—agree that, to receive protection, the private sector whistleblower should work first within the internal channels of the employer's organization.

True—Courts, legislatures, and the IMA Standards recognize that employees have duties of obedience, loyalty, and confidentiality to their organizations. These duties compete with an individual's sense of public responsibility. In addition, an isolated incidence or action may be corrected easily within the organization. For these reasons, the employer usually should be given an opportunity to address a problem before it is made public.

Question 10—True or false?—Even if the accountant is prima facie protected by statute or the common law, he or she still may fail to obtain legal protection.

True—Even if the accountant falls under the statutory or common law protective umbrella, certain defenses generally are available to the employer. The employer can prevail if evidence discloses that the accountant would have been discharged even if the whistleblowing had not occurred. This is a "mixed motive" case—action was taken against the employee for more than one reason.

The employer also could admit that the action was taken solely because of the whistleblowing but contend that the whistleblowing was performed in an unreasonably disruptive manner. Some courts have allowed this defense, particularly in cases where the disclosure was made to the news media or the employee was otherwise indiscreet.

Question 11—Assume that the accountant's allegations in the hypothetical situation ultimately prove to be false—management's representations were neither mislead-

ing nor material. *True or false?*—Under this assumption, the accountant's whistleblowing is never protected.

False—Most jurisdictions require a good faith belief. Because there is encouragement to disclose for the public interest, if allegations ultimately prove to be false the whistleblower still should recover.

Scoring—If you answered all of these questions correctly, congratulations! You are aware of the factors influencing whistleblower legal protection, and your decision to blow the whistle can be made with an appreciation for the possible legal consequences of the decision.

If you scored nine or 10, your legal awareness is sophisticated but incomplete. What you do not know can hurt you. A score of less than eight indicates an incomplete understanding of the legal state of affairs regarding whistleblowing. Although legal consequences should not drive ethical decisions, the costs and benefits should be considered. Incomplete factual knowledge can result in poor decision making.

To blow the whistle always will be a difficult decision. Even without considering whether the whistleblower will be legally protected from retaliation, a management accountant must consider loyalty to the organization, personal conscience, and the requirements of codes of conduct such as the IMA Standards. Add the real risk of unrecoverable loss resulting from demotion or firing, and the decision to blow the whistle becomes complex.

This article does nothing to alleviate that complexity. In fact, the risk of unrecoverable loss is made enigmatic by the present uncertainty in whistleblower protection law, an area of law that remains in a state of constant flux. Nevertheless, the act of whistleblowing has legal ramifications that management accountants have a right to know.

Yet these ramifications will depend on the facts of each case, possibly on federal law, and certainly on the law of the state in which the management accountant resides. Outcomes in individual cases cannot be predicted, but we have attempted to highlight factors that courts and legislatures consider important when drawing distinctions in such cases.

Glenn Rechtschaffen, J.D., CPA, is an auditor with the United States Audit Agency in Hanover, Md. He can be reached at (301) 604-7519.

James A. Yardley, Ph.D., CPA, is professor of accounting at Virginia Polytechnic Institute and State University in Blacksburg, Va. He can be reached at (703) 231-7352.

Whistleblowing inside or outside an organization evinces opposition to employer conduct. The Standards of Ethical Conduct of the Institute of Management Accountants (IMA) provide guidance for management accountants faced with a whistleblowing situation. Management accountants are advised to resolve their conflicts within the organization. If a satisfactory resolution cannot be obtained in this manner; the alternative sanctioned by the Standards (SMA Number 1C, 1983) is "to resign from the organization and to submit an informative memorandum to an appropriate representative of the organization." This action, is a form of internal whistleblowing. According to the Standards, communication of such problems to "authorities or individuals not employed or engaged by the organization [external whistleblowing] is not considered appropriate," unless required by law.

From Rechtschaffen, G. S., and J. A. Yardley, "Whistleblowing and the Law," *Management Accounting* (March 1995): 38–41. Reprinted with permission.

Question

15.1 In Rechtschaffen and Yardley's article, what does the term "misprison" mean? Is it a crime? Explain.

15.2 A Framework for Successful Adoption and Performance of Japanese Manufacturing Practices in the United States

By S. Mark Young

University of Southern California

Japanese manufacturing practices are being implemented widely in the United States. However, firms are experiencing a variety of problems, indicating that these methods may have only limited success in the U.S. manufacturing environment. I suggest that modifications to both Japanese manufacturing practices and features of the U.S. manufacturing environment should be made before Japanese practices can be successfully adopted and performed. A framework for research is developed from which testable propositions are derived.

In the transfer of organizational patterns across societies, both conscious innovations and unconscious innovations produce departures from the original model. No matter how much a new organization's founders may want to build an exact copy of a model drawn from another society, they can never replicate it completely in the new setting. . . . We would expect that changes would be necessary when social structures are transferred across cultures. . . . By identifying more precisely the range of factors behind these departures, we can grasp more clearly how culture and new organizational patterns interact and how the processes of cross-societal emulation shape the development of organizations. (Westney, 1987: 25)

Over the last decade, Japanese manufacturing methods such as *Kaizen*, total quality control (TQC), and just-in-time (JIT) production have assumed a significant role in U.S. manufacturing (Dertouzos, Lester, & Solow, 1989; Hall, 1983; Hayes, Wheelwright, & Clark, 1988; Schonberger, 1982). American firms are implementing Japanese manufacturing practices because these practices have contributed to Japanese preeminence in many areas, including automobile manufacturing and consumer electronics production (Abegglen & Stalk, 1985; Cusumano, 1985; Womack, Jones & Roos, 1990). In the 1980s, hundreds of books and articles were written by both academics and practitioners extolling the virtues of Japanese manufacturing practices (Hay, 1988; Schonberger, 1982; Susaki, 1985).

Japan has a unique cultural and geographical history that affects its institutions assumptions about employee behavior, business relationships, cost management, and performance evaluation systems. These systems differ sharply from those in the United States (McMillan, 1984). These differences led observers to question whether Japanese practices should be modified in order for them to be successful in the United States (Klein, 1989; Zipkin, 1991). The thesis of this article is that U.S. firms and Japanese-owned firms in the United States will be much more successful in adopting and implementing Japanese manufacturing practices, respectively, if they pay more attention to the differences in practices and modify them accordingly.

In reviewing the literature, I found three strategies currently used to introduce Japanese manufacturing practices into the United States.[1] These strategies are (a) to maintain Japanese manufacturing practices as they are employed in Japan, but to modify the current features of the U.S. manufacturing environment (e.g., employee work attitudes and behavior, business relationships, and cost management and performance evaluation systems), (b) to modify some or all of the Japanese practices, but to maintain the current features of the U.S. manufacturing environment noted above, or (c) to modify some or all of the Japanese practices as well as the current features of the U.S. manufacturing environment. To date, it appears that many firms (especially Japanese-owned automobile manufacturers) follow the, first strategy. This approach seems to be largely responsible for problems, such as the current work force's lack of acceptance of Japanese practices (Fucini & Fucini, 1990). Based on a review of the evidence, I believe that the third strategy may be the most viable for firms to successfully adopt and perform these practices in the United States. However, only through systematic research can the three strategies (mentioned above) be reconciled.

Although there is an enormous amount of information and much opinion about the relative success or failure of Japanese manufacturing practices in the United States, the majority of information is derived from anecdotes and small sample studies (Fucini & Fucini, 1990; Gelsanliter, 1990; Junkerman, 1987; Krause, 1986). Both the controversy over whether the practices are successful and the lack of systematic evidence indicate that a research framework, from which testable propositions can be derived, will help to determine the conditions under which the adoption of Japanese manufacturing practices will be successful.

In the next section, characteristics of U.S. repetitive manufacturing systems (those most directly affected by Japanese manufacturing methods) are described (Chase & Aquilano, 1989; Karmarker, 1989; Krajewski & Ritzman, 1990). *Repetitive manufacturing* is defined as medium to high volume production of few product types. Assumptions about expected behavior, cost management and performance evaluation systems, and other features of the system also are presented. This section provides a baseline for discussion and represents the environment into which Japanese manufacturing practices will be implemented. Next, six factors relating to Japanese production practices are presented with an emphasis on the most widely implemented method for repetitive manufacturing—the JIT manufacturing system. The other five factors, *Kaizen,* TQC, JIT purchasing, the underlying behavioral control system, and the development of cost management and performance evaluation systems congruent with Japanese manufacturing practices, also are introduced. Propositions relating to how each of these factors can lead to successful adoption and performance of Japanese practices in the U.S. manufacturing environment are developed. Finally, further implications for theory building and testing are discussed.

REPETITIVE MANUFACTURING IN THE UNITED STATES
Repetitive Manufacturing in the United States—A Typical System
The typical U.S. manufacturing system works in the following manner: The manufacturing process usually begins with the delivery of materials. Materials are supplied to manu-facturing facilities by vendors who rely on the competitive bidding process in order to supply the manufacturer. Considerations of the number of vendors and their proximity to plants are usually less important than prices (Ansari & Modarress, 1990). Manufacturing firms purchase materials in large quantities to avoid running out of stock and facing other disruptions, and these materials are stored by manufacturers in on-site warehouses.

Production begins with each worker producing a subassembly using the raw materials. Workers "push" their subassemblies into a work-in-process (WIP) location where they are stored until needed (Chase & Aquilano, 1989; Krajewski & Ritzman, 1990). Other workers continue this process until the product is completed. Workers are assigned production targets and produce units at their own pace. In some instances, materials requirements planning, a push system, is used for forward planning of the flow of work and to control production (Karmarker, 1989). At the end of the process, a sample of the finished output is inspected by quality control personnel.

In the push system, workers tend to use highly specialized skills in order to produce a discrete part of the final product. Workers do not usually perform the tasks of other workers, and work rules and job classifications often forbid individuals from assisting one another (Drucker, 1987; Walton & Susman, 1989). Generally, workers are compensated through hourly wages or on a piece-rate basis.

In some cases, compensation systems such as piece rates often lead workers to maximize output, rather than to focus on quality. Workers are not held directly responsible for the quality of subassemblies they produce, and the high levels of WIP inventory decouples the process and creates slack in the system. The existence of WIP makes it difficult for management to determine which workers are producing good or bad output, especially if output is not tagged by quality control personnel to indicate specific flaws. Further, if a large amount of WIP accumulates and quality is not assessed at the work station, greater effort and cost are incurred when a defective unit is reworked.

The costing system generates production-variance reports that compare the actual and standard costs of production and serve as the central feedback mechanism for cost control. Usually such feedback is not provided until well after production has occurred; therefore, tracing errors to specific individuals or machines (in order to correct them) is often difficult (Johnson & Kaplan, 1987).

Many of these practices and attitudes are influenced significantly by factor costs such as the low cost of labor, energy, materials, and manufacturing space. These influences led to the attitude of discarding defective products rather than focusing on producing high-quality products (Dertouzos et al., 1989). Due to their relatively high incomes, U.S. consumers also have become more complacent about defects and less prone to appreciate high-quality products (Halberstam, 1986).

Expectations of Behavior and Primary Control
Weisz, Rothbaum, and Blackburn (1984) suggested that con-

trol systems in the United States are designed under the assumption that workers and management seek primary control over their work environments. Primary control is manifested when employees with individualistic tendencies (see Bellah, Madsen, Sullivan, Swidler, & Tipton, 1987) attempt to shape the existing social and behavioral factors surrounding them, including co-workers, specific events, or their environments, with the intention of increasing their rewards. Thus, many employees exhibit behaviors and establish goals that may diverge from those desired by the firm.

Research on manufacturing and control systems in the United States supports the view of Weisz and his colleagues regarding primary control. This research documents how workers attempt to shape their environments by manipulating work standards, incentive systems, and each other to gain desired ends (Mayo, 1933; Roethlisberger & Dickson, 1939; Walker & Guest, 1952). Well-known ethnographic studies by Burawoy (1979), Mathewson (1931), Roy (1952, 1955), and Whyte (1955) document the so-called "making out" process, in which workers circumvent work rules and outwit management and the time-and-motion personnel, as well as provide some minimal job satisfaction for themselves. Group norms relating to behavior under the piece-rate system foster an adversarial relationship between workers and management. The ultimate struggle for control of the shop floor, though, resides with external company unions representing the formal voice of labor, as is evident in the history of labor relations in the United States (Kochan, Katz, & McKersie, 1986). For these reasons, control systems consisting of rules, standards, and norms of behavior are established to guide, motivate, and evaluate employees behavior and performance (Giglioni & Bedeian, 1974; Hopwood, 1976; Lawler & Rhode, 1976; Quchi, 1977).

Despite improvements in U.S. manufacturing environments due to the Neo-Human Relations (Hackman & Oldham, 1980; Herzberg, 1958; McGregor, 1960), Sociotechnical (Emery & Trist, 1960), and Quality of Work Life movements (Davis & Cherns, 1975), the underlying assumptions and norms of primary control regarding traditional, repetitive U.S. manufacturing systems have not changed dramatically (Burawoy, 1979). Rather, the typical system, described above, in many cases is the environment into which many firms will attempt to implement Japanese manufacturing practices.

RESEARCH FRAMEWORK

The research framework presented in Figure 1 centers around the six factors relating to Japanese manufacturing practices: the JIT manufacturing system, *Kaizen,* TQC, JIT purchasing, the underlying behavioral control system, and the use of cost management and performance evaluation systems congruent with Japanese manufacturing practices. As shown in Figure 1, the cost management and performance evaluation systems encompass the other five factors and are used to assess their performance. Propositions relating to

how each factor leads to successful adoption and performance of Japanese practices in the United States will be developed in later sections of this article. Although specific operationalization of the dependent variables is beyond the scope of this article, readers are referred to Damanpour's (1991) comprehensive discussion of measures of the adoption of innovations and Boyd's (1991) thorough review of the literature on performance measures.

Japanese Manufacturing Methods and JIT—A Typical System

In comparison to the U.S. push manufacturing system that begins with the delivery of raw materials, customer demand triggers production in the JIT system. This demand for products "pulls" subassemblies through the system as workers in the final stage of production dictate the flow of these subassemblies through the process. This process continues upstream to the beginning of the line, and beyond, to the suppliers of raw materials. Suppliers deliver materials to the beginning of the line just as workers need them through a just-in-time-purchasing (JITP) system. This system eliminates the need for storing raw materials.

Unlike the push system in which a worker can usually work at his or her own pace, a worker's pace is disciplined by the *Kanban* or signaling system (Hall, 1983; Lu, 1989; Ohno, 1988). The *Kanban* system controls the WIP inventory and slack between stations because workers must wait to begin production until they receive a *Kanban* signal. When the demand pattern fluctuates and when multiple parts are produced on the same machines, multiple *Kanban* are used. Reducing WIP inventory also allows greater visibility regarding any production problems. Workers are taught to act cooperatively and are cross-trained so that they can perform all tasks in their group. This cross-training provides them with greater flexibility. Each worker is held personally responsible for the quality of the subassembly he or she produces and the orderliness and cleanliness of his or her work station.

Integrally tied to the JIT system is the philosophy of *Kaizen,* or continuous improvement (Imai, 1987), and total quality control (TQC) or *Jidoka* system (Chase & Aquilano, 1989; Schonberger, 1982). Whereas the JIT system focuses a worker's attention, *Kaizen* instills in the worker the habit of continually improving the production process and reducing waste. According to the TQC system, workers are trained to halt production if a defect is found and to resolve all problems immediately. TQC also encompasses methods such as statistical process control (SPC) and eliminates the need for a separate quality inspection department.

Compensation under the JIT system usually begins with a flat salary, which may be tied to individual or group performance. Other factors such as seniority within the firm or special knowledge can increase compensation (Lincoln & Kalleberg, 1990; Weitzman, 1985). Though little is known about Japanese cost management systems, they have been designed to be congruent with the JIT and TQC manufacturing process

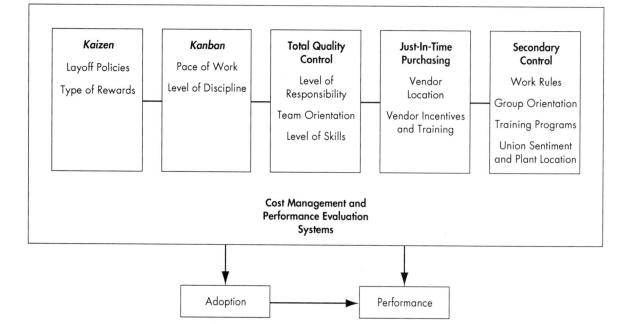

and provide immediate feedback about the functioning of the production process. In general, in Japan methods of cost management and performance evaluation are significantly simpler than those used in the United States (Kanatsu, 1990; Monden & Sakurai, 1990).

The development of Japanese manufacturing practices also has been tied directly to much higher factor costs than those in the United States. For instance, the cost of energy, manufacturing space, raw materials, and labor were significantly higher in Japan after World War II. Because Japan was resource poor, its survival as a nation after World War II was contingent on its competing through manufacturing (McMillan. 1984). Further, the much lower per capita income of Japanese consumers, the overall mind set of the Japanese people not to be complacent about quality, and the importance the Japanese people placed on their quest to become world economic leaders changed the way in which this society viewed manufacturing (Halberstam, 1986).

Expectations of Behavior and Secondary Control
In contrast to their characterization of push manufacturing as operating in a primary control environment, Weisz and his colleagues (1984) characterized Japanese manufacturing methods as relying on secondary control. Under secondary control, individuals increase their rewards by accommodating themselves to the existing environment through an adjustment of their expectations, goals, and attitudes. Secondary control systems induce individuals to subordinate their needs to a more powerful individual or force, such as the work group or the company.

These authors (Weisz et al., 1984) discussed two forms of secondary control in Japanese firms that are relevant for this discussion—the vicarious form and the predictive form. The vicarious form of control consists of aligning oneself with other individuals, groups, or institutions in order to participate psychologically in the control they exert. Acts of loyalty such as singing the company song, wearing the company uniform, and following company slogans are examples of the vicarious form of behavior. The predictive form of control relates to anticipating events in order to control their impact on oneself. An example of predictive control is the *Ringi* system through which the Japanese arrive at consensus. Under this system, middle management submits a proposal to all individuals and subunits that would be affected by it. Everyone is permitted to submit changes to the proposal, although clear lines of authority and status are followed in order to avoid anxiety, uncertainty, and conflict. It is understood that individuals subordinate any control that they might have under this system to their superiors.

IMPLEMENTATION OF JAPANESE PRACTICES IN THE UNITED STATES
Kaizen
In Japan, *Kaizen,* or continuous improvement, is a pervasive concept linked to all Japanese manufacturing practices. Imai (1987) described *Kaizen* as the driving force behind Japan's manufacturing success in eliminating worker complacency. However, implementation of *Kaizen* at the New

United Motor Manufacturing Company (NUMMI) caused Parker and Slaughter (1988: 2) to coin the term *management by stress*:

> Thus, no matter how well the workers learn their jobs, there is always room for Kaizen, or continuous improvement. At Nummi recently, slow sales caused the company to slow the line speed to reduce inventories of unsold cars. Instead of letting those on the line enjoy the slightly more relaxed pace, some workers were removed from the line and the jobs rebalanced so that the pace was as killing as before....Management-by-stress managers understand that workers continue to know more about the actual performance of their jobs than higher management does, and so make the process of appropriating that knowledge a never ending one.

Under *Kaizen*, workers are required to make production improvements and to impart their local information to management. Such improvements and information can be programmed into software that is used to drive industrial robots that replace the workers (Sayer, 1986; Young & Davis, 1990). Further, because of recent downsizing, many employees believe that adopting *Kaizen* means that they will ultimately lose their jobs or that their jobs will become even more demanding (Young & Davis, 1990). Risen (1989s) reported that at a GM plant in California where *Kaizen* is practiced, auto workers became outraged after GM announced a 20 percent layoff of workers despite "Japanese-style labor agreements" defining long-term employment and no layoff policies.

Layoffs are less commonplace in Japan for those employed under Japanese-style tenured employment. In Japan, because many employees generally are not afraid of losing their jobs, they are not opposed to learning about new technology and suggesting process improvements (Johnson, 1988). However, Junkerman (1982) stated that there is strong social pressure in Japan to make "voluntary" suggestions for improvements in the work place. He recounts the story of a Toyota worker who committed suicide when he was unable to think of an efficiency suggestion in his quality circle. Some companies such as Nissan (Japan) have a quota of suggestions for each employee that must be met each month (*Frontline*, 1984). In Japan, to encourage suggestions, both monetary and nonmonetary rewards are given to workers for suggesting improvements, and such policies can be encouraging for workers (Imai, 1987).

In the United States, employees are uncertain if management will use *Kaizen* for their benefit unless no layoff policies are used. Because few jobs carry tenure and few long-term employment contracts are made, some firms have instituted no layoff policies. Propositions 1a and 1b summarize this discussion.

When *Kaizen* is implemented:

Proposition 1a: The lower the likelihood that workers will be laid off from their jobs, the faster its rate of adoption and

the better the firm's performance.

Proposition 1b: The higher the likelihood that both monetary and nonmonetary rewards are given for improving the manufacturing process, the faster its rate of adoption and the better the firm's performance.

The JIT System and Pace of Work[2]

The most consistent source of concern and the greatest source of confusion regarding the implementation of Japanese manufacturing practices are the JIT system and the pace of work. First, the JIT system does reduce the level of inventory; however, low levels of inventory do not *necessarily* increase the pace of work. Domingo (1985) believes that low levels of inventory continuously create a small crisis in the mind of workers, by forcing them to create a perfect subassembly unit every time. As a result, workers develop stronger work discipline and concentration.

The negative reaction to JIT by U.S. workers may be the result of U.S. workers' not being accustomed to such stringent disciplinary practices. The JIT system provides little opportunity for workers to build any kind of slack, or relief (through WIP) into the production process (Sayer, 1986). Slack may be beneficial because it serves as a buffer against uncertainty and provides workers with more autonomy and time to resolve production problems (Klein, 1989).

In the United States, Japanese-owned firms using JIT systems have increased the pace of work so significantly that workers in many of these firms have voiced strong complaints (Fucini & Fucini, 1990). It seems that the pace demanded from workers in these plants is tied directly to the Japanese work ethic. The Japanese work ethic is explained as (a) a cultural phenomenon in which the historical legacies of Confucianism, Shintoism, and collective farming have fostered strong feelings of cooperation, group cohesiveness, and work norms (Ouchi, 1981; Schein, 1981); (b) a phenomenon based on the post-World War II economic necessity to rebuild Japan and the societal mind set that was created because of the war (Shimada, 1983); and (c) direct coercion and exploitation of Japanese cultural norms of collectivism by Japanese firms who force long hours of work at a frenetic pace (Briggs, 1988; Kamata, 1982; Sayer, 1986; Sethi, Namiki, & Swanson, 1984; Turnbull, 1986).

Though all three explanations are plausible, very little is documented about the third view. Some evidence supporting this view comes from Japanese sociologist, Satoshi Kamata, who was employed in the 1970s as a seasonal worker at Toyota. Kamata reported that Toyota created a cruel work environment due to its tough work rules and extremely fast work pace, and that a large number of work-related injuries were reported. The picture painted by Kamata is bleak compared to most reports of life in Japanese factories. Whereas Dore (1982) cautioned readers against putting too much credence in Kamata's book, other confirming stories about the pressures of working in Japanese automobile firms have been reported. Junkerman's interviews (1982, 1987) revealed similar findings at Nissan, where workers considered the work pace excessive. In general, workers were very hesitant to speak out against their firms, a finding that is still very prevalent (*Japan Behind the Mask,* 1990).

Helm and Edid (1985) followed the daily routine of Tomiki, a typical Japanese (permanent) worker at Toyota. Tomiki's work day is approximately 11 hours long with two 10-minute breaks plus lunch. Tomiki must be careful not to get ill because Toyota does not grant sick leave, so any days off must be taken from vacation time. In describing the pace of work and the stress of maintaining quality demands, Helm and Edid (1985: 77) wrote:

> *There is little room for error. Once or twice an hour, a mistake is made or a machine sticks, causing the next machine in line to stop. A yellow light flashes. Tomiki runs over. The squad must fix the part and work faster to catch up. A red button halts the production line if the problems are severe, but there's an unspoken rule against pushing it.*

Many firms operating in the United States try to emulate the pace of work in Japan, and workers in all of the Japanese-owned U.S. automobile plants (and some electronics plants) have complained about the strenuous pace. For instance, Buss and Bussey (1985: 10) watched as U.S. workers were unable to keep up with the flow of production. They reported that "on the production line, workers are often closer to a run than a walk as they rush between the parts benches and car bodies moving down the line." Also, Flint (1989: 94) quoted a worker at Mazda in Flatrock, Michigan, as saying, "We are building 1,000 good cars per day, an incredible effort. But, if we learn to do it with 90% (of the parts, resources or manpower) they go to 80%. They take away another person, they take away another part."

Krause (1986), Junkerman (1987), Turque and Copeland (1987), Levin (1985), and Risen (1989a) cited a number of instances at the Honda plant in Marysville, Ohio; the Nissan plant in Smyrna, Tennessee; NUMMI in Freemont, California; and Mazda in Flat Rock, Michigan, where many workers were unable to cope with the intensity of the work. Krause (1986: 44) was able to interview workers at the Honda plant in Marysville. He wrote:

> *Yet it is the workload that seems to frustrate the workers most....[E]very worker I talked to said that there are plenty of areas where the workload is unreasonable. . . . Pace on the line is too great. One man got crushed on the rear-door welding line due to a speed up in production. There are also dangerous work conditions.*

Some authors (Hay, 1988; Schonberger, 1982) have argued that JIT enriches jobs for workers by using techniques such as job rotation and cross-training. Both of these factors can create greater job enrichment by increasing the worker's skills and job scope, but an alternative view is that creating such a system of shop floor generalists gives firms more freedom to downsize their work forces, using remaining workers to perform a wider variety of tasks, often at a faster pace (Hout & Stalk, 1987; McCune, Beatty, & Montagno, 1988).

Thus, there is some evidence that Japanese workers experience the same problems with the pace of work in Japan that U.S. workers do, and because U.S. workers are not motivated or bound by any of the three previously stated explanations relating to work ethic, emulating this pace in the United States may be highly dysfunctional. Perhaps, and more important, the JIT system becomes confounded with the pace-of-work issue. This issue, in turn, can reduce acceptance of such a system by the work force. Quite surprisingly, both opponents and proponents of JIT seem to agree that the pace of the JIT system as practiced by the Japanese represents a return to turn-of-the-century U.S. production. Ichiyo (1984: 46) remarked that the trend toward quality circles and new methods of production in Japan is "the application of Taylorism by workers themselves," and even Schonberger (1982:196) stated that "the Japanese out-Taylor us all." The previous discussion is summarized by the following propositions:

When the JIT system is implemented:

> *Proposition 2a: The faster the pace of work, the slower its rate of adoption and the poorer the firm's performance.*
> *Proposition 2b: The stronger the level of concentration and work discipline among workers, the faster its rate of adoption and the better the firm's performance.*

TQC and Increased Worker Responsibility

Reports on the TQC system indicate that Japanese workers are encouraged to report quality problems and to stop the production line to make corrections if necessary (Susaki, 1985). Peer pressure is used both to ensure that errors are reported and to force employees to master their jobs in order not to call attention to themselves too often.

The literature in industrial sociology suggests that not all workers will be eager to embrace the kind of responsibility required under a JIT system. For instance, some workers appear to have a preference for monotonous work with little task variety (Hulin & Blood, 1976; Turner & Lawrence, 1965). Some earlier research, though, shows that workers will prefer jobs with autonomy (Chinoy, 1955; Walker & Guest, 1952) as long as the benefits of such job enlargement (e.g., relieving boredom) are greater than the costs of having greater responsibility (e.g., being held responsible for errors). Cole's (1990) observation of a GM plant indicates that both workers and the UAW were very enthusiastic about the new focus on quality. Determining high-quality standards provides workers with feelings of self-worth and dignity. Brown and Reich (1989) stated that at NUMMI potential workers are rigorously screened before they are hired. One of the key aspects to this screening involves how team oriented workers will be. This is an important concern given the high degree of reliance on the team concept employed at NUMMI.

Another issue related to TQC is the lack of math skills among U.S. workers. Thurow (1988) cited the case of

Matsushita in Japan, which employs high school graduates to perform statistical process control (SPC), a part of a total quality control program, as part of their jobs on the line.

When Matsushita attempted to use high school or college students in its North Carolina plant, it found few qualified applicants and ended up using employees with graduate degrees to perform SPC. Hiring employees with such skills and devoting sufficient resources for their education seems critical to the success of TQC. This discussion is summarized in Propositions 3a and 3b.

When TQC is implemented:

Proposition 3a: The greater the number of employees who are team oriented rather than individualistically oriented and who are willing to accept responsibility for quality, the faster its rate of adoption and the better the firm's performance.

Proposition 3b: The higher the level of mathematics skills of the work force, the faster its rate of adoption and the better the firm's performance.

Just-in-Time Purchasing

Ansari and Modarress (1990) stated that the benefits of just-in-time purchasing (JITP) include overall quality and productivity improvement, as well as paperwork and cost reductions. The initial development of the JITP system evolved with the "Toyota City" model in Tokyo, Japan; vendors were located within a two-mile radius of the central manufacturing plant and could supply the plant many times a day. The burden on the part of suppliers to deliver materials in the system was minimal (Armstrong, 1985).

American firms attempting to implement JITP face many problems. In the United States, the distance between many suppliers and manufacturing plants can be hundreds of miles. Many automobile manufacturing plants may be poorly located for JITP to work. Many vendors construct factories in the South where labor is cheaper and nonunionized, but many automobile manufacturing plants are located in the North, which poses a major problem for JIT delivery.

Another aspect of JITP relates to the huge subcontracting network that operates in Japan. By some estimates there are thousands of subcontractors who produce parts for large Japanese manufacturers and deliver these parts when needed (McMillan, 1990; Sakai. 1990). Such a network does not exist in the United States. One proposed solution is to develop long-term commitments with transportation firms so that parts are delivered on time (Ansari & Modarress, 1990).

Another problem relates to a general misunderstanding of JITP. In their survey of 25 firms in the United States, Ansari and Modarress (1986) found that lack of support and understanding from vendors was the most significant problem with JITP. It appears that many U.S. manufacturers do not fully understand the implications that JITP can have for their vendors. According to Frazier, Spekman, and O'Neal (1988), the key problem relating to manufacturers and suppliers in a JITP environment is the inability to collaborate

due to varying expectations. Manufacturers see JITP as a way for them to move inventory holding costs to suppliers, but suppliers view JITP as a way to guarantee high sales volume. Hutchins (1986) reported that many U.S. manufacturing firms that have adopted this view have met with great resistance from suppliers. Thus, a lack of understanding between manufacturing and suppliers seems to exist. The following proportions summarize this discussion.

When JITP is implemented:

Proposition 4a: The closer vendors are located to manufacturing plants and/or the better the transportation and material handling systems, the faster its rate of adoption and the better the firm's performance.

Proposition 4b: The greater the incentives for vendors for on-time, high-quality delivery, and the better the vendor training, faster its rate of adoption and the better the firm's performance.

Behavioral Control

Japanese manufacturing practices are most effective when teams of workers act cooperatively. The secondary control system described previously evolved because of the requirements of Japanese manufacturing practices. Firms implementing Japanese manufacturing practices have either tried to develop a secondary control environment in the United States or have tried simply to impose manufacturing practices in a primary control environment. As a result, many problems relating to plant location, union job classifications and work rules, greater reliance on teamwork, and worker empowerment arose.

Many Japanese-owned auto firms in the United States have taken great precautions in deciding where to locate the plants. Typically, such plants are located in "right to work" or antiunion states and areas where unemployment is high (Cole & Deskins, 1989). Although such locations may be very cost effective, it appears that a key recruiting strategy is to hire workers without any union experience because union experience hinders assimilation into the desired culture of the firm.

A few years ago, Honda of America used this strategy to hire primarily from a young, rural, predominantly white population of Marysville, Ohio, where unionism is not consistent with the farm culture. In this case, blacks and women fought Honda and won an out-of-court settlement due to these hiring practices (McQueen & White, 1988).

As further evidence of such strategy, Cole and Deskins (1989) showed that many Japanese auto plants in the United States are located in areas that have very low ratios of black to white populations in comparison to their sample of U.S. auto plants. Most Japanese-owned firms spend an enormous amount of time screening workers for their plants in the United States in the hope of developing as homogeneous a work force as possible (Hampton, 1988). Kraar (1989) reported that hiring practices at a Toyota plant in Kentucky required applicants to undergo at least 18 hours of exams, interviews, and attitude measurements. This process is consistent with Koshiro's (1983:85) statement that Japanese firms in Japan are extremely careful regarding who they will hire, and that they will eliminate "highly individualistic personalities from the communal society and segregate 'strangers' or the unqualified."

Drucker (1987) discussed the problem of existing union work rules and job classifications and the implementation of JIT systems. Because union rules forbid workers from performing tasks that are not in their job description, workers must wait until the appropriately classified worker is available to work. Such rules hold up production and complicate the implementation of cross-training. For example, McGune and his colleagues (1988) cited a UAW contract that called for three workers with different job classifications to move parts to the assembly plant at the American Motors Jeep plant. At Honda, only one cross-trained "associate" is needed to perform the same task.

In the U.S. auto industry, the UAW has loosened its hold on the number of job classifications and the kinds of work rules that it will accept. Part of the reason for this change is that since 1979 the UAW has lost more than 400,000 members (Forbes, 1987). It could be that those automobile plants (both Japanese-owned and the U.S.–Japan joint ventures) in which the UAW has been unsuccessful at gaining control have a predominance of employees who do subscribe to the notion of secondary control.

Other authors (Sethi et al., 1984) are highly skeptical that Japanese manufacturing systems can succeed in the United States, given the group-orientation culture in Japan. They make the case that Americans join group activities voluntarily, "on the basis of enlarged benefits that will accrue to them from participation, balanced against the loss of individual freedom that is surrendered to the group" (Sethi et al., 1984:243). The Japanese, however, are forced, in many instances, to join groups that others feel are appropriate for them. At the same time, the Japanese have designed a number of mechanisms in their firms that are based on "a set of reciprocal obligations between the group and the individual" (Sethi et al., 1984:244). For instance, in some applications of JIT and group technology (Hyer & Wemmerlov, 1984), individual incentives have been replaced by group-based incentive schemes (Barefield & Young, 1988). Each group member's compensation is based on the finished output of the group and not on the number of individual subassembly units each member has produced. There is disagreement, however, over whether performance-based incentives should be used at all (Hall, 1987; Schonberger, 1986).

Another difficult issue for many American workers to understand is the power shifting that can occur among employees. Chapman (1984) suggested that both first- and middle-line managers may resist Japanese practices when they realize that they are losing power due to the increased ability of workers to make decisions. One firm studied by Barefield and Young (1988) indicated that a number of first-

line managers quit within two months of a JIT system's being installed in their firm because they perceived that they were losing power and authority.

In the United States, workers are given much more power under JIT applications than management may realize. The implications of this are pointed out by Hudson (1988), who reported that at a Ford plant in the United Kingdom (where a JIT application had recently been implemented), management worried about the new empowerment of the work force. These managers believed that without large stockpiles of parts and other inventories, a workers' strike could cripple the firm. Wilkinson and Oliver (1989) analyzed the power implications of JIT purchasing and came to the conclusion that the JIT system is vulnerable to a number of problems because of its tight coupling.

Using a power model, Wilkinson and Oliver (1989) suggested that workers had the ability to halt manufacturing organizations under the JIT system, and that the effects of such a slowdown would be felt quickly and pervasively throughout the organization. Thus, workers are provided with much more power than they would have under a more traditional system. Evidence of this was recently reported in Mexico when a Mexican labor union won large wage improvements by targeting their strikes in U.S.-owned maquiladora plants that used the JIT manufacturing system. Labor unions know that such companies are vulnerable due to their low levels of inventories (*Bureau of National Affairs, Inc. Daily Labor Report*, 1991).

Empowering workers also means that the relative power of first-line managers and supervisors will be reduced. Hirschhorn and Gilmore (1989) indicated that such a power shift and cultural change can cause increased aggression for all parties and severe problems with authority relationships.

When a secondary control system is implemented:

Proposition 5a: The faster that work rules and job classifications are eliminated, the faster its rate of adoption and the better the firm's performance.
Proposition 5b: The greater the group orientation of workers and the more homogeneous the group members, the faster its rate of adoption and the better the firm's performance.
Proposition 5c: The greater the number of high-quality training programs related to power shifting between management and workers, the faster its rate of adoption and the better the firm's performance.
Proposition 5d: The higher the level of unemployment and antiunion sentiment surrounding a plant site, the faster its rate of adoption and the better the firm's performance.

Cost Management and Performance Measurement Systems

The previous discussion has centered on elements of Japanese manufacturing systems and the nature of secondary control. Another dimension of the research framework (in Figure 1) is tied to the performance of the manufacturing methods and individual performance measurement. In

318

many U.S. firms that have implemented Japanese practices, problems have arisen because they attempted to use existing cost management systems that were designed for traditional U.S. repetitive manufacturing. Such systems, according to Johnson and Kaplan (1987), were developed around the turn of the century and are now highly inappropriate for use in manufacturing environments employing new production methods. Kaplan (1986) investigated a U.S. firm that had just implemented a JIT system. The JIT system was working effectively; however, the company still relied on an obsolete cost accounting system to allocate its costs and assess its performance. The results were miscosted products and an overall system in which performance was not being measured accurately.

Kaplan's findings are not unusual. Barefield and Young (1988) found that in the firms they visited, the development and implementation of JIT systems was done initially by industrial and systems engineers. Cost accounting and internal auditing departments, which have a large responsibility for developing control and performance evaluation systems, had very little to do with how the system was planned and implemented. In some cases, JIT systems were implemented for well over two years before an effective cost management system was installed.

Clearly, without using the appropriate kinds of information to control and evaluate the performance of the system, Japanese practices could be rejected due to poor performance. To be congruent with Japanese manufacturing practices, cost management systems must be changed in the following ways. First, the Japanese align their cost management systems with the corporate strategy of the firm (Hiromoto, 1988). Cost management systems must measure the key indicators by which manufacturing performance is based, such as continuous improvement, the cost of quality, flexibility, customer satisfaction, value-added and non-value-added activities, product life cycle costs, and other measures of strategic success (Kanatsu, 1990; Kaplan, 1990; Monden & Sakurai, 1989; Shields & Young, 1991). Such measures are being developed, but there is still a focus on using only financial performance measures.

Second, because users of a JIT system require no physical counts of inventory, have no WIP inventory, use few to no purchase orders, make no hard copy reports for shipping and receiving, and do not need traditional labor reporting and variance analysis, they can design very simplified cost management systems (Foster & Horngren, 1988).

Finally, as shown in Figure 1, because information about performance is always fed back to employees, a cost management and performance evaluation system that inaccurately measures performance can cause misperceptions of employees' contributions to the firm. Such misperceptions can lead to negative changes in employees' attitudes and behavior. Because cost and performance management for Japanese practices are significantly different from traditional cost management, it appears that congruence between Japanese practices and cost management may be relatively more

important than for congruence between traditional manufacturing methods and cost management. The overall discussion is summarized in the next proposition:

When Japanese manufacturing practices are implemented:

> *Proposition 6: The more congruent the cost management and performance evaluation systems are with Japanese manufacturing practices, the faster the rate of adoption of Japanese practices and the better the firm's performance. Such congruence is relatively more important for the success of Japanese practices compared to non-Japanese practices.*

SUMMARY AND DISCUSSION

In the introduction to this paper, I contend that both Japanese-owned firms operating in the United States and American-owned firms implementing Japanese manufacturing practices have encountered difficulties. The goal of the article is to develop a theoretical framework that integrates the literature; from this, propositions outlining the problems and difficulties can be derived and tested before Japanese practices can be successfully adopted and performed. The information summarized in this article indicates that the third implementation strategy outlined in the introduction—to modify some or all of the Japanese manufacturing practices as well as current features of the U.S. manufacturing environment—is the most promising. Researchers should carefully study the six factors identified—*Kaizen*, TQC, the *Kanban* system, JIT purchasing, expectations about secondary control, and the current U.S. cost management and performance evaluation systems—so that they can advise firms of the best way to successfully implement these manufacturing practices. Further, because the Japanese are continuously experimenting with and modifying their manufacturing practices based on the principles of *Kaizen* (Chandler & Ingrassia, 1991; Technical Insights, 1990), it does not seem prudent to simply accept current Japanese practices and the U.S. manufacturing environment as they exist without working toward improvement.

Further theory development and testing should proceed on several fronts. First, rigorous cross-sectional and longitudinal case and field studies of U.S. firms that have switched to Japanese manufacturing practices and Japanese firms that have implemented their manufacturing practices in the United States are greatly needed. Case and field studies provide a richness that cannot always be gained from other research methods, and recent literature provides sound guidance for theory building from case studies (Eisenhardt, 1989; Yin, 1989). One recent example of a case study relating to Proposition 6 in this article is presented by Young and Selto (1991), who conducted a field study that addressed the changing role of cost accounting and other performance evaluation information in a Fortune 500 JIT manufacturing facility. A significant finding was the lack of training that employees received regarding changes to the cost management and performance evaluation system and the effects this lack of training had on their understanding of the changes and their related performance.

Other more traditional types of research methods are also being applied to theory testing in this area. A survey study by Brown and Mitchell (1991) investigated changes in employee perceptions when a firm changed half of its plant from a batch-processing to a JIT facility (Proposition 5c). While benefits such as improvements in material delivery, information quality, and resource availability occurred, many workers in the JIT system noted performance obstacles relating to their lack of training, problems in adjusting to new scheduling, and more interdependence on co-workers. Laboratory experiments are also being used in theory testing regarding Japanese manufacturing practices. Young, Shields, and Wolf (1988) manipulated the traditional U.S. push system versus the JIT system and worker responsibility versus no responsibility for quality control. Results showed that, as hypothesized, the greatest amount of good-quality output occurred for the interaction of the JIT system and when workers had responsibility for quality control (Proposition 2a and Proposition 3a).

The three studies cited above represent the beginnings of theory testing and building in this area. The research framework proposed in this article is a first step toward providing guidelines for such research, and as testing proceeds, clearer theoretical and practical recommendations regarding the successful adoption and performance of Japanese manufacturing practices will be made.

References

Abegglen, J. C., & Stalk, G. 1985. *Kaisha—The Japanese corporation.* New York: Basic Books.

Ansari, A., & Modarress, B. 1990. *Just-in-time purchasing.* New York: Free Press.

Ansari, A., & Modarress, B. 1986. JIT purchasing: Problems and solutions. *Journal of Purchasing and Materials Management,* 22(2):11–15.

Armstrong, L. 1985. Toyota's fast lane. *Business Week,* November 4, 42–46.

Barefield, R. M., & Young, S. M. 1988. *Internal auditing in a just-in-time environment.* Altamonte Springs, FL: The Institute of Internal Auditors.

Bellah, R. N.. Madsen. R., Sullivan. W. M.. Swidler. A., & Tipton, S. M. (Eds.). 1987. *Individualism and commitment in American life.* New York: Harper & Row.

Boyd, B. K., 1991. Strategic performance and financial performance: A meta-analytic review. *Journal of Management Studies,* 28: 353–374.

Briggs. P. 1988. The Japanese at work: Illusions of the ideal. *Industrial Relations Journal,* 19(2): 24–30.

Brown, C., & Reich, M. 1989. When does union-management cooperation work? A look at NUMMI and GM-Van Nuys. *California Management Review,* 32(4): 26–34.

Brown. K. A., & Mitchell, T. R. 1991. A comparison of just-in-time and batch manufacturing: The role of performance obstacles. *Academy of Management Journal,* 34: 906–917.

Burawoy, M. 1979. *Manufacturing consent—Changes in the labor process under monopoly capitalism.* Chicago: University of Chicago Press.

Bureau of National Affairs. Inc. *Daily Labor Report.* 1991. Mexican labor union wins big gains by striking low-inventory maquiladoras: A7.

Buss. D. D., & Bussey, J. 1985. Japanese management confronts U.S. unions in elections at Honda. *Wall Street Journal,* October 12:10.

Chandler. C., & Ingrassia. P. 1991. Shifting gears—Just as U.S. firms try Japanese management, Honda is centralizing. *Wall Street Journal.* April 11: Al.

Chapman, S. N. 1984. Japanese manufacturing systems: Implications to the organization. *Academy of Management Proceedings:* 300–304.

Chase, R., & Aquilano, N. 1989. *Production and operations management* (5th ed.). Homewood, IL: Irwin.

Chinoy. E. 1955. *Automobile workers and the American dream.* Boston: Beacon.

Cole, R. E. 1990. U.S. quality improvement in the auto industry: Close but no cigar. *California Management Review,* 33(5): 71–85.

Cole, R. E.. & Deskins. D. 1989. Racial factors in site location and employment patterns of Japanese auto firms in America. *California Management Review,* 32(1): 9–22.

Cusumano, M. A. 1985. *The Japanese automobile industry: Technology and management at Nissan and Toyota.* Cambridge. MA: Harvard University Press.

Damanpour, F. 1991. Organizational innovation: A meta-analysis of effects of determinants and moderators. *Academy of Management Journal,* 34: 555–590.

Davis, L. E.. & Cherns, A. B. (Eds.). 1975. *The quality of working life.* (Vols. 1–2). New York: Free Press.

Dertouzos, M. L. Lester, R. K., & Solow, R. M. 1989. *Made in America—Regaining the productive edge.* Cambridge, MA: MIT Press.

Domingo, R. 1985. "Kanban": Crisis management Japanese style. *Euro-Asia Business Review,* 4: 22–24.

Dore, R. 1982. Introduction. In S. Kamata (Ed.), *Japan in the passing lane:* ix- xi. New York: Pantheon Books.

Drucker, P. F. 1987. Workers' hands bound by tradition. *Wall Street Journal,* August 2:18.

Eisenhardt, K. M. 1989. Building theories from case study research. *Academy of Management Review,* 14: 532–550.

Emery, F. E., & Trist, E. L. 1960. Socio-technical systems. In C. W. Churchman & M. Verhulst (Eds.), *Management sciences, models and techniques,* vol. 2: 83–97. London: Pergamon Press.

Flint, J. 1989. Constant improvement? Or speedup? *Forbes,* April 17: 92–94.

Forbes, D. 1987. The lessons of NUMMI—GM and Toyota say the plant's a success, but it's no worker's paradise. *Business Month,* June 5: 34–37.

Foster, G., & Horngren, C. T. 1988. Cost accounting and cost management in a JIT environment. *Journal of Cost Management* 2(4): 4–14.

Frazier, G. L., Spekman, R. E., & O'Neal, C. R. 1988. Just-in-time exchange relationships in industrial markets. *Journal of Marketing,* 52: 52–67.

Frontline. 1984. The darker side of Japanese management. PBS News Documentary.

Fucini, J. J. & Fucini, S. 1990. *Working for the Japanese—Inside Mazda's American auto plant.* New York: Free Press.

Gelsanliter, D. 1990. *Jumpstart—Japan comes to the heartland.* New York: Farrar, Straus & Giroux.

Giglioni. G. B., & Bedeian, A. 1974. A conspectus of management control theory: 1900-1972. *Academy of Management Journal,* 17: 292–305.

Hackman, J. R., & Oldham, G. R. 1980. *Work redesign.* Reading, MA: Addison-Wesley.

Halberstam, D. 1986. *The reckoning.* New York: Morrow.

Hall, R. W. 1987. *Attaining manufacturing excellence.* Homewood, IL: Dow Jones-Irwin.

Hall, R. W. 1983. *Zero inventories.* Homewood, IL: Dow Jones-Irwin.

Hampton, W, 1988. How does Japan Inc. pick its American workers? *Business Week,* October 3: 84–85.

Hay. E. 1988. *The just-in-time breakthrough.* New York: Wiley.

Hayes, R. H., Wheelwright, S. C., & Clark, K. 1989. *Dynamic manufacturing.* Cambridge, MA: Harvard Business School Press.

Helm. L., & Edid, M. 1985. Life on the line: Two auto workers who are worlds apart. *Business Week,* September 30: 76–78.

Herzberg, F. 1958. *Work and the nature of man.* Cleveland, OH: World.

Hiromoto, T. 1988. Another hidden edge-Japanese management accounting. *Harvard Business Review,* 88(4): 22–27.

Hirschhorn, L., & Gilmore, T. N. 1989. The psychodynamics of a cultural change: Learnings from a factory. *Human Resource Management,* 28: 211–233.

Hopwood, A. 1976. *Accounting and human behavior.* New York: Prentice-Hall.

Hout. T. M., & Stalk, G. 1987. Working better and faster with fewer people. *Wall Street Journal,* May 15:10.

Hulin. C. L., & Blood, M. R. 1976. Job enlargement, individual differences, and worker responses. *Psychological Bulletin,* 69: 41–55.

Hutchins, D. 1986. Having a hard time with just-in-time. *Fortune,* June 9: 64–66.

Hyer, N. L., & Wemmerlov, U. 1984. Group technology and productivity. *Harvard Business Review,* 72(4): 140–149.

Ichiyo, M. 1984. Class struggle on the shopfloor—The Japanese case. *Ampo: Japan-Asia Quarterly Review,* 16: 38–49.

Imai, M. 1987. *Kaizen—The key to Japan's competitive success.* New York: Random House.

Japan Behind the Mask. 1990. Coronet Film & Video. Northbrook, IL: Simon & Schuster.

Johnson, C. 1988. Japanese-style management in America. *California Management Review,* 31(4): 34–45.

Johnson, H. T. & Kaplan. R. 1987. *Relevance lost: The rise and fall of management accounting.* Cambridge, MA: Harvard Business School Press.

Junkerman, J. 1982. We are driven. *Mother Jones:* 21–40.

Junkerman, J. 1987. Nissan, Tennessee—It ain't what it's cracked up to be. *Progressive:* 16–20.

Kamata, S. 1982, *Japan in the passing lane—An insider's account of life in a Japanese auto factory.* New York: Pantheon Books.

Kanatsu, T. 1990. *TQC for accounting—A new role in company wide improvement.* Cambridge, MA: Productivity Press.

Kaplan, R. S. 1986. Accounting lag: The obsolescence of cost accounting systems. *California Management Review,* 29(2): 174–199.

Kaplan, R. S. (Ed.). 1990. *Measures for manufacturing performance.* Cambridge, MA: Harvard Business School Press.

Karmaker, U. 1989. Getting control of just-in-time. *Harvard Business Review,* 77(5): 122–131.

Klein, J. A. 1989, The human costs of manufacturing reform. *Harvard Business Review,* 77(1): 60–66.

Kochan, T. A., Katz, H. C., & McKersie, R. R. 1986. *The transformation of American industrial relations.* New York: Basic Books.

Koshiro, K. 1983. The quality of working life in Japanese factories, In T. Shirai (Ed.), *Contemporary industrial relations in Japan:* 63–88, Madison: University of Wisconsin Press.

Kraar, L. 1989. Japan's gung-ho U.S. car plants. *Fortune,* January 30: 98–108.

Krajewski, L. J. R., & Ritzman, L. P. 1990. *Operations management—Strategy and analysis.* Reading, MA: Addison-Wesley.

Krause, K. 1986. Americans can build good cars—They're doing it in Marysville, Ohio. *Washington Monthly* (4): 41–46.

Lawler, E. E., & Rhode, J. G. 1976. *Information and control in organizations.* San Francisco: Goodyear.

Levin, R. P. 1985. GM—Toyota venture will test ability of workers in U.S. to match Japanese. *Wall Street Journal,* March 5:12.

Lincoln, J. R., & Kalleberg, A. L. 1990. *Culture, control and commitment.* Cambridge: Cambridge University Press.

Lu, D. J. 1989. *Kanban—Just-in-time at Toyota.* Cambridge, MA: Productivity Press.

Mathewson, S. B. 1931. *Restriction of output among unorganized workers.* Carbondale: Southern Illinois University Press.

Mayo. E. 1933. *The human problems of an industrial civilization.* New York: MacMillan.

McGregor, D. 1960. *The human side of enterprise.* New York: McGraw-Hill.

McCune, J. T., Beatty, R. W., & Montagno, R. V. 1988. Downsizing: Practices in manufacturing firms. *Human Resource Management,* 27:145–161.

McMillan, C. J. 1984, *The Japanese industrial system.* New York: Walter de Gruyter.

McMillan, J. 1990. Managing suppliers: Incentive systems in Japanese and U.S. industry. *California Management Review,* 34(5): 38–55.

McQueen, M., & White, J. B. 1988. Blacks, women at Honda unit win back pay. *Wall Street Journal,* March 24: 2.

Milbank, D. 1990. Culture clash—Making Honda parts, Ohio company finds, can be road to ruin. *Wall Street Journal,* October 5: Al, A6.

Monden, Y., & Sakurai, M. (Eds.). 1990. *Japanese management accounting: A world class approach to profit management.* Cambridge, MA: Productivity Press.

Ohno, T. 1988. *Toyota production system: Beyond large scale production.* Cambridge, MA: Productivity Press.

Ouchi, W. G. 1977. The relationship between organizational structure and control. *Administrative Science Quarterly,* 22: 95–113.

Ouchi, W. G. 1981. *Theory Z—How American business can meet the Japanese challenge.* Reading, MA: Addison-Wesley.

Parker, M., & Slaughter, J. 1988. Management by stress—Behind the scenes at Nummi Motors. *New York Times,* December 4: 2.

Risen, J. 1989a. Dissidents win at Mazda—Plant stung, UAW firm. *Los Angeles Times,* May 11: Part 4:1.

Risen, J. 1989b. Japanese labor policies stirring U.S. rebellion, *Los Angeles Times,* May 20: Part 1:1.

Roethlisberger, F. J., & Dickson, W. J. 1939. *Management and the worker.* Cambridge, MA: Harvard University Press.

Roy, D. 1952. Quota restriction and goldbricking in a machine shop. *American Journal of Sociology,* 17: 427–442.

Roy, D. 1955. Efficiency and "the fix": Informal intergroup relations in a piecework machine shop. *American Journal of Sociology,* 20: 255–266.

Sakai, K. 1990. The feudal world of Japanese manufacturing. *Harvard Business Review,* 78: 38–49.

Sayer, A. 1986. New developments in manufacturing: The just-in-time system. *Capital and Class,* 11: 43–72.

Schein, E. H. 1981, Does Japanese management style have a message for American managers? *Strategic Management Review,* 23: 55--67.

Schonberger, R. J. 1982. *Japanese manufacturing techniques—Nine hidden lessons in simplicity.* New York: Free Press.

Schonberger, R. J. 1986. *World class manufacturing.* New York: Free Press.

Sethi, S. P., Namiki, N., & Swanson, C. L. 1984. *The false promise of the Japanese miracle: Illusions and realities of the Japanese management system.* London: Pitman.

Shields, M. D., & Young, S. M. 1991. The management of product life cycle costs. *Journal of Cost Management for the Manufacturing Industry,* 5(3): 39–52.

Shimada. H. 1983. Japanese industrial relations—A new general model? A survey of the English-language literature. In T. Shiral (Ed.). Contemporary industrial relations in Japan: *233–254, Madison: University of Wisconsin Press.*

Susaki, K. 1985, Japanese manufacturing techniques: Their importance to U.S. manufacturers. Journal of Business Strategy, 5:10–19.

Technical Insights, Inc. *Inside R&D.* 1990. Japanese scramble for technical power. November 21: 2.

Thurow, L. 1988. America's economy: A formula for recovery. *Financial Executive* (3): 38–43.

Turnbull, P. J. 1986. The "Japanization" of production and industrial relations at Lucas Electrical. *Industrial Relations Journal*, 17: 193–-206.

Turner, A. N., & Lawrence, P. R. 1965. *Industrial jobs and the worker.* Cambridge, MA: Harvard University, Graduate School of Business Administration.

Turque, B., & Copeland, J. B. 1987. Life at Nissan: Paradise lost? *Newsweek*, August 10: 50.

Walker, C. R., & Guest, R. H. 1952. *The man on the assembly line.* Cambridge, MA: Harvard University Press.

Walton, R., & Susman, G. 1987. People policies for the new machines. *Harvard Business Review*, 66(2): 98–106.

Weisz, J. R., Rothbaum, F. M., & Blackburn, T. C. 1984. Standing out and standing in—The psychology of control in America and Japan. *American Psychologist*, 39: 955–969.

Weitzman, M. 1985, *The share economy—Conquering stagflation.* Cambridge, MA: Harvard University Press.

Westney, D. E. 1987, *Imitation and innovation.* Cambridge: Cambridge University Press.

Whyte, W. F. 1955. *Money and motivation.* New York: Harper & Brothers.

Wilkinson, B., & Oliver, N. 1989. Power, control and the kanban. *Journal of Management Studies*, 26(1): 47–58.

Womack, J. P., Jones, D. T., & Roos, D. 1990. *The machine that changed the world.* New York: Rawson Associates.

Yin, R. 1989. *Case study research: Design and methods.* Beverly Hills, CA: Sage.

Young, S. M., & Davis, J. S. 1990. Factories of the past and of the future: The implications of robotics on workers and management accounting systems. In D. Cooper & T. Hopper (Eds.), *Critical Accounts*: 87–106. London: Macmillan.

Young, S. M., Shields, M. D., & Wolf, G. 1988. Manufacturing controls and performance: An experiment. *Accounting, Organizations and Society*, 13: 607–618,

Young, S. M., & Selto, F. S. 1991. *The roles of accounting, production and behavioral variables in determining manufacturing performance in a just-in-time environment.* Working paper, University of Southern California,

Zipkin, P. H. 1991. Does manufacturing need a JIT revolution? *Harvard Business Review*, 72: 40-50.

I would like to thank Jacob Birnberg, Jon Davis, Robert Hall, Anthony Hopwood, Jim Lincoln, C. J. McNair, Heidi Pate, Charles Perrow, Linda Price, Mike Shields, Gerrit Wolf, workshop participants at the London School of Economics and Political Science and the University of Limburg, The Netherlands, and especially Sarah Bonner and Frank Selto for their comments on previous drafts of this article. I also thank the KMPG Peat Mawick Foundation for its financial support.

S. Mark Young received his doctorate from the University of Pittsburgh. He is an associate professor of accounting, in the School of Accounting, at the University of Southern California. His research interests focus on the effects of new manufacturing and service practices on the design and implementation of cost management and management control systems.

Notes

1. I thank one of the reviewers for suggesting this organizing framework.

2. Thanks to Robert Hall and one of the reviewers for clarifying this discussion.

From S. M. Young, "A Framework for Research on Successful Adoption and Performance of Japanese Manufacturing Methods," *Academy of Management Review* (1992): 677-700. Reprinted with permission.

Question

15.2 What are the six factors relating to Japanese manufacturing practices that Young discusses? Describe the variables that have to be managed with each of the six practices for successful implementation in the U.S. to occur.

15.3 Tapping the Full Potential of ABC

By Joseph A. Ness and Thomas G. Cucuzza

Chrysler and Safety-Kleen are models for how to get employees to embrace activity-based management.

Many companies have used activity-based costing (ABC) in one-time profitability studies to help them decide which products or customers to cut or keep. But ABC can be much more than a superior accounting technique that shows how much money individual products are really making or losing. When ABC is woven into critical management systems, it can serve as a powerful tool for continuously rethinking and dramatically improving not only products and services but also processes and market strategies.

To use ABC in that fashion involves managing in a radically different way. And that, of course, means the people in a business—from the CEO to frontline workers—must change radically, too. No wonder so many companies have found *activity-based management* so much more difficult to implement than they had imagined.

Thousands of companies have adopted or explored the feasibility of adopting ABC. However, we estimate that no more than 10% of them now use activity-based management in a significant number of their operations. The other 90% have given up, or their programs are stagnating or floundering.

The problem is that managers often do not think of activity-based management as a major organizational-change program. It is. Combing the organization to pinpoint all the useful information about the direct and indirect costs of a product or service is a huge undertaking. So is setting up an information system that can track those cost-contributing activities and present them in formats that employees can use.

Educating employees at all levels about the principles and the mechanics of ABC may be the most difficult task of all. Employees must understand thoroughly what the company is trying to achieve through ABC as well as how to use it in their jobs. They must be convinced that ABC can succeed and that it is worth the effort. To win over employees, each company needs a carefully crafted rollout that takes into account its culture and operating idiosyncrasies.

Finally, other management systems need to be overhauled to ensure that employees fully incorporate ABC into their work practices and do not retreat to their old practices in times of stress and self-doubt. The old accounting system has to be rooted out as quickly as possible. Measurement and incentive systems have to be tied to the ABC numbers. And the daily decision-making process—including which managers are involved in making decisions and how they make them—often must be significantly altered, too. A major reason so few efforts have succeeded is that managers fail to take all those steps. Admittedly, they are difficult steps to take.

Like any major organizational-change program, ABC invariably runs up against employee resistance. Indeed, in the companies we have worked with, employee resistance has been the single biggest obstacle. Such resistance is natural. Managers of a unit—whether a function, a division, or a plant—are understandably nervous about revealing detailed information that could be used to attack their practices or undermine their authority. It would be naive to expect managers to rejoice at being asked to replace a cost-accounting system they are used to with one that could dramatically change the definitions of success and failure. And after having been downsized, TQMed, and reengineered, managers and nonmanagers alike, not surprisingly, often greet ABC as the latest threat to their jobs.

Nonetheless, the effort required to weave activity-based thinking into the fabric of a company's way of managing is worth it. When managers adopt activity-based management, they use ABC to find answers to questions such as the following: What should a given product or process cost? What are the non-value-adding activities that contribute to its current cost? If a given distribution channel or market is unprofitable, where can the company reduce costs to make it profitable? If the company eliminates an unprofitable product or customer, how much will it save in costs? If the company lowers the price of a product to increase sales volume, what will the impact on the cost per unit be? And what can the company do during the design and engineering stages of a product to avoid unnecessary costs in the first place?

For many managers, the standard approach for improving a business is to benchmark each function or process against the company they think is the best in that function or process. But activity-based management enables companies to leapfrog the best—to become the company everyone else is copying. Activity-based management makes possible dramatic, rather than incremental, improvements. Consider the benefits reaped by two companies: Chrysler Corporation, a company whose ABC implementation effort we have studied, and Safety-Kleen Corporation, a client that we helped with installing ABC.

Chrysler estimates that, since it began implementing ABC in 1991, the system has generated hundreds of millions of dollars in benefits by helping simplify product designs and eliminate unproductive, inefficient, or redundant activities. The benefits have been 10 to 20 times greater than the company's investment in the program. At some sites, the savings have been 50 to 100 times the implementation cost.

Since Safety-Kleen, a mid-size waste-recycling company, introduced ABC into its organization, also in 1991, it has reaped more than $12.7 million in cost savings, cost avoidance, and increased revenues—more than 14 times its investment in the program. The company, based in Elgin, Illinois, has used ABC to prune product lines, rationalize operations, and expand into new markets. Even more important, ABC has helped Safety-Kleen transform itself from an organization whose individual operations made decisions based on what each one—rightly or wrongly—thought best for itself into an organization whose operations now make day-in, day-out decisions that are best for the whole company.

To illustrate the obstacles that managers are likely to encounter when they try to install ABC and the ways in which they might overcome those hurdles, we will look at Chrysler and Safety-Kleen in detail. The outstanding success of their ABC programs is not the only reason we chose them as models.

Another is that they have more operations using ABC and have integrated ABC into critical management systems to a greater degree than most other companies. More than two-thirds of Chrysler's manufacturing and assembly plants in the United States, all of its Mopar replacement-parts operations, its finance arm, and the company's well-known cross-functional platform teams now use ABC. And plans call for the whole company to use performance measures based on—ABC-generated numbers by the year 2000. At Safety-Kleen, the corporate laboratory and 7 of its 11 recycling operations have integrated ABC totally into their financial and performance-measurement systems.

A third reason we focused on Chrysler and Safety-Kleen is to illustrate the range of approaches a company can take. At Chrysler, Robert A. Lutz, the company's president and chief operating officer, decided that he wanted the organization to use ABC and then made sure it did every step of the way. At Safety-Kleen, a middle manager initiated a pilot project at one plant and then used its success to win over executives and other plants' managers.

Although the two companies arrived at the decision to adopt ABC by different paths, both believed that a new approach to cost management was necessary to achieve their long-term strategies. Both understood that, instead of an accounting system designed to control expenditures, they needed a system that would help managers make better decisions about which products or services to offer and how to make and sell them. Both ran into many of the obstacles that other companies have encountered. Unlike many companies, Chrysler and Safety-Kleen recognized that they were not merely changing their accounting systems; they were changing their organizations. That understanding heavily influenced the way they rolled out ABC, and it is why their stories offer valuable lessons for other companies interested in activity-based management.

TURNING TO ABC

Chrysler, which has $52 billion in revenues and 123,000 employees, 97,000 of those in the United States, turned to ABC to help transform a bureaucratic organization set in its ways. During the 1980s, the automotive giant made enormous strides in improving its operating efficiency, slashing costs, boosting quality, and rejuvenating its product line. Nonetheless, Chrysler ended the decade still playing catch-up to such formidable competitors as the Japanese automakers and Ford Motor Company. Chrysler's financial crisis in the late 1980s, its second in a decade, underscored how much work remained to be done.

Chrysler's leaders were determined to replace the company's hierarchical functional structure with one that was much more flexible, efficient, cross-functional, and process oriented. To that end, they pushed the company to create its platform teams for developing new vehicles and to forge closer links with suppliers and distributors. Encouraged by the teams' initial successes in the late 1980s, they decided to transform the entire company into a process-focused organization.

Lutz, who had championed the platform teams and was the driving force behind the decision to structure the whole company around processes, became the leading advocate for using ABC to help with the transformation. He knew how difficult getting employees to change would be, especially with the auto market beginning to rebound and the company's profits rising. He believed that ABC would buttress the process approach by showing how much each process actually cost and by exposing inefficiencies.

The main purpose of the old cost-accounting system had been to help the finance department monitor operations and value inventory. However, outside of finance, few people believed the old system provided an accurate picture of the company's costs. One of the skeptics was Lutz. During his career at Ford, BMW, and Chrysler, he had often been annoyed when his creative proposals for product designs and manufacturing-process improvements were rejected. Because the companies' financial systems focused on direct costs and relied on arbitrary cost allocations, such as labor-based overhead rates, he felt they were incapable of evaluating his proposals fairly. His frustrations resurfaced during the rollout of the platform teams at Chrysler. Once again, Lutz saw clearly that the company's cost-accounting system could not report costs by process, much less separate value-added from non-value-added activities. When he came across an article about activity-based costing, he said, "This is the system for me."

In contrast, Safety-Kleen, a relatively young, fast-growing company, turned to ABC because it had out-grown its accounting system. Safety-Kleen was founded in 1968 in response to companies' crying need to find safe ways to remove and recycle their hazardous wastes. The company started out processing one type of waste—mineral spirits—in one plant in Illinois and needed only a basic cost-accounting system that could provide sufficient information to satisfy internal financial controls and investors. The company's main challenge was how to exploit the vast opportunities in an undeveloped market. It was a marketing-driven company focused on environmental compliance; efficiency of operations was a secondary concern.

By 1991, however, Safety-Kleen had become much bigger and much more complex. The number of hazardous chemicals it handled had grown to more than 100, and the number of product lines had grown to ten, including used motor oil, antifreeze, oil filters, paint, and dry-cleaning solvents. And its number of plants had grown to 12 in eight states and Puerto Rico, and most of them handled multiple types of waste. (One plant has since been closed.) By the early 1990s, the market had also become more complex. Growth had slowed, competition had increased, and some states had begun imposing taxes of up to 25% on hazardous-waste generators and recyclers.

Safety-Kleen, which currently has 6,600 employees and revenues of $800 million, achieved its rapid growth by encouraging the managers of its facilities to act like entrepreneurs. Plant managers were responsible for deciding how to handle the wastes shipped to their facilities; they could process the material themselves or ship it to another facility or, in some cases, to a third-party processor. But usually, wastes were simply shipped to the nearest Safety-Kleen plant, whether or not it was the one that could process them at the lowest cost. In fact, Safety-Kleen did not know the true costs of its services and products. The main purpose of the cost-accounting numbers was to help the accounting department keep the books, not to help operations do its job.

As the pressure on profits intensified, so did operations' and marketing's animosity toward accounting because they didn't trust its numbers. Operations and marketing began to develop their own numbers to support decisions about capital expenditures, pricing, plant utilization, and process improvements. Top management gradually realized that the company needed to start basing waste-handling decisions on what would generate the most profits for the whole company rather than what would be best for an individual plant. In order to make decisions that way, the company needed much more detailed information about its operational costs, including how much processing, shipping, and handling a given batch of materials would cost at each plant. In short, the company needed a radically new cost-accounting system.

INTERNAL RESISTANCE

When Safety-Kleen and Chrysler first introduced ABC, they both quickly discovered that many employees—from frontline workers to senior managers to entire departments—resisted. Some feared ABC would change the existing power structure. Some felt threatened because they knew ABC would reveal inefficient practices that had been hidden by the traditional cost-accounting systems. Others did not like ABC, simply because it was new. And many managers, especially those who felt ABC was being imposed on their operations, resisted because they knew installing it was a tremendous amount of work. (See the insert "Why Collecting ABC Information Is Such a Big Job.")

The deep skepticism with which Chrysler employees greeted the ABC initiative at some of the first work sites where it was installed was hardly surprising. Chrysler had a long history of flavor-of-the-month performance improvement programs that never seemed to deliver what they promised and were replaced as soon as a new program came along. The fact that one division had briefly tried a form of ABC in the mid-1980s and had abandoned it after a change in management only fed the skepticism.

As Lutz had anticipated, once the market had rebounded, employees questioned why the company needed to change at all. Furthermore, with all plants operating at full tilt, line and middle managers questioned whether they had the time to collect the necessary data. Many employees also feared that an unspoken motive for introducing ABC was to eliminate jobs. Some of the corporate controller's staff and some operations managers were equally unenthusiastic. The old cost-accounting system had shaped their skills and their way of thinking about costs. They, too, assumed that ABC was just the latest fad and that once it had passed, life would continue relatively unchanged.

The initial resistance at Safety-Kleen was different, partly because a middle manager in accounting was the effort's champion. The notion that ABC might greatly help Safety-Kleen originated with C. James Schulz, the controller of North American operations, who recruited William J. Chaika, the assistant controller of the recycling centers, to undertake a pilot project. Schulz and Chaika's bosses—the corporate controller and the chief financial officer—approved and supported the project, but Chaika was the one who actively championed the effort.

Senior managers had chosen a plant in New Castle, Kentucky, as the pilot because they wanted to use it to enter a new growth market. Before plunging ahead, they wanted to make sure they knew the actual costs of processing materials with new multimillion-dollar equipment at the plant. Chaika assembled a team of three Safety-Kleen regional controllers, one financial analyst, and two consultants from Price Waterhouse to join him in installing an ABC system. When they arrived at the plant, the trouble began. The manager told them to get lost. As far as he was concerned, accounting had no business telling him how to run his plant.

Chaika also ran into resistance from the vice president of recycle-center operations, to whom all the plant managers reported, and the five marketing vice presidents, who were each responsible for one or more lines of hazardous waste. Operations and marketing agreed that the company needed to change the way it made decisions, but they had different priorities. Marketing wanted information on product costs, and operations wanted information on operating performance. Neither department was happy that the initiative had come out of accounting. In addition, each feared the other would use the numbers to invade its turf. And the five marketing vice presidents were fearful that ABC would change the ground rules for calculating profits and, as a result, might reduce their pay.

After some initial struggles, both Chrysler and Safety-Kleen overcame internal resistance in ways that serve as a model for other companies. First, both companies persuaded critical employees to give ABC a fair shake and, ultimately, to embrace the system. Second, both mounted major programs to educate employees at all levels in the principles and mechanics of ABC. Third, both began with one plant and then rolled out the program throughout their organizations, making sure that local managers were involved and that there were visible successes. Finally, once ABC had been introduced at a facility, they quickly dumped the old accounting system.

GETTING WIDESPREAD ACCEPTANCE

At many companies, top management delegates the implementation of ABC to the accountants. We think that practice is a mistake. At Chrysler, executives got involved from the start, a commitment that continues today. For example, Chrysler's operating committee of senior executives which Lutz chairs, has taken responsibility for tracking and guiding the ABC program on a regular basis. In addition, Chrysler's officers—its top 32 executives—spend half a day once a year in a workshop in which they receive in-depth briefings on the rollout's progress and deliberate about where the company should install ABC next.

Lutz also decided that finance alone should not control the emerging ABC system. Instead, he gave joint responsibility for the system to James D. Donlon III, the controller, and James P. Holden, the vice president who is in charge of continuous improvement and the move to process management. The project team that has spearheaded the implementation program reports to both executives. In addition, both Lutz and Robert J. Eaton, Chrysler chairman and CEO, became vocal advocates of ABC throughout the company. At work site after work site, both have preached that a process-based structure using ABC could make Chrysler the most agile, lowest-cost automaker in North America by 1996 and in the world by 2000.

Safety-Kleen used a different approach to gain employee acceptance. First, Chaika pacified the manager of the New Castle plant by promising that if he didn't agree that ABC helped him make better decisions by the end of the pilot project, he could abandon it. Within three months, everyone could see that ABC would help the plant cut costs significantly. (In the first year, ABC helped the plant identify a hefty $3.5 million in potential annual cost savings.) Equally important, the ABC numbers were extremely helpful in figuring out the amount of new materials that the plant needed to process in order to be competitive and profitable. The plant's manager was sold.

Chaika then orchestrated special meetings with operations and marketing and with senior executives, a group that included the vice president of recycle-center operations and the five marketing vice presidents. Chaika and his team went over the plant's 150-page cost book in great detail, showing how costs had been allocated to different processes and how the cost of each product had been derived. No one could argue with the numbers. Everyone realized that such

numbers would help them make better decisions, which would quickly generate higher profits.

Chaika did not have to woo the managers of the other plants. After seeing the difference ABC was making at New Castle, they clamored to get on board.

TRAINING THE WORKFORCE

No company that we know of has invested the time and effort that Chrysler has in educating employees about ABC. More than 18,000 Chrysler employees have attended one of the company's formal ABC training courses. Many union officials and suppliers' employees have taken the courses, too. From the outset, the courses have had two main purposes: to explain why ABC is necessary and to instruct employees in how to set it up and use it. Chrysler created three groups of courses.

The courses in the first group, which introduce the basic concepts of ABC, are for employees at a wide range of levels—from top management down to some hourly workers. The half-day courses explain what ABC is, how it differs from the traditional cost-accounting system, and what Chrysler hopes to get out of it. The message, reinforced with examples, is that ABC's purpose is to help employees make better decisions, not to get them to work harder or to eliminate their jobs.

The courses in the second group are for managers who will have responsibility for implementing ABC at their work sites. The two-day courses make heavy use of case studies and cover the practical application of ABC information in making decisions. For example, a computerized simulation lets people tackle realistic business problems, such as whether the company should start manufacturing a part that it now buys from a supplier. The computer program first uses traditional financial information, which allocates many costs arbitrarily, and then ABC information. Most participants figure out the best solution when they use the ABC numbers. In contrast, the answers—and the outcomes—vary widely when they use the numbers from the old accounting system. "Those with good intuition do well, while those without good intuition go bankrupt," says David E. Meador, the Chrysler manager who heads the company's ABC implementation team.

The courses in the third group, which last three to five days, are highly technical and specialized. Their purpose is to teach employees such as industrial engineers, controllers, and investment analysts how to set up and use an ABC-based system—in other words, the skills needed to collect the data, build the models, set up the computer systems, and analyze the information.

Safety-Kleen never offered formal classroom training in ABC. Instead, it put employees through a three-month, intensive, on-the-job training program—an approach that makes sense for many smaller companies. After the first-day fiasco at New Castle, Chaika realized that he could not impose ABC on a plant. Every aspect—from collecting the data, to designing the system, to training the workforce to interpret and use the data—had to be done in partnership with the plant's management. So, at New Castle and later at other plants, the implementation team first spent two days explaining to the plant's managers all the steps involved in installing ABC, emphasizing that the process would be a joint effort. The team also stressed that the main reason for installing ABC was to help managers expand the business, not shrink it, and it pointed to how ABC had led to hiring, not firing, at the first plants.

After the data had been collected and the system had been designed at a particular plant, the team and the plant's managers made a top-ten list of ways they thought that efficiency could be improved. The team then helped the plant's personnel analyze the projects, in the process teaching them how to use ABC and showing how it could help them make better decisions. For example, the Safety-Kleen plant in Linden, New Jersey, analyzed the company's practice of temporarily storing used motor oil at hazardous-waste-process centers before shipping it to its oil-recycling plant in East Chicago, Indiana. When Safety-Kleen entered the market for recycling motor oil, it used available tank capacity at hazardous-waste centers in order to reduce transportation costs. Using small trucks, the centers collected the oil from service stations within a 150-mile radius. Once a center had enough to fill a big tanker truck, it loaded the oil again and transported it 10 to 25 miles to a rail yard, where it was shipped to East Chicago. Because Safety-Kleen had tank capacity available at its centers, managers considered it a free resource. But an ABC-based analysis showed that the cost of using it certainly was not free. First, the company had not calculated the costs of testing each batch of oil in the truck, unloading it, testing it again in the tank, reloading it into a larger truck, and retesting it in that truck. Second, the company had not considered the cost of unnecessary paperwork: Although oil is not a hazardous material, the company had to document its handling as if it were in order to comply with regulations for hazardous-waste centers. Once the company tallied all of those costs and charged them to the oil-recycling business, the practice quickly stopped. The small trucks began taking the oil directly to the rail yard.

At every plant where ABC was implemented, the team stayed until the staff was able to put at least two or three items on its top-ten list into action. It made sure that the benefits were quantified—both to drive home to the plant's employees the difference that ABC had made and to win over people at other plants. In instance after instance, plant managers said that ABC helped them make decisions that they previously had had a gut feeling were right but had been reluctant to make without hard data. ABC, they said, gave them the data they needed.

THE ROLLOUT

Chrysler's managers, like Safety-Kleen's, realized fairly quickly that they had to take great care to make sure that employees felt involved in ABC's introduction and saw proof that it really worked. Chrysler's first step was to expose top-level managers to the concept in a series of seminars. Then, in 1991, Chrysler launched a pilot project at its high-volume stamping plant in Warren, Michigan. Chrysler's managers chose Warren because it looked like a sure win. The plant had a progressive manager, and company executives believed that its product mix could be improved. Over time, the plant had been pressed into making some low-volume parts, and executives had strong hunches that their true costs were much higher than the traditional cost-accounting system indicated.

The pilot was extremely successful. The ABC numbers showed that the actual costs of some low-volume parts were as much as 30 times the stated costs, which made clear that the company would be much better off outsourcing those parts and making more high-volume parts. In addition, the pilot helped uncover pockets of waste and inefficiency, which plant managers attacked immediately. Finally, it helped the plant redesign both its products and processes so that it could make parts for the company's next minivan model much more efficiently.

Two-thirds of the way into the rollout at Warren, the results were already so impressive that Lutz decided to introduce ABC at six more plants. He assigned Donlon, the controller, the job of getting the effort under way. Donlon handpicked 6 young, aggressive employees to be on the initial ABC implementation team. All came from the finance department. But as the rollout began to pick up steam over the next year, the team's full-time staff was increased to 20. To reinforce the message that the motive for installing ABC was to help the managers run their operations better, the team's membership also was broadened to include people from manufacturing, engineering, and information systems. The team's composition certainly helped the ABC program achieve the high level of acceptance that it has won throughout the company.

Chrysler refined the introduction process into a science and methodically rolled out ABC into all areas of the company in order to emphasize that it was for everyone, not just manufacturing. The entire rollout at a work site takes 6 to 15 months, depending on the size of the facility. First, an advance group conducts 12 weeks of training to pave the way for the actual installation of ABC. During that period, everyone at the work site takes one or more of the courses the company offers, and managers widely distribute videos and newsletter articles on what is to come. They also encourage the people who will be responsible for setting up and using the ABC system to attend sessions aimed at making them receptive to new ideas. Next, two other groups arrive on the scene to implement the ABC system and to give the operation's managers and professionals hands-on training in using its information and maintaining and updating the system. The first group oversees the efforts to collect data and build the ABC computer model.

The second helps with the technical work required to link the ABC model with the general ledger, the manufacturing-planning system, and other support systems. Both groups work closely with the managers of the operation—to tap their knowledge and to instill in them a sense of ownership of both the rollout and the new ABC system.

Chrysler's managers also realized that they had to show, rather than merely tell, employees that ABC would help them make better decisions. For example, ABC helped Chrysler tackle a long-standing problem: how to determine the optimal number of wiring harnesses—the wiring packages used for a vehicle's electrical systems—that it should design and produce for a new minivan. The alternatives ranged from one to nine. If the company produced only one, that harness would have to contain wires for all the possible options. On the other hand, if the company produced nine harnesses, each one tailored to a particular type of van, it would waste less material but would incur greater costs and make the design and production processes more complex. Because design engineers were measured by how well they kept down the materials costs for each vehicle, they voted for nine. Because manufacturing plant managers were rewarded for minimizing inventory and labor, they wanted to produce only one. But the ABC team showed that making two harnesses would strike the best balance between minimizing waste and maximizing productivity. Once they saw the ABC numbers, neither the design engineers nor the manufacturing managers could dispute that conclusion.

After Safety-Kleen had installed the ABC pilot at its New Castle plant, operations and marketing executives took a strategic approach to selecting the next plants. The goal was to use the rollout to get an overview of the relative costs and profitability of each recycling process and line of business. If the decision between two plants utilizing the same process was a toss-up, they chose the plant whose manager seemed more enthusiastic.

Safety-Kleen tried to strike a balance between maximizing the speed of the rollout and minimizing the number of people on the implementation teams. To that end, the company limited the number of work sites at which ABC was being introduced at any one time to two and staggered the two efforts. A core team of three people—the regional controller, an accounting analyst, and, until the company felt it had mastered the process, a Price Waterhouse consultant—oversaw each introduction from the beginning to the end. Five others—analysts who assisted with process mapping, data collection, and activity costing—performed their tasks and then left. A typical implementation took three months at the plant and a week to tie in the plant's new ABC system to corporate headquarters.

Because of the plant-by-plant approach, the corporate accounting department was not able to convert to ABC all at once. Only after all the targeted plants had been converted could the controller's staff stream-line and automate its own closing process. The result: Even though ABC requires more data collection, reporting, and analysis than the traditional accounting system did, closing the books each month now takes no longer than before.

Within 15 months of the pilot's launch, operations, marketing, and accounting executives had begun to use ABC information to make strategic decisions. And within 18 months of the launch, Safety-Kleen's five largest plants had adopted it.

FINAL INTEGRATION

The final hurdle in implementing ABC is integrating it into the organization's financial systems and performance measures. Many companies have tried to implement ABC as a shadow or secondary system. But ABC won't take root if its numbers are not integrated into the company's mainstream financial-reporting system. When the ABC data are not kept up to date, can't be reconciled with the financial reports, or are not distributed widely as the official numbers, managers often retreat to the old numbers. "If two sets of numbers exist, one set will ultimately dominate," says Donlon, the controller at Chrysler, which tried using ABC as a shadow system at some of its first sites.

Most companies develop standalone ABC models, which they install on off-line personal computers. Those models often can't be integrated into the official financial results, are difficult to maintain, and usually do not follow generally accepted accounting principles, which means they cannot be used for external financial reporting. As a result, they quickly become obsolete.

Precisely because maintaining one set of numbers is difficult enough, let alone two, Safety-Kleen's management decided that as soon as an ABC system had been introduced into a work site, it should become the sole source of financial-reporting numbers. In the recycling centers, the company installed a new data-collection system that could update the ABC numbers each month. It also built automatic links between its corporate general ledger and the ABC system to ensure that the numbers reconciled in both systems every month.

Safety-Kleen now uses ABC numbers to develop its annual budget and to make strategic decisions about closing plants and adding and cutting product lines. Safety-Kleen also has adopted ABC-based performance measures, which involved a fundamental rethinking of the old system. As Safety-Kleen rolled out ABC, its top-level managers realized that some of the old performance measures were not motivating plant managers to make decisions that were best for the company as a whole. For example, plant managers were still rewarded based on how they performed against an operating budget set at the beginning of each year, which did not take into account processing efficiency or unit costs. The measures were changed to reward managers for reducing the unit costs of the materials processed at their plants.

When used in a onetime analysis of products' costs, ABC can make a big difference. But it is a onetime big difference. After a company has integrated ABC into all of its main-stream financial systems, and ABC numbers have become the yardsticks of performance, the system dramatically changes the way an organization's people think. Then, the average quality of the decisions made day in and day out will be vastly higher than before. When that happens, you can bet that the company's performance will show it.

Joseph A. Ness is a partner and Thomas C. Cucuzza is a senior manager in Price Waterhouse's financial- and cost-

management consulting practice and are based, respectively, in St. Louis, Missouri, and Cleveland, Ohio. They advise manufacturing and service companies on how to implement advanced cost-management systems.

WHY COLLECTING ABC INFORMATION IS SUCH A BIG JOB

Most companies seriously under-estimate how big a job gathering the information needed to set up an ABC system is. One reason is that ABC is much more detailed and complex than standard cost accounting. Traditional systems lump together many costs into a few heterogeneous overhead pools, or categories. Under ABC, each of those pools are often broken into scores of ABC *activities,* and it may take hundreds of inquiries to identify and gather the information on them. Similarly, an ABC system uses many more statistical measures to assign the overhead costs to products, processes, distribution channels, customers, and markets than a traditional system does. A standard system typically uses one or two statistical measures, such as the number of hours of direct labor required to make each product, to allocate overhead costs to products. A typical ABC system uses dozens of *cost drivers,* ranging from the number of

parts to the number of sales calls, to allocate activity costs.

Another reason collecting data is so time-consuming, especially in the beginning, is that figuring out precisely what kind of information is required to set up an ABC system and where to find it takes a while. Most companies go overboard at first and end up with a mountain of excruciatingly detailed information, which overwhelms both their people and their computer systems. When Chrysler installed ABC at its first factory, a stamping plant in Warren, Michigan, it gathered three times the information it could use practically. Because of that overkill, collecting the information took twice the resources that it would now, given Chrysler's knowledge and experience. Similarly, Chrysler's Mopar replacement-parts operation found itself overwhelmed by data when it attempted to construct ABC costs for

each of the 250,000 parts that it stocks. Mopar ultimately decided to construct the costs of 60 major and minor product groups, which reduced the amount of data to a manageable level but was still extremely useful.

Safety-Kleen also found that less could be more. When its ABC implementation team was helping plants set up ABC systems, many of the plants' managers pressed the team to include an extraordinary amount of detail in the ABC models. The team, however, grew worried that the detail would overwhelm the ABC systems and also concluded that much of the requested information was not important for determining costs. When the managers persisted, the ABC team got them to accept a compromise: 75% of the information would be included in the ABC model, and the team would set up another statistical performance-reporting system to track the rest.

From "Tapping the Full Potential of ABC," by J. Ness and T. Cucuzza, *Harvard Business Review* (July–August 1995): 130–138. Copyright © 1995 by the President and Fellows of Harvard College; all rights reserved.

Question

15.3 According to Ness and Cucuzza, why is collecting ABC information such a big job? Explain.

15.4 Implementing Activity-Based Costing Systems Successfully

By Michael D. Shields and Michael A. McEwen

Executive Summary

- Behavioral and organizational factors play a critical role in implementing ABC. This article outlines steps to take to ensure that behavioral and organizational factors are being taken into account.

- According to a recent survey of companies that have implemented ABC, 25 percent reported that they did not receive financial gains from the implementations.
- An important reason for unsuccessful implementations of ABC is that many companies have emphasized the architectural and software design of ABC systems at the expense of behavioral and organizational issues.

- A model based on the survey identifies and describes specific behavioral and organizational factors that are important to a successful implementation.
- The top factors include top management support, linkage to competitive strategy, linkage to quality initiatives, linkage to JIT and speed initiatives, linkage to performance evaluation and compensation, and consensus about ABC objectives

Although activity-based costing (ABC) has been widely accepted in recent years as a better system for measuring resource consumption than traditional cost accounting systems,[1] many companies have experienced significant problems with ABC.[2] Exhibit 1 shows the results of a survey discussed throughout this article. Of 143 companies responding to the survey, 75 percent reported that their company had received a financial benefit from ABC, while 25 percent indicated that they had not.

This article discusses the results of the survey and points out that one important reason for unsuccessful implementations of ABC is that many companies have overemphasized the architectural and software design of ABC systems and failed to pay adequate attention to behavioral and organizational issues.[3] The article uses the survey results to develop a model for implementing new cost management systems based on certain critical behavioral and organizational factors that affect implementations of any new administrative innovation.[4]

THE SURVEY

Here are the important facts about the survey:

- *Purpose and coverage:* The survey was mailed to companies that have implemented ABC to determine how successful the implementations proved to be and which implementation factors were most associated with success.
- *Technical advice:* The survey was developed in consultation with representatives of the Consortium for Advanced Manufacturing-International (CAM-I), software companies that sell ABC software, and consultants from the Big-Six accounting firms.
- *Survey date and number of responses:* The mailing occurred in September 1993; 143 usable responses had been received by November 1993.
- *Analysis:* Information from the survey was analyzed statistically using several techniques, including correlation analysis, step-wise regression analysis, and factor analysis. (The results of the analysis can be obtained from Michael D. Shields at 901 678-5387.)
- *Annual sales of respondents:* From $1 million to $33 billion (median $250 million, mean $2.15 billion)

- *Number of employees:* Mean of 15,944 employees and a median of 1,500.

EXHIBIT 1
ABC SUCCESS

Extremely Low				Extremely High			
1	2	3	4	5	6	7	Mean
7%	7%	16%	15%	31%	15%	9%	4.35

Industries (measured by mean revenue):
- Commercial manufacturing (72 percent)
- Commercial nonmanufacturing (22 percent)
- Defense contracts (5 percent)
- Nondefense government contracts (2 percent)
- *Respondents' job titles:*
  - Accounting manager or controller (80 percent)
  - Operations managers (9 percent)
  - CFO or vice-president of finance (7 percent)
  - Vice-president of operations (5 percent)
- *Respondents' job positions:*
  - Financial (48 percent)
  - Operational (22 percent)
  - Financial and operational (30 percent)
- *Respondents' roles in the ABC implementation:*
  - Facilitator (44 percent)
  - Leader (52 percent)
  - Mentor (4 percent)
- *Respondents' professional worth experience:* Range from 2-40 years (mean 15 years, median of 14 years)
- *Respondents' experience with ABC:* Range from 1-20 years (mean 2.65 years, median 2 years)

Satisfaction with ABC systems. Respondents were asked to rate their perception of the satisfaction of four employee groups:

1. Accounting and finance employees;
2. Top management;
3. Users of ABC; and
4. Initiators of ABC.

Of these, accounting and finance employees had the highest mean level of satisfaction, followed by top management, users of ABC, and initiators of ABC. There also was wide dispersion in the degrees of satisfaction.

Use of consultants. The companies surveyed used from 0–4,000 hours of external consultant time to implement ABC, with a mean of 467 hours and a median of 95 hours.

Ages and number of ABC systems. The ages of the ABC systems ranged from 1–74 months, with a mean and median of 19 months. Each company had (or still has) from 0–23 ABC systems, with a median of 1 and a mean of 2.

Total costs processed. Exhibit 2 shows the median percentage of annual total costs processed by ABC each year after it was implemented.

Two results in Exhibit 2 are noteworthy. First, the median percentages in each row increase from right to left, which indicates that companies that began using ABC more recently have processed more of their costs with ABC in the first year it was used than did the companies that began using ABC earlier. Second, within each column, the median percentage increases each year ABC is used (i.e., the percentages increase from the top to the bottom of each column). These results show that, on average, later adopters of ABC started with relatively larger-sized implementations and that adopters have increased their use of ABC over time.

Objectives—original and revised. According to the survey, the original objectives of implementing ABC were as follows:

- Better cost information (mean 35 percent)
- Product cost information (32 percent)
- Process cost information (16 percent)
- Improve cost systems (15 percent)
- Performance measurement (2 percent)
- Quality or time management (1 percent)

The current objectives are similar to the original objectives except that the importance of process cost information has increased to the levels of product costing and better cost information.

Current status of ABC projects. The current work status of the companies' ABC initiatives range from activity analysis (the most frequently completed), followed by product costing, reengineering, and performance measurement. Product costing is the highest future objective of ABC, followed by activity analysis, reengineering, and performance measurement.

IMPORTANT IMPLEMENTATION FACTORS

A review of the literature on implementing ABC and other administrative innovations has identified 17 implementation factors that might affect the success of an ABC implementation.[5] The survey used seven-point scales to measure the extent to which each of these 17 implementation factors is present. The survey results showed considerable variation in the degree to which the 17 implementation factors were present. Their rank-order degree of presence is as follows:

1. Standalone system
2. Top management support
3. Commercial software
4. Accounting ownership
5. Link to competitive strategy
6. Clear and concise objectives
7. Implementation training
8. Consensus about objectives
9. Training in using ABC
10. Training in designing ABC systems
11. Link to quality initiatives
12. Nonaccounting ownership
13. Resource adequacy
14. External consultants
15. Link to JIT and speed initiatives
16. Custom software
17. Link to performance evaluation and compensation

ABC IMPLEMENTATION MODEL

The implementation model developed based on this survey uses only 12 of the 17 implementation factors—i.e., those that the survey showed to be significantly correlated with ABC success. Their inclusion in the model is supported by literature on implementing ABC and other administrative innovations.[6]

For convenience, these 12 factors have been combined in the ensuing discussion into only seven factors:

1. Top management support;
2. Linkage to competitive strategy, especially quality and JIT/speed;
3. Linkage to performance evaluation and compensation;
4. Training;
5. Nonaccounting ownership (i.e., the belief by nonaccountants that the ABC system is of practical use to people throughout the company, not just to the accounting department);
6. Internal resources; and
7. Consensus and clarity of the objectives of ABC.

The remaining 5 of the original 17 factors showed no significant correlation with ABC success, namely:

1. Accounting ownership;
2. Commercial software;
3. Custom software;
4. External consultants; and
5. Standalone system.

EXHIBIT 2
MEDIAN PERCENTAGE ANNUAL TOTAL COSTS PROCESSED BY ABC EACH YEAR SINCE BEGAN USING ABC

		Years Since Began				
	Year	1	2	3	4	5
% Costs	1	50%	30%	10%	6%	4%
Processed	2		65%	50%	10%	15%
Each Year	3			70%	15%	20%
	4				28%	30%
	5					40%
% of						
Companies		36%	36%	19%	4%	5%

The remainder of this article discusses each of the implementation factors found to be significantly correlated with ABC success.[7]

TOP MANAGEMENT SUPPORT

The survey results show that top management support is the most important factor in determining how successful an ABC implementation is (see the list of seven factors listed previously). In a related question, the respondents were asked to rate the degree to which each of the 17 implementation factors was present in their own implementations. Consistent with the perceived importance of top management support to the success of ABC, top management support came near the top of the list of the factors most present in the respondents' own ABC initiatives ("standalone systems" was first, followed by "top management support," as shown in the rank-order list of the 17 factors given previously).

These results are consistent with the more general finding that almost all successful administrative innovations require the support of top management. Most successful administrative innovations start with top management and cascade down the hierarchy.[8] Top management support for ABC is crucial for at least three reasons:[9]

1. Top management can focus resources (e.g., money time, and talent), goals, and strategies on those innovations they deem worthwhile and deny resources for innovations they do not support;
2. They can provide the political help needed to push aside or motivate employees who try to sabotage innovations they want to succeed; and
3. Since ABC maps the internal economics of a company's resources, products, activities, and organizational units, it plays a key role in the development of organizational goals and strategies (e.g, for performance measurement, control, and evaluation).

Top management must demonstrate a Commitment to ABC by using it as the basis for decision making. It is especially important for top management to use ABC information in communications and agreements with other employees to encourage (or force) them to use ABC information.

LINKAGE TO COMPETITIVE STRATEGY

An important way for top management to use ABC in their analysis and action is in the formulation and evaluation of competitive strategy. The survey results indicate that the linkage of ABC to competitive strategy is an important determinant of the success of an ABC implementation. Fortunately, the linkage between ABC and strategy is the fifth highest factor present during implementation according to the survey results.

ABC should be linked to a company's competitive strategy regarding organizational design, new product development, product mix and pricing, and technology. Here are some examples:

- *Competing based on cost or custom design.* If a company chooses to compete based on the design of custom or low-cost products, its ABC systems should provide designers with accurate estimates of product or process costs. These costs should be available both before and during the design process. Designers should also know the costs of customization.
- *Competing based on scale economies.* If a company competes based on manufacturing scale economies and efficiencies for commodity products, its ABC systems should focus on measuring the costs of manufacturing activities and plant capacity.
- *Competing based on distribution and logistics.* If a company competes based on superior distribution and logistics, its ABC systems should focus on measuring the costs of those activities rather than manufacturing costs.

ABC systems can be easily tailored to satisfy the information demands of these competitive strategies. The tighter the linkage between ABC and competitive strategy, the more effective an ABC implementation will be.

Linkages to continuous improvement. Especially important is the link of ABC to continuous improvement of quality and time. The survey shows that the linkage of ABC with quality initiatives and with initiatives on JIT and speed are important determinants of ABC success. Given their importance, these linkages are not present as much as they should be; many companies have no linkage between ABC and continuous improvement strategies.

ABC information can play important roles in helping a company achieve continuous improvement. It can be used to identify potential economic gains from improving quality and speed. It also can be used to measure economic progress toward improving quality and time-based performance.

LINKAGE TO PERFORMANCE EVALUATION AND COMPENSATION

The survey indicates that the degree of linkage between ABC and performance evaluation and compensation is an extremely important determinant of a successful ABC implementation. Unfortunately, the survey indicates that out of the 17 implementation Factors, this one is least present—i.e., for most companies, there is little or no linkage between performance evaluation and compensation and ABC.

The importance of the linkage between performance evaluation and compensation and ABC implementation is natural because employees pay attention to those things that affect their welfare. The welfare of most employees is affected by the system used to evaluate and compensate them. Therefore, when ABC is linked to performance measurement and compensation—and provided that employees believe that the resulting system fairly represents their performance—they will be motivated to help it succeed.

Sabotage or indifference. If employees believe that an ABC system is detrimental to their performance evaluations and future compensation, they may try to sabotage the implementation. If, however (as in most companies), there is no link between ABC and performance evaluation and compensation, most employees, will, at best, be indifferent to ABC. Key ways to reduce the potential for problems caused by poor measurement or employees' lack of confidence in ABC is to provide training in ABC and involve nonaccountants in the design and implementation of ABC.

TRAINING

The survey found that training is extremely important to the success of an ABC implementation. Unfortunately, training in the design, implementation, and use of ABC was only in the middle of the 17 factors in terms of the degree of presence during implementation.

These types of training provide important ways to link ABC to competitive strategy, continuous improvement programs, and performance evaluation and compensation. Training can include:

- Readings;
- Lectures;
- Hands-on projects; and
- On-the-job training.

Training in the logic and operation of ABC is important because it helps people understand how ABC differs from traditional cost accounting and why ABC provides a superior economic measurement and information system. If people do not understand why or how ABC works, they are likely to ignore or misunderstand it. Training in how to design ABC systems is important because it reduces the chance that an ABC system will provide inaccurate measurements of resource consumption and supply. Training also helps increase nonaccounting ownership.

Training in how to implement ABC can include the following:

- Pilot systems;
- Cross-functional teams;
- Early user involvement;
- Coordination and integration with other initiatives (e.g., JIT, TQM, and reengineering); and
- Broad-based ownership.

Training of employees in how to use ABC information can include how to interpret an ABC printout and how to use ABC information for product design, product pricing, and process improvement.

Performance measurement and compensation. Especially important is training in how ABC will affect performance evaluation and compensation. For example, if a manager is paid based on how actual costs compare to standard costs, the manager should be trained on how ABC provides different cost estimates than a traditional cost system does for the same level of performance. Employees must be told how the compensation system will be adjusted to incorporate this difference in measured performance for the same actual performance. If people do not understand how ABC affects their performance evaluation, pay, and other prospects, they may resist its introduction and use.

NONACCOUNTING OWNERSHIP

The survey found that nonaccounting ownership of ABC was an important determinant of ABC success, while accounting ownership was unimportant. Unfortunately, the survey found that nonaccounting ownership was present during implementation to a much lesser extent than was accounting ownership.

A broad cross-section of employees should be involved in decisions about all the following:

- The initial decisions to invest in ABC;
- The design and implementation of ABC systems; and
- The use of ABC information for analysis and action.

Because ABC can provide important economic information about all parts of a company, broad ownership increases the chances that nonaccountants will support and promote ABC and be committed to its use and success.

When ABC is owned only by accountants, there is the danger that it might be used only to satisfy their needs, which often relate to status within the accounting profession and external reporting. An important reason why some companies have not had good implementation experiences is that the accountants have retained ownership or have not succeeded in sharing ownership with nonaccountants.[10] The consequence can be a repeating cycle of ABC designs without corresponding management action.

Identifying owners. Implementation success critically depends on early identification of targeted individuals or groups who are expected to become owners of ABC through their use of ABC information for decision making. These targets should primarily be nonaccountants—e.g., design engineers, production managers, product managers, and top executives.

When broad-based ownership of an ABC system is not present, there is the danger that other employees will not support or use ABC. They may believe that ABC is just another "new toy" for accountants and that, like most accounting "products," it is intended for financial managers and external constituents.

RESOURCES

Designing and implementing an ABC system requires having adequate resources. The internal resources primarily include time and the commitment of accountants, top management, and operating employees. External resources include commercial software and consultants. Implementations in some companies were hindered by lack of resources, especially accounting and management information systems (MIS) staff, managers, and computer resources.[11]

The survey found that having at least adequate employee resources is one of the most important determinants of ABC success. Significantly, however, other types of resources (such as either commercial or custom-designed ABC software and also external consultants) did not prove to be important to the success of an ABC implementation. The survey found that most companies do not spend much on consultants, custom software, or internal resources (e.g., employee time). Given the importance of having adequate internal resources to successfully implementing ABC, most companies should focus more on these resources.

Most companies surveyed use commercial software to help structure their ABC design and to process ABC information. The availability and use of commercial vs. custom software did not prove important to the success of ABC in the long run, however, because it is not related to the behavioral and organizational issues involved. The choice of software as a technical information system is important for accountants and MIS specialists, but evidently this choice is relatively unimportant to nonaccountants or to the ultimate success of an ABC project.

Use of consultants. The use of external consultants can be important because most companies have little internal expertise with ABC. Using external consultants can provide a big benefit to the design of an ABC system and in providing training about ABC. But the key to making ABC successful depends more on effectively dealing with the behavioral and organizational issues discussed above.

There also is a potential danger in relying too much on external consultants. Consultants cannot substitute for the support of top management and the linkage of ABC to competitive strategy, continuous improvement, performance measurement, compensation. Successful implementations of ABC require the presence of these other factors. The implementation process must create internal ownership, knowledge, and action. Ideally, an external consultant should be used to facilitate an ABC initiative. A consultant is a source of knowledge that should be used to increase the knowledge and expertise within a company for selling, designing, implementing, and using ABC.

OBJECTIVES OF ABC

The survey found that consensus and clarity of objectives for ABC are important determinants of ABC success. In most companies, however, the clarity of purpose and consensus about the objectives of ABC are not what they should be.

When the objectives of ABC are precisely known (e.g., to improve the accuracy of cost estimates for customized products), ABC designers and users can develop a clear understanding of how an ABC system should be designed and how its information should be used. When the objectives are not well specified, designing an ABC system becomes more difficult.

To clarify objectives, the following questions should be asked:

- What are the cost objects?
- What resources in a company should be included?
- How accurate should the measurements be?
- How frequently should the measurements be made?
- Who should the information be reported to?
- What is the information intended to be used for?

Not knowing the answers to these questions makes success with ABC elusive. When everyone agrees on a particular objective, their efforts and resources are aligned so that they do not work at cross purposes. Consensus between the designers and users of ABC is particularly important.

The final implementation factor included in the survey is whether the ABC system stands alone or is integrated with other accounting systems. Although the survey indicates that having ABC as a standalone system is the least important determinant of ABC success, almost all of the companies used standalone ABC systems. Many companies have used a standalone ABC system in part because they use commercial software that is designed to run as a standalone program.[12]

When first starting with ABC, having a standalone system is often prudent. A standalone system can provide a relatively quick and cheap way to experiment with pilot systems while a company learns how best to use ABC. Besides, companies have to be careful about making changes to their mainframe accounting systems for reasons of cost, compatibility, and internal control. The problem with a standalone system stems from extended reliance on standalone pilot systems and from failure to eventually integrate ABC with other information systems that are important to nonaccountants.

CONCLUSION

The implementation factors included in the survey can be statistically summarized by a model with two important dimensions that are labeled below based on the implementation factors associated with them. In order of statistical importance, they are as follows:

Organizational support and integration:

1. Top management support;
2. Link to competitive strategy;
3. Link to quality initiatives;
4. Link to JIT/speed initiatives;
5. Link to performance evaluation and compensation; and
6. Consensus about ABC objectives.

Training:

7. Training in designing ABC Systems;
8. Training in implementing ABC systems; and
9. Training in using ABC information.

The other 8 out of the total of 17 implementation factors can play a supporting role but—in the absence of the important nine factors listed above—they are unlikely to lead to success with ABC. These eight relatively unimportant factors are as follows:

1. Standalone system;
2. Commercial software;
3. Accounting ownership;
4. Clear and concise objectives;
5. Nonaccounting ownership;
6. Resource adequacy;
7. External consultants; and
8. Custom software.

Unfortunately, this survey found that many of the nine important implementation factors were not present to the extent they should be, while some of the relatively unimportant factors (e.g., a standalone system, commercial software, and accounting ownership) are present more than is warranted by their importance to the ultimate success of an ABC initiative.

Michael D. Shields is Arthur Andersen Professor of Accounting at the University of Memphis. Michael A. McEwen is director of area information technology at KPMG Peat Marwick LLP in San Francisco.

Notes

1. For a representative sample of this literature, see J. Brimson, *Activity Accounting: An Activity-Based Costing Approach* (New York: John Wiley & Sons, 1991); C. Cokins, A. Stratton, and J. Helbling, *An ABC Manager's Primer* (Montvale, NJ: institute of Management Accountants, 1993); R. Cooper and K. Kaplan, *The Design of Cost Management Systems* (Englewood Cliffs, NJ: Prentice-Hall, 1991); P. Turney, *Common Sense: The ABC Performance Breakthrough* (Hillsboro, OR: Cost Technology, 1991).

2. K. Cooper, R. Kaplan, L. Maisel, E. Morrissey, and R. Oehm, *Implementing Activity-Based Cost Management* (Montvale, NJ: Institute of Management Accountants, 1992); C. Argyris and R. Kaplan, "Implementing New Knowledge: The Case of Activity Based Costing," *Accounting Horizons* (September 1994): 83–105; I. Cobb, J. Innes, and F. Mitchell, "Activity-Based Costing Problems: The British Experience," *Advances in Management Accounting* (1993): 6B–83; J. Innes and F. Mitchell, "ABC: A Survey of CIMA Members," *Management Accounting* (U.K.) (October 1991): 28–30.

3. Cooper, Kaplan, Maisel, Morrissey, and Oehm, see note 2; H. Hankinson and S. Lloyd, "Change Management," in B. Brinker (ed.) *Handbook of Cost Management* (New York: Warren, Gorham & Lamont, 1995) and P. Frost and C. Egri, "The Political Process of Innovation," *Research in Organizational Behavior* (1991): 229–295.

4. M. Shields, and S. Young, "A Behavioral Model for implementing Cost Management Systems," *Journal of Cost Management* ("Winter, 1989): 17–27; M. Shields and S. Young, "Behavioral and Organizational Issues," in B. Brinker (ed.), *Handbook of Cost Management* (1995).

5. See notes 3 and 4 for references to this literature.

6. See notes 3 and 4.

7. See note 4 for more detailed reviews and analyses.

8. For both Shields and Young (1989) and (1995), see note 4; Frost and Egri, see note 3; A. Meyer and J. Goes, "Organizational Assimilation of Innovation: A Multilevel Contextual Analysis," *Academy of Management Journal* (1988): 897–923.

9. Hankinson and Lloyd, see note 3.

10. Cooper, Kaplan, Maisel, Morrissey, and Oehm, see note 2.

11. Cobb, Innes, and Mitchell, see note 2.

12. J. Borden, "Cost Management Software," in B. Brinker (ed.) *Handbook of Cost Management* (New York: Warren, Gorham & Lamont, 1995); J. Borden, "Activity-Based Management Software, Journal of Cost Management (Winter 1994): 39–49.

From M. D. Shields, and M. A. McEwen, "Implementing Activity-Based Costing Systems Successfully," *Journal of Cost Management* (Winter 1996): 15–22. Reprinted with permission.

Question

15.4 In Shields and McEwen's article, why is top management support so important for the success of ABC? Explain.